T0215770

Communications
in Computer and Information Science   917

Commenced Publication in 2007
Founding and Former Series Editors:
Phoebe Chen, Alfredo Cuzzocrea, Xiaoyong Du, Orhun Kara, Ting Liu,
Dominik Ślęzak, and Xiaokang Yang

More information about this series at http://www.springer.com/series/7899

Yuqing Sun · Tun Lu
Xiaolan Xie · Liping Gao
Hongfei Fan (Eds.)

Computer Supported Cooperative Work and Social Computing

13th CCF Conference, ChineseCSCW 2018
Guilin, China, August 18–19, 2018
Revised Selected Papers

 Springer

Editors
Yuqing Sun
Shandong University
Jinan, China

Tun Lu
Fudan University
Shanghai, China

Xiaolan Xie
Guilin University of Technology
Guilin, China

Liping Gao
University of Shanghai for Science
and Technology
Shanghai, China

Hongfei Fan
Tongji University
Shanghai, China

ISSN 1865-0929   ISSN 1865-0937 (electronic)
Communications in Computer and Information Science
ISBN 978-981-13-3043-8   ISBN 978-981-13-3044-5 (eBook)
https://doi.org/10.1007/978-981-13-3044-5

Library of Congress Control Number: 2018959137

This Springer imprint is published by the registered company Springer Nature Singapore Pte Ltd.
The registered company address is: 152 Beach Road, #21-01/04 Gateway East, Singapore 189721, Singapore

Preface

Welcome to ChineseCSCW 2018, the 13th CCF Conference on Computer Supported Cooperative Work and Social Computing. ChineseCSCW 2018 was sponsored by the China Computer Federation (CCF), and co-organized by the Technical Committee on Cooperative Computing (TCCC) of CCF and Guilin University of Technology. The ChineseCSCW 2018 proceedings are published by Springer, which is a fantastic opportunity for the conference to attract worldwide attention and to connect global scholars in related fields.

ChineseCSCW (initially titled CCSCW) is a highly reputable conference series on computer supported cooperative work (CSCW) and social computing in China with a long history. It aims at bridging Chinese and overseas CSCW researchers, practitioners, and educators, with a particular focus on innovative models, theories, techniques, algorithms, and methods, as well as domain-specific applications and systems, from both technical and social aspects in CSCW and social computing. The conference was initially held biennially from 1998, and has been held annually since 2014.

ChineseCSCW 2018 received 150 submissions, and after a rigorous double-blind peer–review process, only 33 were accepted as full papers for oral presentation, resulting in an acceptance rate of 22%. The program also included 13 short papers, which were presented as posters. In addition, the conference featured four keynote speeches, eight technical seminars, and a special panel discussion on "Social Computing and AI for Legal Affairs." We are grateful to the keynote speakers, Prof. Tianyou Chai (member of the Chinese Academy of Engineering) from Northeastern University, Prof. Dajun Zeng from the Chinese Academy of Sciences, Prof. Zhiwen Yu from Northwestern Polytechnic University, and Prof. Xiaofei Liao from Huazhong University of Science and Technology.

We hope that you enjoy ChineseCSCW 2018.

October 2018

Ning Gu
Xiaohui Cheng

Organization

ChineseCSCW 2018 was held in Guilin, China, during August 17–19, 2018.

Steering Committee

Ning Gu	Fudan University, China
Bin Hu	Lanzhou University, China
Xiaoping Liu	Hefei University of Technology, China
Yong Tang	South China Normal University, China
Weiqing Tang	Chinese Academy of Sciences, China
Shaozi Li	Xiamen University, China
Yuqing Sun	Shandong University, China
Xiangwei Zheng	Shandong Normal University, China

General Chairs

Ning Gu	Fudan University, China
Xiaohui Cheng	Guilin University of Technology, China

Program Committee Chairs

Yuqing Sun	Shandong University, China
Tun Lu	Fudan University, China
Xiaolan Xie	Guilin University of Technology, China

Organizing Committee Chairs

Xiaoping Liu	Hefei University of Technology, China
Xiangwei Zheng	Shandong Normal University, China
Haiping Yu	Guilin University of Technology, China

Publicity Chairs

Yong Tang	South China Normal University, China
Minggang Dong	Guilin University of Technology, China

Publication Chairs

Bin Hu	Lanzhou University, China
Yuqing Sun	Shandong University, China
Chaoquan Chen	Guilin University of Technology, China

Finance Chair

Shouxue Chen   Guilin University of Technology, China

Paper Award Chairs

Shaozi Li   Xiamen University, China
Yichuan Jiang   Southeast University, China
Hailong Sun   Beihang University, China

Program Committee

Hongming Cai   Shanghai Jiao Tong University, China
Jian Cao   Shanghai Jiao Tong University, China
Buqing Cao   Hunan University of Science and Technology, China
Donglin Cao   Xiamen University, China
Chao Chen   Chongqing University, China
Liangyin Chen   Sichuan University, China
Qingkui Chen   University of Shanghai for Science and Technology, China
Qingzhang Chen   Zhejiang University of Technology, China
Yuan Cheng   Wuhan University, China
Shiwei Cheng   Zhejiang University of Technology, China
Xiaohui Cheng   Guilin University of Technology, China
Longbiao Chen   Xiamen University, China
Lizhen Cui   Shandong University, China
Weihui Dai   Fudan University, China
Xianghua Ding   Fudan University, China
Wanchun Dou   Nanjing University, China
Hongfei Fan   Tongji University, China
Shanshan Feng   Shandong Normal University, China
Liping Gao   University of Shanghai for Science and Technology, China
Qiang Gao   Beihang University, China
Ning Gu   Fudan University, China
Kun Guo   Fuzhou University, China
Yinzhang Guo   Taiyuan University of Science and Technology, China
Fazhi He   Wuhan University, China
Haiwu He   Chinese Academy of Sciences, China
Bin Hu   Lanzhou University, China
Yanmei Hu   Chengdu University of Technology, China
Changqin Huang   South China Normal University, China
Huan Huo   University of Shanghai for Science and Technology, China
Bo Jiang   Zhejiang Gongshang University, China
Bin Jiang   Hunan University, China
Weijin Jiang   Xiangtan University, China
Yichuan Jiang   Southeast University, China
Lanju Kong   Shandong University, China

Yi Lai	Xi'an University of Posts and Telecommunications, China
Fangpeng Lan	Taiyuan University of Technology, China
Feng Li	Jiangsu University, China
Li Li	Southwest University, China
Jianguo Li	South China Normal University, China
Renfa Li	Hunan University, China
Shaozi Li	Xiamen University, China
Shiying Li	Hunan University, China
Taoshen Li	Guangxi University, China
Xiaoping Li	Southeast University, China
Lu Liang	Guangdong University of Technology, China
Hong Liu	Shandong Normal University, China
Dongning Liu	Guangdong University of Technology, China
Shijun Liu	Shandong University, China
Xiaoping Liu	Hefei University of Technology, China
Li Liu	Chongqing University, China
Tun Lu	Fudan University, China
DianJie Lu	Shandong Normal University, China
Huijuan Lu	China Jiliang University, China
Qiang Lu	Hefei University of Technology, China
Li Pan	Shandong University, China
KeJi Mao	Zhejiang University of Technology, China
Chunyu Miao	Zhejiang Normal University, China
Haiwei Pan	Harbin Engineering University, China
Youtian Qu	Zhejiang University of Media and Communications, China
Limin Shen	Yanshan University, China
Yuliang Shi	Dareway Software Co., Ltd, China
Xiaoxia Song	Datong University, China
Kehua Su	Wuhan University, China
Hailong Sun	Beihang University, China
Ruizhi Sun	China Agricultural University, China
Yuqing Sun	Shandong University, China
Yuling Sun	East China Normal University, China
WenAn Tan	Nanjing University of Aeronautics and Astronautics, China
Shan Tang	Shanghai Polytechnic University, China
Yong Tang	South China Normal University, China
Yan Tang	Hohai University, China
Weiqing Tang	Chinese Academy of Sciences, China
Yiming Tang	Hefei University of Technology, China
Yizheng Tao	Chinese Academy of Engineering Physics, China
Shaohua Teng	Guangdong University of Technology, China
Lei Wang	Dalian University of Technology, China
Li Wang	Taiyuan University of Technology, China
Tong Wang	Harbin Engineering University, China
Hongbo Wang	University of Science and Technology Beijing, China
Hongjun Wang	Southwest Jiaotong University, China

Xiaodong Wang	National University of Defense Technology, China
Yijie Wang	National University of Defense Technology, China
Wei Wei	Xi'an University of Technology, China
Yiping Wen	Hunan University of Science and Technology, China
Jiyi Wu	Hangzhou Normal University, China
Chunhe Xia	Beihang University, China
Yong Xiang	Tsinghua University, China
Yu Xin	Harbin University of Science and Technology, China
Meng Xu	Shandong Technology and Business University, China
Xiaolan Xie	Guilin University of Technology, China
Zhiqiang Xie	Harbin University of Science and Technology, China
Jianbo Xu	Hunan University of Science and Technology, China
Jiuyun Xu	China University of Petroleum, China
Bo Yang	University of Electronic Science and Technology of China, China
Chao Yang	Hunan University, China
Gang Yang	Northwestern Polytechnical University, China
Jing Yang	Lanzhou University, China
Xiaochun Yang	Northeastern University, China
Xiaojun Zhu	Taiyuan University of Technology, China
Dingyu Yang	Shanghai Dianji University, China
Yang Yu	Sun Yat-sen University, China
Lei Yu	PLA Information Engineering University, China
Changyou Zhang	Chinese Academy of Sciences, China
Xianchuan Yu	Beijing Normal University, China
Guijuan Zhang	Shandong Normal University, China
Guangquan Zhang	Soochow University, China
Liang Zhang	Fudan University, China
Jifu Zhang	Taiyuan University of Science and Technology, China
Shaohua Zhang	Shanghai Software Technology Development Center, China
Wei Zhang	Guangdong University of Technology, China
Zili Zhang	Southwest University, China
Zhiqiang Zhang	Harbin Engineering University, China
Qiang Zhao	Chinese Academy of Engineering Physics, China
Junlan Zhao	Inner Mongolia University of Finance and Economics, China
Yifeng Zhou	Southeast University, China
Zhengtao Yu	Kunming University of Science and Technology, China
Xianjun Zhu	Jinling Institute of Technology, China
Xiangwei Zheng	Shandong Normal University, China
Qiaohong Zu	Wuhan University of Technology, China
Ning Zhong	Beijing University of Technology, China

Contents

Collaborative Models, Approaches, Algorithms, and Systems

A Role-Based Semantic Framework for Collaborative Socialized
Process Model Reconstruction 3
   Wenan Tan, Li Huang, Lu Zhao, and Shan Tang

MCPS2: Intention Maintenance of Structure Document Based MCPS
Under Mobile Platform 20
   *Dan Wang, Sizheng Zhu, Liping Gao, Shanshan Wang, Xiaofang Xu,
   and Changqing Tao*

Research on Data Provenance Model for Multidisciplinary Collaboration 32
   Fangyu Yu, Beisi Zhou, Tun Lu, and Ning Gu

Mobile Agent-Based Mobile Intelligent Business Security
Transaction Model 50
   Wei-Jin Jiang, Jia-Hui Chen, Yu-Hui Xu, and Yang Wang

A Novel Strategy for Complex Human-Agent Negotiation 66
   Lichun Yuan, Siqi Chen, and Zili Zhang

Multi-strategy Mutation Constrained Differential Evolution Algorithm
Based on Replacement and Restart Mechanism 77
   Lyuyang Tong, Minggang Dong, and Chao Jing

Consistency Maintenance of CRDT-Based File Management System
in Cloud Environment 87
   Liping Gao and Changqing Tao

A Generic Arrival Process Model for Generating Hybrid Cloud Workload . . . 100
   Chunyan An, Jian-tao Zhou, and Zefeng Mou

Cost-Effective Coupled Video Distribution Network 115
   *Jing Chen, Zhigang Chen, Dianjie Lu, Chen Lyu, Guijuan Zhang,
   Xiangwei Zheng, and Hong Liu*

Optimal Design of Obstacles in Emergency Evacuation Using
an Arch Formation Based Fitness Function. 129
   Liang Li, Hong Liu, and Yanbin Han

Web Service Composition with Uncertain QoS: An IQCP Model 146
   Hengzhou Ye and Taoshen Li

A Fast Neighbor Discovery Algorithm in WSNs..................... 163
Liangxiong Wei, Weijie Sun, Haixiang Chen, Ping Yuan, Feng Yin,
Qian Luo, Yanru Chen, and Liangyin Chen

FCI-Outlier: An Efficient Frequent Closed Itemset-Based Outlier Detecting
Approach on Data Stream 176
Shangbo Hao, Saihua Cai, Ruizhi Sun, and Sicong Li

Multi-model Hybrid Traffic Flow Forecast Algorithm Based on
Multivariate Data 188
Jie Zhou, Yuling Sun, and Liang He

A New Algorithm for Real-Time Collaborative Graphical Editing System
Based on CRDT.. 201
Liping Gao and Xiaofang Xu

Throughput-Guarantee Resource Provisioning for Streaming Analytical
Workflows in the Cloud....................................... 213
Yan Yao, Jian Cao, and Shiyou Qian

A Probabilistic and Rebalancing Cache Placement Strategy for ICN
in MANETs... 228
Cheng Zhang, Chunhe Xia, and Haiquan Wang

Social Computing

Detect Cooperative Hyping Among VIP Users and Spammers
in Sina Weibo 241
Ziyu Guo, Shijun Liu, Yafang Wang, Liqiang Wang, Li Pan,
and Lei Wu

A Relationship-Based Pedestrian Social Groups Model 257
Guang-peng Liu, Hong Liu, and Liang Li

Socio-Technical System Design Framework for People with Disability 272
Peng Liu, Tun Lu, and Ning Gu

An Overlapping Community Detection Algorithm Based on Triangle
Coarsening and Dynamic Distance 285
Bingjie Xiang, Kun Guo, Zhanghui Liu, and Qinwu Liao

Identifying Potential Experts on Stack Overflow..................... 301
Zihan Ban, Jiafei Yan, and Hailong Sun

Predicting Students' Mood Level Using Multi-feature Fusion Joint
Sentiment-Topic Model in Mobile Learning........................ 316
Xianqing Wang, Meihua Zhao, Changqin Huang, Jia Zhu,
and Yong Tang

Identification of Influential Users in Emerging Online Social Networks
Using Cross-site Linking   331
    Qingyuan Gong, Yang Chen, Xinlei He, Fei Li, Yu Xiao, Pan Hui,
    Xin Wang, and Xiaoming Fu

LSTM Sentiment Polarity Analysis Based on LDA Clustering   342
    Zechuan Chen, Shaohua Teng, Wei Zhang, Huan Tang, Zhenhua Zhang,
    Junping He, Xiaozhao Fang, and Lunke Fei

Data Analysis and Machine Learning for CSCW and Social Computing

Anomaly Detection Algorithm Based on Cluster of Entropy   359
    Wenan Tan, Xi Fang, Lu Zhao, and Anqiong Tang

Abnormal Detecting over Data Stream Based on Maximal Pattern
Mining Technology   371
    Saihua Cai, Ruizhi Sun, Jiayao Li, Chao Deng, and Sicong Li

Spatial Task Allocation Based on User Trajectory Prediction   386
    Yun Jiang, Wei He, Lizhen Cui, Qian Yang, and Zhaohui Peng

Study on Learner's Interest Mining Based on EEG Signal Analysis   398
    Yonghui Dai, Junjie Chen, Haijian Chen, Shengqi Lu, Ye Fu,
    and Weihui Dai

Research on Cross-Media Retrieval of Collaborative Plotted Multimedia
Data Based on Container-Based Cloud Platform and Deep Learning   410
    Xiaolan Xie, Qiangqing Zheng, Xinrong Li, Xiaochun Cheng,
    and Zhihong Guo

A Fast Feature Selection Method Based on Mutual Information in Multi-
label Learning   424
    Zhenqiang Sun, Jia Zhang, Zhiming Luo, Donglin Cao, and Shaozi Li

Multi-kernel Collaboration-Induced Fuzzy Local Information C-Means
Algorithm for Image Segmentation   438
    Yiming Tang, Xianghui Hu, Fuji Ren, Xiaocheng Song, and Xi Wu

Chinese-Vietnamese Word Alignment Method Based on Bidirectional RNN
and Linguistic Features   454
    Shengxiang Gao, Haodong Zhu, Zhuo Wang, Zhengtao Yu,
    and Xiaohan Wang

Short Papers

Facial Expression Recognition Algorithm Based on Equal Probability
Symbolization Entropy. 469
  Fa Zheng, Bin Hu, and Xiangwei Zheng

Automatic Sleep Stage Classification Based on LSTM. 478
  Peiying Shi, Xiangwei Zheng, Ping Du, and Feng Yuan

Overlapping Community Detection Algorithm Based on Spectral and Fuzzy
C-Means Clustering. 487
  Xiaoshan He, Kun Guo, Qinwu Liao, and Qiaoling Yan

Watershed Flood Forecasting Based on Cluster Analysis
and BP Neural Network. 498
  Wangsong Wang and Yan Tang

Academic News Text Classification Model Based on Attention Mechanism
and RCNN. 507
  *Ronghua Lin, Chengzhou Fu, Chengjie Mao, Jingmin Wei,
  and Jianguo Li*

Energy-Efficiency for Smartphones Using Interaction Link Prediction
in Mobile Cloud Computing. 517
  Jiuyun Xu, Chao Guan, and Xiangrui Xu

MDIS: A Node Localization Algorithm Based on Multi-region Division
and Similarity Matching. 527
  *Hao Wang, Haixiang Chen, Ping Yuan, Feng Yin, Qian Luo,
  and Liangyin Chen*

An Efficient Graph-Search Algorithm for Full Link
Application Suggestion 536
  *Haijie Zhang, Nan Zeng, Hu Song, Menghan Xu, Huiyu Wang, Bo Yang,
  and Chen Lyu*

An Adaptive k-NN Classifier for Medical Treatment Recommendation
Under Concept Drift 546
  Nengjun Zhu, Jian Cao, and Yan Zhang

Evaluating the Impacts of Concurrency Control over User Experience
in Feature-Based Collaborative Designing 557
  Yuan Cheng, Fazhi He, Xiao Lv, and Weiwei Cai

A Concurrency Benchmark Tool for Cloud Storage. 567
  Weiwei Cai, Agustina Ng, and Chengzheng Sun

Task Assignments in Complex Collaborative Crowdsourcing 574
  Wei He, Lizhen Cui, and Cheng Huang

A Collaboration Services Scheduling Method Based on Intelligent
Genetic Algorithm.   581
    Wei Guo, Meng Xu, Weixia Xu, and Lizhen Cui

Author Index   589

Collaborative Models, Approaches, Algorithms, and Systems

A Role-Based Semantic Framework for Collaborative Socialized Process Model Reconstruction

Wenan Tan[1,2], Li Huang[1,3(✉)], Lu Zhao[1], and Shan Tang[2]

[1] School of Computer Science and Technology,
Nanjing University of Aeronautics and Astronautics, Nanjing, Jiangsu, China
wtan@foxmail.com, huangli713@126.com
[2] School of Computer and Information Engineering,
Shanghai Polytechnic University, Shanghai, China
[3] School of Information and Electromechanical Engineering,
Jiangsu Open University, Nanjing, Jiangsu, China

Abstract. Collaborative socialized process model reconstruction plays important roles in social network management. Group multi-role identification aims to the optimal collaboration performance by assigning potential roles to candidates. It could improve social process services management. In this work, we pay a specific attention to the challenge of the lack of formalization to describe human resources in business process. Based on Social Network Analysis (SNA), a semantic framework provides semantic description of human resources for social business process reconstruction. The main contributions of this paper includes: (1) By formalizing the semantic collaborative social process model for collaborative task assignment, a role-based semantic framework for Social Process Modeling Ontology (SPMO) is proposed; (2) A series of computational solutions for measuring multi-group collaboration performance and interaction cost are proposed for combinatorial optimization problem; and (3) two algorithms, SSPGC (semantic social process graph construction) and CSNRC (collaborative socialized network reconstruction) are proposed for semantic analysis on collaborative social process models. Finally, the experimental results show that our solution is a scalable framework and can be efficiently applied in reconstructing collaborative process model in real-world networks and obtaining optimal performance.

Keywords: Social collaboration · Process model reconstruction
Role identification · Task assignment

1 Introduction

Collaborative socialized process model reconstruction is a complex and important project in social business management, because it involves many factors that should be considered, such as resource assignment, team efficiency, and collaborative cost. Enterprises are searching for good services to migrate and integrate in social collaboration networks, as well as to reduce the costs of process development and

© Springer Nature Singapore Pte Ltd. 2019
Y. Sun et al. (Eds.): ChineseCSCW 2018, CCIS 917, pp. 3–19, 2019.
https://doi.org/10.1007/978-981-13-3044-5_1

maintenance. Recently many research efforts have been made to improve the efficacy of Business Process Management (BPM). For example, some reports suggest utilizing restructuring techniques centered on the organizational perspective or people to achieve it [1–3]. The new paradigm Social Computing has recently been payed more attention to Knowledge Discovery in Database with theoretical basis, methods and researches.

Business Process as a Service (BPaaS) is a cloud-based business process model, which has attracted much attention due to the adoption of cost-effective business process solutions [4, 5]. The analysis of social network graphs and complex network model aims to study complex human and natural phenomena, especially the reconstruction of roles, that is to group activities according to the skills needed for the project [6]. Based on detection for roles handover, roles identification could indicate realistic or potential relations among social members [7, 8]. Scientific cooperation and open-source software projects development are typical combinatorial optimization problem with wide application. They are characterized as self-organizing and dynamic, in which cooperators primarily driven by similar research field and self-motivation contribute and collaborate to the projects. Social relationship among people or organizations in collaborative networks affect the overall performance of the BPM. Resource description in cross-organization intranet and open source project are unstructured and heterogeneity due to the lack of unified formal definitions. Ontologies could help to ensure the interoperability of communities or organizations. So a unified consensus between entities and organizations is necessary. For instance, a project manager should understand pivotal employees, core team, leaders and communication bridge in social environment, and search for potential cooperators. Another example is when a team member stops work in certain case force majeure, it must be substituted by cooperators automatically and quickly to satisfy project. So, it's necessary to find a well-connected performer from the structural aspect and who has similar profiles in the semantic aspect. By exploring the semantic perspective of business process model, role in social collaboration networks could be reconstructed, in turn, both the structural and semantic information within cross-organization or communities are correlated and influence each other.

This paper proposes a role-based semantic framework for collaborative socialized process model. It uses the theoretic of BPaaS and semantic web technology to discover well-collaborative process model under the perspective of personal role [9]. The framework includes: (1) a high-level abstract representation of social process models based on ontology is enriched with semantic role reconstruction; (2) a computational solution for detecting collaborative communities and entities for measuring multi-group collaboration performance and interaction cost; and (3) two algorithms, SSPGC and CSNRC are generated. Concretely, SPMO based on Business Process Modeling Ontology (BPMO) [10] is built to recognize roles, resources and strategies with similar profiles, as well as lots of social relations and interaction performance between components of BPs in potential cooperation groups. Furthermore, a set of strategies on SNA-based collaborative criteria for evaluating the collaboration of social process (SPs) is defined. Finally, a series of computational solutions for measuring multi-group collaboration performance and interaction cost are designed for combinatorial optimization problem.

2 Motivation

Generally, a scientific cooperation project consists of complex sub-projects and tasks, potential experts and teams with different resources and skills are deemed necessary in professional fields. So personal human resource and sub-process in organization should be reconstructed to fulfil the complex project. This work pays emphasis on "role" resources, particularly depicting skills in professional research field. Let us consider two social organizations for potential collaboration *SPM provider*1 and *SPM provider*2 providing cross-organization task assignment solutions. An open project manager could choose *SPM provider*1 and *SPM provider*2 to participate in the social collaborative project depend on their suitable role resources and services of sub-process model.

The *SPM provider*1 and SPM *provider*2 process models are illustrated in Fig. 1 with BPMN notations, including four main control flow elements: *event, activity, connector* and *resource*. Blue ovals represent human resource to perform tasks, dotted lines represent tasks assigned to experts, so there are expert set $\{h_1, h_2, h_3, h_4\}$ in Fig. 1 (a), and $\{h_5, h_6\}$ in Fig. 1(b), supposing part of this process is taken into account. These experts are able to participate in the SNA research project on the condition that they have suitable skills. For example, skills set of expert h_1 is $S_1 = \{Data\ Classification, Pattern\ Recognition, Semantic\ Web\}$, and h_5 has $S_5 = \{Semantic\ Web, Ontology, Knowledge\ description\}$. Without considering interaction relation, $\{h_1, h_4, h_5\}$ could be an available collaborative group. Besides that, collaborative relationship and interaction cost among process model services in social network should be considered. Ideally, since expert h_1 and h_5 have some similar skills such as $\{Semantic\ Web\}$, and they and their group could provide the skills required by the SNA project.

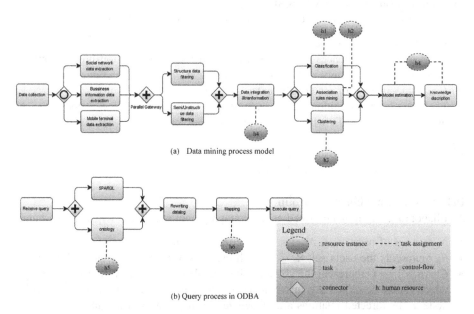

(a) Data mining process model

(b) Query process in ODBA

Fig. 1. BPMN example: (a) Data mining process model & (b) Query process in ODBA (Color figure online)

It often happens that SPs collaboration fail or are inefficient when resource is invalid and thus the requirements of cross-organization social collaboration may not be satisfied. We illustrate some of the concerns about the resource requirements in SPs that we are aiming to address:

Firstly, human resources h_1 and h_5 come from different organizations, their profiles and specialties may be represented with different patterns and semantics. To avoid ambiguity, our goal is to supply a general semantic description for human resources.

Secondly, in a complex project, manager should discover and schedule associated groups to provide special service for skills request. It is necessary to identify roles and search for potential cooperators. h_1 and h_5 worked as potential cooperators based on the correlation between them, so they may be the bridges. Thus, organizing teams based on roles distribution aims to enhance organization collaboration.

Thirdly, considering the interaction cost, the weight on the edge of social network should be calculate to minimize the cost among cross- and inner-organization.

3   Problem Definition

3.1   Collaboration in Social Network

Social networks are graphic structures comprised of participants (individuals or organizations) and collaboration links. Some special organizations could provide service by business process reconstructing [11, 12]. The lower interaction cost between two candidate experts, the more easily they cooperate so much as their sub-groups.

Definition 1: Social Process Graph
A social process graph $G_p = (U, S, E, T, R)$ is a labeled directed graph where:

- U represents the set of social users;
- $S \subseteq U \times U$ is a sequences set that connects two users (i.e. relationships or dependencies), and the weight w represents the incident value for the connector;
- $E = U \cup S$ is a set of model elements;
- $T : E \rightarrow t$ In the definition we set a function in which a type t is assigned for each model element $e \in E$, where t depends on types of elements described by each standard;
- $R : U \rightarrow role$ is a function that assigns a given role r_i for each node $u \in U$, where $r_i \in R$ depends on the shared features.

Definition 2: Collaborative Group
A collaborative group is described as a subgraph, denoted as $G_c = (N_c, R_c, C)$ where:

- N_c is a set of users, $u_i \in N_c$, $i = 1...n$ represents a node in G_c;
- R_c represents the users set, $R_c \subseteq S$, each user has a directed relation with others;
- $C : (u, u') \rightarrow C$ represent the collaborative membership of users (u, u') in a group, which can be described as a matrix in a centralized group. Each group has a centroid node u_i. Its directed relations are recognized by the matrix of neighbors.

Definition 3: Role
Given a set of roles $R = \{r_1, ..., r_n\}$ in a group $g \subseteq G_c$, each role can be expressed as $r_i = (A_r, L_r)$, where:

- A_r is a set of attributes (i.e. skills) represented by $A_r = \{a_1, ..., a_n\}$;
- L_r is a weight of role's level. It is a vector of a weight, $L_r[j] \in [0, +\infty)$ $j(0 \leq j \leq n)$.

Definition 4: Cross-organization Task Assignment
A complex project P can be described as $P = <X, A, R, G, s_0>$. Given a cross-organization task assignment project P, it requires a set of skills $X = \{x_1, ..., x_n\}$. A is a set of agents (performers), R is a set of roles, and $G = \{g_1, ..., g_m\}$ is a set of candidate professional sub-group, where $g_i = \{e_1, ..., e_t\}$ is composed of many candidate experts, and each experts e_i has one or more kinds of skills $e_i = \{s_1, ..., s_u\}$. Obviously, $e_i \subseteq X$. s_0 is an initial status of the system. A human user will play a certain role in a task, and each group works in a certain environment.

In formalizing task assignment problem, actors and roles are the main assignments, and we can utilize the vectors and matrices to express the environments and sub-groups. Where, nonnegative integers $m = |A|$ and $n = |R|$ represent the size of and respectively, i is the indices of agents, and j is the indices of roles. Remark. $N \subseteq N^+$ represents a non-negative integers set.

Definition 5: Candidate Matching Matrix
A complex project candidate matching matrix Q_m is an $m \times n$ matrix, where $Q_m[i,j] = \omega \in [0, 1]$ denotes the matching value of agent $i \in \mathcal{N}(0 \leq i \leq m)$ for role $j \in \mathcal{N}$ $(0 \leq j \leq n)$.

Definition 6: Interaction Cost Matrix
A candidate interaction cost matrix Q_c is defined as an $m \times n$ matrix, where $Q_c[i,j] = \omega'(0 \leq i \leq m, 0 \leq j \leq n)$ is the interaction cost weight of agent $i \in \mathcal{N}$ $(0 \leq i \leq m)$ for role $j \in \mathcal{N}$ $(0 \leq j \leq n)$.

As defined above, a group can be expressed by Q, L, T, Q_m, and Q_c [13], in which L is a vector of role range, Q is a qualification matrix, T is a role assignment matrix, σ and $\sum_{i=0}^{m-1} T[i,j]$ measures group performance and each role workability, respectively. Two kinds of thresholds $\tau_0 \in (0, 1]$ and $\tau_1 \in [0, 1)$ are used to denote the limit of qualified agents and matching extent of candidate, where $\tau_1 < \tau_0$. If $Q[i,j] \geq \tau_0 (0 \leq i \leq m, 0 \leq j \leq n)$ then it means that agent i is qualified for role j, otherwise not. If $Q_m[i,j] \geq \tau_1 (0 \leq i \leq m, 0 \leq j \leq n)$, then candidate agent i is qualified to involve in role j, otherwise not.

In fact, the problem of cross-organization task assignment is to find a feasible T by using multirole assignment while minimizing cost can be calculated by Eq. (2) under the above constrained conditions.

$$max\,\sigma = \begin{cases} \sum_{i=0}^{m-1} \sum_{j=0}^{n-1} Q_c[i,j] \times L_r(j) \times T[i,j], \text{ if } Q[i,j] \geq \tau_0 \\ \sum_{i=0}^{m-1} \sum_{j=0}^{n-1} Q_c[i,j] \times Q_m[i,j] \times L_r(j) \times T[i,j], \text{ else if } \tau_1 \leq Q_m[i,j] \leq \tau_0 \\ 0, \quad \text{else if } Q_m[i,j] < \tau_1 \end{cases}$$

$$(1)$$

$$min \ \delta = \sum_{i=0}^{m-1} \sum_{j=0}^{n-1} Q_m[i,j] \times T[i,j] + \sum_{i=0}^{m-1} \sum_{j=0}^{n-1} Q_c[i,j] \times T[i,j] \qquad (2)$$

Subject to,

$$T[i,j] \in \{0,1\}(0 \leq i \leq m, 0 \leq j \leq n) \qquad (3)$$

$$\sum_{i=0}^{m-1} T[i,j] \leq L[j](0 \leq j \leq n) \qquad (4)$$

$$Q[i,j] \times T[i,j] \geq \tau_0 \times T[i,j](0 \leq i \leq m, 0 \leq j \leq n) \qquad (5)$$

$$Q_m[i,j] \times T[i,j] \geq \tau_1 \times T[i,j](0 \leq i \leq m, 0 \leq j \leq n) \qquad (6)$$

3.2 Semantic Business Process Model

To formalize the description of resources in social process management and realize the semantic of SP modeling in reality, we capitalize the Web Ontology Language to represent ontologies for resources in SPs.

Definition 7: Semantic Social Process Graph

A semantic social process graph $P_s = (U, S, E, T, R, C, I, I_m, I_o, I_R)$ is annotated from the perspective of an ontology O semantically, and it is denoted as:

- C is a concept set and I represents the instances set in O;
- $I_m: I \rightarrow E$ In the definition we set a function assigning for each instance $i \in I$ a model element $e \in E$, and i annotates to e;
- $I_o: I \rightarrow C$ In the definition we set a function assigning for each instance $i \in I$ a concept $c \in C$, and i is instantiated from c.
- $I_R: I \rightarrow R$ In the definition we set a function assigning for each instance $i \in I$ a role $r \in R$, and i annotates to r.

Remark. the interpretation of U, S, E, T, R has been presented in Definition 1.

3.3 SNA-Based Collaboration Criteria

Series of criterion for the complete process aims at evaluating the collaboration of SPs, they are based on SNA measure, including coordination, interactivity, egalitarianism.

Collaboration. The rationale represents a collaboration between experts working together to achieve a common goal. The participants could provide many opportunities for the collaboration. The more skills an expert has in his/her field, the more opportunities he/she could offer for collaboration. Therefore, egalitarianism and interactivity should be considered as criteria when tasks assigned to participants. Degree of node and weight of edge could evaluate the strength of a connection or tie.

Core-Periphery. A core-periphery pattern is made up with two classes of nodes, i.e., core and periphery. Core node denotes the dominant and leadership. The experts worked with many others and are closely linked to the core. Peripheral nodes have fewer connections and influence. The closeness centrality measures the connection, the closer participant is to the others, the easier he/she contacts to the partners. It means that the higher closeness centrality a participant has, the more opportunities to coordinate with others he/she has. It is useful to understand critical or most connected members and identify leaders in the social environment.

4 Semantic Analysis for Collaborative Social Process Models

4.1 Social Process Modeling Ontology (SPMO)

The structured nature of BPs and the unstructured nature of social world in terms of relations between social entities are focused. We reuse Definition 7 to represent the elements in social process model with a domain-specific ontology semantically, and provide sets of concepts and instances to annotate the social process model elements. We formalize the SPMO as an extension based on *CloudPrO* [2] to conceptualize the elements' functionality in social process modeling. In fact, SPMO consider more about human resources, in this way, structured property of business world in terms of SPs and unstructured property of social world according to relations between human resource and BP, are both covered by SPMO.

Ontology Concepts. SPMO is denoted as a 3-tuple $<C_{SPMO}, A_{SPMO}, R_{SPMO}>$, where C_{SPMO} is a concept set, A_{SPMO} is attribute set, and R_{SPMO} is a set of rules based on current relationships. Core concepts in BPMO abstract expression of concepts and relations are depicted in Fig. 2. We are particularly interested in human resource, so the main concept is *SPMO:Human resource* denotes an additional concept for *BPMO:Task* by *SPMO:Allocate*. *SPMO:Human resource* represents profile of task performer. It includes several sub-concepts:

- *SPMO:Resource* refers to resource attributes, especially the human resource attributes to accomplish a certain task.
- *SPMO:Action* refers to the human resource assigned to work items or operations via *SPMO:Allocate*.
- *SPMO:Link* refers to the human resource linked to other resources.

Ontology Attributes. The next step is to detail *SPMO:Resource structure*, it has three attributes: *SPMO:Skill*, *SPMO:Education* and *SPMO:Work*.

- *SPMO:Skill* means professional abilities that candidate experts have.
- *SPMO:Education* depicts education experience, it has two sub-concepts: *SPMO: Name* and *SPMO:Type* (e.g. *Education: Name: NUAA, Education: Type: Graduate School*).
- *SPMO:Work* represents working background, it is also divided into two sub-concepts: *SPMO:Affiliation* and *SPMO:Position* (e.g. *Work: Affiliation: Google, Work: Position: AI expert*).

In this paper, we aim to identify the roles and relations among social networks, so our rationale is that all the participants collaborated share their ties or relationships.

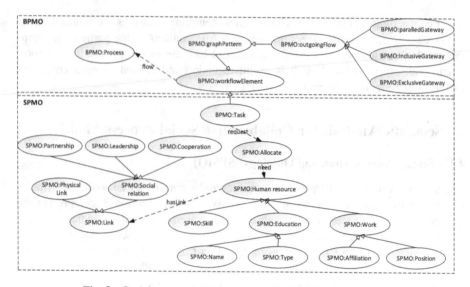

Fig. 2. *Social process modeling ontology(SPMO)* representation

Another important concept *SPMO:Link*, is also defined to represent relations among human resources. And *SPMO:Social relation* is extended by relation type into three types: *SPMO:Cooperation, SPMO:Leadership*, and *SPMO:Partnership*.

- *SPMO:Cooperation*: to allocate a task between e_1 and e_2, denoted as cooperation (e_1, e_2), e_1 and e_2 are providing resources and skills to the same task.
- *SPMO:Leadership*: a task is mastered by a core member e_1, it is the dominant and well connected the others.
- *SPMO:Partnership*: denoted as partnership (e_1, e_2), e_1 and e_2 are both to the same task and they are linked through physical link.

A case in point is the Fig. 3, the social process model detail of a domain-specific ontology for task assignment.

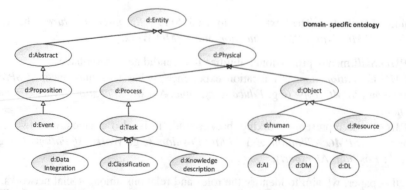

Fig. 3. Sematic annotation of social process model based on domain-specific ontology

Figure 3 depicts an instance of social process model with annotations of domain-specific ontology for task assignment processing. The prefix "d" cites as the namespace of the domain-specific ontology, and relation between concepts is "sub-concept-of" relation. [: *name*] represents the instance from *CloudPro* concept and domain experts.

In order to annotate social process model with SPMO, we show the details to construct a semantic social process graph in Algorithm 1. Given a social process model $G_p = (N, S, M, T, R)$, SPMO ontologies $O_{(c)spmo} = O_{bpmo} \cup O_{CloudPro} \cup O_{spmo}$, then we can annotate each model element $e \in U \cup S$ with concepts from $O_{(c)spmo}$ to construct a semantic social process model P_S^D. First, each model element e in G_p is iterated over and its $O_{(c)spmo}$ is get (Lines 1–3). During the iteration, if the element e's type matches the notation element x in a special modeling language X, i.e., $T(e) = x$, a new instance i with related data properties is created by the element e and the concept c in $O_{(c)spmo}$ (Lines 4–5). Then, the constructed instance is added to the set of instances (Line 6). At last, a semantic social process graph P_S^D is built.

Algorithm 1 SSPGC(Semantic Social Process Graph Construction) algorithm

Input: A social process graph G_p, and ontology $O_{(c)spmo}$

Output: A semantic social process model P_S^D

1: $M \leftarrow ExtractModelElements(G_p)$
2: for $e \in E$
3:   for $(c, x) \in O_{(c)spmo}$ /* $c \in O_{spmo}, x \in X$ */
4:     if $T(e) = x$ then
5:       $i \leftarrow Instantiation(e,c)$ /* According to model element e and concept c, the instance i with the associated properties is generated.*/
6:       $I \leftarrow i$ /* add instance i to the set of instances I */
7:     end if
8:   end for
9: end for
10: $P_S^D \leftarrow ConstructedSemanticSPG(G_p, O_{(c)spmo}, I)$
11: return P_S^D

4.2 Role Identification in Collaborative Network

Users engage in social cooperation (e.g. crowdsourcing) and their activity are primary attributed to a fraction of the individuals participating. So, social relationships among the organizational actors are focused on in organization restructuring by using context concept and structural information to promote cross-organizational collaboration.

Semantic Role Identification. To achieve an affiliation of well-connected actors and potential collaborators which have similar profiles, social knowledge of discovery and rediscovery can be used. Several new distances are defined accounting for the structural and semantic information to measure the relationship among the performers (actors and/or organizational groups). Among the performers the structural dependencies are significantly influenced by the connection, but the similarities of profile shows semantic relations among them. As defined in SPMO, each process instance could be achieved by different performers, which is affiliated to different roles. That's mean, one actor that may be qualified with one or more roles, which it may be involved in several event activities. Collaborative semantic annotation on consensus-based SNA provide context to specify human-resource entities and relations according to ontology.

In the process model of semantic, we utilize the semantic information (denoted as C) to describe the personal information of each actor in BPM. Specifically, certain task was performed by specific actor and it's relationships. A matrix (*nodes* × *features*) is defined in Table 1, whose features with the row is the instance that described each node (i.e. performer) in the business process. Where, the features belong to the semantic information C, such as information, function, organization and behavior context and a combination of them. Thus, this matrix can be defined as a feature matrix F, where $F(i,j) \in \{0,1\}$ is mean that if performer i is capable of task j that is described in semantic concept features.

Table 1. Semantic information C in social network process model

Nodes	Features			
	Task1	Task2	...	TaskM
Performer1	1	0	...	0
Performer2	0	1	...	0
...	...			
PerformerN	0	1	...	1

Given a project vector P is a n-vetor, it contains several tasks to assign, $P = \{T_1, T_2, \ldots, T_n\}$, where T_i represent a task, $T_i = \{f_1, f_2, \ldots, f_m\}$, f_i represents a skill feature needed in task T_i. And given a performer vector Pf_j, where $Pf_j = \{s_1, s_2, \ldots, s_t\}$, where s_i represents profile of performer based on SPMO. To search a candidate performer for the task, it is necessary to calculate the semantic relevance between task vector and performer vector by cosine similarity distance, then normalize the similarity distance to be a posterior probability computed by *softmax* function, denoted as follows,

$$R(Pf, T) = cosine(Pf_i, T_j) = \frac{PF_i^T T_j}{\|Pf_i\|\|T_j\|} \tag{7}$$

$$P(Pf^+|T) = \frac{\exp(\gamma R(T, Pf^+))}{\sum_{Pf' \in Pf} \exp(\gamma R(T, Pf'))} \tag{8}$$

Where γ is smoothing factor, Pf^+ and Pf' is positive and negative sample respectively, and Pf is the whole sample. $P(Pf^+|T) \in [0, 1]$, if $P(Pf^+|T) \in [0, 1] > \lambda$, then it could be a candidate for the task. Thus, a set of candidate performers could be obtained as $C_p = \{\omega_1, \omega_2, \ldots, \omega_l\}$, where $\omega_i(1 < i < l)$ equals $P(Pf^+|T)$. So the candidate matching matrix in definition 5 can be denoted as follow, that is, candidate Pf_i matches task T_j.

$$Q_m[i,j] = P(Pf^+ | T) \tag{9}$$

Interaction Cost Computing among Candidates. After we get the set of candidates for a project, interaction cost needs to compute to measure the budget of a project. To minimum interaction cost, SNA-based collaboration criteria mentioned in Sect. 3.3 must be concerned. Authority, betweenness centrality and knowledge exclusivity are also evaluate the trust degree.

Given a set of candidates N_c for a project based on above semantic role identification, there are some interoperate among collaborators in the inner-organization or cross-organization, so these candidates can be seen as nodes in networks, interoperate can also be seen as edges, and the frequency of interoperate can evaluate the weight of edge. $Gc = (N_c, S, M, T, R)$, $Gc \square Gp$, represents social process graph consisted of the candidates. The rationale represents a collaboration between candidates who work together or interact with each other to pursue a common goal.

First, according to the core-periphery criteria, the core nodes denote the authority and leadership. The core or leader node work with many others and are well connected. The closeness centrality C_v measures the connection between node v and i,

$$C_v = \frac{|N_c| - 1}{\sum_{i \neq v} d(v, i)} \tag{10}$$

According to the values of C_v, Top-k leaders are collected to be a set of leaders, and the k is determined by the quality of sub-projects in the partitioned complex project.

Second, according to the collaboration criteria, complex project requires team collaboration under leader, so interaction cost is represented as a weighted sum of the shortest path between candidate nodes and leader node, the formula is,

$$G_c Cost = \sum_{i=1}^{|N_c|} \sum_{j=1}^{k} d(n_i, n_{leaderj}) \tag{11}$$

where $d(n_i, n_{leaderj})$ denotes the sum of weight w of edge on the shortest path between candidate n_i and leader $n_{leaderj}$, w can be measured by the role interaction between two candidates r_i and $r_{leaderj}$, it is denoted as conditional probability under the same task t,

$$w = similarity(r_i, r_{leaderj}) = \frac{p(r_i, r_{leaderj}|t)}{p(r_i|t)p(r_{leaderj}|t)} \tag{12}$$

Where $p(r_i|t)$ denotes the probability of role r_i participate in task t, and $p(r_i, r_{leaderj}|t)$ denotes the probability of role r_i and $r_{leaderj}$ collaborate in task t. Finally, interaction cost weight of agent $Q_c[i,j] = \omega'$ in definition 6 can be calculated as $Q_c = G_c Cost$.

4.3   Social Networks Reconstruction for Collaboration

Cross-organization task assignment aims at solving the social networks reconstruction for collaboration. The method starts with the semantic annotation for social process graph by using Algorithm 1. After element is annotated concept information based on SPMO, many semantic measure methods can be used to evaluate multi-role assignment and find proper candidates. While the minimum interaction cost is satisfied with the candidate of matched team from cross-organization, collaborative social network is indeed constructed. Collaborative social network reconstruction algorithm based on semantic role identification can be described as follows.

Algorithm 2 CSNRC(Collaborative Social Network Reconstruction) algorithm

Input: A semantic social process model P_s^D, a set of skills $X=\{x_1,..,x_n\}$ in complex P, thresholds $\tau_0 \in (0,1]$ and $\tau_1 \in [0,1)$

Output: A collaborative social process model CP

1: for $n \in N$ do
2:    for $r \in R$ and $x_i \in X$ do
3:      *build qualification matrix Q, $Q[i, j \in [0, 1]$*
4:      *build role assignment matrix T, $T[i, j] \in \{0, 1\}$*
5:      *build Candidate matching matrix Q_m, $Q_m[i,j] = P\left(Pf_i^+ | T_j\right) \in [0,1]$ /* compute semantic
relevance between skills in x_i and n */
6:      if $Q[i, j] \geq \tau_0$ then /* compute maximum group performance σ */
7:        $\sigma \leftarrow \sum_{i=0}^{m-1} \sum_{j=0}^{n-1} Q_c[i,j] \times L_p(j) \times T[i,j]$
8:      else if $\tau_1 \leq Q_m[i,j] \leq \tau_0$ then
9:        $\sigma \leftarrow \sum_{i=0}^{m-1} \sum_{j=0}^{n-1} Q_c[i,j] \times Q_m[i,j] \times L_r(j) \times T[i,j]$
10:      else if $Q_m[i,j] < \tau_1$ then
11:        $\sigma \leftarrow 0$
12:      end if
13:      $Q_c = G_c Cost = \sum_{i=1}^{|N_c|} \sum_{j=1}^{k} d(n_i, n_{leaderj})$
14:      $\delta = \sum_{i=0}^{m-1} \sum_{j=0}^{n-1} Q_m[i,j] \times T[i,j] + \sum_{i=0}^{m-1} \sum_{j=0}^{n-1} Q_c[i,j] \times T[i,j]$ /* minimum interaction cost */
15:    end for
16: end for
17: $CP \leftarrow (\boldsymbol{max\, \sigma, min\, \delta})$
18: return CP

The space complexity and time complexity of leader node evaluation are $O(n + m)$ and $O(nm + n^2 \log n)$ respectively under a weighted social process graph. Where, n and m are the node number and edges respectively. With the constraints of budget of the project, this proposed algorithm of collaborative social network reconstruction could have best performance while minimizing the cost. By changing the threshold values τ_0 and τ_1, the matching degree of agent for a role in task assignment could search an optimal value. Assuming that n is the number of the skills and r is the number of the role included in the project; m is the number of agents (performers) that are candidates for the tasks. Our proposed algorithm runs in $O(mr + nr)$ time. As discussed in the above algorithm, the proposed algorithm supporting the collaborative social network reconstruction is feasible and runs more efficient.

5 Experiment and Evaluation

We conduct a simulation experiment to solve the problem of collaborative socialized process reconstruction, to validate the efficiency in dealing with the real world problems. Next, we will discuss our approach from two aspects, including the effect of SNA-based semantic measures on collaboration process, and the performance in cross-organization collaboration based on role identification. Specifically, we utilize the DBLP data as our experimental dataset to build the social graph. Where, the node represents expert and the weight of edge depicts the communication cost between two experts. Expert nodes in the DBLP social networks describes personal profiles, including skills, works, affiliation and position, et al. For this, two collaborative *groupsA* (Fig. 4(a)) and *groupsB* (Fig. 4(b)) are used to accomplish a project. Each group has 30 members, and *groupA* has 43 relations between experts, while *groupB* has only 30. In both networks, the core member is *Pieter Abbeel*. Each member can interact with those who has relationships.

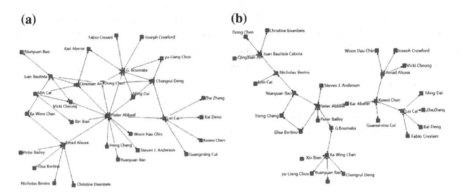

Fig. 4.   (a). Collaborative *groupA* (b). Collaborative *groupB*

5.1 Evaluation Method

The consensus quality in *groupsA* and *groupsB* are compared for the evaluation of the effect of SNA-based semantic measures on collaborative quality. As presented in [14] and [15], the consensus quality is described as follows.

Theorem 1. Let $X \in \prod(U)$, $C \in Con(U)$, and $x \in C(X)$. By the quality of consensus x in profile X, we can have the follows,

$$\hat{d}(x,X) = 1 - \frac{d(x,X)}{card(X)} \tag{13}$$

where U is a universe, $Con(U)$ is all consensus functions set for profile $\prod(U)$.

Obviously, the more collaborative quality, the more consensus quality. It can evaluate the collaboration process based on SNA and our semantic methodology.

To evaluate accuracy of the role identification, the result of identifying potential collaborative groups was compared with expert confirmation. On the basis of concept c, the feature vector of candidate expert can be calculated by Eq. (14) as following,

$$\vec{F} = (id, v) \tag{14}$$

where, id is expressed as a unique identifier for the instance in SPMO concept repertory, while v can be described as value of the instance of an expert's profile. Therefore, the accuracy of the role identification by group i is calculated by Eq. (15).

$$accuracy\left(\vec{F_i}, \vec{F_e}\right) = \frac{\sum (F_i, F_e)}{\sqrt{\sum (F_i)^2} * \sqrt{\sum (F_e)^2}} \tag{15}$$

5.2   SNA-Based Semantic Evaluation of Collaboration Process

By the Eq. (13), we can obtain the consensus quality for each collaborative group. It can be utilized to verify the SNA-based sematic evaluation of collaboration process. As shown in Fig. 5, the result of average quality of consensus improves the consensus quality in collaborative process due to the semantic concept is annotated to the attributes of participants, who leverage their human resources in social process. Where, *groupA* convergences faster and shows better consensus quality than *groupB*. Because *groupA* has greater density than *groupB*, that is, there are more ties in *groupA*. The former has more collaborative opportunities and generate more collabora-tive relations than the latter. Therefore, *groupA* has better consensus quality.

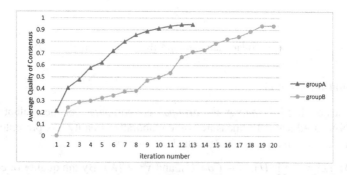

Fig. 5. Consensus quality for collaborative groups

On the other hand, we utilize the closeness centrality to assess the influence of SNA-based collaboration. As shown in Fig. 6, the nodes of *groupA* are closer to one another than those of *groupB*. The greater closeness centrality of a node, the more prestige he/she has, so the members with higher closeness centrality are more collaborative and get more support for accomplishing project.

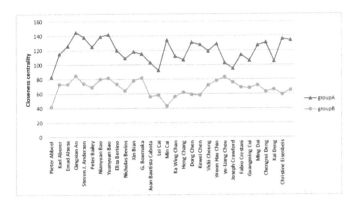

Fig. 6. Comparison of closeness centrality of *groupA* and *groupB*

5.3 Performance Evaluation in Cross-Organization Collaboration Process

To further verify efficiency and effective of our algorithm, we conduct scale experiment of the cross-organizational interaction cost evaluation and algorithm. Note that, (1) each scale experiment is executed for 20 times; (2) the size of the agent (performer) set, $m \in N, 30 \leq m \leq 500$ with steps of 20; (3) the scale $k \in N, 3 \leq k \leq 10$ randomly, and the size of the role set, $n = m/k$; (4) the limit of role that can be assigned to agent, L_a, it is from 1 to 5; and (5) the limit of role level $L_r \in [0, +\infty)$ should be normalized as follows,

$$L'_r = \frac{L_r - min\, L_r}{min\, L_r - min\, L_r} \tag{16}$$

Thus, L'_r can be limit in [0, 1]; (6) the threshold τ_0 and τ_1 are used according to ROC curve, which means the performance of prediction algorithm. Leveraging such method, τ_0 and τ_1 can be obtained. More than 7000 subjects with matching values and predicted samples, the corresponding threshold τ_0's value of each agent exactly reaches 0.65, 0.7, 0.75, 0.8, 0.85, 0.9, 0.95, and threshold τ_1's value is also obtained as follows: 0.04, 0.13, 0.17, 0.21, 0.05, 0.12, 0.23.

Interaction cost among cross-organization candidates decides the reconstructing collaborative group members for a complex project. Evaluation experiments select five tasks, compares and analyses the results of the proposed model(SRA) with Random, PuLP, ILOG. As shown in Figs. 7 and 8, Random model selects a group of candidates randomly, that travers every skill for the collaborative project. PuLP, ILOG are the Linear Programming method to find optimization solution, but the parameter and weight cannot be controlled. With the threshold τ_0 and τ_1 are continually changing, the interaction cost for collaboration in cross-organization is minimum.

The interaction cost influenced by threshold τ_0's and τ_1's variation. The value changes between 0 and 1, which affect interaction cost. Furthermore, with the cost constraint, the model will continuous change the threshold value to response to the interaction cost for the project and performers better than other methods. Shown in the Figs. 7 and 8, when $\tau_0 = 0.8$ and $\tau_0 = 0.21$, the interactive cost is minimum.

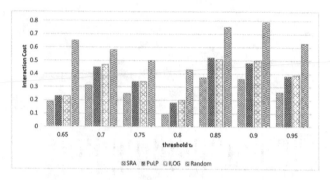

Fig. 7. Comparison of interactive cost with threshold τ_0

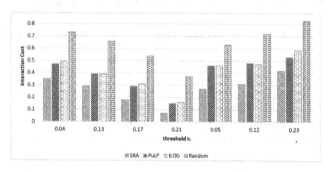

Fig. 8. Comparison of interactive cost with threshold τ_1

6 Conclusion

The paper aims to argue a semantic framework to reconstruct the socialized process for cross-organization collaboration. First, we formalize the cross-organization task assignment problem. Next, SPMO is defined for constructing semantic social process graph. Especially, we focus on organizational perspective especially the human resource, and build semantic concept architecture for the description of human profile. In addition, SNA-based collaboration criteria are discussed to measure the relations among social network members. Then, we improve the role identification method based on RBC and GRA via semantic SNA.

In future, we will perform the optimization of socialized collaboration performance in inter-group and super-group computational quality. The semantic annotation architecture for human resource needs to be improved. Other constraint logics in environment, declarative approaches, heuristics and others will also be concerned.

Acknowledgments. The paper is supported in part by the National Natural Science Foundation of China under Grant No. 61672022, Key Disciplines of Software Engineering of Shanghai Polytechnic University under Grant No. XXKZD1604, University Natural Science Foundation of Jiangsu Province under Grant No. 18KJB520008, and 13th Five-year Youth special project of Jiangsu Open University under Grant No. 17SSW-J-Q-005.

References

1. Oinas-Kukkonen, H., Lyytinen, K., Yoo, Y.: Social networks and information systems: ongoing and future research streams. J. Assoc. Inf. Syst. **11**(2), 61–68 (2010)
2. Hachicha, E., Gaaloul, W., Maamar, Z.: Social-Based Semantic Framework for Cloud Resource Management in Business Processes. In: IEEE International Conference on Services Computing, pp. 443–450 (2016)
3. Brambilla, M., Fraternali, P., Vaca Ruiz, C.K.: Combining social web and BPM for improving enterprise performances. Eval. Program Plan. **2**(1), 5–6 (2012)
4. Wang, M., Bandara, K.Y., Pahl, C.: Process as a service. In: 2010 IEEE International Conference on Services Computing, SCC 2010, pp. 578–585(2010)
5. Khlif, W., Ben-Abdallah, H.: Integrating semantics and structural information for BPMN model refactoring. In: International Conference on Computer and Information Science, pp. 656–660(2015)
6. Song, M., Van der Aalst, W.M.P.: Towards comprehensive support for organizational mining. Decis. Support Syst. **46**(1), 300–317 (2008)
7. Burattin, A., Sperduti, A., Veluscek, M.: Business models enhancement through discovery of roles. Comput. Intell. Data Min. **8174**, 103–110 (2013)
8. Mahyar, H., et al.: Identifying central nodes for information flow in social networks using compressive sensing. Soc. Netw. Anal. Min. **8**(1), 33 (2018)
9. Yongsiriwit, K., Assy, N., et al.: A semantic framework for configurable business process as a service in the cloud. J. Netw. Comput. Appl. **59**, 168–184 (2016)
10. Ranjan, R., Benatallah, B., Dustdar, S., et al.: Cloud resource orchestration programming: Overview, issues, and directions. IEEE Internet Comput. **19**(5), 46–56 (2015)
11. Kargar, M., An, A., Zihayat, M.: Efficient bi-objective team formation in social networks. Eur. Conf. Mach. Learn. Knowl. Discov. Databases **7524**, 483–498 (2012)
12. Kargar, M., Zihayat, M., An, A.: Finding affordable and collaborative teams from a network of experts. In: Proceedings of the 2013 SIAM International Conference on Data Mining (2013)
13. Zhu, H., Zhou, M.C., Alkins, R.: Group role assignment via a kuhn–munkres algorithm-based solution. IEEE Trans. Syst., Man, Cybern.-Part A: Syst. Hum. **42**(3), 739–750 (2012)
14. Nguyen, N.T.: Advanced methods for inconsistent knowledge management. Springer, London (2008). https://doi.org/10.1007/978-1-84628-889-0
15. Mcauley, J., Leskovec, J.: Learning to discover social circles in ego networks. In: International Conference on Neural Information Processing Systems, pp. 539–547 (2012)

MCPS2: Intention Maintenance of Structure Document Based MCPS Under Mobile Platform

Dan Wang[1]([✉]) [iD], Sizheng Zhu[1], Liping Gao[2], Shanshan Wang[1] [iD],
Xiaofang Xu[2], and Changqing Tao[2] [iD]

[1] Computer Center, University of Shanghai for Science and Technology,
Shanghai 200093, China
wangdandjxy@sina.com
[2] School of Optical-Electrical Computer Engineering, University of Shanghai for
Science and Technology, Shanghai 200093, China

Abstract. In order to meet the intentions of multi-user to the maximum extent possible, and enhance the meaning of collaborative works. We improve an intention maintenance algorithm called MCPS2, which based on the MCPS algorithm in the last paper. The MCPS2 algorithm uses the P2P network connection method to construct a cooperative customer network, and all cooperative clients participate in a collaborative editing according to requesting structured documents by partial replication strategy. At the same time, combined with user liveness, giving master attribute to collaborative sites, and add the Title Creator (TC) attribute to title-node, reasonable arrangements for new nodes, editing, request and other rights. Finally, we support permission transfer dynamic control mechanism to ensure the user's immediate demand.

Keywords: P2P · Partial replication architecture · Structured document
Liveness · Permissions allocation

1 Introduction

With the vigorous developing of the computer industry, promote and affect people's daily work and life, especially the emergence of the Internet, help them across the area and culture to implement online and real-time communication. In recent years, the increasingly scale of work in some industry, is difficult to handle a huge job on individual efficiently and qualitatively. Therefore, a new working mode called CSCW [1] (Computer Supported Cooperative Work) have been improved.

The appearance of CSCW significantly changes the traditional way of working, highly improves the efficiency. It supports the users to deal with the same collaborative work at the same time by using different equipment even in the different areas.

After that, multiple collaborative algorithms, systems and applications [2–5] related to CSCW be supported, and in the research and development process, also emerged a

Y. Sun et al. (Eds.): ChineseCSCW 2018, CCIS 917, pp. 20–31, 2019.
https://doi.org/10.1007/978-981-13-3044-5_2

series of conflict and consistency problems [2]. Later, researchers put forward and improved a variety of algorithms around conflict resolution and consistency mainte-nance. It is important to point out that the research of consistency maintenance mainly solves the problem of differences within documents between the collaborative users, finally confirm each collaborator holds the same copy; Conflict resolution mostly intended to maintain the intentions of every collaborative user and reflect the signifi-cance of collaborative work. At present, according to many researchers deep work, the achievements about consistency maintenance algorithms and methods is relatively mature, but there are relatively few studies involved in the intention maintenance. In one collaborative work, how to maintain the intention of each cooperative user to the maximum level is important to improve the significance of collaborative work.

In recent years, the emerge of mobile devices and the fast development of mobile terminals technology, platforms and applications in endlessly, urge the traditional collaborative applications and algorithms supporting PC side gradually transplant to mobile applications in order to adapting to the trend of technology development. The differentiation of network, storage and device with PC side in the process of trans-plantation are the key problems to be resolved urgently.

Structured documents, we can simply understand it as a context structured by text content and hierarchical organization [7]. For example, the word document editing templates that we frequently use at work, headlines, tables and pictures have strict style and hierarchy, in which the title level can clearly reflect the structure of the content in the document. Combine the structured documents with collaborative editing work, and store related context in a structured way. On the one hand, it refines the integral conflict to part conflicts, improves the efficiency of collaboration; on the other hand, we give corresponding authority to content of different levels, as much as possible to ensure all collaborative users' intention; moreover, the structured storage mode more suitable for mobile terminals to solve the shortcomings of limited storage space. Therefore, how to optimize the storage mode of the structure document at the mobile end, how to rationally design the user's editing authority, and ultimately improve the cooperation efficiency, is of great significance.

The rest parts of this paper contains: First, overview the MCPS algorithm [6], and define the document structure, node attributes, node type, and the network connection mode. Next, we present the MCPS2 algorithm and give the detail algorithm description of the initialization of documents, the mode of arbitration, the transfer of authority and so on. Then, analyze the complexity of the core algorithm and present a motivating example for implementing the MCPS2's processing mechanism, to verify its accuracy. Finally, we give the conclusion of this work and discuss future work.

2 Background Knowledge

In 1988, Sun [2] supplemented the standard of intention maintenance based on the consistency maintenance model CCI (Convergence Causality Intention) that proposed in the original dPOT [1] (distributed Operational Transformation) algorithm, emphasized the importance of collaborators' intention in a collaborative work. In terms of consistency maintenance, the most representative algorithms are roughly divided into two classes, the OT [1] (Operation Transformation) algorithm based on operation transformation and the AST [4] (Address Space Transformation) algorithm based on address space transformation. So far, many concurrency control algorithm and scheme based OT or AST derived, as GOTO [1], SCOT4 [8], ABST [9], TIBOT [10] and so on. At the same time, these two kinds of technology are widely used in the development of collaborative applications and systems, such as the distributed sketching system called SketchPad [11] supports multi user collaborative editing and the Co-CAD [12] collaborative system plunks for product design. In the aspect of intention maintenance, some conflict resolution strategies had been proposed to solve the problems appear in editing of different types of documents, like the multi version strategy [13] to solve the intention conflict of text, and the semantic conflict resolution strategy based on the two-dimensional graphics editing proposed by Ignat [14]. However, most of these studies are based on fully replication architecture [2], and rely on the state of optimism, it is necessary to ensure that the network is continuous and communication is unhindered, and the storage space is sufficient and so on. Once the scale of document becomes lager or the number of operations is rising, even the network interrupted suddenly, if we cannot provide appropriate resolved scheme, it must lead to failure of collaborative working and collaborative strategy. However, limited storage and network instability are the characteristics of mobile terminals. In response to this problem, in 2014, Huanhuan Xia [15] et al. proposed the partial replication architecture, which not only saves storage space, but also saves the update time of the copy and is more suitable for mobile terminals than the full replication architecture. Then, Sun proposed the CSOT [16] (Cloud storage Operational Transformation) in 2016, first transplanted the consistency maintenance ability of OT algorithm into the shared space of cloud storage, and achieved an ideal combination of concurrent operation and effect, which lays a foundation for the development of cloud based collaborative technology.

Based on the research of Huanhuan Xia and Sun, we put forward a conflict resolution algorithm in last article to resolve the problem of structured document collaborative editing based on the partial replication architecture in cloud platform called MCPS algorithm. We summarize several conflicts may occur in the collaborative editing of structured document, and give each of them the appropriate algorithm of resolution. Innovatively proposed two concepts of TLV (Tree liveness) and NLV (Node liveness) to solve conflicts of collaborative users' conflicts dynamically, to some extent, the intention of cooperative users maintained objectively. Nevertheless, the entire collaborative system of structured document still needs to be refined, such as how to control the user's entry and exit, as well as how to distribute the privileges of different cooperative users. In previous intention maintenance algorithms, more of them solve the conflicts by comparing priority of cooperative sites or comparing the timestamp of conflict operations or use the version control method and so on. In this paper, we modify the mode of network connection, add the attributes of title-master and site-master, give permission to all collaborators in the work. In order to realize the characteristics of the user that comes and go, we design a reasonable control mechanism of authority transferring according to the user's editing liveness in the shared document. We propose an intention maintenance algorithm of structured document based on collaborators' liveness, which is called MCPS2 algorithm.

3 Preparatory Works

3.1 Review of MCPS Algorithm

1. CIB: InsertBefore()_InsertBefore(), when the cloud server receives two operations of InsertBefore, they point to the same parent node, and the value of refId is the same.
2. CII: Insert()_Insert(), like the condition of CIB, it may get distinct results if the operations executed in different orders.
3. CD: Delete(), when a client wants to delete a title.
4. CDI: Delete()_InsertBefore(),when a delete operation is allowed, the cloud server receives a InsertBefore operation at the same time, they have a common parent node, and the refId of the deleted node is the same as the refId of the InsertBefore operation.
5. CUN: UpdateName()_UpdateName(), when the two operations change the name of the same node at the same time.
6. CUD: UpdateData()_UpdateData(), similar to CUN, when two operations want to change the text content of the same node, different executed sequence may occur conflicts.

In the Fig. 1, we give the basic definition involved in the node properties designed by the MCPS algorithm, in which the node set in the dashed box is the subtree of the StrTree. We define it as skeleton tree that the collaborative clients can request from the server. The detailed replica request policy of partial replication architecture can refer to the article [15]. In order to maintain the collaborative users' intention to the maximum extent, we propose the definitions of NLV: Node liveness and TLV: Tree liveness to record and update the editing liveness of each collaborative users at all title nodes dynamically. Once the editing conflict appearing, we judge the priority sequence of operation execution by comparing the liveness of the conflict sites. This method is more objective and fair than the previous way of judging operation order by judging the priority and timestamp of the conflict sites. This paper will improve and refine the communication mode, collaborative editing process, user permission, definition of structured document, and method of intention maintenance based on the previous MCPS algorithm, so as to improve the availability of the algorithm in the system development.

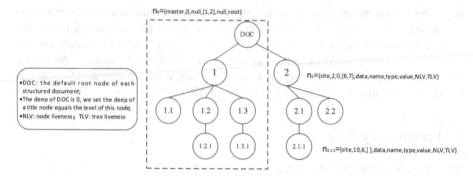

Fig. 1. A figure introduces the Structured Document Tree (StrTree) and skeleton tree.

3.2 Basic Definition

Mode of Network Connection

This article does not follow the connection mode of MCPS, instead of selecting the connection mode using P2P. We set up a master for each collaboration team. When the collaboration work begins, master is the sponsor of the collaborative editing of the structure documents. Once the master is withdrawn from the collaborative work, a new master will be selected from the collaboration team according to the membership liveness, and the detailed selection process will be given in the next design of the algorithm (Fig. 2).

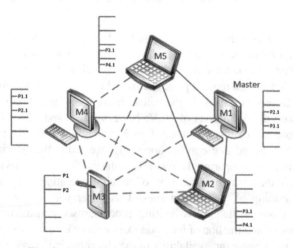

Fig. 2. The P2P connection of collaborative sites

The main work of Master is to initiate the structured document to the cooperative users at the beginning of the collaborative work, and have the authority to merge the structured documents. In this system, the combination of document is a timing triggered process, that is, requests and merges the data before the intercepting point of each cooperative user automatically after a specific time interval. If other collaborative users (is not the master) want to merge the structured document, he must post merging request to the master, the merging operation can be executed only after the master passing the request.

The Definition of Document and Node

The definition of document structure follows the definition in the MCPS algorithm. The main replica is stored as a tree structure, and the sub parent relationship in the tree represents the hierarchy of the title nodes.

The Definition of Node Types

1. Title-Root-Node: we call it TRN, as the parent node of all first class titles, stored to constructs the tree storage structure, it can be null or store the name of the structured document.
2. Title-Node: called TN, it is the request node of collaborative client.
3. Str-Parent-Node: called SPN, it is the parent node of request node of collaborative client, and the parent node doesn't be requested by collaborative client, it just maintains the tree structure of copy and doesn't contain any text content.
4. Str-Brother-Node: simply called SBN, it as the brother node of request node of collaborative client, and the brother node doesn't be requested by collaborative client, it likes Str-Parent-Node does not contain detail text content.

The Definition of Node Attributes

We add two new node attributes based on the basic definition of node attribute in the last paper:

1. CE: Current Editors Numbers, the number of collaborative users currently participating in document editing under the title node.
2. TC: Title Creator, it is in each title node to record the creator of this node, in order to be used in the process of requesting judge and combining the document.

The Definition of Operation

1. Append (N): Locally incrementally requesting data for each node's Title Creator in the node set N.
2. Delete (id, site): collaborative site delete the one node which has specify id.
3. InsertTitle (parentId, id, site, data, name): insert a new title node after the tail of child node which the parent id is parentId.

4. InsertTitleBefore (parentId, refId, id, site, data, name): insert one new node that id is id, title name is name and text content is data front of the refId which is in the child node queue of parentId.
5. UpdateName (id, newName, oldName, site): updating the oldName of node which identifier is id to newName.
6. UpdateData(id, newData, oldData, site): updating the old text content oldData of node which identifier is id to newData.

4 The MCPS2 Algorithm

4.1 The Request Node Process of Collaborative Sites

We provide a node attribute called TC (the creator of the title node) to mark the collaborative site who insert this title node. Suppose in Fig. 3, collaborative site M2 requests for editing the title node set P = [p3.1, p4.1], the TC value of title node p3.1 and p4.1 are the same as M1, so post request node to site M1, the detail operating process please refer to Algorithm 1. After receive the request node operation at site M1, determine whether the requested title node has reached the upper limit of the number of editors. If so, refuse the request, otherwise the request has to wait for the judgment of all collaborative editors of this node. And the TC has a vetoed right, if TC pass the request, the other sites in the CE has to arbitrate this request, and we give a time limit in the arbitrate process, if overtime, the site gives up the arbitrate right, judgement standard is: comparing with the sum of NLV (node liveness) at agree sites and refuse sites, the result of high node liveness is effective, in summary, more contribution higher arbitration power. The detail arbitration process refer to Algorithm 2.

Algorithm 1. RequesetNodes(P)
1.   **for** i←0 to P.length **do**
2.   request for site of P[i].TC
3.   **end for**

Algorithm 2. Arbitration(id):n /*this site is M， the node set is N */

1.   **for** i←0 to N.length **do**
2.   **if** (N[i].id==id) **then**
3.   n←N[i]
4.   **end if**
5.   **end for**
6.   **if** (n.CE.length>=MaxCE) **then**
7.   post refuse to the request site
8.   return n←null
9.   **else**
10.   **if** (site M agree)
11.   **for** (j←0 to n.CE.length) **do**
12.   Ask for arbitration from collaborative sites in n.CE[j]
13.   **if** (n.CE[j] agree) **then**
14.   NLVa←n.CE[j].NLV
15.   **else if** (n.CE[j] refuse) **then**
16.   NLVr←n.CE[j].NLV
17.   **else**
18.   j←j+1
19.   **end if**
20.   **end for**
21.   **else**
22.   post refuse to the request site
23.   return n←null
24.   **end if**
25.   **end if**
26. /*comparing of node liveness*/
27. **if** (NLVa>= NLVr) **then**
28.   n.CE.add(M)
29.   post node n to the request site
30. **else**
31.   post refuse to the request site
32.   n←null
33. **end if**
34. return n

4.2   Permission Transfer of Master

Before master withdraws, he needs to decide to transfer the master permission to which site, the basis of selection of the next master is: "In a tree structured document, the site with the highest liveness and the largest contribution will be the next master", that is, which site has the highest tree liveness TLV on the title root node DOC is selected as the next master.

Algorithm 3. masterChange(M₁ , Str): M
1.   sites←Str.DOC.CE
2.   result←-1
3.   **if** master exsit **then**
4.   **for** i←0 to sites.length **do**
5.   result←Max(result , Str.DOC.sites[i].TLV)
6.   **end for**
7.   **for** j←0 to sites.length **do**
8.   **if** (Str.DOC.sites[j].TLV==result) **then**
9.   M←sites[j]
10.   break;
11.   **end if**
12.   **end for**
13.   **end if**
14.   grant privilege to site M

5 An Example

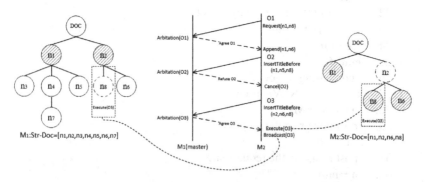

Fig. 3. The example of requesting nodes at M1 and M2

In Fig. 3 contains two collaborative sites M1 and M2, and the M1 sponsor the collaborative editing work of structured document as the master, it provide the initial copy Str-Doc = [n1, n2, n3, n4, n5, n6, n7], M1 is the creator of all nodes in Str-Doc, so the value of TC of the nodes in Str-Doc is M1. The operation O1 generated at site M1 only request to edit the title node n1 and n2, so n1.CE = [M1], n2.CE = [M1].

M2 Requests to Execute O1 = Request (n1, n6): M2 participates in the collaborative work, and request node set N = [n1, n6] from master, because the TC of n1 and n6 is M1, M1 arbitrates O1 directly, the detail arbitration process as follows:

Step 1: Determining whether the number of edited users in the CE of each of the two nodes reaches the upper limit, if not, accepting arbitration of M1, M1 agrees to send node data to M2.

Step 2: M1 agrees and request for arbitration of the site in CE of n1 and n6, because n1.CE = [M1], n6.CE = [], the arbitration is passed by default.

Step 3: After executing the step 2, M1 modifies the attributes of n1 and n6 locally, as n1.CE = [M1, M2], n6.CE = [M2].

Step 4: According to the partial replicated architecture, M1 will return the node set N' = [DOC, n1, n2, n6] to M2 in order to guarantee the tree structure of replica, and the n2 just contain the parameters of storage structure.

M2 requests to execute O2 = InsertTitleBefore(n1, n5, n8, M2, data, name): The detail execute process refer to follow steps:

Step 1: Firstly find the parent node of n5 is n1, so n1.TC = M1

Step 2: Post InsertTitleBefore request to M1

Step 3: M1 refuse the request and return the result to M2

Step 4: O2 become a waste operation

M2 requests to execute O3 = InsertTitleBefore(n2, n6, n8, M2, data, name):

Step 1: Find the parent node of n6 is n2, so n2.TC = M1

Step 2: post InsertTitleBefore request to M1

Step 3: M1 agrees and post arbitration request to other collaborative editors (the sites in n2.CE) who join in the n2 collaborative editing, that is request to M1, the arbitration is passed by default;

Step 4: O3 is executed at M1, and Str-Doc = [n1, n2, n3, n4, n5, n6, n7, n8], n8. TC = [M2], n8.CE = [M2] and update the value of NLV and TLV at these nodes, the value of NLV and TLV in changed node record as Fig. 4.

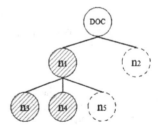

Node		DOC	n1	n2	n6
M1	NLV	0	0	0	0
	TLV	0	0	0	0
M2	NLV	0	0	0	0
	TLV	1	0	1	0

After Executing O3

M3:Str-Doc=[n1,'n2',n3,n4,'n5']

Fig. 4. The TLV and NLV of at M1 and M2

6 Conclusion and Future Work

In this paper, we support a new intention maintenance algorithm of structure document based MCPS under mobile platform called MCPS2, uses the P2P network connection mode to construct the collaborative work sites. Creatively put forward definitions of site's master and title creator. The reasonable distribution of permissions about node editing, request operation, to maximum maintain the intention of multi-user. In order to satisfy the needs of collaborators' coming and going, a dynamic control mechanism of permission transfer is given, which ultimately enhances the significance of the completely collaborative work.

The following research work includes: (1) optimize the efficiency of the algorithm, improve the permission transfer control process; (2) combine the MCPS2 algorithm with the MCPS algorithm, develop a collaborative editing APP for supporting structured document's editing work; (3) introducing the editing content of image [17, 18], form and text in the application.

Acknowledgement. We would like to thank the reviewers, whose valuable critique and comments helped to improve this paper. Moreover, this work is supported by the Innovation and entrepreneurship project of University of Shanghai for Science and Technology under Grant No. XJ2018371, National Science Foundation of China (NSFC) under Grant No. 61202376 and 61572325, Shanghai Natural Science Foundation under Grant No. 17ZR1419100, the Open Project Program of Shanghai Key Laboratory of Data Science (No. 201609060003).

References

1. Ellis, C.A., Gibbs, S.J.: Concurrency control in groupware systems. In: ACM SIGMOD Conference on Management of Data, New York, pp. 399–407 (1989)
2. Sun, C.Z., Ellis, C.: Operational transformation in real-time group editors: issue, algorithms, and achievements. In: ACM Conference on Computer Supported Cooperative Work, Seattle, pp. 59–68 (1998)
3. Shi, M., Xiang, Y., Yang, G.: The Theory and Application of Computer Supported Cooperative Work. Publishing House of Electronics Industry, Beijing (2000)
4. Gu, N., Yang, J.M., Zhang, Q.W.: Consistency maintenance based on the Mark & Retrace technique in groupware systems. In: ACM SIGGROUP Conference on Supporting Group Work, Sanibel Island, pp. 264–273 (2005)
5. Gao, L.P., Fu, Q.Q., Gao, L.L., et al.: Research on consistency maintenance of right management operations in real time collaboration environments. Int. J. Database Theory Appl. **7**(3), 255–264 (2014)
6. Wang, D., Gao, L., Zhu, S.: Research on consistency maintenance in three-stage network supporting operation re-transferring. J. Chin. Comput. Syst. **2018**(1), 128–133 (2018)
7. Wang, D., Zhu, S., Gao, L.: Conflict resolution of structured document collaborative editing based on the partial replication architecture in cloud platform. In: Chinese Conference on Computer Supported Cooperative Work and Social Computing, pp. 221–224. ACM, Chongqing (2017)
8. Vidot, N., Cart, M., Ferrie, J., et al.: Copies convergence in a distributed real-time collaborative environment. In: Computer Supported Cooperative Work, New York, pp. 171–180 (2000)

9. Shao, B., Li, D., Gu, N.: A fast operational transformation algorithm for mobile and asynchronous collaboration. IEEE Trans. Parallel Distrib. Syst. **21**(12), 1707–1720 (2010)
10. Li, R., Li, D., Sun, C.Z.: A time interval based consistency control algorithm for interactive groupware applications. In: the 10th International Conference on Parallel and Distributed Systems, Newport Beach, pp. 429–436 (2004)
11. SketchPad. http://www.dynamicgeometry.com/
12. Zheng, Y., Shen, H.F., Sun, C.Z.: Leveraging single-user AutoCAD for collaboration by transparent adaptation. In: the 13th International Conference on Computer Supported Cooperative Work in Design, pp. 78–83 (2009)
13. Sun, C., Chen, D.: Consistency maintenance in real-time collaborative graphics editing systems. ACM Trans. Comput. Hum. Interact. (TOCHI) **9**(1), 1–41 (2002)
14. Ignat, C.-L., Norrie, M.C.: Draw-together: graphical editor for collaborative drawing. In: Proceedings of the 20th Anniversary Conference on Computer Supported Cooperative Work, Canada, pp. 269–278 (2006)
15. Xia, H.H., Lu, T., Shao, B.: A partial replication approach for anywhere anytime mobile commenting. In: The CSCW 2014, Baltimore, Maryland, USA, pp. 15–19 (2014)
16. Ng, A., Sun, C.: Operational transformation for real-time synchronization of shared workspace in cloud storage. In: Proceedings of the 19th International Conference on Supporting Group Work, pp. 61–70 (2016)
17. He, F., Han, S.: A method and tool for human-human interaction and instant collaboration in CSCW-based CAD. Comput. Ind. **57**(8), 740–751 (2006)
18. Cheng, Y., He, F., Cai, X., et al.: A group undo/redo method in 3D collaborative modeling systems with performance evaluation. J. Netw. Comput. Appl. **36**(6), 1512–1522 (2013)

Research on Data Provenance Model
for Multidisciplinary Collaboration

Fangyu Yu[1,2,3], Beisi Zhou[1,2,3], Tun Lu[1,2,3(✉)], and Ning Gu[1,2,3]

[1] School of Computer Science, Fudan University, Shanghai, China
{16110240028,17210240028,lutun,ninggu}@fudan.edu.cn
[2] Shanghai Key Laboratory of Data Science, Fudan University, Shanghai, China
[3] Shanghai Institute of Intelligent Electronics and Systems, Shanghai, China

Abstract. Provenance, which can be applied to assure quality, to reinforce reliability, to track fault, and to reproduce process in the end product, refers to record the lifecycle of a piece of data or thing that accounts for its generation, transformation, manipulation, and consumption, together with an explanation of how and why it got to the present place. Recently, due to its extensive applicative domains, the provenance modeling problems have brought to attention of scientific researchers significantly. In this paper, an overview of core components regarding provenance models in existing literature is presented, with a wide width from modelling methods, model comparison, and model practice, to specified issues. In addition, a collaborative model called CollabPG, was built based on the characteristics of multidisciplinary collaboration. Finally, we discussed several issues in relevance with provenance models. This paper mainly presents an overall exploration and analysis, so that potential insights could be provided for both expert and common users to select or design a provenance-based model in arbitrary applications especially multidisciplinary collaboration.

Keywords: Provenance model · Core components · Model comparison
Model practice · Multidisciplinary collaboration

1 Introduction

Different researchers interpreted definitions for provenance from different perspective. Wherein, Davidson et al. defined provenance as the data's documentation history, which includes each of conversion process's steps for the data source [1]. Herschel et al. considered provenance as "information describing the production process of some end product" [2]. Similarly, Freire et al. quoted the provenance concepts of the Oxford English Dictionary as "its history and pedigree; the source or origin of an object; a record of the ultimate derivation and passage of an item through its various owners" [3]. Ragan et al. indicated that provenance has been be used to depict the histories and origins of various types in different ways [4]. Moreover, Uri et al. depicted that provenance is a causality graph with certain nodes and edges, elucidating the process by which an object became its current state [5]. Almeida et al. mentioned that provenance, sometimes based on scientific workflows, could be utilized to preserve

Y. Sun et al. (Eds.): ChineseCSCW 2018, CCIS 917, pp. 32–49, 2019.
https://doi.org/10.1007/978-981-13-3044-5_3

particular data's execution log history as a traceable resource [6]. Allen et al. referred provenance as the record of creation, update and activities that influence a piece of data, which aids to facilitate trust in cross-organizational collaboration [7]. In this paper, a relatively common definition of provenance is proposed, which refers to record the lifecycle of a piece of data or thing that accounts for its generation, transformation, manipulation, and consumption, together with an explanation of how and why it got to the present place.

According to diverse application scenarios, provenance is mainly categorized into four categories, containing data provenance, workflow provenance, information systems provenance, and provenance meta-data [2], with a hierarchy from most general to specific ones. In the context of workflow domains, provenance possesses three types diversely: retrospective, prospective, and evolution [8–11].

In scientific researches, provenance could be employed for several purposes. For instance, scientists and engineers track provenance information to identify its contributors, occurred time, and execution process, etc., for certain data product [12]; provenance assists us to assess, maintain and improve the quality of products [13]; provenance can be used to enhance the transparency, authenticity, and integrity of a piece of data [6, 14]; In particular, scientists expend substantial effort tracking provenance data so as to ensure the repeatability and reproducibility of production process in scientific experiments [15]; It is perhaps more significant that scientists could gain insights into the chain of reasoning facilitated to discover, analyze, and explain unexpected results [16]. In a nutshell, diverse purposes provide provenance with multiple applications.

Many scholars have tackled issues with provenance across numerous domains, such as, Medical Sciences [6], Biology [17], Biomedicine [18], Genomics [19], Geography [20], and Geoinformatics [21], which were exploited in scientific workflow [22], medical records [6], financial reports [4], supply chains [23], data exploration [1], and network diagnosis [24], etc.

As illustrated in various literature, the problem of systematically modeling [25], capturing [26], storing [27], and querying [28] provenance have attracted extensive attention of scientific researchers in a wide broad of applications. In this article, we emphatically concern provenance-modeling issues in multidisciplinary collaboration applications. The aim of this article is to provide users with potential principles and sound tradeoffs while designing or choosing their peculiar provenance model. The contributions of this work are threefold. One is that we identify critical components of the provenance model and compare diverse methodologies used in them. Secondly, we conceive a collaborative model for provenance practice in multidisciplinary collaboration. Finally, we conclude certain problems existed in current model-centric provenance researches.

We organize the rest of this paper as follows. An essential outline on comparison among existing provenance-inspired models is elucidated in Sect. 2. Section 3 designs a provenance model for multidisciplinary collaboration comprehensively. Several open-ended issues on provenance models, systems, and practice are illuminated in Sect. 4. Finally, we conclude this paper with a brief conclusion of main contributions and further work.

2 Core Components of Provenance Model: An Overview

2.1 Two Classical Model Specifications

In current literature, various researchers have proposed different provenance models and relevant solutions in their respective fields. However, differences between those models make it arduous to understand the expressiveness of provenance representations, access and utilize provenance unimpededly, especially exchange information between provenance-enabled systems. Against this background, the scientific community began to emerge a consensus on provenance standardization in 2007, thus releasing and revising the open provenance model (OPM) [29] to resolve provenance-related challenges and issues. Subsequently, furtherly inspired by OPM, another conceptual model named PROV-DM [30] was endorsed by the World Wide Web consortium (W3C) in 2013, which provided well-established concepts and definitions to achieve information's interchangeable interoperability in heterogeneous contexts.

In OPM, three types and their dependencies are constituted, as shown in Fig. 1(a). Wherein, Artifact represents an immutable object during process execution, which can be expressed in physical carrier (such as device), or digital representation (such as data). Process can be considered as a range of actions to act on artifacts, and thus new artifacts may be entailed. As a contextual entity, Agent could enable, facilitate, control, and influence the execution of processes. In terms of causal relationships, one artifact, being triggered by the other, can be used or generated by a process, which may be triggered by another process, under the control of one or more agents. Similarly, PROV-DM contains core types and their relationships, forming the essence of provenance information. As depicted in Fig. 1(b), there are three element types and seven relationships. Hereinto, we consider an Entity, either real or imaginary, as something with certain fixed aspects that can be physical, digital, or conceptual. Activity performs upon or with entities during a period, and it may include generating, transforming, modifying, processing, and consuming entities. Agent is responsible for an activity's happening, the existence of an entity, or the activities of other agents.

2.2 Characteristic Comparison Among Existing Models

The OPM and PROV-DM have been currently regarded as fundamental model specifications. Despite all this, the provenance models have the variation tendency with applications and user requirements in practical usage. Instead of recreating the wheel, numerous researchers have exploited and even extended either OPM or PROV-DM to build their unified provenance model. In this section, we identify relevant studies on existing provenance models, intended to illuminate potential principle of provenance-oriented models for users, so that they could obtain insight into making informed decisions while designing or selecting a provenance model.

Review Method. In our study, an explicit strategy for literature search and selection was adopted to explore existing research works. Next, we would elaborate it gradually.

Search Strategy. First, we framed the research question (RQ) to explore focused aspects of existing provenance models, which aims at facilitating users to gain

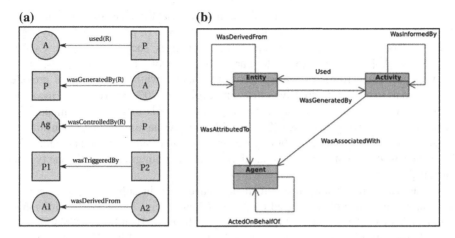

Fig. 1. (a) The OPM core composition [29], (b) The PROV-DM core composition [30]

comprehensive perspectives about the provenance-based model's principles. Further, we identified relevant studies (RS). Wherein, six databases were searched altogether in the search scope (SS): (1) IEEExplore; (2) ACM Digital Library; (3) Scopus; (4) Springer Database; (5) ScienceDirect; (6) CNKI. Based on Title, Abstract, or Keywords match, the search string (SS) was ("provenance model" OR "lineage model" OR "derivation model" OR "pedigree model") in English. Likewise, the Chinese search string was ("起源模型" OR "溯源模型" OR "世系模型"). In the filtering criteria (FC), articles pertaining to provenance model were included, and articles in the form of abstracts, summary of workshops, or systematic reviews only were excluded. We mainly surveyed outcomes of literatures between January 2014 and January 2018.

Study Selection. Initially, we obtained 608 articles from six databases via matching search strings in titles, abstracts, or keywords. Second, duplicated works (93) were excluded, with 515 articles remained. Third, we performed screenings of abstract relevance to remove 456 articles. At this point, 59 articles remained. Fourth, we reviewed the remaining articles, focusing especially on excluding those that were not related to provenance model. That is, articles (38) with no evidence of implementation, such clear statement, enforcement method, and model analysis, were removed. At this step, 21 articles remained. Finally, we used an inductive codification methodology to further analyze all full-text articles, excluding articles that were not suitable for classification. Each article used the predefined categories, including specification, type, domain, purpose, etc. As a result, 20 articles were selected totally for subsequent analyses.

Comparative Results of the Search. As depicted in Table 1, twenty provenance models are mainly surveyed. We can see from nine properties that most models [11, 31–47] utilize or extend PROV (57%) or OPM (33%), which consider their respective field features, with only rare percentages (nearly 10%) of these are built proprietarily [48] or based on other standards, such as RWS (Read-Write-Reset) [49]. In terms of element types, these are all the models pertaining to workflow (25%) or data provenance (75%). That is to say, those models usually own specific modeling structure with certain domain, specialize on particular type of process, and apply high-level instrumentations such as structured query languages, such as SQL [50], Cypher [51], SPARQL [52], ProQL [53], etc. Particularly, in workflow-based models, all of them support some forms of retrospective provenance, whilst few of those provide related means to collect prospective (40%) and evolution (20%) provenance. However, recent literature has revealed that researchers turn towards extensions to models for capturing prospective provenance [36, 50–52], and few have proposed extensions to integrate retrospective, and evolution provenance both in design-time and run-time [11, 54]. Whereas, it is pointed that the transition is not sharp but gradient from one type to another [9].

Additionally, provenance-inspired models have been in applied various applications, under the usage of diversified purposes. Wherein, Fig. 2 indicates a wide range of domains, of which the most frequent are Biomedicine or Healthcare (20%) [32, 34, 36, 46], Security-related (15%) [33, 41, 45], Data Analysis (15%) [39, 42, 43], and Web-based (15%) [40, 47, 48], together with Domain-Agnostic (10%) and Collaboration (10%) areas [31, 36]. As shown in Fig. 3, the purpose of existing models includes Data Quality (nearly 21%), Replication (nearly 21%), Recall (nearly 18%), Data Security (nearly 15%), and Presentation (nearly 15%) dominantly.

Moreover, almost all models support compatibility (75%) and interoperability (90%), in which scalability (20%) are rarely carried. Amongst those traits, compatibility is evaluated based on its coincidence degree with these standards. For a model-enabled system with good scalability, it has the capacity to manipulate large amounts of provenance at back-end [55] and front-end [56], respectively. Interoperability is the ability to exchange provenance information within multiple systems [15, 29, 30, 54], and it is measured basically whether it is in accordance with these standards or not in this paper.

Finally, the result shows that there are three types of publications, in which large percent (75%) of them were published as conferences, 20% as journals, and one Ph.D. thesis (5%) was also covered. There is evidence that the numbers of publications remained relatively increasing (267%) from 2014 to 2017.

Be noted that, those selected models are not intended to be complete but to induce certain insight in model properties and construction for reference only, which may not cover or represent all-encompassing situations in current literature.

Discussion and Analysis. Due to space constraints, other provenance-oriented models are not enumerated in this article. However, we can probably draw three conclusions from existing literature that: (1) the majority models are core and extension of OPM or PROV-DM standards, which have been applied in a broad spectrum of domains such as biomedicine or healthcare, data analyses, web-based, security-related areas, etc., with diverse purposes of data quality, replication, recall, data security, presentation, etc. (2) almost all of available models emphasize on their compatibility, scalability, and interoperability, in which information exchange amongst systems receive attention in emerging researches. (3) existing models are mostly focused on specific discipline, whose ingredients are related to structured provenance information, with a lack of researches on unstructured collaboration especially interdisciplinary collaboration.

Table 1. Characteristic dimensions of existing provenance models (the check "$\checkmark$" denotes a clear statement, whilst the star "*" indicates no explicit expression in related full-text article)

No.	Name	Specification	Type				Domain	Purpose	Compatibility	Scalability	Interoperability	Publication	Year
			Workflow provenance		Evolution provenance	Data provenance							
			Prospective provenance	Retrospective provenance									
1	Interaction PM [33]	PROV				$\checkmark$	Service-Oriented Security	Data Security (Security Concerns, Secure Interaction)	$\checkmark$	*	$\checkmark$	Journal	2017
2	HyperFlow [49]	RWS		$\checkmark$			Workflow Programing	Data manipulations; Replication; Recall	*	*	$\checkmark$	Journal	2016
3	CRIM [36]	OPM	$\checkmark$	$\checkmark$			Biomedical Domain	Understandability; Replication; Presentation	*	$\checkmark$	$\checkmark$	Journal	2014
4	Uniform PM [11]	PROV	$\checkmark$	$\checkmark$	$\checkmark$		Domain-Agnostic	Replication; Presentation	$\checkmark$	*	$\checkmark$	Conference	2017
5	GeoPROV-LM [37]	PROV		$\checkmark$			Land Administration	Data Quality; Data Security (Access Control)	$\checkmark$	*	$\checkmark$	Conference	2015
6	SimP [38]	OPM & PROV				$\checkmark$	Scientific Data Management	Replication; Data Quality (Creditability)	$\checkmark$	*	$\checkmark$	Conference	2016
7	DPM [39]	OPM				$\checkmark$	Time Series Analysis; Data Preprocessing	Data manipulations; Replication; Recall	$\checkmark$	*	$\checkmark$	Conference	2014
8	Sensor Web-based PM [40]	PROV				$\checkmark$	Sensor Web	Data Quality (Usability, Reliability); Presentation	*	*	$\checkmark$	Conference	2017
9	Bioprov [34]	PROV				$\checkmark$	Biodiversity Datasets	Presentation	$\checkmark$	*	$\checkmark$	Conference	2015
10	PBAC [41]	OPM				$\checkmark$	Securing Provenance	Data Security (Access Authorization)	*	*	$\checkmark$	Conference	2015
11	CoHeal [32]	OPM				$\checkmark$	Healthcare Management	Data Quality	$\checkmark$	$\checkmark$	$\checkmark$	Conference	2017
12	Associated PM [42]	PROV				$\checkmark$	Statistical Analyses; Data Journalism; Scientific Research	Replication	$\checkmark$	*	$\checkmark$	Conference	2017
13	Data Point (DP) [48]	*				$\checkmark$	Internet of Things (IoT)	Data Quality (Trustworthiness, Dependability; Data Security	*	*	*	Conference	2017
14	Quantified Self Ontology [43]	PROV	.			$\checkmark$	Quantified Self	Data Quality (Trustworthiness); Data Security; Presentation	$\checkmark$	*	$\checkmark$	Conference	2016

(continued)

Table 1. (*continued*)

No.	Name	Specification	Type				Domain	Purpose	Compatibility	Scalability	Interoperability	Publication	Year
			Workflow provenance			Data provenance							
			Prospective provenance	Retrospective provenance	Evolution provenance								
15	CDPM [35]	OPM				√	Collaboration Design Process	Recall (Process Analysis)	√	*	√	Conference	2015
16	Data Supply Chain Model [44]	PROV				√	Domain-Agnostic	Recall (Process Analysis)	√	√	√	Conference	2015
17	HACCP [45]	PROV		√			Food-Safety Monitoring	Recall (Process Analysis, Process Inferring)	√	*	*	Conference	2016
18	ProvCaRe [46]	PROV				√	Biomedical Domain; Healthcare Domain	Replication; Reproducibility	√	√	√	Conference	2017
19	ROV-Model [47]	PROV				√	Social Media (Weibo)	Data Quality (Trustworthiness)	√	*	√	Journal	2017
20	CPM [31]	OPM				√	Biosciences Collaboration	Understandability: Recall (Process Analysis)	√	*	√	Phd.Thesis	2014

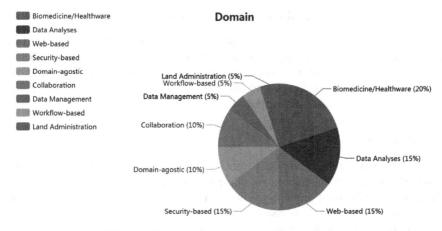

Fig. 2. Domains of existing provenance models

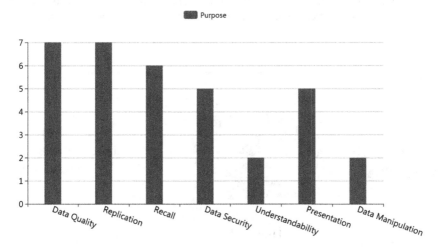

Fig. 3. Purposes of existing provenance models

3   A Collaborative Provenance Model for Multidisciplinary Applications

In the field of multidisciplinary collaboration, it is requisite that multiple researchers from different disciplines, such as physics, chemistry, computer, medicine, etc., complete creative and intellectual labor together by means of exchanging and sharing various resources. In this section, we summarize specific characteristics of multidisciplinary collaboration, and design a provenance model to record collaborative process and its associated data evolution for research collaboration across disciplines. On this basis, we also concisely evaluate the proposed model's effectiveness.

3.1 Multidisciplinary Collaboration Characteristics

Here, four features are identified by categorizing varying collaboration patterns, complex team composition, different communication schema, and dynamic collaborative process, and each of them is ever-changing in collaboration process. All those characteristics enable it challenging to design one provenance-base model that could depict the process of human interaction and data evolution wholly.

3.2 Typical Scenario

For ease of exposition in a review paper such as this, we simplified the actual scenario of multidisciplinary collaboration. As illustrated in Fig. 4, the multidisciplinary collaboration is a process of problem-solving to work together towards a common goal, via exchanging and sharing diverse resources such as hardware devices, system software, and information technologies among cross-disciplinary researchers, during which relevant scientific data would be generated, transformed, modified and consumed continually by those collaborators. Overall, this kind of collaboration consists two sub-processes, i.e., human interaction and data evolution, whose influence acts upon each other.

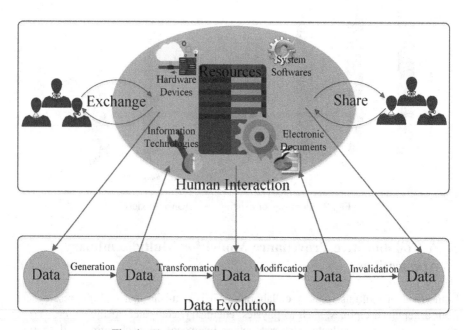

Fig. 4. The multidisciplinary collaboration scenario

3.3   A Collaborative Provenance Model: CollabPG

Based on PROV-DM [30], we further extend our collaborative provenance model, which constitutes two kinds of information: components and dependencies. In this method, we utilize a directed acyclic graph CollabPG(R, A, RE, RU, E) to collect associated provenance information, in which R, A, RE, RU are vertex sets in triple expression and E are edge sets. As shown in Fig. 5, we give an example of this model. Here, Resources (R) is expressed in yellow ovals, Activities (A) in blue rectangles, Researchers (RE) in orange pentagons, and Rules (RU) in green circles. The attributes of each element are shown in gray. In two blue cloud-patterned scopes, we can observe scientific collaboration among multidisciplinary researchers under various rules. The Black scope reveals data evolution process, including its generation, transformation, and modification.

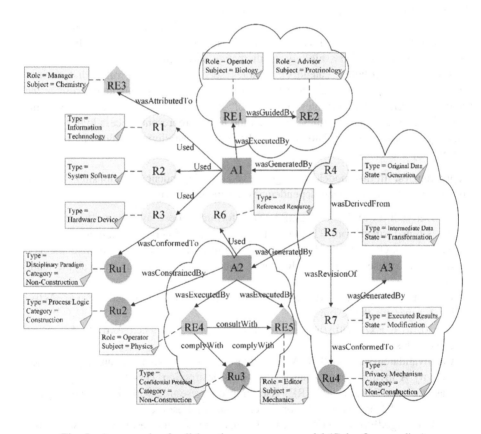

Fig. 5. An example of collaborative provenance model (Color figure online)

Components. There are four element types, including:

Resource(rid, attributes, state): denotes multiple resources that can be any physical, digital, or conceptual artifacts with certain utility values, where rid is a unique identifier. Attributes are sets of attribute-pairs representing fixed aspects of this resource, such as the type attribute, which contains information resource (hardware devices, information technologies, system software, etc.) and scientific data (referenced resource, intermediate data, executed results, etc.) that may be collected in electronic documents. State is the resource's lifecycle phase, including generation, transformation, modification, and invalidation. The generated resource begins to be utilized, and is no longer available for use after invalidation.

Activity(aid, attributes, timeRange): refers to the collaborative activity, acting upon or with resources, which happens during a period of time. Wherein, aid is the unique identifier, and attributes are sets of attribute-pairs, such as the type attribute. Besides, the timeRange, written by [startTime, endTime], denotes the time interval (includes the beginning and end time) that an activity occurs.

Researcher (reid, attributes, subject): denotes scientific researchers responsible for the occurrence of an activity, or certain resource's existence. Wherein, reid is the unique identifier, attributes are sets of attribute-pairs such as the type attribute, which contains role, level, etc., and subject is the discipline that one researcher belongs to, such as physics, chemistry, biology, mathematics, mechanics, etc.

Rule (ruid, attributes, category): denotes sets of restriction rules that various resources, activities, or researchers have to obey. Amongst of all items, ruid is the unique identifier, and attributes are sets of attribute-pairs. The category contains structured and unstructured rules, in which the former represent process logics such as causality and concurrency. The latter are disciplinary paradigm, confidential protocol, and privacy mechanism.

Dependencies. In this model, the edge E expresses dependency relationships between above vertices. Here, sixteen dependencies are included primarily:

wasDerivedFrom(r2, r1) $\in$ R2xR1: Transforming one resource into another, i.e., R2 is transformed from R1, together with changes of certain attributes.

wasRevisionOf(r2, r1) $\in$ R2xR1: Modifying from the resource to a newest one, i.e., R2 is the revised version of R1, only minor values being updated at the same attributes.

wasGeneratedBy(r, a) $\in$ RxA: Producing one resource by an activity, i.e., Activity A generates the resource R.

Used(r, a) $\in$ RxA: Utilizing one resource by an activity, i.e., Activity A uses an existing resource R.

wasInvalidatedBy(r, a) $\in$ RxA: Invalidating the resource by an activity, i.e., Activity A invalids an existing R, due to its destruction, cessation, or expiry.

wasAttributedTo(r, re) $\in$ RxRE: Ascribing one resource with the researcher, i.e., Researcher RE is responsible for the existence of Resource R.

wasExchangedBy(a2, a1) $\in$ A2xA1: Exchanging specific resources by two activities, i.e., Activity A2 uses some resources generated by Activity A1.

wasExecutedBy(a, re) $\in$ AxRE: Executing an activity by the researcher, i.e., Researcher RE plays a role in Activity A.

dependOn(re2, re1) $\in$ RE2xRE1: Researcher RE2's outcome depends on importing contributions of RE1.

consultWith(re2, re1) ∈ RE2xRE1: Researcher RE2 carries out activities together with RE1 via joint supervision, consultation, and decision-making.

wasGuidedBy(re2, re1) ∈ RE2xRE1: Researcher RE2 directly acts on activities under the guidance of RE1.

wasConformedTo(r, ru) ∈ RxRU: Conforming one resource to certain rule, i.e., Resource R conforms to the Rule RU, such as disciplinary paradigm.

wasConstrainedBy(a, ru) ∈ AxRU: Restricting an activity to certain rule, i.e., Activity A was constrained by Rule RU, such process logic.

complyWith(re, ru) ∈ RExRU: Complying researcher's behavior with certain rule, i.e., Researcher RE complies with Rule RU, such as confidential protocol.

exclusiveWith(ru2, ru1) ∈ RU2xRU1: Rule RU2 and RU1 is mutually exclusive.

Precede(ru2, ru1) ∈ RU2xRU1: Rule RU2 have priority over RU1, whatever they are exclusive or not.

3.4 Evaluation of the CollabPG Model

Here, we mainly focus three evaluation criteria on our model, which contains compatibility, scalability, and interoperability.

The PROV-DM [30] defines some conceptual standards, such as information collection, storage methods, and query technologies, aiming to achieve the goal of exchanging information between heterogeneous systems. The proposed CollabPG model has the compatibility with it. Wherein, the resource, activity, and researcher have similar functionality to entity, activity, and agents in PROV-DM. Considering such factors as privacy, sensitivity, and control-flow of provenance information, we add the element of rule and related dependencies in our model. The relationships, such as wasExchangedBy and wasExecutedBy, correspond to wasInformedBy and wasAssociatedWith, while dependOn, consultWith, and wasGuidedBy can be viewed as extends of actedOnBehalfOf. Through the analysis above, we can build a mapping from the collaborative provenance model to the PROV-DM, so that our model ensures its compatibility, which supports exchanging information with other provenance-enabled models. Specially, collaboration characteristics have been reflected explicitly in our model, whose comparison with PROV-DM is shown concretely in Table 2.

Besides, it can be observed that our model has the interoperability to support exchange information amongst multiple systems, due to its accordance with the PROV-DM standard. Moreover, we would pursue good scalability in subsequent model-based system design as well.

4 Challenges and Opportunities on Provenance Model in Multidisciplinary Collaboration

After surveying the state of the art, this section would concern specific research issues on the balance between models, systems, and practice in provenance exploration of multidisciplinary collaboration. We would introduce each of them separately.

Table 2. Comparison of collaborative provenance model with PROV-DM

		CollabPG	PROV-DM
Ingredients	Basic elements	Resource	Entity
		Activity	Activity
		Researcher	Agent
	Extended element	Rule	–
Dependencies	Data-evolution-related relationships	wasDerivedFrom	wasDerivedFrom
		wasRevisionOf	wasRevisionOf
		wasGeneratedBy	wasGeneratedBy
		Used	Used
		wasInvalidatedBy	wasInvalidatedBy
	Basic relationships	wasAttributedTo	wasAttributedTo
		wasExchangedBy	wasInformedBy
		wasExecutedBy	wasAssociatedWith
	Collaborative relationships	dependOn	actedOnBehalfOf
		consultWith	actedOnBehalfOf
		wasGuidedBy	actedOnBehalfOf
	Rule-based relationships	wasConformedTo	–
		wasConstrainedBy	–
		complyWith	–
		exclusiveWith	–
		Precede	–

Trade-Off Between Core Principles and Extension Requirements for Provenance-Bound Models. Concerning the core criteria of a provenance model to be quality-guaranteed, several researchers have summarized related criteria for evaluating the quality of models. Examples include Completeness, Correctness, Clarity, Consistency, Simplicity and Comprehensibility. That is, the model should contain all ingredients of the domain that are relevant, conformed to the syntax of modeling language together with authentic and correct information. Moreover, the statements in the model are not uncontested, contradictory, and redundant. Lastly, the model should be effortless to be understood by its users and developers. Meanwhile, it may be inevitable to adjust provenance via extending original components of models to satisfy specific needs in practical applications. Under this circumstance, qualified requirements such as compatibility, scalability, and interoperability, could enhance the capacities of models. Therefore, it is anticipant that core and extension in provenance models are considered comprehensively in the future approach.

Trade-Off Between General Models and Specific Systems. On one hand, a desired model is versatilely used, domain-agnostic, loosely-coupled with systems, and supports interoperability and interchange among systems as well. On the other hand, no any model is likely to be self-contained and represent all provenance-inspired systems. Sometimes, the representativeness of one model is more imperative than its completeness. In practical exploration, the model should be integrated with specific application system. For instance, there is a correlation between provenance models and capture systems, in which the information granularity of models mobilizes diverse grained-level systems to be adopted. However, we have to take integration efforts, provenance granularity, false positives, and analysis scope into count in terms of choosing appropriate capture methods and systems [26]. Specifically, the granularity of capture encounters provenance costs, i.e., fine-grained capturing approaches aggravate the issues of information overload, performance influence, and memory workload. Therefore, we should pertinently select coarse-grained, fine-grained, or hybrid-enabled systems based on actual models and scenarios.

Trade-Off Between Privacy and Utility of Information in Provenance Model. Several studies have indicated that attentions with provenance-centric disclosure are linked to issues of security and privacy concerns [16, 22], due to part of provenance's sensitivity and confidentiality, particularly for individual interaction from different disciplines in collaborative environments. When it comes to security, researchers exploit diverse access control strategies, such as authentication, authorization, and sandboxing, aiming to pinpoint which view of provenance that particular users can access. As elucidated in existing literature, customized techniques, including sanitization, abstraction, obscuring, and redaction, are employed to render an abstracted overview of provenance by omitting sensitive pieces of its information. However, those pruning methods inevitably yields varying degree of utility loss for provenance usage, which may pose possibly undesirable side-effects while exploring provenance details. As a consequence, it remains to be explored to consider double-side factors about balancing an appropriate threshold of confidentiality protection and utility preservation in provenance information. More specifically, we could reveal partial provenance to targeted users varying with their ownership roles, trust levels, and access privileges. At the same time, fractional information could be concealed according to its sensitive attributes, privacy requirements, and application propensity.

In the domain of multidisciplinary collaboration, challenges mentioned above involve only some issues of models, whose proposals may be applicable to arbitrary applications as well. In provenance practice, one important point is that choice of what model-based solution is most appropriate depends on different needs.

5 Conclusion and Future Work

In this paper, we revealed underlying overview that constitute core components of provenance model, such as, model specification, characteristic comparison, and model analysis. We conceived a collaborative model with multi-faceted factors in multidisciplinary applications, designed to depict cross-disciplinary scientists' collaboration process through exchanging and sharing diverse resources, together with its associated provenance data evolution. We summarized fundamental issues in existing provenance models to facilitate the understanding of model dimensions and construction. A recapitulative research in this article was designed to facilitate to make reasonable decisions about which model-based provenance solution to choose for both domain experts and common users in interdisciplinary applications.

In the future research, we intend to further explore dependency path calculations, tracking mechanisms, storage methods, query technologies, and access visualization of provenance applied in multidisciplinary applications, combined with their collaborative characteristics and attributes.

Acknowledgment. This work was supported by the Joint Fund of National Natural Science Foundation of China and the China Academy of Engineering Physics (NSAF) under Grant No. U1630115, and the National Key Research and Development Program of China under Grant No. 2018YFC0381402.

References

1. Davidson, S.B., Freire, J.: Provenance and scientific workflows: challenges and opportunities. In: Proceedings of the 2008 ACM SIGMOD International Conference on Management of Data, pp. 1345–1350. ACM, London (2008)
2. Herschel, M., Hlawatsch, M.: Provenance: on and behind the screens. In: Proceedings of the 2016 International Conference on Management of Data, pp. 2213–2217. ACM, London (2016)
3. Freire, J., Koop, D., Santos, E., Silva, C.T.: Provenance for computational tasks: a survey. Comput. Sci. Eng. **10**(3), 11–21 (2008)
4. Ragan, E.D., Endert, A., Sanyal, J., Chen, J.: Characterizing provenance in visualization and data analysis: an organizational framework of provenance types and purposes. IEEE Trans. Vis. Comput. Graph. **22**(1), 31–40 (2016)
5. Braun, U., Shinnar, A., Seltzer, M.: Securing provenance. In: Proceedings of the 3rd Conference on Hot Topics in Security, p. 4. USENIX Association (2008)
6. Almeida, F.N., Tunes, G., da Costa, J.C.B., Sabino, E.C., Junior, A.M., Ferreira, J.E.: A provenance model based on declarative specifications for intensive data analyses in hemotherapy information systems. Future Gener. Comput. Syst. **59**, 105–113 (2016)
7. Allen, M.D., Chapman, A., Seligman, L., Blaustein B.: Provenance for collaboration: detecting suspicious behaviors and assessing trust in information. In: International Conference on Collaborative Computing: Networking, Applications and Worksharing, pp. 342–351. IEEE, Washington (2012)
8. Zafar, F., et al.: Trustworthy data: a survey, taxonomy and future trends of secure provenance schemes. J. Netw. Comput. Appl. **94**, 50–68 (2017)
9. Herschel, M., Diestelkämper, R., Lahmar, H.B.: A survey on provenance: what for? What form? What from? VLDB J. **5**, 1–26 (2017)
10. Pimentel, J.F., Freire, J., Braganholo, V., Murta, L.: Tracking and analyzing the evolution of provenance from scripts. International Provenance and Annotation Workshop (2016)
11. Duan, X., et al.: Linking design-time and run-time: a graph-based uniform workflow provenance model. In: IEEE International Conference on Web Services, pp. 97–105. IEEE, Washington (2017)
12. Cheney, J., Chiticariu, L., Tan, W.C.: Provenance in databases: why, how, and where. Found Trends Databases **1**(4), 379–474 (2009)
13. Ross, S.: Digital preservation, archival science and methodological foundations for digital libraries. New Rev. Inf. Netw. **17**(1), 43–68 (2012)
14. Boose, E.R., Ellison, A.M., Osterweil, L.J., Clarke, L.A., Podorozhny, R., Hadley, J.L., Wise, A.E., Foster, D.R.: Ensuring reliable datasets for environmental models and forecasts. Ecol. Inform. **2**(3), 237–247 (2007)

15. Groth, P., Moreau, L.: PROV-overview: an overview of the PROV family of documents (2013)
16. Bachour, K., Wetzel, R., Flintham, M., Huynh, T.D., Rodden, T., Moreau, L.: Provenance for the people: an HCI perspective on the W3C PROV standard through an online game. In: Proceedings of the 33rd Annual ACM Conference on Human Factors in Computing Systems, pp. 2437–2446. ACM, London (2015)
17. Zhao, J., Miles, A., Klyne, G., Shotton, D.: Provenance and linked data in biological data webs. Brief. Bioinform. **10**(2), 139–152 (2008)
18. Masseroli, M., Canakoglu, A., Ceri, S.: Integration and querying of genomic and proteomic semantic annotations for biomedical knowledge extraction. IEEE/ACM Trans. Comput. Biol. Bioinf. **13**(2), 209–219 (2016)
19. Ocaña, K.A., Silva, V., De Oliveira, D., Mattoso, M.: Data analytics in bioinformatics: data science in practice for genomics analysis workflows. In: IEEE International Conference on e-Science, pp. 322–331. IEEE, Washington (2015)
20. Zhao, H., Zhang, S., Zhang, Z.: Relationship between multi-element composition in tea leaves and in provenance soils for geographical traceability. Food Control **76**, 82–87 (2015)
21. Yue, P., He, L.: Geospatial data provenance in cyberinfrastructure. In: 2009 17th International Conference on Geoinformatics, pp. 1–4. IEEE, Washington (2009)
22. Holten Møller, N.L., Bjørn, P., Villumsen, J.C., Hancock, T.C.H., Aritake, T., Tani, S.: Data tracking in search of workflows. In: The ACM Conference on Computer-Supported Cooperative Work and Social Computing. ACM, New York (2017)
23. Li, P., Wu, T.Y., Li, X.M., Luo, H., Obaidat, M.S.: Constructing data supply chain based on layered PROV. J. Supercomput. **73**(4), 1509–1531 (2016)
24. Chen, A., Wu, Y., Haeberlen, A., Zhou, W., Loo, B.T.: The good, the bad, and the differences: better network diagnostics with differential provenance. In: Conference on ACM SIGCOMM 2016 Conference, pp. 115–128. ACM, New York (2016)
25. Bowers, S., McPhillips, T., Ludäscher, B., Cohen, S., Davidson, Susan B.: A model for user-oriented data provenance in pipelined scientific workflows. In: Moreau, L., Foster, I. (eds.) IPAW 2006. LNCS, vol. 4145, pp. 133–147. Springer, Heidelberg (2006). https://doi.org/10.1007/11890850_15
26. Stamatogiannakis, M., et al.: Trade-offs in automatic provenance capture. In: Mattoso, M., Glavic, B. (eds.) IPAW 2016. LNCS, vol. 9672, pp. 29–41. Springer, Cham (2016). https://doi.org/10.1007/978-3-319-40593-3_3
27. https://www.w3.org/TR/2013/REC-prov-o-20130430/
28. Wylot, M., Cudremauroux, P., Hauswirth, M., Groth, P.: Storing, tracking, and querying provenance in linked data. IEEE Trans. Knowl. Data Eng. **29**, 1751–1764 (2017)
29. Moreau, L., et al.: The open provenance model core specification (v1.1). Fut. Gener. Comput. Syst. **27**(6), 743–756 (2011)
30. Missier, P., Belhajjame, K., Cheney, J.: The W3C PROV family of specifications for modelling provenance metadata. In: Proceedings of EDBT, pp. 773–776 (2013)
31. Huang, X.: Research on biology collaboration: scientific software sharing, selection and recommendation. Ph.D. thesis, Fudan University (2014) (in Chinese)
32. Sun, Y., Lu, T., Gu, N.: A method of electronic health data quality assessment: enabling data provenance. In: Proceedings of CSCWD 2017. IEEE, Washington, pp. 233–238 (2017)
33. Hasan, R., Khan, R.: Unified authentication factors and fuzzy service access using interaction provenance. Comput. Secur. **67**, 211–231 (2017)
34. Amanqui, F.K., et al.: A model of provenance applied to biodiversity datasets. In: 2016 IEEE 25th International Conference on Enabling Technologies: Infrastructure for Collaborative Enterprises (WETICE), pp. 235–240. IEEE, Washington (2016)

35. Sun, X., Gao, X., Kang, H., Li, C.: A data provenance model for collaboration design process. In: International Conference on Information Sciences, Machinery, Materials and Energy (2015)
36. Curcin, V., Miles, S., Danger, R., Chen, Y., Bache, R., Taweel, A.: Implementing interoperable provenance in biomedical research. Future Gener. Comput. Syst. **34**, 1–16 (2014)
37. Sadiq, M.A., West, G., McMeekin, D.A., Arnold, L., Moncrieff, S.: Provenance ontology model for land administration spatial data supply chains. In: International Conference on Innovations in Information Technology, pp. 184–189. IEEE, Washington (2016)
38. Jabal A A., Bertino E.: SimP: secure interoperable multi-granular provenance framework. In: International Conference on E-Science, pp. 270–275. IEEE (2017)
39. De Souza, L., Vaz, M.S.M.G., Sunye, M.S.: Modular development of ontologies for provenance in detrending time series. In: International Conference on Information Technology: New Generations, pp. 567–572. IEEE Computer Society, Washington (2014)
40. Jiang, L., Kuhn, W., Yue, P.: An interoperable approach for Sensor Web provenance. In: International Conference on Agro-Geoinformatics, pp. 1–6 (2017)
41. Mohy, N.N., Mokhtar, H.M.O., El-Sharkawi, M.E.: Delegation enabled provenance-based access control model. In: Science and Information Conference, pp. 1374–1379. IEEE, Washington (2015)
42. Trinh, T.D., et al.: Linked data processing provenance: towards transparent and reusable linked data integration. In: The International Conference, pp. 88–96 (2017)
43. Schreiber, A.: A provenance model for quantified self data. In: International Conference on Human–Computer Interaction (2016)
44. Lan, J., Liu, X., Luo, H., Li, P.: Study of constructing data supply chain based on PROV. In: Wang, Yu., Xiong, H., Argamon, S., Li, X., Li, J. (eds.) BigCom 2015. LNCS, vol. 9196, pp. 69–78. Springer, Cham (2015). https://doi.org/10.1007/978-3-319-22047-5_6
45. Markovic, M., Edwards, P., Kollingbaum, M., Rowe, A.: Modelling provenance of sensor data for food safety compliance checking. In: Mattoso, M., Glavic, B. (eds.) IPAW 2016. LNCS, vol. 9672, pp. 134–145. Springer, Cham (2016). https://doi.org/10.1007/978-3-319-40593-3_11
46. Valdez, J., Rueschman, M., Kim, M., Arabyarmohammadi, S., Redline, S., Sahoo, S.S.: An extensible ontology modeling approach using post coordinated expressions for semantic provenance in biomedical research. In: Panetto, H., et al. (eds.) On the Move to Meaningful Internet Systems, OTM 2017 Conferences, OTM 2017. LNCS, vol. 10574. Springer, Cham (2017). https://doi.org/10.1007/978-3-319-69459-7_23
47. Zhang, Z., Dong, H., Tan, C., Yi, Y.: Evaluation of Weibo credibility based on data provenance. In: Application Research of Computers (2017) **(in Chinese)**
48. Olufowobi, H., Engel, R., Baracaldo, N., Bathen, Luis Angel D., Tata, S., Ludwig, H.: Data provenance model for Internet of Things (IoT) systems. In: Drira, K., et al. (eds.) ICSOC 2016. LNCS, vol. 10380, pp. 85–91. Springer, Cham (2017). https://doi.org/10.1007/978-3-319-68136-8_8
49. Balis, B.: HyperFlow: a model of computation, programming approach and enactment engine for complex distributed workflows. Future Gener. Comput. Syst. **55**, 147–162 (2016)
50. Barga, R.S., Digiampietri, L.A.: Automatic capture and efficient storage of eScience experiment provenance. Concurr. Comput. Pract. Exp. **20**(5), 419–429 (2008)
51. https://neo4j.com/developer/cypher-query-language/
52. https://www.w3.org/TR/rdf-sparql-query/
53. Karvounarakis, G., Ives, Z.G., Tannen, V.: Querying data provenance. In: ACM Conference on the Management of Data (SIGMOD), pp. 951–962 (2010)

54. Bowers, S., McPhillips, T., Riddle, S., Anand, M.K., Ludäscher, B.: Kepler/pPOD: scientific workflow and provenance support for assembling the tree of life. In: Freire, J., Koop, D., Moreau, L. (eds.) IPAW 2008. LNCS, vol. 5272, pp. 70–77. Springer, Heidelberg (2008). https://doi.org/10.1007/978-3-540-89965-5_9
55. Akoush, S., Sohan, R., Hopper, A.: HadoopProv: towards provenance as a first class citizen in MapReduce. In: Usenix Workshop on the Theory and Practice of Provenance. USENIX Association (2013)
56. Deutch, D., Gilad, A., Moskovitch, Y.: selP: selective tracking and presentation of data provenance. In: International Conference on Data Engineering, pp. 1484–1487. IEEE, Washington (2015)

Mobile Agent-Based Mobile Intelligent Business Security Transaction Model

Wei-Jin Jiang[1,2,3](✉), Jia-Hui Chen[1](✉), Yu-Hui Xu[1](✉),
and Yang Wang[1](✉)

[1] Institute of Big Data and Internet Innovation, Mobile E-Business Collaborative
Innovation Center of Hunan Province, Hunan University of Commerce,
Changsha 410205, China
jlwxjh@163.com, 18508488203@163.com, 810663304@qq.com,
363168449@qq.com
[2] Key Laboratory of Hunan Province for New Retail Virtual Reality
Technology, Hunan University of Commerce, Changsha 410205, China
[3] School of Computer Science and Technology,
Wuhan University of Technology, Wuhan 430073, China

Abstract. The flexibility and convenience of mobile commerce is more in line
with the needs of e-commerce in the new era, but it also brings a series of unique
security issues in the mobile environment. The serious information asymmetry
between the two sides of the transaction creates more opportunities for fraud.
This has caused consumers to lose trust in the mobile commerce market. The
phenomenon of mobile commerce fraud and lack of trust has become one of the
main factors hindering the development of mobile commerce. The paper proposes a dynamic trust computing model which is based on mobile agent, which
realizes the qualitative and quantitative conversion of trust. To stop malicious
users from credit hype and deception, a special attribute evaluation method and
trust punishment method are proposed. The new user trust degree assignment
method has been improved, and a method of dynamically setting the initial trust
degree of new users based on the minimum trust degree of the previous system
is proposed, which resists the ruin behavior of abandoning the reputation data at
random. By adopting the transaction evaluation system and weights. The system
introduces a multi-factor mechanism. The model better reflects the influence of
subjective factors such as individual preference and risk attitude on trust calculation, and enhances the sensitivity of trust algorithm in trading individual
attributes. Detailed theoretical analysis and a large number of simulation
experiments verify the mechanism can solve the problem of trust computing in
mobile network transactions.

Keywords: Mobil internet · Mobil commerce · Dynamic trust model
Mobil system (MAS)

1 Introduction

In pace with the development of mobile Internet (Mobil Internet (MI) technology and
applications, MI-based mobile e-commerce (M-Commerce) is booming in the late years.
Also, mobile Internet promotes sharing of consumption model, intellectualization of

© Springer Nature Singapore Pte Ltd. 2019
Y. Sun et al. (Eds.): ChineseCSCW 2018, CCIS 917, pp. 50–65, 2019.
https://doi.org/10.1007/978-981-13-3044-5_4

equipment and diversification of scene. Mobile commerce is growing far faster than traditional e-commerce. According to the 41st "China Internet development statistics report", the number of Internet users in China has reached 750 million, the Internet penetration rate has reached 53.2%, and the number of mobile phone users reached 695 million, accounting for 95.1% by the end of December 2017. Mobile phone online payment users grows rapidly, reaching 489 million, and offline mobile payment habits have been formed. 50.3% of netizens use mobile phone to pay and settle their accounts when shopping at a store. The number of online booking users for special bus is 168 million, the number of online booking for air, hotel and train tickets has reached 594 million, and the number of online group-buying users is also close to 200 million. The number of online payment users is has increased at an annual rate of 46.1%., and the number of online stock transactions has increased by nearly 48.8%. It can be said that the center of mobile Internet has shifted from "wide" to "deep" [1], and various mobile applications have penetrated into every corner of people's lives, and become a new engine to stimulate the growth of "Internet +" network economy and the transformation and upgrading of new market. However, the rapid development of anything is accompanied by unforeseen problems and unpredictable potential risks [2]. The security problem of mobile commerce is gradually emerging with the development of mobile commerce. According to the China electronic commerce complaints and the rights of the public service platform statistics [3], Complaints about national e-commerce services through various forms such as mail, micro-blog, WeChat and so on. are received in the second half of 2017, which are increased by 2.18% in the second half of 2016. On the New Year's day of 2018, a woman in Changsha was tricked into buying a 100-yuan snack online for 80,000 yuan after receiving a "post-sale refund" phone call and being asked to provide alipay information. Compared with the electronic commerce security mechanism under the traditional Internet environment, most of the functions are virtualized because the mobile network is not the real name authentication, and has the topology change, the discrete uncertainty, the information anonymity and the asymmetry. There are also problems such as wireless eavesdropping, identification, mobile payment, etc., so its security and reliability are relatively low, making mobile traders have no sense of security and trust between each other [5].

More and more people pay attention to the trust mechanism of mobile commerce. In this regard, many scholars in the related fields have put forward a trust model. The model is based upon the corresponding theory which is aimed at settleing many problems existing in the trust computing approach and promote the smooth progress of the mobile business online transactions. At present, the existing C2C website mainly adopts the method of accumulation or average value, but this calculation model does not take into consideration the number of transactions into consideration, the degree of trust between the two parties, so it is easily affected by the malicious bad behavior of the evaluation party [6]. These are the existing problems as follows. First, when modeling and evaluating trust relationship, the factors of evidence change in the interaction process are not fully considered, resulting in insufficient ability of the model to dynamically perceive evidence changes. Second, most of the models adopt a simple evaluation strategy, which only evaluates the success of the service provided by the user. It does not consider the characteristics of trust multi-dimensionality. And, it can not comprehensively and personally evaluate trust, and lacks a multi-dimensional evaluation mechanism for service quality. After n times of convergence, all users who successfully provide services have the same degree of trust, resulting in lower accuracy of user trust calculation. Third, trust is context dependent and transactions are subject to location and time constraints. Therefore, user reputation feedback generated in different trading environments can not be treated equally. Fourth, Trust mapping, transaction context factors will affect consumers' perception of transaction risk, and then affect the value of different contextual feedback. Thus, solving context trust mapping will be more reasonable for trust evaluation. Fifth, existing models can only identify and protect against simple attacks and deceptive behaviors, but it lacks effective identification and protection mechanisms for complex and concealed cheating behaviors such as spy attacks, collusion group attacks and strategic attacks, leading to poor security and robust of the model. Therefore, the process is more complex, and the security of mobile transaction is more severe and more difficult to solve [3].

In view of the above shortcomings, based on the long-term research on trust management, the paper presents a dynamic trust computing model which is based upon mobile (service) business transaction (mobile interactive service), and integrate transaction context factor and trust mapping mechanism to evaluate seller trust. A dynamic trust computing mould is proposed to realize the qualitative and quantitative conversion of trust. A special attribute evaluation method and a trust punishment method are proposed to prevent malicious users from credit hype and deception. This paper raises an approach to dynamically set the initial trust of new users based on the minimum trust degree of the previous system. Besides, it averts the behavior of abandoning the credit message at will.

2 Related Work

Trust relationship is a complex social relationship, which is abstract and difficult to quantify. Without trust, the relationship between participants in social activities is difficult to identify and maintain. At the same time, the uncertainty and variability of trust relationships make it difficult to model, manage, and maintain trust [7]. The main task of trust modeling is to measure trust relationship and to construct computing engine. In recent years, domestic and foreign scholars have carried out trust modeling suitable for various application fields from the perspectives of inaccuracy theory such as average model, Bayes theory, fuzzy logic, subjective logic, cloud model, evidence theory, interval number theory and intuitionistic fuzzy theory. Such research has laid a solid theoretical foundation for the development of trust management.

At the end of the twentieth century, the concept of network trust emerged. It was first proposed by Marsh. For the trust and cooperation problems in the subject, some basic attributes of trust were defined by formal symbols. The trust metric algorithm based on linear equations lays the foundation for the application of trust model in the computer field [8]. Subsequently, references [9, 10] proposed trust management as an important part of information system in the study of communication system security issues, and proposed the basic concept of trust management, which demonstrated the relationship between trust behavior and trust through a simple language. The relationship and the trust management mechanism are introduced into the distributed system, and the first generation trust management system PolicyMaker is constructed for the authority allocation and management in the distributed system. They use some special formal symbols to give a definition of the trust-related attributes in the subject. In the process of its definition, a linear algorithm that can quantitatively analyze trust is given.

The traditional trust model treats a single transaction as a whole, and only gives a single evaluation value for the transaction itself. The trust model established by Griffiths [11] is more diversified than before, considering many factors. Combining these factors, the related task assignment is carried out. The model he established is mainly aimed at different requirements of the services provided by different users in a single transaction, and the related solutions are given. Considering the different proportions of different factors in this system and the user's satisfaction with the success or failure of the transaction, related expenses, trust quality, trust time, etc. In addition, it analyzes the characteristics that trust may decrease with time, making the establishment of the model easy to implement and practical. However, the shortcoming is that the model does not consider the recommendation trust into the trust system.

Reference [12] proposed that the mobile P2P network trust model introduces the distance factor and recommendation factor to control the impact of indirect trust and improve the accuracy of recommendation trust. Reference [13] proposed the multi-granularity trust model in the mobile environment by using the concept of clustering and time factor to effectively resist the deception of malicious nodes. Reference [14] proposed a dynamic security trust model DSTM_MP2P in a mobile network environment. The model considers the case where the node trust information is known or unknown, and improves the success rate of resource download. Reference [15] proposed the trust model Mob Trust of the mobile network by using the message forwarding capability of the node. The model introduces the K bucket theory and stores the evaluation data forwarded by the node in the K bucket, which expands the storage range of the evaluation data. Reference [16] proposed the MT-RBAC access control framework, which implements the access control mechanism of mobile networks based on spatial context, trust constraints and resource control strategies. The above mobile network trust model considers the difference between the mobile network and the network in different aspects, and improves the transaction success rate of the mobile network to some extent.

Reference [17] proposed a method of reputation measurement and trust evaluation. This method comprehensively considers six factors such as evaluation satisfaction, positive feedback ratio, feedback credibility, transaction amount, time decay and party length. The collusion node and the malicious node are identified with the honest node. However, the credibility of the feedback measured by the trust of the party has limitations. In order to evaluate trust more accurately and prevent trust deception, Reference [17] proposed a trusted service selection algorithm based on preference recommendation. The algorithm first searches for a group of recommended users with similar preferences, then uses the Pearson correlation coefficient to calculate the user's evaluation similarity and domain relevance, and combines the user's recommendation level to filter the user's recommendation information, which will be more accurate and more in line with the user's personality. The information is highlighted, not submerged in useless and inaccurate recommendation information, so that users can get the recommendation information they want, so as to better solve the problem that the recommendation information is not recognized by the user.

Although the above models partially solve the problems of modeling and evaluation of trust in different contexts, and propose trust assessment models, evaluation ways or evaluation mechanisms, the models have lots of shortcomings. For example, due to the randomness, fuzziness and unpredictability of trust in the complex network environment, depicting it accurately is not a easy thing. In most of the cases, however, models describe and measure the trust relationship between entities by using classical mathematical theories (such as probability theory, fuzzy theory). Therefore, the models are not perfect in terms of trust (reasonable) expression, trust measurement (theory), etc. It is hard to find an effective solution to the impact of bad recommendation on trust assessment. It can not reflect the personality characteristics of different entities in the evaluation of trust due to lack of flexible trust evaluation mechanism. Moreover, as the number of e-commerce transaction entities continues to increase, the time complexity and spatial complexity of trust calculations will increase exponentially. How to reduce the time and space complexity of trust calculation and guarantee the real-time, dynamic and accuracy of trust calculation is the key to the further practical application of trust metrics. At present, the reputation based trust evaluation mechanism of large e-commerce websites (such as eBay Jingdong and Taobao) is relatively simple, just through the reputation evaluation results given by each buyer after a transaction is completed by the seller. It does not take into account the support of social relations networks, such as friends, friends, colleagues, neighbors, communities, and the role of reputation (Word-of-Mouth). Sellers are not excluded from fraud by registering multiple buyers' accounts, making multiple purchases and giving themselves high reputation ratings, so the seller's total credit evaluation results are less credible.

In view of the above problems, the paper draws on the existing research study, combines the author's research results in the literature [17], and introduces some attributes of social trust into the virtual e-commerce environment by using the mobile commerce in the complex mobile Internet environment as the research background. By analyzing the factors of trust influence and trading mechanism in the mobile network environment, the paper pays attention to the essential connotation of the trust relationship network under the mobile business environment. Besides, a cooperative computing theory is introduced, and a dynamic trust model based on MAS co operation for complex mobile network environment is proposed. A set of trust model and secure transaction mechanism for mobile e-commerce is established, which reduces the time complexity and space complexity of trust calculation and increases the accuracy and practicability of trust evaluation.

3   MAS Trust Model for Mobile Network Transaction

3.1   The Trust and Credibility of the Mobile Agent Business System

In the field of P2P, Web services, cloud computing, e-commerce, mobile commerce, Internet of Things, autonomic computing, collaborative computing, trust is the basis of cooperation. If there is no trust, there is basically no possibility of cooperation. Since an

Agent-based computing and modeling method is the natural computing model of these systems, their research on trust can usually be carried out in the perspective and perspective of multi-agent system (MAS) [18].

The definition of trust and reputation is as follows:

Definition 1. (Trust [19]) In the context of mobile commerce, trust assessment users (Agent$_e$) are trusted to infer Agent$_p$ from their own reasoning judgment and some relevant experience accumulated before. Hence we can see the subjective view of Agent. Generally speaking, trust is a judgmental belief of the trustee on the ability and reliability of the trusted person. Trust includes many connotations. Trust relationship is an important basis for the choice of Agent partners.

Definition 2. (Reputation [20]) Under the condition of mobile commerce, it is not based on his own point of view, but the trust gained after processing the views of other agents.

Definition 3. (Trust degree [21]) The trustworthy customer (Agent$_c$) quantifies the trust degree of the merchant (Agent$_p$).

Definition 4. (Trust management [22]) The main meaning of this concept is to complete the trust and reputation of the entire cooperation in the modern open network. Finally, the results of these processes are archived, protected and transmitted to each other. At the same time, it is guaranteed that at the same time, it is guaranteed that in the case of an interactive agent, mutual trust communication can be carried out or a recommendation for related trust can be made without an interactive agent.

The key task in the trust management system is to build a dynamic trust model [23]. The role of this model is to calculate the degree of trust between the participants in real time, and to obtain their potential trust. The model ultimately rely on these results for reference and decision making. For the premise of an open dynamic environment, in this case, some relevant researchers will use mathematical modeling or some related tools to conduct corresponding research. And these mathematical models need to be described by the ultimate trust. In response to the open dynamic environment, some related researchers have established their own trust models based on a variety of methods and tools. These models use the various elements in the quantitative trust relationship to characterize the trust.

3.2 Mobile Business Transaction Dynamic Trust Computing Model (CFBCDT)

The trust value of a user u at a certain time t is calculated by:

$$\tau_t(u) = \begin{cases} \alpha\tau_{t-1}(u) + \beta \cdot \bar{f}(x,u) \cdot e^{\sum_{k \in N(u)} w[p(x,u)] \cdot Cr[\tau_{t-1}(x)] \cdot \rho(t_x,t)} & , \quad N(u) \neq 0 \\ \tau_{t-1}(u), & \quad N(u) = 0 \end{cases} \quad (1)$$

$N(u)$ represents a set that is bought and sold with user u when it is in the interval $[t-1, t]$. $\tau_{t-1}(u)$ indicates the trust of user u at $t-1$. For $\forall x \in N(u)$, $\tau_{t-1}(x)$ indicates the trust of use x at $t-1$. $W[p(x, u)]$ is the weight function of the transaction value:

$$w[p(x, u)] = \frac{p(x, u)}{200} \tag{2}$$

In the above functions, $p(x, u)$ is a function for x and u, two independent variables. Specifically, it refers to the corresponding transaction value. Among the provisions of this transaction value, 200 is the downline of the specified transaction value, and is also the lowest price. Such value must be subject to the corresponding specific provisions on insurance claims. For the minimum educational value of this regulation, each company has its own set of relevant operational rules. For example, the eBay service only targets customers who have a transaction value of more than \$200, and eBay has its own regulations. That is to meet the 100 US dollars before the corresponding transaction. According to such regulations, the relevant agencies have conducted a period of investigation report published in the "China Online Transaction Research Report", which indicates that the average transaction in China meets eBay's service requirements.

$Cr[\tau_{t-1}(x)]$ represents the weight of x, indicating the credibility of x. $t_x \in [t-1, t]$ indicates the time when the user x and u conduct the transaction. $\rho\ (t_x, t)$ is a time discount function, which represents the time weight of the reputation feedback evaluation score. When the tx is closer to t, the weight of the reputation feedback evaluation score given by the user agent x to the user agent u is higher.

$$\rho(t_x, t) = \rho^{t-t_x}, \quad 0 < \rho < 1, \text{ (where } \rho \text{ is the time weighting factor)} \tag{3}$$

After the transaction is completed, Agent x's average reputation feedback score for Agent u can be represented by $\bar{f}(x, u)$

$$\bar{f}(x, u) = \frac{\sum\limits_{i=1}^{|C|} \omega_{ci} f_{ci}(x, u)}{\sum\limits_{i=1}^{|C|} \omega_{c_i}} c_i \tag{4}$$

Among them, $|C|$ is the number of the key factors of reputation (such as the quality or price of the traded item). $f_{c_i}(x, u)$ is the credit feedback evaluation of the agent Agent x in the case of a certain credit factor ci to another party Agent u. $f(x, u) = (f_{c_1}(x, u), f_{c_2}(x, u), \ldots, (x, u))$ is an n-dimensional vector under the condition of c_1, $c_2, \ldots, c_n$, that is, $f(x, u)$ is the credit feedback evaluation given by x to u after the transaction with u. $f_{c_i}(v, u) \in [-1, 1]$. $\omega_{c_i} \in [0, 1]$ is the weight value of ci, indicating the general goodwill of each participating trader Agent to ci.

α indicates the trust degree in the recent period. β represents the credit rating feedback given by $X \in N(u)$ that has traded with u.

We use a collaborative filtering-based approach to calculate the weight of users' trust. The specific implementation process is as follows. First, Agent u trades separately with its trading partners, then Agent u and Agent x deal with the trading partner at the same time. Compare the two transaction records and see the difference in scores to evaluate the weight $Cr[\tau_t(x)]$ of the trust value of the rating user Agent x.

Assume that Agent u is the target user, the score is Agent x. Let N(u) be the set of partners in the Agent u trading process, and N(X) be the set of trading partners of the Rating User Agent x, *CN(X, u)* a collection of partners who trade with both at the same time. The key problem is how to score the reputation. The feature of this score is that it is not a simple one-dimensional vector problem, but a lot of dimensions, which causes certain difficulties in the calculation. A solution to this problem is the cosine angle. This method solves a certain degree of similarity problem in the rating of credit feedback.

The cosine angle method is used to solve the similarity of the vector x and y, which is expressed as follows.

$$sim(x,y) = \cos(\bar{x}, \bar{y}) = \frac{\bar{x} \cdot \bar{y}}{\|\bar{x}\| \cdot \|\bar{y}\|} = \frac{\sum x_j y_j}{\sqrt{[\sum x_j]^2 \cdot [\sum y_j]^2}} \tag{5}$$

Assuming that Agent u and Agent x are known, the trust value weight of Agent x is calculated and updated as:

$$Cr(\tau_t(x)) = sim(x, u) = \frac{\sum_{k \in CN(x,u)} \cos[f(x,k), f(u,k)]}{|CN(x,u)|}$$

$$= \frac{\sum_{k \in CN(x,u)} \frac{\sum_{i=1}^{|c|} f_{c_i}(x,k) \cdot f_{c_i}(u,k)}{\sqrt{\left[\sum_{i=1}^{|C|} f_{c_i}(x,k)\right]^2 \left[\sum_{i=1}^{|C|} f_{c_i}(u,k)\right]^2}}}{|CN(x,u)|} \tag{6}$$

Where $|CN(x, u)$ is the number of common transaction partners for Agent u and Agent x. $k \in CN(x, u)$is a common trader of Agent u and Agent x. $f(x, k)$ and $f(u, k)$ are the reputation feedback evaluation (vector) of Agent x and Agent u for common traders based on reputation key factors. The closer the evaluation scores of Agent x and Agent u are, the greater the weight $Cr[\tau_t(x)]$ of the trust value $\tau_t(x)$ of the rating user Agent x is. The trust calculation method based on collaborative filtering can not only calculate the weight of the scorer x (Agente) trust degree, but also calculate the score similarity of the scorer x (Agente), the graded U (Agentp), which can better reduce or eliminate the negative effects of credibility and fraud. The scorer x (Agente) is a conspiracy participant, that is, x (Agente) only gives positive reputation evaluation to the gang members and negative or even malicious reputation evaluation to other trader (agent).

3.3   Dynamic Setting Method of Initial Trust Degree

With the rapid development of mobile Internet, a problem that often arises is the evaluation of online reputation, which is a very important and necessary step for new users to determine the trust value of their credibility first when they first use the network. There are two situations here. The first is that the user trust is higher than or equal to the initial trust, so that the user can continue to use the original information. The second is that the user trust is lower than the initial trust degree. The user can only abandon the original account, unless it is re-registered. In fact, the advantage of this is to prevent users from negatively affecting the reputation evaluation after multiple transactions, to supervise the reputation of each user, and to ensure that the Internet maintains a trust and harmony in the whole process of use.

In this regard, we propose a method to dynamically set the initial trust of new users. The calculation process is as follows.

After the new user u registers and logs in at t time, the initial trust degree is specifically expressed as:

$$\tau_t(u) = \min(\tau_{t-1}) - \frac{1}{\theta}\Phi[\min(\tau_{t-1})] \tag{7}$$

Among them, $\min(\tau_{t-1})$ is the minimum trust in the system at $t-1$. θ indicates the number of traders with a degree of trust $\min(\tau_{t-1})$. Damping function is

$$\Phi[\min(\tau_{t-1})] = 1 - \frac{1}{1 + e^{-\frac{[\min(\tau_{t-1})(i) - \max(\tau_t)]}{\sigma}}}$$

The advantage of this method is to crack down on the corrupt moral behavior that undermines the reputation, effectively guaranteeing the credibility of the network. It solves many trust problems that new models do not solve in trust models, and prevents them from taking advantage of this opportunity to conduct large-scale fraud.

3.4   The Method of Trust Punishment

Assume that a user has recently failed due to bad intentions, so that punishment should be severely punished to ensure the stability and security of the entire environment. Of course, the strength of the punishment will be related to the amount of the transaction. Do not blindly. The specific basis can be based on the comparison of the amount with the historical average, and the difference is very large, so that the greater the possibility of potential fraud, the greater the degree of punishment for such malicious behavior. According to research, the new punishment system is the degree to which the existing trust value is reduced by one penalty to achieve the punishment. The details are as follows.

$$\tau_t(i) = \tau_0 - (R_i^{\max} - R_i^{\min}) \times \left(1 - \frac{\sigma}{10}\right) \tag{8}$$

Among them, τ_0, τ_t is the representative of the trust value before and after the punishment. $R_i^{\min}$ and $R_i^{\max}$ are their minimum values, respectively. σ is the grade score of the transaction amount, which can be calculated according to formula (9). Let a certain attribute have a total of W evaluation levels, wherein the evaluation score interval of the i-th level is $[R_i^{\min}, R_i^{\max}]$, $R_i^{\min}$, $R_i^{\max}$ is its minimum maximum value, and the evaluation score value σ of the interval is:

$$\sigma = R_i^{\min} + \theta \times (R_i^{\max} - R_i^{\min}) \tag{9}$$

In formula (9), when $i \geq W/2$, θ is the weighted percentage of the entity above the I level; when i < W/2, θ is lower than its weighted percentage.

For example, the following can be divided into three different levels of criteria, which are described in terms of bad, medium, and good. They correspond to three different intervals of [0, 4], [4, 7], and [7, 10]. Just as the user has 100 evaluations, the number of these three regions is 30, 40 and 30 respectively. There is a rule that the weight of the evaluation is 1, and the above is all the prerequisites for the evaluation. The scores obtained by calculating these basic conditions against the correlation of Eq. (9) are 2.9, 5.5, and 7.3, respectively. Through this series of problems, the qualitative to quantitative conversion is realized.

The adoption of this new method has brought about a change in the entity evaluation. This change is converted from the previous fixed evaluation to non-fixed. The occurrence of this change is reasonable. There is a case in which the trust level is the same, but different trust values will appear after the corresponding calculation. The essence is that the users who get the high score value get a high evaluation value, which is directly proportional.

4   Simulation Experiments and Performance Analysis

4.1   Simulation Environment and Experimental Steps

In order to simulate the real mobile business environment as far as possible, we configure the client and local server, the Internet server space of China Wan network, and use NetLogo network simulation software to simulate the mobile communication environment and scene. Taobao trust accumulation and averaging, E-FIRE model [22], Travos model were selected, and they were simulated with our online transaction trust model (CFBCDT). The experimental results were compared with the average mean square error which is regarded as the standard.

In the whole simulation environment system, different users constitute a complete transaction scenario. These include an $Agent_c$, 10 scoring Agente and 41 merchants ($Agent_p$). Among these so-called scoring users, it is composed of honesty and malicious users, while malicious users include lying, random noises, defamation and reputation exaggeration.

Assume that the Pi of 41 merchants (the probability of conducting an honest trade) obeys a uniform distribution in the interval [0, 1], and is set to [0, 0.025, 0.05, ..., 0.975, 1] respectively. Assuming that the estimated probability is $\widehat{P}_i$, the mean square deviation can be calculated to measure the performance and effectiveness of the trust model (Np is the number of merchants).

$$\Phi = \frac{1}{N_p} \sum_{i=1}^{N_p} (P_i - \widehat{P}_i)^2 \qquad (10)$$

The execution steps of the simulation system are as follows.

(1) The system randomly selects a pair of scoring users $Agent_e$ to interact with the merchant $Agent_p$ for $41 \times 10 \times 20 = 8200$ times, that is, the average each rating user $Agent_e$ interacts 20 times with each merchant Agentp to produce the interactive history of the rating user $Agent_e$ and the merchant $Agent_p$, initializing the cyclic variable i = 1.

(2) Each scorer $Agent_e$ submits its own evaluation of each merchant Agentp to the user $Agent_c$.

(3) Scoring user $Agent_e$ constructs a query that responds to user $Agent_c$ based on its interaction history data with merchant $Agent_p$.

(4) Based on the received evaluation, the user $Agent_c$ estimates the reputation value of each merchant $Agent_p$ according to a malicious behavior prevention method.

(5) The system obtains the average mean square error Φi of the estimate according to Eq. (42).

(6) User $Agent_c$ interacts with each merchant $Agent_p$ once and saves the interaction result i++.

(7) If i < 41, enter step (2).

(8) At the end, the output is Φi.

The running cycle of each experiment is generally twenty times. The average value of these twenty data is calculated as the basis of evaluation and measurement.

The experiment is split into two conditions. The first case focuses on the prevention performance of the system in a good faith environment (scoring user $Agent_e$ is all honest) and a malicious environment (50% evaluation user $Agent_e$ takes malicious behavior). In the second case, all the scoring users $Agent_e$ take bad behavior, and a user $Agent_c$ will add its own direct experience when calculating the merchant's reputation. This case is mainly to compare the robustness of the trust model in special cases.

4.2   Performance Test of Reputation System for Malicious Behavior When Credit Environment or Probability is 0.5

It can be seen from Fig. 1 that if 10 $Agent_e$ akes honest fair responsible behavior, the Taobao system will consider all $Agent_e$ to be completely honest and trustworthy. There will be no introduction errors, which can be regarded as the theoretical optimal value. Square error is also minimal. In the paper, the average mean square deviation curve of the trust computing model system is basically coincided with the Taobao. It can be seen that this model does not have any effect on the fair trader $Agent_c$, but the recognition rate of the dishonest maliciously scorer $Agent_e$ is very high. For the Travos trust computing system, when the number of transactions between $Agent_c$ and $Agent_p$ is not much, because it can't judge whether Agente is trustworthy, the Travos system has filtered most of the $Agent_e$'s evaluation. Of course, with the increasing frequency of $Agent_c$ and $Agent_p$ transactions, the effect of this error filtering problem will gradually decrease. Until more than 20 times, the problem will basically disappear (Table 1).

Table 1. The number of Agent$_e$ users in each experiment in case 1.

The type of rating user Agent$_e$	Number of rating users Agent$_e$				
	1	2	3	4	5
Fair	10	5	5	5	5
Lying	0	5	0	0	0
Noisy	0	0	5	0	0
Badmouthing	0	0	0	5	0
Bragging	0	0	0	0	5

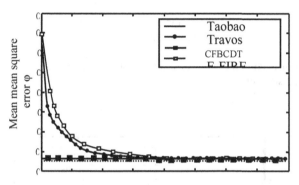

The number of transaction times between user
Agent$_c$ and merchant Agent$_p$

Fig. 1. Impact of trust model on fair scorer

Figures 2, 3, 4 and 5 compares the corresponding filtering and prevention effects for different user types. It can be seen from the diagram that the biggest difference is the Taobao (Taobao) system. Therefore, once a malicious Agent$_e$ is encountered, it will affect the trust model system to make an effective evaluation of its credibility. The trust calculation model established in this paper has the same practicability as Travos and E-FIRE.

When the historical transaction between Agent$_c$ and Agent$_p$ reaches a certain number of transactions, the corresponding filtering effect will be better. The number of transactions is generally 30 to 40 times. However, the average mean square error of the trust system in this paper is generally much smaller than that of the Travos and E-FIRE trust systems. The Travos trust system is less effective against the attack of the noisy user Agent$_e$. When the number of historical interactions between Agent$_c$ and Agent$_p$ is not much N (1–10 times), the mean square error of Taobao and this model is significantly lower than that of Travos. E-FIRE is close to Travos. For online transactions, this comparison is more practical because of the small number of historical transactions between buyers and sellers in the actual environment.

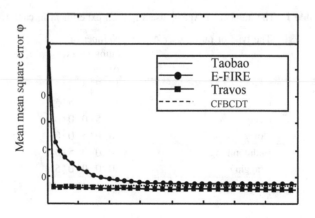

The number of transaction times between user
Agent$_c$ and merchant Agent$_p$

Fig. 2. Comparison of the preventive performance of 50% of the scorers Agent$_e$ taking the opposite of the real situation

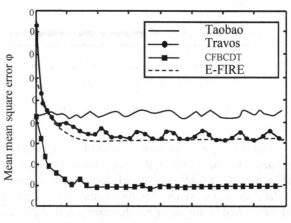

The number of transaction times between user
Agent$_c$ and merchant Agent$_p$

Fig. 3. Comparison of the preventive performance of randomness (noisy) malicious behavior of 50% of the scorers Agent$_e$

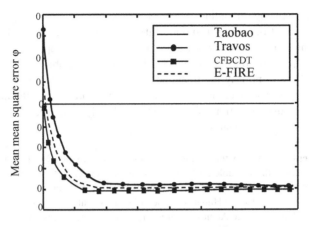

Fig. 4. Comparison of the preventive performance of 50% scoring user $Agent_e$ adopting badmouthing malicious behavior

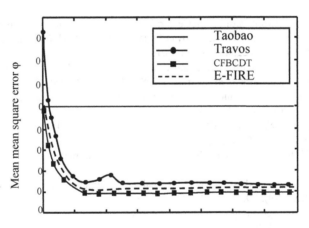

Fig. 5. Comparison of the prevention performance of reputation fraud (bragging) malicious behavior of the 50% scoring user $Agent_e$

5 Conclusions and Further Work

In the open and transparent mobile business environment, building and perfecting the trust reputation evaluation system between entities is an effective way to solve the transaction security means under the large data environment. This paper is based on many problems existing in online transaction trust management, especially for the current dynamic trust modeling in mobile Internet transactions. A flexible trust transaction management method based on multi-agent system is proposed.

The next step is to consider using cloud theory and mobile agent collaborative filtering technology to portray the dynamic attributes and reputation of trust. In addition, a global trust fusion computing method with more flexibility and resistance capability, a type discrimination of user nodes and a dynamic reconfiguration mechanism of the topology are established.

Acknowledgement. Thanks to the online transaction data provided by Taobao Kaiwen Fila billion store. Thanks to the valuable comments from the review experts, which will improve the quality of this article. This work was supported by the National Natural Science Foundation of China (61472136; 61772196), the Hunan Provincial Focus Social Science Fund (2016ZDB006), Hunan Provincial Social Science Achievement Review Committee results appraisal identification project (Xiang social assessment 2016JD05) The authors gratefully acknowledge the financial support provided by the Key Laboratory of Hunan Province for New Retail Virtual Reality Technology (2017TP1026).

References

1. China Internet Network Information Center: The 41st Statistical Report on the Development of China's Internet. http://www.cac.gov.cn/2018-01/31/c_1122347026.htm. http://www.cac.gov.cn/2018-01/31/c_1122346138.htm (2018)
2. Ae, K.Y., Rasik, P.: A trust prediction framework in rating-based on experience sharing social networks without a Web of Trust. Inf. Sci. **191**(3), 128–145 (2012)
3. Nan, H., Ling, L., Sambamurthy, V.: Fraud detection in online consumer reviews. Decis. Support Syst. **50**(3), 614–626 (2011)
4. Zhang, Z.Q., Xie, X.Q., et al.: CRank: a credit assessment model in C2C e-Commerce. Inf. Syst. Dev. **5**, 333–343 (2011)
5. Yun, Y.: C2C transactions in the dynamic credit evaluation model. Inf. Sci. **28**(4), 563–566 (2010)
6. Yaghoubi, N.: Trust models in e-Business: analytical-compare approach. Interdiscip. J. Contemp. Res. Bus. **2**(9), 398–416 (2011)
7. Zhang, X.: A strengthening of security solutions C2C transaction integrity. Microelectron. Comput. **27**(5), 194–198 (2010)
8. Marsh, S.: Formalising trust as a computational concept. Ph.D. thesis, University of Stirling (1994)
9. Blaze, M., Feigenbaum, J., Lacy, J.: Decentralized trust management. In: Proceedings of the Symposium on Security and Privacy, Oakland, pp. 164–173 (1996)
10. Blaze, M., Feigenbaum, J., Keromytis, A.D.: Keynote: trust management for public-key infrastructures. In: Proceedings of the 1998 Security Protocols International Workshop, Cambridge, England, pp. 59–63 (1998)
11. Griffiths, N.: Task delegation using experience based multi-dimensional trust. In: Proceedings of the 4th International Joint Conference on Autonomous Agents and Multiagent Systems, Netherlands, pp. 489–496. ACM Press, London (2005)
12. Zhang, Q., Zhang, X., Wen, X.Z., Liu, J.R., Ting, S.: Construction of peer-to-peer multiple-grain trust model. J. Softw. **17**(1), 96–107 (2006)

13. Wang, X., Liang, P., Ma, H., Xing, D., Wang, B.: A P2P trust model based on multi-dimensional trust evaluation. In: Li, K., Fei, M., Irwin, G.W., Ma, S. (eds.) LSMS 2007. LNCS, vol. 4688, pp. 347–356. Springer, Heidelberg (2007). https://doi.org/10.1007/978-3-540-74769-7_38

14. Guo, L., Yang, S., Wang, J., Zhou, J.: Trust model based on similarity measure of vectors in P2P networks. In: Zhuge, H., Fox, Geoffrey C. (eds.) GCC 2005. LNCS, vol. 3795, pp. 836–847. Springer, Heidelberg (2005). https://doi.org/10.1007/11590354_103

15. Reece, S., Rogers, A., Roberts, S., Jennings, N.R.: Rumours and reputation: evaluating multi-dimensional trust within a decentralized reputation system. In: Proceedings of the 6th International Joint Conference on Autonomous Agents and Multiagent Systems, pp. 1–8. ACM Press, Honolulu (2007)

16. Reece, S., Roberts, S., Rogers, A., Jennings, N.R.: A multi-dimensional trust model for heterogeneous contract observations. In: Proceedings of the 22th AAAI Conference on Artificial Intelligence, pp. 128–135. AAAI Press, London (2007)

17. Wang, S., Zhang, L., Li, H.-S.: Evaluation approach of subjective trust based on cloud model. J. Softw. 21(6), 1341–1352 (2010)

18. Shao, K., Luo, F., Mei, N.X., Liu, Z.T.: Normal distribution based dynamical recommendation trust model. J. Softw. 23(12), 3130–3148 (2012). http://www.jos.org.cn/1000-9825/4204.htm. (in Chinese)

19. Ashtiani, M., Azgomi, M.A.: Trust modeling based on a combination of fuzzy analytic hierarchy process and fuzzy VIKOR. Soft Comput. 20(1), 399–421 (2016)

20. Wu, T., Xiao, J., Qin, K., et al.: Cloud model-based method for range constrained thresholding. Comput. Electr. Eng. 42(2), 33–48 (2015)

21. McCole, P., Ramsey, E., Williams, J.: Trust considerations on attitudes towards online purchasing: the moderating effect of privacy and security concerns. J. Bus. Res. 63(9/10), 1018–1024 (2010)

22. Jun, X.: Survey of trust model based on uncertainty theory. J. Chin. Comput. Syst. 38(1), 99–106 (2017)

23. Jiang, W., Xu, Y., Guo, H., Zhang, L.: Multi agent system-based dynamic trust calculation model and credit management mechanism of online trading. Sci. China Inf. Sci. 44(9), 1084–1101 (2014)

A Novel Strategy for Complex Human-Agent Negotiation

Lichun Yuan[1], Siqi Chen[1,2], and Zili Zhang[1,3(✉)]

[1] College of Computer and Information Science, Southwest University,
Chongqing 400715, China
wjsylc@email.swu.edu.cn, {siqichen,zhangzl}@swu.edu.cn
[2] School of Software, Tianjin University, Tianjin 300072, China
[3] School of Information Technology, Deakin University,
Locked Bag 20000, Geelong, VIC 3220, Australia

Abstract. The problem of human-agent negotiation is still not well understood, mainly because human players are not fully rational from game theory's perspective and thus the interaction in such context is hard to model using traditional ways. This paper proposes a novel strategy for complex human-agent negotiation – that is – multiple issues, unknown opponent preferences as well as real-time constraints. This novel strategy is able to model opponent behaviour during negotiation session and make reasonable decisions to establish agreements with human players. We analyze the results of extensive experiments, and show that it is able to outperform human counterparts, in both high and low conflictive negotiation scenarios.

Keywords: Human-agent negotiation · Opponent modeling
Multi-agent systems

1 Introduction

The research of human-agent negotiation (HAN) aims at constructing sensible and skillful agents whose primary purpose is to negotiate well with humans. The main motivation behind the study of HAN is the wide-ranging of its values, among the traditional business, conflict-resolving and artificial intelligence area. Features in HAN include partial offers and emotions exchange, preferences elicitation strategies, favors-and-ledgers behaviour and so on [9,12,16], that are not often seen in the traditional agent-agent negotiation.

This new class of negotiation has drawn recent interest since they can be used as conflict resolvers or educational tools to improve negotiation skills [3]. The value and moral complexities of lying during negotiation are well discussed and established [1,8,17]. To avoid being disrupted by the unreal information, many negotiation researchers prefer to model opponent preferences [2].

During the negotiation session, players' (human and agent) actions are driven by their own hidden utilities and bidding strategies. The agent can reach better

Y. Sun et al. (Eds.): ChineseCSCW 2018, CCIS 917, pp. 66–76, 2019.
https://doi.org/10.1007/978-981-13-3044-5_5

(higher self utility or social welfare) final agreement by exploring the baseline, if given the behaviour model of human. However, negotiating with human is not a straightforward work since (i). individuals have their own behaviours, and each opponent model can only be detected indirectly through the offers exchange part with various offers proposed by the human end, (ii). the diversity of opponents require a more general and robust strategy for offer creating and decision making.

Aiming to provide a solution that can clarify these two problems, we make use of the *Gaussian Processes (GPs)* to learn the behaviour model, and transit it to *Simulated Annealing* for a decision. *Simulated Annealing* exploits the idea of annealing, a technique initially used in metallurgy, to find the lowest cost results for sequential arrangement problems, which appropriates to the settings in HAN. This technique makes it possible to reach a final agreement with higher social welfare (the sum of players' utilities) by exploiting the counter offers made by opponent. To achieve a better agent in HAN session, this work contributed by (i). introducing a generic framework of human-agent negotiation strategy that can observe opponent's behaviour model over time, (ii). modifying a simulated annealing algorithm for multi-issue HAN offer selection. To make the proposed algorithms easier to explain, the paper focuses on offers exchange part of the bilateral multi-issue HAN even though this work are applicable to a well-developed HAN agent.

The rest of this paper provides the necessary knowledge for the reader in Sect. 2. Section 3 details the modeling and offering strategies. Section 4 explains the design of the experiments, evaluates each agent with its performance. A conclusion of this work is made in Sect. 5.

2   Background Knowledge

Background knowledge is provided to the reader for the remainder of this paper in this section. Firstly, the framework of bilateral human-agent negotiations is introduced. Secondly, it presents the regression technique of *Gaussian Processes*. The technique of *Simulated Annealing* is then discussed.

2.1   Bilateral Human Agent Negotiations

Let $I = \{a, h\}$ be the agent and human negotiator and $i(i \in I)$ be the particular negotiator. The two players negotiate several rounds to make an agreement including a set of values, each value is assigned to a distinct item such as gold, fruit or other properties. J is described as the issues to be negotiated, and each particular issue is specified by $j(j \in \{1, ..., n\})$. The minimum expectation of each player is called reserved utility u_{res}. A value O_j is assigned to the issue j at the beginning of the negotiation. The tuple $O = (O_1, ..., O_n)$ is called an offer. Each side makes an offer in turn, an agreement is said to be reached if both sides agree on an offer [15].

The player can make an agreement or send a new offer after receiving the opponent's offer. Negotiation continues until the offer is accepted or ends due to deadline t_{max} is reached.

The weight of each issue $j \in \{1, ..., n\}$ is described by a preference vector $p^i = (P^i_1, ..., P^i_n)$. Players make decisions following their own preference vector. An offer's utility for negotiator i can be calculated as follows:

$$U^i(O) = \sum_{j=1}^{n} \left(p^i_j \cdot V^i_j(O_j) \right) \qquad (1)$$

where O and p^i_j are defined above. The evaluation function V^i_j is used to map each selection of issue j to a real number.

If no acceptance due to timeout, both sides will get their reserved utility u_{res}. If the agent knows opponent's utility function, the Pareto-optimal contract [13] can be predicted to improve the final result. However negotiators avoid revealing their own information.

2.2   Gaussian Processes

Gaussian Processes (GPs) have been widely used in agent-agent negotiation fields [4–7]. Readers can refer to [14] for a better understanding of the GPs. By maximizing the marginal likelihood of the following:

$$\log p(\mathbf{y}|\mathbf{X}) = -\frac{1}{2}\mathbf{y}^T(\mathbf{K} + \sigma_n^2\mathbf{I})^{-1}\mathbf{y} - \frac{1}{2}\log|\mathbf{K} + \sigma_n^2\mathbf{I}| - \frac{n}{2}\log 2\pi \qquad (2)$$

a *GP* is said to be learned. $\mathbf{X} \in R^{m \times d}$ is the matrix of all input data, $y \in R^{m \times 1}$ is the vector of output data, $\mathbf{K} \in R^{m \times m}$ represents the covariance and $|.|$ is the determinant. Θ is a vector of all hyperparameters, by maximizing the marginal likelihood in relation to Θ, the hyperparameters can be fitted to suit the available data. Formally, the result of the derivatives of Eq. 2 is required for this maximization. These derivatives are then used to perform the updates according to the following:

$$\frac{\partial}{\partial \theta_j} \log p(\mathbf{y}|\mathbf{X}, \Theta) = \frac{1}{2}\mathbf{y}^T \mathbf{K}^{-1}\frac{\partial \mathbf{K}}{\partial \theta_j}\mathbf{K}^{-1}\mathbf{y} - \frac{1}{2}\mathrm{tr}\left(\mathbf{K}^{-1}\frac{\partial \mathbf{K}}{\partial \theta_j}\right)$$
$$= \frac{1}{2}\mathrm{tr}\left(\left(\alpha\alpha^T - \mathbf{K}^{-1}\right)\frac{\partial \mathbf{K}}{\partial \theta_j}\right) \text{ with } \alpha = \mathbf{K}^{-1}\mathbf{y} \qquad (3)$$

2.3   Simulated Annealing

Simulated Annealing [10] exploits the idea of annealing to find the lowest cost solutions. In this work we focus on agent's offer generating and selecting through *Simulated Annealing*. Our main focus here is to reach a higher social welfare with different opponents. In other words, we make use of already learned model through *Gaussian Processes*, pass the history data into *Simulated Annealing* algorithm to find an offer with higher social welfare. In this work we modify a *Simulated Annealing* algorithm for HAN named *Simulated Annealing.HAN*, the technicalities of this algorithm are explained and discussed next.

3   Agent Design

This section details the proposed algorithm of the agent for HAN. A generic strategy framework for HAN is first given, which makes it possible to model opponents in ongoing negotiation session. The features of the decision making and offer generating strategy based on the already learned model are then detailed.

3.1   The Strategies of Human-Agent Negotiation

The agent utility $U(O_{opp})$ of a particular offer O can be computed by the agent's utility function, corresponding time stamp t_c with $U(O_{opp})$ are then recorded. These data will be added as input to the learner GPs, a linear concession strategy based on the output of GPs is adapted to reduce the complexity in computing. More specifically, the ultimate utility from opponent's offer $\hat{u}$(i.e. the final concession of the opponent) is provided by GPs, the current utility u' can be calculated:

$$u' = \hat{u} + (u_{max} - \hat{u})(\hat{t} - t_c)^\alpha \tag{4}$$

where t_c is the current time, u_{max} describes the theoretical maximum that can be reached, $\hat{t}$ is the corresponding time stamp of $\hat{u}$. α is used to describe the way that agent concedes. These are described in lines 1–5 of Algorithm 1.

Algorithm 1. The strategies of HAN is described. Opponent's behaviour model Θ is observed and updated through the offers exchange.

1:**while** $t^{(c)} < T_{max}$ **do**
2:      $D_o(o) \Leftarrow$ receive opponent's offer o
3:      $U(O_{opp}) \Leftarrow$ calculate utility
4:      $\Theta \Leftarrow GPs(t^{(c)}, U(O_{opp}))$
5:      $u' \Leftarrow$ setTarget(Θ)
6:      if Acceptable then
7:            an agreement reached
8:      else
9:            *Simulated Annealing.HAN*(D_o, u')
10:End **while**
11:Terminate the negotiation session

The agent's decision is driven by the current u'. After receiving an offer from the human player, two conditions will be checked firstly (i) the agent utility of this offer $U(O_{opp})$ is not smaller than the current utility u'; (ii) the agent used to propose this offer during this negotiation. The agent makes a agreement and terminates the process if any of these two conditions is fulfilled, lines 6–7 of Algorithm 1.

Otherwise, the agent loads the best opponent's offer from the history data, checks whether the utility of this offer is over the u'. If this holds, this offer will be re-proposed. Re-proposing the best history offer is reasonable because it not only achieves the opponent's expectation but also improves the efficiency. If no agreement is reached, a new offer will be generated following the *Simulated Annealing.HAN* algorithm, lines 8–9.

3.2   Learning During the Negotiation Session

The unknown opponents model can be learned over time. Once a counter offer is sent by the human end, the agent utility is calculated with utility function and provided to the data set $D_1 = \{t_1^{(i)}, u_1^{(i)}\}_{i=0}^{t_{1_{max}}}$, with i representing the time step from the beginning to a maximum of $t_{1_{max}}$. As the negotiation continues, the human's behaviour model is indirectly observed from the dynamically increased data set.

The model is trained when a new instance is obtained to update the best suitable model. A target utility u' is proposed by this new model to select the next offer through *Simulated Annealing.HAN* algorithm. Typically, the utility $u_1^\star$ at time $t_1^\star$ can be predicted as follows:

$$
\begin{aligned}
&u_1^\star | \Gamma_1, \mathbf{u}_1, t_1^\star \sim N(\bar{\mathbf{u}}_1^\star, cov(\mathbf{u}_1^\star)) \\
&with \\
&\bar{\mathbf{u}}_1^\star = \mathbf{K}_1(t_1^\star, \Gamma_1)[\mathbf{K}_1(\Gamma_1, \Gamma_1) + \sigma_1^2 \mathbf{I}]^{-1} \mathbf{u}_1 \\
&cov(\mathbf{u}_1^\star) = \mathbf{K}_1(t_1^\star, t_1^\star) - \mathbf{K}_1(t_1^\star, \Gamma_1)[\mathbf{K}_1(\Gamma_1, \Gamma_1) + \sigma_1^2 \mathbf{I}]^{-1} \mathbf{K}_1(\Gamma_1, t_1^\star)
\end{aligned}
\tag{5}
$$

where $u_1^\star$ is the prediction at time $t_1^\star$, matrix Γ_1 is the history of inputs, vector $\mathbf{u}_1$ presents the utilities collected till $t_1^\star$, $\mathbf{K}_1$ describes the covariance and $\sigma_1^2 \mathbf{I}$ is the noise.

GPs' hyperparameters describe the opponent's model, the model is stored for future use. The negotiation session will be ended when either the maximum available time of an agreement is reached.

3.3   Offer Construction

Simulated Annealing is a technique used to solve the combinatorial optimisation problems such as the travelling salesperson problem. To fit the settings of the human-agent negotiation, a modification of the *Simulated Annealing* algorithm is adapted. This new algorithm *Simulated Annealing.HAN* is detailed in Algorithm 2.

There are two input data sets required by *Simulated Annealing.HAN*. D_o represents the history of opponent's offers. Although the player is not fully rational, it is still acceptable to assume that array of the historical data is in line with the discounting pleasure. Then, the frequency and alternative time of a value in issue j reflects the importance to the opponent's overall utility. The second data set is the target utility u', agent only creating offer with utility between a narrow range of u' to reduce the time consumption in calculation.

A random offer with not less than target self utility u' is generated and selected as the candidate to be proposed. Then the agent starts tuning this random offer into a new offer, lines 1–3 of Algorithm 2. Function *SelfUtil* is used to predict preferences through the opponent's history action and calculate a total points(the sum of utilities in both sides) E with input offer. If the new offer has a higher total points E than the candidate, or the exponential of E divided current $Temp_{curr}$ is bigger than a random value, the candidate offer will be replaced by the new one, lines 5–10. $Temp_{curr}$ will be reduced and offer be proposed when $Temp_{curr}$ is smaller than a threshold, lines 11–13.

Algorithm 2. *Simulated Annealing.HAN(D_o, u')*

1: $O_{prop} \Leftarrow$ random offer based on u'
2: **while** $Temp_{curr} > Temp_{min}$ **do**
3:      $O_{curr} \Leftarrow$ tune the offer(O_{prop})
4:      **if** $SelfUtil(O_{curr}) >= u'$
5:           $E = TotalPoints(D_o, O_{curr}) - TotalPoints(D_o, O_{prop})$
6:           **if** $E >= 0$
7:                $O_{prop} \Leftarrow O_{curr}$
8:           **else**
9:                **if** $exp(E/T_{curr}) > Random(0, 1)$
10:                    $O_{prop} \Leftarrow O_{curr}$
11:      $T_{curr} \Leftarrow r * T_{curr}$
12: End **while**
13: Propos O_{prop}

---

4   Results and Analysis

Experiments of the agent was done and results were collected with the IAGO (Interactive Arbitration Guide Online) [11], that is selected by the international Automated Negotiation Agents Competition(ANAC) as a negotiation platform. IAGO allows an agent negotiate with human in a specified gamespace, where the preferences define the utility function of both sides. The performance can be evaluated by the final points achievements.

4.1   Experimental Design

The gamespace was configured to be a 4-issue multi-issue bargaining task, with each issue having 6 levels(5 items). Each item was assigned a point value between 1 and 4. All point accruals were linear, meaning that gaining 1 of the 1-point item was worth 1 point, 2 was worth 2 points, etc. The game was casted as a "Resource Exchange Game", items were described as "bars of gold", "bars of iron", "shipments of bananas" and "shipments of spices". Players took on the role of negotiators determining how to split the items between them.

   The agent player was assigned 4 points for each bar of iron, 3 points for each bar of gold, 2 points for each shipment of bananas, and 1 point for each shipment of spice. Two various preferences named "High Conflict Player" and "Low Conflict Player" assigned to the human players separately to explore agent's performance under different situations. These values are summarized in Table 1.

Table 1. Item payoffs

	Agent player	High conflict player	Low conflict player
Shipments of spices	1	1	4
Shipments of bananas	2	2	3
Bars of gold	3	3	2
Bars of iron	4	4	1

To evaluate the proposed methods, 3 agents with different algorithms were coded, under name of GPAgent, SAAgent and MXAgent.

GPAgent uses *GPs* as modeling strategy to get a target utility u', the concession factor is set to $\alpha = 0.5$. GPAgent generates and proposes offers randomly with utility between a range around target utility u'.

SAAgent uses a linear concession policy ($\alpha = 1$) and generates offers through *Simulated Annealing.HAN* in order to reach a higher total points.

MXAgent uses both of the proposed methods. A target utility u' is calculated with the concession factor $\alpha = 0.5$ through *GPs*, offers with higher total points are selected and proposed through *Simulated Annealing.HAN*. Strategies of each agent are summarized in Table 2.

Table 2. Agent strategies

	Modeling strategy	Offering strategy
GPAgent	*Gaussian Processes*	Random
SAAgent	Linear	*Simulated Annealing.HAN*
MXAgent	*Gaussian Processes*	*Simulated Annealing.HAN*

4.2   Result and Analysis

In this set of experiments, we recruited 186 participants for our sample study. The participants were all over 18 years old undergraduates and were assigned one of the two preferences in Table 1, had an approximately 10 min negotiation with one of the three virtual agents.

Figure 1 shows the performance of GPAgent playing against participants in both high and low conflictive domain. The x-axis represents the preferences of the participants and y-axis presents the utility by the points of each side. Because of the high conflict players share the same preferences with agent, the average of total points with high conflict player should be a fixed 50 points. But a loss of total points occurred owing to the increased amount of negotiations that timed out, forced both player to take their u_{res}, thus reducing the total value to a mere 8 points. Figure 4 demonstrates a case that GPAgent negotiates with high conflict player, GPAgent reaches a agreement with higher self points than

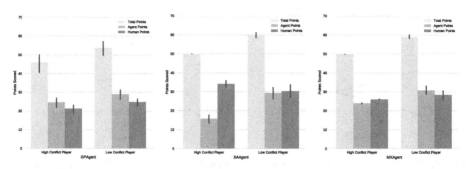

Fig. 1. The performance of GPAgent.

Fig. 2. The performance of SAAgent.

Fig. 3. The performance of MXAgent.

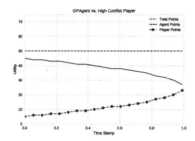

Fig. 4. A case of GPAgent negotiate with high conflict player.

Fig. 5. A case of GPAgent negotiate with low conflict player.

its opponent. A case of GPAgent against low conflict player is shown in Fig. 5, a unstable fluctuation of the total points occurs during the whole negotiation session, this may be caused by the strategy that GPAgent only controls its baseline but selects offers randomly without calculating the social welfare.

Figure 2 is the results of SAAgent playing against human. With linear concession, altruistic offer strategy and no opponent modeling, SAAgent reached the highest average of total points, but sacrificed itself in games especially with the high conflict players. The agent reaches a lower points than both types of players in Figs. 6 and 7. Total points have a steady growth when SAAgent negotiate with low conflict player, the result is shown in Fig. 7. These two figures show that the agent can reach a better social welfare with *Simulated Annealing.HAN* technique, but the linear concession strategy will keep pulling back and reducing agent's self points.

The performance of MXAgent is presented in Fig. 3. By combining *Gaussian Processes* with *Simulated Annealing.HAN*, MXAgent reaches a approximate result with GPAgent, adjustes the sightless self utility sacrifice in high conflictive domain, shown in Fig. 8. And achieves a close copy of SAAgent's total points in low conflictive domain, shown in Fig. 9.

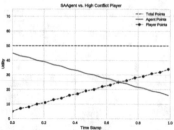

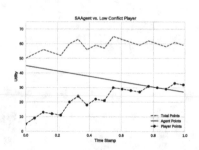

Fig. 6. A case of SAAgent negotiate with high conflict player.

Fig. 7. A case of SAAgent negotiate with low conflict player.

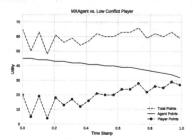

Fig. 8. A case of MXAgent negotiate with high conflict player.

Fig. 9. A case of MXAgent negotiate with low conflict player.

5   Conclusions and Future Work

In this paper, a generic framework has been presented for human-agent negotiation. We make use of gaussian processes and simulated annealing algorithms to improve the final results when negotiating with humans. A set of three experiments in both high and low conflictive negotiation domains were conducted to testify the efficiency of our strategies.

In our future work we will run a more widespread experiments to improve the efficiency and robustness of our agent among different opponents. Then, we plan to migrate our work under multi-human-agent negotiation settings.

Acknowledgment. This work is supported by National Natural Science Foundation of China (Grant number: 61602391). The authors also thank to the anonymous reviewers of this article for their valuable comments.

References

1. Aquino, K., Becker, T.E.: Lying in negotiations: how individual and situational factors influence the use of neutralization strategies. J. Organ. Behav. **26**(6), 661–679 (2005)
2. Baarslag, T., Hindriks, K.V.: Accepting optimally in automated negotiation with incomplete information. In: Proceedings of the 2013 International Conference on Autonomous Agents and Multi-agent Systems, pp. 715–722. International Foundation for Autonomous Agents and Multiagent Systems (2013)
3. Broekens, J., Harbers, M., Brinkman, W.-P., Jonker, C.M., Van den Bosch, K., Meyer, J.-J.: Virtual reality negotiation training increases negotiation knowledge and skill. In: Nakano, Y., Neff, M., Paiva, A., Walker, M. (eds.) IVA 2012. LNCS (LNAI), vol. 7502, pp. 218–230. Springer, Heidelberg (2012). https://doi.org/10.1007/978-3-642-33197-8_23
4. Chen, S., Ammar, H.B., Tuyls, K., Weiss, G.: Optimizing complex automated negotiation using sparse pseudo-input Gaussian processes. In: Proceedings of the 2013 International Conference on Autonomous Agents and Multi-agent Systems, pp. 707–714. International Foundation for Autonomous Agents and Multiagent Systems (2013)
5. Chen, S., Hao, J., Weiss, G., Tuyls, K., Leung, H.: Evaluating practical automated negotiation based on spatial evolutionary game theory. In: Lutz, C., Thielscher, M. (eds.) KI 2014. LNCS (LNAI), vol. 8736, pp. 147–158. Springer, Cham (2014). https://doi.org/10.1007/978-3-319-11206-0_15
6. Chen, S., Hao, J., Weiss, G., Zhou, S., Zhang, Z.: Toward efficient agreements in real-time multilateral agent-based negotiations. In: 2015 IEEE 27th International Conference on Tools with Artificial Intelligence (ICTAI), pp. 896–903. IEEE (2015)
7. Chen, S., Weiss, G.: An intelligent agent for bilateral negotiation with unknown opponents in continuous-time domains. ACM Trans. Auton. Adapt. Syst. (TAAS) **9**(3), 16 (2014)
8. Gratch, J., Nazari, Z., Johnson, E.: The misrepresentation game: How to win at negotiation while seeming like a nice guy. In: Proceedings of the 2016 International Conference on Autonomous Agents & Multiagent Systems, pp. 728–737. International Foundation for Autonomous Agents and Multiagent Systems (2016)
9. Keenan, P.A., Carnevale, P.J.: Positive effects of within-group cooperation on between-group negotiation. J. Appl. Soc. Psychol. **19**(12), 977–992 (1989)
10. Kirkpatrick, S., Gelatt, C.D., Vecchi, M.P.: Optimization by simulated annealing. Science **220**(4598), 671–680 (1983)
11. Mell, J., Gratch, J.: Grumpy & pinocchio: answering human-agent negotiation questions through realistic agent design. In: Proceedings of the 16th Conference on Autonomous Agents and Multiagent Systems, pp. 401–409. International Foundation for Autonomous Agents and Multiagent Systems (2017)
12. de Melo, C.M., Carnevale, P., Gratch, J.: The effect of expression of anger and happiness in computer agents on negotiations with humans. In: The 10th International Conference on Autonomous Agents and Multiagent Systems-Volume 3, pp. 937–944. International Foundation for Autonomous Agents and Multiagent Systems (2011)
13. Raiffa, H.: The Art and Science of Negotiation. Harvard University Press, Cambridge (1982)
14. Rasmussen, C.E.: Gaussian processes in machine learning. In: Bousquet, O., von Luxburg, U., Rätsch, G. (eds.) ML -2003. LNCS (LNAI), vol. 3176, pp. 63–71. Springer, Heidelberg (2004). https://doi.org/10.1007/978-3-540-28650-9_4

15. Rubinstein, A.: Perfect equilibrium in a bargaining model. Econ.: J. Econ. Soc. **50**, 97–109 (1982)
16. Van Kleef, G.A., De Dreu, C.K., Manstead, A.S.: The interpersonal effects of emotions in negotiations: a motivated information processing approach. J. Pers. Soc. Psychol. **87**(4), 510 (2004)
17. White, J.J.: Machiavelli and the bar: ethical limitations on lying in negotiation. Law & Soc. Inq. **5**(4), 926–938 (1980)

Multi-strategy Mutation Constrained Differential Evolution Algorithm Based on Replacement and Restart Mechanism

Lyuyang Tong[1,3], Minggang Dong[1,2(✉)] 🆔, and Chao Jing[1,2]

[1] College of Information Science and Engineering, Guilin University of Technology, Guilin 541004, China
d2015mg@qq.com
[2] Guangxi key Laboratory of Embedded Technology and Intelligent System, Guilin University of Technology, Guilin, China
[3] School of Computer Science, Wuhan University, Wuhan, China

Abstract. In order to balance relationships between objective functions and constraints, this paper proposes a multi-strategy mutation constrained differential evolution algorithm based on the replacement and restart mechanism (MCODE). Due to the feasible rule as the constraint processing technology, MCODE utilizes multi-strategy mutation to balance the relationship between the constraints and the objective functions. Moreover, MCODE employs the replacement and restart mechanism to improve the diversity for jumping out of the local solution of the infeasible area. The comparison with the other four constrained optimization methods on the 18 CEC2010 test functions shows that MCODE achieves a relatively competitive result.

Keywords: Differential evolution (DE) · Constrained optimization
Multi-strategy mutation

1 Introduction

On the field of evolutionary computation, many researchers are paying more and more attention to applying the evolutionary algorithms (EAs) to settle the constrained optimization problem. Since the existence of constraints, some constraint processing methods have already been mentioned and integrated with EAs. Therefore, various constraint optimization evolution algorithms (COEAs) have been designed. The current popular COEAs can be simply divided as follows:

(1) Penalty-based methods. In terms of the penalty function technique, a penalty function is constructed via constraints and objective functions. Then individuals are compared using the penalty function. ($(u + \lambda)$-CDE [1] and CMA-ES [2])

Supported by the National Natural Science Foundation of China (61563012, 61203109), Guangxi Natural Science Foundation (2014GXNSFAA118371, 2015GXNSFBA139260).

(2) Methods of taking priority of the feasible rather than the infeasible. In this method, objective functions or constraints are applied to compare individuals, but feasible solutions are usually chosen rather than infeasible solutions. (εDE [3] and εDEag [4])

(3) Multi-objective optimization based approach. In the multi-objective optimization technique, the constrained optimization problem makes a transformation into the multi-objective optimization problem. After transformation, Pareto dominance is often used to choose individuals. (DyHF [5] and CMODE [6])

In general, COEAs require to obtain two objectives. The one needs to quickly find the feasible domain. The other is to obtain the optimal function value after evolution. The importance has been revealed that COEAs can make a trade-off between constraints and objective functions. We propose a multi-strategy mutation constrained differential evolution algorithm based on the replacement and restart mechanism (MCODE). MCODE adopts a feasibility rule as a constraint processing technique. Furthermore, MCODE proposes a multi-strategy mutation strategy to balance the relationship between the constraints and the objective functions. Also, MCODE applies the replacement and restart mechanism to increases the diversity for jumping out of the local solution of the infeasible area, and finally achieves the goals of quickly searching for a feasible domain and finding the optimal solution.

2 Related Work

2.1 Constrained Optimization Problems

Taking the form of minimization as an example, the constraint optimization problem is described as following:

$$\begin{aligned} & \text{minimize} f(\boldsymbol{x}), \boldsymbol{x} = (x_1, x_2, ..., x_D) \in S, L_i \leq x_i \leq U_i \\ & \text{subject to} : h_j(\boldsymbol{x}) = 0, j = 1, 2, ..., k \\ & \qquad\qquad g_j(\boldsymbol{x}) \leq 0, j = k+1, k+2, ..., q \end{aligned} \quad (1)$$

where $f(\boldsymbol{x})$ indicates the fitness value, $\boldsymbol{x} = (x_1, ..., x_D) \in S$ represents the decision vector, S is regarded as the decision domain. The jth equality constraints or inequality constraints are called $h_j(\boldsymbol{x})$ or $g_j(\boldsymbol{x})$, respectively. For COPs, the jth constraint violation degree can be described as following:

$$G_j(\boldsymbol{x}) = \begin{cases} \max\{|h_j(\boldsymbol{x}) - \delta|, 0\}, 1 \leq j \leq k \\ \max\{g_j(\boldsymbol{x}), 0\}, k+1 \leq j \leq q \end{cases} \quad (2)$$

where δ represents the transformed threshold. All constraints are described as following:

$$G(\boldsymbol{x}) = \sum_{j=1}^{q} G_j(\boldsymbol{x}) \quad (3)$$

If $G(\boldsymbol{x}) = 0$, $\boldsymbol{x}$ is feasible; otherwise $\boldsymbol{x}$ is infeasible.

2.2 Feasible Rule

Deb designed a feasibility rule as a constraint processing technique [7], which belongs to a method of taking the priority of the feasible rather than the infeasible. Individuals take the following comparisons: (1) From two solutions in the infeasible domain, the solution is chosen on the lower constraint violation degree. (2) If two solutions are infeasible and feasible respectively, it is selected in feasible domain. (3) If the both are in the feasible domain, the solution is selected on the better function value.

2.3 FROFI

A novel COEA (FROFI) which combines objective function information with the feasible rule was presented by Wang et al. [9]. Moreover, the replacement mechanism is utilized to replace some individuals from the archive A. Furthermore, FROFI proposes the mutation strategy to improve the diversity. In the above strategy, objective function is applied to compare the individuals and its information may be helpful for jumping out of the local solution in the infeasible zone.

3 Multi-Strategy Mutation Constrained Differential Evolution Algorithm Based on Replacement and Restart Mechanism

3.1 Multi-strategy Mutation Operation

Due to the feasible rule as the constraint technique, it is more biased toward constraints and often ignoring the effects of the objective functions in terms of selection. To make up for this deficiency, MCODE proposes the multi-strategy mutation operation to balance the constraints and the objective functions. Multi-strategy mutation operation (1) includes two kinds of differential mutation strategy and the improved BGA mutation operation [8]. In the early stage of evolution, individuals are basically infeasible solutions. Using the above two differential mutation strategies can enhance the global exploration. During the late evolutionary period, some individuals evolve from infeasible solutions into feasible ones. "DE/rand-to-pbest/1" can direct solutions in the feasible domain towards the best function value. Also, "DE/current-to-rand/1" has effective effects in solving rotation problems. The differential mutation strategies are described below:
   "DE/rand-to-pbest/1":

$$v_{i,G} = x_{r_1,G} + F \cdot (x_{pbest,G} - x_{r_1,G}) + F \cdot (\tilde{x}_{r_2,G} - x_{r_3,G}) \tag{4}$$

"DE/current-to-rand/1":

$$v_{i,G} = x_{i,G} + rand \cdot (x_{r_1,G} - x_{i,G}) + F(x_{r_2,G} - x_{r_3,G}) \tag{5}$$

where rand denotes a random parameter and its value is within the range of $[0,1]$. $X_{pbest,G}$ is regarded as the 100p%$(p \in (0,1])$ best individual of present population. F represents the mutation coefficient from 0 to 1. $\tilde{x}_{r2,G}$ stands for an individual of the archive A and the present population. The multi-strategy mutation operation (1) also applies the improved BGA mutation operation to increase population diversity. Among them, the improved BGA is described as follow:

$$v_{i,j} = \begin{cases} v_{i,j} \pm rang_i * \sum_{s=0}^{15} \alpha_s * 2^{-s}, rand < 1/n \\ v_{i,j}, \qquad\qquad\qquad otherwise \end{cases} \tag{6}$$

$$randg_i = (U_i - L_i) * (1 - \frac{gen}{total\_gen})^6 \tag{7}$$

where $randg_i$ is range of mutation, $total\_gen$ denotes the total generation, and gen denotes the present generation. The parameter $a_s \in \{0,1\}$ is chosen on the probability $p_r(\alpha_s = 1) = 1/16$. The symbol "+" or "-" is selected with the probability of 0.5. The multi-strategy mutation operation (1) is given in Algorithm 1:

Algorithm 1 The multi-strategy mutation operation (1)

1: **if** $rand \leq 0.5 + 0.3*(FEs/MaxFEs)$ **then**
2:     Implement the differential mutation operation based on formula (4);
3: **else**
4:     Implement the differential mutation operation based on formula (5);
5: **end if**
6: Individuals who are generated by "DE/rand-to-pbest/1" utilize the crossover operation;
7: Implement the improved BGA mutation operation based on formula (6) and formula (7);

In order to further search a feasible solution for the population that is trapped in the infeasible solution region, the multi-strategy mutation operation (2) is applied to increase the probability of searching a feasible domain [9]. Algorithm 2 describes the multi-strategy mutation operation (2) as following:

Algorithm 2 The multi-strategy mutation operation (2) [9]

1: **if** (All Individuals are infeasible solutions) **then**
2:     Randomly select an individual x_a in population P_{t+1}, and then generate a new individual x'_a by creating a new value in a random dimension;
3:     Calculate the constraints G and the fitness value f for the new individual x'_a;
4:     Select x_b according to maximum constraints in P_{t+1};
5:     **if** $f(x'_a) < f(x_b)$ **then**
6:         $x_b = x'_a$;
7:     **end if**
8: **end if**

3.2   Replacement and Restart Mechanism

In order to reduce the constraint-biased greediness of the feasibility rule, replacement and restart mechanism is applied to balance the constraints and the objective functions. From replacement mechanism [9], the individual with the highest constraints and relatively high fitness value is replaced by the one with the least constraints and relatively low fitness value in archive A. On the one hand, it increases the diversity. On the other hand, from the perspective of the objective function, it can make it possible to search an optimal solution for individuals who have low objective function at the boundary of the feasible domain. The replacement mechanism is given in Algorithm 3:

Algorithm 3 Replacement mechanism [9]

1: The population P_{t+1} is sorted in ascending fitness value, then divided into M parts on average;
2: $i = 1$;
3: **while** $|A| > 0 \& i \leq M - 1$ **do**
4:    Select x_c according to the highest constraints in the ith part;
5:    Select x_d according to the lowest constraints in archive A;
6:    **if** $f(x_d) < f(x_c)$ **then**
7:        $x_c = x_d$;
8:        Delete the individual x_d in archive A
9:    **end if**
10:    $i = i + 1$;
11: **end while**

In addition, restart mechanism [10] is used to solve the complex constraints to escape the local solution of the infeasible solution region and determine whether the population is trapped in the local solution of the infeasible solution region by the standard deviation of constraints. If the whole individuals are infeasible solutions and the standard deviation of the constraints is less than δ (δ is usually set to 10^{-8}), the restart mechanism is performed. The restart mechanism is described in Algorithm 4:

Algorithm 4 Restart mechanism [10]

1: **if** $std(G) < \delta \& isempty(find(G == 0))$ **then**
2:    $x_{i,j} = rand_j(0, 1) \cdot (U_j - L_j) + L_j$;
3: **end if**

3.3   MCODE

The general idea of MCODE is: first, population is randomly initialized. Second, if the population satisfies the restart condition, the restart mechanism will be performed. Third, the population P_{t+1} is generated by the multi-strategy mutation operation (1), and then replaced by the replacement mechanism. Fourth, the multi-strategy mutation operation (2) is utilized. Eventually, if the stop condition is reached, MCODE stops and outputs the best solution, otherwise back to step two. The pseudocode of MCODE is described in Algorithm 5:

Algorithm 5 The pseudocode of MCODE

1: Set the population number N and the maximum function evaluations MAX_FES, and randomly initialize the population P_t;
2: Compute fitness value f and constraints G about the population P_t;
3: $FES = NP$, $P_{t+1} = \emptyset$ and $A = \emptyset$;
4: **while** $FES < Max\_FES$ **do**
5:    if the population satisfies the restart condition, the restart mechanism will be performed;
6:    **for** $i = 1 : NP$ **do**
7:       Utilize the multi-strategy mutation operation (1);
8:       Compute fitness value f and constraints G about the ith individual of population P_t;
9:       $FES = FES + 1$;
10:       Save the best individual into the next generation P_{t+1} according to the feasibility rule;
11:       If u_i cannot enter to P_{t+1} and $f(u_i) < f(x_i)$, then $A = A \cup u_i$;
12:    **end for**
13:    Utilize replacement mechanism;
14:    Utilize the multi-strategy mutation operation (2) and $FES = FES + 1$;
15:    $t = t + 1$;
16: **end while**

3.4 Complexity Analysis

In a classic DE, the runtime complexity is $O(D \cdot NP \cdot G_{max})$, where D denotes dimension, NP represents the population number, and G_{max} is maximum generations number. MCODE just extends a classic DE in terms of the multi-strategy mutation operation and replacement and restart mechanism. So MCODE does not add the complexity of the overall algorithm. In terms of the runtime complexity, MCODE is approximately equal to the classic DE.

4 Performance Evaluation

4.1 Benchmark Functions and Parameters Settings

The 18 CEC2010 constrained optimization benchmark functions are utilized to test effectiveness of MCODE [11]. The comparison algorithms are as follows: εDEag [4]; ECHT-DE [12]; AIS-IRP [13] and FROFI [9]. We use Matlab R2016a to implement the algorithm and the system configuration is 2.8 GHz Intel(R) Core(TM)i7-7700HQ CPU computer with 16G of memory under window10. All the algorithms run independently 25 times on 18 benchmark functions of 30 dimensions. The total function evaluations (FES) are set to 600000. In MCODE, corresponding parameters are set as: $NP = 80$, the scale factor pool $F_{pool} = [0.6, 0.8, 1.0]$ and the crossover probability pool $CR_{pool} = [0.1, 0.2, 1.0]$.

4.2 Experimental Results Analysis

The proposed MCODE is evaluated by the average fitness value and its standard deviation and compared with εDEag, ECHT-DE, AIS-IRP, FROFI. Notations "+","−", and "≈" represent that the competitive algorithm is significantly superior to, inferior to, and similar to MCODE, respectively. Notation "*" indicates that the related algorithm cannot obtain the feasible solution at some cases.

Table 1. Testing results for 30 dimensional CEC2010 benchmark function

Functions	εDEag [4]	ECHT-DE [12]	AIS-IRP [13]	FROFI	MCODE
C1	−8.21E−01 (7.10E−04)+	−8.00E−01 (1.79E−02)−	−8.20E−01 (3.25E−04)−	−8.21E−01 (1.86E−03)−	−8.21E−01 (1.64E−03)
C2	−2.15E+00 (1.20E−02)+	−1.99E+00 (2.10E−01)−	−2.21E+00 (2.84E−03)+	−2.01E+00 (3.20E−02)−	−2.05E+00 (2.55E−02)
C3	2.88E+01 (8.05E−01)−	9.89E+01 (6.26E+01)−	6.68E+01 (4.26E+02)−	2.64E+01 (7.94E+00)+	2.87E+01 (2.85E−07)
C4	8.16E−03 (3.07E−03)−	−1.03E−06 (9.01E−03)−	1.98E−03 (1.61E−03)−	−3.33E−06 (2.74E−10)−	−3.33E−06 (5.28E−11)
C5	−4.50E+02 (2.90E+00)−	−1.06E+02 (1.67E+02)−	−4.36E+02 (2.51E+01)−	−4.81E+02 (1.77E+00)−	−4.82E+02 (2.45E+00)
C6	−5.28E+02 (4.75E−01)−	−1.38E+02 (9.89E+01)−	−4.54E+02 (4.79E+01)−	−5.28E+02 (8.10E−01)−	−5.30E+02 (5.11E−01)
C7	2.60E−15 (1.23E−15)−	1.33E−01 (7.28E−01)−	1.07E+00 (1.61E+00)−	0.00E+00 (0.00E+00)≈	0.00E+00 (0.00E+00)
C8	7.83E−14 (4.86E−14)−	3.36E+01 (1.11E+02)−	1.65E+00 (6.41E−01)+	1.18E+01 (3.28E+01)−	3.67E+00 (1.84E+01)
C9	1.07E+01 (2.82E+01)+	4.24E+01 (1.38E+02)−	1.57E+00 (1.96E+00)+	3.53E+01 (3.45E+01)−	3.17E+01 (4.11E+01)
C10	3.33E+01 (4.55E−01)−	5.34E+01 (8.83E+01)−	1.78E+01 (1.88E+01)+	5.46E+01 (1.16E+02)−	3.13E+01 (4.21E−03)
C11	−2.86E−04 (2.71E−05)−	2.60E−03 (6.00E−03)*−	−1.58E−04 (4.67E−05)−	−3.92E−04 (5.04E−08)+	−3.92E−04 (2.37E−06)
C12	3.56E+02 (2.89E+02)*−	−2.51E+01 (1.37E+02)*−	4.29E−06 (4.52E−04)−	−1.99E−01 (1.32E−06)+	−1.99E−01 (5.66E−06)
C13	−6.54E+01 (5.73E−01)−	−6.46E+01 (1.67E+00)−	−6.62E+01 (2.27E−01)−	−6.83E+01 (2.63E−01)−	−6.84E+01 (2.03E−01)
C14	3.09E−13 (5.61E−13)−	1.24E+05 (6.77E+05)−	8.68E−07 (3.14E−07)−	0.00E+00 (0.00E+00)≈	0.00E+00 (0.00E+00)
C15	2.16E+01 (1.10E−04)−	1.94E+11 (4.35E+11)−	3.41E+01 (3.82E+01)−	2.16E+01 (8.06E−05)−	2.16E+01 (7.64E−05)
C16	2.17E−21 (1.06E−20)−	0.00E+00 (0.00E+00)≈	8.21E−02 (1.12E−01)−	0.00E+00 (0.00E+00)≈	0.00E+00 (0.00E+00)
C17	6.33E+00 (4.99E+00)−	2.75E−01 (3.78E−01)−	3.61E+00 (2.54E+00)−	4.25E−01 (6.62E−01)−	1.95E−01 (4.02E−01)
C18	8.75E+01 (1.66E+02)−	0.00E+00 (0.00E+00)+	4.02E+01 (1.80E+01)−	1.35E−01 (6.75E−01)+	4.14E−01 (1.39E+00)
+/−/≈	3/15/0	1/16/1	4/14/0	4/11/3	

From Table 1, MCODE is superior to εDEag, ECHT-DE, AIS-IRP, FROFI on 15 (C3-C8 and C10-C18), 16 (C1-C15 and C17), 14(C1, C3-C7 and C11-C18), 11(C1-C2, C4-C6, C8-C10, C13, C15 and C17) benchmark functions, respectively. It is inferior to εDEag, ECHT-DE, AIS-IRP, FROFI on 3(C1-C2 and C9), 1(C18), 4(C2 and C8-C10), 4(C3, C11-C12, C18) functions, while similar

84   L. Tong et al.

to ECHT-DE and FROFI on 1(C16) and 3(C7, C14 and C16) functions, respectively.

Since the robustness of the algorithm is also a key metric, we have evaluated the robustness of FROFI and MCODE from Figs. 1, 2, 3, 4, 5, 6, 7, 8, 9, 10, 11, 12, 13, 14, 15, 16, 17 and 18. It shows that X axial represents for the algorithm and Y axial stands for the fitness function value. From figure 1 to 18, the robustness of MCODE is better than FROFI on 11 test functions, especially on C2, C4, C5, C6, C9, C13, C15 and C17 test functions. However, the robustness of MCODE is inferior to FROFI on C3, C11-C12, and C18 test functions, especially due to slight differences on C3, C11, and C18 test functions. On the C7, C14, and C16 test functions, the fitness function values of MCODE and FROFI are dense around the optimal solution, and the robustness of the two algorithms are approximated. The results of figure show that the proposed MCODE achieves the outstanding robustness than FROFI.

In summary, from Table 1 and Figs. 1, 2, 3, 4, 5, 6, 7, 8, 9, 10, 11, 12, 13, 14, 15, 16, 17 and 18, MCODE outperforms than εDEag, ECHT-DE, AIS-IRP,

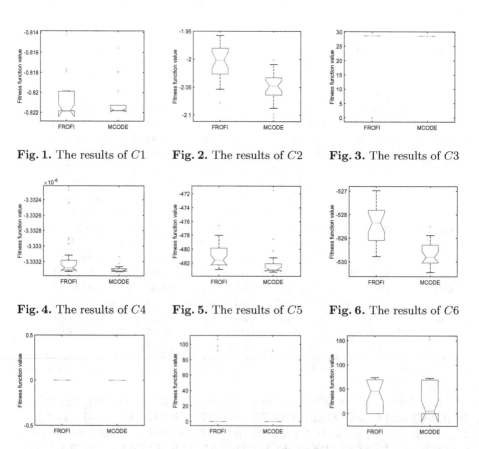

Fig. 1. The results of $C1$ **Fig. 2.** The results of $C2$ **Fig. 3.** The results of $C3$

Fig. 4. The results of $C4$ **Fig. 5.** The results of $C5$ **Fig. 6.** The results of $C6$

Fig. 7. The results of $C7$ **Fig. 8.** The results of $C8$ **Fig. 9.** The results of $C9$

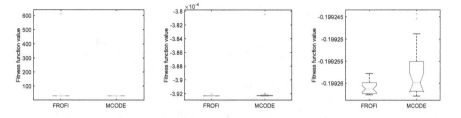

Fig. 10. The results of C10 **Fig. 11.** The results of C11 **Fig. 12.** The results of C12

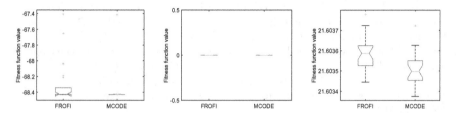

Fig. 13. The results of C13 **Fig. 14.** The results of C14 **Fig. 15.** The results of C15

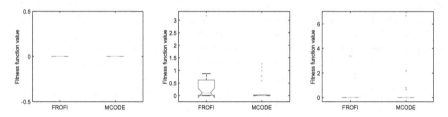

Fig. 16. The results of C16 **Fig. 17.** The results of C17 **Fig. 18.** The results of C18

FROFI. Also, it demonstrates that MCODE has strong robustness and achieves the goal of finding a better objective function solution while entering the feasible domain.

5   Conclusion

For constrained optimization, this paper proposes a multi-strategy mutation constrained differential evolution algorithm based on the replacement and restart mechanism (MCODE). MCODE adopts the multi-strategy mutation operation to consider the influence of objective information under the feasibility rule to balance the relationship between the constraints and the objective functions. Furthermore, MCODE utilizes the replacement and restart mechanism to improve the diversity for jumping out of the local solution of the infeasible zone to further balance the constraints and the objective functions. The proposed MCODE algorithm is evaluated on the 18 CEC2010 test functions and demonstrates effectiveness and robustness.

References

1. Wang, Y., Cai, Z.: Constrained evolutionary optimization by means of $(u + \lambda)$-differential evolution and improved adaptive trade-off model. Evol. Comput. **19**, 249–285 (2011)
2. Kusakci, A.O., Can, M.: An adaptive penalty based covariance matrix adaptation-evolution strategy. Comput. Oper. Res. **40**, 2398–2417 (2013)
3. Takahama, T., Sakai, S.: Efficient constrained optimization by the ε constrained adaptive differential evolution. In: IEEE Congress on Evolutionary Computation (CEC), pp. 1–8 (2010)
4. Takahama, T., Sakai, S.: Constrained optimization by the ε constrained differential evolution with an archive and gradient-based mutation. In: IEEE Congress on Evolutionary Computation (CEC), pp. 1–9 (2010)
5. Wang, Y., Cai, Z.: A dynamic hybrid framework for constrained evolutionary optimization. IEEE Trans. Syst. Man Cybern. Part B (Cybern.) **42**, 203–217 (2012)
6. Wang, Y., Cai, Z.: Combining multiobjective optimization with differential evolution to solve constrained optimization problems. IEEE Trans. Evol. Comput. **16**, 117–134 (2012)
7. Deb, K.: An efficient constraint handling method for genetic algorithms. Comput. Methods Appl. Mech. Eng. **186**, 311–338 (2000)
8. Wang, Y., Cai, Z., Guo, G., Zhou, Y.: Multiobjective optimization and hybrid evolutionary algorithm to solve constrained optimization problems. IEEE Trans. Syst. Man Cybern. Part B (Cybern.) **37**, 560–575 (2007)
9. Wang, Y., Wang, B.C., Li, H.X., Yen, G.G.: Incorporating objective function information into the feasibility rule for constrained evolutionary optimization. IEEE Trans. Cybern. **46**, 2938–2952 (2016)
10. Wang, B.C., Li, H.X., Li, J.P., Wang, Y.: Composite differential evolution for constrained evolutionary optimization. IEEE Trans. Syst. Man Cybern.: Syst. 1–14 (2018)
11. Mallipeddi, R., Suganthan, P.N.: Problem definitions and evaluation criteria for the CEC 2010: competition on constrained real-parameter optimization. Nanyang Technological University, Singapore, vol. 24 (2010)
12. Mallipeddi, R., Suganthan, P.N.: Differential evolution with ensemble of constraint handling techniques for solving CEC 2010 benchmark problems. In: IEEE Congress on Evolutionary Computation, pp. 1–8 (2010)
13. Zhang, W., Yen, G.G., He, Z.: Constrained optimization via artificial immune system. IEEE Trans. Cybern. **44**, 185–198 (2014)

Consistency Maintenance of CRDT-Based File Management System in Cloud Environment

Liping Gao[1,2] and Changqing Tao[1(✉)]

[1] School of Optical-Electrical Computer Engineering,
University of Shanghai for Science and Technology, Shanghai 200093, China
912935395@qq.com
[2] Shanghai Key Laboratory of Data Science, Fudan University,
Shanghai 200093, China

Abstract. With the rapid development of cloud services, a growing number of applications are being migrated to the cloud to provide better collaboration support. In the face of the ever-increasingly large number of documents, the way of single person management documents seem to be incapable, and the efficiency of document management is imminent. Multi-user real-time collaborative management of documents can not only improve the efficiency of document management, but also clearly understand the willingness of peers and improve the user experience. The biggest challenge in real-time multi-user collaborative management files is to maintain consistent maintenance of the file management system. Traditional consistency maintenance methods are usually based on complex control mechanisms and conversion functions to maintain the consistency of collaborative text, which is not ideal for collaborative management in the cloud environment. In recent years, CRDT (Commutative Replicated Data Type) has been proposed as a new consistency maintenance mechanism in collaborative text editing, but it is rarely applied to scenarios such as cloud environments and file management. This paper proposes a new CRDT-based conflict detection and resolution method to maintain the ultimate consistency of file collaborative management. Firstly, the relationship between operations is defined, and the conflict detection mechanism is proposed. Secondly, an effective scheme for conflict resolution is proposed. Finally, the correctness of the proposed scheme is proved and the time complexity and space complexity are theoretically analyzed. Therefore, the method proposed in this paper can greatly improve the correctness and efficiency of file collaborative management in the cloud environment.

Keywords: Cloud · Collaboration · File · CRDT

1 Introduction

Cloud storage is one of the important core in cloud computing for data sharing and collaboration. Users can access and modify replicated files on a cloud storage system as if they were operating on a local computer and synchronize to the data center and other user sites in real time. The consistency maintenance technology in the cloud environment is still not very common. Xia [1] has studied the application of AST

© Springer Nature Singapore Pte Ltd. 2019
Y. Sun et al. (Eds.): ChineseCSCW 2018, CCIS 917, pp. 87–99, 2019.
https://doi.org/10.1007/978-981-13-3044-5_7

technology in the mobile cloud environment, and proposed a synchronization protocol based on scalar timestamp and global identifier. The address space conversion strategy implements asynchronous collaboration of user pictures in a mobile cloud environment. The real-time file system is an important branch in the field of CSCW. In recent years, many scholars have also carried out related research. For example, Sun [2] studied the real-time synchronization of shared workspaces in cloud storage. The COT algorithm is used to maintain the consistency of the shared space and achieve the desired ideal result. Gao [3] made a discussion on the consistency maintenance of file management of real-time cloud office systems, and proposed an improved COT algorithm designed on the basis of CSOT to adapt to the new centralized architecture in the cloud environment. The operation conversion function solves the conflicts generated when the basic operations are concurrent, so that the file management in the office system in the cloud environment can meet higher real-time requirements.

The consistency maintenance technology of the replicated files in the real-time collaborative editing system is fundamental to ensure the correctness of the system. The commonly used consistency maintenance technologies include OT (Operation Transformation) [4–6], AST(Address Space Transformation) [1, 7], and CRDT [8–10]. CRDT technology is a type of replicated data that can be exchanged for design operations. Each object is assigned a globally unique identifier in the collaborative editing process, so that the interchangeability between objects can be achieved and the consistency of the final result can be maintained. At present, CRDT technology is widely used in the consistency maintenance of collaborative editing systems for 2D graphics and 3D graphics, which has not been applied to complex environments such as cloud storage and file management systems. The literature [10, 11] applies the CRDT algorithm to real-time collaborative CAD systems and linear texts in large-scale situations, and designs conflict detection and solutions to maintain consistent maintenance of collaborative spaces. This paper focuses on the use of CRDT consistency maintenance technology in file management systems in cloud storage, designing reasonable interchangeable data types and algorithms to resolve conflicts between concurrent operations to maintain consistency of shared documents at each site. This paper make important contributions in the following three areas:

(1) Defining the dependency conflict relationship, non-dependency conflict relationship and compatibility relationship of the operation, and designing the operation relationship detection algorithm;
(2) Design a CRDT-based conflict resolution to maintain the ultimate consistency of each copy while maintaining as much user intent as possible;
(3) Illustrate and analyze its efficiency.

2 Data Model and Operational Model

2.1 Basic Data Structure

The replicated workspace of the file management system can be defined as a tree model: $T = \{N, A\}$, where $N = \{N0, N1, N2,...\}$ represents the set of nodes in the tree, and it is also the file or folder of file management system. A is represent the set of arrows in the tree, that is, the relationship between the nodes in the storage space. Each node N has a name and an attribute N.OID, which for the sake of simplicity is represented by capital letters 'A', 'B',…, etc. And the attribute N.OID represents the unique identifier of the most recent operation acting on the node. The path of a node refers to the combination of names from the root node in the tree structure to the parent node. As shown in Fig. 1, the path of the file E is A/D.

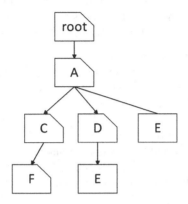

Fig. 1. Basic structure of file

2.2   Basic Definition

Definition 1: Feature Dependency ($\propto$)
Given any two nodes N1 and N2 in the file tree model, N1 is said to be dependent on N2. It is called N1c $\propto$ N2 when:

(1)   N1 and N2 belong to the parent-child relationship, that is, N1.parentname = N2.name;
(2)   There is a node Nx, such that N2.name $\subset$ Nx.path and Nx.name $\subset$ N1.path

Definition 2: Dependency conflict relationship ($\oplus$)
Given the same two operations O1 and O2 of the state vector SV, O1 and O2 have a dependency conflict relationship if and only if the target nodes of O1 and O2 have dependencies and the results obtained are different after execute O1 and O2 by different orders, recorded as O1 $\oplus$ O2.

Definition 3: Non-dependent conflict relationship ($\times$)
Given two operations O1 and O2 of the same state vector SV, the paths of target node of O1 and O2 have non-dependencies and the results obtained are different after execute O1 and O2 by different orders. It is said that O1 and O2 belong to a non-dependent conflict relationship and are recorded as O1 $\times$ O2.

Definition 4: Compatibility relationship ()
O1 and O2 are compatible operations when the target nodes of the given operations O1 and O2 do not have any dependencies, that is, the target nodes are in different subtree streams, and the execution order of the two does not affect their operation results. Recorded as O1 O2.

Definition 5: Unique identifier for operation (OID)
The unique identifier for the operation is a triplet <session, sumsv, site>, where session represents the identifier of the session between the sites, sumsv represents the sum of the state vectors carried by the operation, and site represents the identifier of the site generated by the operation. OID(O1) < OID(O2) when:

(1) OID(O1)[s] < OID(O2)[s], or
(2) When OID(O1)[s] = OID(O2)[s], OID(O1)[sumsv] < OID(O2)[sumsv], or
(3) When OID(O1)[s] = OID(O2)[s] and OID(O1)[sumsv] = OID(O2)[sumsv], OID (O1)[site] < OID(O2)[site].

Definition 6: Global order of operations ($\Rightarrow$)
Given any two operations O1 and O2 in a double-linked list, position(O) represents the position of the operation O in the double-linked list, if P(O1) > P(O2), position (O1) < position(O2) or OID (O1) > OID(O2), then O1 $\Rightarrow$ O2.

2.3   Basic Operation

This article mainly analyzes and studies on the basis operation, such as create, delete, and rename and update. The definition of operations and the basic operation model are as follows:

Definition 7: Operation (O)
In the file management system, operation O is an octet <T, l, T-OID, OID, next, prior, link, s>, where T represents the type of operation, such as create, delete, and rename operations; l represents whether the operation is local or remote, true local, False represents remote; T-OID represents the unique identifier of the target operation of operation O; OID represents the unique identifier of the operation; next represents the pointer that point to the next operation in the double-linked list; prior represents the pointer that point to the previous operation in the double-linked list; link represents the pointer used for the single-linked list in the hash table; the state s represents the state when the operation is executed.

(1) O = Create(p, C, N): Create a subtree T rooted at node N under the folder named p. The subtree can be a folder node or a file. C represents the node type, file or folder.
(2) O = Delete (p, C, N): Delete node N in the folder with path p.
(3) O = Rename (p, C, N.name, N.nameNew): In the folder with the path p, the name of the name N.name is the folder or the file is renamed to N.nameNew.
(4) O = update(p, N, d): The content of the file node N under the update path p is d.

3   Conflict Detection and Conflict Resolution

3.1   Operational Conflict Detection

In the file management system, the basic operations include four basic operations of creating, deleting, renaming, and moving. Due to the dependencies between the objects targeted by the operations and the complex relationships between the operations, the concurrent operations are generated. And the different execution orders will produce different operational effects, that is, conflicts. Therefore, when integrating remote operations, there will be dependency conflicts, non-dependency relationships, and compatibility relationships. Before executing the operation, the relationship between concurrent operations needs to be detected.

Given operations O1 and O2 acting on nodes N1 and N2, respectively, for the four basic operations defined above, there may be conflicts between different pairs of operations. As shown in Table 1, since the table contents are symmetrical, only the upper triangular information of the table is displayed.

Table 1.   List of possible conflict types for operations

	create	delete	rename	update
create	$\times$	$\oplus$	$\oplus_{or}\times$	$\ominus$
delete		$\oplus_{or}\times$	$\oplus_{or}\times$	$\oplus$
rename			$\oplus_{or}\times$	$\oplus_{or}\times$
update				$\ominus$

(1) O1 = create,   O2 = create,   if   and   only   if   p1 = p2,   C1 = C2   and   N1.name = N2.name, O1 and O2 are mutually exclusive conflicts, called O1 $\times$ O2, and other cases are compatible, then called O1 O2.

(2) O1 = create, O2 = rename, if N1 $\propto$ N2, then O1 and O2 are dependent conflict relationships, called O1 $\oplus$ O2; if p1 = p2 and N1.name = N2.nameNew, then O1 and O2 are non-dependent conflicts. It is called O1 $\times$ O2; otherwise, it is a compatible relationship, so it is called O1 O2.

(3) O1 = delete, O2 = delete, if N1 $\propto$ N2, then O1 and O2 are dependent conflict relationships. If p1 = p2 and N1 = N2, O1 and O2 belong to a non-dependent conflict relationship.

(4) O1 = delete, O2 = rename, if N1 $\propto$ N2, then O1 and O2 are dependent conflict relationships, O1 $\oplus$ O2; if p1 = p2, and N1 = N2, then O1 and O2 are non-conflicting conflict relationships, called O1 $\times$ O2; In other cases, it is a compatible relationship, so it is called O1 O2.

(5) O1 = rename, O2 = rename, if N1 $\propto$ N2, then O1 and O2 are dependent conflict relationships, O1 $\oplus$ O2; if p1 = p2 and N1.nameNew = N2.nameNew or N1 = N2 and N1.nameNew != N2.nameNew, O1 and O2 are non-dependent conflict relationships, called O1 $\times$ O2; in other cases, they are all compatible, then called O1 O2.

(6) O1 = delete, O2 = update. If N2 $\propto$ N1, then O1 and O2 are dependent conflict relationships, O1O2; in other cases, they are compatible, then O1O2.

(7) O1 = rename, O2 = update, if N2 $\propto$ N1, then O1 and O2 are dependent conflict relationships, O1 $\oplus$ O2; if p1 = p2 and N1 = N2, then O1 and O2 are non-dependent conflict relationships; Compatible relationship, then called O1 O2.

(8) In other cases, the operation is a compatible relationship, which is called O1 O2.

3.2 Operational Conflict Resolution

In a real-time file management system, the consistency requirement is to maintain the CCI (Consistence, Convergence, Intention) model. The CRDT data model will converge automatically, while consistency requirements and intent maintenance require need to achieve as far as possible to meet the intent of all users. For the detection of the relationship between the above operations, the requirements are as follows:

(1) Compatible relationship: the effect of all operations should be achieved;
(2) Non-dependent conflict relationship: user's intentions should be maintained as much as possible;
(3) Dependency conflict relationship: Maintain the effect of all users' operations as much as possible.

Dependency conflict resolution: Given any two operations O1 and O2, where O1 is an already executed operation and O2 is a remote operation, and O1 and O2 belong to a dependency conflict relationship, the solution to the conflict relationship is as follows: if the object that operates O1 and O2 has a dependency conflict, or the operation depends on a conflict, or the ID of the operation O1 is greater than the ID of O2, then the operation O2 is undo, O1 is executed, O2 is re-executed, and the operation O1 is linked. Go to the front of O2; otherwise, link operation O2 directly to the right side of operation O1.

Non-dependency conflict resolution: If operation O1 and operation O2 belong to a non-dependent conflict relationship and the id of operation O1 is smaller than O2, operation conversion is performed on operation O2, and operation O1 is linked to the front of operation O2, otherwise, operation O1 is undo, and the O2 is executed, O1 is transformed and executed. Operate O2 is put into double-linked list at the right of O1.

Compatible operational relationship solutions: If the operation O1 and the O2 are compatible, and the OID of the operation O1 is smaller than O2, O2 is undo, the operation O1 is executed and O2 is re-executed, and then O1 is linked to the front of the operation O2. Otherwise, O1is directly executed, and then put it into double-linked list at the right of O2.

3.3   Local Operation Integration Process

When the local operation is generated, it is directly executed, and the operation is directly linked to the back of the double-linked list. If a remote operation is received, its target operation is found, and it is detected whether there is an operation with the same target operation as it is, and their relationship. And based on their relationship, determine their correct position in the double-linked list. The local operation execution process is as follows:

Algorithm1: LocalOperation(O)
Execute a local operation O directly
If head.next == null then
O is double linked next to head
Else
O double linked next to last operation in Li
SV[i]=SV[i]+1
OID stored in Hi
End if

3.4   Remote Operation Integration Process

In Algorithm 2, when the remote operation O is integrated, the target operation needs to be found in the double-linked list. If there is an operation after the target operation, it is necessary to detect the relationship between the operation and the operation O, and find the correct position of operation O in the double-linked list. The function FindPosiong () referenced in the algorithm is responsible for finding the position of the operation O in the double-linked list.

Algorithm2: RemoveOperation(O)
Receive a remote operation O
tar=Hi.get(N.OID); nextTar=tar.next;
If nextTar=null then
O is double linked after nextTar in Li
Else
FindPosition(nextTar, O)
Execute the operation O
O is double linked in Li
SV[i]=SV[i]+1
OID is stored in Hi
End if

Algorithm 3 finds the concurrent operation according to the state vector, and finds the correct link position in the double-linked list according to the relationship between the concurrent operations.

Algorithm3: FindPosition(O1, O2)

While(O1.next != null) then
  if O1.s == O2.s then
    If FindRelation(O1,O2)=O1 $\oplus$ O2 then
      If N1 α N2 then
        O1=O1.next, continue
      Else
        Undo O1, execute O2, redo O1
        O2 is double-linked before O1,break
      End if
    Else if FindRelation(O1,O2)=O1 $\times$ O2 then
      If OID(O1)>OID(O2)

        O2=Tranform(O1 $\times$ O2)
        O1=O1.next, continue
      Else
        O1=Transorm(O1 $\times$ O2)
        O2 is double-linked before O1,break
      End if
    Else if FindRelation(O1,O2)=O1 $\ominus$ O2 then
      If OID(O1) > OID(O2)
        O1 = O1.next, continue
    else
        O2 is double-linked before O1,break
      End if
    End if
  Else if O1.s !=O2.s && OID(O1)<OID(O2) then
    O1=O1.next,continue
  Else
    undo O1, executed O2, redo O1,break
  End if
End while
If O1.next = null then
  O2 is double linked after O1
End if

---

4   Consistent Maintenance Based on CRDT in Cloud

This paper studies the consistency maintenance of collaborative file management system based on cloud environment. The design is based on CRDT data type to design and store user operations, making it suitable for file management systems in cloud environments. The cloud environment mainly adopts the C/S architecture. The consistency maintenance of file management in the design cloud environment must take into account the structural changes. Therefore, this section designs reasonable server and client algorithms based on the C/S architecture, and concentrates the analysis and calculation work on the server. The client only needs to process the locally generated operations and the operation server calculated and analyzed. Analyzed.

The main tasks of the client are: executing and sending local operations to the server; receiving remote operations, finding the correct location in the singly linked list and executing it.

Algorithm9: ControlPro on client
Get the latest workspace status from the server
Thread1:
Generate a local operation O
LocalOperation(O)
Send O to server
Thread2:
Receive remote operations sequence T
For(i=0;i<T.length;i++)
O = T[i]
RemoveOperation(O)
end

The main task of the server is: thread 1 handles the new connection request and sends the latest copy to the new site; thread 2 receives and performs the remote operation, and updates the target operation of the remote operation to be the OID of operation in front of it in the double-linked list. Thread 3 is responsible for forwarding the updated remote operations to other sites.

Algorithm10: ControlPro on Server
Init()
Li=[]; Hi=[];
Thread1:
handling new connection requests
Thread2:
Receive remove operations sequences RS from clients
RS =[T1,T2,...Tn]
For(i=0;i<RS.length;i++)
For(j=0;j<RS[i].length;j++)
O=RS[i][j]
RemoveOperation(O)
T-OID(O)=OID(O.jprior)
End
Send updated operations sequence Ti to other client   than i
End

5 Efficiency Analysis and Case Verification

5.1 Efficiency Analysis

Time complexity: As shown in the local operation execution algorithm, the time complexity of directly querying for the target operation of local operation according to the hash table and the unique identifier is $O(1)$. When the session begins, the last operation to be performed is found in the double-linked list, in which case the time complexity is $O(n)$, where n represents the number of operations that have been performed in the double-linked list. In the case of integrated remote operations, the time complexity is $O(1)$ at best. In this case, the target operation is found in the hash table through the unique identifier t-oid, while the remote operation is located right next to the target operation, only if there is no other operation after the target operation, or if the remote operation needs to be directly linked to the target operation. When considering the worst case, the integrated remote operation calls the FindPosition function to find the correct position of the operation, and the worst time complexity of the FindPosition function is $O(m)$, where m is the operation that exists after the target operation.

Space complexity: In our proposed method, each operation O is an eight tuple <T, l, T-OID, OID, next, prior, link, s>, assuming its length is Q and there are n operations in the double-linked list, and then the space complexity in this case is $(Q \times n)$, Suppose the hash table has the same space overhead as the double-linked list, and the total number of files or folders per site is P, certainly not more than the number of operations in the double-linked list. Each file or folder has a name attribute and Maintain an operation identifier, assuming that the occupied space is L. So in our proposed method, the total space complexity is $(2Q \times n + P \times L)$.

5.2 Case Verification

This section mainly designs a collaborative file management scenario to verify the correctness of the proposed algorithm. Suppose there are three sites collaboratively managing files. The initial file system space is as shown Fig. 2 and the initial session is 1 and there already have folder A and folders B and C in it. The relationship between the two sites is ID(site0) < ID(site1), Li. On behalf of the site i, a double-linked list for storing operations that have been performed, for the sake of convenience, the positional relationship between operations in the double-linked list is indicated by $\rightarrow$. Site 1 generates 2 operations: O1 = create(A/B, 'E'), O3 = create(A/B/E, 'F'). Site 2 generates 1 operations: O4 = rename(A/B, 'E', 'M'). Site 3 generates 3 operations: O2 = create(A/B, 'E'), O5 = delete(A/B, 'E1'). Where sv(O1) = (1, 0, 0), OID (O1) = (1, 1, 1), sv(O2) = (0, 0, 1), OID(O2) = (1, 1, 3), sv(O3) = (2, 0, 1), OID (O3) = (2, 3, 1), sv(O4) = (1, 1, 1), OID(O4) = (2, 3, 2), and sv(O5) = (1, 0, 2), OID (O5) = (2, 3, 3).

At Site 1, the local operation O1 is executed immediately and directly linked to the last of the double-linked list, that is, the double-linked list of the site 1 is L1 = O1; the remote operation O2 arrives, and the target operation of O2 is the same as that of O1, and the relationship between O1 and O2 needs to be detected that is the non-dependent

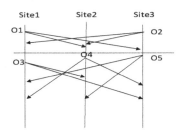

Fig. 2. Operation sequence diagram

conflict relationship, and OID(O1) < OID(O2). The conversion operation O2 is create (A/B, 'E1') and is linked after the operation O1. The local operation O3 is executed immediately, and the double linked list at this time is L1 = O1 → O2 → O3. The remote operation O5 arrives, and its target operation is O1, which is not in the same session with O2, so it should compared with O3. The relationship of them is a dependency conflict relationship, so O5 is executed according to the dependency and put O5 at after O3. Remote operation O4 arrives, its target operation is the same as O1, and it is not compared under different sessions. O4 has the same state as O3 and O5. O4 and O3 are dependency conflict. According to the relationship between O3 and O4, O4 is executed. O4 and O5 are compatible and OID(O4) < OID(O5), so O5 is undo, O4 is executed, and O5 is re-executed. The double-linked list at this time is L1 = O1 → O2 → O3 → O4 → O5.

At Site 2, the remote operation O2 arrives. There is no concurrent operation with it after the target operation. It is directly linked to the current double-linked list. The remote operation O1 arrives. It is the same as the target operation of operation O1. They belong to the non-dependent conflict relationship. O2 is converted to create(A/B, 'E1') and linked after operation O1. The local operation O4 is executed immediately and is directly linked at the end of the double-linked list. The double-linked list at this time is L1 = O1 → O2 → O4. The remote operation O5 arrives and its target operation is the same as O1. It is not in the same session as O1 and O2 and will not be detected. O5 is in the same state as O4 and they are compatible with OID(O4) < OID(O5), so O5 is behind O4 in the double-linked list. Remote operation O3 arrives, its target operation is O1, O2 is not considered, O3 and O4 belong to the dependency conflict relationship. According to the dependency, O4 is undo, O3 is executed, and O4 is re-executed. The double-linked list at this time is L2 = O1 → O2 → O3 → O4 → O5.

At Site 3, similarly, the execution order of the operations is O2, O1, O5, O4, O3, and the operation sequence stored in the double-linked list is L2 = O1 → O2 → O3 → O4 → O5 (Fig. 3).

It can be seen from the above case analysis that Site 1, Site 2 and Site3 are executed in different orders, and the result of consistency as shown in the figure can be obtained.

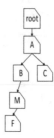

Fig. 3. State diagram maintained by each site after collaborative work

6 Conclusion

In the paper, a new CRDT-based conflict detection and solution is proposed for real-time file management system in cloud environment maintain consistent maintenance of collaborative work. Firstly, the basic operation and the relationship between operations are defined, and the conflict detection mechanism is proposed. Secondly, the effective solution of conflict resolution is proposed. Finally, the correctness of the proposed scheme is proved and the time complexity and space are theoretically analyzed. Complexity, the conflict detection and solution proposed in this paper can effectively maintain the consistency of the final text and ensure the correct execution of the operation. In future research, we will focus on fine-grained research, that is, on the operation of file content, and improve the algorithm to adapt to the study of fine-grained consistency maintenance. At the same time, with the rise of cloud environment and the popularity of mobile, the research in mobile cloud environment is also becoming more and more popular. The next work can apply file collaborative management to mobile cloud environment and design according to new application scenarios. Reasonable algorithms to maintain consistency of collaborative work.

Acknowledgments. We would like to thank the reviewers, whose valuable critique and comments helped to improve this paper. Moreover, this work is supported by the Shanghai Natural Science Foundation under Grant No. 17ZR1419100, and the Open Project Program of Shanghai Key Laboratory of Data Science (No. 201609060003).

References

1. Xia, H., et al.: A partial replication approach for anywhere anytime mobile commenting. In: ACM Conference on Computer Supported Cooperative Work and Social Computing, pp. 530–541. ACM (2014)
2. Ng, A., Sun, C.: Operational transformation for real-time synchronization of shared workspace in cloud storage. In: The International Conference, pp. 61–70 (2016)
3. Gao, L., Qiang, Z., Xin, Z.: Research on consistency maintenance of file management in real-time cloud office system. In: The Chinese Conference, pp. 245–246 (2017)

4. Sun, C., Xia, S., Zhang, Y., et al.: Achieving convergence, causality-preservation, and intention-preservation in real-time cooperative editing systems. Proc. ACM Trans. Comput.–Hum. Interact. **4**, 63–108 (1998)
5. Bin, S., Du, L., Tun, L., et al.: An operational transformation based synchronization protocol for Web 2.0 applications. In: Proceedings of ACM Conference on Computer-Supported Cooperative Work, vol. 4, pp. 563–572 (2011)
6. Gao, L., Xin, Z., Qiang, Z.: Research for consistency maintenance of real-time collaborative associated graph model in the mobile platform. In: Chinese Conference on Computer Supported Cooperative Work and Social Computing, pp. 243–244. ACM (2017)
7. Ning, G., Yang, J., Zhang, Q.: Consistency maintenance based on the mark & retrace technique in groupware systems. In: Proceedings of GROUP 2005, November 2012
8. Preguica, N., et al.: A commutative replicated data type for cooperative editing. In: IEEE International Conference on Distributed Computing Systems, pp. 395–403. IEEE (2009)
9. Ahmednacer, M., Martin, S., Urso, P.: File system on CRDT. Comput. Sci. (2012)
10. Lv, X., et al.: CRDT-based conflict detection and resolution for massive-scale real-time collaborative CAD systems. In: The Chinese Conference, pp. 185–188 (2017)
11. Lv, X., He, F., Cai, W., et al.: A string-wise CRDT algorithm for smart and large-scale collaborative editing systems. Adv. Eng. Inform. **33**, 397–409 (2016)

A Generic Arrival Process Model for Generating Hybrid Cloud Workload

Chunyan An[ID], Jian-tao Zhou[✉], and Zefeng Mou

Inner Mongolia University, Huhhot 010021, China
cszhoujiantao@qq.com

Abstract. In cloud computing, the arrival process of user requests is becoming more diversiform with the globalization of users and the popularization of mobile technology. Moreover, the workloads in cloud computing are tending towards a hybrid of more applications types. It is hardly for the traditional arrival process models to cover the ever-increasing new arrival processes in reality. For that, we propose a general and flexible arrival process model to describe various arrival processes. At the same time, we present a unified generation algorithm to generate the corresponding workload arrival instance based on the arrival process model automatically. The model defines the arrival process by four steps: firstly defines the number of intervals during the workload lifetime, then defines the length of each time interval, next defines the number of requests arriving during each time interval, lastly defines the arrival time points during each time interval. In the case study, we use the generic arrival process model to describe three arrival process models of typical cloud application types and a custom arrival process model, and present corresponding arrival instances using the generation algorithm. The cases showed the flexibility and extensibility of the model. The model and algorithm are simple and generic and are more approaching to realistic hybrid arrival processes.

Keywords: Cloud computing · Cloud workload generation
Generic arrival process

1 Introduction

Cloud applications are reaching more and more industries, such as online social network services, user data processing services, online videos, customer relationship management applications, online mass games, online booking and online banking. Different cloud applications have different workload patterns. At the same time, the global distribution of cloud users and the continuous development of mobile technology make workload patterns more complex. For example, because the users are in different time zones, the new diurnal pattern may become a superposition of multiple traditional diurnal patterns. In most real-world cloud scenarios, the workload population is hybrid with more than one cloud applications, and the workload patterns are more and more diversified. To mimic the cloud workloads closer to reality, a generic workload model is needed. A generic arrival process model plays a key role which should cover a variety of arrival processes and independent of application types.

© Springer Nature Singapore Pte Ltd. 2019
Y. Sun et al. (Eds.): ChineseCSCW 2018, CCIS 917, pp. 100–114, 2019.
https://doi.org/10.1007/978-981-13-3044-5_8

The limitations of existing arrival process models for cloud workload generation can be broadly classified into two types. One limitation is the arrival process models are too unitary, for example only for specific applications or mimic some specific scenario such as burst. Another limitation is the arrival process models are not general and scalable enough to cover a variety of arrival processes. For instance, most current arrival models are defined as arrival time points that are consistent with an independent and identical distribution like possion process mostly. These models lack the time-dependent characteristics such as periodicity. Though in recent years, the arrival process models based on MAP (Markov arrival process) were studied to describe some time-dependent characteristics. Unfortunately, the number of states and the generation matrix of MAP models depend on different applications or different scenarios. As a result, the arrival models lack generality and calculations for workload generation will multiply as the number of states increases. Therefore, the MAP model is not suitable for use as a generic arrival process model to generate hybrid workloads.

In this paper, a hierarchical generic arrival process model was developed. The main characteristics of various arrival process models were captured and were independent of different applications types. At the same time, we proposed a unified algorithm to automatically generate arrival process instances that conform to the arrival model definition.

The arrival process model is defined by four steps: (1) the duration of workload which is defined as the number of time intervals, (2) the variation of each time interval, (3) the variation of the requests numbers within each time intervals, (4) each arrival time points within each metering interval in final.

Our generation algorithm supports that each step can be defined as a constant, or a statistical distribution/process, or a self-defined function. Then the algorithm automatically generates an arrival process instance based on the defined arrival process model. The generation of sample arrival time points conforms to the corresponding definition and has random characteristics. The option of self-defined function further enhances the extensibility and flexibility of the generic arrival process model.

In the case study following the model definition, we demonstrated how to use the generic arrival model to define the arrival process models for three representative cloud applications types. A Web application, a batch application and a MapReduce application were picked. Additionally, an arrival process model included a self-defined function was illustrated. Furthermore, the corresponding four arrival process instances were generated based on their arrival process models.

The rest of this article is organized as follows: Sect. 2 analyses the related works involved in arrival process models and generation algorithms. Section 3 details the generic arrival process model and its generation algorithm, as well as four example demonstrations. Section 4 summarizes our work and future directions.

2 Related Works

A number of researchers have investigated modeling and simulation of arrival processes. There are three typical representations of arrival process: point process, count process and rate process [1]. The random variable in point process is the interval between adjacent arrival time points. The random variable in count process is the number of points arrived at each equally spaced interval T. The random variable in rate process is the normalized count, which equals to the number of points in each time interval divided by time interval T. The point process is the most accurate because it requires all the arrival time points. Count process and rate process lose the accurate time points with interval T. However, if the research problem does not care about the accurate arrival time points, the latter two processes could be chosen. For instance, in [2] different arrival rates were defined for different types of jobs. In the existing studies about arrival process model, some studies adopted one representation, others mentioned above combined representations.

Next, the related works about arrival process model are classified into three types: i.i.d. first-order model, temporal dependent model and hierarchical model.

At present, the first-order arrival models mostly adopted point process representation. That is, the intervals sequence conforms to some distribution or some statistical process. The most common assumption was the arrival process followed the Poisson Process [3, 4]. Some researchers argued that this assumption are unrealistic. They built their arrival process models by fitting real data. For example, in [5] the arrival of batch jobs conformed to Weibull distribution. In [6] the arrival intervals were in accordance with Pareto distribution by fitting the traces from the Google internal data center. In [7] the interarrival times in private cloud workloads were well modeled by a 3-phase Hyper-Exponential distribution. The author found the model with 5 parameters was more realistically than the lognormal and Pareto models with 2 parameters. And in [8] the author used a queueing system to model a cloud system with a lot of servers, and interarrival times were denoted as a phase-type distribution. The phase-type distribution is composed of adjustable number of exponential phases. This phase-type arrival process model is a general i.i.d. first-order model because any distributions can be generated closely by a combination of these exponential phases [9].

The i.i.d. first-order arrival process models describe the statistical distribution of interarrival times within a period of time, but not the temporal dependence between different time periods. Namely, they cannot define the temporal features such as periodicities, burstiness and self-similarity. To address these shortcomings, a MAP (Markov Arrival Process) model was proposed in [10] to represent the distribution and correlation of arrival times. Meantime, the author [10] pointed out that the MAP model is a superset of i.i.d. first-order models, and also gave a method to fit the MAP model. MAP models define that arrival process can be in different states. During each state holding period, the arrival process conforms to a certain distribution, which is generally exponential distribution [11], called MMPP (Markov Modulated Poisson Process), or other distribution [12], called semi-Markov process, and the state transition is defined by an intensity matrix. In recent years, some researchers believe MAP models are more realistic than the i.i.d. first-order processes. In [13], the arrival process of a Web application was modeled by MAP. The work in [14] fitted the interarrival times for Grid level jobs through Poisson, Interrupted Poisson Process (IPP), MMPP2, MMPP3, and MMPP4 models. The result was that MMPP2 is closer to the real data in changeability than Poisson and IPP. Although MAP model introduces more realistic temporal correlation, the state definitions and generation matrix are dependent on applications and workload scenarios. Moreover, the complexity of model definition will be multiplied with the increase of the number of states. Therefore, MAP models are not suitable for generating diverse hybrid cloud workloads in terms of generality and scalability.

In order to more accurately grasp the characteristics of the arrival process, some studies have adopted hierarchical models. This is similar to our modeling approach. In [15] the author built a two-level arrival process model to describe the access to a file system. Firstly the access times were divided into groups by clustering method. Then three features were used to define arrival process: the interval between clusters, the number of accesses within a cluster and the interarrival times within a cluster. Lastly, the arrival process model was proved to synthesize access instances of a distributed replicated file system close to the original data. Another research [1] fitted a LRD (Long Range Dependent) arrival process model in two steps. First, the arrival rate process was fitted by a multifractal wavelet model. Second, Controlled-Variability InF was made to convert rate process to arrival time points. After the two steps a completely determined LRD arrival instance were generated. Strictly speaking, the above two studies only gave the hierarchical method to generate arrival process instances which could be close to real trace logs. Neither of them proposed arrival process model formally. Besides, they cannot be general applicable in other types of applications or scenarios. The hierarchical arrival process model we proposed combines the counting process with point process, captures the main characteristics of the arrival process, and maximizes the flexibility of the model with time-section and hierarchical methods. This model can be used to specify diverse arrival scenarios for different applications.

At present, most cloud workload generation tools are built in the Benchmarks. These workload generators typically enable users to generate the required workloads by defining the distributions or parameter values of the arrival process. Most arrival process models in Benchmarks are i.i.d. first-order model. For example, a popular Web Benchmark: Rubis [16] defined that user session length and think time between sessions conformed to negative exponential distributions. Some researchers [17] adjusted the arrival process model of Rubis, where the request arrival rates can be set. And at a request arrival rate, the requests arrived accord with uniform distribution. A "standard" Benchmark for NOSQL cloud system is: Yahoo! Cloud Serving Benchmark (YCSB) [18]. The total number of operations and different throughputs can be configured before workload generation. Then during each timeframe, the interarrival times are generated conformed to uniform distribution. The generated arrival process based on arrival rate lost the variability of arrival time points within a timeframe. SPEC Cloud ™ IaaS 2016 [19] use open source CBTool [20] to generate workload. CBTool allows users to set the duration of a workload, the maximum number of requests, and the distribution of arrival process. Our workload generation tool is more flexible than CBTool. Four features can be configured: the number of intervals during the workload lifetime, the length of each time interval, the number of requests arriving during each time interval and the arrival time points during each time interval.

We noticed there are some recent Benchmarks turned to generate workloads based on MAP models. For example, BURSE [21] was proposed to generate workloads with spikes and self-similarity according to a MMPP model. However, MMPP model is complex and not intuitive for users. And one model is only true usually of one specific application or some specific scenarios. As a consequence, MMPP model is not suitable for a general workload generation tool. By contrast, our arrival process model and generation algorithm are more simple, general and intuitive. Our work laid a solid foundation for generating hybrid cloud workloads. The work about a general workload model and generation tool in cloud computing can be referred to [22].

3   A Generic Arrival Process Model

For simplicity and generalization of the arrival process model, the inner features which are specific to applications are out of the question. For example, for web applications, only the arrival time points of the first request in each session are considered. The other requests in sessions are taken no account because the requests arrived interdependently. Similarly, for MapReduce application, only the arrival time points of each job are included. The start-times of mapper and reducer in each job are excluded. In other words, our model is concerned only the variations in the number and frequency of user requests which are common for different applications. A generic model defined the interdependencies of a cloud application you can refer to our work [22]. Another aspect requires further explanation, the generic arrival model defined one arrival at a time, but it can easily be extended to the batch arrival process by adding a bulk-number parameter.

In this section, the generic arrival process model will be reported in three parts: (1) the mathematical specification of the general arrival process model, (2) the instances generation algorithm based on the arrival process model, (3) case study for three typical cloud applications and one arrival process model with self-defined function.

3.1   Formal Specification of a Generic Arrival Process Model

In this section the arrival process is formally defined by a hierarchical mathematical model. For the convenience of the reader, Table 1 lists a summary of the main annotations in the order introduced in the paper.

Table 1. The annotations in the model

Annotation	Data type	Definition
Duration	Integer	The duration of workload
$F(\Delta T_x)$, $\{\Delta T_x, x = 1, 2, \cdots, \text{Duration}\}$	Stochastic process	ΔT_x is the length of xth time interval
$\theta(.)$	Function	ΔT_x conforms to function $\theta(.)$, $\Delta T_x \sim \theta(.)$, $x = 1, 2, \cdots, \text{Duration}$
$FN^{R-U}(\Delta T_x)$, $\{N^{R-U}(\Delta T_x), x = 1, 2, \cdots, \text{Duration}\}$	Stochastic process	$N^{R-U}(\Delta T_x)$ is the quantity of arrived requests in ΔT_x (the xth interval)
$\delta(.)$	Function	$N^{R-U}(\Delta T_x)$ conforms to function $\delta(.)$, $N^{R-U}(\Delta T_x) \sim \delta(.)$
$F(T(x, k))$, $\{T(x, k), k = 1, 2, \cdots N^{R-U}(\Delta T_x)\}$	Stochastic process	$T(x, k)$ is the kth arrival time point within the xth time interval
$\{\text{Func}_x(), x = 1, 2, \cdots, \text{Duration}\}$	A set of functions	$\text{Func}_x()$ is the function that the arrival time points within the xth time interval conforms to

A generic arrival process model that can be used to generate hybrid cloud workload requires two conditions as follows

- ☐ Generality: the model can grasp the essential characteristics of the arrival process for different cloud applications. And more complex and diverse arrival processes can be generated by superposition.
- ☐ Accuracy: the arrival process model combines counting process and point process to generate time-dependent workloads without losing the accurate arrival time points.

In this model, firstly the total time of the workload is defined in terms of the number of time intervals included. Then, the length of each time interval and the number of requests arrived within each time interval can be constant or variable. And the arrival time points within each time interval can be defined individually. This enables the arrival process model not only to describe the accurate arrival points within a time interval but also to describe the temporal dependence among different time intervals, such as periodicity, bursty, variability and self-similarity. The generic arrival process model is defined in four steps as follows.

1. The total time: *Duration*

   An arrival process is divided into several time intervals. The total time of an arrival process is defined as a positive integer *Duration*, which represents the number of time intervals included in an arrival process. The length of each time interval could be unequal.

2. The length of each time interval

   A total arrival process is split into *Duration* continuous and disjoint time intervals. The length of each time interval could be equal, noted as a constant ΔT. It can also be variable, the variation of the lengths can be represented as a stochastic process $F(\Delta T_x)\{\Delta T_x, \quad x = 1, 2, \ldots, Duration\}$, where ΔT_x is a random variable which represents the length of x th time interval. Let $\theta(.)$ be a function used to determine the variation of the interval lengths. The relationship between $F(\Delta T_x)$ and $\theta(.)$ is denoted as

$$F(\Delta T_x) \sim \theta(.) \tag{1}$$

3. The quantity of arrivals in each interval

   The variation of the arrival numbers in each time interval is denoted as a stochastic process $FN^{R-U}(\Delta T_x), \{N^{R-U}(\Delta T_x), x = 1, 2, \ldots, Duration\}$, where $N^{R-U}(\Delta T_x)$ is the number of arrived requests within ΔT_x (the xth time interval). Let $\delta(.)$ be a function used to determine the variation of the arrival numbers in each time interval. The relationship between $FN^{R-U}(\Delta T_x)$ and $\delta(.)$ is denoted as

$$FN^{R-U}(\Delta T_x) \sim \delta(.) \tag{2}$$

A special case is that all time intervals are equal, so we simplified the stochastic process as $FN^{R-U}(x), \{N^{R-U}(x), x = 1, 2, \cdots\}$, where $N^{R-U}(x)$ is the quantity of arrivals in the xth interval. Let $\delta(.)$ be a function used to determine the variation of the arrival numbers in each time interval. The relationship between $FN^{R-U}(x)$ and $\delta(.)$ is denoted as

$$FN^{R-U}(x) \sim \delta(.) \tag{3}$$

4. The arrival time points in each time interval.
The arrival point process for each time interval can be defined individually. For each time interval ΔT_x, $x = 1, 2, \cdots,$ Duration, an arrival point process composed of $N^{R-U}(\Delta T_x)$ time points is denoted as a stochastic process

$$F(T(x, k)), \; \{T(x, k), k = 1, 2, \cdots N^{R-U}(\Delta T_x)\} \tag{4}$$

where $T(x, k)$ is the kth arrival time point within the xth time interval. $T(x, k), k = 1, 2, \cdots N^{R-U}(\Delta T_x)$ should be satisfied with

$$\sum_{l=1}^{x-1} \Delta T_x < T(x, k) \le \sum_{l=1}^{x-1} \Delta T_x, k = 1, 2, \cdots N^{R-U}(\Delta T_x) \tag{5}$$

We denote a set of functions $\{Func_x(), x = 1, 2, \cdots,$ Duration$\}$, where $Func_x()$ is the function that the arrival time points within the xth time interval conforms to. Namely,

$$F(T(x, k)) \sim Func_x(), x = 1, 2, \cdots, Duration, \; k = 1, 2, \cdots N^{R-U}(\Delta T_x) \tag{6}$$

A special case is that each arrival point process is consistent, so we simplified the stochastic process and the function as $F(T(k))$ and $Func()$ respectively. And they have

$$F(T(k)) \sim Func(), k = 1, 2, \cdots N^{R-U}(\Delta T_x) \tag{7}$$

3.2   A Generation Algorithm Based on Arrival Process Model

The input parameters of the generation algorithm are on basis of the generic arrival process model, include: (1) the number of time intervals *Duration*, (2) the function $\theta(.)$ determining the variation of the interval lengths, (3) the function $\delta(.)$ determining the variation of the arrival numbers in each time interval, (4) a set of functions $\{Func_x(), x = 1, 2, \cdots, Duration\}$ determining the arrival time points within each time interval conforms to. Here $\theta(.)$, $\delta(.)$ and every $Func_x(), x = 1, 2, \cdots, Duration$ can be assigned by three methods: constant, statistical distribution or process and self-defined function. Any statistical distribution can be assigned, such as exponential distribution, Weibull distribution. The steps of the algorithm are consistent with the steps of the generic arrival process model. Firstly, a list of $\{\Delta T_x, x = 1, 2, \cdots, Duration\}$ are generated randomly according to $\theta(.)$. Secondly, a list of $\{N^{R-U}(\Delta T_x), x = 1, 2, \cdots, Duration\}$ are generated randomly according to $\delta(.)$. Lastly, arrival time points $\{T(x, k), x = 1, 2, \cdots, Duration, k = 1, 2, \cdots, N^{R-U}(\Delta T_x)\}$ are generated randomly according to the corresponding $Func_x()$, $x = 1, 2, \cdots, Duration$. Table 2 showed the pseudo-code for generating the arrival process instance based on the arrival process model.

Table 2. Pseudo-code of generation algorithm

```
Input: Duration, θ(.),  δ(.),  Funcₓ( ), x = 1,2,⋯, Duration
Output: { T(x, k), x = 1,2,⋯, Duration, k = 1,2,⋯ N^(R_U)(ΔTₓ) }
----------------------------------------------------------------------------------------------------

--------------------
Begin
i←1
T(1,1) ←0
while (i<=Duration)
{
      ΔTᵢ ←θ(.)
}
   if (δ(ΔTₓ) is not defined)
{
   i←1
      while (i<=Duration)
      { k←1
         while (T(i, k)<ΔTᵢ)
          {
             T(i, k + 1)←T(i, k)+ random number that matches the random process Funcₓ( )
             k←k+1
          }
         i←i+1
      }
}
   else
   {
     i←1
       while(i<=Duration)
       {
          N^(R_U)(ΔTᵢ)←δ(ΔTᵢ)
          k←1
while(k<=N^(R_U)(ΔTᵢ))
          {
              T(i, k + 1)←T(i, k)+random number that matches the random process Funcₓ( )
             k←k+1
          }
          i←i+1
       }
}
End
```

3.3 Case Study

To explain the generality of the arrival process model for different cloud applications in detail, we take three typical cloud applications: Web applications [23], MapReduce applications [24] and batch applications [5] as examples. We explained in detail the definitions of the three arrival processes using our generic model, and gave three generated arrival process instances applying our generation algorithm. At the same time, we presented an extra example on the definition of an arrival process model with self-defined function as well as the generated arrival process instance.

Web Application Arrival Process Model Example

In this web application workload, the arrival process was divided into rounds. The time of each round is unequal. Within one round, the number of active users is denoted as *Concurrent_Users*, and each active user initiated one session. *Ramp_Up_Period* specifies the time to initiate all the sessions in one round. If all sessions are created at the same time, then $Ramp\_Up\_Period = 0$. Otherwise, the sessions are created one after another at regular intervals. The interval between two adjacent sessions is *Ramp_Up_Period/Concurrent_Users*. For example, there were 5 active users in a round and 10 s of *Ramp_Up_Period*, it will take 2 s between each session creation. The length of each session conforms to the negative exponential distribution Exp(15). Thus, the time of each round is defined as

$$F(\Delta T_x) \sim \theta(.) = Ramp\_Up\_Period + Exp(15) \tag{8}$$

Because in one round each active user can only create one session, the number of sessions in one round $N^{R-U}(\Delta T_x)$ is the number of active users. According to the specification in [23], the variation of the arrival numbers in each round is defined as

$$FN^{R-U}(x) \sim \delta(.) = N(10, 3) \tag{9}$$

The arrival time points in round x is defined as

$$T(x, k) = (k - 1) * \left(\frac{Ramp\_Up\_Period}{Concurrent\_Users} \right), \; k = 1, 2, \ldots N^{R-U}(\Delta T_x) \tag{10}$$

We use the following steps to generate the arrival process instance.

1. Give *Duration* a value
2. Generate *Duration Concurrent_Users* which are random sampled by normal distribution $N(10, 3)$
3. Generate *Concurrent_Users* session lengths which are random sampled by negative exponential distribution Exp(15). In each round, the length of a round is given by the sum of Ramp_Up_Period and the maximum session length of the samples.
4. In each round, Ramp_Up_Period is set as 800 s, then the interarrival time is (*Ramp_Up_Period/Concurrent_Users*)

Because of limited space, Fig. 1 showed an arrival process instance with *Duration* = 4, the number of sessions in 4 rounds are 9, 11, 13, 5, the 4 session lengths are 823.6955 s, 849.5503 s, 826.9957 s, 826.9957 s. We take the start time of the round as the first arrival point. And the interarrival time in each round is in turn Ramp_Up_Period/Concurrent_Users = 88.8889 s, 72.7273 s, 61.5385 s, 160 s.

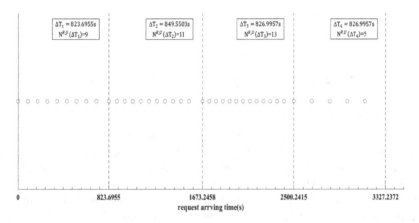

Fig. 1. A web application arrival process instance

MapReduce Application Arrival Process Model Example
The arrival process model [24] is first-order. The interarrival time conformed to *Weibull*(20, 0.5). As a result, it is not necessary to divide the arrival process model into time intervals, then *Duration* = 1;And the interarrival time Δt_k conforms to *Weibull*(20, 0.5), that is Func( ) $\sim$ *Weibull*(20, 0.5), thus, the kth arrival time point is equal to

$$T(1,\ k) = T(1, (k-1)) + \Delta t_k,\ k = 1, 2\ldots \tag{11}$$

We use the following steps to generate the arrival process instance.

1. *Duration* = 1, ΔT = 6000 s
2. Randomly generate sample points conforming to *Weibull*(20, 0.5) as interarrival times until the arrival time point is beyond ΔT.

Figure 2 shows an instance of the arrival process, which generates 20 arrivals within 6000 s.

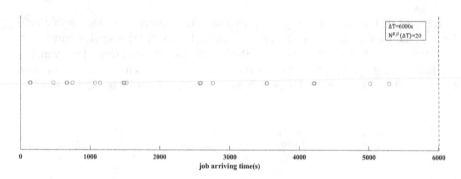

Fig. 2. A MapReduce application arrival process instance

Batch Application Arrival Process Model Example

The arrival process model [5] appears Daily-cycle pattern. The day is first divided into 48 intervals by half an hour, i.e. $\Delta T = 1800$ s. Then the variation of the number of arrivals during each of 48 intervals is defined to conform to Weibull distribution, i.e. $\delta(.) \sim W(1.79, 24.16)$. The hours from 8AM to 5PM are called "peak hours". The variation of the interarrival time Δt_k conforms to also Weibull distribution with different parameters, i.e. $Func() \sim W(4.25, 7.86)$. Thus, the arrival time points in each interval can be defined as

$$T(x, k) = T(x, k-1) + \Delta t_k \tag{12}$$

We use the following steps to generate the arrival process instance.

1. *Duration* $= 48$, $\Delta T = 1800$ s
2. Randomly generate 48 sample points conforming to $W(1.79, 24.16)$ as the number of arrivals within each of 48 intervals
3. During the peak hours, the interarrival times in each interval are generated randomly according to the Weibull distribution $W(4.25, 7.86)$. The numbers of sample points within each interval are determined by step 2. And in each interval the first arrival time point is the start time of the interval.

Because the author only gave the interarrival time during the peak hours, also the space is limited, we showed an instance of the arrival process during only the first four time intervals (that is, from 8 to 10) in Fig. 3. A batch arrival process is multiple arrivals at a time. However, we are more concerned with the arrival times in this work, so that the number of jobs in an arrival is not defined.

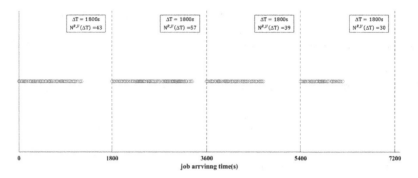

Fig. 3. A batch application arrival process instance

An Example of Arrival Process Model with Self-defined Functions

The arrival process model introduces more flexibility by supporting self-defined functions. We presented an example of the arrival process including self-defined functions. Firstly, we gave the specification of the self-define arrival process.

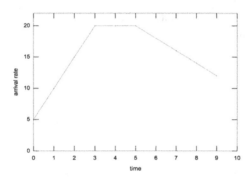

Fig. 4. Arrival rate function example

$$\delta(x) = \begin{cases} 5 + 5x & (0 \le x \le 3) \\ 20 & (3 \le x \le 5) \\ 20 - 2(x - 5) & (5 \le x \le 9) \end{cases} \quad \text{且} \quad \delta(x) = \delta(x - 9) \quad (13)$$

As can be seen from Fig. 4, the arrival rate increases linearly from 8 am to 11 am, from average 5 arrivals per hour to 20 arrivals per hour. From 11 pm to 1 pm, the arrival rate remains at average 20 arrivals per hour. From 1 pm to 5 pm, the arrival rate drops linearly until 12 arrivals per hour. After 5 pm it is closed. The time is divided into hours, i.e. $\Delta T = 1$ h. The arrival time point in an interval conforms to the poisson process, and λ_i of the possion process is set to the mean number of arrivals in the *ith* interval. In Fig. 4, horizontal axis is time with hour as the unit, and vertical axis is arrival rate. 8 am corresponds to the value 0 on the x-axis. The mathematical function of the variation of arrival rate is defined in Eq. 13.

We specify the access process with our model as follows:

1. The time is divided into hours, i.e. $\Delta T = 1\,h$.
2. The mean number of arrivals in the *ith* interval is

$$E\left(N^{R-U}(i)\right) = \int_{i-1}^{i} \delta(x)dx \qquad (14)$$

3. The arrival time points in the *ith* interval are

$$\left\{T(i,k),\; k = 1,2,\cdots N^{R-U}(i)\right\},\; F_x() \sim Possion\left(E\left(N^{R-U}(i)\right)\right) \qquad (15)$$

We use the following steps to generate the arrival process instance.

1. *Duration* $= 9$, $\Delta T = 1\,h$.
2. The number of arrivals in each interval is randomly generated according to the mean number of arrivals in this interval. As shown in Fig. 5, the nine samples are 6, 11, 16, 20, 19, 18, 15, 12.
3. The interarrival times in each interval are generated randomly according to the passion process with their parameter λ_i.

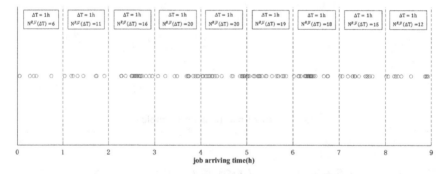

Fig. 5. A self-defined arrival process instance

4 Conclusion

This paper presented a general hierarchical arrival process model and an algorithm for generating arrival process instances based on the arrival model.

The general arrival process model was specified in four steps, had two advantages. (1) It captured the essential features of arrival process models, was independent of application and workload scenario. (2) It combined the advantages of point process and count process, can not only describe accurate time points in each interval but also describe temporal dependence of intervals.

Our corresponding generation algorithm supports that each of four steps can be defined as a constant, or a statistical distribution/process, or a self-defined function. The option of self-defined function further enhances the extensibility and flexibility of the generic arrival process model. Compared with the existing generation tools, our algorithm is simple and effective, and has stronger scalability.

The case study showed the generality, flexibility and effectiveness of our works. In sum, the generic arrival process model and generation algorithm will provide a solid foundation for generating more realistic hybrid cloud workloads.

In the future, we will further study how to formally define a more complex arrival process model by combined multiple general arrival process models in vertical and horizontal axis of time. In vertical axis of time, a complicated arrival process model can be the superposition of multiple parallel arrival processes model. In horizontal axis of time, a time-dependent arrival process model can be defined by multiple consecutive arrival process models. We believe that the study will make the general arrival process model more comprehensive.

Acknowledgement. The authors wish to thank Natural Science Foundation of China under Grant No. 61662054, 61262082,61562064 and 61462066, Natural Science Foundation of Inner Mongolia under Grand No.2015MS0608 and 2018MS06029, Inner Mongolia Science and Technology Innovation Team of Cloud Computing and Software Engineering and Inner Mongolia Application Technology Research and Development Funding Project "Mutual Creation Service Platform Research and Development Based on Service Optimizing and Operation Integrating", Inner Mongolia Engineering Lab of Cloud Computing and Service Software and Inner Mongolia Engineering Lab of Big Data Analysis Technology.

References

1. Li, H.: Realistic workload modeling and its performance impacts in large-scale escience grids. IEEE Trans. Parallel Distrib. Syst. **21**(4), 480–493 (2010)
2. Guo, M., Guan, Q. Ke, W.: Optimal Scheduling of VMs in Queueing Cloud Computing Systems with a Heterogeneous Workload, vol. 6 (2018)
3. Vakilinia, S., Ali, M.M., Qiu, D.: Modeling of the resource allocation in cloud computing centers. Comput. Netw. **91**, 453–470 (2015)
4. Lin, A.D., Li, C.S., Liao, W., Franke, H.: Capacity optimization for resource pooling in virtualized data centers with composable systems. IEEE Trans. Parallel Distrib. Syst. **29**(2), 324–337 (2018)
5. Iosup, A., Sonmez, O., Anoep, S., Epema, D.: The performance of bags-of-tasks in large-scale distributed systems. In: Proceedings of the 17th International Symposium on High Performance Distributed Computing—HPDC 2008, p. 97 (2008)
6. Costa, G.D., Grange, L. Courchelle, I.D., Costa, G.D., Grange, L., Courchelle, I.D.: Modeling and generating large-scale google-like workload (2016)
7. Wolski, R., Brevik, J.: Using parametric models to represent Private cloud workloads. IEEE Trans. Serv. Comput. **7**(4), 714–725 (2014)

8. Atmaca, T., Begin, T., Brandwajn, A., Castel-Taleb, H.: Performance evaluation of cloud computing centers with general arrivals and service. IEEE Trans. Parallel Distrib. Syst. **27**(8), 2341–2348 (2016)
9. Bolch, et al.: Queueing Networks and Markov Chains. Wiley, New York (1998)
10. Casale, G.: Building accurate workload models using Markovian arrival processes. In: Proceedings of the ACM SIGMETRICS Joint International Conference on Measurement and Modeling of Computer Systems - SIGMETRICS 2011, p. 357 (2011)
11. Meier-Hellstern, K., Fischer, W.: The Markov-modulated Poisson process (MMPP) cookbook. Perform. Eval. **18**(18), 149–171 (1993)
12. Wang, E., Yang, Y., Wu, J., Liu, W., Wang, X.: An efficient prediction-based user recruitment for mobile crowdsensing. IEEE Trans. Mob. Comput. **17**(1), 1 (2017)
13. Pacheco-Sanchez, S., Casale, G., Scotney, B., McClean, S., Parr, G., Dawson, S.: Markovian workload characterization for QoS prediction in the cloud. In: Proceedings—2011 IEEE 4th International Conference on Cloud Computing CLOUD 2011, pp. 147–154 (2011)
14. Li, H., Muskulus, M., Wolters, L.: Modeling job arrivals in a data-intensive grid. Job Sched. Strateg. Parallel Process. **4376**, 210–231 (2007)
15. Ware, P.P., Page, T.W., Nelson, B.L.: Automatic modeling of file system workloads using two-level arrival processes. ACM Trans. Model. Comput. Simul. **8**(3), 305–330 (1998)
16. RUBiS. http://rubis.ow2.org/ (2018)
17. Wilkes, J.: PRESS: PRedictive Elastic ReSource Scaling for cloud systems. In: 2010 International Conference on Network and Service Management, pp. 9–16 (2010)
18. YCSB. https://github.com/brianfrankcooper/YCSB/wiki
19. Cloud, S., et al.: SPEC Cloud ^{TM} IaaS 2016 Benchmark Design Overview, pp. 1–37 (2016)
20. CBTOOL. https://github.com/ibmcb/cbtool/tree/master/scripts
21. Yin, J., Lu, X., Zhao, X., Chen, H., Liu, X.: BURSE: a bursty and self-similar workload generator for cloud computing. IEEE Trans. Parallel Distrib. Syst. **9219** (2014)
22. An, C., Zhou, J., Liu, S., Geihs, K.: A multi-tenant hierarchical modeling for cloud computing workload. Intell. Autom. Soft Comput. 1–8 (2016)
23. The Apache Olio Project. http://incubator.apache.org/olio/
24. Chen, Y., Ganapathi, A., Griffith, R., Katz, R.: The case for evaluating MapReduce performance using workload suites. In: 2011 IEEE 19th Annual International Symposium on Modelling, Analysis, and Simulation of Computer and Telecommunication Systems, pp. 390–399 (2011)

Cost-Effective Coupled Video Distribution Network

Jing Chen[1], Zhigang Chen[2], Dianjie Lu[1(✉)], Chen Lyu[1,3],
Guijuan Zhang[1], Xiangwei Zheng[1], and Hong Liu[1]

[1] School of Information Science and Engineering, Shandong Normal University,
Jinan, China
ludianjie@sina.com
[2] State Grid JIANGSU Electric Power Co. LTD, Nanjing, China
[3] Luoyang Institute of Information Technology Industries, Luoyang, China

Abstract. Faced with emerging demands such as massive online video and
multiple terminals access, Video Distribution Networks (VDNs) effectively
alleviate the conflict between online video increasing and response time of users
accessing video content. Most existing works are focused on the popularity of
video content to determine which video should be pushed to users. However, in
these works, personalized demands of users such as bandwidth, delay and other
factors influenced on distribution cost are not comprehensively taken into
account. To overcome this problem, we propose a Cost-Effective Coupled Video
Distribution model which couples active distribution method and negative distribution method to improve the rate of video hitting and reduce the delay of
user access. In this model, we formulate the coupled video distribution process
as a cost minimizing problem by considering the bandwidth consumption
together with the delay performance and construct a multicast distribution tree
for the video delivery. Since solving this problem is NP-hard, we develop a
Heuristic Multicast Distribution Tree (HMDT), to provide more efficient
approximate cost. The extensive simulations show that our proposed HMDT can
yield strategies with smaller expected cost than previous algorithms on bandwidth and delay.

Keywords: Cost-effective coupled video distribution · Bandwidth
Delay · Heuristic multicast distribution tree

1 Introduction

With the rapid upgrading of the network environment and the popularity of smartphones, video has become a conveniently way to delivery information. As reported by
a survey [1], online video has been the dominant application of network traffic due to
social media sharing. In 2015, global video traffic accounted for 70% of all Internet
traffic. By 2019, global video traffic will increase by approximately 80% since mobile
devices and applications should increase by 10 times [2]. For example, as the most
popular online video site, YouTube has more than 1 billion users per month. With the
surge of massive online video and majority terminal access, video streaming multimedia objects are taking a large portion of network traffic and its quality of service is

© Springer Nature Singapore Pte Ltd. 2019
Y. Sun et al. (Eds.): ChineseCSCW 2018, CCIS 917, pp. 115–128, 2019.
https://doi.org/10.1007/978-981-13-3044-5_9

influenced by factors such as bandwidth, delay, packet loss, and jitter. How to increase the video content hitting rate, reduce bandwidth consumption, minify video access delay and improve user experience on the internet has become a challenging topic in the field of video streaming multimedia technology.

Video Distribution networks (VDNs) play a vital role in content distribution between final users and origin servers because they can effectively reduce response time of users accessing video content and bandwidth consumption by deploying servers closer to the users. In addition, even if the origin server malfunctions, users can also obtain video content from the surrogate servers, and the reliability of video distribution is enhanced. However, VDNs also have some limitations. On the one hand, the storage constraint of surrogate server cache has limited storage capacity and it is impossible to replicate all the video objects; on the other hand, because of the limited bandwidth of backbone network, origin server is infeasible to send all video streaming multimedia objects to each surrogate server. Consequently, how to effectively distribute video streaming multimedia objects while ensuring service quality and providing an optimal distribution cost is a hot topic in wireless network research. The work [3] contribute to analyze the strategy in which the most popular contents are pushed, and design of push-based content delivery to alleviate the burden of bandwidth in cellular network and converged broadcasting network. Caching strategies introduced in [4] provide an effective mechanism for alleviating massive bandwidth requirements by caching the most popular video objects closer to the network edge. The popularity of most videos is well studied on the temporal evolution [5, 6]. Popularity-driven content caching [7] studies the popularity of content and uses it to determine which content it should cache and which it should remove. This algorithm can effectively improve the cache hitting rate. However, they do not consider the personalized demands of users. In particular, randomly request of video streaming multimedia objects need to be fast and efficient allocation from origin server. Due to the storage limit of surrogate server and the pressure of bandwidth, it opens a new challenge to increase the hitting rate of video streaming multimedia and minimize the distribution cost.

In this paper, we present a novel model called Cost-Effective Coupled Video Distribution Model which aims at satisfying the personalized needs of users, improving the video hitting rate, and achieving effective cost of consider bandwidth and delay. The Coupling Video Distribution model combines coupled active video distribution and coupled negative video distribution. Before the user requests arise for video streaming multimedia objects, coupled active video distribution selectively deliver video objects to the surrogate servers based on the quantification for video objects of user interested. Besides, when the requests arrives at the request servers that have not replicate the relevant video objects in advance, coupled negative video distribution forward the request and replicate the requested video objects from the origin server. And then request servers deliver video objects to clients. For the cost-effective of coupled video distribution, we jointly consider distribution cost of both bandwidth consumption and delay performance and construct a multicast distribution tree to delivery video objects. Therefore, we formulate the coupled distribution as a problem of a minimizing cost problem. Since solving the problem is NP-hard, an efficient algorithm HMDT (Heuristic Multicast Distribution Tree) is proposed toward the optimization problem. Finally, the comparison is executed between our proposed

HMDT algorithm and the Approximate Steiner Tree Distribution (ASTD) algorithm. The effectiveness of HMDT algorithm is justified through extensive simulations, from which we demonstrate that HMDT algorithm yield strategies with smaller expected cost than ASTD algorithm.

The organization of the paper is as follows. First, we give a brief review of the related studies in Sect. 2. Then, we introduce our network model in Sect. 3 and formulate the optimization cost problem in Sect. 4 respectively. Next, we present the heuristic multicast distribution tree algorithm in Sect. 5 and conduct simulations to compare the performance of our proposed HMDT algorithm with the ASTD algorithm. In Sect. 6, we. Finally, the conclusion is given in Sect. 7.

2 Related Work

Recently, many of the work focuses on the allocation of video streaming multimedia content and the quality of service to satisfy users. In the wireless sensor network, the minimum energy consumption transmission from origin to multiple receivers is explored by constructing a minimum multicast tree [8]. According to the battery status and information of content popularity, proactive caching are implemented to satisfy the random energy arrival and requests of user content, and to provide more multicast opportunities [9]. The authors in [10] introduced a method of session based cloud content delivery network by considering the mobility and the dynamic demands of users in the mobile Internet. Wang et al. optimized the dynamic content replication and resource allocation by using a controller of software defined network [11]. The authors in [12] minimized the energy consumption in a multicast situation where the information should be disseminated to several destinations in the limited delay. Aram et al. [13] considered the problem of replica placement and the server selection together, and proposed an optimal scheme to minimize deployment cost of servers. Mukerjee et al. [14] proposed a centralized VDN that allows network operators to control video layout and allocate bit rate on a precise time scale while optimizing the quality of real-time video delivery.

Users are assigned to a surrogate server in a QoS-based surrogate server prioritization techniques [15–17]. In order to meet the needs of user, Zeng et al. [18] proposed a QoS-based greedy heuristic algorithm to optimize the replica placement of cloud storage content delivery networks. In [19, 20], the authors proposed an optimal video placement strategy according to analyze the deployment of video distribution services based on cloud-assisted and formulated deployment problem which considers user experience together with operational cost. In [21, 22], the authors indicated that mapping users' request to an adjacent surrogate server can significantly improve the QoS in a mobile network, such as delay and jitter. However, in the mobile wireless network, because of the uncertainty of the distribution surrogate server and the personalized demand for video streaming multimedia objects, we design cost-effective coupled video distribution model. Coupled video distribution effectively distribute video streaming multimedia objects according to users' interests and requests for video objects, reducing user access delay and bandwidth consumption. In addition, we construct multicast distribution tree to delivery video objects, considering cost with bandwidth consumption and delay performance. Since minimizing coupled distribution cost are proven NP-hard, we design a heuristic multicast distribution tree algorithm to solve it.

3 Network Model

3.1 Coupled Video Distribution Model

Dynamic multicast is required in the coupled multicast video distribution application. Since the users of group often join or leave timely, the network topology changes constantly in the distribution group. Hence, continuous dynamic process is truncated into a series of static graphs $G = \{g_1, g_2, \ldots, g_n\}$. Therefore, the surrogate servers may vary over time in coupled video distribution.

In our model, we assume that the origin server stores all video streaming media objects. Each surrogate server covers at least one area, and users can request and offload videos from surrogate servers closer to them. To meet the demands of users with limited capacity of surrogate servers, a novel video distribution method coupled active distribution and negative distribution is adopted.

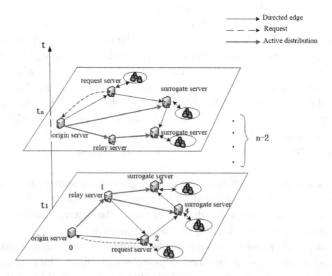

Fig. 1. Coupling video distribution model: taking the snapshot at time t_1 as an example. The origin server, 1 is the relay server, 2 is the request server, and 3, 4 represent the surrogate servers. The solid red directed edges corresponds to coupled active video distribution process in the figure; the dashed directed edge corresponds to the process of request server sends queries for video objects to origin server when there is not cache user requested video objects.

In the Coupled Video Distribution Model (see Fig. 1), when users send request to surrogate servers, the surrogate servers may cache the video objects or not. The active video distribution strategy allows the origin server distribute the relevant video objects that users are interested to the surrogate servers closer to the client before requests arise for those video objects. O_{ij} indicates the number of video streaming media object j in the surrogate server i and O_j represents the total number of video objects j in all stored video streaming multimedia objects. The origin server evaluates ratio O_{ij}/O_j to quantify interested degree of users for video objects j in the surrogate server i. According to the ratio, the origin server distributes the video objects to the surrogate servers through the multicast distribution tree. Several relay servers can be added during the multicast distribution process to enhance performance of video distribution. The process of coupled negative video distribution strategy is as follows: when the user send request to the video objects, disappointedly, the request servers does not cache those video objects and cannot satisfy users requested. Then, request servers will send requested to origin server and it sends video objects to the request servers through the multicast distribution tree according to the received video request. Finally, request servers delivery those video objects to the requesting user. Coupled active video distribution can effectively reduce the user access delay and improve hitting rate of video streaming multimedia objects in the surrogate servers. Coupled negative video distribution relieve bandwidth consumption by transmitting only the request video objects in the network.

3.2   Constructing Multicast Distribution Tree

The popularity of smart devices for video multimedia induces great demand of bandwidth and lower access delay in mobile network. In term of cost on coupled video distribution, we consider video distribution cost on bandwidth and delay. In the coupled video distribution model, the origin server distributes video objects to surrogate servers by constructing multicast distribution tree. During construction of the multicast distribution tree, we add several relay servers to optimize the performance and minimize the cost of video distribution. In the multicast distribution tree model (see Fig. 2), red node 0 represents the origin server, blue nodes 1, 2, 3, 4, 6 represent surrogate servers or request servers, and black nodes 5, 7 represent the relay surrogate servers. The directed edge between the two nodes corresponds to the communication edge among servers, and the number on the directed edge indicates cost of considering bandwidth and delay. The red edge indicates the path we are looking for with the effective cost from origin server to each surrogate or request server.

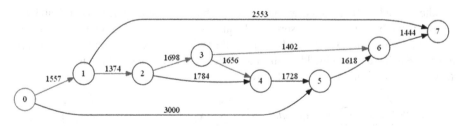

Fig. 2. Multicast distribution tree model

4 Problem Formulation

Here, we assume the performance of the video distribution network do not include the cost of delay and bandwidth among the terminal users and the surrogate servers. Because users usually request video from a surrogate server in their own area, the access time and bandwidth costs are not effected by allocation of video objects replica.

4.1 Minimizing Coupled Distribution Cost

In the process of coupled video distribution, the problem of minimizing the coupled distribution cost is designed to satisfy the demand for video objects of user requests and the minimization of bandwidth and delay.

The video streaming multimedia in origin server is divided into n different video stream objects, and each video stream object is represented by e. Then the video stream object can be expressed by $E = \{e_1, e_2, e_3, \ldots, e_n\}$. We denote the storage constraint of each surrogate server i ($i = 1, 2, \ldots, m$) as l_i. λ_i represents the number of requested video objects that the surrogate server i forwards. In the process of coupled active distribution, θ_{ij} indicates the interested degree of users for video object j in the surrogate server i, then $\theta_{ij} = O_{ij}/O_j$. The variable x_{ij} indicates whether the video object j is cached in the surrogate server i.

$$x_{ij} = \begin{cases} 1, & \text{Video object } j \text{ is active distributed to surrogate server } i \\ 0, & \text{Video object } j \text{ is negative distributed to request server } i \end{cases}$$

The coupled video distribution delay cost can be expressed by

$$\sum_{i=1}^{m} \sum_{j=1}^{n} (1 - x_{ij}) \lambda_i d_{ij} \tag{1}$$

In the formula (1), d_{ij} represents retrieval delay of the surrogate server i for the video object j

The coupled video distribution bandwidth cost can be formulated as

$$\sum_{i=1}^{m} \sum_{j=1}^{n} (x_{ij} c_j b_{ij} \theta_{ij} + (1 - x_{ij}) \lambda_i c_j d_{ij}) \tag{2}$$

For the formula (2), c_j indicates the size of the video streaming object j and b_{ij} represents the bandwidth of the surrogate/request server i requesting for video object j.

When considering cost of bandwidth together with delay, using coefficients α and β to balance delay and bandwidth to meet a variety of applications and requirements, the subject of minimization cost is as follows:

$$Min \left(\alpha \sum_{i=1}^{m} \sum_{j=1}^{n} (1 - x_{ij}) \lambda_i d_{ij} + \beta \sum_{i=1}^{m} \sum_{j=1}^{n} (x_{ij} c_j b_{ij} \theta_{ij} + (1 - x_{ij}) \lambda_i c_j b_{ij}) \right) \tag{3}$$

Similarly,

$$Min \sum_{i=1}^{m} \sum_{j=1}^{n} \left(\alpha(1 - x_{ij})\lambda_i d_{ij} + \beta c_j b_{ij}(x_{ij}\theta_{ij} + \lambda_i(1 - x_{ij})) \right) \tag{4}$$

The constraints of formula (4) are as below:

$$\sum_{j=1}^{n} x_{ij} c_j \leq l_i, \quad i = 1, 2, \ldots, m \tag{5}$$

$$b_{ij} \leq b \tag{6}$$

$$0.1 \leq \alpha < 1, \quad 0.1 \leq \beta < 1 \tag{7}$$

$$\alpha + \beta \geq 1 \tag{8}$$

Formula (5) is the storage capacity constraint of surrogate/request server i, Bandwidth of the surrogate/request server delivery video objects cannot over the maximum bandwidth b is shown as Eq. (6). Formulas (7) and (8) are constraints for balance factor α and β.

4.2 Problem Complexity

Next, we review the problem of minimizing coupled distribution cost. Given the size of different video stream objects and the number of requested video objects, is there an allocation strategy such that the total cost in (4) is less than a threshold? Meanwhile, video stream capacity stored in the surrogate server i is not more than l_i as in Eq. (5). The bandwidth satisfies the Eq. (6), and the relationship of the balanced coefficients satisfy the constraints of the Eqs. (7) and (8).

For the convenience, we only consider a special scenario where single surrogate server with the storage capacity l is considered. Then, the cost minimization problem is mapped to a set coverage problem and is proven NP-hard. Its complete proof is available in [23]. In the following part, we will give a heuristic algorithm to solve this problem.

5 Heuristic Multicast Distribution Tree Algorithm

The previous section analysis of the NP-hard problem showing that addressing the problem of minimizing coupled distribution cost lead to tremendous cost. Hence, we propose an effective algorithm, which we called Heuristic Multicast Distribution Tree (HMDT), to obtain better approximate cost. The weight of a node is assigned by the density of the subtree which is rooted at the node and extended the minimal cost path to each terminals [24]. HMDT algorithm continuously adds the minimal weight node and effective cost terminal to this node. Eventually, a cost-effective distribution tree will be constructed where all terminals are included.

We regard the servers in the network as node $V(v_1, v_2, .., v_m)$ and the origin server as root node r. The terminals represents surrogate/request servers and terminalSet indicates terminal set. Additionally, we generate a directed network graph file, which include root node r, the number of node, node set V, terminalSet, the number of directed edges and the edges cost between the two nodes.

Algorithm 1 Heuristic Multicast Distribution Tree Algorithm

Input: root node r in the directed network graph G file, node set V, K terminals in V, number of directional edges and cost of each edge

Output: cost effective delivery path and cost

1 Initialize: $T \leftarrow \varnothing$, cost(T) $\leftarrow 0$

2 while terminalSet not empty

3    $W_{best} \leftarrow \infty, V_{best} \leftarrow \varnothing$

4   for each node v in G do

         rc $\leftarrow$ The lowest cost of reaching v nodes from r

         n $\leftarrow$ n+1

5   for (each k in terminalSet, $1 \leq k \leq K$) and ($c_j \leq$ available storage of v_i)

           Calculate the cost rc(v_i, k) from v_i to each terminal

           rc $\leftarrow$ rc+rc(v_i, k)

6   end for

7   if (rc*n$<W_{best}$)

           $W_{best} \leftarrow$ rc*n

           $V_{best} \leftarrow v_i$

8   end if

9   end for

10 for each k in terminalSet, $1 \leq k \leq K$

       calculate the cost of k to V_{best}

       $k_{min} \leftarrow$ terminal with the lowest cost in terminalSet

11 end for

12 terminalSet $\leftarrow$ terminalSet-k_{min}, $V \leftarrow V - k_{min}$, $T \leftarrow T \cup \{<V_{best}, W_{best} >\}$

13 end while

14 return T and cost(T)

---

6 Experimental Results

In this part, we perform extensive simulations to show the improvement of our proposed HMDT algorithm. We compare our algorithm with the generally used Approximate Steiner Tree Distribution (ASTD) [25] in various performance. The ASTD algorithm selects the optimal path according to the density of the Steiner tree [25]. Given a tree T and the cost of the tree $c(T)$, the density of the Steiner tree is defined as: $\rho(T) = c(T)/k(T)$, where $k(T)$ represents the number of terminals in the tree T. To build this tree, the subtree with the minimal density is selected as the first level of the selection tree in ASTD algorithm. Then, the algorithm selects the minimal density subtree from remaining terminal set nodes and add this subtree to the previous level of the selection tree. Next, we repeat the selection until enough terminals are contained in the tree. In our simulation, the size of the video streaming is distributed with the normal distribution N(20 k, 1 GB).The servers deployment obey the uniform distribution U (100, 1000), and surrogate servers are randomly selected among these servers.

We first analyze the cost affected by the balance coefficient α and β (see Fig. 3). In the simulation, we deploy 15 servers and select 10 surrogate/request servers among these servers. The bandwidth was randomly allocated from 800 to 3000 bps, and the delay was randomly distributed between 1000 and 2500 ms. Figure 3(a) and (b) show the influence of the balance coefficient on the cost from the three-dimensional surface map and the three-dimensional contour map respectively. As can be seen from Fig. 3 (a), when the sum of α and β becomes larger, the cost of distribution rises. Especially, the yellow area of cost reaches the highest value. We can observe the effect of α and β more intuitively in Fig. 3(b). When the sum of α and β remains unchanged, the cost of distribution fluctuates within a smaller range. In addition, when the sum of α and β remains 1, the cost is low; particularly, when α and β vary from 0.5 to 0.7, the consumed bandwidth and the produced delay can achieve a better balance which is acceptable for the users.

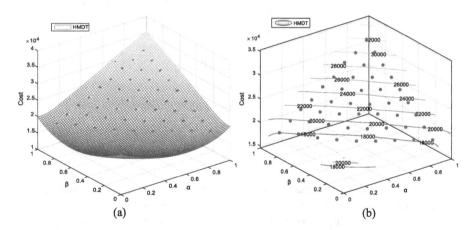

(a)   (b)

Fig. 3. Impact of the coefficient α and β

Next, we evaluate the influence on bandwidth cost according to the balance coefficient, the number of surrogate server and the directed edges (see Fig. 4). In this simulation, the delay is randomly allocated between 1000 and 2500 ms, and the specific parameter settings are given for each figure (see Table 1). It can be seen from the comparison between Fig. 4(a) and (b) that the cost of Fig. 4(b) increase slowly as the bandwidth becoming larger. We can note that the balanced cost of $\alpha = 0.5$, $\beta = 0.5$ is better than that of $\alpha = 0.2$, $\beta = 0.8$. This result shows that the balanced distribution cost is optimal when the sum of coefficient is 1 and the difference between α and β is small. Additionally, we explore how the number of surrogate servers affect the distribution cost when different number of surrogate servers is deployed in Fig. 4(b) and (c). Experimental analysis shows that the increased number of surrogate servers leads to larger cost when the number of servers is fixed. Then, we change the number of directed edges to explore whether the number of edges has an impact on the distribution cost. By comparing Fig. 4(b) and (d), we can see that the distribution cost is relatively lower with more edges. The analysis results of the above experimental results show that parameter setting of different have a greater impact on distribution cost. Importantly, our proposed HMDT algorithm exhibits effective performance and achieves lower cost than ASTD algorithm. In Fig. 5, we study the influence of the number of directed edges. We set $\alpha = 0.5$, $\beta = 0.5$ and deploy 20 servers and 15 surrogate servers in the scenario. The bandwidth was randomly allocated between 800 and 3000 bps, and the delay is distributed within 1000 ms and 2500 ms. As we can see from Fig. 5, the distribution cost is declining as the number of edges increases. Consequently, the distribution cost of the HMDT algorithm is lower than ASTD algorithm.

Table 1. Parameter settings.

Experimental figure	α, β	Number of server	Number of surrogate server	Number of edge
(a)	$\alpha = 0.2$ $\beta = 0.8$	20	10	40
(b)	$\alpha = 0.5$ $\beta = 0.5$	20	10	40
(c)	$\alpha = 0.5$ $\beta = 0.5$	20	15	40
(d)	$\alpha = 0.5$ $\beta = 0.5$	20	10	60

In Fig. 6, we explore the delay effect on cost. We set $\alpha = 0.5$, $\beta = 0.5$, and deploy 20 servers, randomly selected 10 surrogate servers, 40 directed edges. The bandwidth ranges between 800bps and 3000bps. It can be seen from the graph that the distribution cost keeps rising as the delay increases. In other words, the longer delay leads to higher cost. Moreover, our proposed HMDT algorithm achieves lower distribution cost than the ASTD algorithm.

Figures 7 and 8 show the effect on distribution cost of the number of surrogate server and the number of serve respectively. In this simulation, we set $\alpha = 0.5$, $\beta = 0.5$, and randomly deploy 200 directed edges. The bandwidth ranges from 800 to 3000 bps, and the delay is randomly allocated between 1000 ms and 2500 ms. As for the influence of the number of surrogate servers, we randomly deploy 100 servers and select surrogate servers based on demands of users among servers. Figure 7 shows that the distribution cost is rising when the number of surrogate servers increases. In Fig. 8, we randomly deploy 15 surrogate servers and keep the number of surrogate servers unchanged. As demonstrated in this figure, the distribution cost grows rapidly as the number of servers increases. During the simulation, we can find that the increasing of the number of surrogate servers or the number of servers will result in higher distribution cost, and our proposed HMDT algorithm is superior to the ASTD algorithm in performance.

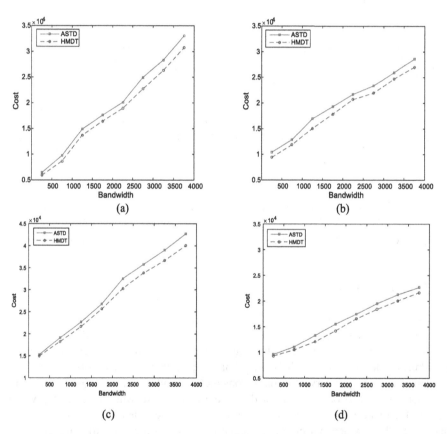

Fig. 4. Influence on the bandwidth cost

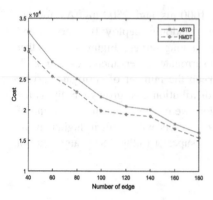

Fig. 5.   Cost vs. number of directed edges

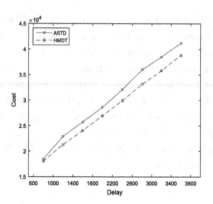

Fig. 6.   Cost vs. delay

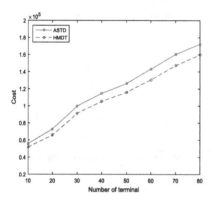

Fig. 7.   Cost vs. number of terminals

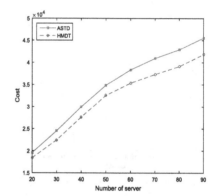

Fig. 8.   Cost vs. number of servers

7   Conclusion

In this paper, we propose a Cost-Effective Coupled Video Distribution model, which combines coupled active video distribution and coupled negative video distribution. On one hand, the process of coupled active video distribution is that origin server advanced distributes video objects which is according to quantification video objects of users interested to surrogate servers through constructing multicast distribution tree, before the user send video objects requested; On the other hand, when users query video objects for request servers which has not replicate those video objects, origin server distributes those video objects to the request servers through constructing multicast distribution tree. The process of this is coupled negative video distribution. Hence, users can request video stream multimedia objects from surrogate/request servers closer to users, relieving access delay.

To meet the demand of users for video objects and minimize the distribution cost, we formulate the coupled video distribution process as problem of minimizing coupled distribution cost by considering the bandwidth together with delay. Due to the problem is NP-hard, we propose a heuristic multicast distribution tree (HMDT) algorithm to provide an optimal approximately cost. The simulation results show that HMDT algorithm reduce distribution cost of considering bandwidth and delay effectively. Additionally, we demonstrate effective performance and lower cost of HMDT algorithm compared with ASTD algorithm in bandwidth, delay, the number of surrogate server and number of server etc. Whatever, cost-effective coupled video distribution proposed in this paper significantly improves the accuracy rate of delivery video objects and achieves an optimal minimum cost of consider bandwidth and delay.

Acknowledgments. This work is supported by the Project of Science and Technology of State Grid (No. SG[2017]179), National Natural Science Foundation of P. R. China under Grant Nos. 61572299, 61602286, 61402270, 61373149, Natural Science Foundation of Shandong Province, China under Grant Nos. ZR2016FB13, ZR2014FQ009.

References

1. White paper: Cisco Visual Networking Index: Forecast and Methodology, 2015–2020. 1 June 2016
2. Cisco Systems: Cisco Visual Networking Index: Forecast and Methodology, 2014–2019. Cisco, San Jose, CA (2015)
3. Wang, K., Chen, Z., Liu, H.: Push-based wireless converged networks for massive multimedia content delivery. IEEE Trans. Wirel. Commun. **13**(5), 2894–2905 (2014)
4. Borst, S., Gupta, V., Walid, A.: Distributed caching algorithms for content distribution networks. In: Proceedings of IEEE International Conference on Computer Communications, pp. 1478–1486. IEEE Press (2010)
5. Zhou, Y., Chen, L., Yang, C., et al.: Video popularity dynamics and its implication for replication. IEEE Trans. Multimed. **17**(8), 1273–1285 (2015)
6. Brodersen, A., Scellato, S., Wattenhofer, M.: YouTube around the world: geographic popularity of videos. In: Proceedings of International Conference on World Wide Web, pp. 241–250 (2012)
7. Li, S., Xu, J., Schaar, M., et al.: Popularity-driven content caching. In: Proceedings of IEEE International Conference on Computer Communications, pp. 1–9. IEEE Press (2016)
8. Gong, H., Fu, L., Fu, X., et al.: Distributed multicast tree construction in wireless sensor networks. IEEE Trans. Inf. Theory **63**(1), 280–296 (2016)
9. Zhou, S., Gong, J., Zhou, Z., et al.: Green delivery: proactive content caching and push with energy-harvesting-based small cells. IEEE Commun. Mag. **53**(4), 142–149 (2015)
10. Lu, D., Hu, B., Zheng, X., et al.: Session-based cloud video delivery networks in mobile internet. J. Internet Technol. **18**(7), 1561–1571 (2017)
11. Wang, K., Li, H., Yu, F., et al.: Virtual resource allocation in software-defined information-centric cellular networks with device-to-device communications and imperfect CSI. IEEE Trans. Veh. Technol. **65**(12), 10011–10021 (2016)
12. Fu, X., Xu, Z., Peng, Q., et al.: ConMap: a novel framework for optimizing multicast energy in delay-constrained mobile wireless networks. In: Proceedings of the ACM International Symposium, pp. 1–10. ACM (2017)
13. Aram, O., Yousefi, S., Solimanpur, M.: Joint server selection and replica placement in urban content delivery networks. Int. J. Oper. Res. **25**(3), 288–306 (2016)

14. Mukerjee, M., Naylor, D., Jiang, J., et al.: Practical, real-time centralized control for CDN-based live video delivery. In: Proceedings of ACM SIGCOMM, pp. 311–324 (2015)
15. Zhao, T., Lu, D., Zheng, X., et al.: Priority-oriented cloud video delivery networks. In: Proceedings of IEEE 8th International Conference on Information Technology in Medicine and Education (ITME2016), pp. 662–667 (2016)
16. Hu, H., Wen, Y., Chua, T.S., et al.: Community based effective social video contents placement in cloud centric CDN network. In: Proceedings of IEEE International Conference on Multimedia and Expo, pp. 1–6 (2014)
17. Papagianni, C., Leivadeas, A., Papavassiliou, S.: A cloud-oriented content delivery network paradigm: modeling and assessment. IEEE Trans. Dependable Secure Comput. 10(5), 287–300 (2013)
18. Zeng, L., Xu, S., Wang, Y., et al.: Toward cost-effective replica placements in cloud storage systems with qos-awareness. Softw. Pract. Exp. 47(6), 813–829 (2017)
19. He, J., Wu, D., Zeng, Y., et al.: Toward optimal deployment of cloud-assisted video distribution services. IEEE Trans. Circuits Syst. Video Technol. 23(10), 1717–1728 (2013)
20. Gao, L., Yu, F., Chen, Q., et al.: Consistency maintenance of do and undo/redo operations in real-time collaborative bitmap editing systems. Cluster Comput. 19(1), 255–267 (2016)
21. Xu, Q., Huang, J., Wang, Z., et al.: Cellular data network infrastructure characterization and implication on mobile content placement. ACM Sigmetrics Perform. Eval. Rev. 39(1), 277–288 (2011)
22. Gao, L., Gao, D., Xiong, N., et al.: CoWebDraw: a real-time collaborative graphical editing system supporting multi-clients based on HTML5. Multimed. Tools Appl. 77(4), 5067–5082 (2018)
23. Guan, X., Choi, B.: Push or pull? Toward optimal content delivery using cloud storage. J. Netw. Comput. Appl. 40, 234–243 (2014)
24. Hsieh, M., Wu, H., Tsai, M.: FasterDSP: a faster approximation algorithm for directed Steiner tree problem. J. Inf. Eng. 22(6), 1409–1425 (2006)
25. Charikar, M., Chekuri, C., Cheung, T., et al.: Approximation algorithms for directed Steiner problems. J. Algorithms 33(1), 73–91 (1999)

Optimal Design of Obstacles in Emergency Evacuation Using an Arch Formation Based Fitness Function

Liang Li[1,2], Hong Liu[1,2(✉)], and Yanbin Han[1,3]

[1] School of Information Science and Engineering, Shandong Normal University,
Jinan 250014, China
{1161787,lhsdcn}@126.com, hyb309@163.com
[2] Shandong Provincial Key Laboratory for Distributed Computer Software
Novel Technology, Jinan 250358, China
[3] School of Information Science and Engineering, University of Jinan,
Jinan 250014, China

Abstract. Congestion in pedestrian crowds is a critical issue for evacuation management and it is possible to alleviate crowd congestion by appropriately placing obstacles in the evacuation scene. To alleviate the crowd congestion by suitably placing obstacles, it is important to extract the characteristics of the evacuation process to improve the evacuation efficiency. In this paper, an arch formation based obstacle optimization approach is firstly employed to get the suitable characteristics of obstacles in a evacuation scene. Concretely, the arch formation in a dense crowd is used to guide the crowd congestion alleviation. The radial pressure, which can represent the strength of arch formation, is used to build a new fitness function for the PSO. The proposed approach can guide the design of pedestrian facilities to achieve a better management of evacuation. In this paper, the effectiveness, and quality of the proposed approach are validated through analysis and simulations.

Keywords: Evacuation simulation · Particle swarm optimization
Crowd congestion · Arch formation

1 Introduction

For the few decades, dynamic characteristics of pedestrians in panic evacuation has attracted many attentions because the increase of congestion situations and mass events in reality. The incessant developments in evacuation research will bring significant benefits in public traffic management, architecture design and risk avoidance. Therefore, it is necessary to improve the research of emergency evacuation to achieve a better management and control on evacuation for safety and comfort reasons.

Although the emergency evacuation is a critical issue for crowd safety management, the relative rarity of crowd accidents creates several issues related to these researches. Since occurrence of crowded situation is still mostly unpredictable, data considering those accidents are very scarce. For this reason, simulation modeling and

© Springer Nature Singapore Pte Ltd. 2019
Y. Sun et al. (Eds.): ChineseCSCW 2018, CCIS 917, pp. 129–145, 2019.
https://doi.org/10.1007/978-981-13-3044-5_10

experiments are the primary approaches for modeling crowd evacuation behavioral during emergency evacuation.

In this paper, we focus on improving the evacuation effect by changing the design of pedestrian facilities, which is achieved by set obstacles in the evacuation scene. With the development of the evacuation researches, many scholars have found that obstacles near the exit can influence the outflow and the crowd congestion. So it is important to set the obstacles correctly to achieve a better management of evacuation.

Although a lot of researches have already been developed on how to improve the evacuation by obstacles, there are still limitations for application because it is difficult to obtain the optimal characteristics of obstacles. For example, configurations of obstacles are complicated, and it is hard to distinguish effects of different character-istics. Therefore, the optimization of obstacles in evacuation is a topic worthy of exploration.

This paper proposes an approach to optimize the obstacles in evacuation scene to alleviate the crowd congestion in a dense crowd. The main contributions in this paper are shown as follows:

1. It proposed that the arch formation in a dense crowd can alleviate the crowd congestion. The arch formation, which is a result of self-organized motion of evacuation crowd, has potentials to influence the crowd congestion, and it can be adjusted by the obstacles. Therefore, it is possible to optimize the configurations of obstacles according to the arch formation to improve the evacuation.
2. We put forward that the radial pressure of the arch formation in a dense crowd is a suitable index to assess the adjustment effect of obstacles. The radial pressure is a characteristic of the arch formation and is changes with the crowd congestion. By using the radial pressure as an index, it is possible to study the relationship between the arch formation and the configuration of obstacles and assess the state of arch formation, which is important for crowd congestion alleviation.
3. Based on the calculating of radial pressure, a fitness function for Particle Swarm Optimization (PSO) algorithm is proposed to improve the optimization of obstacles. This new fitness function can improve the efficiency of obstacle optimization to achieve the congestion alleviation.

The rest of this paper is organized as follows. Section 2 introduces related literature on the social force model, obstacle configuration optimization, arch formation and PSO algorithm. Section 3 describes the arch formation based congestion alleviation approach and the radial pressure based fitness function. Simulation setups, results, and an in-depth discussion are provided in Sect. 4. The concludes is given in Sect. 5.

2   Related Works

2.1   Social Force Model (SFM)

Emergency evacuation is a complex process because crowd behavior usually seems to be irregular, chaotic, and unpredictable [1]. There are many factors that will restrict and influence the dynamic adjustments of evacuation. Therefore, modelling interactions among a crowd and the states of pedestrian individuals is important for management of evacuation. Simulation modeling is the main method for understanding evacuations, and many evacuation models have been proposed by scholars, such as the social force model (SFM) [2, 3], cellular automata model [4–6], fuzzy logic-based model [7], and agent-based model [8]. Many typical self-organized phenomena and collective behaviors can be reproduced by these models [9].

The SFM proposes a way to illustrate the exclusive interactions among crowd pedestrians and the interactions between pedestrians and obstacles. In this model, every pedestrian has a desired velocity which illustrates his destination, and acceleration (deceleration) is decided by different forces. As a microscopic continuous evacuation model, the SFM can reproduce many self-organizing crowd motion, such as oscillatory effects at bottlenecks and lane formation in bidirectional flows.

The SFM is used to simulate many scenarios, such as crowds in densely situation and panic escape [10]. Given that the SFM is suitable to simulate the characteristics of evacuation pedestrians, it has attracted many attentions to be used to simulate more phenomena in crowds [11–13].

As a microscopic model, the SFM has great potential for providing high-quality motion details for crowd evacuation. For example, by using the SFM, Helbing et al. proposed a "crowd pressure" to quantitate and represent congestion in crowds. Their works have illustrated that the SFM can simulate crowds in very crowded dangerous situations [1]. In this paper, the SFM was used to conduct the evacuation simulation.

2.2 Research on Obstacles in Emergency Evacuation

In emergency situations, it is feasible to increase the evacuation efficiency by suitably placing obstacles near the exit. Helbing et al. found that the outflow can be increased by appropriately placing obstacles near the exit [14]. In their follow-up work, Helbing also found that obstacles may increase pedestrian flow by 30% compared to that without the obstacle [1]. Yanagisawa et al. found that the mean traveling time of pedestrians was reduced by 25% in an experiment when an obstacle was arranged for actual pedestrians [15]. However, obstacles with inappropriate configurations negatively affect the evacuation efficiency. Zhao et al. simulated an evacuation and found that placing obstacles symmetrically near the exit door may be harmful for evacuation [16].

The obstacle's configuration should be properly adjusted to get an optimal improvement in crowd evacuation. Therefore, a significant amount of research has already been conducted to determine the proper configuration of the obstacles (i.e., position). Jiang et al. used a genetic algorithm to achieve a layout design of the obstacles [17]; however, they only considered pillar-like obstacles. Other differently shaped obstacles, such as thin, flat panels, can also enhance the evacuation efficiency. Frank et al. studied the pedestrian behavior on an escape situation obstructed by a panel and pillar near the door [18]. Zhao et al. employed a modified differential evolution (DE) to optimize the characteristics of differently shaped obstacles and thus achieved a minimum evacuation time for all pedestrians [16].

Obstacle placement has been proven to be a suitable approach to improve the evacuation effect. However, this topic is worthy of further exploration because the applications of obstacles are still limited.

2.3   Research of Arch Formation in Crowd Evacuation

An arch-shaped structure (or arching phenomena) at bottlenecks is a typical phenomenon in systems such as traffic, civil engineering, granular flow through a hopper
and escape evacuation [19]. In some situations, evacuation crowds exhibit collective
phenomena similar to those observed in granular experiments, for example, evacuation
flows at bottlenecks [20]. In this paper, the arching effect in an evacuation crowd is
called an arch formation. An arch formation is difficult to avoid when panic pedestrians
gather at an exit, see Fig. 1. The arch formation is formed and broken repeatedly, and
this phenomenon may decrease the outflow rate and increases congestion. Therefore, it
is necessary to develop an approach to solve the arch formation problem as much as
possible.

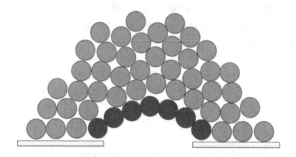

Fig. 1. The diagram of an arch formation in a dense crowd

Many studies have been conducted to study arch formation. Suzuno et al. discuss
the arch formation in an evacuation process with the social force model [19]. They
discussed the physical mechanism of obstacles in a evacuation system and showed that
the obstacle affects arch formation in three ways. Twarogowska et al. analyzed two
macroscopic crowd dynamic models and studied the pedestrians evacuation in a room
with one exit [21]. They discussed the crowd motions such as clogging at bottlenecks
and stop-and-go waves. In their simulations, the density profiles of the crowd showed a
congestion situation with an arch formation.

In summary, the arch formation, which is a typical phenomenon in pedestrian
evacuation systems, has direct or indirect relations with the flow rate and congestion of
a crowd. This phenomenon may hinder an evacuation and increase crowd congestion.
This limitation motivates the authors to develop a possible method that can solve the
arch formation problem.

2.4   Particle Swarm Optimization (PSO)

Particle swarm optimization (PSO), which was firstly proposed to model the behaviors
of bird, is a famous approach for optimization problems. As a population-based optimization approach, PSO has attracted many research attention, and a large number of
modifications had been conducted to modify the basic algorithm, comprehensive

surveys of which can be found in [22, 23]. Nowadays, it has been well recognized as an efficient approach for intelligent search and optimization.

PSO has attracted many attentions in engineering problem optimization because it has powerful search performance and algorithmic simplicity. PSO maintains many good solutions as the leaders to guide the optimization process, which is different from differential evolution and genetic algorithms. For these reasons, the PSO was also applied to optimize the configurations of obstacles in an evacuation scene. For example, Cristiani et al. introduced a new approach that guarantees both the opacity of the obstacles and impermeability, and the PSO was used to optimize the configurations of obstacles. The simulation result showed that the model can increase the evacuation efficiency by adding multiple optimally placed and shaped obstacles in the walking area [24].

In this paper, the PSO algorithm is used to guide the configuration optimization of obstacles in a evacuation scene.

3 Optimal Design of Obstacle for Emergency Evacuation

3.1 Arch Formation Based Congestion Alleviation for Emergency Evacuation

In this section, we focus on the relation between crowd congestion and arch formation. Previous studies have reported that the density at bottlenecks in a crowd has a characteristic that it will oscillatory changes in the flow direction [1, 10]. In fact, it is obvious that there are many self-organized motion in a dense crowd, among them oscillating flows, which is an inevitable phenomenon caused by crowd congestion [1, 25]. The arch formation, which is formed and broken repeatedly, is a kind of self-organized motion caused by the oscillatory changes. Therefore, arch formation is a common phenomenon in crowds and is hard to avoid because it is caused by crowd congestion.

The arch formation, which is formed and broken repeatedly, is a kind of self-organized motion caused by the oscillatory changes in an evacuating crowd. The arch formation, which is formed and broken repeatedly, will hinder the evacuation process when it is formed. Congestion will increase because pedestrians behind the arch are still pushing each other to get close to the exit, which is dangerous for the pedestrians. Therefore, the critical problem of an arch formation is that it hinders the evacuation process.

Given that the arch formation is a common phenomenon in crowds and is harmful to evacuation, solving the negative effect caused by arch formation in crowds is a critical issue for dense crowds.

Although the arch formation hinders the evacuation process and increases congestion, it can also endure external pressure from outside pedestrians, which is a positive effect for evacuation. Therefore, it is important to find an approach that makes use of advantageous effects and solves disadvantageous effects to solve the arch formation problem.

Figure 1 shows a situation where an arch formation has formed at an exit. In this situation, the arch formation has only a negative effect on the crowd because it is too close to the exit. Although the arch formation can still endure external pressure, it does not benefit the evacuation because there are no pedestrians inside the arch formation. Even worse, external pressure will increase the duration of the arch formation. However, there will be several positive effects if an arch formation is formed at an outer position, see Fig. 2. First, the arch formation at an outer position can protect pedestrians near the exit. If the arch formation endures external pressure, the pedestrians inside it will not suffer from overcrowding. Second, the arch formation at an outer position is wider and endures less pressure than the one in Fig. 2, and thus, it is unstable and collapses easily. This situation will benefit the evacuation because the shorter the duration of the arch formation, the more rapid the evacuation is and the less congestion that occurs.

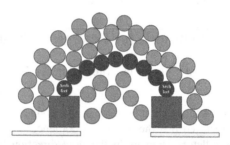

Fig. 2. An outer-arch (pedestrians with dark color) and arch feet.

The above idea inspires the authors to devise an approach to solve the arch formation problem in evacuation by changing the position of the arch formation. This approach, which uses self-organized motion to solve the congestion problem, is different from existing approaches.

3.2   Radial Pressure Based Fitness Function for PSO

In this paper, we use the radial pressure of the arch to evaluate the effect of arch formation and obstacles. The benefits include: In this paper, we focus on the optimization of obstacles in evacuation scene to achieve the crowd congestion alleviation, and the PSO is used to get the optimization configuration. As mentioned above, adjusting the arch formation by obstacles may be a suitable approach to alleviate the crowd congestion. Therefore, the concrete target of the proposed approach is to adjust the arch formation by the optimization of obstacles.

The radial pressure of the arch formation in a crowd is used to evaluate the effect of arch formation and obstacles and build a new fitness function for the PSO in this paper. According to the references [26, 27], the radial pressure of the arch formation is an index of the strength of an arch formation. This variable can evaluate the state of an arch formation, which is suitable to analyze the adjustment effect of obstacles. Thus, this radial pressure based fitness function has great potential to guide the optimization process of obstacles.

This paper proposes an approach to calculate approximately the radial pressure based on a reasonable arch axis. Although arch formation in crowds has various shapes, relevant research shows that it is possible to analyze arch formation by a static mode [20]. In this paper, the reasonable arch axis is used to analyze arch formation. This model is extensively used in research on the arching effect in civil engineering, and it provides a theoretical basis and design method for the application of the arching effect. In this work, the reasonable arch axis is considered as a static model of the arch formation during a crowd evacuation. This hypothesis allows us to ignore the concrete detail of the arch formation and focus on the relation between the obstacles and arch formation. The structure of the reasonable arch axis is shown in Fig. 3, and the formula for this model is as follows [28, 29]:

$$y = 4 \cdot r / \left(s^2 \left(s \cdot x - x^2 \right) \right), \tag{1}$$

where S is the arch span, r is the rise of the arch, x is the abscissa of the arch axis and p is the pressure act on the arch formation.

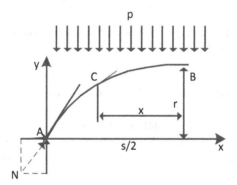

Fig. 3. Computation model of the reasonable arch axis

The horizontal thrust and vertical bearing force at a random point on the axis of arch are respectively:

$$N = p \cdot s^2 / (8h), \tag{2}$$

$$N_2 = p \cdot x, \tag{3}$$

The radial pressure at a random point on the arch axis is:

$$N_c = \left(p \cdot \sqrt{s^4 + 64 \cdot x^2 \cdot h^2} \right) / (8h), \tag{4}$$

The radial pressure at point A is the biggest and at point B is the least.

$$N_A = \left(p \cdot \sqrt{s^4 + 16 \cdot h^2} \right)/(8h), \tag{5}$$

$$N_B = (p \cdot S^2)/(8h), \tag{6}$$

In this paper, the congestion alleviation ability of obstacles increases with the decrease of the radial pressure. This is because the radial pressure represents the strength of arch formation, and the crowd congestion varies inversely with the strength of arch formation. However, there are still many limitations on the radial pressure because there will be no arch formation when the radial pressure is too small. Therefore, it is necessary to set several constraints to ensure the effect of the radial pressure. In this paper, we introduce a condition to limit the spacing of the obstacles.

$$s < s_{max} = 4 \cdot d \cdot cos\varphi/(p \cdot (1 - sin\varphi)), \tag{7}$$

where d is the length of the obstacle, φ is the internal friction angle and is usually be set to 15°–20°. Therefore, the final fitness function is:

$$F = \lambda_0 \cdot N_A + \lambda_1 \cdot N_B, S < S_{max}, \tag{8}$$

where N_A and N_B are the radial pressure of the arch formation in the crowd, λ_0 and λ_1 are weight coefficients and default is 1.

4   Simulation Design and Analysis of Results

In this paper, the PSO was used to optimize the configurations of obstacles to alleviate the crowd congestion. First, we will demonstrate the evacuation simulation that we designed to test the effect of obstacles. Second, the simulation result and the analysis are given.

4.1   Simulation Design

The original evacuation scene is a room with one exit, see Fig. 4. In this paper, we use the diameter of the particle as the length units. The room is 150 d long and 100 d wide. The length of the door is 6 diameters. Pedestrian initialization position is random distributes uniformly in the evacuation scene.

The social force model is used to conduct the evacuation simulation. The central position of the door is used to represent the direction of driving force. We put forward a new method which is similar to the density to quantify the effect of obstacles. According to the characteristics of the social force mode, there is an overlap between two pedestrians when they compress each other, as shown in Fig. 5(a). The radial

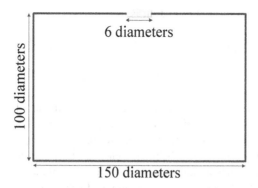

Fig. 4. The original evacuation scene.

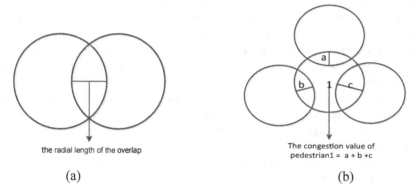

the radial length of the overlap

(a)

The congestion value of
pedestrian1 = a + b +c

(b)

Fig. 5. (a) Congestion value between two pedestrians; (b) Congestion value of a pedestrian.

length of the overlap is used to represent the congestion value. The whole congestion value of a pedestrian is the sum of the overlaps, see Fig. 5(b). The congestion value of the crowd is the average of the congestion value of all the pedestrians.

First, the hypothesis that the arch formation in a dense crowd can be used to alleviate the congestion was tested by a simulation. We used the average congestion value of crowd as the index to illustrate the comparison result. There are 500 pedestrians in the evacuation scene. The obstacle we used to control the arch formation is a square with a width of 4 diameters. A 3-diameter distance is designated between the obstacle and the front wall to allow many pedestrians inside the outer-arch. The obstacles are placed symmetrical with spacing of 8 diameters. In this section, the scene without obstacles is the original scene and the scene with obstacle is the modified scene. We ran each specific condition several times and use the average as the final result. Second, the hypothesis that the radial pressure can be used to build a fitness function to guide the optimization of obstacles was also tested.

The formulation of the PSO iteration is as follows:

$$V_i^{k+1} = V_i^k + C_1^k \cdot N_1 \cdot \left(P_i^k - X_i^k\right) + C_2^k \cdot N_2 \cdot \left(P^k - X^k\right), \tag{9}$$

$$X_i^{k+1} = X_i^k + V_i^{k+1}. \tag{10}$$

where k is the iteration number, X_i is the position of the ith particle of the swarm, P_i is the best point ever met by the *i*th particle in the previous iterations (corresponding to the personal best value of the objective function), P^k is the global best point ever experienced by the whole swarm, V_i is the velocity of the *i*th particle, C_1 and C_2 are two weight coefficients which influence the balance between the global and local search phase, ω is the inertia effect, χ is a speed limiter. In this paper, the values are set as follows: $C_1 = 2$, $C_2 = 1.494$, $\chi = 1.0$, $\omega = 0.729$.

The arch formation in a dense crowd is used to guide the design of the obstacle. Therefore, we focus on the variables that can influence the arch formation. In this paper, the approach that adjusting the arch formation by the obstacles is inspired by the usage of anti-slide piles in civil engineering. Anti-slide piles are a common tool to adjust the soil arching effect in civil engineering. The principle of the anti-slide pile is that it changes the position of the arch feet [27–29]. The spacing between the anti-slide piles, the size of the piles and the spacing between the piles and the exit are key configurations that influence the adjustment effect of the anti-slide piles. Therefore, we changed the corresponding variables of obstacles to adjust the effect of obstacles, which is similar with the usage of anti-slide piles. It is consist of the distance between the obstacle and the front wall and the distance between the symmetrical obstacles, see Fig. 6. The original scene is the same as the scene in the previous simulation, and the number of pedestrians is 300.

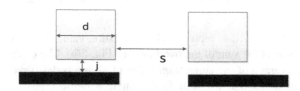

Fig. 6. The optimization variables of obstacles in our method.

The state vector is as follows:

$$x = [s|j|d]. \tag{11}$$

In this paper, the radial pressure is used to build a fitness function to guide the optimization of obstacles in evacuation scene to alleviate the crowd congestion. To demonstrate the effect of the new fitness function, a comparison test which used the average congestion value as the fitness function is given.

We use the evacuation process that pedestrians evacuate the scene as the objective function. To simplify the calculation process, a simplified method for the optimization was proposed in this paper. See Fig. 7, the red line is the congestion value in evacuation without obstacles, and the green line and blue line are congestion values in evacuation with different obstacles. It is obvious that different congestion values have a similar downtrend, which means that the congestion in a period of evacuation process can represent the congestion of the whole evacuation. Therefore, the congestion value during the 100th frame to the 120th frame is used to represent the congestion value of the whole evacuation process.

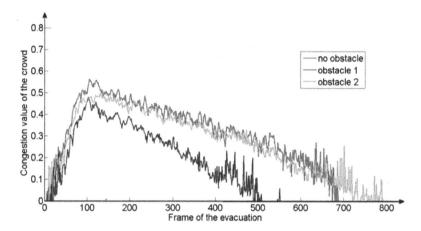

Fig. 7. The horizontal axis indicates frame numbers of the running simulation, the vertical axis indicates the average congestion value. The red line is the congestion value in evacuation without obstacles, the green line and blue line are congestion values in evacuation with different obstacles. (Color figure online)

We used the number of iterations and objective congestion value as termination conditions for the PSO. In this paper, the number of iterations we used is 10 and the objective congestion value is 0.1

4.2   Simulation Results Analysis

Here, results of simulation and analysis are given to demonstrate the effect of our approach. In Fig. 8(a), the average congestion value in different scenes are given. Obviously, the average congestion value in the modified scene is lower than it in the original scene. This result illustrates that the obstacles set according to the arch formation can truly alleviate the congestion. In Fig. 8(b), the evacuation efficiency in different scenes are presented. The frame number is corresponding with the time and number of pedestrians is used to represent the evacuation efficiency. In Fig. 8(b), the pedestrians number in the modified scene is declining more quickly than that in the original scene. It is obvious that arch formation controlled by the obstacles can increase the evacuation efficiency. Therefore, the arch formation in a dense crowd can be used to alleviate the congestion and improve the evacuation efficiency.

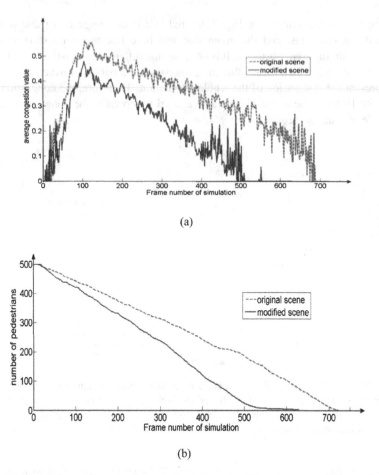

Fig. 8. (a) Comparison of average congestion values in different scenes. This result is the average of all congestion values of pedestrians. The horizontal axis represents frame numbers of the running simulation, and the vertical axis indicates the average congestion value. The red dash line is the average congestion value in the original scene, and the blue solid line is the average congestion value in the modified scene. (b) Comparison of evacuation efficiency in different scenes. Horizontal axis is the number of frame, and the vertical axis is the number of pedestrians in the scene. The red dash line is the number of pedestrians in the original scene, and the blue solid line is number of pedestrian in the modified scene. (Color figure online)

Figure 9 is a distribution diagram, which is drawn by our previous testing data, of the congestion value. It is used to illustrate the relations between control variables and the fitness value. The variation of congestion value of crowd is indicated by the change of color. The congestion value changes obviously when the spacing between obstacles and spacing between obstacles and the wall change and changes little with the size of obstacle. This phenomenon shows that the size of obstacles has less influence on congestion alleviation than the spacing. The distribution diagram of the congestion value can provide prior information to guide the optimization process.

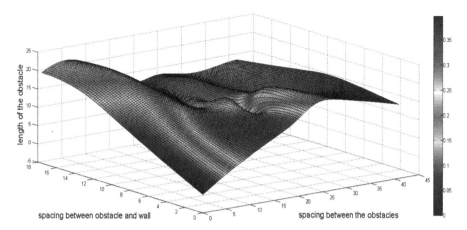

Fig. 9. Distribution diagram of the congestion value. The x axis is spacing between obstacle and the wall, the y axis is spacing between obstacles and the z axis is the size of obstacle. The different colors in the diagram indicate different congestion values. As shown in the color-bar, red color demonstrates high congestion value; blue color demonstrates low congestion value. (Color figure online)

The optimization result that guided by the fitness function which is based on the congestion value is shown in the Fig. 10. Figure 10(a) to (d) are evolution process of the spacing between obstacles, the spacing between the obstacle and the wall, the size of the obstacle and the congestion value of the crowd. The lines from p1 to p5 are different particle swarms that with different state vectors. Figure 10 shows that the optimization results of state vector are divided into two groups. The reason is that the congestion alleviation can be achieved by different approaches. Obstacles with suitable configurations may alleviate the crowd congestion without adjusting the arch formation. Although the obstacle, which would not adjust the arch formation, can also alleviate the congestion, it increases the probablity that the optimization result is trap in local optimum. Therefore, the fitness function based on the congestion value has limitation in guiding the optimization of obstacles.

The optimization result that guided by the new fitness function which is based on the radial pressure is given in the Fig. 11. Figure 11(a) to (d) are evolution process of the spacing between obstacles, the spacing between the obstacle and the wall, the size of the obstacle and the congestion value of the crowd. The lines from p1 to p5 are different particle swarms that with different state vectors. The Fig. 11 shows that the optimization results of state vector are uniformly converges to a stable value, and average congestion value is lower than that in Fig. 10. This is because the optimization guided by the new fitness function can find the suitable configuration of obstacle to adjust the arch formation, and the congestion alleviation is achieved by the arch formation. Therefore, the fitness function based on the radial pressure is suitable to guide the optimization of obstacles to adjust arch formation for crowd congestion alleviation.

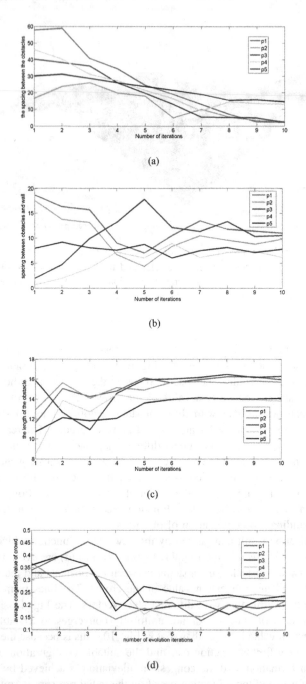

(a)

(b)

(c)

(d)

Fig. 10. These pictures show the variation of configurations of obstacles calculated by the direct fitness function. (a) the y axis is the spacing between obstacles, (b) the y axis is the spacing between the obstacles and the wall, (c) the y axis is the size of the obstacle (d) the y axis is the crowd congestion. The x axis is the number of evolution. Different colors representing different particle populations. (Color figure online)

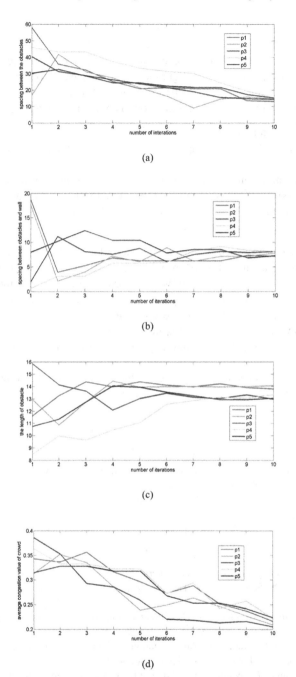

(a)

(b)

(c)

(d)

Fig. 11. These pictures show the variation of configurations of obstacles calculated by the indirect fitness function. (a) the y axis is the spacing between obstacles, (b) the y axis is the spacing between the obstacles and the wall, (c) the y axis is the size of the obstacle (d) the y axis is the congestion value of the crowd. The x axis is the number of evolution. Different colors representing different particle populations. (Color figure online)

5   Conclusion

In this paper, we pay attention to the crowd congestion by the adjustment of arch formation in a dense crowd. The configurations of obstacles are optimized by the PSO to achieve a better adjustment of arch formation, and a radial pressure based fitness function is proposed to guide the optimization. The simulation results are as follows:

1. The arch formation in a dense crowd can be adjusted by the obstacles in evacuation scene to alleviate the crowd congestion. Therefore, the arch formation can be used to
2. The arch formation can be used to guide the optimization of obstacles. Concretely, the radial pressure, which is an index of the strength of arch formation, can be used to build a new fitness function for the PSO, and it can improve the convergence speed of the optimization process.

In summary, the proposed approach is suitable to optimize the configurations of obstacles to achieve an alleviation of crowd congestion. However, there are unresolved issues for this approach too. Although the arch formation can modify the optimization of obstacles, the adjustment is too simple for the evacuation. Since obstacles are tools for us to adjust the arch formation, the configuration of the obstacle needs further research. Our simulation environment is just a simple scene. There is a necessary for better methods to achieve the modeling and simulation of complex environments.

Acknowledgments. This research is supported by the National Natural Science Foundation of China (61472232, 61572299, 61373149 and 61402270).

References

1. Helbing, D., Johansson, A., Al-Abideen, H.Z.: Dynamics of crowd disasters: an empirical study. Phys. Rev. E Stat. Nonlinear Soft Matter Phys. **75**(2), 046109 (2007)
2. Helbing, D., Farkas, I., Vicsek, T.: Simulating dynamical features of escape panic. Nature **407**(6803), 487–490 (2000)
3. Helbing, D., Molna, T.: Social force model for pedestrian dynamics. Phys. Rev. E Stat. Phys. Plasmas Fluids **51**(5), 4282 (1995)
4. Schadschneider, A.: Bionics-Inspired Cellular Automaton Model for Pedestrian Dynamic. In: Fukui, M., Sugiyama, Y., Schreckenberg, M., Wolf, D.E. (eds.) Traffic and Granular Flow'01, pp. 499–509. Springer, Heidelberg (2002). https://doi.org/10.1007/978-3-662-10583-2_52
5. Tang, T.Q., Rui, Y.X., Zhang, J.: A cellular automation model accounting for bicycle's group behaviour. Phys. A Stat. Mech. Appl. **492**, 1782–1797 (2018)
6. Tang, T.Q., Chen, L., Guo, R.Y.: An evacuation model accounting for elementary students' individual properties. Phys. A Stat. Mech. Appl. **440**, 49–56 (2015)
7. Zhou, M., Dong, H., Wang, F.Y., Wang, Q., Yang, X.: Modeling and simulation of pedestrian dynamical behavior based on a fuzzy logic approach. Inf. Sci. **360**, 112–130 (2016)
8. Ha, V., Lykotrafitis, G.: Agent-based modeling of a multi-room multi-floor building emergency evacuation. Phys. A Stat. Mech. Appl. **391**(8), 2740–2751 (2012)

9. Liu, H., Liu, B., Zhang, H., Li, L., Qin, X.: Crowd evacuation simulation approach based on navigation knowledge and two-layer control mechanism. Inf. Sci. **436–437**, 247–267 (2018)
10. Helbing, D., Buzna, L., Johansson, A., Werner, T.: Self-organized pedestrian crowd dynamics: experiments, simulations, and design solutions. Transp. Sci. **39**(1), 1–24 (2005)
11. Han, Y., Liu, H., Moore, P.: Extended route choice model based on available evacuation route set and its application in crowd evacuation simulation. Simul. Model. Pract. Theory **75**, 1–16 (2017)
12. Liu, H., Zhang, P., Hu, B., Moore, P.: A novel approach to task assignment in a cooperative multi-agent design system. Appl. Intell. **43**(6), 162–175 (2015)
13. Li, Y., Liu, H., Liu, G.P.: A grouping approach based on grid density and relationship for crowd evacuation simulation. Phys. A Stat. Mech. Appl. **473**, 319–336 (2017)
14. Johansson, A., Helbing, D.: Pedestrian flow optimization with a genetic algorithm based on Boolean grids. In: Waldau, N., Gattermann, P., Knoflacher, H., Schreckenberg, M. (eds.) Pedestrian and Evacuation Dynamics, pp. 267–272. Springer, Heidelberg (2006). https://doi. org/10.1007/978-3-540-47064-9_23
15. Yanagisawa, D., Nishi, R., Tomoeda, A., Ohtsuka, K., Kimura, A.: Study on efficiency of evacuation with an obstacle on hexagonal cell space. SICE J. Control Meas. Syst. Integr. **3**, 395–401 (2010)
16. Zhao, Y.X., Li, M., Lu, X.: Optimal layout design of obstacles for panic evacuation using differential evolution. Phys. A Stat. Mech. Appl. **465**, 175–194 (2017)
17. Jiang, L., Li, J., Shen, C., Yang, S., Han, Z.: Obstacle optimization for panic flow—reducing the tangential momentum increases the escape speed. PLoS ONE **9**, e115463 (2014)
18. Frank, G., Dorso, C.: Room evacuation in the presence of an obstacle. Phys. A Stat. Mech. Appl. **390**, 2135–2145 (2011)
19. Suzuno, K., Tomoeda, A., Iwamoto, M.: Dynamic structure in pedestrian evacuation: image processing approach. In: Chraibi, M., Boltes, M., Schadschneider, A., Seyfried, A. (eds.) Traffic and Granular Flow '13, pp. 195–201. Springer, Cham (2015). https://doi.org/10. 1007/978-3-319-10629-8_23
20. Masuda, T., Nishinari, K., Schadschneider, A.: Critical bottleneck size for jamless particle flows in two dimensions. Phys. Rev. Lett. **112**(13), 138701 (2014)
21. Twarogowska, M., Goatin, P., Duvigneau, R.: Macroscopic modeling and simulations of room evacuation. Appl. Math. Model. **38**(24), 5781–5795 (2014)
22. Banks, A., Vincent, J., Anyakoha, C.: A review of particle swarm optimization. Part I: background and development. Nat. Comput. **6**(4), 467–484 (2007)
23. Alrashidi, M.R., El-Hawary, M.E.: A survey of particle swarm optimization applications in electric power systems. IEEE Trans. Evol. Comput. **13**(4), 913–918 (2009)
24. Cristiani, E., Peri, D.: Handling obstacles in pedestrian simulations: models and optimization. Appl. Math. Model. **45**, 285–302 (2016)
25. Feliciani, C., Nishinari, K.: Measurement of congestion and intrinsic risk in pedestrian crowds. Transp. Res. Part C **91**, 124–155 (2018)
26. Jia, H.L., Wang, C.H., Li, J.H.: Discussion on some issues in theory of soil arch. J. Southwest Jiao Tong Univ. **38**(4), 398–402 (2003)
27. Jiang, L.W., Huang, R.Q., Jiang, X.: Analysis of soil arching effect between adjacent piles and their spacing in cohesive soils. Rock Soil Mech. **27**(3), 445–450 (2006)
28. Yang, M., Yao, L.K., Wang, G.J.: Study on effect of width and space of anti-slide piles on soil arching between piles. Chin. J. Geotech. Eng. **29**(10), 1477–1482 (2007)
29. Zhao, M.H., Chen, B.C., Liu, J.H.: Analysis of the spacing between anti-slide piles considering soil-arch effect. J. Cent. South Highw. Eng. (2006)

Web Service Composition with Uncertain QoS: An IQCP Model

Hengzhou Ye[1,2]($\boxtimes$) and Taoshen Li[3]

[1] Guangxi Key Laboratory of Embedded Technology and Intelligent System,
Guilin University of Technology, No. 12, Jiangan Road, Qixing District,
Guilin 541004, China
2002018@glut.edu.cn
[2] College of Electrical Engineering, Guangxi University,
No. 100, Daxue Street, Xixiangtang District, Nanning 530004, China
[3] School of Information and Engineering, Guangxi University, Nanning, China
tshli@gxu.edu.cn

Abstract. Quality of Service (QoS) is commonly employed to represent non-functional web service (WS) characteristics for the purpose of optimizing WS composition. As a departure from most of the extant research on QoS aggregations, where QoS is typically represented deterministically, we hypothesize the QoS to a WS as a random variable that follows a normal distribution. A serial of formulas are proposed to calculate the expectation and variance of the QoS of a composite service; this yields four QoS criteria suited to workflow described by a directed acrylic graph (DAG). The Web service composition problem with uncertain QoS is then modeled as an integer quadratically constrained program (IQCP). Finally, a series of experimental results obtained in CPLEX and Java illustrate that our model has favorable robustness and can estimate composite service QoS rapidly and accurately.

Keywords: Uncertain QoS · Service composition
Integer quadratically constrained program · Directed acyclic graph

1 Introduction

The coarse-grained, loosely coupled service-oriented architecture (SOA) processes communication among services through simple and well-defined interfaces independent of the underlying implementation platform or network communication module. WS and SOA-based software systems are often combined with various other services to realize SOA. The WS composition problem has received a great deal of research attention, to this effect. With the proliferation of WSs on the Internet, QoS is commonly adopted to describe non-functional WS characteristics. Optimizing the QoS-aware service composition (QSC) is an especially popular research subject in this field. The goal is to select a composite WS that maximizes certain aggregated-quality functions while implementing the desired user functionalities and preserving several QoS constraints.

© Springer Nature Singapore Pte Ltd. 2019
Y. Sun et al. (Eds.): ChineseCSCW 2018, CCIS 917, pp. 146–162, 2019.
https://doi.org/10.1007/978-981-13-3044-5_11

The workflow-based QSC problem has been extensively studied as well [1–4]. However, most previous researchers consider each WS to have a deterministic QoS. In actuality, the QoS measure of a WS is intrinsically probabilistic due to the complexity and dynamic nature of the network environment [5] and is very challenging to accurately estimate. For example, the response time for a WS is dependent upon the number of requests invoking it. As discussed by Wang et al. [6], the QoS obtained by the service provider's description (or the QoS value calculated through historical information) does not truly reflect the performance of the service. For scientific computing tasks, service oriented applications, and MapReduce applications in cloud environment, research has shown that the CPU, network, and I/O performance may fluctuate significantly in the short term [7, 8]. Armbrust et al. [9] found that the performance of a service can fluctuate by 4–16% due to network and disk I/O interference. The QoS of a WS should be described in an uncertain form in order to ensure an accurate and workable QSC problem model [10].

Previous researchers have represented the QoS of a WS as a single value, multiple values [11], standard statistical distribution [12, 13], and any probability distribution [14]. QoS, when represented as a constant value, does not contain quality variations. It is more reasonable to model QoS as a standard statistical distribution (e.g., normal distribution) than several values with different frequencies. Though not every QoS measure of a WS follows a normal distribution, taking any probability distribution into consideration will increase the difficulty of the problem significantly.

In this study, we assumed that the QoS to a WS follows a normal distribution. In an attempt to design a DAG-based workflow, we established QoS aggregation methods for several QoS criteria and built an IQCP to tackle the QSC problem with uncertain QoS. The main contributions of this work are as follows.

- We use an original and efficient aggregation approach for maximum/min-type and product-type QoSs. Compared to representing QoSs in any probability distribution, the proposed method estimates QoS aggregation quicker and more accurately.
- We built the QSC problem with uncertain QoS into the well-known IQCP model, which is promising for exactly solving the composition problem with uncertain QoS.

The remainder of this paper is structured as follows. An overview of the research on Web service composition with uncertain QoS is conducted in Sect. 2. Section 3 lists the necessary assumptions and theorems. Section 4 describes the workflow and QoS model. Section 5 details QoS aggregation calculation process. Section 6 proposes the WS composition model with uncertain QoS; Sect. 7 describes its performance in detail. Section 8 provides a brief summary and conclusion.

2 Related Work

The global constraint decomposition strategy [15–17] can be adopted to tackle with the QSC problem by considering the uncertainty of QoS. This typically involves dividing the WS composition process into two phases: decomposition of global constraints and local optimization selection. In the former phase, the global constraints are decomposed into a series of constraints imposed on each subtask only. Using these local constraints, the local selection process is carried out via optimization to quickly select best services while ensuring that global constraints are satisfied. When exceptions occur during running time, an appropriate substitution can be quickly identified by simply repeating the local selection process. The strategy is thus adaptable to dynamic environments to a certain extent. Chen et al. [18] proposed the instant recommendation approach to deal with manage uncertain QoS, which works by revealing the most reliable and robust services per the execution log of composite services, therefore, user demands can be fulfilled with higher probability. Hyunyoung et al. [19] also estimated actual QoS performance to a service based on the real transaction history rather than the QoS information published by its provider.

Representing QoSs as multiple values or probability distributions may be a more straightforward way to resolve the uncertain QoS service composition problem. Wang et al. [6] and Shen et al. [20] used the cloud model to evaluate QoS uncertainty; three key parameters(expected value, entropy and hyper entropy) were used to characterize the stability of QoS, then to decrease the number of candidate or composite services, redundant services were pruned by Skyline computing. Skyline computing was also adopted by following work. Fu et al. [21] used an empirical distribution function to describe QoS uncertainty with special focus on stochastic dominance (SD) theory. The method discussed by Fu et al. [22] does not require the assumption that QoS has a specific distribution, and focuses on aggregating the QoS in a cumulative manner. Yu et al. [23] developed the novel p-dominant service skyline concept, which is computed based on a p-R-tree indexing structure and a dual-pruning scheme.

Some researchers have calculated the QoS of a composite service, called QoS aggregation, which is one of the core issues relevant to the QSC problem. Hwang et al. [5] presented a uniform probabilistic model to denote the QoS of atomic or composite WSs with corresponding computation algorithms. The method is precise, but extremely time-consuming. Zheng et al. [14] developed a set of formulas for QoS aggregation according to four typical patterns: sequential, concurrent, selection, and loop. As opposed to the method presented by Hwang et al. [5], its numerical computation algorithms stipulate that the starting point and width of the intervals must be consistent for all QoS distributions – this unfortunately makes QoS monitoring and parameter-setting more difficult. They also ignore QoS aggregation for multiplicative QoS (e.g., reliability) to avoid any combinatorial explosions. Chellammal et al. [15] also denotes QoS denoted as a Probability Mass Function (PMF). By introducing the global constraint decomposition strategy, QoS aggregation is only calculated when the composite service selected via local optimization is unfit for user requests. This reduces the high time overhead on QoS aggregation. By modeling QoS values in normal distribution, Schuller et al. [24] selected the optimized service combination at minimal cost under QoS requirements; they used a simulation approach for QoS estimation. Wang et al. [25] focused on the uncertainty of service execution rather than the uncertainty of QoS. Du et al. [26] and George et al. [27] only used one QoS criterion each: the former used response time, the latter used cost.

3 Underlying Assumptions and Theorems

We held the following assumptions in conducting this study:

(1) The QoS to a WS follows a normal distribution and the QoS of one WS is unrelated to the QoSs of other WSs.
(2) When QoSs to each WS follow normal distributions, the QoS aggregation to a composite service combined by these WSs follows a normal distribution.
(3) For a given workflow F, let $s = (s_1, s_2, ..., s_n)$ be an arbitrary composite service to F and the response time of s_i $(i = 1, 2, ..., n)$ follow a normal distribution $N(\mu_i, \sigma_i^2)$. There are two non-negative real number sequences $(x_1, x_2, ..., x_n)$ and $(y_1, y_2, ..., y_n)$ which can be used to calculate the expectation $E(s)$ and variance $D(s)$ of the response time of s as follows:

$$E(s) = \sum_{i=1}^{n} x_i \cdot \mu_i, \quad D(s) = \sum_{i=1}^{n} y_i \cdot \sigma_i^2 \tag{1}$$

Assume that X_i is a random variable, and $X_i \sim N(\mu_i, \sigma_i^2)$ $(i = 1, 2,...,n)$, and X_i is independent of X_j $(i \neq j)$. Let $Y_n = \prod_{i=1}^{n} X_i$. The expectation and variance of Y_n are denoted as $E(Y_n)$ and $D(Y_n)$, respectively.

Theorem 1. $E(Y_n) = \prod_{i=1}^{n} \mu_i$.

Proof: Because $X_1, X_2, ..., X_n$ are independent of each other, $E(Y_n)$ can be obtained as follows:

$$E(Y_n) = E\left(\prod_{i=1}^{n} X_i\right) = \prod_{i=1}^{n} E(X_i) = \prod_{i=1}^{n} \mu_i$$

Theorem 2. If $\mu_i = \varepsilon\sigma_i$, then $(Y_n) = \left[\left(1 + \frac{1}{\varepsilon^2}\right)^n - 1\right] \prod_{i=1}^{n} \mu_i^2$

Proof: Apply mathematical induction to n.

(1) When $n = 2$,

$$D(Y_2) = D(X_1 X_2) = \sigma_1^2 \sigma_2^2 + \sigma_1^2 \mu_2^2 + \sigma_2^2 \mu_1^2$$

$$= (2\varepsilon^2 + 1)\sigma_1^2 \sigma_2^2 = \left[\left(1 + \frac{1}{\varepsilon^2}\right)^2 - 1\right] \mu_1^2 \mu_2^2$$

(2) Let us assume that when n is equal to k, the theorem is true. That is,

$$D(Y_k) = \left[\left(1 + \frac{1}{\varepsilon^2}\right)^k - 1\right] \prod_{i=1}^{k} \mu_i^2.$$

When $n = k + 1$,

$$D(Y_{k+1}) = D(Y_k)D(X_{k+1}) + D(Y_k)[E(X_{k+1})]^2 + D(X_{k+1})[E(Y_k)]^2$$

$$= \left\{ \left[\left(1 + \frac{1}{\varepsilon^2}\right)^k - 1 \right] \prod_{i=1}^{k} \mu_i^2 \right\} (\sigma_{k+1}^2 + \mu_{k+1}^2) + \sigma_{k+1}^2 \prod_{i=1}^{k} \mu_i^2$$

$$= \left[\left(1 + \frac{1}{\varepsilon^2}\right)^{k+1} - 1 \right] \prod_{i=1}^{k+1} \mu_i^2$$

These two steps yield the conclusion.

4 Workflow and QoS Model

A workflow represents how to constitute the capabilities of different WSs in four basic patterns (sequence, concurrency, selection, and loop). The labeled graph [28], numbered graph [20], and DAG [29] are common ways to represent a workflow. In the resource allocation field, DAG is used to represent the workflow [30, 31]. DAG cannot directly denote the selection and loop patterns. However, the loop pattern can be regarded as a special sequential one. A workflow with selection patterns can be broken up into several workflows without any selection pattern. Therefore, a workflow with selection and loop patterns can be transformed into several workflows that can be represented by DAG. Consider the workflow shown in Fig. 1, which can be split into the two workflows shown in Fig. 2a and b, respectively. Here, we only consider workflows that can be represented with DAG.

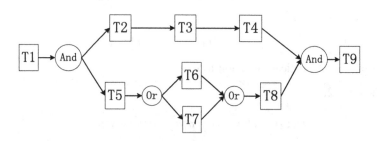

Fig. 1. Workflow with selection pattern

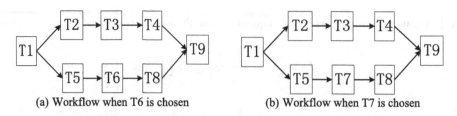

(a) Workflow when T6 is chosen   (b) Workflow when T7 is chosen

Fig. 2. Equivalent workflow to Fig. 1 represented by DAG

The QoS is used to measure the performance of candidate services. The most commonly used QoS criteria include cost, response time, reliability, availability, reputation, and throughput. According to the aggregation method, these criteria can be divided into four classes: sum-type (e.g., cost), min/max-type (e.g., response time), product-type (e.g., reliability), and average-type (e.g., reputation). Similar to [14], the aggregation rules for sequence and concurrency patterns and different types of QoS criteria are summarized in Table 1.

5 Expectation and Variance of QoS for Composite Services

Assume that there are n tasks $T = \{T_1, T_2,\ldots, T_n\}$ in a workflow F. Each task Ti, $i \in [1,n]$ has m number of candidate WSs $s_i = \{s_{i1}, s_{i2},\ldots, s_{im}\}$. A set of 0–1 variables $x = \{x_{ij}\}(1 \leq i \leq n, \ 1 \leq j \leq m)$ represent a combination $cs(x)$ of F. When the task t_i chooses the service s_{ij}, $p_{ij} = 1$, otherwise $p_{ij} = 0$. Let the cost, response time, reliability, and reputation of s_{ij} follow normal distributions $N\left(\mu p_{ij}, \sigma p_{ij}^2\right)$, $N\left(\mu t_{ij}, \sigma t_{ij}^2\right)$, $N\left(\mu r_{ij}, \sigma r_{ij}^2\right)$ and $N\left(\mu c_{ij}, \sigma c_{ij}^2\right)$, respectively. According to our assumptions, the cost, response time, reliability, and reputation of $cs(x)$ will also follow normal distributions. Their corresponding expectation and variance are discussed below.

Table 1. Aggregation rules for different patterns and types of QoS

QoS type	Pattern	Aggregation rules
Sum-type	Sequence/concurrency	Addition of their QoS values
Min/max-type	Sequence concurrency	Addition of their QoS values maximum of their QoS values
Product-type	Sequence/concurrency	Multiplication of their QoS values
Average-type	Sequence/concurrency	Average of their QoS values

5.1 Expectation and Variance of Cost

According to Table 1, the cost of a composite service can be summed by the cost of all its components. The linear combination of a set of independent normal random variables still obeys a normal distribution, so the cost of $cs(x)$ is distributed from a normal distribution. Thus, the expectation $E_p(cs(x))$ and variance $D_p(cs(x))$ of $cs(x)$ can be obtained by Formulas (2) and (3), respectively:

$$E_p(cs(x)) = \sum_{i=1}^{n} \sum_{j}^{m} p_{ij} \cdot \mu p_{ij} \tag{2}$$

$$D_p(cs(x)) = \sum_{i=1}^{n} \sum_{j=1}^{m} p_{ij} \cdot \sigma p_{ij}^2 \tag{3}$$

5.2   Expectation and Variance of Response Time

Let j represent an arbitrary composite service of F which consists of a series of services $(s_{1j_1}, s_{1j_1}, \ldots, s_{nj_n})$. Under our assumptions, the existence of two non-negative real number sequences $(x_1, x_2, \ldots, x_n)$ and $(y_1, y_2, \ldots, y_n)$ yields the following two formulas:

$$\sum_{i=1}^{n} x_i \cdot \mu t_{1j_1} = \mu t_j, \quad \sum_{i=1}^{n} y_i \cdot \sigma t_{1j_1}^2 = \sigma t_j^2 \tag{4}$$

where μt_j, σt_j denote the expectation and mean square deviation of j, respectively. Their values can be calculated as follows by sampling:

$$\mu t_j = \sum_{i=1}^{Times} t_{ij_i}(k), \quad \sigma t_j^2 = \sum_{i=1}^{Times} \left[t_{ij_i}(k) - \mu t_j \right]^2 \tag{5}$$

where $t_{ij_i}(k)$ denotes the k-th response time of s_{ij_i} and Times is the number of sampling iterations.

Select q number of different composite services $(j_1, j_2, \ldots, j_q)$ by random for F and let:

$$x = (x_1, x_2, \ldots, x_n)^{\mathrm{T}}, \quad u = (\mu t_{j1}, \mu t_{j2}, \ldots, \mu t_{jn})^{\mathrm{T}} \tag{6}$$

$$U = \begin{pmatrix} \mu t_{1j_{11}} & \mu t_{2j_{12}} & \cdots & \mu t_{nj_{1n}} \\ \mu t_{1j_{21}} & \mu t_{2j_{22}} & \cdots & \mu t_{nj_{2n}} \\ \cdots & \cdots & \cdots & \cdots \\ \mu t_{1j_{q1}} & \mu t_{2j_{q2}} & \cdots & \mu t_{nj_{qn}} \end{pmatrix} \tag{7}$$

yielding the following expression:

$$Ux = u \tag{8}$$

When $q > n$, Formula (8) is a non-negative overdetermined linear equation system. Its solution, that is, the value of x, can be calculated by a known method.

Similarly, let:

$$y = (y_1, y_2, \ldots, y_n)^{\mathrm{T}}, \quad o = (\sigma t_{j1}, \sigma t_{j2}, \ldots, \sigma t_{jn})^{\mathrm{T}} \tag{9}$$

$$O = \begin{pmatrix} \sigma t_{1j_{11}}^2 & \sigma t_{2j_{12}}^2 & \cdots & \sigma t_{nj_{1n}}^2 \\ \sigma t_{1j_{21}}^2 & \sigma t_{2j_{22}}^2 & \cdots & \sigma t_{nj_{2n}}^2 \\ \cdots & \cdots & \cdots & \cdots \\ \sigma t_{1j_{q1}}^2 & \mu t_{2j_{q2}}^2 & \cdots & \sigma t_{nj_{qn}}^2 \end{pmatrix} \tag{10}$$

This allows us to obtain following equation:

$$Oy = o \tag{11}$$

y can be obtained by solving Eq. (11).

Calculating the value of x or y are time consuming. However, the calculation process can be completed offline because it depends only on the workflow and candidate services, and is independent of user requirements. Hence, this process does not affect the time overhead of combining services.

After determining values of x and y, the expectation and variance of the response time of $cs(x)$, denoted as $E_t(cs(x))$ and $D_t(cs(x))$, respectively, can be calculated as follows:

$$E_t(cs(x)) = \sum_{i=1}^{n} \left(x_i \sum_{j=1}^{m} p_{ij} \cdot \mu t_{ij} \right), \quad D_t(cs(x)) = \sum_{i=1}^{n} \left(y_i \sum_{j=1}^{m} p_{ij} \cdot \sigma t_{ij}^2 \right) \tag{12}$$

5.3 Expectation and Variance of Reliability

According to Table 1, the reliability of a composite service can be achieved by multiplying the reliability of all its components. Based on Theorem 1, the expectation of reliability of $cs(x)$, denoted as $E_r(cs(x))$, can be calculated as follows:

$$E_r(cs(x)) = \prod_{i=1}^{n} \sum_{j=1}^{m} p_{ij} \cdot \mu r_{ij} \tag{13}$$

According Theorem 2, the variance of reliability of $cs(x)$, denoted as $D_r(cs(x))$, can be calculated approximately by Formula (14):

$$D_r(cs(x)) = \left[\left(1 + \frac{1}{\varepsilon^2} \right)^n - 1 \right] \prod_{i=1}^{n} \sum_{j=1}^{m} p_{ij} \cdot \mu r_{ij}^2 \tag{14}$$

where the parameter ε can be obtained as follows:

$$\varepsilon = \frac{1}{n \cdot m} \sum_{i=1}^{n} \sum_{j=1}^{m} \frac{\mu r_{ij}}{\sigma r_{ij}} \tag{15}$$

5.4 Expectation and Variance of Reputation

According to Table 1, the reputation of a composite service can be calculated by averaging the reputation of all its components. The expectation and variance of the reputation of $cs(x)$, denoted as $E_c(cs(x))$ and $D_c(cs(x))$, respectively, can be calculated as follows:

$$E_c(cs(x)) = \frac{1}{n}\sum\nolimits_{i=1}^{n}\sum\nolimits_{j=1}^{m} p_{ij} \cdot \mu c_{ij}, \quad D_c(cs(x)) = \frac{1}{n^2}\sum\nolimits_{i=1}^{n}\sum\nolimits_{j=1}^{m} p_{ij} \cdot \sigma c_{ij}^2 \quad (16)$$

6 Web Service Composition Model with Uncertain QoS

Without loss of generality, our aim is to minimize the cost while satisfying QoS constraints in regards to response time, reliability, and reputation. Our model is described in detail below.

$$\text{Object:} \quad \min\left(\sum\nolimits_{i=1}^{n}\sum\nolimits_{j}^{m} p_{ij} \cdot \mu p_{ij} + \beta \sum\nolimits_{i=1}^{n}\sum\nolimits_{j=1}^{m} p_{ij} \cdot \sigma p_{ij}^2\right) \quad (17)$$

$$\text{s.t.:} \quad P(q_t \le C_t) \ge p_t, \quad P(q_r \ge C_r) \ge p_r, \quad P(q_c \ge C_c) \ge p_c \quad (18)$$

$$p_{ij} \in \{0,1\}, 1 \le i \le n, 1 \le j \le m \quad (19)$$

$$\sum\nolimits_{j=1}^{m} p_{ij} = 1, 1 \le i \le n \quad (20)$$

where β is a tunable parameter, $P(X \le x)$ is the probability that the value of X falls into the interval $(-\infty, x]$, C_t, C_r, and C_c respectively represent the constraints of response time, reliability, and reputation, and p_t, p_r, and p_c are given constants.

Considering that the QoS of composition services are subject to normal distributions, Inequation (18) can be converted into Inequations (21)–(23) in accordance with the 3σ principle:

$$\mu_t + 3\sigma_t \le C_t \quad (21)$$

$$\mu_r - 3\sigma_r \ge C_r \quad (22)$$

$$\mu_c - 3\sigma_c \ge C_c \quad (23)$$

where μ_t, σ_t, μ_r, σ_r, μ_c, and σ_c respectively represent the expectation and mean variance of the response time, reliability, and reputation of a composite service.

Inequation (21) is equivalent to the following two inequations:

$$0 \le C_t - \mu_t \quad (24)$$

$$9\sigma_t^2 \le (C_t - \mu_t)^2 \quad (25)$$

Substituting Formula (12) into in Inequation (25), and introducing the tunable parameters β_1 and β_2 (considering that there exists some error in the expectation and variance of the response time), yields the following:

$$9\beta_2 \sum_{i=1}^{n} \left(y_i \sum_{j=1}^{m} p_{ij} \cdot \sigma t_{ij}^2 \right) \le \left(C_t - \beta_1 \sum_{i=1}^{n} \left(x_i \sum_{j=1}^{m} p_{ij} \cdot \mu t_{ij} \right) \right)^2 \qquad (26)$$

Introduce a variable $\gamma = \sqrt{\left(1 + \frac{1}{\varepsilon^2}\right)^n - 1}$, Substituting Formulas (13) and (14) into inequation (22), and introducing the tunable parameters β_3 (considering that there exists some error in the variance of the reliability), yields the following:

$$\prod_{i=1}^{n} \sum_{j=1}^{m} p_{ij} \cdot \mu r_{ij} - 3\beta_3 \gamma \sqrt{\prod_{i=1}^{n} \sum_{j=1}^{m} p_{ij} \cdot \mu r_{ij}^2} \ge C_r \qquad (27)$$

Note that $\sqrt{p_{ij}} = p_{ij}$. After some simplifications, Inequation (27) is equivalent to the following inequality:

$$(1 - 3\beta_3 \gamma) \cdot \prod_{i=1}^{n} \sum_{j=1}^{m} p_{ij} \cdot \mu r_{ij} \ge C_r \qquad (28)$$

Taking the logarithm of both sides of Inequality (28) yields the following:

$$\sum_{i=1}^{n} \sum_{j=1}^{m} p_{ij} \cdot \log(\mu r_{ij}) \ge \log(C_r/(1 - 3\beta_3 \gamma)) \qquad (29)$$

Inequality (23) is equivalent to the following condition:

$$\mu_c - C_c \ge 0, \quad (\mu_c - C_c)^2 \ge 9\sigma_c^2 \qquad (30)$$

Substituting Formula (16) into Inequality (30) yields:

$$\left(\frac{1}{n} \sum_{i=1}^{n} \sum_{j=1}^{m} p_{ij} \cdot \mu c_{ij} - C_c \right)^2 \ge \frac{3}{n^2} \sum_{i=1}^{n} \sum_{j=1}^{m} p_{ij} \cdot \sigma c_{ij}^2 \qquad (31)$$

In summary, the problem with WS composition for uncertain QoS can be represented as an IQCP model.

$$\text{Object:} \quad \min \left(\sum_{i=1}^{n} \sum_{j}^{m} p_{ij} \cdot \mu p_{ij} + \beta \sum_{i=1}^{n} \sum_{j=1}^{m} p_{ij} \cdot \sigma p_{ij}^2 \right) \qquad (32)$$

$$\text{s.t.:} \quad 0 \le C_t - \beta_1 \sum_{i=1}^{n} \left(x_i \sum_{j=1}^{m} p_{ij} \cdot \mu t_{ij} \right) \qquad (33)$$

$$9\beta_2 \sum_{i=1}^{n} \left(y_i \sum_{j=1}^{m} p_{ij} \cdot \sigma t_{ij}^2 \right) \le \left(C_t - \beta_1 \sum_{i=1}^{n} \left(x_i \sum_{j=1}^{m} p_{ij} \cdot \mu t_{ij} \right) \right)^2 \qquad (34)$$

$$\sum_{i=1}^{n} \sum_{j=1}^{m} p_{ij} \cdot \log(\mu r_{ij}) \ge \log(C_r/(1 - 3\beta_3 \gamma)) \qquad (35)$$

$$\sum_{i=1}^{n} \sum_{j=1}^{m} p_{ij} \cdot \mu c_{ij} - n \cdot C_c \ge 0 \qquad (36)$$

$$\left(\sum_{i=1}^{n}\sum_{j=1}^{m}p_{ij}\cdot\mu c_{ij}-n\cdot C_c\right)^2 \geq 3\cdot\sum_{i=1}^{n}\sum_{j=1}^{m}p_{ij}\cdot\sigma c_{ij}^2 \qquad (37)$$

$$p_{ij}\in\{0,1\}, 1\leq i\leq n, 1\leq j\leq m \qquad (38)$$

$$\sum_{j=1}^{m}p_{ij}=1, \ 1\leq i\leq n \qquad (39)$$

7 Experiments

7.1 Robustness Metrics

Several previous researchers have explored temporal robustness metrics for resource scheduling or service composition problems. There is no consensus on which metric should be adopted, but instead it is up to the scholar's discretion per the problem at hand. Tolerance time [30], makespan mean [31], slack time [32], and robustness probability [33] are commonly used metrics. In this study, we established the following two metrics according to these metrics.

The first is robust probability R_p, which represents the probability that the selected composite service satisfies the stated constraints. Let *TotalTimes* represent the total number of tests and *FailedTimes* represent the total number of defaults. R_p is calculated as follows:

$$R_p = (\text{TotalTimes} - \text{FailedTimes})/\text{TotalTimes} \qquad (40)$$

The other is relaxation metrics R_s, which represents the gap between user constraints and the aggregated QoS of the selected composite service:

$$R_s = (C_t - t)/C_t + (r - C_r)/C_r + (c - C_c)/C_c \qquad (41)$$

where C_t, C_r, and C_c respectively denote the restrictive conditions of response time, reliability, and reputation, while t, r, and c respectively denote the response time, reliability, and reputation of the selected composite service. The values of t, r, and c are random, so the R_s value is the minimum value of multiple measurements.

7.2 Simulation Environment and Parameter Settings

We conducted experiments on a PC which has a 2.4 GHz CPU and 4 GB of memory installed with win7 and JRE6. We used CPLEX to solve the IQCP model and the function lsqnonneg in Matlab to solve the non-negative overdetermined linear equation system. The expectations of response time, reliability, and reputation to a candidate service were taken from the QWS database [34]. The expectation of cost was randomly evaluated on the interval [100, 200] due to the lack of information about cost in this database. As pointed out by Armbrust et al. [9], the fluctuation range of response time can reach 4–16%. For the response time, we let the mean variance be times the expectation where is a random value on [0.1, 0.2]. We took a similar approach to the mean variance of cost and reputation. The reliability criterion belongs to product-type. If the magnitude of fluctuation is relatively large, the reliability to a composite service including a lot of component services may tend towards zero. Thus, the reliability criterion is a random value on [0.001, 0.015]. And the maximum reliability and reputation criteria were set to 1.

If a candidate service is selected for each task of the workflow, its QoS is the average expectation of the QoS for all its candidate services. The response time, reliability, and reputation of this composite service are denoted as BC_t, BC_r, and BC_c, respectively, then the values of C_t, C_r, and C_c are set to 1.2 * BC_t, 0.8 * BC_r, and 0.8 * BC_c, respectively. We set the number of samples to 10000, $\beta = 0$, and $\beta_1 = \beta_2 = \beta_3 = 1$.

The DAGs in our experiments were randomly generated. The number of nodes starts at 10 and increases to 100 in intervals of 10. In DAG, there is an initial node and a termination node. Each node has 1–4 direct child nodes except the termination node at a ratio of 6:3:2:1. The number of candidate services per task also starts at 10 and increases to 100 by intervals of 10.

7.3   Robustness Analysis

When number of tasks was assigned 20 and number of WSs varied between 10 and 100, values of R_p and R_s were as shown in Table 2. Table 3 shows these values when number of WSs was assigned 20 and number of tasks varied between 10 and 100. The R_p values in both tables are approximately 99.9% for different number of tasks and WSs, i.e., more than 99.74% as determined by the 3σ principle. The value of R_s is around 0.7, indicating that there were still some gaps between user constraints and the aggregated QoS of the selected composite service in our experiment. The values of R_p and R_s were less affected by the scale of the problem, indicating that our model has good stability.

Table 2. R_p and R_s over WSs with 20 tasks

Number of WSs	R_p	R_s
10	0.9995	0.7008
20	0.9995	0.6452
30	0.9992	0.6885
40	0.9997	0.6893
50	0.9996	0.6932
60	0.9993	0.6549
70	0.9995	0.6573
80	0.9994	0.6243
90	0.9989	0.5602
100	0.9990	0.7446

Table 3. R_p and R_s over tasks with 20 WSs

Number of tasks	R_p	R_s
10	0.9997	0.7198
20	0.9981	0.6110
30	0.9989	0.6946
40	0.9990	0.6536
50	0.9993	0.5923
60	0.9995	0.6926
70	0.9978	0.6191
80	0.9989	0.6471
90	0.9996	0.7206
100	0.9999	0.7221

The results shown in Figs. 3 and 4 indicate that the time overhead increases rapidly with the number of tasks and the number of services when using CPLEX. More efficient algorithms are yet necessary.

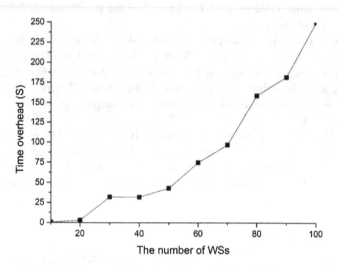

Fig. 3. Time overhead over a range of WSs with 20 tasks

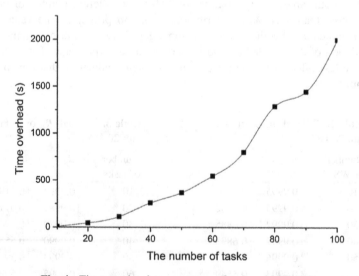

Fig. 4. Time overhead over a range of tasks with 20 WSs

7.4 QoS Estimation of Composite Services

Accurate and rapid estimation of QoS is the key to resolving the large-scale WS composition problem with uncertain QoS. We evaluated the QoS distribution and time overhead of our approach (labeled as M1) compared to the method adopted by Hwang et al. [5] (labeled as M2) and the simulation method adopted by Zheng et al. [14] (labeled as M3). The number of tasks and WSs are assigned 20 and 100, respectively.

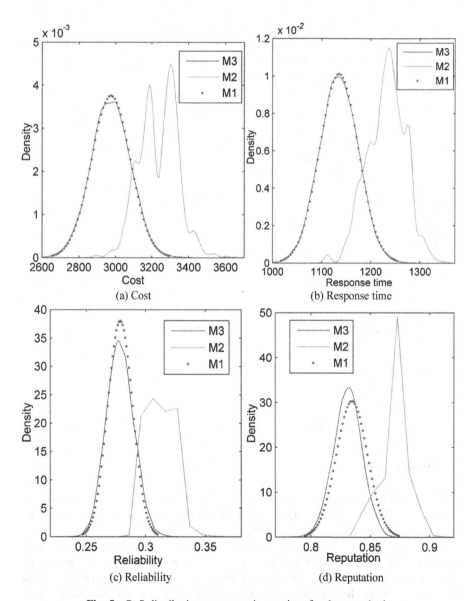

Fig. 5. QoS distribution to composite services for three methods

For M2, we adopted the algorithm and parameters recommended by Hwang et al. [5]; that is, the aggregate random variable discovery problem (ARVD) used the greedy strategy, the sample space of a single random variable was set to 20, and the aggregate size of the sample space was set to 30. For M3, number of samples was 10000.

We estimated the QoS distribution for any composite service for a given workflow with 20 tasks using the above three methods; the results are shown in Fig. 5. Generally, when the number of samples was large enough, the results obtained by M3 were very close to the actual. The distributions of cost (Fig. 5a), response time (Fig. 5b), reliability (Fig. 5c), and reputation (Fig. 5d) obtained by our method were approximately the same as M3. The results obtained by M2 deviated substantially.

As shown in Fig. 6, the time complexity of M1 was far less than M2 or M3 for the number of tasks. In effect, our method is better suited to solving large-scale service composition problems with uncertain QoSs.

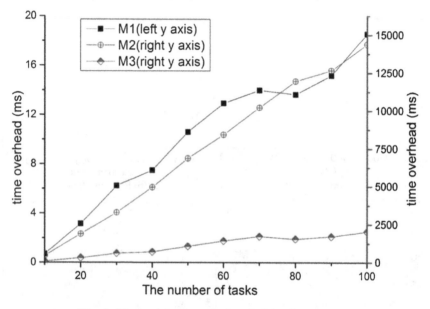

Fig. 6. Time overhead to calculate QoS for three methods

8 Conclusions

As distributed and integrated applications, WSs are invoked over a network (usually the Internet). The corresponding QoS is affected by many factors including the network environment, hardware facilities, user behavior, and others, making it very challenging to accurately estimate. The model used to describe the WS composition problem with uncertain QoS must be sufficiently robust – in other words, the selected composite services should have a high probability of meeting user requirements even if the QoSs of WSs are volatile. In this study, we represented the WS composition problem with uncertain QoS as an IQCP model based on some assumptions and approximations. We validated the proposed model by a series of simulations.

In the future, we plan to further optimize the IQCP model and its parameters. We also plan to find more effective algorithms to solve the model and to apply to other types of QoS probability distributions.

Acknowledgment. This work is supported by Guangxi Universities key Laboratory Director Fund of Embedded Technology and Intelligent Information Processing (Guilin University of Technology) under Grand No. 2018A-05.

References

1. Ramírez, A., Parejo, J.A., Romero, J.R., et al.: Evolutionary composition of QoS-aware web services: a many-objective perspective. Expert Syst. Appl. **72**, 357–370 (2017)
2. Zhou, J., Yao, X.: A hybrid artificial bee colony algorithm for optimal selection of QoS-based cloud manufacturing service composition. Int. J. Adv. Manuf. Technol. **88**(9–12), 3371–3387 (2017)
3. Zou, G.B., Lu, Q., Chen, Y.X., et al.: QoS-aware dynamic composition of web services using numerical temporal planning. IEEE Trans. Serv. Comput. **7**, 18–31 (2014)
4. Karimi, M.B., Isazadeh, A., Rahmani, A.M.: QoS-aware service composition in cloud computing using data mining techniques and genetic algorithm. J. Supercomput. **73**(4), 1387–1415 (2017)
5. Hwang, S.Y., Wang, H.J., Tang, J., et al.: A probabilistic approach to modeling and estimating the QoS of web-services-based workflows. Inf. Sci. **177**, 5484–5503 (2007)
6. Wang, S.G., Sun, Q.B., Zhang, G.W., et al.: Uncertain QoS-aware skyline service selection based on cloud model. J. Softw. **23**(6), 1397–1412 (2012)
7. Alexandru, I., Simon, O., Nezih, Y., et al.: Performance analysis of cloud computing services for many-tasks scientific computing. IEEE Trans. Parallel Distrib. Syst. **22**(6), 931–945 (2011)
8. Jiang, D.J., Guillaume, P., Chi, C.H.: Ec2 performance analysis for resource provisioning of service oriented applications. In: Proceedings of the 2009 International Conference on Service-Oriented Computing, pp. 197–207 (2009)
9. Armbrust, M., Fox, A., Griffith, R., et al.: A view of cloud computing. Commun. ACM **53**(4), 50–58 (2010)
10. Li, Z., Yang, F.C., Su, S.: Fuzzy multi-attribute decision making-based algorithm for semantic web service composition. J. Softw. **20**(3), 583–596 (2009)
11. Hwang, S.Y., Hsu, C.C., Lee, C.H.: Service selection for web services with probabilistic QoS. IEEE Trans. Serv. Comput. **8**(3), 467–480 (2015)
12. Zhu, X.L., Wang, B.: Web service selection algorithm based on uncertain quality of service. Comput. Integr. Manuf. Syst. **17**(11), 2532–2539 (2011)
13. Kattepur, A., Georgantas, N., Issarny, V.: QoS composition and analysis in reconfigurable web services choreographies. IEEE Int. Confer. Web Serv. **125**(3), 235–242 (2013)
14. Zheng, H.Y., Yang, J., Zhao, W.L.: Probabilistic QoS aggregations for service composition. ACM Trans. Web **10**(2), 1–34 (2016)
15. Chellammal, S., Gopinath, G., Manikandan, S.R.: An approach for selecting best available services through a new method of decomposing QoS constraints. SOCA **9**(2), 107–138 (2015)

16. Liu, Z.Z., Xue, X., Shen, J.Q., et al.: Web service dynamic composition based on decomposition of global QoS constraints. Int. J. Adv. Manuf. Technol. **69**(9), 2247–2260 (2013)

17. Ye, H.Z., Li, T.S., Jing, C.: Decomposition of global constraints for QoS-aware web service composition. Int. J. Innov. Comput. Inf. Control **12**(6), 2053–2066 (2016)

18. Chen, L., Wu, J., Jian, H.Y., et al.: Instant recommendation for web services composition. IEEE Trans. Serv. Comput. **7**(4), 586–598 (2014)

19. Hyunyoung, K., Reeseo, C., Wonhong, N.: Transaction history-based web service composition for uncertain QoS. Int. J. Web Grid Serv. **12**, 42–62 (2016)

20. Shen, L.M., Chen, Z., Li, F.: Service selection approach considering the uncertainty of QoS data. Comput. Integr. Manuf. Syst. **19**(10), 2652–2663 (2013)

21. Fu, X.D., Yue, K., Liu, L., et al.: Discovering admissible web services with uncertain QoS. Front. Comput. Sci. **9**(2), 265–279 (2015)

22. Fu, X.D., Yue, K., Liu, L., et al.: Admissible composition plans of web service with uncertain QoS. Comput. Integr. Manuf. Syst. **22**, 122–132 (2016)

23. Yu, Q., Bouguettaya, A.: Computing service skyline from uncertain QoWS. IEEE Trans. Serv. Comput. **3**, 16–29 (2010)

24. Schuller, D., Lampe, U., Eckert, J., et al.: Cost-driven optimization of complex service-based workflows for stochastic QoS parameters. In: IEEE International Conference on Web Services, pp. 66–73 (2012)

25. Wang, P.W., Ding, Z.J., Jiang, C.J., et al.: Automatic web service composition based on uncertainty execution effects. IEEE Trans. Serv. Comput. **9**(4), 551–565 (2016)

26. Du, Y.H., Tan, W., Zhou, M.C.: Timed compatibility analysis of web service composition: a modular approach based on Petri nets. IEEE Trans. Autom. Sci. Eng. **11**(2), 594–606 (2014)

27. George, M., Ioannis, R.: Cost-sensitive probabilistic contingent planning for web service composition. Int. J. Artif. Intell. Tools **25**, 1–20 (2016)

28. Farhad, M., Naser, N., Kamran, Z., et al.: QoS decomposition for service composition using genetic algorithm. Appl. Soft Comput. **6**(5), 3409–3421 (2013)

29. Gabrel, V., Manouvrier, M., Murat, C.: Web services composition: complexity and models. Discrete Appl. Math. **196**(2), 100–114 (2015)

30. Ding, Y.S., Yao, G.S., Hao, K.R.: Fault-tolerant elastic scheduling algorithm for workflow in cloud systems. Inf. Sci. **393**, 47–65 (2017)

31. Chirkin, A.M., Belloum, A.S.Z., Kovalchuk, S.V., et al.: Execution time estimation for workflow scheduling. Future Gener. Comput. Syst. **75**, 376–387 (2017)

32. Deepak, P., Saurabh, K.G., Rajkumar, B., et al.: Robust scheduling of scientific workflows with deadline and budget constraints in clouds. In: Proceedings of the 2014 IEEE 28th International Conference on Advanced Information Networking and Applications, pp. 858–865 (2014)

33. Mark, A.O., Sudeep, P., Anthony, M., et al.: Makespan and energy robust stochastic static resource allocation of a bag-of-tasks to a heterogeneous computing system. IEEE Trans. Parallel Distrib. Syst. **26**(10), 2791–2805 (2015)

34. Eyhab, A.M., Qusay, M.H.: QoS-based discovery and ranking of web services. In: Proceedings of the International Conference on Computer Communications and Networks, pp. 529–534 (2007)

A Fast Neighbor Discovery Algorithm in WSNs

Liangxiong Wei[1], Weijie Sun[1], Haixiang Chen[1], Ping Yuan[2], Feng Yin[3], Qian Luo[4], Yanru Chen[1(✉)], and Liangyin Chen[1(✉)]

[1] College of Computer Science and Technology, Sichuan University, Chengdu, China
echochen.cyr@foxmail.com, chenliangyin@scu.edu.cn
[2] School of Mathematics and Information Engeerging,
Chongqing University of Education, Chongqing, China
pypingyuan@163.com
[3] School of Computer Science and technology,
Southwest University for Nationalities, Chengdu, China
yf_eagle@aliyun.com
[4] Second Research Institute,
General Administration of Civil Aviation of China, Chengdu, China
caacsri_luoqian@163.com

Abstract. The existing deterministic neighbor discovery algorithms in WSNs ensure that successful discovery can be obtained within a certain time, but the average discovery delay is long. It is difficult to meet the need for rapid discovery in mobile low duty cycle environments. This paper proposes a group-based fast neighbor discovery algorithm (GBFA). By carrying neighbor information in beacon packet, GBFA knows in advance some potential neighbors and select more energy efficient potential neighbors and actively make nodes wake up to verify whether these potential neighbors are true neighbors, thereby speeding up neighbor discovery and improving energy utilization efficiency. The evaluation results indicate the mean delay and extra energy consumption of the GBFA algorithm are lower than Group-based method up to 10.58% and 18.88% respectively.

Keywords: Neighbor discovery · WSNs · Energy efficiency

This work was supported by the National Natural Science Foundation of China (grant no. 61373091); NNSFC&CAAC U1533203; the key Technology R&D program of Sichuan Province (grant no. 2016GZ0068, Science & Technology Department of Sichuan Province, China); the Collaborative Innovation of Industrial Cluster Project of Chengdu (grant no. 2016-XT00-00015-GX); Civil Aviation Airport United Laboratory of Second Research Institute, CAAC & Sichuan University of Chengdu (grant no. 2015-YF04-00050-JH).
L. Wei and W. Sun—Equal contribution

© Springer Nature Singapore Pte Ltd. 2019
Y. Sun et al. (Eds.): ChineseCSCW 2018, CCIS 917, pp. 163–175, 2019.
https://doi.org/10.1007/978-981-13-3044-5_12

1 Introduction

With the quick development of Internet of Things, one of its important supporting technologies, *i.e.* wireless sensor networks (WSNs), gets much more attentions. WSN is a self-organizing network which contains many sensors. Because of its ubiquitous perceptual characteristics, it is widely used in the fields of environmental monitoring, target tracking, data acquisition, structural health detection, emergency rescue, animal habit monitoring and so on. As a prerequisite for networking and routing, neighbor discovery is a key procedure [1]. Neighbor discovery is indispensable not only in the initial phase but also at any time when the network is beginning to work, since new sensors may be placed in the network anytime [2,3]. In addition, neighborhoods between nodes change quickly in mobile WSNs, as a result neighbor discovery operation needs continue in the whole network lifetime [4].

Due to limited power of sensor nodes in WSNs, to prolong the service life, node usually works in low duty cycle (LDC) mode. It means that nodes are awake in several slots and asleep during the remaining slots. In LDC case, it is difficult to make two nodes lying in communication range of each other remain active at the same time. Or say, achieving fast neighbor discovery in LDC is very challenging. Many neighbor discovery algorithms have been proposed to reply this issue. The existing algorithms are split into probabilistic algorithms and deterministic ones. In probabilistic neighbor discovery algorithm, the state of node, *i.e.* active or asleep state, follows a probabilistic distribution of time. This kind of algorithms can get a shorter average discovery delay, but can't guarantee the detection of a neighbor within a given delay. In the deterministic discovery algorithm, node adopts the fixed wake-up scheduling model to ensure that all the neighbors are discovered in the specified delay, but the average discovery latency is often longer.

In recent years, more and more researchers have presented some neighbor discovery middlewares, which uses transitivity of neighbor relations to speed up neighbor discovery by sharing neighbor information, such as Group-based [4] and Acc algorithm [5]. These algorithms greatly accelerate the neighbor discovery by increasing some energy-efficient active time slots. Now, such algorithms are often idealized, and there are still many difficulties in implementation. Their energy utilization and discovery delay still have room for further improvement.

Based on the existing group-based neighbor discovery method, this paper proposes a group-based fast neighbor discovery, *i.e.* GBFA. For one sender, its beacon packet contains its neighbor information. When another node receives the beacon packets, the receiver will know the wake-up schedules of the sender's neighbors. The neighborhood between the receiver and sender's neighbors will be verified when sender's neighbors wake up in next time. In GBFA, low efficient verifications are filtered as much as possible. Our main contributions are as follows:

- Node can broadcast its neighbor information. The node that receives the neighbor information can early verify whether the receiver and sender's neighbors are neighbors.
- We quantify the contribution of each verification to discovery delay reduction and filter the unnecessary verifications that have less contribution degree.
- We evaluated and compared GBFA with the existing algorithms. The results show our method performs others in various cases.

2   Related Work

In the early development of WSNs, sensor nodes mainly work in the way of always wakeup since the application environment is relatively single. During this period, there are many neighbor discovery algorithms suitable for this situation, such as [6]. These algorithms require nodes to be active all the time and are not suitable for LDC WSNs. To meet the demand of LDC, many researchers have proposed some synchronous algorithms based on clock synchronization, such as S-MAC [7]. Although the synchronous algorithm is simple, it needs to consume a lot of energy for clock synchronization. Unfortunately, it is difficult to synchronize the nodes without knowing other nodes in advance.

Many asynchronous neighbor discovery algorithms have emerged. Based on whether the discovery latency is limited or not, existing pair-wise asynchronous protocols are divided into the probabilistic algorithms [8,9] and deterministic ones [2,10–16].

The probabilistic algorithms includes Birthday [8], Panda [9] and so on. In Birthday, node selects one work state (*i.e.* active or sleep state) in each slot with a probability. A latest probabilistic protocol is Panda [9]. In Panda, sensor remain sleep in initial step. The sleep time of node follows an exponential distribution. Following sleep step, sensors wake up and listen for a changeless time. If no packet is received in the listen state, the node broadcasts one packets to others.

The earliest deterministic neighbor discovery protocols are quorum-based ones [10,11], where time is divided into m^2 slots. These slots can be regarded as a two-dimensional array. Node can randomly select 1 row and 1 column to be active. This pattern ensures that the overlap of active slots between two nodes within m^2 slots. Another kind of earlier protocols is prime-based ones, like Disco [12] and U-connect [13]. Although quorum-based and prime-based methods obtain small worst bound, they are worse than the probabilistic protocol in the average case. In response to that, Searchlight [1] was proposed. It employs two active slots, *i.e.* anchor slot (A slot) and probe slot (P slot) in one period. A slot is fixed in the first slot in each period. Since the length of any period is the same, the offset between the A slots of any two nodes remains unchanged. Then, P slot is introduced to probe the A slot the other node. The later researchers find that employing unequal-sized slots can obtain good discovery performance. Searchlight-Striped [1], Non-integer [14] and Lightning [15] are included. There are other related methods, *i.e.* block-based methods [2] and Nihao [16]. In block-based methods, block theory are used to obtain a wakeup schedule. Nihao defines dedicated listen and transmitting slots. In each listen slot, the radio remain listening during the whole slot. In each transmitting slot, one beacon is sent at the beginning, then the node goes back to sleep.

In recent years, more and more researchers have proposed some neighbor discovery middleware that use the transitivity of neighbor relationships to accelerate neighbor discovery by sharing neighbor information. In WiFlock algorithm [17], all nodes in the range of one-hop neighbors are regarded as one group. By uniformly adjusting distribution of the nodes's active slots in the group, the nodes outside the group can be found more quickly, thereby speeding up the neighbor discovery process. But in fact, this homogenization is difficult to implement in practical application scenarios, and it is difficult to deal with asymmetric environments. Acc algorithm [5] inserts a partial wake-up slot to accept the neighbor information recommended by the neighbor node, thereby speeding up the discovery and achieving better discovery performance, but Acc directly receive the recommendation from its one-hop nodes. It is not applicable to multi-hop applications. EQS method [3] uses quorum graph theory proposed by themselves to remove the unnecessary working slots to improve energy efficiency. The Group-based algorithm [4] adds small amount of additional wake-up slots, used to recommend and verify neighbor relationships, which greatly speeds up neighbor discovery. But Group-based is not very efficiency in the selection of verification node. There is still room for further improvement in latency and energy usage efficiency.

3   Method Design

3.1   System Assumptions

Similarly to most existing methods, we make some assumptions below:

- Nodes randomly deploy in a two-dimension area;
- Each node owns one and only identification (ID) to distinguish it from others;
- All nodes are homogenous, namely their physical characteristics are the same;
- The signal coverage area of any node is a fixed circle;
- The transmitted power and signal frequency of all nodes are the same respectively;
- Each node works in a slot-based and LDC way. We ignore the time and energy consumption of transient state, *i.e.* power-up and power-down state;
- All nodes employ identical neighbor discovery method.

3.2   Core Idea of GBFA

Our method can be regarded as a neighbor discovery middleware. In underlying tier, any pair-wise neighbor discovery method can be used. GBFA efficiently schedules a small amount of additional wake-up slots to accelerate neighbor discovery process. For any four nodes (see Fig. 1, the four black circles denote

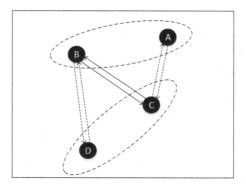

Fig. 1. The discovery process of GBFA

node A, node B, node C and node D respectively), assume that the neighbor table of B contains A, the neighbor table of C contains D. In other words, A and B have discovered each other, C and D also have discovered each other through pair-wise neighbor discovery. Next, GBFA will work. Specifically, when B and C discover each other, they will send their neighbor information to each other. Therefore, B and C will know the wake-up schedule of D and A respectively. Since B and C recommend their neighbor information to each other, B and C are called recommenders. A and D are included in the neighbor information of C, B respectively and will be recommended in next successfully discovery time. A and D are called recommended nodes. If any node, *i.e.* B, sends its neighbor information to another, *i.e.* C, C is called accepted node of B. Because we can't make sure that whether one recommended node is the neighbor of its accepted node, it is necessary to verify whether they are neighbors or not. Since C knows the wake-up schedule of A after recommending, C will proactively wake up when A wakes up in next time to receive beacon packet of A. B also can verify whether D is its neighbor by the same way.

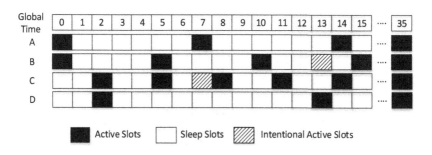

Fig. 2. An example of GBFA

Next, we give an example to describe the working process. As Fig. 2 shows, A, B, C, D denote four nodes, any of which can receive the RF signals from the others. The four nodes employ Disco pair-wise method in the underlying layer. Their duty cycle (for short, DC) are: $DC_A = \frac{1}{7}$, $DC_B = \frac{1}{5}$, $DC_C = \frac{1}{3}$ and $DC_D = \frac{1}{11}$ respectively. Firstly, both A and B wake up in slot 0 and discover each other. Next, C and D discover each other in slot 2. Then, B can C discover each other in slot 5, meanwhile B recommends its neighbor information (including A's) to C. As a result, C knows the wake-up schedule of A and wakes up in A's next active slot, namely slot 7, to verify whether A is its neighbors. Since C can receive the beacon packet of A, C has confirmed that A is its neighbor. So, A and C achieve successful neighbor discovery in advance. But, if only the pair-wise method is used, the successful discovery between A and C is obtained in slot 14, which is 7 slots behind of the time when GBFA is used. Similarly, C will recommend its neighbor information (including node D's) to B at slot 5. B and D can achieve successful neighbor discovery in advance at slot 13, which is faster 22 slots than the time when only Disco method is used.

3.3   Selection of Verification Node

From Subsect. 3.2 we can see that accepted node is required to verify its recommended nodes, since there is no information to confirm that recommended nodes are the neighbors of the accepted node before verification. Unfortunately, when accepted node and recommended node are far apart from each other, they are no probability to become neighbors. The advantage of verification in this case is inadequate. Therefore, it is necessary to carefully select appropriate recommended nodes that have much contribute to advanced discovery latency reduction. Next, we will select appropriate verification node by two ways. One is estimating the distance between two nodes based on the number of their common neighbors. Another one is to select the recommended node if the advanced discovery time when GBFA used is much than a certain value.

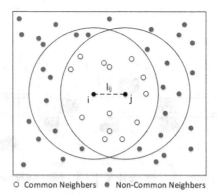

O Common Neighbors   ● Non-Common Neighbors

Fig. 3. Random node distribution

Since nodes are uniformly deployed in an area, the number of common neighbors of node i and j is directly proportional to the overlapping area between the communication area of i and j, denoted by S_{ij} (see Fig. 3). Next, we will deduce that S_{ij} is also proportional to the distance between i and j (denoted by l_{ij}). As Fig. 4 shown, S_{ij} can be denoted by the equation below.

$$S_{ij} = S_{AO_iB} + S_{AO_jB} - S_{AO_iBO_j}, \tag{1}$$

where S_{AO_iB} and S_{AO_jB} represent the area of sector AO_iB and AO_jB respectively, $S_{AO_iBO_j}$ denotes the area of rhombus AO_iBO_j. Suppose that l_{ij} is the distance between O_i and O_j. R is the radius of circle. Then,

$$S_{ij} = 2R^2 cos^{-1} \frac{l_{ij}}{2R} - l_{ij} \sqrt{R^2 - \frac{l_{ij}^2}{4}}, \tag{2}$$

From Eq. (2), S_{ij} monotonically decreases with the increase of l_{ij}. When $l_{ij} = R$, $S_{ij} = 0.391\pi R^2$. It means that i and j may not be neighbors when $S_{ij} < 0.391$ and they are likely neighbors when $S_{ij} \geq 0.391$. So, $S(l_{ij} = R) = 0.391$ is regarded as a threshold value of verification node selection. In WSNs, to get the value of S_{ij} is very difficult. We use the common neighbor number of i and j to roughly represent S_{ij}.

$$D_{ij} = \frac{2N_c}{N_i + N_j}, \tag{3}$$

where N_c represents the common neighbor number, N_i and N_j represents i and j's neighbor number respectively.

Suppose that D_u is the distance threshold value for whether the recommended node needs to be verified. When the receiving node receives the recommended node, it calculates the overlap ratio D. When $D > D_u$, it indicates the node is close to the receiving node, and is likely a neighbor, which is verified, and vice versa.

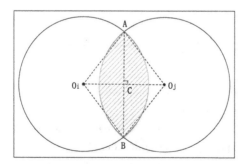

Fig. 4. The relationship between S_{ij} and l_{ij}

Through the verification of recommended nodes stated above, GBFA achieves some advanced discoveries. But there is one problem: the advanced time may be

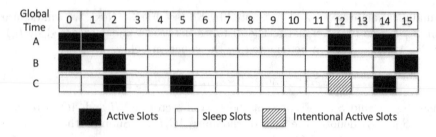

Fig. 5. The benefit of advanced discovery

very smaller in some cases, which is not very energy efficiency. Take Fig. 5 for example. A, B and C are three sensor nodes. They all employ Searchlight pair-wise method and GBFA to achieve discovery. Their DCs are all $\frac{1}{12}$ in Searchlight pair-wise method. C discovers B and knows the wake-up schedule of A in slot 2. C wakes up to verify A at slot 12 and discover A in advance. If only Searchlight is used. C and A discover each other in slot 14, which is 2 slots behind of slot 12, the time of successful discovery when both Searchlight and GBFA are used. The advanced time is 2 slots and is very small. So, this verification is unworthy.

We use gain ratio P_{ij} to quantify the performance of each verification.

$$P_{ij} = \Delta L_{ij} \sqrt{DC_i DC_j} , \tag{4}$$

where ΔL_{ij} is the advanced discovery time of nodes i and j, and DC_i, DC_j represent the duty ratios of nodes i, j, respectively. We set a yield threshold P_u. If $P \geq P_u$, this recommended node is selected to verify. We can change the threshold based on the network environment and energy budget. When the energy budget is high, the value can be appropriately lowered to speed up neighbor discovery. Conversely, when the energy budget is lower, the value is enlarged to save energy.

Table 1. Simulation parameters

Parameters	Descriptions
Network area size	$500\,\mathrm{m} \times 500\,\mathrm{m}$
Node communication radius	$50\,\mathrm{m}$
Node number	Default value: 200, variation range: [32,640]
Node movement speed	Default value: $5\,\mathrm{m/s}$
Average DC	Default value: 2%, variation range: [0.02,0.1]
Slot length	Default value: $25\,\mathrm{ms}$

4   Evaluation and Performance Analysis

In the simulations, all nodes are randomly deployed in $500\,\text{m} \times 500\,\text{m}$ two-dimensional rectangular monitoring area. The random node movement model [18] is used to simulate the movement of the sensor nodes. GBFA and Group-based are both middleware algorithms applied over the underlying pair-wise discovery algorithm and the more classic Disco is selected as the underlying discovery algorithm. The simulation result of the algorithm is the average value calculated after 20 times. We list the main evaluation parameters in Table 1.

4.1   CDF Comparison

We simulated three algorithms in the static scenario and compared the change of their CDFs with increase of time slots. To be fair, we adjusted the threshold value of node verification to make the additional wake energy consumption of both group-based and GBFA about 8%, as shown in Fig. 6.

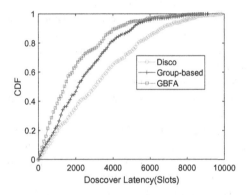

Fig. 6. CDF comparison

We can see from Fig. 6, over time, the algorithm discovers all neighbors in certain time. Disco finished all discoveries in $9854 - th$ slot. Group-based and GBFA respectively completed all discoveries in 9127 and 8818 time slot. From Fig. 6 we can see, before 1000 slot, the change of the three methods are similar, and in $1000 - 4000$ slot, Group-based's convergence speed are more quickly than Disco, the convergent speed of GBFA is faster than the Group-based again. For example, the $3500 - th$ slot, Disco found 57.8% of neighbors, Group-based found 74.2% of neighbors, and GBFA found 83.2% of neighbors. This is because nodes at the beginning of the algorithm are almost haven't found each other, the number of recommended neighbors is small. But with the passage of time, the number of neighbors to recommend each other increases and the discovery process accelerated accordingly.

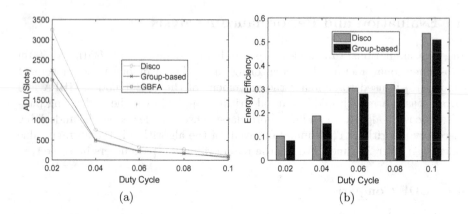

Fig. 7. Impact of DC

4.2 Impact of DC

The node movement speed is set to 0. By setting the DC for change from 2% to 10%, we respectively compare both the average latency and additional energy cost influenced by DC.

In figure Fig. 7(a), the average discovery latency of GBFA is significantly lower than Disco and Group-based method. This effect is especially significant when the DC is low. For example, when the DC is 2%, Disco's average latency is 3247, Group-based method's average discovery latency is 2240, and GBFA's average latency is 2003. Compared with Group-based, GBFA decreases the average latency approximately 10.58%. Group-based method requires an additional active slot for transmitting recommendation information. GBFA may verify before Group-based method's transmission slot and discovered neighbors. The lower the DC, the more obvious the differences are.

Figure 7(b) presents Group-based and GBFA's additional energy cost under the average discovery delay of Fig. 7(a). From the figure we can see that with the increase of DC, Group-based and GBFA's extra energy consumption increases, because when the nodes are more likely to discover each other when the DC is higher, the node has more neighbor information for recommendation, and the node needs to increase the number of active slots to verify more neighbors. In addition, GBFA's additional energy consumption is less than Group-based, especially in the case of lower DC, which shows that GBFA is more energy efficient than Group-based. For example, compared with Group-based, GBFA lows additional energy consumption roughly 18.88% when $DC = 0.02$.

4.3 Impact of Node Density

We placed 32 nodes in the initial network, adding 32 nodes each time, up to 640 nodes, that is, the node density is from 1 to 20. We compare the mean discovery delay and the additional wake-up energy of each algorithm with the increase of node density.

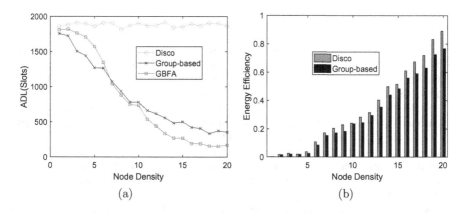

Fig. 8. Node density's impact

In Fig. 8(a), the mean latency of Disco remains almost unchanged when node density enlarges, while Group-based and GBFA decrease the average delay with the increase of node density. The reason is as the node density enlarges, the more neighbors of the node, the more neighbor information can be used for recommendation between nodes to speed up discovery. When node density is more than 5, the average discovery delay of GBFA has been lower than Group-based, which indicates that the performance of GBFA is better than Group-based when the node density is larger. When node density is not more than 5, Group-based's average latency is lower than GBFA. It is likely because, effective recommendations number is smaller in GBFA in these cases.

Figure 8(b) shows the additional energy consumption of Group-based and GBFA. We find that as the node density enlarges, the energy consumption of Group-based and GBFA increase, because the higher the node density is, the more neighbor information is recommended between the nodes, causing the node to need more active wake-up time slots to verify more neighbors. In addition, it can be seen that GBFA's average additional wake-up energy consumption is lower than Group-based and energy utilization is higher under various node densities.

5   Conclusion

This paper proposes a group-based fast neighbor discovery algorithm GBFA for LDC WSNs, which filters low efficient verifications as much as possible, reduces the discovery delay and improves the energy efficiency. However, it still has some disadvantages. For example, when node is leaving, the TTL is set according to the maximum speed of the node. In the case of a large differences in node speed, sometimes the TTL value is too short and the discovery performance is reduced. In the future, we use the specific motion model to accurately estimate the neighbor's hold time and set the corresponding TTL value.

References

1. Bakht, M., Trower, M., Kravets, R.: Searchlight: won't you be my neighbor? In: MobiCom 2012 Proceedings of the 18th Annual International Conference on Mobile Computing and Networking, pp. 185–196 (2012). https://doi.org/10.1145/2348543. 2348568
2. Lee, W., Youn, I.H., Song, T., Kim, N., Youn, J.H.: Prime block design for asynchronous wake-up schedules in wireless sensor networks. IEEE Commun. Lett. **20**, 1437–1440 (2016). https://doi.org/10.1109/LCOMM.2016.2564971
3. Zhang, D., He, T., Ye, F., Ganti, R.K., Lei, H.: EQS: neighbor discovery and rendezvous maintenance with extended quorum system for mobile sensing applications. IEEE Trans. Mob. Comput. **16**(7), 72–81 (2017). https://doi.org/10.1109/TMC.2016.2612200
4. Chen, L., et al.: Group-based neighbor discovery in low-duty-cycle mobile sensor networks. IEEE Trans. Mob. Comput. **15**(8), 1996–2009 (2016). https://doi.org/10.1109/TMC.2015.2476471
5. Zhang, D., et al.: ACC: generic on-demand accelerations for neighbor discovery in mobile applications. In: Proceedings of SenSys (2012). https://doi.org/10.1145/2426656.2426674
6. Vasudevan, S., Kurose, J., Towsley, D.: On neighbor discovery in wireless networks with directional antennas. In: INFOCOM 2005 (2005). https://doi.org/10.1109/INFCOM.2005.1498535
7. Ye, W., Heidemann, J., Estrin, D.: Medium access control with coordinated adaptive sleeping for wireless sensor networks. IEEE/ACM Trans. Netw. (TON) **12**, 493–506 (2004). https://doi.org/10.1109/TNET.2004.828953
8. McGlynn, M.J., Borbash, S.A.: Birthday protocols for low energy deployment and flexible neighbor discovery in ad hoc wireless networks. In: MobiHoc 2001: Proceedings of the 2nd ACM International Symposium on Mobile Ad hoc Networking & Computing, pp. 137–145 (2001). https://doi.org/10.1145/501416.501435
9. Margolies, R., Grebla, G., Chen, T., Rubenstein, D., Zussman, G.: Panda: neighbor discovery on a power harvesting budget. IEEE J. Sel. Areas Commun. (2016). https://doi.org/10.1109/JSAC.2016.2611984
10. Lai, S., Ravindran, B., Cho, H.: Heterogenous quorum-based wake-up scheduling in wireless sensor networks. IEEE Trans. Comput. (2010). https://doi.org/10.1109/TC.2010.20
11. Tseng, Y.C., Hsu, C.S., Hsieh, T.Y.: Power-saving protocols for IEEE 802.11-based multi-hop ad hoc networks. In: INFOCOM (2002). https://doi.org/10.1109/INFCOM.2002.1019261
12. Dutta, P., Culler, D.: Practical asynchronous neighbor discovery and rendezvous for mobile sensing applications. In: ACM Conference on Embedded Network Sensor Systems, pp. 71–84 (2008). https://doi.org/10.1145/1460412.1460420
13. Kandhalu, A., Lakshmanan, K., Rajkumar, R.: U-connect: a low latency energy-efficient asynchronous neighbor discovery protocol. In: Proceedings of International Conference on Information Processing in Sensor Networks (IPSN 2010), pp. 350–361 (2010). https://doi.org/10.1145/1791212.1791253
14. Chen, S., Russell, A., Jin, R., Qin, Y., Wang, B., Vasudevan, S.: Asynchronous neighbor discovery on duty-cycled mobile devices: integer and non-integer schedules. In: MobiHoc 2015 Proceedings of the 16th ACM International Symposium on Mobile Ad Hoc Networking and Computing, pp. 47–56 (2015). https://doi.org/10.1145/2746285.2746297

15. Wei, L., et al.: Lightning: a high-efficient neighbor discovery protocol for low duty cycle WSNs. IEEE Commun. Lett. **20**(5), 966–969 (2016). https://doi.org/10.1109/LCOMM.2016.2536018

16. Qiu, Y., Li, S., Xu, X., Li, Z.: Talk more listen less: energy-efficient neighbor discovery in wireless sensor networks. In: IEEE Conference on Computer Communications (INFOCOM) (2016). https://doi.org/10.1109/INFOCOM.2016.7524336

17. Purohit, A., Priyantha, N., Liu, J.: WiFlock: collaborative group discovery and maintenance in mobile sensor networks. In: IPSN (2011)

18. Johnson, D.B., Maltz, D.A.: Dynamic source routing in ad hoc wireless networks. In: Imielinski, T., Korth, H.F. (eds.) Mobile Computing. Springer, Boston (1996). https://doi.org/10.1007/978-0-585-29603-6_5

FCI-Outlier: An Efficient Frequent Closed Itemset-Based Outlier Detecting Approach on Data Stream

Shangbo Hao[1], Saihua Cai[1], Ruizhi Sun[1,2(✉)], and Sicong Li[1]

[1] College of Information and Electrical Engineering,
China Agricultural University, Beijing 100083, China
{hao_caumail, caisaih, sunruizhi, lsc}@cau.edu.cn
[2] Scientific Research Base for Integrated Technologies of Precision Agriculture
(Animal Husbandry), The Ministry of Agriculture, Beijing 100083, China

Abstract. In the era of information and technology, sensors are widely used to monitor the measured information to support decision making. However, the abnormal data (outlier) is existing in the collected data stream and it would mislead the accuracy of decision making, thus, it is necessary to be detected effectively. Aiming at the problem that the frequent itemset-based outlier detecting method will cost much time in outlier detecting phase, we propose the frequent closed itemset-based outlier detecting method to improve the efficiency of outlier detecting and save much time in outlier detecting stage. Specifically, we mine the frequent closed itemsets with the existing CLOSET algorithm and then design three outlier factors to measure the abnormal degree of each transaction. Then, we propose an outlier detecting method called FCI-Outlier that based on the mined frequent closed itemsets and the designed outlier factors, and the top k transactions that sorting in descending order according to their transaction outlier factor value are judged as the outliers. At last, the public dataset and real data stream are used to verify the efficiency of FCI-Outlier method, and the experimental results show that it is effective in outlier detecting.

Keywords: Outlier detecting · Frequent closed itemset mining
Data stream · Outlier factors

1 Introduction

The widely use of sensors makes people can better grasp the information of monitored object, it is benefit for decision making. The collected sensors data is existing with the form of data stream, and its scale is very huge due to each sensor transports the monitoring data to computer terminal in short time interval, therefore, it is much more difficult to discover the useful data information from huge-scale data stream.

However, the outlier usually exists in the collected data, and it is a main factor that will influence the accuracy of data prediction and analysis, therefore, detecting and eliminating the outliers before prediction and analysis process will improve the data quality. Compared with traditional distance-based outlier detecting methods [1–3] and density-based outlier detecting methods [4, 5], the frequent itemset-based methods [6, 7]

© Springer Nature Singapore Pte Ltd. 2019
Y. Sun et al. (Eds.): ChineseCSCW 2018, CCIS 917, pp. 176–187, 2019.
https://doi.org/10.1007/978-981-13-3044-5_13

are more suitable for large scale of data due to it needn't to calculate the distance between each element in data stream. The frequent itemset mining-based method can be divided into: (1) frequent itemset mining phase, and (2) outlier detecting phase. However, the frequent itemset-based outlier detecting method, FindFPOF [6], is not suitable in data stream environment due to the huge scale of data stream makes the mined frequent itemsets is very large, which will result the outlier detecting phase cost much time. The LFP method [7] changed some abnormal judgment conditions and obtained the good performance in some datasets, however, the problem of high time cost haven't been solved.

In the frequent itemset mining phase, due to the frequent closed itemsets are the lossless compression manifestation of all frequent itemsets and their number is much smaller [8], therefore, the frequent closed itemset-based outlier detecting method can be more effective than that based on the frequent itemsets. In outlier detecting phase, the outlier factor is the core factor to influence the accuracy of outlier detecting, therefore, design an efficient outlier factor determining method is crucial for outlier detecting.

Based on the above idea, this paper proposes an efficient Frequent Closure Itemset-based Outlier detecting method (FCI-Outlier) to detect the implicit outliers existing in data stream. To our best knowledge, it is the first frequent closed itemset-based outlier detecting method. The major contributions of this paper can be listed as follows:

(1) We define three outlier factors to measure the abnormal degree of each transaction, and then propose the FCI-Outlier algorithm to discover the implicit outliers.
(2) It is easy to realize our approach due to the existing fast itemset mining method of CLOSET [9] is adopted to effectively mine frequent closed itemsets.
(3) We use public dataset and real data stream to test the validity of FCI-Outlier method.

The remaining parts can be organized as follows. The preliminaries are given in Sect. 2. The outlier detecting method including: (1) frequent closed itemset mining method, and (2) outlier detecting method are presented in Sect. 3. The experimental analysis is stated in Sect. 4. The conclusion of our study is discussed in Sect. 5.

2 Preliminaries

This section mainly introduces some concepts and properties used in this paper to more clearly explain the proposed method.

Let itemset $S = \{s_1, s_2, s_3, ..., s_n\}$ and $S_k = \{s_1, s_2, ..., s_k\}$ is a k-itemset ($k < n$), where $S_k \subseteq S$. Then, S_k is called the subset of S and S is called the superset of S_k. Data stream $DS = (t_m, t_{m+1}, ..., t_n)$ contains a collection of infinite transactions t_j and each t_j is composed of a subset of itemset S. The sliding window (SW) model [10] is used for conveniently handling data stream, it supporting process the most recent transactions and the dimension of sliding window is $|SW|$.

Definition 1. *Support:* The frequency of itemset A that existing in DS is defined as *support*.

Definition 2. *Frequent itemset (FI):* the itemset A is a FI must satisfy its *support* value is not smaller than the predefined threshold of minimum support (*min_sup*).

Definition 3. *Frequent closed itemset (FCI):* The itemset A is the FCI must satisfy no frequent superset (denoted as B) of A can make *support* $(A) = $ *support* (B).

In frequent closed itemset mining phase, several properties including pruning strategy [8] need to be used to further improve the mining efficiency.

Property 1. If FI A and itemset B are contained in transaction t_j, and any superset of B is not contained in t_j, $A \cup B$ is a FCI.

Property 2. If FI A is the true subset of FCI B and $support(A) = support(B)$, then, any offspring of the itemset A and B in the tree is not FCI.

Property 3. Itemsets A and B are two FIs and $support(A) = support(B)$, if A is a subset of B and B is a FCI, then, there exists no FCI containing A but not $(B{-}A)$.

3   Our Proposed FCI-Outlier Approach

This section mainly presents a frequent closed itemset-based outlier detecting method called FCI-Outlier to discover the outliers on data stream. FCI-Outlier method can be roughly divided into: (1) frequent closed itemset mining phase, and (2) outlier detecting phase.

In frequent closed itemset mining phase, we use the existing CLOSET [9] algorithm and sliding window model to realize the frequent closed itemset mining on data stream environment. In outlier detecting phase, we first design three outlier factors and then propose the FCI-Outlier algorithm to detect the abnormal transactions, and the top k transactions are judged as outliers.

3.1   Frequent Closed Itemset Mining Method

CLOSET algorithm is a famous FCI mining algorithm, it uses FP-tree structure to conduct the mining process. In this subsection, we introduce the main idea of CLOSET algorithm and then use the sliding window model to accomplish it in stream environment.

The CLOSET algorithm can be included into next three steps: (1) Search for frequent 1-itemsets; (2) Divide the search space; and (3) Mine frequent closed itemsets. In order to explain the CLOSET algorithm more clearly, we use the following example to illustrate it. The information of transactions is listed in Table 1, and the predefined *min_sup* value is 2 in this example.

Table 1. Information of transactions

id	Transaction	id	Transaction	id	Transaction
t_1	$\{s_1,s_3,s_4,s_5,s_6\}$	t_2	$\{s_1,s_2,s_5\}$	t_3	$\{s_3,s_5,s_6\}$
t_4	$\{s_1,s_3,s_4,s_6\}$	t_5	$\{s_3,s_5,s_6\}$	...	... ...

(1) Search for frequent 1-itemsets. The transactions are scanned for one time to calculate the *support* value of each 1-itemset, and the frequent 1-itemsets are stored in a created frequent item list in decreasing order according to their *support*. In this example, the frequent 1-itemsets are $<s_3:4, s_5:4, s_6:4, s_1:3, s_4:2>$.

(2) Divide the search space. After finding the frequent 1-itemsets, the search space can be divided into 5 duplicate spaces in this example: (i) contains item s_4; (ii) contains item s_1 but not contains item s_4; (iii) contains item f but not contains item s_1 or s_4; (iv) contains item s_5 but not contains item s_6, s_1 or s_4; (v) only contains item s_3.

(3) Mine frequent closed itemsets. When the search space is divided, the frequent closed itemset mining process is conducted with each search space.

For space (i), generate the conditional database of item s_4 ($TDB(s_4)$), the itemsets in $TDB(s_4)$ is $\{s_3s_5s_6s_1\}$ and $\{s_3s_5s_1\}$, check $TDB(s_4)$ with the *min_sup* of 2. Then, the frequent closed itemset is $\{s_3s_6s_1s_4:2\}$.

For space (ii), generate the conditional database $TDB(s_1)$, the itemsets in $TDB(s_1)$ are $\{s_3s_5s_6, s_5, s_3s_6\}$. Continue generating frequent itemsets of item s_1 ($<s_3:2, s_5:2, s_6:2>$) due to no itemset has appeared in every record in the condition database s_1, then divide the frequent itemsets into 3 sub search spaces: (1) contains s_1s_6 but not s_4; (2) contains s_1s_5 but not s_4 or s_6; (3) contains s_1s_3 but not s_4, s_6, or s_5. In the sub search space, the itemsets of s_6s_1 and s_3s_1 need to be discarded due to they are the sub-itemsets, the itemset s_5s_1 is the frequent close itemset. Then, the frequent closed itemset is $\{s_1:3, s_5s_1:2\}$.

For space (iii), the conditional database of item s_6 is $\{s_3s_5:3, s_3\}$, item s_3 is in every itemset of this conditional database and $\{s_3s_6\}$ is not the subset of any subset that has existed. Then, $\{s_3s_6:4\}$ is the frequent closed itemset, the same as the frequent closed itemset $\{s_3s_5s_6:3\}$.

For space (iv), the conditional database of item s_5 is $\{s_3:3\}$, but itemset $\{s_3s_5:3\}$ is subset of $\{s_3s_5s_6:3\}$. Then, the itemset $\{s_5:4\}$ is the frequent closed itemset.

After the above 3 steps, the frequent closed itemsets of $\{s_1s_3s_4s_6:2, s_1:3, s_1s_5:2, s_3s_6:4, s_3s_5s_6:3, s_5:4\}$ are mined, they are stored in frequent closed itemset library FCI_L. The detail mining process of CLOSET algorithm is shown in Fig. 1.

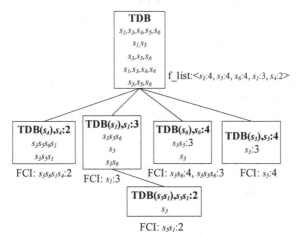

Fig. 1. The detail process of CLOSET algorithm

3.2   Outlier Detecting Method

It can be known from the definition of outlier proposed by Hawkins [11] that the data is judged as the outlier must meet the condition that it is obviously different to most data, therefore, the core idea of outlier detecting is to discover the data information that with a significant difference with most data.

In 2005, He et al. [6] presented a novel frequent itemset-based outlier detecting method called FindFPOF to detect the implicit outliers. It took the proportion of the *support* value of containing *FIs* to the total number of mined *FIs* as the judgment for outlier detecting. Though it can detect the outlier relatively accurate, but the detecting phase would cost much time for the huge scale of mined *FIs*. Besides that, such a situation need cause our attention that if a transaction contains much frequent itemsets but the length of this transaction is very long, which causes the proportion of frequent itemsets to the length of transaction is relatively small. This kind transaction would be judged as the outlier by FindFPOF method, but it is not fair due to more itemsets in these transactions are different with most data.

Aimed at the problems existing in FindFPOF method, the first important task is to design the efficient outlier indexes to guide the specific operation of outlier detecting. First, the transaction is less like an outlier if the containing transactions having larger *support* value, the reason is that the itemsets is less abnormal if they are more frequent. Second, the transaction is less like an outlier if the containing transactions having longer closed frequent itemsets, the reason is that more frequent itemsets are contained into longer closed frequent itemsets. Third, the transaction is more like an outlier if more infrequent 1-itemsets are contained into the transactions, the reason is that the infrequent can be extended by infrequent 1-itemsets and the infrequent itemset means the appearing frequency is lower than the predefined *min_sup*. Fourth, the transaction t_1 is more like an outlier than t_2 if transactions t_1 and t_2 contain same maximal frequent patterns (where $len(t_1) > len(t_2)$), the reason is that the frequent density of t_1 is smaller than t_2. The specific outlier factors are listed as follows.

Definition 4. *FCIOF* (*Frequent Closed Itemset Outlier Factor*): For each frequent closed itemset X, its length is $len(X)$. then, *FCIOF* is defined as

$$FCIOF(X) = support(X) * len(X) \tag{1}$$

Definition 5. *MiIOF* (*Minimal infrequent 1-Itemset Outlier Factor*): Let $DS = (t_1, t_2, ..., t_n)$ be n transactions in the sliding window. For each transaction t_i, the number of infrequent 1-itemsets is $M(m_i)$. Then, *MiIOF* is defined as:

$$MiIOF(t_i) = M(m_i) + 1 \tag{2}$$

If the $MiIOF(t_i)$ value is much larger, the transaction t_i is much more likely an outlier due to less frequent 1-itemsets are contained in t_i.

Definition 6. *TOF (Transaction Outlier Factor)*: Let $DS = (t_1, t_2, ..., t_n)$ be n transactions in the sliding window. For each transaction t_i, the number of contained frequent closed itemset is $N(t_i)$, the length of t_i is $len(t_i)$. Then, *TOF* is defined as:

$$TOF(t_i) = \frac{MiIOF(t_i)}{(N(t_i)+1) * len(t_i) * \sum_{X \subseteq t_i, X \in FCI\_L} (FCIOF(X)+1)} \qquad (3)$$

After the construction of three outlier factors, the top k transactions (sorting in descending order with $TOF(t_i)$ value) are judged as outliers. The specific process of FCI-Outlier is presented in Algorithm 1.

Algorithm 1: FCI-Outlier

Input: Data stream, *FCIs*, n (the size of sliding window)
Output: Outliers

---

1. **foreach** transaction t_i in sliding window **do**
2. $FCIOF(X) = support(X)*len(X)$
3. **for** frequent closed itemset X in t_i **do**
4. $MiIOF(t_i) = M(m_i) + 1$
5. $TOF(ti) = \frac{MiIOF(t_i)}{(N(t_i)+1)*len(t_i)* \sum_{X \subseteq t_i, X \in FCI\_L}(FCIOF(X)+1)}$
6. **end for**
7. **end for**
8. sort t_i in descending order by $TOF(t_i)$ value
9. take top k t_i as outliers

To describe the proposed FCI-Outlier method more clearly, the example listed in Table 1 is used as a sample, and the *min_sup* value is also set in 2. In frequent closed itemset mining phase, the mined *FCIs* are $\{s_1s_3s_4s_6:2\}$, $\{s_1:3\}$, $\{s_1s_5:2\}$, $\{s_3s_6:4\}$, $\{s_3s_5s_6:3\}$, $\{s_5:4\}$. Then, the *FCIOF* value, *MiIOF* value and *TOF* value are calculated to determine the abnormal degree of each detected transaction.

$FCIOF(s_1s_3s_4s_6) = 2*4 = 8$, $FCIOF(s_1) = 3*1 = 3$, $FCIOF(s_1s_5) = 2*2 = 4$,
$FCIOF(s_3s_6) = 4*2 = 8$, $FCIOF(s_3s_5s_6) = 3*3 = 9$, $FCIOF(s_5) = 4*1 = 4$.
$MiIOF(t_1) = 1 + 1 = 2$, $MiIOF(t_2) = 0 + 1 = 1$, $MiIOF(t_3) = 0 + 1 = 1$,
$MiIOF(t_4) = 0 + 1 = 1$, $MiIOF(t_5) = 0 + 1 = 1$.
$TOF(t_1) = 2/((6 + 1)*4*(8 + 3 + 4 + 8 + 9 + 4 + 1)) = 0.001931$,
$TOF(t_2) = 1/((3 + 1)*3*(3 + 4 + 4 + 1)) = 0.003787$,
$TOF(t_3) = 1/((3 + 1)*3*(8 + 9 + 4 + 1)) = 0.016129$,
$TOF(t_4) = 1/((3 + 1)*4*(8 + 3 + 8 + 1)) = 0.003125$,
$TOF(t_5) = 1/((3 + 1)*3*(8 + 9 + 4 + 1)) = 0.003787$.

Therefore, the probability that the transactions being outliers in decreasing order is t_3, t_2, t_5, t_4, t_1.

4   Experiment Results and Discussions

A comprehensive performance study is conducted to evaluate the proposed FCI-Outlier algorithm. It is conducted to test its performance against FindFPOF method [6], LFP method [7] and OODFP method [12] on public dataset of Wisconsin Breast Cancer Data (WBCD) [13] and real data stream of the agricultural sensors.

The experiments are implemented in python 3.5 with a machine of i3-2020 2.93 GHz. The compared performance is conducted with different value of *min_sup* and different size of sliding window (|*SW*|), and the selected top *k* transactions are statistics when all the outliers are found in current sliding window.

4.1   Detection Efficiency of FCI-Outlier Method on Dataset WBCD

The WBCD dataset has 699 instances with 9 attributes, in which 458 transactions are marked as *benign* and 241 transactions are marked as *malignant*. In this experiment, the |*SW*| is 20, 30 and 40 separately, and the ratio of *min_sup* value to |*SW*| is 30%, 40%, 50% and 60%. The top *k* transactions selected when all *malignant* are found are recording in this experiment. The performance of FCI-Outlier, FindFPOF, LFP and OODFP is shown in Figs. 2, 3 and 4.

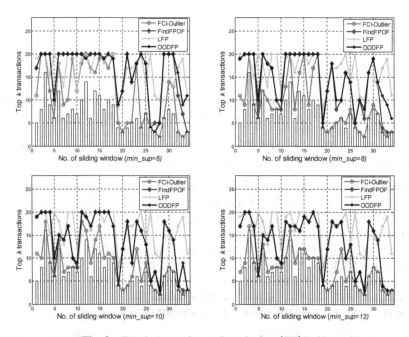

Fig. 2. Top *k* transactions selected when |*SW*| is 20

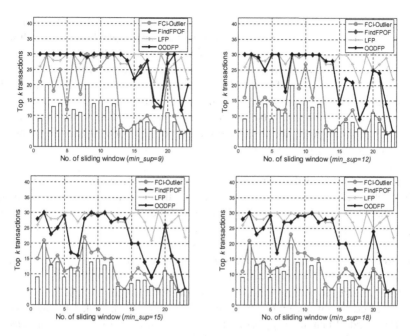

Fig. 3. Top k transactions selected with the $|SW|$ is 30

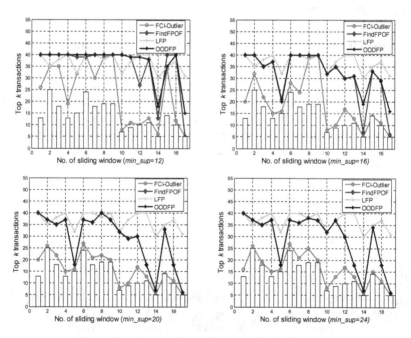

Fig. 4. Top k transactions selected with the $|SW|$ is 40

We can see from Fig. 2 that when $|SW|$ is 20, the proposed FCI-Outlier method performs better than FindFPOF method, LFP method and OODFP method in different *min_sup* values. With the increasing value of *min_sup*, the outlier detecting efficiency of FCI-Outlier method show an increasing trend and it also reach into 100% in most situations. The performance of OODFP method is the same with FindFPOF method in most situations, and the FindFPOF performs better than OODFP method in few cases. In the compared four methods, the performance of LFP method is the worst in most situations, and the selected number of transactions of LFP method is equal to the total transactions in current sliding window when all true outliers are discovered in some situation.

We can see in Fig. 3 that when $|SW|$ is 30, the outlier detecting efficiency of FCI-Outlier method also shows an increasing trend with the increasing of *min_sup* value, and the outlier detecting efficiency of FCI-Outlier method is the highest of the compared four methods. When the *min_sup* value is not less than 15, the number of selected transactions of FCI-Outlier method is close to the number of true outliers in most sliding window. When the *min_sup* value is 15 and 18, the outlier detecting efficiency of FindFPOF method and OODFP method is almost the same.

When the size of sliding window is 40, the outlier detecting efficiency of FCI-Outlier method is always higher than that of FindFPOF method, LFP method and OODFP method. When the *min_sup* value is selected in 12 and 16, the outlier detecting efficiency of FCI-Outlier method is not high in many sliding window, and the outlier detecting efficiency of FindFPOF method and OODFP method is equal when the *min_sup* value is 20 and 24.

4.2   Detection Efficiency of FCI-Outlier Method on Agricultural Data Stream

The agricultural data stream is collected from 30 agricultural sensors that distributed in the greenhouse, and the measured attributes including: air temperature, air humidity, soil temperature, soil humidity and CO_2 concentration. If the measured value is within a certain range, it is recorded as the normal element, otherwise, it is likely the outlier. To better illustrate the results of outlier detecting, we first marked the abnormal transactions. Due to the amount of distributed sensors is 30, therefore, the $|SW|$ is set in 30 in this experiment. The experiment is conducted in different value of *min_sup*, and the final results are shown in Fig. 5.

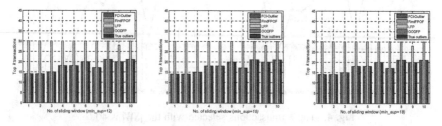

Fig. 5. Top k transactions selected on agricultural data stream

We can know from Fig. 5 that FCI-Outlier method can effectively discover the implicit outliers in the sliding window when the *min_sup* value is selected in 12, 15 and 18. When all outliers are discovered, the number of selected transactions of FCI-Outlier method, FindFPOF method and OODFP method is equal to the number of true outliers, it indicates that the outlier detecting efficiency of FCI-Outlier method can reach in 100%. However, the outlier detecting efficiency of LFP method is relatively lower than the compared three methods in different *min_sup* values. Therefore, the proposed FCI-Outlier method can be used in outlier detecting for the agricultural data stream environment.

4.3 Time Cost of FCI-Outlier Method in Outlier Detecting

The time cost in outlier detecting phase is another important index to evaluate the proposed FCI-Outlier method, it determines the efficiency of outlier detecting directly. In this subsection, the time cost of FCI-Outlier method is evaluated on dataset WBCD and agricultural sensor data stream, and the FindFPOF method and OODFP method are used as the compared methods to further compare the efficiency. On dataset WBCD, the time cost is conducted with different *min_sup* value and |*SW*| is selected in 50, the experimental result is shown in Table 2. On agricultural data stream, the time cost is also conducted with different *min_sup* value, and |*SW*| is selected in 30 due to the number of distributed sensors is 30, the experimental result is listed in Table 3.

Table 2. Time cost of FCI-Outlier on WBCD dataset (ms)

No. SW	*min_sup* = 25			*min_sup* = 30		
	FCI-Outlier	FindFPOF	OODFP	FCI-Outlier	FindFPOF	OODFP
1	0.349	0.597	0.265	0.596	0.964	0.512
2	0.299	0.515	0.224	0.328	0.553	0.257
3	0.332	0.564	0.231	0.437	0.64	0.363
4	0.299	0.526	0.246	0.428	0.694	0.383
5	0.268	0.453	0.189	0.501	0.811	0.427
6	0.384	0.65	0.289	0.492	0.802	0.411
7	0.279	0.484	0.194	0.48	1.107	0.429
8	0.489	0.775	0.356	0.742	1.075	0.606
9	0.368	0.555	0.278	0.743	1.059	0.603
10	0.311	0.517	0.237	0.442	0.766	0.413
11	0.28	0.484	0.197	0.863	1.191	0.674
12	0.309	0.54	0.232	0.425	0.587	0.332
13	0.256	0.433	0.178	0.453	0.669	0.365

Table 3. Time cost of FCI-outlier on agricultural data stream (ms)

No. SW	min_sup = 20			min_sup = 25		
	FCI-Outlier	FindFPOF	OODFP	FCI-Outlier	FindFPOF	OODFP
1	1.828	7.106	1.527	0.621	1.496	0.522
2	1.694	8.102	1.424	0.699	3.035	0.534
3	1.356	7.141	1.127	0.413	1.775	0.347
4	2.258	4.867	1.739	0.445	0.863	0.321
5	2.699	5.258	1.973	0.374	0.682	0.257
6	0.955	2.715	0.902	0.245	0.56	0.205
7	2.126	4.932	1.738	0.433	0.805	0.324
8	2.487	5.58	2.032	0.75	1.442	0.539
9	1.998	4.455	1.632	0.623	1.199	0.459
10	2.55	4.881	1.876	0.481	0.906	0.353

It can be seen in Table 2 that on dataset WBCD, the time cost of FCI-Outlier method is smaller than that of FindFPOF method and larger than that of OODFP method. Due to the OODFP method is based on the mined maximal *FIs* and the scale of maximal *FIs* is much smaller than the numbers of *FIs* and *FCIs*, therefore, the time cost of OODFP method is smallest in the compared three methods.

We can see from Table 3 that the time cost of FCI-Outlier method is little larger than that of OODFP method, and it is much less than that of FindFPOF method. The time cost of the compared three methods is decreasing gradually accompanied with the increasing value of *min_sup*, the reason is that the scale of mined *FIs*, *FCIs* and maximal *FIs* is reducing much accompanied with the increasing value of *min_sup*.

5   Conclusion

With the widely distributed use of sensors, the data stream is transferred to the computer terminal in real-time to provide the data support to the production in every field. However, the outliers are usually in the collected data stream, and they will mislead the accuracy of data-based predicting, therefore, the implicit outliers need to be detected as soon as possible to improve the reliability of the data. In recent years, the scale of generating data shows an exponential growth trend, which results the frequent itemset-based outlier detecting methods will face great challenges, such as: the huge amount of mined frequent itemsets makes much time is cost in outlier detecting phase, and the accuracy of outlier detecting need to be further improved. Aiming at the existing problems, we propose the frequent closed itemset-based outlier detecting method called FCI-Outlier to effectively detect the implicit outliers. Specifically, we use the CLOSET method to mine the frequent closed itemsets first, and then design three outlier factors to measure the abnormal degree of the detected transactions, and the top *k* transactions are judged as the outliers.

The extensive experiments verify the FCI-Outlier method is more effective than the compared FindFPOF method, LFP method and OODFP method in outlier detecting, and in large min_sup value, the outlier detecting efficiency of FCI-Outlier method can reach in 100%. Besides that, the time cost of FCI-Outlier method is much less than FindFPOF method.

The uncertain data stream is a new research hot spot and it has attracted more attention in recent years. In the future, the frequent closed itemset-based outlier detecting method to detect the implicit outliers on uncertain data stream is a noteworthy research direction.

Acknowledgements. This work was supported by Scientific and technological key projects of Xinjiang Production and Construction Corps (Grant No. 2015AC023).

References

1. Cao, L., Yang, D., Wang, Q., Yu, Y., Wang, J.: Scalable distance-based outlier detection over high-volume data streams. In: 30th International Conference on Data Engineering, pp. 76–87. IEEE, Chicago (2014)
2. Angiulli, F., Fassetti, F.: Distance-based outlier queries in data streams: the novel task and algorithms. Data Min. Knowl. Disc. **20**(2), 290–324 (2010)
3. Kontaki, M., Gounaris, A., Papadopoulos, A.N., Tsichlas, K., Manolopoulos, Y.: Efficient and flexible algorithms for monitoring distance-based outliers over data streams. Inf. Syst. **55**, 37–53 (2016)
4. Tang, B., He, H.: A local density-based approach for outlier detection. Neurocomputing **241**, 171–180 (2017)
5. de Vries, T., Chawla, S., Houle, M.E.: Density-preserving projections for large-scale local anomaly detection. Knowl. Inf. Syst. **32**(1), 25–52 (2012)
6. He, Z., Xu, X., Huang, Z.J., Deng, S.: FP-Outlier: frequent pattern based outlier detection. Comput. Sci. Inf. Syst. **2**(1), 103–118 (2005)
7. Zhang, W., Wu, J., Yu, J.: An improved method of outlier detection based on frequent pattern. In: 2th WASE International Conference on Information Engineering, pp. 3–6. IEEE, Beidaihe (2010)
8. Nori, F., Deypir, M., Sadreddini, M.H.: A sliding window based algorithm for frequent closed itemset mining over data streams. J. Syst. Softw. **86**(3), 615–623 (2013)
9. Pei, J., Han, J., Mao, R.: Closet: an efficient algorithm for mining frequent closed itemsets. In: ACM SIGMOD Workshop on Research Issues in Data Mining and Knowledge Discovery, vol. 4, no. 2, pp. 21–30 (2000)
10. Cai, S., Sun, R., Cheng, C., Wu, G.: Exception detection of data stream based on improved maximal frequent itemsets mining. In: Xu, M., Qin, Z., Yan, F., Fu, S. (eds.) CTCIS 2017. CCIS, vol. 704, pp. 112–125. Springer, Singapore (2017). https://doi.org/10.1007/978-981-10-7080-8_10
11. Hawkins, D.M.: Identification of Outliers, 11th edn. Chapman and Hall, London (1980)
12. Lin, F., Le, W., Bo, J.: Research on maximal frequent pattern outlier factor for online high dimensional time-series outlier detection. J. Converg. Inf. Technol. **5**(10), 66–71 (2010)
13. Wisconsin Breast Cancer Data (WBCD) Webpage. https://archive.ics.uci.edu/ml/machine-learning-databases/breast-cancer-wisconsin. Accessed 12 June 2018

Multi-model Hybrid Traffic Flow Forecast Algorithm Based on Multivariate Data

Jie Zhou, Yuling Sun[✉], and Liang He

East China Normal University, Shanghai 200062, China
jzhou@ica.stc.sh.cn, {ylsun,lhe}@cs.ecnu.edu.cn

Abstract. Traffic flow forecast is a fine-grained task in urban intelligent transportation systems. Accurate traffic flow forecast can effectively support the development of intelligent transportation systems, reduce congestion, and improve the quality of residents' travel. The forecast of traffic flow is affected by many random factors such as weather, holidays and seasons. It has a certain degree of randomness and uncertainty, which makes the traditional single model prediction result extremely unstable, and the consideration of random factors is incomplete. As a result, the final forecast results are quite different from the actual situation. To address this problem, this paper proposes a multi-model hybrid traffic flow forecast algorithm based on multivariate data, which considers various random factors from multiple aspects, and captures different features through multiple models to improve the accuracy. The experiments on the dataset of KDD CUP 2017 demonstrate the effectiveness of our approach.

Keywords: Traffic flow forecast · Multivariate data · Multi-model-based

1 Introduction

The continuous construction of digital cities and the rapid development of various high-tech have spawned the birth of various smart city construction concepts [1, 2]. Among them, smart transportation is the inevitable trend of the development of traditional transportation system under the background of informatization [3–6]. Smart transportation refers to the full use of modern electronic information technology such as Internet of Things and mobile Internet in the transportation field, collecting various types of traffic information through analyzing, mining and applying data processing technologies such as data modeling and data mining [3, 5, 7, 8], in order to realize the systematic and real-time nature of intelligent transportation, and enhance the interactivity of information exchange and the extensiveness of services.

The idea of intelligent transportation provides a revolutionary solution to many problems in traditional transportation systems. Taking the congestion problem of expressways as an example, the congestion problem of high-speed toll stations has always been a pain point in traditional transportation networks. In recent years, with the exponential growth of private cars, congestion of toll stations has become the norm of highways, greatly reducing the high-speed travel experience of residents. The construction and development of the smart transportation system provides an innovative solution to this problem. The development of various Internet of Things and mobile

© Springer Nature Singapore Pte Ltd. 2019
Y. Sun et al. (Eds.): ChineseCSCW 2018, CCIS 917, pp. 188–200, 2019.
https://doi.org/10.1007/978-981-13-3044-5_14

Internet devices, such as GPS-based Google Map, Waze, Baidu Map, and Gaode Map, provides a comprehensive and real-time way for crowdsourced traffic data collection; it is possible to effectively analyze and predict future high-speed traffic conditions and Estimated Time of Arrival (ETA) by constructing a variety of targeted data models based on these real-time data. On the one hand, it can provide users with real-time travel guides, which can effectively avoid the peak traffic and improve the travel experience. On the other hand, it also provides data basis for the real-time effective traffic supervision program design of the traffic control department, so that the traffic control department can real-time, effective staffing and traffic grooming based on the forecast results to avoid large-scale congestion.

Traffic flow and ETA prediction are the basic functions of the intelligent transportation system, and also the research focus and difficulty in the field of urban computing and social computing [7, 8]. At present, a large number of domestic and foreign researchers have studied this problem and proposed a series of algorithms for traffic flow prediction [9], such as historical trend method [10], nonparametric regression method [11], neural network based prediction methods [12], etc. These algorithm models can obtain better prediction results without emergency traffic events, special weather and special time, but the model results are extremely unstable in the case of many interference factors. However, the actual high-speed traffic speed will be affected by various random factors such as weather conditions, holidays, and commuting peaks, which further makes the final prediction results produced by such algorithms often differ greatly from the actual situation. At the same time, the algorithms such as support vector machine [13], KNN [14], ARIMA prediction algorithm [15], XGBoost [16] are also widely used in traffic flow prediction problems. However, actual high-speed traffic data is a typical multivariate data, and the existing methods tend to focus on single-model prediction. There are various advantages and disadvantages that vary from method to method, and it is difficult to comprehensively mine the characteristics of various aspects of traffic data.

In response to the current research situation, this paper proposes a multi-model-based traffic flow forecast algorithm based on multivariate data. The algorithm models various types of data based on different model angles from multivariate data, and then predicts real-time traffic flow through a combination of multiple model advantages. The algorithm proposed in this paper effectively combines the advantages of various models, and avoids the shortcomings of different models, and the effect is greatly improved.

2 Problem Description

2.1 Problem Definition

Traffic flow refers to the number of vehicles passing through a certain monitoring point or section within a unit time [9]. Affected by a variety of random factors such as weather, holidays, time, etc., traffic volume often has a large degree of suddenness and randomness. According to the prediction time span, the forecast of traffic flow can be divided into long-term forecast, medium-term forecast and short-term forecast: long-term forecast is generally based on the year, medium-term forecast is generally based on month, day and hour, and the forecasting unit short-term forecast is generally 5–15 min; according to the different forecasting objects, the traffic flow forecast can be further divided into the traffic flow forecast of the road section and the forecast of the monitoring point [9]. This paper focuses on the short-term traffic forecast problem for toll stations.

The research data comes from 1 month's traffic data of a high-speed road section, involving the inflow and outflow historical data of the three stations of the toll station 1, the toll station 2 and the toll station 3, and the road network topology of the target area (e.g. Figs. 1, 2 and 3), vehicle trajectory, toll station historical traffic volume, weather data, etc. We conduct model training based on historical data from last month to predict traffic conditions at specific peak hours in the next month. As shown in Fig. 4, the specific research question can be described as how to design the algorithm and model based on the historical data of the previous month. Based on the model, the traffic data of the green time slot is given in the next month (06:00–08:00, 16:00–18:00), the traffic volume in the time slot of the red mark (08:00–10:00, 17:00–19:00) is predicted in each 20 min. Which means to predict the inflow and outflow of the toll station 1, the toll booth 2, and the toll booth 3. Among them, the toll gate 2 is a one-way toll gate that can only be entered, and the other ports are two-way toll gates that can enter and exit.

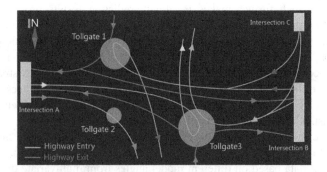

Fig. 1. Road network topology of target area

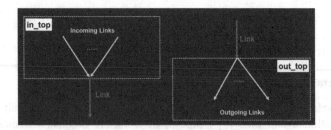

Fig. 2. In_top and Out_top for a road link

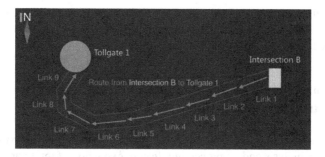

Fig. 3. Link sequence for the route from intersection B to tollgate 1

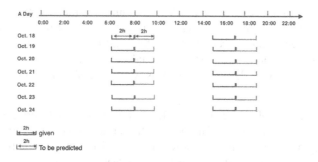

Fig. 4. Time windows for traffic prediction (Color figure online)

2.2 Data Description

In traffic flow forecasting, road network traffic information is typical multivariate information, mainly reflected in different sources, different environments, different spatial locations, and so on. In the source, it includes vehicle flow information, vehicle attribute information, weather information, and so on; in spatial location, the information comes from different toll stations, different areas, and so on; in data collection, there are also different sources, different sensors such as ETC, video and GPS. In order to improve the correctness and reliability of traffic information, it is necessary to analyze and process data such as traffic and weather from multiple sources. The multi-transportation data involved in this paper mainly includes the following parts:

- Road data, including the length, width, number of ramps, ramp widths, links to toll stations, toll stations, and so on;
- Vehicle data, including the time the vehicle entered the route, the vehicle's travel path, vehicle capacity and vehicle type, and so on;
- Vehicle trajectory data, including vehicles, toll stations, intersections, entry path times, travel times, and so on;
- Weather data, including air pressure, wind speed, wind direction, temperature, humidity and precipitation in the selected area.

The algorithm will use this data for feature extraction and model training, so that the multivariate data can be reasonably coordinated and the useful information can be fully integrated.

3   Multi-model Hybrid Traffic Flow Forecast Algorithm Based on Multivariate Data

The multi-model hybrid traffic flow forecast algorithm proposed in this paper includes three steps: data analysis and preprocessing, feature extraction of multivariate data, and multi-model fusion. This chapter will introduce the proposed algorithm with examples.

3.1   Data Analysis and Data Preprocessing

Data analysis and preprocessing are mainly to obtain the initial awareness of the data, and provide the basis for the subsequent feature extraction and mining. In this paper, we mainly analyze and pre-process the traffic flow statistics of each site at a fixed time period, the time-continuous traffic flow of a single site, and the traffic flow of a single site on random extraction dates. The analysis results are shown in Figs. 5, 6 and 7, specifically:

- Statistical analysis of traffic flow at each station for a fixed period of time: We analyze the time distribution of traffic flow from 6 to 10 o'clock every day at a toll station. The analysis results are shown in Fig. 5. The results mainly confirm the abnormal factors such as holidays have strong interference effects on traffic flow. As can be seen from the figure, since the traffic volume has changed suddenly during the National Day from October 1 to October 7, we define this part of the data as an outlier. In the final training data, the algorithm deletes the data during this period to reduce noise.

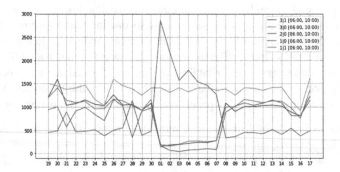

Fig. 5.   Traffic statistics for each station from 6:00–10:00 daily

- Time-continuous traffic analysis at a single site: We performed a time-continuous traffic analysis on toll station 3-0. The results are shown in Fig. 6. The results confirm the periodic characteristics of the traffic data, such as daily periodicity, weekly periodicity, and so on. It can be seen from the figure that the flow curve has a relatively obvious periodicity, and the traffic flow distribution of the station is also relatively close, which provides a basis for the feature extraction of the model.

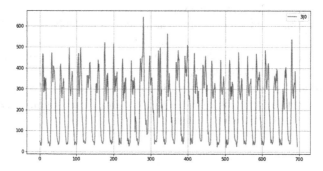

Fig. 6. Traffic flow statistics for every 20 min imported from toll station No. 3

– Traffic analysis of individual sites on a random pick date: We randomly analyzed traffic flow data of four days at toll station 3-0 (September 20, October 11, September 27, and October 21). The analysis results are shown in Fig. 7. The results mainly confirm the interference effect of the daily time period characteristics on the vehicle traffic flow. It can be seen from the figure that the traffic flow distribution from 6:00 to 10:00 in the four days of random selection is basically the same: the traffic volume at 6 o'clock starts to increase slowly, and the highest peak of traffic flow is reached from 8:00 to 9:00, what we usually call the peak hours of work. This is also very consistent with people's travel rules.

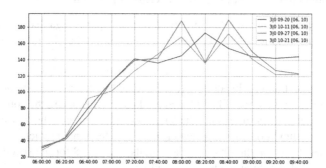

Fig. 7. Traffic statistics for the In_top of the No. 3 toll station from 6:00 to 10:00 of September 20, October 11, September 27, and October 21 four days

3.2   Feature Extraction of Multivariate Data

The forecast of traffic flow is not only related to people's work schedule, but also related to weather, road structure, emergencies, and so on. For this reason, multiple data needs to be considered in extracting features. Through the data analysis of the previous step, we confirmed the interference effects of random factors such as holidays, weather, and time periods on traffic flow. For example, in sunny weather, more people would like to go out and play, and holidays often cause high traffic, 8:00–10:00 am and 5:00–7:00 pm is the peak period of commuting, and so no, and the periodicity of traffic flow is also found. Therefore, we propose a multi-model-based forecast method based on multivariate data. The multivariate data here refers to traffic flow data that combines various factors such as weather, holidays, time periods, dates, etc. The second step of the algorithm is feature extraction from multivariate data. Based on the above analysis, we mainly extracted the following features:

- Toll_id;
- Direction;
- Week;
- Weather characteristics;
- Traffic flow every 20 min for the first two hours;
- Statistics of two-hour traffic (including maximum, minimum, median, average, variance, and so on);
- Statistics of traffic flow per hour (including maximum, minimum, median, average, variance, and so on);
- Special date, including whether it is a working day, whether it is the first day of work, whether it is the first day of vacation, whether it is the first day of work, whether it is the last day of work, whether it is a holiday, and so on;

   For discrete variables, we convert them to one-hot vector processing.

3.3   Multi-model-Based Traffic Flow Forecast Algorithm

The traffic flow prediction algorithm proposed in this paper is regarded as a regression problem and uses historical data to establish a model to predict the future traffic flow. To enable us to capture the characteristics of more dimensions, we used three different machine learning models: LightGBM, XGBoost, GBRT, and selected three different strategies for model training. In addition to the overall training prediction, the algorithm also uses the tollgate-direction-differentiated prediction scheme and the combination of the predictions of the morning and the afternoon to carry out the model training. Finally, the algorithm performs weighted ensemble on the three prediction schemes of the three models to obtain the final forecast results, see Fig. 8 for the specific process.
   An overview of the three models is as follows:

- LightGBM: Microsoft's gradient boosting framework uses a learning algorithm based on decision tree, which has the advantages of fast training efficiency, low memory usage, high accuracy, support for parallel learning, and processing of large-scale data.

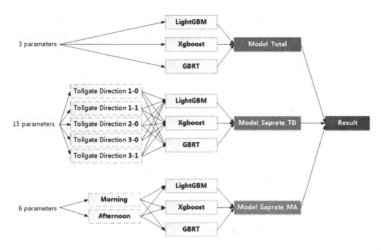

Fig. 8. The framework of ensemble

- XGboost: A tree learning algorithm for processing sparse data. Using approximate tree learning theory to use fractional descriptions, a reasonable weighting weight can be given to each training strength. Parallel and distributed design makes the algorithm very fast learning and modeling speeds, end-to-end systems can process large amounts of data with minimal cluster resources.
- GBRT: A promotion of boosting, which can deal with regression problems, can directly deal with the characteristics of mixed types, and has better robustness to outliers in output space.

We will explain in detail the multi-model fusion traffic flow prediction algorithm flow proposed in this paper below.

For a data set with n samples and m features $D = \{(x_i, y_i)\}(|D| = n, x_i \in R^m, y_i \in R)$, a model containing K trees can be expressed as:

$$\tilde{y}_i = \phi(x_i) = \sum_{k=1}^{K} f_k(x_i), f_k \epsilon F \tag{1}$$

where $F = \{f(x) = w_{q(x)}\}(q : R^m \to T, w \in R^T)$ represents the function space composed of trees, q represents the mapping of x to leaf nodes, and w represents the weight of leaf nodes.

Loss function is defined as:

$$L(\phi) = \sum_i^l (\tilde{y}_i, y_i) + \sum_k \Omega(f_k) \tag{2}$$

Where $\Omega(f) = \lambda T + \frac{1}{2}\lambda w^2$ is the regular term which aims to reduce the complexity of the model. T is the number of leaf nodes, and w is the weight of the leaf nodes.

The model uses the Taylor formula of the loss function to obtain the loss approximation representation at step t to find the optimal submodel. The formula is:

$$L^{(t)} \simeq \sum_{i=1}^{n} \left[l\left(y_i, \tilde{y}^{t-1}\right) + g_i f_t(x_i) + \frac{1}{2} h_i f_t^2(x_i) \right] + \Omega(f_t) \tag{3}$$

where $g_i = \partial_{\tilde{y}^{t-1}} l(y_i, \tilde{y}^{t-1})$, $h_i = \partial_{\tilde{y}^{t-1}}^2 l(y_i, \tilde{y}^{t-1})$ represents the first derivative and the second derivative of the loss, respectively, after removing the constant:

$$\tilde{L}^{(t)} = \sum_{i=1}^{n} \left[g_i f_t(x_i) + \frac{1}{2} h_i f_t^2(x_i) \right] + \Omega(f_t) \tag{4}$$

The algorithm defines $I_j = \{i | q(x_i) = j\}$ as the sample set of leaf node j. The above formula can be used to sum each leaf node:

$$\begin{aligned} \tilde{L}^{(t)} &= \sum_{i=1}^{n} \left[g_i f_t(x_i) + \frac{1}{2} h_i f_t^2(x_i) \right] + \gamma T + \frac{1}{2} \lambda \sum_{j=1}^{T} w_j^2 \\ &= \sum_{j=1}^{T} \left[\left(\sum_{i \in I_j} g_i \right) w_j + \frac{1}{2} \sum_{i \in I_j} h_i + \lambda w_j^2 \right] + \gamma T \end{aligned} \tag{5}$$

For a given tree structure q(x), when the derivative of the above formula is 0, the minimum value can be obtained to obtain the value of the leaf node:

$$w_j^* = -\frac{\sum_{i \in I_j} g_i}{\sum_{i \in I_j} h_i + \lambda} + \gamma T \tag{6}$$

Furthermore, when the tree is q, the optimal value of the loss function is:

$$\tilde{L}^{(t)}(q) = -\frac{1}{2} \sum_{j=1}^{T} \frac{\left(\sum_{i \in I_j} g_i \right)^2}{\sum_{i \in I_j} h_i + \lambda} + \gamma T \tag{7}$$

Since the complexity of traversing all possible tree structures to get the optimal loss is too high, the algorithm adopts a layer-by-layer construction method. That is, a root node is continuously split in the construction. The process of splitting is subject to the change of loss:

$$L_{split} = \frac{1}{2} \left[\frac{\left(\sum_{i \in I_L} g_i \right)^2}{\sum_{i \in I_L} h_i + \lambda} + \frac{\left(\sum_{i \in I_R} g_i \right)^2}{\sum_{i \in I_R} h_i + \lambda} - \frac{\left(\sum_{i \in I} g_i \right)^2}{\sum_{i \in I} h_i + \lambda} \right] - \gamma \tag{8}$$

After building the tree model, we can use this model for regression prediction.

The multi-model-based traffic flow forecast algorithm based on multivariate data uses three different models to build the model. Three different strategies are also selected for model training, as follows:

- Strategy 1: All the data of the toll stations are trained in a model, which can increase the amount of data, and learn the common characteristics of the traffic flow distribution of different toll stations, such as 6:00–8:00 in the morning. Traffic increases, but the characteristics of each site are weakened.
- Strategy 2: Different models are used for training in the morning and afternoon. The morning traffic is trained with morning data, while the afternoon traffic is trained with afternoon data, so that the distribution characteristics of the previous and afternoon predictions can be obtained separately, but This reduces the amount of data.
- Strategy 3: For each site, we use a separate model to train. In this way, we can learn the individual characteristics of each site well, and will not affect the distribution characteristics of the site because of the overall data. For example, the traffic volume of this site is much larger than other sites.

In addition, because of the small number of training samples, we use time window sliding to greatly increase the data sample.

4 Experiments and Analysis

4.1 Metric Function

In this paper, we choose Mean Absolute Percentage Error (MAPE) to evaluate the result. The MAPE for traffic flow forecast is defined as

$$MAPE = \frac{1}{C}\sum_{c=1}^{C}\left(\frac{1}{T}\sum_{t=1}^{T}\left|\frac{f_{ct} - p_{ct}}{f_{ct}}\right|\right) \tag{9}$$

where C is the number of tollgate-direction pairs (as aforementioned: 1-entry, 1-exit, 2-entry, 3-entry and 3-exit), T be the number of time windows in the testing period, and f_{ct} and p_{ct} be the actual and predicted traffic volume for a specific tollgate-direction pair c during time window t.

The classical regression loss function adopted by most machine learning package:

$$MSE = \frac{1}{2}(f_{ct} - p_{ct})^2 \tag{10}$$

$$MAE = |f_{ct} - p_{ct}| \tag{11}$$

We take a log-transform of target y, we can obtain a sample mathematical approximation:

$$|logp_{ct} - logf_{ct}| = \left|log\frac{p_{ct}}{f_{ct}}\right| = \left|log\left(1 + \frac{p_{ct} - f_{ct}}{f_{ct}}\right)\right| \approx \left|\frac{p_{ct} - f_{ct}}{f_{ct}}\right| \tag{12}$$

Through the log-transform, the measure MSE and MAE become relatively measure close to the spirit of MAPE.

4.2   Experiment Analysis

In order to verify the effectiveness of our proposed algorithm, we use the data of KDD CUP 2017 to conduct experiments. Table 1 shows our experimental results on KDD CUP 2017 data. As can be seen from the table, our multi-model fusion strategy has a significant effect on improving the prediction results. First, from the results of models 1, 2, and 3, it can be seen that each model has different learning ability for the same data, and can capture different features, and performance also is different. When the results of the three models are merged, the results obtained by the model 4 are significantly better than those of the single model. The model 8 combined by models 5, 6, and 7 and the model 12 combined by models 9, 10, and 11 also can verify such conclusions. At the same time, we can also find from the data that the same model can learn different characteristics when using different strategies. Compared with models 1, 5 and 9, we find that the results of the three models are different. Finally, when we fuse the results of models 4, 8, and 12 to get model 13, the results of the model are improved again, and nearly 10% improvement is achieved compared to the single model. Therefore, it can be seen from the experimental results that the multi-model fusion strategy used in this paper can effectively improve the accuracy and robustness of prediction.

Table 1. The results of the experiment

#	Model	MAPE
1	lightgbm	0.1213
2	xgboost	0.1216
3	gbrt	0.1210
4	ensemble_3model (ensemble of model1, 2 and 3)	0.1187
5	lightgbm_separate_tollgate_direction	0.1154
6	xgboost_separate_tollgate_direction	0.1170
7	gbrt_separate_tollgate_direction	0.1149
8	ensemble_eparate_tollgate_direction (ensemble of model 5, 6 and 7)	0.1133
9	lightgbm_separate_morning_afternoon	0.1180
10	xgboost_separate_moring_afternoon	0.1181
11	gbrt_separate_moring_afternoon	0.1214
12	ensemble_separate_morning_afternoon	0.1160
13	ensemble_3ensemble (ensemble of mode 4, 8 and 12)	0.1125

In addition, in order to view the learning effect of the proposed model, we show the forecast results of the toll station 1-1 on October 26th in Fig. 9. As can be seen from the figure, the models 4, 8, and 12 are overall. The trends are consistent, but there are large differences, and the combined results can be a good synthesis of the characteristics of these models, making the results more stable and reliable. The experimental results show that the fusion model integrates the advantages of other single model predictions, with small errors and high prediction accuracy, and has great advantages in traffic flow prediction tasks. In addition, we used this method to participate in the KDD CUP traffic flow prediction competition, and obtained the second price of the competition, which further verified the feasibility and effectiveness of the proposed method.

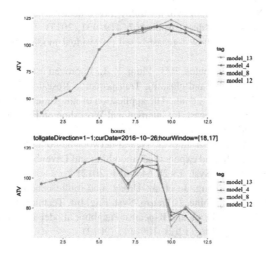

Fig. 9. One example of the forecast

5   Conclusion

In this paper, we propose a multi-model hybrid traffic flow forecast algorithm based on multivariate data. This approach comprehensively mines the characteristics of various aspects from multivariate data, models various types of data based on different model, and then predicts real-time traffic flow through a variety of model ensemble methods. The experimental results show that the approach can effectively combines the advantages of various models, and avoids the shortcoming of different models and the results obtains a greatly improvement.

References

1. Zhang, J., Zheng, Y., Qi, D.: Deep spatio-temporal residual networks for citywide crowd flows prediction. In: AAAI (2017)
2. Zhang, S., et al.: Effective and efficient: large-scale dynamic city express. IEEE Trans. Knowl. Data Eng. **28**(12), 3203–3217 (2016)
3. Zheng, Y.: Methodologies for cross-domain data fusion: an overview. IEEE Trans. Big Data **1**(1), 16–34 (2015)
4. Zheng, Y.: Trajectory data mining: an overview. ACM Trans. Intell. Syst. Technol. (TIST) **6** (3), 29 (2015)
5. Ma, S., Zheng, Y., Wolfson, O.: T-share: a large-scale dynamic taxi ridesharing service. In: ICDE (2013)

6. Ma, S., Zheng, Y., Wolfson, O.: Real-time city-scale taxi ridesharing. IEEE Trans. Knowl. Data Eng. **27**(7), 1782–1795 (2015)
7. Qiao, S., et al.: Short-term traffic flow forecast based on parallel long short-term memory neural network. In: 2017 8th IEEE International Conference on Software Engineering and Service Science (ICSESS). IEEE (2017)
8. Yuan, P.C., Lin, X.X.: How long will the traffic flow time series keep efficacious to forecast the future? Physica A: Stat. Mech. Appl. **467**, 419–431 (2017)
9. Zhao, Z., Yang, Z.: Traffic flow forecast based on residual modification GM(1, 1) model. Comput. Sci. (2017)
10. Stephanedes, Y.J., Michalopoulos, P.G., Plum, R.A.: Improved estimation of traffic flow for real-time control (discussion and closure). Transportation Research Record (1981)
11. Wang, X., Zhicai, J., Miao, L., et al.: The application of nonparametric regressive algorithm for short-term traffic flow forecast. In: International Workshop on Education Technology and Computer Science, pp. 767–770. IEEE (2009)
12. Chan, K.Y., Dillon, T.S., Singh, J., et al.: Neural-network-based models for short-term traffic flow forecasting using a hybrid exponential smoothing and Levenberg–Marquardt algorithm. IEEE Trans. Intell. Transp. Syst. **13**(2), 644–654 (2012)
13. Rong, Y.U., Wang, G., Zheng, J., et al.: Urban road traffic condition pattern recognition based on support vector machine. J. Transp. Syst. Eng. Inf. Technol. **13**(1), 130–136 (2013)
14. Yu, B., Wu, S., Wang, M., et al.: K-nearest neighbor model of short-term traffic flow forecast. J. Traffic Transp. Eng. **12**(2), 109–115 (2012)

A New Algorithm for Real-Time Collaborative Graphical Editing System Based on CRDT

Liping Gao[1,2(✉)] and Xiaofang Xu[1]

[1] School of Optical-Electrical Computer Engineering, University of Shanghai for Science and Technology, Shanghai 200093, China
lipinggao@usst.edu.cn, 450190073@qq.com
[2] Shanghai Key Laboratory of Data Science, Fudan University, Shanghai 200093, China

Abstract. With the rapid development of collaborative applications, real-time collaborative graphical editing systems will face many new challenges in the future. The key technology to guarantee the correctness in the graphical editing system is consistency maintenance. It is also a core topic in the field of collaborative computing and a basic research in many scientific and engineering collaboration systems. However, over the past years, the complexity of graphics has produced much problems for the real time editing field, including methods of operational transformation (OT) and conflict resolution strategy with multi-version replication, etc. Recently, CRDT (Exchanged Copy Data Type) has been proposed as a new alternative mechanism in collaborative text editing with much higher efficiency. However, the CRDT-based real-time graphics editing system consistency maintenance method has rarely been studied in the previous literature. In the paper, a kind of CRDT algorithm is proposed, and the complex constraint relationship between the graphics and the dynamic rule library is used to divide the graphic operation into operation, which the relevant solutions are given. The algorithm integrates different types of graphics operations for First, the algorithm guarantees the convergence of the coordinated users and maintains the operational intent under the integrated framework. Secondly, a CRDT-based algorithm is designed. Thirdly, the time complexity and space complexity of the put forward algorithm are theoretically analyzed, which is further verified the feasibility of the algorithm. Finally, The direction of future solution is given.

Keywords: Consistency maintenance · Real-time collaboration
CRDT · Graphical editing

1 Introduction

With the development of big data and cloud computing, real-time graphics editing systems are more inclined to collaborate on a large scale. A complex project typically involves hundreds of designers collaborating on a common task. In this case, two issues need to be considered further. One is that a large number of concurrency conflicts may occur inevitably, which poses a higher challenge for consistency maintenance. Another is that for large-scale collaboration where large numbers of users simultaneously edit shared documents [1], shared documents are updated frequently. This situation usually

© Springer Nature Singapore Pte Ltd. 2019
Y. Sun et al. (Eds.): ChineseCSCW 2018, CCIS 917, pp. 201–212, 2019.
https://doi.org/10.1007/978-981-13-3044-5_15

leads to a decline in collaborative computing performance [2]. Another key challenge for the success of intelligent collaborative editing systems is to improve computational efficiency. Recently, CRDT technology has been proposed as a new concurrency control mechanism for collaborative text editing. The main task of the paper is to raise a new algorithm for real-time graphic editing system to adapt to the basic operation of graphic editing system. The core idea of the CRDT algorithm is to plan exchange concurrency operations. Therefore, conversions are no longer needed and concurrent operations can be performed in any order [7]. This paper mainly proposes a string CRDT algorithm for intelligent graphics editing systems, which is face to new challenges. The performance of the CRDT algorithm has proven to be superior to traditional methods and is applicable to large-scale distributed environments [7]. The organization structure of this paper is as belows: The second part raises the research related work; The third part proposes the CRDT-based conflict resolution in real-time graphics editing system; the fourth part is analyze the complexity of time and space. The Fifth part is gives summary.

2 Related Work

In the collaborative graphics editing system, the consistency maintenance mostly uses the multi-version mechanism [14] to solve the concurrency control problem. For example, Sun et al. proposed a cloud storage operation transformation (CSOT) in the literature [4]. The convergence of real-time synchronous shared tree document structure in cloud storage system; Sun et al. [4] proposed a new collaborative object grouping technology called CoGroup, which is based on operation conversion (OT) technology and TA. Based on previous work], someone has proposed an optimized version to optimize the number of object versions. Gao et al. [5, 14] used a multi-version strategy to solve the problem of execution and undo/redo consistency maintenance in real-time collaborative bitmap editing systems. There are also many studies that apply a series of changes to the dott algorithm in OT in a collaborative graphics editing system. These methods based on OT [13] do not have good execution efficiency in collaborative editing group editing under large-scale data. Recently, CRDT (Commutative Replicated Data Type) was proposed as a new concurrency control mechanism to achieve the ultimate consistency of collaborative text editing. Since the first work in [6], a representative CRDT algorithm has been proposed and applied to collaborative text editing. [7] HE et al. proposed String-wise in large-scale collaborative editing system. The CRDT algorithm solves the consistency maintenance in intelligent and large-scale data environments, and its correctness has been verified. In past studies [15, 16], some people used traditional algorithms to solve real-time collaborative CAD system. Others have propose the CRDT model into the real-time collaborative CAD [11] system. In both of these articles, the advantages of CRDT in large-scale data processing are highlighted, and the efficiency is higher, and the time complexity and space complexity are well optimized. However, in collaborative graphics editing systems, there is little research based on CRDT, which has great advantages over multi-version mechanisms and tree-based mechanisms.

Compared with the traditional OT algorithm, the algorithm based on CRDT has great advantages. For example, the COT (Context-Based Operational Transformation) algorithm improvement was previously applied to the graphics editing scenario. In this case, the execution condition of O is to compare the operation of DS with C(O) [12]. In C(O), all operations in C (O) need to do the operation conversion, then in the one-time operation transmission, the DS and C(O) front operations will perform the useless comparison once and for all, which costs time waste and transmission overhead. The CRDT-based algorithm proposed in this paper is based on unique ID number to find the operation object to operate directly, especially during the delete operation.

3 Proposed Algorithm

In the work of documentstring editing [7], we extend and advance the data structure so that we can get good use in the Co-PAINT system based on real-time graphics. The real-time collaborative graphics editing system composes mass collaborative sites. Each site maintains the CoRDG (dynamic rule library), a hash table, a double linked list and an interactive view. CoRDG is used to store association relationships between predefined objects. The hash table stores the operations of all objects. Double linked list is links all graphic operations, including visible and invisible modeling operations, from the beginning to the end. Each graphic object operation is regarded as the operation node of double linked list. View can provide interactive interfaces for collaborative users. The whole frame is shown as shown in Fig. 1.

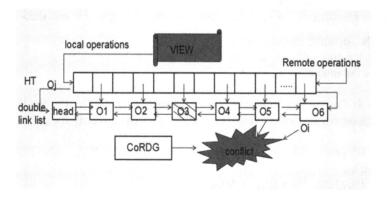

Fig. 1. Overall framework

The whole control process is shown as shown above. Collaborative designers can perform create, delete, update operations on local sites at the same time, and receive remote graphics object operations from other sites. A local operation generation, the local operation is executed promptly and the operation is directly linked to the last operation of the double linked list by using the identifier of the last operation. The integration process of remote operations consists of two steps. First, remote operations require a target image object operation to be found in a hash table with a unique identifier. Second, the location of the target graphical object operation needs to be found in the double-linked list. It is probably that operation may be performed after the alike target object operation. When there are conflicts, the priority of their association in the CoRDG and their identifiers need to be used to resolve conflicts. Finally, the effect of the integrated update appears in the interactive view.

Definition 1: Graphic object operation (Oa)

In real-time collaborative image editing system, an Oa consists of a 14-element < t,,k, (x,y),l,O[i],Obji,visible,flag,key,c_key,pre_key,next,prior,link,s > ,with t representing the type of operation, (x, y) representing the position of the center point of the graphic object in the implicit coordinate system of the graphic document, and 0 = true representing the local operation. l = false represents a remote operation, and O(i) represents a set of graphical state associations generated, where O[k] = (i,j), $0 \le k \le i$.

Definition 2: (Oa $\prec$ Ob) given two Oa and Ob in the double-linked list, the position of Oa is denoted as pos(Oa), the position of Ob is denoted as pos(Ob), if pos(Oa) < pos (Ob) (The position of Oa in the double linked list is in front of Ob, then Oa $\prec$ Ob.

Based on the above definition, we can get Oa $\prec$ Ob between two graphics operations due to different target operation locations in the double-linked list. However, when two concurrent graphics operations may have the same operational position in a double linked list. In this case, we can't get Oa $\prec$ Ob between the two graphics operations, so we need to sort them. Therefore, unique identifiers can determine their order. The unique identifier is defined as follows.

Definition 3: Identifier (ID)

The unique identifier of the graphic object consists of a triple: <s, ssv, site>

(1) s is the identifier of the session
(2) ssv is the sum of the state vectors of an operation
(3) site is the unique identifier of the site symbol

Definition 4: Given the operations of any two graphic objects Oa, Ob, the IDs of the two operations are ID_{Oa} and ID_{Ob}: (1) If $ID_{Oa}[s] < ID_{Ob \to}$ (2) If $ID_{Oa}[s] = ID_{Ob}[s]$, ID_{Oa}
[ssv] = $ID_{Ob}[ssv]$ (3) If $ID_{Oa}[s] = ID_{Ob}[s], ID_{Oa}[ssv] = ID_{Ob}[ssv]$, $ID_{Oa}[ssv] = ID_{Ob}[ssv], ID_{Oa}$
[site] = $ID_{Ob}[site]$ Then $ID_{Oa} \prec ID_{Ob}$

Definition 5: Given any two compatible graphical objectsObj$_i$, and Obj$_j$, ID_{Oa} is the unique identifier of Obj$_i$, ID_{Ob} is the unique identifier of Obj$_j$. When they have the same target operating position in the double linked list, if $ID_{Oa} \prec ID_{Ob}$, then Obj$_i \prec$ Obj$_j$.

To ensure ultimate consistency, we need to ensure that all modeling operations in the double-linked list have the same overall order in each site when all operations are performed in all sites. The definition of the overall order relationship for all modeling operations is given below.

Definition 6: Total ordering of operations (O⇒)
Given any three operations, called O1, O2, O3, if (1) O1 ≺ O2 or O2 ≺ O1 or (2) O1 ≺ O2, O2 ≺ O3, O1 ≺ O3, then here is O⇒

In real-time collaborative text editing, final consistency and intent preservation are two important correctness criteria for the correctness of the CRDT algorithm. Therefore, after the correctness criteria in collaborative text editing, the real-time Co-Drawing system is considered correct if the following criteria are adhered to:

Final Consistency: All operational models from different sites are identical after all modeling operations have been performed in all sites.

Unlike collaborative text editing, in an operation-based Co-RGD system, there are complex relationships between operations, and there is inevitably a modeling conflict between operations between different designers. In this case, some graphics object operations cannot be performed due to operational conflicts, which ultimately leads to the inability of the entire drawing task to be completed. Therefore, conflict resolution is neededed to maintain more design intent and maintain ultimate consistency. Considering the complexity of graphics operations, in order to maintain the final consistency, this article divides operations into basic class operations and predefined relationship class operations.

Basic Class Operation
In the collaborative graphics editing system designed in this paper, the basic class operations are divided into three types: N operation (D), D operation (Delete) and U operation (Update). The following defines the conflict relationship and detection between graphic object operations.

Definition 7: Conflict/Compatibility
Suppose two operations are given, called Oa,Ob.Oa||Ob and the target graphic object identifiers for Oa and Ob operations are the same, if any of the following conditions are met:

(1) $T(Oa) = T(Ob) = Operate.Update \ \& \ K(Oa) \neq K(Ob)$
(2) $T(Oa) = T(Ob) = Operate.Delete$
(3) $T(Oa) = Operate.Update \ \& \ T(Ob) = Operate.Delete$
(4) $T(Oa) = Operate.Delete \ \& \ T(Ob) = Operate.Update$

Then there is a conflict relationship between Oa and Ob, expressed as: Oa ⊗ Ob. If there is no conflict relationship between the two operations Oa and Ob, they are said to be compatible relationships, expressed as: Oa ⊙ Ob. Where T(O) represents the operation type of O. K(O) represents the attached new attribute value of the image object.

Alogrrithm1 ConflictResolve

INPUT:Oa⊗Ob

Int flag=0

If   T(Oa)=T(Ob)=operate.Delete‖

         T(Oa)=T(Ob)=Operate.Update&K(Oa)≠K(Ob)‖

         T(Oa)=Operate.Update & T(Ob)=Operate.Delete‖ID(Oa)<ID(Ob)

then

         Ob is not execute, Ob.visible=0,flag=1

         If Oa.next=null then

             Oa.next=Ob,Ob.prior=Oa

         Else

             Ob.next=Oa.next,Oa.next.prior= Ob ,Oa.next=Ob,Ob.prior=Oa

         End if

Else

         Oa is undone,Ob is execute

         Oa.prior.next=Ob,Ob.prior=Oa.prior,Ob.next=Oa,Oa.prior=Ob,Oa.visible=0

End if

Output:flag

Algorithm 1 describes how to resolve conflicts between basic class operations. Operation Oa is the execution of the operation, and Operation Ob is the remote operation to be performed. There are two situations to be considered. When the operation is the same operation type, the operation is determined according to the priority. The operation with higher priority is linked to the double-linked list, and the operation with lower priority is not executed. It can be seen that the operation flag set to 0 and the lower priority is Set to 1. When the operation is a different type of operation, we specify that the priority of the U operation is greater than the priority of the D operation.

Algorithm 2 describes how to resolve compatible operations between basic operations. Operation Oa is the execution of the operation, and Operation Ob is the remote

Algorithm 2 CompatibleResolve

INPUT:Oa⊙Ob

If   ID(Oa) <ID(Ob)

then

Ob is execute

  If   Oa.next=NULL

  then

    Oa.next=Ob,Ob.prior=Oa

  Else

    Ob.next=Oa.next,Oa.next.prior= Ob ,Oa.next=Ob,Ob.prior=Oa

  End if

Else

  Oa is undone,Ob is execute,Oa is redo

  Oa.prior.next=Ob, Ob.prior=Oa.prior,Ob.next=Oa,Oa.prior=Ob,Oa.visible=0

End if

---

operation to be performed. When the two operations are compatible, the operation with the smaller identifier is performed before the operation with the higher identifier. At the same time, an operation link with a larger identifier in a double-linked list is after an operation with a smaller identifier.

Predefined Relationship Class Operations

In the actual engineering drawing design process, there is an inherent relationship between objects, and the user can define the association relationship between the objects in advance, and add the corresponding constraint rules under the relationship. In this case, for one or more operations, the executed result violates the predefined semantic constraints, which may cause inconsistencies. Therefore, the predefined relationship class operations mainly discuss the relationship between the positions of the graphic objects. As shown in the figure below, the position constraint relationship of "contains" between "door" and "handle" is predefined. If the designer of Site 1 thinks that the position of the "handle" should be to move K2 to the left by a certain distance on the left side of the door (Operation O1), likewise, the designer of Site 2 has this idea, but the operator of Site 2 puts K1 has moved a certain distance to the right (Operation O2). For O1 and O2 operations, it is legal if only consider the consistency of independent operations, because they are operations on different objects without any conflict, although they are concurrent. But this operation violates the requirement of semantic consistency.

The rectangular object K1 represents the door and the circular object K2 represents the door handle. According to the connection between objects, the positional relationship between K1 and K2 can be predefined: the moving range of the door handle should not exceed the size range of the door, otherwise it will not meet the actual design requirements, resulting in semantic illegitimate, as illustrated below (c).

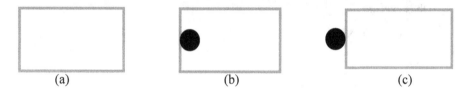

(a)   (b)   (c)

Fig. 2. Example of semantic inconsistency

The Representation of the Association Relationship Between the Graphic Objects

The O(i) in the operation tuple represents the association constraint relationship between the two objects, and the relationship can be represented by Relate-Rule: Relate is the relationship between the objects, the specific representation method An ordered pair of <Obj1, Obj2, r-id, r-describe>. Among them, Obj1 and Obj2 are two related object identifiers, r-id represents the generated constraint rule identification number, corresponding to rule, and r-describe is a description of the specific constraint relationship.

Rule is a constraint rule. It consists of one or more rules. The ordered form is an ordered pair of <r-id, Attributes, and comp>, where r-id is associated with r-id in Relate, and Attributes is associated with the attribute, comp, compares the sign for the value on the specific attribute.

Definition 8: Position constraint

For two different image objects, if there is one or more locations in the spatial location, We call such a position attribute association constraint relationship between two different image objects. To operate on any of these graphical objects, you must first detect the constraint relationship between them. As shown in Fig. 2, K1 and K2 have the associated constraint relationship on the location attribute, which is represented by Relate-Rule: <1.1,2.1,1, "Obj1:1.1(door) Include Obj2:2.1(handle)">. In other words, the K1 of the graphic object Obj1 and the K2 of the graphic object Obj2 are in a constrained relationship. The specific rule number is 1. Therefore, Rule with a sequence number of 1 is: < 1, x1-pos, " $\leq$ ", < 1, y1-pos, " $\geq$ ", < 1, x2-pos " $\geq$ ", < 1, y2-pos, " $\leq$ " $>$ .O(i) is a dynamic addition of various complex relationships between graphical objects to the dynamic rule base according to the actual design requirements. The system will transmit the broadcasts to other sites in time, so that the library of each site keeps up to date.

Definition 9: Predefined action conflict detection
The predefined concurrency conflict operation assumes that the given two operations Oa and Ob are for different objects if the following conditions are met:

(1) Oa||Ob
(2) Oa, Ob∈Relate (the relationship between Oa and Ob operation objects)
(3) Oa, Ob ⊄ Rule (Oa, Ob violates the rule defined by Rule after execution)

Then, Oa and Ob are concurrent conflict operations.

Predefined Concurrency Compatible Operations If Oa and Ob are not concurrent collision operations, Oa and Ob are compatible operations.

Predefined conflict resolution

INPUT Oa⊗Ob

Int flag=0

IF Oa、 Ob∈Relate & Oa、 Ob∉ Rule

then

   Ob is execute

   If ID(Oa)≺ID(Ob)

   then

      Ob is undo,Ob.visible=0 Oa is execute

      Oa.next=Ob.next,Ob.next.prior= Oa ,Ob.next=Oa,Oa.prior=Ob

   Else

      Oa is undo,Oa.visible=0 ,Oa is redo

      Oa.prior.next=Ob,Ob.prior=Oa.prior,Ob.next=Oa,Oa.prior=Ob,

      Oa.visible=0

   Else

      Execute CompatibleResolve

   End if

Definition 10: Integrated local operation

The algorithm gives an integrated local operation Oa. There are two situations to be considered: First, when Oa:pre_key is empty and no modeling operations exist in the double-linked list, Oa is inserted at the head of the double-linked list. Otherwise, the operation is inserted after the last graphical modeling operation of the doubly linked list. In the second case, when Oa:pre_key is not empty, you need to find the graphics modeling operation (pre) that was just executed at the local site. The Oa connection is after the Pre that was just found. Then, broadcast Oa to the remote site.

IntergrateLocal(Oa)

INPUT :Oa

If Oa.pre_key==null

then

If head.next!=null

then

    Nt=head.next

    While nt!=null do

    Nt=nt.next

Else

    Oa is double linked next to head

    End while

      Oa is double linked after NT.prior

  End if

Else

    pre =hash(Oa.pre_key)

    Oa is double linked after tar

End if

    Oa is broadcast to remote site

4   Time Complexity Analysis and Space Complexity

Local modeling operations of the time of complexity in a session is $O(1)$ as the target modeling operations have found directly using the hash table and the unique ID. Only when a session begins, we need to get the last executed operation of the double linked list as the target modeling operation for the first operation issued in each collaborative site. In this case, the time complexity is $O(n)$, where n is the quantity of executed modeling operations in the double linked list.

In ours approach, each operation Oa is a fourteen-tuples $<t,k,(x,y),l,O[i],Obji,visible,flag,key,c\_key,pre\_key,next,prior,link,s>$ The regular part is $<t,k,(x,y),l,Obji,visible,flag,key,c\_key,pre\_key,next,prior,link,s>$. The unregular part is $O[i]$. We suppose that the dimension of the regular part is S. The size of $<O[i]>$ is decided by the quantity of target operations whose the mutual relationship between the objects. If there is no predetermined relationship between the objects, so, the total size of each modeling is S. In the worst situation, there are R target modeling operations and T operations dependent on the by Oa. Assuming that the counts of operations in the links list is N (involving tombstones), the first-rate space complexity is $O(S \times N)$, the worst situation complexity is $O((S + R + T) \times N)$. So far as to the worst case, R and T are typical small. Meanwhile, the space overhead of the hash table is the same as that of the double linked list.

5   Conclusion

This paper proposes to improve CRDT algorithm to solve the consitency maitenance and conflict resolution in the graphics editing systems to support intelligence collaboration in big data. The algorithm can preserve the intention of the operation and ensure the semantic maintenance by ensuring the association relationship between the predefined graphic objects and the position attribute constraint rules. Through the analysis of time complexity and space complexity, the computational property of the algorithm is much better than the existing COT algorithm and AST algorithm. Therefore, ours algorithm is more suitable for intelligent collaborative applications compared to existing algorithm.

In the future of research, we will to quest further issues in this field further. First of all, we will keep on improve the posed algorithm. Then, we will do more detailed experiments to analyze and verify its correctness, and we will put forward reasonable case analysis. At the same time, we can do the related simulation prototype system, which the correctness of the algorithm. Finally, we will explore how to use multi-core CPU/multi-core GPU to accelerate large-scale collaborative application [8–10].

Acknowledgments. We would like to thank the reviewers, whose valuable critique and comments helped to improve this paper. Moreover, this work is supported by the Shanghai Natural Science Foundation under Grant No. 17ZR1419100, and the Open Project Program of Shanghai Key Laboratory of Data Science (No. 201609060003).

References

1. Gu, N., et al.: DCV: a causality detection approach for large-scale dynamic collaboration environments. In: Proceedings of the 2007 International ACM Conference on Supporting Group Work. ACM (2007)
2. Ignat, C.-L., Oster, G., Fox, O., Shalin, V.L., Charoy, F.: How do user groups cope with delay in real-time collaborative note taking. In: Boulus-Rødje, N., Ellingsen, G., Bratteteig, T., Aanestad, M., Bjørn, P. (eds.) ECSCW 2015: Proceedings of the 14th European Conference on Computer Supported Cooperative Work, pp. 223–242. Springer, Cham (2015). https://doi.org/10.1007/978-3-319-20499-4_12
3. Wu, Y., He, F., Zhang, D., Li, X.: Service-oriented feature-based data exchange for cloud-based design and manufacturing. IEEE Trans. Serv. Comput. 11, 341–353 (2018)
4. Ng, A., Sun, C.: Operational transformation for real-time synchronization of shared workspace in cloud storage. In: Proceedings of the 19th International Conference on Supporting Group Work, pp. 61–70. ACM (2016)
5. Gao, L.P., Lu, T.: Maintaining semantic consistency of compound Undo operations in replicated collaborative graphical editing environments. Jisuanji Yingyong Yanjiu 27(9), 3434–3438 (2010)
6. Oster, G., Urso, P., Molli, P., et al.: Data consistency for P2P collaborative editing. In: Proceedings of the 2006 20th Anniversary Conference on Computer Supported Cooperative Work, pp. 259–268. ACM (2006)
7. Lv, X., He, F., Cai, W., et al.: A string-wise CRDT algorithm for smart and large-scale collaborative editing systems. Adv. Eng. Inf. 33, 397–409 (2017)
8. Zhou, Y., He, F., Qiu, Y.: Optimization of parallel iterated local search algorithms on graphics processing unit. J. Supercomput. 72(6), 2394–2416 (2016)
9. Zhou, Y., He, F., Qiu, Y.: Dynamic strategy based parallel ant colony optimization on GPUs for TSPs. Sci. China Inf. Sci. 60(6), 068102 (2017)
10. Melab, N., Talbi, E.G.: GPU Computing for parallel local search metaheuristics. IEEE Trans. Comput. 62(1), 173–185 (2013)
11. Lv, X., He, F., Cai, W., et al.: CRDT-based conflict detection and resolution for massive-scale real-time collaborative CAD systems. In: Proceedings of the 12th Chinese Conference on Computer Supported Cooperative Work and Social Computing, pp. 185–188. ACM (2017)
12. Sun, D., Sun, C.: Operation context and context-based operational transformation. In: Proceedings of the 2006 20th Anniversary Conference on Computer Supported Cooperative Work, pp. 279–288. ACM (2006)
13. Gao, L., Gao, D., Xiong, N., et al.: CoWebDraw: a real-time collaborative graphical editing system supporting multi-clients based on HTML5. Multimed. Tools Appl. 77(6), 5067–5082 (2017)
14. Gao, L., Yu, F., Chen, Q., et al.: Consistency maintenance of Do and Undo/Redo operations in real-time collaborative bitmap editing systems. Cluster Comput. 19(1), 255–267 (2016)
15. Gao, L., Lu, T., Gu, N.: CLAF: Solving Intention Violation of Step-Wise Operations in CAD Groupware. Elsevier Science Publishers B. V., Amsterdam (2010)
16. Gao, L., Lu, T.: Achieving transparent and real-time collaboration in Co-AutoCAD application. J UCS 17(14), 1887–1912 (2011)

Throughput-Guarantee Resource Provisioning for Streaming Analytical Workflows in the Cloud

Yan Yao, Jian Cao[⊠], and Shiyou Qian

Department of Computer Science and Engineering,
Shanghai Jiao Tong University, Shanghai, China
{yaoyan,cao-jian,qshiyou}@sjtu.edu.cn

Abstract. Nowadays, most data analytical applications comprise of multiple tasks, which can be represented as workflow in nature. Some of data analytical applications, the data requests arrived continuously, such as fraud detection application, order application, etc. Generally, such streaming analytical workflow applications have a rigid requirement on throughput. It is critical to provisioning resource for streaming analytical workflows on a cloud platform with financial cost as minimizing as possible while still guaranteeing system throughput. We propose a cost effective resource provisioning algorithm which can guarantee system throughput. Experiments on the Alibaba cloud indicate that our proposed scheduling algorithm can guarantee the workflow throughput under different intensities of the workloads.

Keywords: Analytical workflow · Workflow scheduling
Cloud computing

1 Introduction

Nowadays, large-scale data sets are gathered at a very rapid speed in a broad range of areas, such as commerce, engineering sciences, and bimolecular research [16]. Big data has become a hot topic both in industrial and academic communities. The value of big data is from data analytics, which help knowledge discovery, decision-making, and technological innovation [5]. For example, in business domains, there is a need to investigate and forecast the market demands by analyzing different types of data. In many cases, data analytic tasks should be performed in a real-time way so that decision making can be more efficiently.

Generally, the processing of these data consists of multiple steps that have both inherent logic flow and data flow relationships, which can be described and enabled by a workflow model. We call the workflows that used for big data analytics as analytical workflow [12]. Thereby, the analytical workflow for streaming data processing is called streaming analytical workflow.

On the other hand, over the past few years, tremendous success has been achieved for cloud computing in offering IaaS (infrastructure as a services), PaaS

© Springer Nature Singapore Pte Ltd. 2019
Y. Sun et al. (Eds.): ChineseCSCW 2018, CCIS 917, pp. 213–227, 2019.
https://doi.org/10.1007/978-981-13-3044-5_16

(platform as a service), SaaS (soteware as a service) with a pay-as-you-need fashion [4]. Specifically, the IaaS clouds, providing computational resources in the form of virtual machines (VMs) to cloud users on demand, are gaining popularity in the execution of various applications, including workflow applications. Computing resources can be accessed at a lower cost as well as flexible configurations in IaaS clouds. Moreover, VMs can elastically be used to handle complex workflow systems without much investment in purchasing, managing, and maintaining hardware or software resources by cloud users.

Since there is a cost associated with cloud services, a cost-effective resource provisioning strategy is needed when applications are deployed to the cloud. At the same time, the performances of the applications (e.g., completion time, reliability) should also be assured. Therefore, the underlying focus of any resource provisioning strategy is to lessen the financial cost and improve the performance involved during workflow execution.

Although resource allocation strategies for cloud workflow have been widely addressed in the past years, unfortunately, they cannot yet meet the challenges brought by streaming analytical workflows yet. The main target of most cloud workflow scheduling research is to ensure that each workflow instance can be completed in a given time at the lowest cost. However, for streaming analytical workflows, in addition to ensuring each workflow instance can be finished in a given time, we also need to ensure the throughput of the whole system, i.e., to process workflow instances that continuously arrive with enough speed so that each instance will not be delayed. When workflow instances arrive at a speed faster than the execution speed of every instance, the system has to process multiple workflow instances at the same time. We should exploit the parallelism provided by multicore processor architecture as well as the distributed computing nature of cloud data centers to guarantee the throughput of the whole system [11].

We study the resource provisioning problems for streaming analytical workflow services in cloud environment in this paper. The main contributions of this paper are as follows:

- We propose a co-hosting model to reduce the number of resources required to guarantee the throughput of the analytical workflow system. On the one hand, a virtual machine instance will try to host as many component services as possible in order to increase resource utilization, and on the other hand, resource capability limitations among component services are considered.
- We develop a resource scheduling algorithm for streaming analytical workflow system that can minimize the financial cost while guaranteeing system throughput.
- Extensive experiments are performed using a real analytical workflow application in the Alibaba Cloud.

The rest of this paper is organized as follows. In Sect. 2, related works are summarized. Section 3 introduces the system architecture and models including streaming analytical workflows, resource model, and co-hosting model. In Sect. 4, the formulation of the problem and the details of the scheduling algorithm are given. In Sect. 5, experimental setups and the analysis of the results are provided. The final section is the conclusion.

2   Related Work

In cloud environment, resource scheduling is always an important problem, and still complicated for workflow applications [10]. This problem has been proved an NP-hard problem [9]. A considerable amount of research has been undertaken to solve the cloud workflow scheduling problem in recent years. Specifically, there have been some overview works on the state-of-the-art of the of workflow scheduling algorithms [15].

Based on different performance metrics, there are various ways of classifying algorithms. Such as, resource provisioning algorithms can be categorized as either batch processing [17] or streaming processing [7] according to the workload types. Data is gathered and then processed in batches under batch processing mode. In contrast, streaming processing plays emphasis on the velocity of the data, i.e., data are continual continuously arriving and leaving.

Many studies have tried to improve the latency and throughput of streaming application on various platforms, such as the grid or cloud. In [6], a transformation-based allocation algorithm that tries to minimize the costs of streaming big data processing was proposed. This algorithm is based on the model that resources are not shared among component services for different tasks. In contrast, our algorithm is based on a co-hosting model, i.e., component services that process different tasks can share one resource. Moreover, performance interference between co-running component services has to be considered.

The resource requirement of an application can be load-independent (such as storage, memory, and communication channels) and load-dependent (such as disk activity, CPU cycles, and execution threads numbers) [14]. Different applications have a different type of resource bottlenecks. In this paper, we restrict ourselves to the streaming analytical workflow whose tasks are computation-intensive. Thus, the most constrained resource is CPU. Therefore, we adopt CPU utilization and the number of cores as capacity criteria. In case the total resource requirements of the co-runners are below a server capacity, the performance interference among the component services can be ignored, as no resource contention happened.

3   System Architecture and Models

3.1   System Architecture

There exists two kind servers in our workflow system: a manager server and multiple execution servers. Instanced workflow tasks will be executed by the component services that are hosted in the execution servers. The manager server

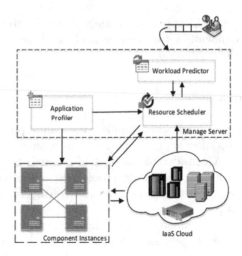

Fig. 1. System architecture.

is in charge of supervising a group of the modules by monitoring the status of all modules in a time interval.

The workflow system comprises of three modular: an workload predictor, an application profiler, and a resource scheduler (as illustrated in Fig. 1). The predictor produces an arrival rate prediction by utilizing historical information. The application profiler predicts the resource requirements of the applications, for example, CPU core numbers.

Based on the predicted workload and the resource requirements, the resource scheduler utilizes queueing theory to estimate the number of instances requirements for each task. Considering the estimated instances for each task, the given capacities of each type of virtual machine, and the scheduler uses the proposed algorithm to calculate an initial placement of the applications.

3.2   Cloud Resource Model

Virtual machines (VMs), which is the minimal computing unit provided by cloud providers, are the commonly form of the cloud resource in IaaS clouds. In general, VM instances are heterogeneous and may belong to different categories based on the business and scenarios, for example, computing optimized, memory optimized, storage optimized, etc. Each category contains multiple instance types with different CPU and memory specifications.

Furthermore, different cloud providers (such as Google Cloud [2] and Amazon Web Services [3]) employ different pricing schemes, such as reserved pricing, 'pay-as-you-need' pricing, and spot pricing. The "pay-as-you go" model is adopted in this paper, which charges users in terms of time units (e.g., minute, hour) and processing power. It is a common practice for cloud providers to round up the time in the charging process. For instance, it will still be charged as one minute if the actual rented time is less than one minute in Google cloud and Alibaba cloud.

3.3   Analytical Workflow Model

By convention, streaming analytical workflows are represented using DAGs (directed acyclic graphs), with nodes denote the tasks and edges denote the data flow between tasks. If task t_i has data dependency with task t_j, then there exist edge between the two nodes in the workflow graph.

In more detail, if the output data of the task t_i is the input of the task t_j, there is an edge e_{ij}. On the contrary, if the output data of the task t_j is the input of the task t_i, there is an edge e_{ji}. we can say there is data And edge e_{ij} exists if there is a data dependency between and, t_i is said to be the parent task of t_j and t_j is said to be the child task of t_i. A task cannot run until all of its input data are available.

Each individual task in a analytical workflow has a execution time. Therefore, we assign task execution time to individual node of a workflow graph as node weight. Each node consumes data from the others and then produces data. Because that all tasks are run in the same cloud datacenter (or cloud regions), in which data transmission rate is reasonably high and free of charge, the data transmission time and cost are ignored.

3.4   Co-hosting Model

Analytical workflows can be executed in a distributed manner in the cloud environment. In other words, workflows are deployed in a decentralized fashion. For streaming analytical workflows, requests arrive continuously. When the arrival rates of requests are higher than the execution rate of every task in an instance, the system will process multiple workflow instances at the same time to meet the throughput requirement. Thereby multiple component services for each analysis task will be deployed.

To fully utilize the cloud resources and therefore reduce cost, this paper employs the service deployment model we call a co-hosting model, that is, one VM is able to host multiple component services simultaneously, as shown in Fig. 2. This can be contrasted with a dedicated deployment model, where the entire virtual machine runs a single service (application or component). The number of services typically exceeds the number of the rented virtual machines in a co-hosting model, t. Therefore, the co-hosting model will be much more cost-effective.

However, co-running component services on the same virtual machine will cause performance degradation because of resource contention. Some research works [8,13] have prove that the performance interference among the co-running applications on the same VM can be ignored when the number of co-runners is less than the number of vCPU (virtual CPU) in a VM. Therefore, we further assume that each vCPU (virtual CPU) in a VM serves only one task at a time. In other words, a VM with two vCPUs may serve at most two tasks concurrently.

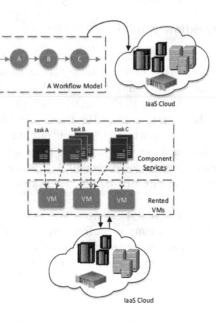

Fig. 2. Co-hosting model in cloud.

4   Throughput-Guarantee Resource Scheduling

Streaming analytical workflows can be computation-intensive or communication-intensive (i.e., data-intensive). In this paper, computation costs of streaming analytical workflows are comparatively higher than that of communication costs. And the computational cost are the rental cost of VMs, which are used to execute the workflow tasks.

For a given analytical workflow application, $A =< a_1, a_2, ..., a_N >$, and S type virtual machines $VM = \{vm_1, vm_2, ..., vm_S\}$, we propose a cost-effective resource scheduling algorithm.

4.1   Performance Metric - Throughput

To better understand the problem, we firstly give the definition of throughput. The number of jobs processed over a given interval of time is called throughput. In this paper, we define two kinds of throughput: *workflow throughput* and *component throughput*. Workflow throughput is the number of requests processed by the overall workflow system per unit time. The number of jobs processed by a component service in the workflow system over unit time is denoted as component throughput.

We estimate throughput using queueing modeling theory. We model the entire workflow system as an open queueing network, with each component service as a $G/G/M$ queue [14]. For an individual component service a_i, the time it takes to process a job request (only the time it takes to process it, not including the time it has been waiting in the queue) on virtual machine vm_j is equal to t_{ij}. The mean service rate $\mu_{ij} = 1/E\left[t_{ij}\right]$. The component throughput χ is defined as the summation of the mean service rate of all allocated virtual machines.

$$\chi(a_i) = \sum_{j=1}^{S} (m_j \cdot \mu_{ij}) \tag{1}$$

where m_j is the number of vm_j type virtual machines on which component service a_i is placed on. Workflow throughput is given by

$$\chi = min(\chi(a_i)) \tag{2}$$

where $i = \{1, 2, ..., n\}$. According to the queueing theory, the queueing system is stable if traffic intensity ρ is less than 1. That is, $\rho = \lambda/\chi(a_i)$. In other words, $\chi(a_i) > \lambda$ the queueing system is stable if the mean arrival rate λ is less than the mean service rate of the individual component service, otherwise, the queue grows without bounds.

4.2   Problem Formulation

As the communication costs between virtual machines in the same datacenter are free of charge, we only consider computing cost, which is $cost = \sum_{j=1}^{S} num_j \times price_{vm_j}$, where num_j is the total number of vm_j type virtual machines allocated for the entire workflow. We formulate the resource provisioning problem as:

$$\textit{Minimize} : \sum_{j=1}^{S} num_j \times price_{vm_j} \tag{3}$$

$$\textit{Subject to} : \sum_{j=1}^{S} (m_{ij} \cdot \mu_{ij}) \geq \lambda \tag{4}$$

$$num_j \leq \sum_{i=1}^{N} m_{ij} \tag{5}$$

$$i \in (0, N], j \in (0, S]$$

where m_{ij} is the number of vm_j type VMs that provioned for task a_i. In the co-hosting provisioning model, multiple component services can be co-located into one virtual machine.

4.3   Scheduling Algorithm

In general, optimally resource scheduling in a distributed computing environment has turned out to be an NP hard problem. In this section, a heuristic algorithm to find a optimal resource provisioning solution is explored.

Algorithm 1. Algorithm Design

Input:
1) λ: average arrival rate of jobs
2) $VM[S]$: VM type list, with S type VMs
3) $A[N]$: Analytical workflow Graph, with N components
Output:
1) VM provisioning plan *mapping*
1 Initialize *mapping* $\leftarrow$ *null* **for** *each component services a_i in workflow W* **do**
2   **for** *each VMvm$_j$ type* **do**
3   get $a_i.time\,[vm_j]$;
4   get $a_i.cpuUti\,[vm_j]$;
5   **end**
6   get initialized $\overline{time},\overline{cost}$
7 **end**
8 queue=Sort($a_i,\overline{time}$);
9 **while** *component service queue is not empty* **do**
10     $a_current$=queue.first;
11   candidateList=coRunning(component,$vm_{a_{current}}$);
12   **for** *each component service in candidateList* **do**
13   select the service with maximize service rate;
14   remove from the candidataList;
15   **end**
16   queue.remove($a_current$);
17 **end**
18 **return** *mapping*

Parameters Profiling. Given a task component with full queued input data set, tasks are profiled by ran alone on a single VM instance for each type of VMs. Here, profiling overhead can be well constrained as two reasons. One is that the number of VM type is limited in an IaaS cloud provider. Another, the task profiling only needs to be executed only once for each type of component service. The profile information involves the CPU utilization of the component service, the average execution time of the component service, the CPU utilization of VM instances, the average CPU load of the VM instances, etc.

    The next step is to undertake resource allocation.

1. Component services are sorted according to the unit cost, that is, to take the first component service in the queue out and then assign it to the virtual machine with the highest performance/price ratio of type vm_{ca}. The number of virtual machines of the type vm_{ca} is determined according to queueing theory, i.e., $num = round(\lambda/t_1 \cdot \mu\,[vm_{ca}])$.
2. Select the co-running component services to fully utilize the resources in order to reduce financial cost.
3. Determine the co-running component services. The policy to determine the co-runners is based on two parameters: the average CPU utilization of individual task and the number of virtual CPU cores. Given a rented virtual machine

instance, we can allocate the co-runners based on the minimum value of CPU utilization and the number of CPU cores, i.e., $capacity = min(cpuUti, cores)$. Under the co-hosting resource model, if the total resources required by all co-located tasks are under the VM capacity, the performance degradations of all co-running tasks, hich are produced due to resource contention, can be ignored (be considered as zero).

4. Finally, the parameters of the component service queue are updated. The previous steps are repeated until the component services queue is empty.

5   Experiment Evaluation

5.1   Experiment Settings

We implemented a simulator to emulate the performance of the proposed algorithm. The simulator can evaluate a dynamic workload scenario, with the assumption that the workload's arrival rate follows a certain distribution. Once a scheduling event is triggered, the simulator starts execution. The simulator will queries the predictor module with the inputs of all queued tasks add the average service rates of all types of VMs. Then, based on results of the predictor, the scheduler generates an assignment solution.

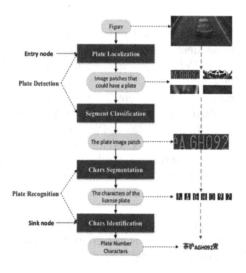

Fig. 3. An example workflow: car plate number recognition.

Figure 3 shows the workflow model of the car plate recognition process, which is developed based on OpenCV [1]. The process of plate recognition consists of four steps: *plate localization, segment classification, char segmentation* and *char identification*. In the plate localization step, all the image patches that could have a plate are located. In the second step, each image patch is classified using the SVM machine learning algorithm and the patch that contain the plate is identified. Next, the plate image patch is passed to char segmentation and seven segments are the outputs. The ANN machine learning algorithm is used to recognize the characters in the last step. All of the four tasks are computation-intensive with small data transfer.

Most big data analysis applications deal with jobs which are arriving dynamically in a real-time fashion. As convention, the arrival of the pictures for the car plate analysis workflows are assumed to be followed a Poisson process, with average λ pictures per second (Fig. 4).

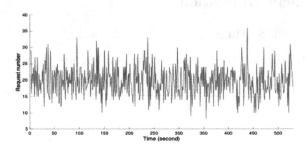

Fig. 4. Workload.

We rented a s1.small type virtual machine instance to host the workload generator, which is implemented using Java. It sends images that contain car plates in the form of the Poisson process. Figure 6 shows the arrival rates of plate pictures over 500 s.

We run simulations on three different "Pay-as-you-go" VM instances in the Alibaba cloud. The configuration parameters of the VMs that are relevant to the experiment are shown in Table 1 [3]. A Pay-as-you-go resource is charged by the second, but settled by the hour. Therefore, the charging unit is an hour in Table. We choose three types of instances: n4.medium, n4.xlarge and n4.2xlarge. The CPU type of all three instances is the Intel Xeon E5-2682 v4 (Broadwell) processor, 2.5 GHz clock speed. And memory is 16 GB, which is sufficient for this experiment.

Each newly provisioned virtual machine needs several minutes to boot-up. Therefore, a boot-up time of 120 s is considered for each instance, which is detailed on the Alibaba cloud website.

Table 1. VM types and price (based on-demand instances offered by *Alibaba* cloud).

VM type	vCPU	Memory	Storage	Price (USD)
n4.medium	2	16 GB	40 GB	$ 0.24
n4.large	4	16 GB	40 GB	$ 0.24
n4.xlarge	8	16 GB	40 GB	$ 0.392

5.2   Evaluation Metrics

We recorded the average execution time of each component service (Table 2). For each request, the execution time may be very different even if they are homogeneous. This is because that there exist performance variations exist even for the same type of virtual machine in different time period. Hence, we count the average execution time for an individual component service to process a single request. For example, the average execution time of the component service locate on a medium type virtual machine is 0.26170 s.

Table 2. The average execution time (*second*).

Components	VM types		
	n4.medium	n4.large	n4.xlarge
Locate	0.2617	0.2231	0.1727
Judge	0.2114	0.1989	0.1787
Segment	0.0876	10.0498	0.0281
Identify	0.0466	0.0232	0.0107

5.3   Results Analysis

First, whether the co-running component services in the co-hosting model will cause performance degradation is investigated. The average rate of Poisson arrival is set to five ($\lambda = 5$). We deploy the plate recognition workflow with a dedicated model and co-hosting model, respectively.

Figure 5 demonstrates the CPU utilization of VMs, which is counted by Alibaba cloud monitoring service. The CPU utilization of each virtual machine instance is very low when it is occupied exclusively by one component service (the average CPU utilization of the four rented virtual machines is 25%, 23%, 11% and 8% respectively). Obviously, the CPU utilization of the virtual machine instance is much higher when it is deployed on multiple component services (Fig. 5(e), i.e., the average CPU utilization is about 60%. However, the average processing time of individual requests is almost the same, as presented in Fig. 6. This indicates there is little performance degradation with our co-hosting model. In other words, the impact of performance interference is avoided by using our co-hosting model.

Next, we analyze the algorithm efficiency under varying workload intensities. We conducted three group experiments with different average request arrival rate ranging from 10 to 100. The observation time window is five minutes. We recorded the execution time and the response time of each arriving picture of the four components. Here, the processing time of a component is the time duration starts from the request be processed to finished. In a similar way, the response time of a component is the time duration starts from the request arrived to finished, i.e., *response time = waiting time + processing time*.

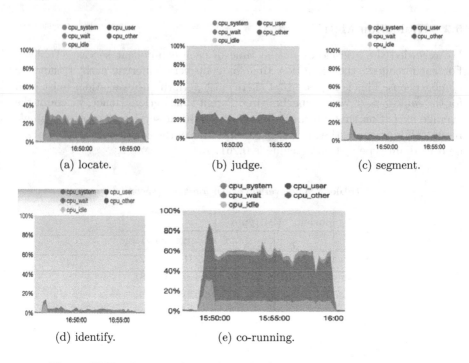

Fig. 5. CPU utilization of VMs from the Alibaba cloud monitoring tool

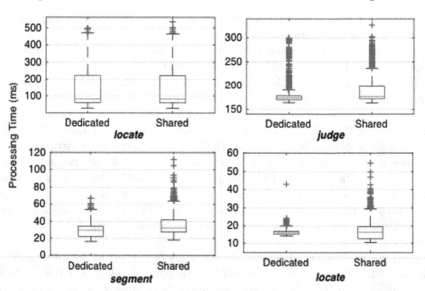

Fig. 6. The comparison of processing time under dedicated model and co-hosting model, respectively.

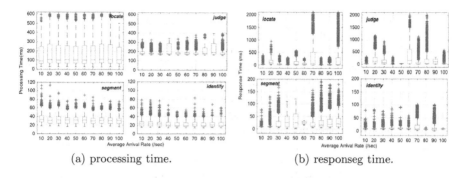

(a) processing time.   (b) responseg time.

Fig. 7. Time changing under different workload

The boxplots in Fig. 7(a) show the distribution of the processing (or execution) time of our proposed algorithm. It can be see that the different average arrival rates of requests have a similar execution time for each request as the median values and the width of the boxes of different average rates are equivalent. These stem from the fact that the execution time of the component is mainly decided by the tasks themselves and the virtual machines that are located. The box plot of the component locate is relatively tall, which indicates a large difference of the execution time. That is, the heterogeneity of the provisioned VMs to the locate component is high.

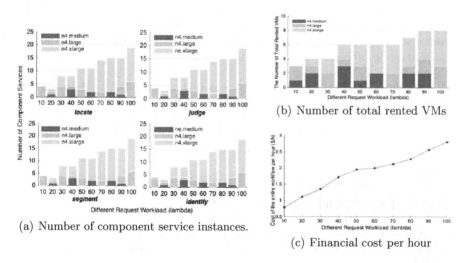

(a) Number of component service instances.

(b) Number of total rented VMs

(c) Financial cost per hour

Fig. 8. The deployed services, rented VMs, and financial cost per unit time of the four components under different workload.

The plots in Fig. 7(b) present the response time distribution of the image requests. Compared to the execution time in Fig. 7(a), the medians are almost equal to each other. This means the response time for most of the image requests equal to the corresponding execution time. As we have defined in previous, the response time of a workflow is equal to the summation the waiting time in the queue and the processing time of the task. The experiment results show that there is no waiting for all new arrival requests, that is, a new arrival request is processed immediately (in a timely manner). However, for the scheduler without considering interference, there exists waiting queues for some requests. Therefore, our approach has a better performance on the latency.

Figure 8(a) shows component services number of the four components and Fig. 8(b) gives the number of total rented virtual machines. It can be seen from the two plots that the number of rented virtual machines is much less than that of component services. For example, there are 76 component services while only rented eight virtual machines altogether, when the workload is 100. Furthermore, the financial cost does not increase exponentially when the load is doubled (Fig. 8(c)).

6   Conclusion

We investigated resource provisioning for individual component services of streaming analytical workflows to minimize the financial cost with throughput constraints. A co-hosting resource model is proposed in order to improve the utilization of the virtual machines, wherefore financial cost is reduced. Under co-hosting resource model, one virtual machine can run multiple component services concurrently while their interference is also elaborately considered. We designed a heuristic resource provisioning algorithm for streaming analytical workflows. The experiment results in the Alibaba cloud demonstrated that the requests can be processed in time.

Acknowledgments. This research was supported in part by the National Key Research and Development Plan of China (No. 2018YFB1003800), the National Natural Science Foundation of China (No. 61472253, 61772334), and the Cross Research Fund of Biomedical Engineering of Shanghai Jiao Tong University (No. YG2015MS61).

References

1. Easypr. https://github.com/liuruoze/EasyPR
2. Google cloud. https://cloud.google.com/compute/
3. Amazon: AWS cloud. http://aws.amazon.com/ec2/instancetypes
4. Armbrust, M., et al.: A view of cloud computing. Commun. ACM **53**(4), 50–58 (2010)
5. Chen, M., Mao, S., Liu, Y.: Big data: a survey. Mob. Netw. Appl. **19**(2), 171–209 (2014)
6. Chen, W., Paik, I., Hung, P.C.K.: Transformation-based streaming workflow allocation on geo-distributed datacenters for streaming big data processing. IEEE Trans. Serv. Comput. 1 (2017)

7. Chen, W., Paik, I., Li, Z.: Cost-aware streaming workflow allocation on geo-distributed data centers. IEEE Trans. Comput. **66**(2), 256–271 (2017)
8. Delimitrou, C., Kozyrakis, C.: Paragon: QoS-aware scheduling for heterogeneous datacenters. In: Architectural Support for Programming Languages and Operating Systems, vol. 48, no. 4, pp. 77–88 (2013)
9. Garey, M.R., Graham, R.L., Johnson, D.S., Yao, A.C.: Resource constrained scheduling as generalized bin packing. J. Comb. Theory Ser. A **21**(3), 257–298 (1976)
10. Guruprasad, H.S., Bhavani, B.H.: Resource provisioning techniques in cloud computing environment: a survey. Int. J. Res. Comput. Commun. Technol. **3**, 395–401 (2014)
11. Hirzel, M., Soulé, R., Schneider, S., Gedik, B., Grimm, R.: A catalog of stream processing optimizations. ACM Comput. Surv. **46**(4), 46:1–46:34 (2013)
12. Khan, S., Shakil, K.A., Alam, M.: Workflow-based big data analytics in the cloud environment present research status and future prospects. CoRR (abs/1711.02087) (2017)
13. Mars, J., Tang, L., Hundt, R., Skadron, K., Soffa, M.L.: Bubble-up: increasing utilization in modern warehouse scale computers via sensible co-locations. In: 44rd Annual IEEE/ACM International Symposium on Microarchitecture, MICRO 2011, Porto Alegre, Brazil, 3–7 December 2011, pp. 248–259 (2011)
14. Raz, T.: The art of computer systems performance analysis: techniques for experimental design, measurement, simulation, and modeling (Raj Jain). SIAM Rev. **34**(3), 518–519 (1992)
15. Rodriguez, M.A., Buyya, R.: A taxonomy and survey on scheduling algorithms for scientific workflows in IaaS cloud computing environments. Concurr. Comput.: Pract. Exp. **29**(8), e4041 (2017)
16. Sandryhaila, A., Moura, J.M.F.: Big data analysis with signal processing on graphs: representation and processing of massive data sets with irregular structure. IEEE Signal Process. Mag. **31**(5), 80–90 (2014)
17. Wen, Y., Chen, Z., Chen, T.: An improved scheduling algorithm for dynamic batch processing in workflows. In: Proceedings of the 2013 International Conference on Cloud and Green Computing, No. 6 in CGC 2013, pp. 502–507 (2013)

A Probabilistic and Rebalancing Cache Placement Strategy for ICN in MANETs

Cheng Zhang[1,2(✉)], Chunhe Xia[1,2], and Haiquan Wang[1,3]

[1] Beijing Key Laboratory of Network Technology, Beihang University,
Beijing, China
zalacheng@foxmail.com
[2] School of Computer Science and Engineering, Beihang University,
Beijing, China
[3] College of Software, Beihang University, Beijing, China

Abstract. Cache placement is a key component of information centric networking (ICN) for optimizing network performance. Previews works on caching placement mainly focus on fixed or semi fixed network. We propose a cache placement/update strategy in a mobile ad hoc network (MANET) environment where content consumer and provider are constantly mobile. Based on hotspot recognition and user requirement modeling, two approaches named *Pcaching* and *Cache Rebalancing* are proposed to settle the cache placement/update problem in one region and between different regions. We evaluate the performance of our approach compared with existing caching scheme and show that *Pcaching* has its advantage in both hit ratio and hop count over previews strategy.

Keywords: Cache placement · ICN · MANET

1 Introduction

Based on named data, Information-Centric Networking (ICN) has become a new way of thinking as traditional Host-Centric Internet communication paradigm lacks efficiency in data access and content distribution measures. ICN uses name-based routing to achieve location independence and enables a series of valuable features such as in-network caching, multicast and mobility support [1]. Therefore, it provides a more efficient means of communication, making it much easier for users to retrieve content. When user requests content, any node receiving the request can act as a server and respond to the request with a copy, thereby reducing the network congestion, access latency, and bandwidth consumption.

As ICN uses name-based routing, it naturally fits the application of mobile peer-to-peer communications where nodes are highly mobile, and in lack of steady network topology. In-network caching mechanism faces the challenge of how to place/distribute contents in a mobile network in order to make the network efficiently working. In this paper, we consider popular content replication and placement problem in a mobile ad hoc network (MANET), so as to optimize network performance as network nodes are constantly moving. We propose a placement/update strategy in a MANET environment

© Springer Nature Singapore Pte Ltd. 2019
Y. Sun et al. (Eds.): ChineseCSCW 2018, CCIS 917, pp. 228–238, 2019.
https://doi.org/10.1007/978-981-13-3044-5_17

where content consumer and provider are both mobile. The model decides where or if a popular content data should be cached or updated in a MANET environment in order to maintain ICN stability and efficiency. We try to address this issue by bringing hot city geographic locations, or hotspots, into consideration, so that our model can place popular data contents according to different hotspots and user requirements. City taxi behavior and geographic features are also studied to help recognize and divide city hotspot regions because taxi moving behaviors are strongly related to their geographic features.

2 Related Works

Most content replication and placement strategy researches have been focused on fixed networks [2–4], which is natural because content caching and placement problems in Web caching and CDNs need to be addressed by taking network topology and throughput into account. However, in a MANET environment, due to dynamic network topology, high provider or consumer mobility and different throughput rate, ICN researchers have to adapt light-weighted caching placement strategies in order to reduce protocol overhead. Due to its host-to-content routing natural, ICN has two basic roles, content consumer and content provider. Paper [5] proposed a content provider mobility scheme in Named Data Networking (NDN), adding a Locator into NDN Interest package and a mapping system which maps identifier to locator. The mapping system is a DNS-like service for users to find out the newest location of content provider on the move. A content consumer mobility ICN scenario is introduced by [6] where mobile users move between different sites while requesting content from caching servers within every site through WIFI connection. A location aided Content Management Architecture for a content-centric MANET is proposed in [7], in which content consumer and provider are both mobile. By binding data to a geographic location, the approach intends to keep a content copy within pre-setup geographic boundaries based on GPS location information. Through proactively replicating the content when needed, the approach can maintain data availability within the boundaries. Different from existing work which mainly studies only one-sided mobility or uniform-distributed geo-location placement strategy, we aim to consider both consumer and provider mobility, as long as the impact of different user request patterns in real city geo-locations, to design an ICN caching update and placement strategy that can work in a highly dynamic MANET environment.

3 Model Overview and Specification

The goal of our model is to manage content placement/update strategy in a MANET environment where content consumer and provider are both mobile. The model decides where or if a popular content data should be cached or updated in a MANET environment in order to maintain ICN stability and efficiency. We try to address this issue by bringing hot city geographic locations, or hotspots, into consideration, so that our model can place popular data contents according to different hotspots and user requirements. City taxi moving behavior and geographic features are also considered in order to recognize and divide city hotspots as taxi behaviors are strongly related to geographic features. The model has three key technologies as shown in Fig. 1 to be further described below:

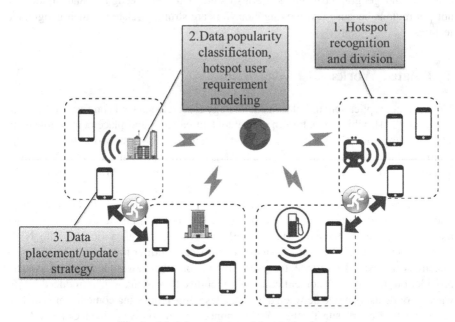

Fig. 1. Model overview and key technologies

Hotspot Recognition and Division

- A city can be divided into two kinds of regions named "load-region" and "drop-region" based on the density of passenger load or drop events extracted from real taxi traces, so we can get load regions and drop regions where the load or drop event happens frequently.

Data Popularity Classification, Hotspot User Requirement Modeling

- Existing caching research [7] tells that the content access rate follows Zipf-like distribution, so we can use this distribution to generally model content popularity.
- In our model, a History Interest Table (HIT) is introduced in order to record historical content requirements of users in a period of time. By using HIT, we can fit a content requirement distribution function (CRF) for a caching node to model user requirement probability distribution.

Data Placement/Update Strategy

- Within one region, users tend to fit with a similar data requirement model. Therefore in order to meet with this requirement, we propose a multi-factor data placement/update strategy in order to cope with HIT, battery status, caching occupation, content time-effectiveness and content popularity.
- With different CRFs, we diverse content requirements in different locations. So we propose an inter-region data update strategy to be adaptable to locations when user moves from one region to another. The strategy makes node periodically updates its own caching in order to fit in with different regions it enters.

3.1 Hotspot Recognition and Division

Through preview researches [8], we found that the taxi moving behaviors or its geographic features are significantly related to the taxi occupation statuses. Instead of dividing the area simply into equally regions, we make the area into two kinds of regions named "load-region" and "drop-region" based on the density of passenger load or drop events extracted from real taxi traces. When a passenger steps into a taxi, the current location is recorded as load-region regions. The destination region, where the passenger steps out, is recorded in the set of drop-region regions. We study the relationship between load-regions and drop-regions, arguing that drop events can better describe passenger moving behaviors, and using drop-regions to form different city hotspots in which data contents are required in respect to user requirement model.

Hotspot Recognition. With real taxi trace data of Beijing city, we analyze the distributions of load-events and drop-events within one week. Through clustering algorithms, we manage to get clustering ranking results, or top hotspots, for both load-events and drop-events, as shown in Fig. 2:

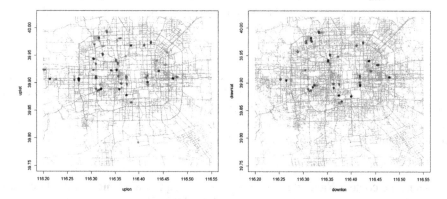

Fig. 2. Hotspot recognition for load and drop events

Hotspot Division. We argue that drop-events are more suitable data to describe people's interest and intention, so in order to simplify calculation we choose top 20 drop-event clusters from Fig. 2 to roughly recognize hotspots. From Fig. 2 we can see that these hotspots include famous scenic spots, large business areas, railway stations and subway stations. After getting clustered hotspots, we have to formally divide those hotspots from the map before we can use them as calculable regions. A Graham's scan method [9] is adopted to find the convex hull of each cluster, and for each convex hull, we calculate its Minimum Bounding Rectangle(MBR) [10] in order to make our division more accurate. With MBR, which is the minimum bounding rectangle for hotspots, we finally get an accurate hotspot region division for MANET.

3.2 Data Popularity Classification and Hotspot User Requirement Modeling

Data Popularity Classification. Inspired by existing researches from Web caching and CDNs, we consider the data access rate by user follows Zipf-like distribution, so we can model content popularity with it. In this distribution, the accessing probability of the r-th $(1 \leq r \leq N_c)$ ranking data from a data-set can be denoted as follows:

$$P_r = \frac{1/i^\alpha}{\sum_{n=1}^{N_c} \frac{1}{n^\alpha}}, r = 1, 2, \ldots, N_c \qquad (1)$$

where $\alpha(0 \leq \alpha \leq 1)$ denotes the value of the exponential parameter of the distribution. When $\alpha = 1$, the distribution follows Zipf's law; and when $\alpha = 0$, it follows Uniform Distribution. N_c is the total number of different contents.

Hotspot User Requirement Modeling. In traditional Content-Centric Networking (CCN) solution, which is a realization of ICN, Forwarding Information Base (FIB), Pending Interest Table (PIT) and Content Store (CS) are three key elements to a node in order to participate in the network [11]. FIB contains content advertisements and their routing information in order to forward Interest packages to the content providers that might hold the matching Data. PIT keeps track of Interest packages so the matching Data returned from content providers can follow the reversed path to the data consumers. CS is a storage cache for the nodes in order to temporarily cache the content Data with respect to different caching schemes. When a data requirement is met in a node, the corresponding entry in Pending Interest Table (PIT) is deleted as shown in Fig. 3. However we argue that PIT is in fact a very important basis in order to get user requirement and interest patterns, so the past PIT entries should be saved instead of deleted.

In our model, a History Interest Table (HIT) is introduced in order to record historical content requirements of within a period of time:

HIT <Name, Time, Location>

Thus, the content **Name** that user requests, the requesting **Time** and the **Location** where the request happens are all recorded by HIT. Hence, we can fit a content requirement distribution function CRF for a node in different locations with respect to Zipf's law: $P_{r,j}$, the probability of r-th ranking content being requested in location j.

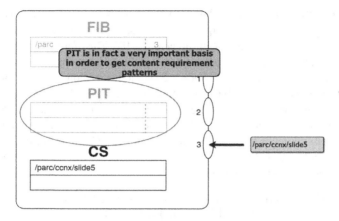

Fig. 3. The importance of PIT

3.3 Data Placement/Update Strategy

The placement/update strategy mainly focuses on optimizing data placement and deciding whether a content data should be replaced by a new one, in order to minimize the access overhead in a dynamic MANET environment. As shown in Fig. 1, we are facing two kinds of problem: placement/update strategy within a single region and between regions. From above user requirement modeling we understand that the requirement pattern tends to be similar within one single region, however differs from different regions. So we consider solving these two problems with *Pcaching* and *Cache Rebalancing*, in both of which HIT plays the key role, as HIT is the most suitable representative to denote user query pattern differences between regions.

Data Placement/Update Strategy Within a Single Region: *Pcaching*. This strategy considers which data should be cached and where to be cached within one region. As the query pattern is similar in a single region, we propose a multi-factor scalable probabilistic cache placement strategy *Pcaching*. *Pcaching* considers HIT, battery status, cache occupation, content time-effectiveness and content popularity to form a Utility Function U that takes the above normalized parameters into account:

$$U = \sum_{i=1}^{N_p} w_i g(x_i) \tag{2}$$

In above function, weights W_i meet $0 \leq W_i \leq 1$ and $\sum_{i=1}^{N} w_i = 1$, and g(x_i) is the normalized parameter from HIT, battery status, and cache occupation, et al. As U has a value within the interval [0:1], it gives a result for caching probability when a node encounters a new data package: if $U \to 1$, the packet is cached with a high probability; on the contrary, if $U \to 0$, the packet is cached with a low probability. Therefore, when a node receives a data packet, it can compute its current caching probability for this packet, which is the *Pcaching* process.

Data Placement/Update Strategy between Different Regions: *Cache Rebalancing.*
As different regions have different query patterns, or request CRFs, we diverse content
requirements in different regions with the help of HIT. Therefore in order to optimize
data placement/update, the strategy must be adaptable to locations. Thus we consider a
Cache Rebalancing approach when node x enters a new region B. The approach asks
any node it encounters for the HIT of region B, which means the node can proactively
get the user requirement patterns of the new region it enters, and add the new regions
CRF to its own one to rebalance its caching table. By periodically *Cache Rebalancing,*
the caching network tends to become a steady state. The *Cache Rebalancing* approach
is detailed described in below:

When Node x enters a new region B,

- x ask for HIT_b to any node y it encounters within region B;
- calculate the content request distribution function CRF_b;
- Using CRF_b, x generates interest package for content C_i with a probability of $P(C_i)$
  for all the i contents of B, and cache all the responded content;

When a content data C passes Node x,

- x checks its own HIT, calculate its content request distribution function CRF;
- with CRF, x uses *Pcaching* process to computes the caching probability of data C;
- As the request arrival time interval fits Poisson distribution:

$$P_n(t) = \frac{1}{n!}(\lambda t)^n e^{-\lambda t} \tag{3}$$

We assume the data update time interval should also fit upper distribution. By
periodically updating its cache, the *Caching Rebalancing* mechanism makes caching
exchanges between different regions smoothly and costless. We can further more get
the steady state for a cache network in a region:

$$R_{r,j} = P_{r,j} + \sum_{i \neq j} R_{r,i} T_{i,j} \tag{4}$$

$R_{r,j}$ denotes the final probability of the r-th ranking content data being requested in
region j, $P_{r,j}$ is the original requesting probability (which can be computed by HIT_j) of
the r-th ranking content data being requested in region j, and $T_{i,j}$ is the transition
probability of node x moves from region i to j.

4 Performance Evaluation

We evaluate the performance of our scheme using ndnSIM [12] simulator based on ns-
3. We also use real city taxi traces of Beijing to best simulate node mobility. Our goal is
to show the benefits of our caching placement strategy by comparing with existing ICN
caching placement approaches (Table 1).

Table 1. Simulation parameters

Parameter	Value
Area size	24 km × 24 km
Time of simulation	7200 s
Number of nodes	3000
Radio range	50 m

Hotspot Recognition and Division. In this section, we use DBSCAN clustering algorithm to analyze city taxi traces in order to get the top ranking clusters of load and drop events. Based on the results of clustering, we take a further step to refine our results by using Graham's scan method to compute the convex hull of each cluster, and for each convex hull, we calculate its Minimum Bounding Rectangle (MBR) in order to make the results more accurate, as shown in Fig. 4.

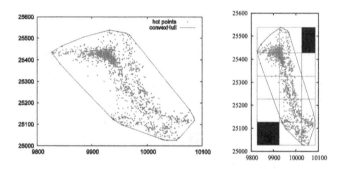

Fig. 4. Minimum bounding rectangle for a hotspot

With MBR, which is the minimum bounding rectangle for hotspots, we finally get an accurate hotspot region division for MANET. In Fig. 5 we can see that these regions include famous scenic spots, large business areas, railway stations and subway stations, which reflex the real social mobility patterns for city taxies.

Data Placement/Update Strategy. In order to demonstrate the benefits of *Pcaching*, we compare *Pcaching* to the default CCN caching strategy LCE (leave copy everywhere) as shown in Fig. 6, which tells the cache hit ratio when Zipf parameter α differs in different cache placement strategies. Large value of Zipf parameter α means a given content gets much higher popularity than others in this region. As can be seen, *Pcaching* shows better cache hit ratio that is nearly two times higher than LCE. This implies that workload of content servers in *Pcaching* is better distributed than LCE. This result is not surprising because LCE strategy caches content chunks aggressively and without any choosing, which could lead to caching redundancy to the whole network, therefore takes down the cache hit ratio of the network. In *Pcaching*, cache hit ratio increases as Zipf parameter increases. This result suggests that the competitive advantage of *Pcaching* comes from those regions that users tend to social and share popular contents through the caching network.

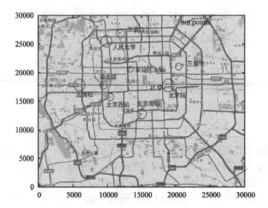

Fig. 5. Top hot regions in a city

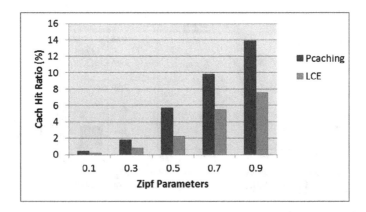

Fig. 6. Cache hit ratio comparison between cache placement strategies

Figure 7 plots the average hop counts by cache size and Zipf parameters. The cache sizes of node ranges from 5 to 25 blocks which represents 5% to 25% of total content number. Compared with the other scheme LCE, we can see that *Pcaching* provides lower average hop counts for different cache sizes. This tells that the *Pcaching* efficiently uses the cache memory to improve the effectiveness of the whole network. We also see that with Zipf parameter increases, average hop counts decreases while *Pcaching* still has advantage to LCE. The results shows hop counts can be reduced by *Pcaching*, and *Pcaching* works better in regions where social communication patterns are frequent.

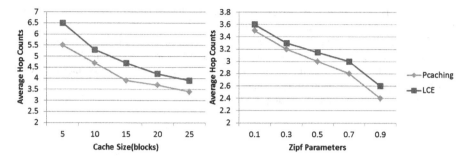

Fig. 7. Hop counts for comparison between cache placement strategies

5   Conclusions

In this article, we study cache placement problem for ICN in a MANET environment. Based on hotspot recognition and user requirement modeling, two approaches named *Pcaching* and *Cache Rebalancing* are proposed to meet the caching placement/update needs for single region and between regions. Through real city taxi mobility trace simulations, we show that our approach outperforms existing CCN traditional caching scheme in both cache hit ratio and hop counts, which indicates that our approach reduces network overhead while maintaining solid performance.

Acknowledgements. This work is supported by these Projects: The National Natural Science Foundation Project of China under Grant No. U1636208; The Co-Funding Project of Beijing Municipal education Commission under Grant No. JD100060630.

References

1. Xylomenos, G., et al.: A survey of information-centric networking research. IEEE Commun. Surv. Tutor. **16**, 1024 (2014)
2. Cohen, E., Shenker, S.: Replication strategies in unstructured peer-to-peer networks. ACM Sigcomm Comput. Commun. Rev. **32**, 177 (2002)
3. Ko, B., Rubenstein, D.: Distributed self-stabilizing placement of replicated resources in emerging networks. IEEE/ACM Trans. Netw. **13**, 476 (2005)
4. Qiu, L., Padmanabhan, N.V., Voelker, M.G.: On the Placement of Web Server Replicas. Cornell University, Ithaca (2000)
5. Jiang, X., Bi, J., Wang, Y., Lin, P., Li, Z.: A content provider mobility solution of named data networking. In: IEEE International Conference on Network Protocols, vol. 1 (2012)
6. Wei, T., Chang, L., Yu, B., Pan, J.: MPCS: A mobility/popularity-based caching strategy for information-centric networks. In: Global Communications Conference, vol. 4629 (2015)
7. Lee, S.B., Wong, S.H.Y., Lee, K.W., Lu, S.: Content management in a mobile ad hoc network: beyond opportunistic strategy. In: IEEE INFOCOM, vol. 266 (2011)
8. Wang, H., Yang, W., Zhang, J., Zhao, J., Wang, Y.: START: status and region aware taxi mobility model for urban vehicular networks. In: Computer Communications Workshops, vol. 594 (2015)

9. Cormen, T.H., Leiserson, C.E., Rivest, R.L., Stein, C.: Introduction to Algorithms, 2nd edn, p. 1297. The MIT Press, Cambridge (2001)
10. Caldwell, D.R.: Unlocking the mysteries of the bounding box. Coordinates Online Journal of the Map & Geography Round Table of the American Library Association (2005)
11. You, W., Mathieu, B., Simon, G.: How to make content-centric networks interwork with CDN networks. In: Network of the Future, vol. 1 (2014)
12. Afanasyev, A., Moiseenko, I., Zhang, L.: ndnSIM: NDN simulator for NS-3 (2012)

Social Computing

Detect Cooperative Hyping Among VIP Users and Spammers in Sina Weibo

Ziyu Guo, Shijun Liu$^{(\boxtimes)}$, Yafang Wang, Liqiang Wang, Li Pan, and Lei Wu

Shandong University, Jinan, China
lsj@sdu.edu.cn

Abstract. Sina Weibo services provide platforms for massive information dissemination and sharing between hundreds of millions of users. The hot topics in this platform attract substantial interest and have enormous potential for business and society. As a result, it has attracted spam teams with malicious intent. In this paper, we study how to detect such opinion spam teams and how do they guide public opinion. Our model is unsupervised and adopts a Bayesian framework to distinguish between spammers and non-spammers. Experiments conducted on a dataset of a Sina Weibo hot topic with a 0.81 F1-measure demonstrate the proposed method's effectiveness. Through further analysis, we found the phenomenon and some methods of the cooperative hyping among VIP users and spammers (in Sect. 3.2). VIP users are small in number but have a great influence due to they have a large number of followers, so VIP users are responsible for hyping topics so that it attract more attention, then a lot of spammers guide public opinion through a lot of manual postings.

Keywords: Hot topics · Spammer detection · Guide public opinion
Bayesian modeling · Cooperative hyping

1 Introduction

Sina Weibo provide platforms for an enormous amount of information sharing and spreading between hundreds of millions of users. This will certainly leed to new opportunities for hyping. The hot topics in Sina Weibo attract substantial interest and have enormous potential for business and society. Therefore, it has attracted spams teams with malicious intent. Spam teams and the hype they create affect people's judgment on information as well as commercial interests.

The existence of VIP users makes this hype much easier. The large number of followers they have allows information to spread faster. VIP users are often the key sparking the public's interest. Therefore, cooperative hyping among VIP users and spammers becomes a common phenomenon.

Through further observation, we discovered some traces of cooperative hyping phenomena between VIP users and spammers. These phenomena manifest in several ways-for example: when some VIP users advertise for certain products, there will be a lot of spammers retweeting related posts and posting buyer reviews. This is the simplest type of cooperative hyping.

© Springer Nature Singapore Pte Ltd. 2019
Y. Sun et al. (Eds.): ChineseCSCW 2018, CCIS 917, pp. 241–256, 2019.
https://doi.org/10.1007/978-981-13-3044-5_18

In this paper, we first propose a model to detect spammers. It should be noted that VIP users are easily identifiable because of the features of a large number of followers and official certification marks. Then the spammers are identified by the model and the VIP users are used to analyze the collaborative hyping phenomenon.

The model is unsupervised and it does not require labeled training data. In this Bayesian model, we treat observed behavioral features as known while modeling the user's *spamicity* as latent. The *spamicity* here refers to the degree of the exhibited behavior being spammed. The key motivation depends on the assumption that the spammers are different from the common user in the behavioral dimension. Inference allows us to learn the distributions of these two classes based on a set of behavioral features.

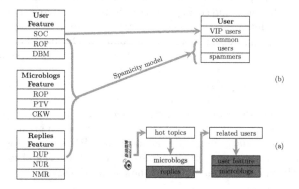

Fig. 1. Data capture and model. In this figure, the features DUP, NUR, NMR, ROP, PTV, CKW, DBM, ROF and ROC were introduced in detail in Sect. 4.2

Figure 1(b) explains our approach. After relevant social media data, we extract features from the user's postings and replies under hot topics as well as the users's profile information,. For user classification, we first identify VIP users based on the official certification. The remaining features are used to train our model to assess a user's degree of spamicity and classify them into the two remaining clusters.

Then we use the "*Wang Baoqiang divorce*" (in Mandarin) case to analyze the popular hype methods, which included the following:

- Whenever a related event occurs, VIP users will post and expand the hot topic's influence. When the influence is expanded, spammers will hype on the basis of facts to guide public opinion. The means by which spammers do this is described as follows:
- Attack each other's weaknesses.
- Combining what happened in the past and making speculations.
- Expanding individuals to groups, with the intent to arouse more resonance and support.

- Explaining the occurrence of new events in an exaggerated fashion to gain public sympathy.
- Talk about it everywhere and anywhere.

In summary, we makes the following contributions:

1. This paper proposes a method that uses observed behavioral characteristics to detect spam teams in an unsupervised Bayesian framework without requiring laborious manual labels.
2. We make a comprehensive experiment to assess the model based on human judgment. The model is also compared against a baseline approaches. The results demonstrate that the proposed model is outperforms.
3. In view of the spam teams detection, we make a diachronic analysis of a specific case, "*Wang Baoqiang's divorce*", to examine the cooperative hyping among VIP users and spammers. The results showcase that the cooperative hyping phenomenon is really exist and the spam teams have formulated rather complicated strategies in reshaping public opinion. We have found some strategies but calls for more academic and industry attention.

2   Related Work

Given the growth of the problem of spamming in large social networks, there has been ample research on detecting spammers, including specifically for Sina Weibo [2,3,15,19], as well as several supervised learning methods [6,18,20] to detect instances of opinion spam. However, such models are largely based on a dichotomy of fake vs. non-fake labels.

Because of a lack of reliable ground truth labels, these previous works relied on fake/non-fake labels for training. For instance, Jindal et al. [9] made the assumption that duplicate or near-duplicate reviews are fake. However, this heuristic is unreliable and overly restrictive. Li et al. [11] used a dataset labeled manually, which also has reliability issues. All these have been suggested that this is difficult, if not impossible for humans to achieve by mere reading [9,18].

Because of the lack of labeled data, unsupervised methods have also been proposed to detect both individual fake review spammers [13,21] and groups of them [16,17]. Relevant methods include time series modeling [22] and distributional analysis [7], mining reviewing patterns as unexpected association rules [10], and detecting review burstiness [5].

Apart from this, [1,4,8] all used graph-based fraud detection and [12,20] used the Markov model. These methods are not suitable for us, they can easily find the spammers in social networks, but it's difficult to find opinion spammers for a specific hot topic, especially guided opinion spammers.

About hyping in Sina Weibo, [23] detected hype users in Sina Weibo. It's a detecting model for spammers rather than detecting the hype methods. In [14], they detected the hype groups based on mining maximum frequent itemsets. This gave us an insight into the discovery of hype. Sina Weibo's hype is often organized and hidden. Discovering these accounts and detecting their hype are effective in stopping them.

3   Data Model

Sina Weibo is one of the most popular social networks in the world, with the vast majority of its user base in China. The network structure is similar to Twitter. Users can follow others and be followed. A user can post or repost postings, and such postings can be reposted, reviewed, or praised.

3.1   Dataset Characteristics

Voting Posts: A voting post consists of a question and some answers. People are able to select one of the answers within a given period. After the user select the answer, he can get the ratio of every answer selected by others. The voting post is often used by some VIP users to survey public opinions or to affirm their own views.

Topic Posts: A topic post is one in which certain keywords are marked with ##. The marked keywords are referred to as the topics of the posting. For example, for a posting such as #Wang Baoqiang divorced#, September 13, the former manager of Baoqiang Wang, Zhe Song was arrested on "job infringement", currently held in Chaoyang police station.), the topic is "Wang Baoqiang divorced" (in Mandarin). Readers may select a topic (e.g., by clicking on it), and they will be led to the topic home page, which lists a number of postings for that topic.

By browsing pages for topics, we can obtain all postings and their respective authors, the number of repostings and applause markings, and all comments on the postings. Additionally, one can select any of the authors of postings to enter their personal home pages.

User Home Pages: A user's home page shows the set of postings that were posted or reposted by the user.

When browsing a user's home page on Sina Weibo, we can only obtain the user's posts, reposts, corresponding replies, and the number of repostings and applause markings. However, it is not possible to obtain the user's replies to other users' posts or reposts.

Relevant Parties for Hot Topics: For a given hot topic, we consider as relevant parties those people who are saliently mentioned in the postings. In some cases, these may be opposing parties. For example, for the topic "Wang Baoqiang divorced", the parties are Baoqiang Wang, his wife Rong Ma, and his agent Zhe Song.

3.2   User Definition

Users participating in a hot topic are categorized into three different subsets: common users, spammers, and VIP users.

Common users are Sina Weibo users who just forward or comment on relevant postings about a hot topic without continuing to follow them.

Spammers for a hot topic are users who are paid posters and seek to promote the hot topic and they behave like common users to avoid being discovered. Their employer may be a party of the hot topic or someone who is hostile toward the party. They create posts or comment on posts posted by others to promote the related topic and guide public opinion on the parties. They are paid based on valid posts as well as the number of those being forwarded, commented on or praised. They typically no longer keep a close eye on the party either before or after the topic has passed.

VIP users are certified by Sina with a special icon on their homepage. For a given hot topic, we can consider VIP users that are often forwarded, commented on or praised by a substantial number of relational users. This also means that they can effectively guide public opinion. Usually the number of VIP users for a particular topic is relatively small, but they have a great impact on the spread of hot topics. Thus, it is very important to identify them.

In addition, it is necessary to mention that the team which guides public opinion generally consists of phantom fans, spammers and some VIP users. *Phantom fans* usually post by machine and are easily identified and deleted by the system, thus we don't care about them. So, in this paper, we first screened out phantom fans through an official plugin provided by Sina. Then we identify spammers (by our spam detection model) and VIP users (by their special features) and use the information on spammers and VIP users to analyze the issues that guide public opinion.

4   Spam Detection Model

4.1   Model Overview

In this paper, spam detection is modeled as an unsupervised problem in Bayesian settings. Specifically, we consider a cluster generation model based on a set of observed features. Each user has a set of behavioral cues that serve as observed features. We assume that these are emitted based on the corresponding latent prior distributions. Model inference involves learning the latent distribution of users in various behavioral dimensions, and clustering users in unsupervised settings based on probabilistic models.

Due to the generation of our model conditions and the labels of user spamicities, inference can also lead to user *spamicity* estimates which is our main focus.

4.2   Features

We have proposed some abnormal behavior characteristics that appear more likely to be related to spamming. Therefore, these characteristics can be exploited as observed features in our model to learn how to distinguish between spam and

Table 1. List of notational conventions.

Variables/functions	Description
u; U	User u; set of all users U
$\pi_U \sim Dirichlet(s, n)$	Spam/Non-spam class label for users based on homepage
α^f	Dirichlet shape parameters (priors) for θ^f for each feature f
β	Dirichlet shape parameters (priors) for π_U of users
θ^f	Per class prob. of exhibiting the user behavior, for $f_1, \ldots, f_8$
π^f	The class each of a user's features belongs to, for $f_1, \ldots, f_8$
$n^{\pi ui}$	Counts of user u being assigned to i
$n_f^{\pi ui}$	Counts of feature f of user u being assigned to i
U^f	Total number of features f

non spam users. We first enumerate a set of user *reply features* and then consider *posting features* and *user features*. The relevant notational conventions are shown in Table 1.

User Reply Features: Replies here refer to the response of a user to the hot topic.

(1) ***Duplicate or Near Duplicate Comments (DUP):*** Spam teams often post multiple replies which are duplicate or near-duplicate with previous replies or others' replies under the same topic. Users that do not have any duplicate comments are referred to as *non-duplicate reply users*, and users that have posted duplicate or near-duplicate replies are called *duplicate or near-duplicate reply users*. To capture this phenomenon, the user's reply feature (f_{DUP}) is calculated as the number of duplicate comments on the same topic via cosine similarity. For a given user, f_{DUP} is the total number of all duplicate replies issued on the hot topic by the user.

(2) ***The Number of User's Replies (NUR):*** Unusually frequent response actions to specific postings constitutes abnormal behavior. Spammers often reply to others multiple times. The sentiment of their replies may also be biased towards one party, which causes many people to reply more and more. These sorts of behaviors can make the topic increasingly hot. We compute a feature f_{NUR}, the number of replies for the target set of postings for a given hot topic.

(3) ***The Number of Postings that the User Responded to (NMR):*** Responding to many postings for a hot topic may be considered abnormal. Spammers respond to many postings about a hot topic in order to support one relevant party with respect to the topic. Similar to the feature f_{NUR}, the feature f_{NMR} is the number of postings the user has responded to for the target set of postings for a given hot topic.

Posting Features: Posting features are based on all postings that a user has made within a given period, not just those related to hot topics being considered.

(4) **Ratio of Original Postings (ROP):** Very few original postings indicates abnormal behavior. Here, original postings refer to postings crafted by users themselves as opposed to repostings. We compute the ratio between original postings and total postings for each user.

(5) **Ratio of User Participating in the Postings about Topic and Voting (PTV):** Spammers tend to post or repost more topic postings and voting postings to highlight their own arguments as being correct.

(6) **Ratio of Postings Containing Keywords (CKW):** The ratio of a user's postings with topic-related keywords (e.g., for the Baoqiang Wang event, these include *Baoqiang Wang, Rong Ma, Zhe Song*, etc.). Spammers tend to post more postings related to hot topics as opposed to other topics. Hence, the ratio of postings containing relevant keywords tends to be higher for them.

User Features:

(7) **Whether the User Deletes all their Postings or is Banned a few months later (DBM):** Some users delete all postings within a certain period, which is also abnormal behavior. Others are banned by Sina. These features were used as spammer labels for supervised classification.

(8) **Ratio of Followers (ROF):** The ratio of the number of a user's followers and followees. Most spammers have fewer followers but more followees.

(9) **Sina Official Certification (SOC):** VIP users have a Sina Official certification. This feature is not considered for the model calculation, but serves as a marker to identify VIP users.

4.3   Process

Spam detection is influenced by replies for a particular hot topic, a user's replies on their posts and user features. We normalize continuous features in [0,1] and make them follow a Dirichlet distribution. This enables the model to capture finer-grained dependencies of user's spamming behavior. θ_k^f for each feature $f \in \{DUP, NUR, NMR, ROP, PTV, CKW, DBM, ROF\}$ denote the per cluster probability of f.

π_U (latent variables) represent the spamicity of a user u. The purpose of the model is learning the *spammers* and *common users*'s latent behavior distributions along with users' spamicity scores π_U. We now detail the generative process (Fig. 2).

4.4   Inference

In complex Bayesian models, exact inference is often difficult to deal with and an approximate method must be used. Gibbs sampling is a Markov chain Monte Carlo algorithm which we use in this paper, because it is easy to derive, the speed is comparable to other estimators, and converges to the global maximum in the limit.

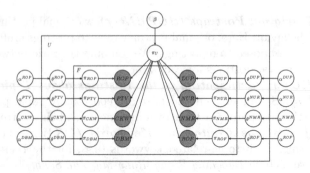

Fig. 2. Plate notation

Algorithm 1. The generation process for users.

1: **for** each cluster π_U **do**
2:    Draw a topic mixture distribution π_U from Dirichlet(β).
3: **for** each user $u \in U$ **do**
4:    **for** each feature $f \in \{1, \ldots, 8\}$ **do**
5:        Draw a multinomial distribution of features θ from Dirichlet(α)
6:        Draw topic assignment π_f from multinomial distribution (θ)
7:        Draw a feature f from topic mixture distribution π_U
8:        $f \in \{DUP, NUR, NMR, ROP, PTV, CKW, DBM, ROF\}$

In each Gibbs sampling iteration, we sample new assignments of π_U with the following equations:

$$p(\pi_U = i | \pi_U = -i) \propto (n^{\pi_{Ui}} + \gamma) \times \prod_f \frac{n_f^{\pi_{Ui}} + \alpha^f}{n^{\pi_{Ui}} + U^f \alpha^f}$$

$$f \in \{DUP, NUR, NMR, ROP, PTV, CKW, DBM, ROF\} \qquad (1)$$

Due to the conjugacy of the Beta (Dirichlet) and binomial (multinomial) distributions, we can integrate out $\theta^f, f \in \{DUP, NUR, NMR, ROP, PTV, CKW, DBM, ROF\}$, and π_U to obtain the equations by Gibbs sampling.

4.5   Hyperparameter EM

We learn hyperparameters α and β by Algorithm 2 that maximize the complete log-likelihood L of the model. We rely on variational optimization for maximization.

5   Experimental

As described in Sect. 4.1, our experiments focus on discovering the classification between common users, spammers and VIP users for a given hot topic. As it is challenging to determine such a classification based only on reply behavior for

---

Algorithm 2. Single-sample EM

Initialize:
1: Start with uninformed priors: $\alpha = 0.5, \beta = 0.5$
2: **repeat**
3:    Run Gibbs sampling to steady state Algorithm (1) using current values of α, β.
4:    Optimize using (4) and using (7)
5: **until** convergence of α, β

---

the hot topic, we also rely on a user's personal information and general postings on their homepage to assist in this assessment. Then, we classify the users by detecting the user's spamicities, that is to say, we generate the user's spamicities through all feature clustering.

5.1 Data

The topic *"Wang Baoqiang divorced"* stems from a posting published by the Chinese actor Baoqiang Wang on August 19, 2016. In this posting, he announced that he was divorcing his wife, Rong Ma, and sacking his agent, Zhe Song. He alleged that his marriage broke down after his wife had an affair with his agent, and that she had also transferred the couple's joint assets. In reaction to this, the posting was reposted and replied to 5 billion times, arousing widespread discussion in the social network.

For our experiments, we crawled the 440 most popular postings about the hot topic *"Wang Baoqiang divorce"*, as well as replies to these posting. We retrieved the replies from all relevant users. From these users' home pages, we then crawled the postings from August to December 2016, which is the most relevant time period for the hot topic *"Wang Baoqiang divorce"*. After data cleaning, we chose 2,000 users to conduct experiments. Their data was crawled in December 2016. The posting features are computed for the postings posted by a user from August to December 2016. In May 2017, we re-crawled the data again to check whether these users were banned or the topic-related postings were deleted.

5.2 Human Evaluation

As noted in Sect. 1, we don't have any gold-standard labeled data on spam teams' user. To assess the user *spamicity* computed, we rely on a human assessment. For this experiment, 15 people participated in the evaluation.

For this work, the judges are first briefed with many signals of opinion spam: The content is unrealistic and full of praise or degrading words. The content is a pure compliment to one party without refutation or is purely negative to the other party without counterarguments. The postings posted before and after do not match. For example, a user has reposted a microblog from Baoqiang Wang and replies "come on, Baby". From this one may conclude that the user is supporting Baoqiang Wang. However, the user used some insulting words to abuse Baoqiang Wang and support Rong Ma in *"Wang Baoqiang divorce"* topic.

It's important to note that the signals provided by previous work and domain experts are provided to the judges without aiming at prejudice, but for better judgment. It's difficult to make a determination by merely reading replies without any signals. It's also challenging for a person to come up with substantial numbers of heuristic signals on their own without extensive experience in detecting spammers.

Given a user, postings and their replies, the judges are asked to check the entire profile independently and provide a label for user's classification.

From these users, we selected 2000 users, including 500 spammers, 500 common users, 70 VIP users and some random users for our experiments. In our supervised experiments, among the spammers and common users, we used 300 for training and reserved 200 for testing, and among the VIP users, we used 50 for training and 20 for testing.

5.3   Generative Models: Model Variants

We focus on classifying users into common users and spammers by evaluating the users' spamicity scores via clustering based on a set of observed features. VIP users can be identified by the *ROF* and *SOC* features.

Model with Estimation (MEM). This setting estimates the hyperparameters $\alpha^f, f \in \{DUP, NUR, NMR, ROP, PTV, CKW, DBM, ROF\}$ and β using Algorithm 3, which learns hyperparameters α and β that maximize the complete log-likelihood L of the model.

SVM. We have manually marked some users, as described earlier in Sect. 5.2. Hence, we can use supervised support vector machines (SVM) as a baseline.

5.4   Results

For our unsupervised experiments, we selected the top 150 spamicities as spammers and the lowest 150 spamicities as common users as well as 60 VIP users. Then we divided the data into three groups randomly for human evaluation. Of course, we also evaluated all the marked data.

Table 2(a) shows the results of each randomization (as the number of users labeled correctly) and the last line is the evaluation of all the marked data. Table 2(b) reports the p, r, F_1 evaluation of using the average human evaluation results (except B_4). Based on Table 2(a) and (b), we note the following observations.

All three judges and the marked data perform similarly with just slight variations. This shows that the human judges have a fairly high degree of consensus. For all experiments, we find that the average recognition accuracy is relatively high and more balanced for buckets B_1, B_2, and B_3, which is in line with expectations. In summary, the proposed MEM is effective and performs better than baselines and other methods. SVM shows that the proposed behavioral features are effective.

Table 2. (a): Number of users detected in each bucket (B_1, B_2, B_3) correctly by each randomization (R_1, R_2, R_3). As the SVMs do not yield spamicity scores, the results are empty. The last line provides the evaluation of all users marked for the SVM baseline experiment across each method. B1:spammers, B2:common users, B3:VIP users. (b): P:Precision, R:Recall and F_1: F_1-Score of using the average human evaluation results, except B_3.

<table>
<tr><td align="center">(a)</td><td></td><td></td><td></td><td></td></tr>
</table>

(a)

	MEM			SVM		
	B_1	B_2	B_3	B_1	B_2	B_3
R_1	42	40	20			
R_2	39	39	20			
R_3	43	39	20			
AVG.	41.3	39.3	20			
total	406	388	70	162	110	18

(b)

	MEM		SVM	
	B_1	B_2	B_1	B_2
P	0.79	0.83	0.65	0.74
R	0.83	0.79	0.81	0.55
$F1$	0.81	0.81	0.72	0.63

5.5 Posterior Analysis of Each Feature

In addition to generate a spamicity score for users (π_U), the model also estimates the latent distributions of users' spamicity (θ^f) corresponding to each observed features f, which is as reflected in the spamicity. Therefore, it's meaningful to analyze the posterior θ^f for each feature f.

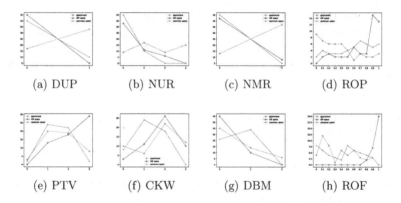

(a) DUP   (b) NUR   (c) NMR   (d) ROP

(e) PTV   (f) CKW   (g) DBM   (h) ROF

Fig. 3. The frequency distribution of arranged events.

Duplicate or Near Duplicate Comments (π^{DUP}). This behavior can detect certain kinds of sock puppets, where a team posts similar replies. In Fig. 3(a), 0 refers to textitnon-duplicate reply users and 1 refers to *duplicate or near-duplicate reply users*. From the densities, we note that many spammers have significant duplicate or near duplicate replies, whereas VIP users and common users have very few such duplicates or near-duplicates. This feature is in line with our expectations and has a very large contribution to the model.

The Number of User Replies (π^{NUR}). In Fig. 3(b), there are three kinds of users with NUR (N_u): 0 ($N_u = 0$), 1 ($0 < N_u \leq 5$), 2 ($5 < N_u \leq 10$), and 3 ($10 < N_u$). The peak of non-spammers' density curve is on the left of the plot, which shows that non-spammers have a lower value for NUR. Spammers generates an ascending curve has obtained a higher NUR value. In addition, the average number of replies of spammers is 9.5, 1.3 for common users and 1.5 for VIP users.

The Number of Postings that the User Responded to (π^{NMR}). This feature is very similar to DUP, as they are all boolean features and the curves are rather consistent. The difference is that almost all common users only reply to one posting and VIP users have a few users replying to more than one posting. This is because that some VIP users also act as spammers for a given hot topic.

Ratio of Original Postings (π^{ROP}). This feature counts the ratio between original postings and all postings. In Fig. 3(d), the scale of $0 \ldots 1$ refers to the ratio. We observe that, unlike previous behaviors, the peak of spammers' density curve is on the left, which shows that spammers have a lower value for ROP. VIP users have a very high percentage of original postings, averaging about 0.95, which means that almost all of their postings are original.

Ratio of Users Participating in the Postings about the Topic and Voting (π^{PTV}). In Fig. 3(e), for spammers, the peak value is smaller and the extreme value is greater than for common users, which indicates that the spammers' PTV values are not concentrated. This may be due to the fact that the number of spammers' followers is different, and spammers with a smaller number of followers tend to post comments instead of postings because their own postings or retweeted postings are not likely to attract more attention. It gave us a lot of inspiration, for example, VIP users may also play the role of spammers, this revelation prompted us to conduct further experiments and analysis.

Ratio of Containing Keywords (π^{CKW}). In Fig. 3(f), there are three kinds of users with CKW (N_k), 0 ($N_k = 0$), 1 ($0 < N_k \leq 5$), 2 ($5 < N_k \leq 100$) and 3 ($100 < N_k$). This feature is not consistent with the previous features. Common users reach their peak on the left, but spammers and VIP users reach theirs on the right. This means that most of the considered users post hot topic-relevant posts, except for common users.

Whether the User Deletes all their Postings or is Banned a few months later (π^{DBM}). In Fig. 3(g), 0 refers to users who have never been banned or deleted all of their postings, 1 refers to users who have been banned and 2 refers to users who delete the postings on their home page. As described in Sect. 5.4, users who have been banned are not typically spammers. However, users who delete all of their postings do tend to be spammers.

Ratio of Followers (π^{ROF}). This feature counts the ratio between followers and followees. In Fig. 3(h), values in $0 \ldots 1$ refer to this ratio. The curves are similar to the curves for ROP, in that the peak of spammers' density curve is on the left, whereas others have their peak toward the right. In other words, most spammers have fewer followers, and vice versa. Apart from this, VIP users have a very high percentage of followers.

6   How VIP Spammers Collaborate with Common Spammers

6.1   The Impact of Public Opinion by VIP Users

VIP Users in Spam Detection Model. We extracted the same features for 70 VIP users and used the previously trained spam detection model (MEM) to predict the *spamicity*. And we also evaluated these VIP users. The results are shown in Table 3.

Table 3. VIP users in MEM and human evaluation.

	MEM	Human evaluation
spammers	20	15
non − spammers	50	47
cadge the hot topic	0	8

Result. From the table, we can see that 20% of VIP users are spammers and 10% cadge the hot topic to attract others. This means that even a small number of VIP users participated in a hot topic, and some of these VIP users are still spammers.

Impact of VIP Users on the Hot Topic. As can be seen from the Fig. 4, VIP users have a greater impact on public opinion in the early days of a hot topic. As the topic deepens, the impact gradually decreases. When there are more serious incidents, the impact will increase again. (In Fig. 4, October 18, 2016 is the first trial of the "*Wang Baoqiang Divorce*" case. And on January 28, 2017, Baoqiang Wang's movie-Buddies in India-was released. In the two months prior to that, extensive publicity for the movie was carried out. The spammers accused him of using the divorce case to hype the new movie. This event greatly promoted hot topics.) In addition, we have found that public opinion in the later period always appears as a double peak, this is a manifestation of the mutual game between every party's spammers and fans of the hot topic.

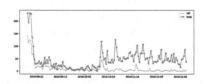

Fig. 4. posting amount of VIP users and all users involved in the event.

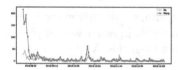

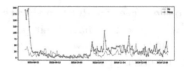

Fig. 5. Posting amount of Rong Ma and Baoqiang Wang's VIP users involved in the event.

Fig. 6. Posting amount of Rong Ma and Baoqiang Wang's spammers involved in the event.

6.2   The Impact of Public Opinion by Spammers

In Fig. 6, two indicative spamming periods have also emerged. The first one, from August 30 to September 20, was in favor of Ma. After witnessing a negative trend that lasted for several days, spammers supporting Wang launched a strong retaliatory campaign (including hiring or coincidence to attract spammers with an unidentifiable stand), which largely prevented the negative trend, until around October 18, when the divorce case first went to court. And with Wang's case of borrowing money to pay legal fees and other manipulating skills, his spammers have managed to control for more than 20 days. In other periods, it belongs to the game time of Wang and Ma's supporters, but overall, Baoqiang Wang has a greater advantage because he stands on the side of moral and legal justice.

6.3   Discussion

Comparing Fig. 6 to Fig. 5, whenever a related event occurs, VIP users will post postings and expand its influence. When the influence is expanded, spammers will hype on the basis of facts to guide public opinion. Through these figures and combining three periods specific posts, we discovered some spammers hyping methods:

Attack each other's weaknesses: Baoqiang Wang's supporters accused Rong Ma chiefly because she had an affair with Wang's agent and the source of economic income after marriage was Baoqiang Wang. The combination of these two conditions made people feel angry. Rong Ma's supporters primarily counterattacked Baoqiang Wang because he put their private affairs on the public platform for discussion, which greatly hurts their children, and the behavior he treated his wife like this is not sufficiently manly.

Combining what happened in the past and making speculations: Baoqiang Wang's supporters guessed that Baoqiang Wang's previous car accident was man-made disaster by Rong Ma and her intent was to try to gain Baoqiang Wang's property. However, Rong Ma and her supporters pointed out that at the beginning of 2016, Baoqiang Wang defrauded the company shares held by her, and he intended to transfer the premarital property.

Expanding individuals to groups, with the intent to arouse more resonance and support: Rong Ma represents family women who have no source of work or income and Baoqiang Wang represented individuals who struggled from the bottom to become individuals with a certain economic and social status. Therefore, their supporters send messages from these aspects to cause resonance and support among people in the same group.

Explaining the occurrence of new events in an exaggerated fashion to gain public sympathy: After exposing that Baoqiang Wang borrowed money to pay for legal fees, his supporters began to speculate that Rong Ma had taken away all their common assets. As a result, Baoqiang Wang had hundreds of millions of assets but could not afford legal fees. At the end of 2016, Baoqiang Wang publicized his new work-"Buddies in India". This incident became a reason why Rong Ma's supporters accused him of using family scandal to hype his new work and they said that Baoqiang Wang was so insidious and honesty was just his superficial image.

Talk about it everywhere and anywhere: Even if they are not releasing new events to fans, keep promoting the project. Send updates, ask for feedback, and do anything and everything to keep people talking about the upcoming release. They do whatever they can to attract others' attention.

7   Conclusions

This paper proposes a model to detect spammers in hot topics of Sina Weibo by using observed Sina Weibo users' posting behavior, and to examine the cooperative hyping among VIP users and spammers. The precision of the model affirmed the estimated characterization of spamming behavior. Based on precise detection of public opinion spammers and VIP users, a diachronic analysis about the cooperative hyping among VIP users and spammers on a widely noted case in China shows that such spam teams subtly manipulated public opinion on Sina Weibo, one of China's top social media platforms. This work sets the path toward new research on cooperative hyping, and potentially, on the social justice and well-being of society.

Acknowledgements. We would like to acknowledge the support provided by the National Key Research and Development Program of China (2017YFA0700601), the Key Research and Development Program of Shandong Province (2017CXGC0605, 2017 CXGC0604, 2018GGX101019, 2016GGX106001, 2016GGX101008, 2016ZDJS01A09), the Natural Science Foundation of Shandong Province for Major Basic Research Projects (No. ZR2017ZB0419), the Young Scholars Program of Shandong University, and the TaiShan Industrial Experts Program of Shandong Province (tscy20150305).

References

1. Beutel, A., Akoglu, L., Faloutsos, C.: Graph-based user behavior modeling: from prediction to fraud detection. In: ACM SIGKDD International Conference on Knowledge Discovery and Data Mining, pp. 2309–2310 (2015)
2. Chen, H., Liu, J., Lv, Y., Li, M.H., Liu, M., Zheng, Q.: Semi-supervised clue fusion for spammer detection in Sina Weibo. Inf. Fusion **44**, 22–32 (2017)
3. Chen, H., Liu, J., Mi, J.: SpamDia: spammer diagnosis in Sina Weibo microblog. In: EAI International Conference on Mobile Multimedia Communications, pp. 116–120 (2016)

4. Fakhraei, S., Shashanka, M., Shashanka, M., Getoor, L.: Collective spammer detection in evolving multi-relational social networks. In: ACM SIGKDD International Conference on Knowledge Discovery and Data Mining, pp. 1769–1778 (2015)
5. Fei, G., Mukherjee, A., Liu, B., Hsu, M., Castellanos, M., Ghosh, R.: Exploiting burstiness in reviews for review spammer detection (2013)
6. Feng, S., Banerjee, R., Choi, Y.: Syntactic stylometry for deception detection. In: Meeting of the Association for Computational Linguistics: Short Papers, pp. 171–175 (2012)
7. Feng, S., Xing, L., Gogar, A., Choi, Y.: Distributional footprints of deceptive product reviews (2012)
8. Hooi, B., Shin, K., Song, H.A., Beutel, A., Shah, N., Faloutsos, C.: Graph-based fraud detection in the face of camouflage. ACM Trans. Knowl. Discov. Data 11(4), 1–26 (2017)
9. Jindal, N., Liu, B.: Opinion spam and analysis, pp. 219–230 (2008)
10. Jindal, N., Liu, B., Lim, E.P.: Finding unusual review patterns using unexpected rules. In: ACM International Conference on Information and Knowledge Management, pp. 1549–1552 (2010)
11. Li, F., Huang, M., Yang, Y., Zhu, X.: Learning to identify review spam. In: International Joint Conference on Artificial Intelligence, pp. 2488–2493 (2011)
12. Li, H., et al.: Bimodal distribution and co-bursting in review spam detection. In: International Conference on World Wide Web, pp. 1063–1072 (2017)
13. Lim, E.P., Nguyen, V.A., Jindal, N., Liu, B., Lauw, H.W.: Detecting product review spammers using rating behaviors. In: ACM International Conference on Information and Knowledge Management, pp. 939–948 (2010)
14. Liu, Y., Zhang, J., Chen, J., Yin, M., Zhang, W.: Detection of hype groups based on mining maximum frequent itemsets in microblogs. Comput. Eng. Appl. (2017)
15. Ma, Y., Yan, N., Yan, R., Xue, Y.: Detecting spam on Sina Weibo. In: CCIS-13 (2013)
16. Mukherjee, A., Liu, B., Glance, N.: Spotting fake reviewer groups in consumer reviews. In: International Conference on World Wide Web, pp. 191–200 (2012)
17. Mukherjee, A., Liu, B., Wang, J., Glance, N., Jindal, N.: Detecting group review spam. In: International Conference Companion on World Wide Web, pp. 93–94 (2011)
18. Ott, M., Choi, Y., Cardie, C., Hancock, J.T.: Finding deceptive opinion spam by any stretch of the imagination, vol. 1, pp. 309–319 (2011)
19. Qiao, Y., Zhang, H., Yu, M., Zhang, Y.: Sina-Weibo spammer detection with GBDT. In: Li, Y., Xiang, G., Lin, H., Wang, M. (eds.) SMP 2016. CCIS, vol. 669, pp. 220–232. Springer, Singapore (2016). https://doi.org/10.1007/978-981-10-2993-6_19
20. Rayana, S., Akoglu, L.: Collective opinion spam detection: bridging review networks and metadata. In: ACM SIGKDD International Conference on Knowledge Discovery and Data Mining, pp. 985–994 (2015)
21. Wang, G., Xie, S., Liu, B., Yu, P.S.: Review graph based online store review spammer detection. In: IEEE International Conference on Data Mining, pp. 1242–1247 (2011)
22. Xie, S., Wang, G., Lin, S., Yu, P.S.: Review spam detection via temporal pattern discovery. In: ACM SIGKDD International Conference on Knowledge Discovery and Data Mining, pp. 823–831 (2012)
23. Zhang, J., Liu, Y., Luo, J., Dong, Y.: Hype user detection based on feature analysis in microblog. In: International Conference on Multimedia Information Networking & Security, pp. 140–143 (2013)

A Relationship-Based Pedestrian Social Groups Model

Guang-peng Liu[1,2,3], Hong Liu[1,2(✉)], and Liang Li[1,2]

[1] School of Information Science and Engineering, Shandong Normal University,
Jinan 250014, China
lhsdcn@126.com
[2] Shandong Provincial Key Laboratory for Distributed Computer Software
Novel Technology, Jinan 250358, China
[3] State Grid of China Technology College, Jinan 250002, China

Abstract. In the crowd evacuation process, pedestrians will produce self-organization phenomenon. Family members, friends and other closely related people will be formed group according to the degree of intimacy. The closer the relationship between people, the higher their aggregation in the group. Although the original social force model can simulate arching in the portals, "faster-is slower" and other phenomena. But in the process of movement, pedestrians are an isolated individuals, who have no association with the rest of surrounding people. This cannot truly reflect the group characteristics during crowd movement process. To simulate this pedestrian behavior in the process of movement, a social groups force model is proposed. However, the social groups model does not take the influence of strength of group membership on the group behavior into account. In view of the above shortcomings, this paper proposes a pedestrian social groups force model based on relationship strength. To consider the influence of the relationship strength on the group attribution force in the model, the model can reflect the features of pedestrian behaviors in the process of movement, and achieve a more efficient and more realistic crowd movement.

Keywords: Social groups · Pedestrian simulation · Social force model
Relationship

1 Introduction

During the development of urban areas, the personnel security issue in crowd intensive public places becomes increasingly serious. Studying the characteristics of crowd evacuation behavior and movement law, then assessing the ability of evacuation in public places is a suitable approach to solve the public security problem. There is been more or less contact between the people of the crowd. People's sociality makes independent people unable to exist independently from the society. Human behavior is governed by their internal psychological activity. Psychologically, most of the individuals in the crowd possess the so-called "herd mentality" features, which makes pedestrian usually spontaneously form a group during the process of movement. Therefore, setting appropriate inducing factors, according to this behavior, can effectively improve the evacuation speed of the crowd.

© Springer Nature Singapore Pte Ltd. 2019
Y. Sun et al. (Eds.): ChineseCSCW 2018, CCIS 917, pp. 257–271, 2019.
https://doi.org/10.1007/978-981-13-3044-5_19

In the process of crowd evacuation, pedestrians will have the self-organizing phenomenon [1, 2]. Pedestrian movement will be affected by the surrounding pedestrian, which can produce phenomenon like bottleneck swing, zipper effect, pedestrian stratification, Mexican wave and group movement [3] etc. At present, we mainly refer to the social psychology model [4]. In the group composed of several people, there is a certain inherent connection among the members. The connection can be divided into family relationships, friend relationships and colleague relationships. Individuals with different types of relationships compose families, friends and colleagues respectively. The intensity of the relationship gradually weakens. The movement of the members in the same group is similar. They will take the approach of mutual assistance, choosing similar walking routes as well as the same export targets. Also, they are able to maintain a certain aggregation in this process. In this way, loose individuals in a group become several small groups that are closely connected.

In order to make evacuation simulation results more realistic, in this paper, we considered the relationship between groups of pedestrian. Groups with large-scale crowd were used as the research object. We used a relationship coefficient to reflect the interaction strength between family members or friends in the process of evacuation. Based on the original pedestrian social groups force model, we proposed a modified pedestrian social groups force model based on relationship strength. It reflects the impact of relationship strength on the social groups attractive force in the model. The results show that the model has great potential to simulate the group behaviors of evacuation pedestrians, and achieve a more efficient and more realistic crowd movement.

The rest of this paper is structured as follows. Section 2 introduces some related works on simulation application of SFM and grouping behavior. Section 3 introduces the SFM and the modified pedestrian social groups model. Section 4 shows and analyzes the simulation results. Conclusion and future works are presented in Sect. 5.

2   Related Work

The security problem of carry out crowd evacuation research under the real scene is difficult to solve. Researchers started to use computer technology and virtual reality technology to simulate crowd movement to research the movement law and characteristics of crowd evacuation model. Researchers have come up with a series of crowd simulation system, such as EXODUS, Myriad, Pathfinder, Guarder [5–9], and etc.

There are two problems needed to be solved in studying the crowd evacuation model, which are path planning and collision avoidance. At present, there are two main types of evacuation models and the first one is macroscopic model. Henderson analogized pedestrian behavior into a gas or liquid molecules motion and proposed pedestrian traffic fluid mechanics model [10, 11]. Another is microscopic model. Helbing analyzed crowd panic then proposed social force model [12, 13]. He thought pedestrian behavior is the result of nonlinear interaction with the surrounding environment. Neuman proposed a cellular automaton model based on discrete model [14, 15]. This model is a dynamical system that divides time and space into discrete states.

2.1 Simulation Application of SFM

SFM has been adjusted to solve many evacuation problems [16–18]. In the crowd movement driven by social force model, Hou [19] introduced trained leaders which the number of leaders was equal to exits. Then analyze the effect of the number of the leaders and leaders' position settings on the crowd evacuation. Wang [20] introduced the exit attraction and the friends attraction while taking the impact of relative velocity on psychological forces into consideration. Shang [21] used self-adaptive ant colony optimization algorithm to choose the best route for movement.

Yang [22] put forward a crowd mechanical model for joining the leader in basic social forces. Individuals were attracted by the leader and move toward the leader's position. As a result, it realized the small-scale aggregation behavior of individuals and accelerated the crowd evacuation process.

The SFM can simulate arching in the portals, "faster-is-slower" and some other phenomena. But in the movement process, pedestrian in the model is an isolated individual that has not associated with the surrounding neighbors. Therefore, it can't truly reflect the group characteristics in the crowd movement.

2.2 Grouping Behavior

In the movement model, the introduction of the group concept can simulate the pedestrian behaviors more realistic. A pedestrian grouping behavior model was proposed based on the combination of microscopic model and some algorithm [23–25]. Through experiment [26, 27] extracted different characteristics to analyses behavior and define its communities.

Kang [28] extracted pedestrian group characteristics from the captured videos and concluded a data-driven pedestrian group behavior model by using machine learning algorithm. Musse [29] considered the influence of both group relationships and originated emergent behaviors on group behaviors. The combination of the group inter-relationship and the collision detection algorithm was used to simulate the behavior of the crowd.

Vizzari [30] established agent groups model by synthetically considering the individual's motive movement and the impact of the groups on individual. Qiu [31] modeled group structures by multi agent method and the simulation was carried out in a hallway. The experimental result showed that, with the intensity of action among the intra-group members and the inter-group members increasing, the movement efficiency of the population decreased.

Grouping behavior has been introduced in above method, but less considered the influence of strength of relationship between groups. Generally, closely related individuals converge more closely to smaller groups resulting in a group phenomenon. Thus, to reflect this influence in Sect. 3 we present a modified pedestrian social groups force model to simulate the group behavior in video surveillance.

3 Modified Pedestrian Social Groups Model

3.1 Original Social Force Model

The social force model was proposed by Helbing [12, 13]. Individual movement is driven by the resultant force includes: its own driving force, the force with other individual, the force with environment, etc. Social force model is based on Newtonian mechanics, and is a continuous micro-simulation model. According to Newton's second law, the mathematical expression of the force for individual can be described as follow:

$$m_i \frac{d\vec{v_i}(t)}{dt} = \vec{f_i^0} + \sum_{j(\neq i)} \vec{f_{ij}} + \sum_w \vec{f_{iw}} \qquad (1)$$

Where:

$$\vec{f_i^0} = m_i \frac{v_i^0(t)\vec{e_i^0}(t) - \vec{v_i}(t)}{\tau_i} \qquad (2)$$

$$\vec{f_{ij}} = \vec{f_{ij}^s} + \vec{f_{ij}^p} = A_i exp\left[\frac{r_{ij} - d_{ij}}{B_i}\right]\vec{n_{ij}} + kg\left(r_{ij} - d_{ij}\right)\vec{n_{ij}} + \kappa g\left(r_{ij} - d_{ij}\right)\Delta v_{ji}^t \vec{t_{ij}} \qquad (3)$$

$$\vec{f_{iw}} = A_i exp\left[\frac{r_i - d_{iw}}{B_i}\right]\vec{n_{iw}} + kg(r_i - d_{iw})\vec{n_{iw}} + \kappa g(r_i - d_{iw})\left(\vec{v_i} \cdot \vec{t_{iw}}\right)\vec{t_{iw}} \qquad (4)$$

For an individual i, m_i is the quality, $\vec{v_i}(t)$ is the current movement speed, $\vec{f_i^0}$ is the target driving force, v_i^0 indicates the desired speed of the individual moving towards to the desired direction $\vec{e_i^0}$, to adapt to the actual walking speed individual i need "relaxation time" τ_i, $\vec{n_{ij}} = \left(n_{ij}^1, n_{ij}^2\right) = (\vec{r_i} - \vec{r_j})/d_{ij}$ indicates the unit vector point from the individual j to the individual i, where $\vec{r_i}$ indicates the location of individual i, $\vec{t_{ij}} = \left(-n_{ij}^2, n_{ij}^1\right)$ indicates the tangential direction, $d_{ij} = \vec{r_i} - \vec{r_j}$, $\Delta v_{ji}^t = \left(\vec{v_j} - \vec{v_i}\right)\vec{t_{ij}}$ indicates the speed difference between two individual in tangential direction. A_i, B_i, k, κ, are constant.

3.2 Modified Social Groups Force Model

Human's social attribute determines there are social groups in the pedestrian flow. Between the social group members will produce some certain movement structure and movement relationship. If we do not consider the influence of group behavior to pedestrian speed, we may underestimate the evacuation time.

Analysis of relevant data found that in pedestrian flow the proportion of two to five walk together in groups is much higher than the proportion of independent walk. By analyzing the trajectory of the pedestrian activity, Moussaid [32] introduced the interaction force between the group members into the social model then generated the social groups force model. In the social groups model, the influence from three factors was considered: pedestrian's visual field, group center and repulsion among the group members. The force among the members of a social groups can be described by three forces: the visual force, the attractive force and the repulsive force among group members (Fig. 1).

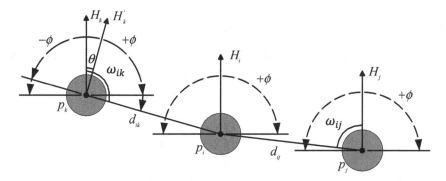

Fig. 1. Rotation angle of social group members.

Social Groups Visual Force. The gazing direction vector of pedestrian i, j, k are respectively H_i, H_j, H_k. The vision angle of pedestrian i is ϕ. It indicates the maximum range of gazing direction that pedestrian can observe to the left and right. Visual force shows the motivation to communicate with other members in the group. To realize the internal communication of the group members, the group members' head need to rotate the corresponding angle θ. Then the center member of social groups can be included in the vision field of group members. However, the greater the angle of head rotation θ is, the less comfort the member feels. In order to increase the comfort of members, members need to constantly adjust their position to enhance the ability of members of the group using visual language to communicate. In the movement process, the greater the angle of head rotation of pedestrian i is, the less comfort he feels when walking. Therefore, the pedestrian i constantly adjust his position through visual force to reduce the rotation angle of the head. And increase the comfort level.

Social Groups Attractive Force. In the initial social force model, the forces between pedestrians are exactly the same, which does not match with the real situation. The social groups attractive force reflects the aspiration of the members in social groups not to deviate from the social groups center. It can be able to distinguish between friends and strangers. The social groups attractive force direction points to the center of the social groups. The magnitude of the force increases with the distance between the social groups' center and the individual.

Social groups force model that proposed by Moussaid makes a distinction between different types of pedestrian movement and reflects the behavior of the group. The model didn't base on the strength of relationship between the members of the group to consider the interaction between the individual. In the pedestrian flow, the aggregation degree for close relationship pedestrian is always higher than estranged relationship pedestrian. Reflecting into the model can be expressed as the greater the relationship value the greater the attractive force of the individual is. Moreover, it has added the contact force in the initial social force model, there is no need to repeatedly add. Integrated above deficiencies, a modified social groups model is proposed. Social groups member i are subjected to group forces which mathematical expression as shown in (5), (6), and (8).

$$\overrightarrow{f_i^{group}} = \overrightarrow{f_i^{vis}} + \overrightarrow{f_i^{att}} \tag{5}$$

In a social groups with N members, social groups visual force of individual i can be expressed as:

$$\overrightarrow{f_i^{vis}} = -m_i \varphi\left(\overrightarrow{V_i}, \overrightarrow{V_h}\right) \beta_1 \theta_i \overrightarrow{V_i} \tag{6}$$

$$\varphi\left(\overrightarrow{V_i}, \overrightarrow{V_h}\right) = \begin{cases} 0, & \omega < 90° \\ 1, & \omega > 90° \end{cases} \tag{7}$$

Where β_1 is a parameter that indicating the social interaction strength between group members. $\overrightarrow{V_i}$ is the current velocity vector of pedestrian i. θ_i is head rotation angle of pedestrian i that is after gazing direction of pedestrian i rotate θ_i the center member can be included in the vision field. Select an individual who has the nearest distance with $C_i' = \frac{1}{n}\sum_{j=1}^{n} P_j$ as a group center C_i. ω is the angle between gazing direction of pedestrian i and line connecting from i to group center C_i. If $\omega > \frac{\pi}{2}$ indicates that C_i is not in the visual field of pedestrian i. Pedestrian i is subjected to social groups visual force. Otherwise if $\omega \le \frac{\pi}{2}$ indicates that C_i is in the visual field of pedestrian i. Pedestrian i is not affected by the social groups visual force.

In reality, there are some relationships between the people of the crowd such as families, friends, colleagues or strangers. These relationships divide people into small groups and different groups have different relationships. In order to quantify the relationship in the pedestrian flow, we define a hyperparameter λ ([0, 1]) [25, 35] to represent the degree of relationship. The value of the relationship between pedestrian i and j is defined as follows:

$$\lambda_{ij} = \begin{cases} 0.7 \sim 0.999, & i \, and \, j \, are \, relatives \\ 0.4 \sim 0.699, & i \, and \, j \, are \, friends \\ 0.001 \sim 0.399, & i \, and \, j \, are \, colleagues \\ 0, & i \, irrelavant \, with \, j \end{cases} \tag{8}$$

The expression of social groups attractive force:

$$\overrightarrow{f_i^{att}} = \lambda_{ic} f(d_{ic}, d_{th}) \beta_2 \overrightarrow{U_{ic}} \tag{9}$$

Where β_2 is a parameter indicating the strength of attraction force between members of social groups. $\overrightarrow{U_{ic}}$ is the unit vector pointing from pedestrian i to the center of a social groups C_i.$f(d_{ic}, d_{th}) = \begin{cases} 0, d_{ic} \le d_{th} \\ 1, d_{ic} > d_{th} \end{cases}$, d_{ic} is the distance between pedestrian i and C_i, threshold $d_{th} = \frac{N-1}{2}$. λ_{ic} is the relationship value between pedestrian i and C_i. The closer the relationship, the greater the value of the weight is. The value of the relationship is defined as follows:

After the modified of the model, individual is subjected to forces as shown in Eq. (10):

$$m_i \frac{d\overrightarrow{v_i}(t)}{dt} = \overrightarrow{f_i^0} + \sum_{j(\ne i)} \overrightarrow{f_{ij}} + \sum_w \overrightarrow{f_{iw}} + \overrightarrow{f_i^{group}} \tag{10}$$

According to their own force situation, individual in a group use the Eq. (10) to calculate its acceleration. The displacement of each step of the individual is obtained after conversion to the speed. Then it realizes the movement of individuals in the scene. The same time as independent individuals not bound by other people's social relations, it does not have a group behavior and movement only reflects the personal behavior.

4   Simulation Results

Through the analysis of surveillance video, we found the individual in the process of movement generated a phenomenon gathered into a group. In which closely related individuals converge more closely to smaller groups resulting in a group phenomenon. The surveillance video in Fig. 2 shows that the group phenomenon had always been existing in the whole movement process. In this paper, through the design of simulation experiments we illustrated the modified pedestrian social groups model can more realistic, more efficient simulated crowd movement.

Fig. 2. Surveillance video.

4.1 Initialization

As can be seen from the surveillance video, near the door can be divided into three regions: the center region of the door, left region of the door, right region of the door. Pedestrians near the exit would choose one of these regions to evacuate. Therefore, for simulating the crowd movement more realistic, the group number was defined as *Groupnum = Doornum * 3*. At the same time, it was stipulated that there need contain at least one family in a group. The number of family members was two, three, four and five. Different family members in the group were defined as friends. Different group members in the groups were defined as colleagues.

Individuals with kinship, friends, colleagues, and isolated individuals with no relationship to all individuals in a group were defined in a group in order to more realistically reflect social relationship characteristics of groups. Assumed that there are 20% of individuals did not contain social relations in a group. The relationship values between the individual were generated in accordance with the definition (9). Divided grid for the scene plane area and then the position of the individual was initialized in a grid. Meanwhile, in order to more real simulate the initial state of the group, a certain number of adjacent grids were merged into one region. The position of the same group was initialized in one region.

The relationships between individuals need to be stored in the corresponding data structure. Figure 3 defines the data structure for storing relational node. Figure 4 defines the data structure of the relational linked list node which is used to store the relationship values between individual and other individuals.

individual No.	Relationship Value

Fig. 3. Relational node.

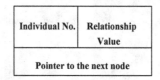

Fig. 4. Linked list node.

In order to describe the process of grouping entire region more detailed, the individual data structures are defined. Individual data structure with the C ++-like language described as follows:

(1) Individual coordinates data structure

```
Struct
{
double dx;
double dy;
} d2dfiled;
```

(2) Individual data structure

```
Struct HMFV_Particle
{
    Ldbl  *lv; // relationship value linked list
    d2dfiled d_pos;//x-axis and y-axis coordinates of the
individual
    double rav;// means of the relationship values
between individual and other individuals
int ord; //individual order
    int group;//individual group number
} Particle;
```

4.2 Emulation Experiment

For verifying the effectiveness of the modified model in this paper and enhance the visualization effect of simulation experiment, and to reflect its practical application value, this paper designed multi groups simulation experiments. In the experiment, the individual information of the same coordinate was read every time. This ensured the consistency of the individual initialization position. The experiment was carried out in a crowd evacuation simulation system designed by ourselves. We used Visual Studio 2012+OSG as the development tool, in Windows7 environment development implementation [17]. The simulation experiment parameters were set as follows (Table 1):

Table 1. The pedestrian and model properties parameters.

Parameters name	Parameter values or range
Pedestrian radius	$r = 0.25$ m
Pedestrian mass	$m = 80$ kg
Desired velocity	$v_i^0 = 0.8$ m s^{-1}
Social force model parameter	$k = 1.2 \times 10^5$ kg s^{-2}
	$\kappa = 2.4 \times 10^5$ kg m^{-1} s^{-1}
	$A = 2000$ N
	$B = 0.08$ m
	$C = 2000$ N
	$D = 0.05$ m

4.3   Simulation Results Analysis

In this paper, the crowd evacuation was simulated in a double-exit room scene. Figures 5 and 6 respectively show the simulation movement process of 200 individuals in the original model and the modified model. Different groups of individuals in the experiment used the color and the style of clothes worn by the individual to distinguish. The individual of the different families in the group used the color and style of the hat worn by the individual to distinguish.

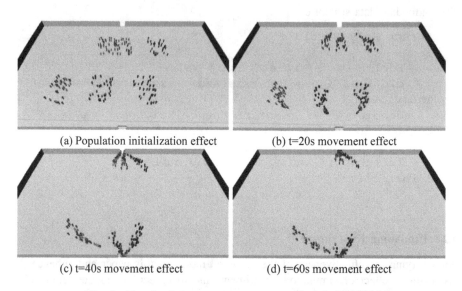

(a) Population initialization effect   (b) t=20s movement effect

(c) t=40s movement effect   (d) t=60s movement effect

Fig. 5. The simulation movement process of original model.

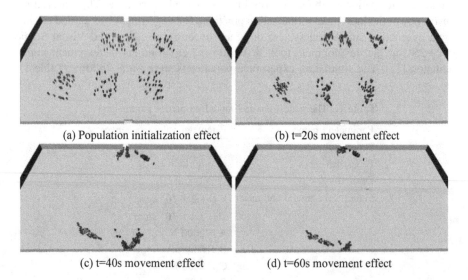

(a) Population initialization effect   (b) t=20s movement effect

(c) t=40s movement effect   (d) t=60s movement effect

Fig. 6. The simulation movement process of modified model

Figure 6a is the initialization effect diagram. The same group of individuals are initialized in a certain range of regions. b, c and d are the effect diagram of group movement of 20 s, 40 s and 60 s respectively. Compared with the state at the same time in Fig. 5, in the process of the whole movement individuals with the same clothing color and style are gradually aggregating. While the individuals which have same color and style of clothes and hats also show aggregation tendency. As individuals with family relationships have larger relationship value than individuals with other types of relationships. The attractive force between family relationships is larger than between other types of relationships. Therefore the aggregating rate between family individuals is higher than between individuals with other types of relationships. The experimental effect well simulates the grouping phenomena appearing in the video. While it is found that the population forms an arch near the exit. Which reflecting the phenomenon in the crowd movement that faster is slower. As shown in the Fig. 7, the effect diagram for the movement of the 1000 individuals in the Matlab. Individuals forming an arch near the exit.

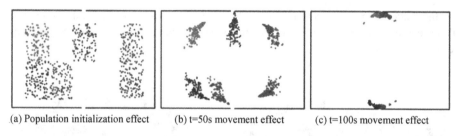

(a) Population initialization effect   (b) t=50s movement effect   (c) t=100s movement effect

Fig. 7. Movement effect in matlab

To reflect the influence of this method on crowd motion, experiments were conducted on a population size from 100 to 1000 respectively. Each group carried out twenty groups of experiments. Then we obtained the average evacuation time of the crowd including different proportions of isolated individuals, see Fig. 8.

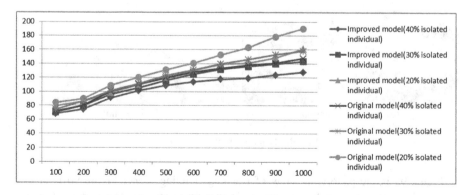

Fig. 8. Average evacuation time

Through the surveillance video, in the case of a certain number of exits with the increasing of individuals, they take more time to evacuate through those exits, in accordance with. From the data analysis in the Fig. 8, with the increasing in the number of individual, groups in both models need more time to complete the evacuation. In the groups with same scale, the evacuation time of our modified model is shorter than the original social force model, which indicates that the modified model can truly improve the evacuation efficiency of the population. While the larger the population size, the more obvious this model for the improvement of evacuation efficiency can be. With the total number of isolated individuals reduced, the evacuation time of groups increased accordingly. This is because the same group of individuals in the evacuation process will first mutual coordination before evacuation, resulting in evacuation efficiency of groups reduced. The result is consistent with the cognition pattern, and more accurately simulate the reality situation.

It is worth noting that the crowd evacuation efficiency increases nearly linearly with the increasing of the number of pedestrians. The reason for this phenomenon is that the evacuation efficiency mostly depends on the pedestrians number, and it is also discussed in literatures [25, 34].

In addition, the modified model algorithm is applied to the teaching building model. The scene and characters are rendered under the 3D simulation platform. Simulation results are shown in Fig. 9.

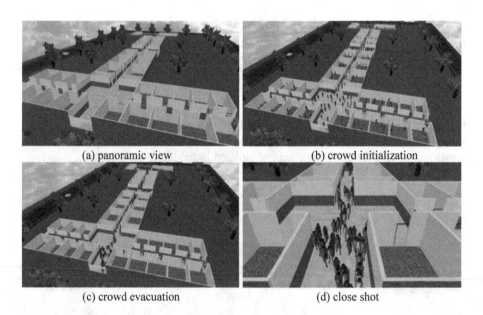

(a) panoramic view   (b) crowd initialization

(c) crowd evacuation   (d) close shot

Fig. 9. Teaching building scenet

Figure 9a is the panoramic view of teaching building scene. Figure 9b is crowd initialization effect. Figure 9c is an effect diagram for evacuation to a certain moment.

Figure 9d is a close shot for evacuation to a certain moment. From Fig. 9c and d can be seen individuals with the same clothing color, that is friends show aggregation trend in the movement. The trend of relatives gathered more obvious and then take into account each other to evacuate jointly to a safe area. A more realistic simulation result has been realized.

It is necessary to notice that modifying the social force model by introducing new forces can simulate the evacuation crowd movement, and is validated in literatures [33–35]. For example, Liu.et al. extracted motion data from video to establish a video data-driven social force model and simulated group movement. Therefore, it is feasible to use the group attribution force to modify the social force model for simulating the group movement, which is shown in the simulation results in this paper.

5   Conclusion

In this paper, a relationship-based pedestrian social groups model is proposed to simulate the group behavior in video surveillance, and the main contributions are summarized as follows:

1. A modified pedestrian social groups force model is proposed to simulate group movement. In the model, we used a relationship coefficient to reflect the relationship strength between individuals in group during the evacuation process and considered the influence of the relationship strength on the social groups attractive force.
2. The simulation experiment added the relationship-based pedestrian social groups model into the 3D simulation experimental platform. Through a high quality and visible way to show a real and vivid crowd evacuation simulation movement, the validity and feasibility of the model are verified, and a more realistic simulation result is achieved. In this manner, it provides a new approach to solve the group problem in emergency crowd evacuation.
3. Multi groups simulations were designed to verify the effectiveness of the proposed approach in this paper.
4. The experimental result show that this modified pedestrian social groups force model has realized the aggregation of individuals with close social relationships during the evacuation process and has modified the group evacuation efficiency. The next step is to extract the pedestrian's coordinates and motion trails from the video, to further improve the relationship-based model of pedestrian social groups and achieve a more realistic simulation result.

Acknowledgments. This research is supported by the National Natural Science Foundation of China (61472232, 61572299, 61373149 and 61402270) and by the Project of Taishan scholarship.

References

1. Porzycki, J., Mycek, M., Lubaś, R., Wąs, J.: Pedestrian spatial self-organization according to its nearest neighbor position. Transp. Res. Procedia **2**(2), 201–206 (2014)
2. Miguel, A.F.: The emergence of design in pedestrian dynamics: locomotion, self-organization, walking paths and constructal law. Phys. Life Rev. **10**(2), 168–190 (2013)
3. Deb, S., Strawderman, L., Dubien, J., Smith, B., Carruth, D.W., Garrison, T.M.: Evaluating pedestrian behavior at crosswalks: validation of a pedestrian behavior questionnaire for the U.S. population. Accid. Anal. Prev. **106**, 191–201 (2017)
4. Sakuma, T., Mukai, T., Kuriyama, S.: Psychological model for animating crowded pedestrians. Comput. Animat. Virtual Worlds **16**(3–4), 343–351 (2005)
5. EXODU. http://fseg.gre.ac.uk. Accessed 28 Dec 2016
6. Myriad. http://www.crowddynamics.com. Accessed 2 Mar 2017
7. Pathfinder. http://www.thunderheadeng.com/pathfinder. Accessed 10 May 2018
8. Wang, Z., Mao, T., Jiang, H., Xia, S.: Guarder: virtual drilling system for crowd evacuation under emergency scheme. J. Comput. Res. Dev. **47**(6), 969–978 (2010)
9. Gomez-Sanz, J., Pax, R., Arroyo, M., Cárdenas-Bonett, M.: Requirement engineering activities in smart environments for large facilities. Comput. Sci. Inf. Syst. **14**, 3 (2017)
10. Henderson, L.F.: On the fluid mechanics of human crowd motion. Transp. Res. **8**(6), 509–515 (1974)
11. Wen, J., Tian, H.H., Xue, Y.: Lattice hydrodynamic model for pedestrian traffic with the next-nearest-neighbor pedestrian. Acta Phys. Sin. **59**(6), 3817–3823 (2010)
12. Helbing, D., Johansson, A., Al-Abideen, H.Z.: Dynamics of crowd disasters: an empirical study. Phys. Rev. E Stat. Nonlinear Soft Matter Phys. **75**(2), 046109 (2007)
13. Helbing, D., Johansson, A.: Pedestrian, crowd, and evacuation dynamics. Encycl. Complex. Syst. Sci. **16**, 697–716 (2012)
14. Von Neumann, J.: The general and logical theory of automata. In: Papers of John Von Neumann on Computing & Computer Theory, vol. 1, no. 41, pp. 1–2 (1951)
15. Chen, C.K., Li, J., Zhang, D.: Study on evacuation behaviors at a t-shaped intersection by a force-driving cellular automata model. Physica A **391**(7), 2408–2420 (2012)
16. Johansson, A., Helbing, D., Shukla, P.K.: Specification of the social force pedestrian model by evolutionary adjustment to video tracking data. Adv. Complex Syst. **10**(Supp 02), 271–288 (2007)
17. Zeng, W., Nakamura, H., Chen, P.: A modified social force model for pedestrian behavior simulation at signalized crosswalks. Procedia Soc. Behav. Sci. **138**, 521–530 (2014)
18. Han, Y., Liu, H.: Modified social force model based on information transmission toward crowd evacuation simulation. Physica A **469**, 499–509 (2016)
19. Hou, L., Liu, J.G., Pan, X., Wang, B.H.: A social force evacuation model with the leadership effect. Physica A **400**(2), 93–99 (2014)
20. Wang, L., Cai, Y., Xu, Q.: Modifications to social force model. J. Nanjing Univ. Sci. Technol. **35**(1), 144–149 (2011)
21. Shang, R., Zhang, P., Zhong, M.: Investigation and analysis on evacuation behavior of large scale population in campus ✰. Procedia Eng. **52**(7), 302–308 (2013)
22. Yang, X., Dong, H., Wang, Q., Chen, Y., Hu, X.: Guided crowd dynamics via modified social force model. Physica A **411**(10), 63–73 (2014)
23. Xi, H., Son, Y.J., Lee, S.: An integrated pedestrian behavior model based on extended decision field theory and social force model. In: Rothrock, L., Narayanan, S. (eds.) Human-in-the-Loop Simulation: Methods and Practice, pp. 824–836. Springer, London (2010). https://doi.org/10.1007/978-0-85729-883-6_4

24. Lu, L., Chan, C.Y., Wang, J., Wang, W.: A study of pedestrian group behaviors in crowd evacuation based on an extended floor field cellular automaton model. Transp. Res. C Emerg. Technol. **81**, 317–329 (2016)
25. Li, Y., Liu, H., Liu, G.P., Li, L., Moore, P., Hu, B.: A grouping method based on grid density and relationship for crowd evacuation simulation. Physica A **473**, 319–336 (2017)
26. Julien, P., Cretual, A.: Experiment-based modeling, simulation and validation of interactions between virtual walkers. In: ACM Siggraph/Eurographics Symposium on Computer Animation, pp. 189–198. ACM, New Orleans (2009)
27. Gonzalez-Pardo, A., Rosa, A., Camacho, D.: Behaviour-based identification of student communities in virtual worlds. Comput. Sci. Inf. Syst. **11**(1), 195–213 (2014)
28. Kang, H.L., Choi, M.G., Hong, Q., Lee, J.: Group behavior from video: a data-driven approach to crowd simulation. In: ACM Siggraph/Eurographics Symposium on Computer Animation, vol. 2007, pp. 109–118. ACM, San Diego (2007)
29. Musse, S.R., Thalmann, D.: A model of human crowd behavior: group inter-relationship and collision detection analysis. In: Thalmann, D. (ed.) Computer Animation and Simulation 1997. EUROGRAPH, pp. 39–51. Springer, Vienna (1997). https://doi.org/10.1007/978-3-7091-6874-5_3
30. Vizzari, G., Manenti, L., Crociani, L.: Adaptive pedestrian behaviour for the preservation of group cohesion. Complex Adapt. Syst. Model. **1**(7), 1–29 (2013)
31. Qiu, F., Hu, X.: Modeling group structures in pedestrian crowd simulation. Simul. Model. Pract. Theory **18**(2), 190–205 (2010)
32. Moussaïd, M., Perozo, N., Garnier, S., Helbing, D., Theraulaz, G.: The walking behaviour of pedestrian social groups and its impact on crowd dynamics. PLoS ONE **5**(4), e10047 (2010)
33. Liu, B., Liu, H., Zhang, H., Qin, X.: A social force evacuation model driven by video data. Simul. Model. Pract. Theory **84**, 190–203 (2018)
34. Liu, H., Liu, B., Zhang, H., Li, L., Qin, X., Zhang, G.: Crowd evacuation simulation approach based on navigation knowledge and two-layer control mechanism. Inf. Sci. **436–437**, 247–267 (2018)
35. Qin, X., Liu, H., Zhang, H., Liu, B.: A collective motion model based on two-layer relationship mechanism for bi-direction pedestrian flow simulation. Simul. Model. Practice Theory **84**, 268–285 (2018)

Socio-Technical System Design Framework for People with Disability

Peng Liu[1,2,3], Tun Lu[1,2,3(✉)], and Ning Gu[1,2,3]

[1] School of Computer Science, Fudan University, Shanghai, China
Liudongping0202@163.com, {lutun, ninggu}@fudan.edu.cn
[2] Shanghai Key Laboratory of Data Science, Fudan University, Shanghai, China
[3] Shanghai Institute of Intelligent Electronics and Systems, Shanghai, China

Abstract. In view of the challenges encountered in the study of the disability system design and the physical and psychological particularity of the disabled, this paper presents a social - technical system design framework for people with disability. The framework is a whole system design process which includes from data collection to behavior analysis, from system design to model mapping. The innovation of this work lies in the following aspects: this framework is used to closely combine social and technological contents at both social and technological levels, to extract design principles based on the new findings of people with disability. It maps the design model of the system based on the theory of social-technical system design, and to obtain the system log and observation data of disabled representatives using the participatory design method. This framework was designed and implemented several service systems for people with disability. It already has more than 1000 disabled users and collected several hundreds of thousands of data.

Keywords: Socio-technical · People with disability · System design
Grounded theory

1 Introduction

Currently, the number of people with disabilities in China is more than 85 million, and the number of disabled families even reaches 17.8% of the total number of households in the country, which means every one in five families around us is a disabled family. With the continuous progress and development of the society, the living condition of the disabled has received more and more attention from the government and the society. Research on the disabled group and related service has always been the research hotspots of computer supported cooperative work, social computing, and human computer interaction fields; utilizing technical means to improve the independence of people with disabilities is worth study [5, 7], but few studies has focused on the self-exploration of the disabled groups to assist them gain more independence. The difference between the disabled group and the ordinary leaves them own special social fact, therefore when analyzing and designing service system aiming to assist people with disabilities to gain more independence, not only key technics and algorithms should be implemented, but also more considerations should be taken for the physical

© Springer Nature Singapore Pte Ltd. 2019
Y. Sun et al. (Eds.): ChineseCSCW 2018, CCIS 917, pp. 272–284, 2019.
https://doi.org/10.1007/978-981-13-3044-5_20

and mental factors of the disabled. Though researchers begin to show interests in social analysis of the disabled community [1, 2], the issues of how to improve the self-independence of people with disabilities, how to explain the reasons behind the behavior of the disabled with the combination of technical facets, understanding the motivation of the self-reliance of the disabled group, and how to design service systems for the people with disabilities to assist them to achieve the goal of self-reliance all remain to be solved.

In view of the above challenges, this paper proposes a social technology system design framework for the disabled group. Within the framework, we adopted Grounded Theory [24] widely used in qualitative study as main method and theoretical basis to study the social factors of the disabled, understanding and analyzing their daily behavior with the combination of data mining, natural language processing, interaction technics. From data collection to data analysis and then to the system design, every period is fully combined with social and technical factors, to obtain the new behavior pattern of the disabled and utilize these findings to help with system model design, making the design of service system better satisfying the needs of the disabled group, meanwhile providing ways for achieving self-reliability.

In summary, the main contribution of this paper is listed below:

(1) It proposes a social-technical system design framework based on the Grounded Theory, from data collection to behavior analysis, then to system design, all periods are closely combined with social and technical contents, making the factors related to both sides to co-act, complement with each other, providing ways for people with disabilities to achieve self-reliability.

(2) It proposes a method to transform social discoveries and behavior patterns to the design of social-technical systems for people with disabilities.

(3) With the close combination of social and technical analysis methods, we introduce the participatory design and system interaction methods to achieve the fast iterations of the prototype system within the framework, solving the problems of the particularity of interactions among the disabled group and the individualized demands.

With the proposed the disabled community oriented social-technical system design framework, multiple service systems for the disabled has been designed and implemented, the number of users with disabilities is more 1000, and hundreds of thousands of related data has been collected. We will discuss the key methods and content of this design framework with details in the following sections.

2 Related Work

2.1 Analysis Framework Based on Grounded Theory

Grounded Theory was first proposed by Barney Glaser and Anselm Strauss in the 60 s of last century, and then through the continuous improvement and formed a set of mature social analysis method. The whole method is composed of the following steps: first, the original scattered data are arranged into open coding, which disrupted the original data and reassemble the data without personal bias to form a new classification. Then the correlative coding is carried out, that is, we explore in great depth the relationship between data classification and establish correlation. Finally, core coding is carried out, that is, according to the correlation relationship through continuous comparison and screening, finally select a core classification which should be related to the most data classification and in order to expand into the new theory [24]. In recent years, many user behavior analysis framework based on this theory were proposed. Wang presents a user behavior analysis system in new Media field, he used it to analysis the users experience and got some suggestion [29]. Zhang used grounded theory in across Social Medias research to analysis how people use internet [30]. These works mainly use this method to analyze users' online behavior, but there is no analysis on the relationship between offline and online. This paper integrates the grounded theory with computational technology analysis method to analyze not only online behavior also offline behavior of the people with disability. The technological and social factors can be effectively combined verified by each other, and the interaction analysis can be used to obtain the behavior pattern and social findings of people with disabilities.

2.2   Behavior Analysis and System Design for People with Disabilities

In the field of computer science and technology, the behavior analysis and system design of people with disabilities mainly research how to use technology and design for compensation. Kristen Shinohara and Josh Tenenberg conducted a 12-hour study and analysis on Sara's home life who is a blind school student, and find that the assistive devices should be easy to control, portable, flexible and interactive [3]. Meg Cramer et al. observed how autistic patients learn with the assistive system in school [4]. For visually impaired people, researchers designed tactile feedback and touchable tablets and watches to get information on screen [5, 6], they also made a hand-held geographic information feedback system that indicate directions by vibrations [7], indoor navigation system with touchable tags [8], and photograph and photo sharing system [9]. The researchers designed mobile social applications for the people with abnormal communication to expand their social network [10, 11], and also designed social emotional analysis systems to help them understand other people's potential awareness in communication with others [12].

In recent years, more and more attention has been paid to social factors in disability studies, which also provides new ways for the design of behavior analysis and service system for the disabled. Liu et al. used qualitative methods to analysis the online and offline social behaviors of extremity disability found that disabled people are more willing to integrate into society in a small group way [13]. Jennifer Mankoff et al. proposed the concept of a cultural model which was composed of everyone's unique experience to guide the design of accessories [14]. Erin Buehler et al. adopted the design concept of open source and sharing, designed and analyzed the open source community of assistive devices for the disabled and provided a new approach for the development and innovation of assistive devices for the disabled [15]. Sun proposed a kind of socio-technical analysis method for vulnerable groups to explain and analysis the relationship between vulnerable groups and technology [28].

Through the above mentioned in the introduction of the behavior analysis and system design of people with disabilities, we can find that the social finding and social theory derived from behavior analysis of people with disabilities were too conceptual to apply to system for people with disabilities. In most research of people with disabilities, the social factor and technical factor are relatively independent of each other, even the two factors are combined, the focus also is the relationship between the group and technology, the way to support people with disabilities help themselves and full participate in society is still underexplored.

3 Social-Technical System Design Framework for People with Disabilities

In this paper, we proposed a social-technical system design framework for people with disabilities, which is based on grounded theory as the theoretical and combines data mining, natural language processing, interactive design and other technologies. It comes from two aspects of social and technology work together and help people with disabilities achieve self-reliance. The whole framework includes three parts: data collection, data analysis and system design (Fig. 1).

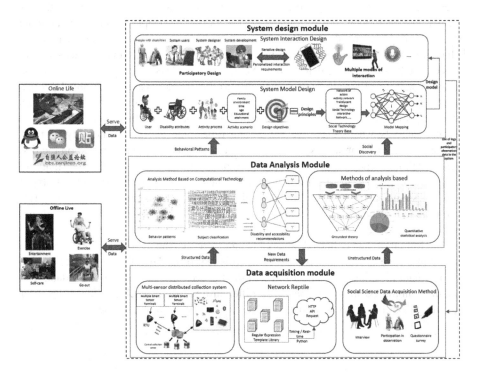

Fig. 1. Social-technical system design framework for people with disabilities

We form a process which can from collecting online data and offline data to constructing a system prototype for people with disabilities by using our system design framework. In each module, the social and technical aspects are well integrated, complementary and supportive to each other. The behavior pattern and new social findings of people with disabilities obtained by our framework analysis can be used to improve or design a new service system for people with disabilities.

3.1   Data Collection

To fully understand the daily life of disabled people and obtain their unique social facts, we need to obtain data from both online and offline. According to the characteristics of daily activities of disabled people, the method based on scene division is used to extract different activity information in different scenes and form the continuous social activities with time series annotation.

Scenario-Based Data Collection Method of People with Disabilities. Due to the psychological and physiological defects, the disabled people's social facts in daily life are totally different, and their life scene is relatively simple and fixed. Based on these characteristics, this paper proposes a Scenario-based data collection method for disabled people. The scene mentioned in this paper mainly refers to the environment where the disabled people perform social activities. Scenes and behavioral activities interact with each other. For example, a severely disabled people who is alone at home on a rainy day will need to contact others to help them close the window, then the behavior activity of closing the window changes the indoor environment, thus showing the continuity of behavioral activities. So the scene plays an important role in the behavior activity of the disabled. According to the characteristics of disabled people, we define the scenes of their activities as indoor, outdoor and online. The indoor scenes refer to indoors environment such as their home, disabled rehabilitation centers, or disabled schools where they live for a long time. Due to limited mobility of most disable people, outdoor scenes mainly refer to a small range of outing based on the first scene. Online scenes refer to disabled community and chat application that are designed friendly to use for disabled people. Then we can collect different data types such as sound intensity, muscle strength, position, chat record, and accessories according to the characteristics of disabled people in different scenarios. The details are show in Fig. 2.

The format of data collected is variable and there may be data noise due to the large variety of offline data in which most of them is real-time. Therefore, it is necessary to perform data cleaning and data format unified processing on the collected data. The post-data should be structured based on different dimensions such as time series, user tags, and disability types to ensure the indexing of behavioral activities.

Data Collection Based on Grounded Theory. In order to better understand the reasons behind disabled people's behavior in the process of collecting data based on scenes, it is necessary to investigate their feelings about the existing related systems and living conditions from the perspective of themselves. In addition to online and offline behavior data, interviews [16], participation observations [17], questionnaires [16], etc., which are commonly used in grounded theory, will be used to obtain real social data of disabled groups in different scenarios.

Because different social science collection methods have their own advantages and disadvantages. For instance, the interviews cannot be carried out in large range, the participation observations cannot be reproduced, and the questionnaires are not flexible enough. Therefore, multiple methods can be used to compensate each other. The data collected by these social science methods are stored with unstructured data format.

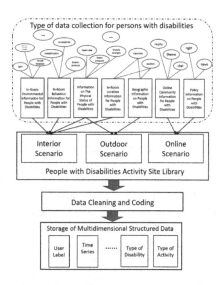

Fig. 2. Scenario-based data collection method of people with disabilities

3.2 Data Analysis

After data collection, a large number of structured and unstructured data are stored as input and used in subsequent data analysis modules to get some new social findings and behavior patterns about people with disabilities. Because of the different sources and structures of data, different data analysis methods are adopted to deal with different data in the process of analysis (Fig. 3).

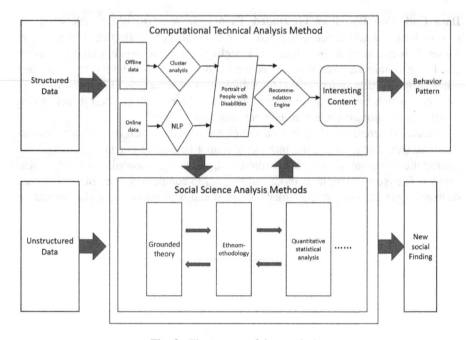

Fig. 3. The process of data analysis

The different kinds of data we collected about people with disabilities include large, multidimensional structured data, although these data seemingly scattered, but contains the behavior patterns of the people with disabilities. In the process of data analysis, we introduce clustering analysis [18, 19], natural language processing [20] and recommendation algorithms [21–23] for computational analysis. Disabled people's Daily behavior has the characteristics of a great variety of data and time series data; therefore, we use clustering algorithm divided into multiple clusters from multiple dimensions and combining it with time series we can obtain behavior patterns of people with disabilities. Natural language processing technology is used to analyze online social information and combine it with behavior patterns generate the user portrait of people with disabilities. This user portrait will be used as data sources to recommend content of interest to disabled users through recommendation engines.

Data Analysis Method Based on Grounded Theory. For interviews and observation data, we use social science analytical method to analysis it. Grounded theory [24] is a mature qualitative research method, which is born for the study of social activities and processes, so it has advantage of analyzing social activities of people with disabilities (Fig. 4).

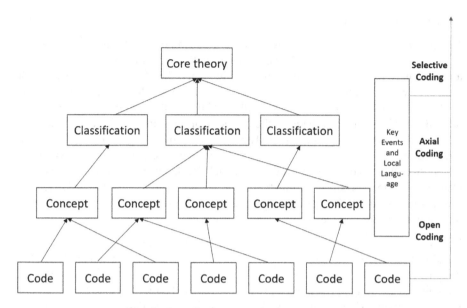

Fig. 4. Encoding process of grounded theory

In the process of using grounded theory analyse people with disabilities, we need to organize data and use key events and words such as "helping each other", "Halfway House", "disabilities friends", "Yellow Mountain climbing" to find content which we interested in. The meaning behind these content are listed to make open coding. After open coding, the relationships between the codes are listed, such as causality, similarity, etc., and analysis the process of creating relationship to form new rules and classifications. Finally, these categories and rules are constantly compared and combined to form one core category that are associated with most categories. The core category have been transformed into new theories of people with disabilities. The whole analysis process is continuous iteration. In the process of classification formation, new data are continuously obtained through interviews and participation observation to help establish the association between classifications.

In data analysis stage, there are interactions of results between analytical methods and methods because of the specifics of the people with disabilities. For example, the analysis result of the grounded theory can be research hypothesis for quantitative analysis. So the whole data analysis is the whole existence of an internal data interaction.

3.3 System Design

Two main problems are faced at the system design section, one is how to apply the new discovery about the people with disabilities in the system analysis stage to the design of the service system for the disabled; the other is how to provide the system interactive personalized service for the disabled group. The following part would talk about how these two problems will be addressed.

System Model Design

Design Principle Extraction. Design principle is proposed basing on the specific activities of people with disabilities, which is not always the same. Different user activities may result in different design requirements, therefore, the design principle shall vary with the different situations and conditions. According to the characteristics of the social activities of the people with disabilities, the design principles can be defined with five elements: the user, the character of disability, the process of activity, the context and the design objective. The user is the main object that the system is designed for, the character of disability refers to the character of disability within the system, like the disability type, type of accessibility, the extent of disability, and etc.; Context refers to the context information when activity happens, like last activity, time, surroundings, and etc. The design objective is to achieve the effects design requires, like helping the disabled to recover, finding a job etc.

Theoretical Model Mapping. With the design principles, they should be mapped as social-technical theories, and with the social-technical theories to guide the system design. The detailed process is like: firstly select users and the process activity according to the design principles, and social-technical theories to guide system design. Like the activity of use and innovation of intelligent assistive devices by disabled groups, the user is the disabled group, assistive device developers, and medical staff, while the design objective is to provide convenience for their usage and learning communication, and to emphasize interaction between roles and roles and devices, Socio-Technical Interaction Networks (STINs) can be adopted to guide the system design [25]. Then map the character of user, the character of disability and context with theories, generating specific system design model. For example, mapping different user characters to subject of behavior, organization and other elements in the STINs theory, mapping the character of disability to device, state in the STINs theory, and mapping activity scenarios to the data, resource and other STINs' elements. With this process, the abstract result generated by data analysis module can be mapped as system design model.

System Interaction Design

Participatory Design. As the interaction requirements for people with disabilities are different with the general public, we introduced participatory design into the implementation of the system [26]. As most of the disabled people are not clear with the implementation process, it's hard to figure out the specific requirements at the beginning of design. Participatory design method selects a few disable representatives, providing the prototype to them, and let them get involved in the system implementation process when using it, as which they can put forward more specific use requirements and changes in their life. Therefore, the developers can make modifications and development with these requirements from the disable group and give the system to the representatives again. The procedure of the system design is a continuous iteration process.

Interaction Method Design. The group of disabled persons is a large general name, which includes the different types of disabled persons, such as limb injuries, blind people, deaf mute people and so on. Therefore, the design of better system interaction is an important part of the system design module. First, select an interaction method from interactive mode library according to the attribute of disability and design goals and implement it within the system. Interactive mode library contains the basic interactive mode like shock, touch, voice, and so on. Then, according to the specific design requirements obtained form the participatory design section, to adjust the system in order to adapt to the individualized interactive experience of the disabled. From the above process, we can see that in the disabled service system, the interaction mode is not single, nor is it static. It should have diversified requirements, and each adaption mode should somehow be able to fit in different conditions. With the process of participatory design, it can be adapted to people with same disability with different disabled levels.

In the system design, the result of data analysis is mapped into an applicable system design model. On the basis of design model, the introduce of participatory design and interactive mode library, and continuous iterations in the system design module, have sufficiently considered the personalized user needs and interaction modes of the disabled group. In the process of participating in the design, analyze the data and field observation data of the disabled representatives, acquiring new requirements and enhancing the system, making iterations of the system framework, improving system progressiveness and scalability.

4   Application of Social - Technical System Design Framework for People with Disabilities

The social-technical system design framework for people with disabilities presented in this paper has been applied to design several service system and has received recognition of some disabled friends, the following will introduce accessible self-care intelligent control monitoring platform for people with disabilities which is one of these systems.

We conducted a half-year study of people with disabilities in the home environment. During this period, we interviewed 11 people with physical disability and collected their behavior data, we also as volunteers for their activities and gatherings to conduct the participant observations. By using analysis methods presented in our framework, we analyzed data from social and technical aspects and find that people with severe physical disability always need others to help them to do some simple things that created a sense of psychological indebtedness can affect their society. this new finding was extracted as a design principle, the people with disabilities, families and caregivers were extracted as user, physical disability, accessibility and severe disability were extracted as character of disability, the simple things like control TV and open window were extracted as the process of activity, home environment was extracted as context, reducing the sense of indebtedness was extract as design objective. Then we mapped this design principle to Activity Theory [27] to generate system model. At the same time, we chosen 4 disabled families to participate in design. According to the feedback of the participatory design, system provide touch, voice and eye control these three interactive ways.

At present the system has been successfully deployed in the 23 families of people with disabilities and collected nearly 50000 data. This system helps people with disabilities to take care of themselves while reducing their psychological indebtedness (Fig. 5).

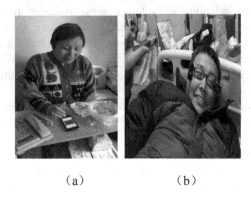

(a)   (b)

Fig. 5. (a) The disabled people who using voice control. (b) The disabled people who using eye control

5 Conclusion

Aiming at the challenges encountered in the systematic study of disabled groups and the physical and psychological specificity of disabled people, this paper proposes a social-technical system design framework for disabled people. The framework includes an entire system design flow from data acquisition, behavior analysis, discovery, system design, and model mapping. In the follow-up study, the influence and relationship between online and offline behaviors of disabled people will be deeply studied on the basis of this framework design. The safety and privacy of disabled people will be fully considered in the system design. The social-technical service system that is more suitable for the disabled people will be developed in topics such as dating and work that disabled people care about.

Acknowledgment. This work was supported by National Natural Science Foundation of China (NSFC) under Grant No. 61332008.

References

1. Goodley, D.: Disability Studies: An Interdisciplinary Introduction. Sage, Thousand Oaks (2016)
2. Shinohara, K., Jacob, O.W.: In the shadow of misperception: assistive technology use and social interactions. In: Proceedings of the SIGCHI Conference on Human Factors in Computing Systems, pp. 705–714. ACM (2011)

3. Shinohara, K., Josh, T.: A blind person's interactions with technology. Commun. ACM **52** (8), 58–66 (2009)
4. Cramer, M., Hirano, S.H., Tentori, M., Yeganyan, M.T., Hayes, G.R.: Classroom-based assistive technology: collective use of interactive visual schedules by students with autism. In: CHI, vol. 11, pp. 1–10 (2011)
5. Kane, S.K., Meredith R.M., Jacob, O.W.: Touchplates: low-cost tactile overlays for visually impaired touch screen users. In: Proceedings of the 15th International ACM SIGACCESS Conference on Computers and Accessibility, p. 22. ACM, (2013)
6. Pasquero, J., Scott, J.S., Noel, S.: A haptic wristwatch for eyes-free interactions. In: Proceedings of the SIGCHI Conference on Human Factors in Computing Systems, pp. 3257–3266. ACM (2011)
7. Yatani, K., Banovic, N., Truong, K.: SpaceSense: representing geographical information to visually impaired people using spatial tactile feedback. In: Proceedings of the SIGCHI Conference on Human Factors in Computing Systems, pp. 415–424. ACM (2012)
8. Fallah, N., Apostolopoulos, I., Bekris, K., Folmer, E.: The user as a sensor: navigating users with visual impairments in indoor spaces using tactile landmarks. In: Proceedings of the SIGCHI Conference on Human Factors in Computing Systems, pp. 425–432. ACM (2012)
9. Harada, S., Sato, D., Adams, D.W., Kurniawan, S., Takagi, H., Asakawa, C.: Accessible photo album: enhancing the photo sharing experience for people with visual impairment. In: Proceedings of the SIGCHI Conference on Human Factors in Computing Systems, pp. 2127–2136. ACM (2013)
10. Hourcade, J.P., Williams, S.R., Miller, E.A., Huebner, K.E., Liang, L.J.: Evaluation of tablet apps to encourage social interaction in children with autism spectrum disorders. In: Proceedings of the SIGCHI Conference on Human Factors in Computing Systems, pp. 3197–3206. ACM (2013)
11. Escobedo, L., et al.: MOSOCO: a mobile assistive tool to support children with autism practicing social skills in real-life situations. In: Proceedings of the SIGCHI Conference on Human Factors in Computing Systems, pp. 2589–2598. ACM (2012)
12. Hong, H., Kim, J.G., Abowd, G.D., Arriaga, R.I.: Designing a social network to support the independence of young adults with autism. In: Proceedings of the ACM 2012 Conference on Computer Supported Cooperative Work, pp. 627–636. ACM (2012)
13. Liu, P., Ding, X., Gu, N.: "Helping others makes me happy": social interaction and integration of people with disabilities. In: Proceedings of the 19th ACM Conference on Computer-Supported Cooperative Work & Social Computing, pp. 1596–1608. ACM (2016)
14. Mankoff, J., Hayes, G.R., Kasnitz, D.: Disability studies as a source of critical inquiry for the field of assistive technology. In: Proceedings of the 12th International ACM SIGACCESS Conference on Computers and Accessibility, pp. 3–10. ACM (2010)
15. Buehler, E., et al.: Sharing is caring: assistive technology designs on thingiverse. In: Proceedings of the 33rd Annual ACM Conference on Human Factors in Computing Systems, pp. 525–534. ACM (2015)
16. Lazar, J., Feng, J.H., Hochheiser, H.: Research Methods in Human-Computer Interaction. Morgan Kaufmann, Burlington (2017)
17. DeWalt, K.M., DeWalt, B.R.: Participant Observation: A Guide for Fieldworkers. Rowman Altamira, Lanham (2011)
18. Xu, R., Wunsch, D.: Survey of clustering algorithms. IEEE Trans. Neural Netw. **16**(3), 645–678 (2005)
19. Berkhin, P.: A survey of clustering data mining techniques. In: Kogan, J., Nicholas, C., Teboulle, M. (eds.) Grouping Multidimensional Data. Springer, Heidelberg (2006). https://doi.org/10.1007/3-540-28349-8_2

20. Jurafsky, D.: Speech and Language Processing: An Introduction to Natural Language Processing. Computational Linguistics, and Speech Recognition. Pearson, London (2000)
21. Ricci, F., Rokach, L., Shapira, B.: Introduction to Recommender Systems Handbook. In: Ricci, F., Rokach, L., Shapira, B., Kantor, P. (eds.) Recommender Systems Handbook. Springer, New York (2011). https://doi.org/10.1007/978-0-387-85820-3_1
22. Balabanović, M., Shoham, Y.: Fab: content-based, collaborative recommendation. Commun. ACM **40**(3), 66–72 (1997)
23. Breese, J.S., Heckerman, D., Kadie, C.: Empirical analysis of predictive algorithms for collaborative filtering. In: Proceedings of the 14th Conference on Uncertainty in Artificial Intelligence, pp. 43–52. Morgan Kaufmann Publishers Inc. (1998)
24. Strauss, A., Corbin, J.: Grounded theory methodology. In: Handbook of Qualitative Research, vol. 17, pp. 273–285 (1997)
25. Kling, R., McKim, G., Fortuna, J., King, A.: Scientific collaboratories as sociotechnical interaction networks: a theoretical approach. arXiv preprintcs arXiv:0005007 (2000)
26. Muller, M.J.: Participatory design: the third space in HCI. In: Human-Computer Interaction: Development Process, pp. 165–185. CRC press, Boco Raton (2003)
27. Leontiev, A.N.: Actividad, consciencia y personalidad. Buenos Aires (1978)
28. Yuling, S.: Socio-technical analysis method and system design for vulnerable group. Ph.D. thesis, Fudan University, Shanghai (2016)
29. Qi, W.: User behavior anaysis and system design in new media systems. Ph.D. thesis, Fudan University, Shanghai (2014)
30. Peng, Z.: User behavior analysis and user identity identification across social medias. Ph.D. thesis, Fudan University, Shanghai (2018)

An Overlapping Community Detection Algorithm Based on Triangle Coarsening and Dynamic Distance

Bingjie Xiang[1,2,3], Kun Guo[1,2,3], Zhanghui Liu[1,2,3(✉)],
and Qinwu Liao[4]

[1] College of Mathematics and Computer Sciences,
Fuzhou University, Fuzhou 350116, China
xiangbj301@163.com, gukn123@163.com, lzh@fzu.edu.cn
[2] Fujian Provincial Key Laboratory of Network Computing and Intelligent
Information Processing, Fuzhou, China
[3] Key Laboratory of Spatial Data Mining and Information Sharing,
Ministry of Education, Fuzhou 350116, China
[4] Power Science and Technology Corporation State Grid Information
and Telecommunication Group, Xiamen 351008, China
liaoqinwu@sgitg.sgcc.com.cn

Abstract. Discoverying hidden communities in various kinds of complicated networks is a considerable research direction in the field of complex network analysis. Its goal is to discover the structures of communities in complex networks. The algorithms devised upon the Attractor dynamic distance mechanism are capable of finding stable communities with various sizes. However, they still have deficiencies in overlapping community discovery and runtime efficiency. An overlapping community discovery algorithm based on triangle coarsening and dynamic distance is posed in this paper. First, a coarsening strategy devised upon triangle is adopted to reduce networks' sizes. Second, for the coarsened networks, a dynamic distance processing mechanism based on overlapping Attractors is used to discover the overlapping communities in the networks. Finally, the communities in the raw networks are obtained through anti-roughening steps. The experiments on different datasets demonstrate that the proposed algorithm not only can discover the overlapping communities accurately but also has low time complexity.

Keywords: Overlapping community · Triangular coarsening
Dynamic distance

1 Introduction

As technology advances rapidly, the connections among things become closer and closer, and the relational networks formed by things also become more complicated. Hence, complex network analysis has become a research hotpot. For example, protein-protein interaction networks, computer server networks, transmission networks of epidemic diseases, and scientific collaboration networks have become the research objects of many scholars. As a considerable feature of complex networks, the community is

© Springer Nature Singapore Pte Ltd. 2019
Y. Sun et al. (Eds.): ChineseCSCW 2018, CCIS 917, pp. 285–300, 2019.
https://doi.org/10.1007/978-981-13-3044-5_21

characterized by tight connections between nodes in the communities and sparse node connections among communities [1]. Discovering the community in complex networks helps researchers comprehend the internal mechanisms of the network better, improve the networks' behavior, which have important application values in the real life.

The algorithms of overlapping community detection are split into clique-based methods [2, 3], methods devised upon label propagation [4–6], link-based methods [7–9], and so on. The clique-based approaches model the community as cliques that identify the overlapping communities by discovering all K-cliques in networks. The representative algorithms include CPM [2], EAGLE [3], etc. The algorithms adopting the idea of label propagation initialize one unique label for every node in networks, and then update the nodes' labels by iterations until the labels become stable. The representative algorithms include RAK [4], COPRA [5], COPRA-EP [6], etc. The algorithms based on link clustering transform the nodes of networks into edges, and convert them into node clusters after discovering the edges clusters. The representative algorithms include DBLINK [7], NMFIB [8], ELCSD [9], etc.

Shao et al. proposed the Attractor algorithm based on dynamic distance in 2015 [10] to achieve better accuracy in community detection. The algorithm considers the influence of nodes' neighbors according to the distance between nodes and iteratively update the distance. After several iterations, the distance will approach 0 or 1. The edge with distance 1 will be cut off, and the corresponding communities will be formed. In 2016, Meng et al. proposed the I-Attractor algorithm [11], which solved one problem of the Attractor algorithm that did not consider the cohesive force difference of each neighbor node and converged slowly. In 2017, Chen et al. proposed the F-Attractor algorithm [12], which aims to overcome the shortcoming of long calculation time of Attractor algorithm and improve the efficiency of community discovery.

An algorithm for detecting the overlapping communities which depends on the ideas of triangle coarsening and dynamic distance (CDTD) is put forward to deal with the drawback that the community discovery algorithms based on dynamic distance cannot find overlapping structures with low time complexity.

The principle contributions about the paper are summed up as follows: (1) before applying the mechanism of Attractor algorithm, the triangle roughening strategy is adopted to utilize the strong community characteristics of triangles, so that the network scale can be enormously decreased and the operating efficiency of the algorithm can be enhanced without losing the information contained in the raw network; (2) the similarity maximization strategy is used to determine which community the node corresponding to the edge with distance 1 belongs to. The similar communities are merged to find overlapping communities.

2   Related Concepts

Definition 1 (Neighbor set of Node h). The neighbor set of node h is

$$NB(h) = \{h \in V | (h, z) \in E\} \tag{1}$$

Definition 2 (Neighbor set of Node h Include Itself). The neighbor set of node h is

$$NA(h) = NB(h) \cup \{h\} \tag{2}$$

Definition 3 (Neighbors of Community C_i). The neighbors of community C_i is

$$NB(C_i) = \cup_{v \in C_i} NB(v) - C_i \tag{3}$$

Definition 4 (Jaccard Distance). The Jaccard distance between nodes h and z is

$$d(h, z) = 1 - \frac{|NA(h) \cap NA(z)|}{|NA(h) \cup NA(z)|} \tag{4}$$

where $|*|$ represents the number of elements in set $*$.
For a weighted undirected graph, the Jaccard distance between nodes h and z is

$$d(h, z) = 1 - \frac{\sum\limits_{r \in (NA(h) \cap NA(z))} (wei(h, r) + wei(z, r))}{\sum\limits_{(r,g) \in E; r,g \in (NA(h) \cup NA(z))} wei(r, g)} \tag{5}$$

where $wei(h, r)$ is the weight of the edge (h, r).

Definition 5 (Common Neighbor Set). The common neighbor set of nodes h and z is

$$CN(h, z) = NB(h) \cap NB(z) \tag{6}$$

Definition 6 (Exclusive Neighbor Set). Node h's exclusive neighbor set is

$$EN(h) = NB(h) - CN(h, z) \tag{7}$$

Definition 7 (Similarity between Node and Community). The affinity between node h and community C_k is

$$sim(h, C_k) = \frac{|NB(h) \cap NB(C_k)|}{|NB(h)|} \tag{8}$$

Definition 8 (Similarity of Communities). The initial communities are denoted as $C = \{C_1, C_2, \ldots, C_m\}$. The affinity between community C_l and community C_k is

$$simcom(C_l, C_k) = \frac{|NB(C_l) \cap NB(C_k)|}{\min(|NB(C_l)|, |NB(C_k)|)} \tag{9}$$

Definition 9 (Influence Factor). The influence factor of node r on distance $d(h, z)$ is

$$inf(r, z) = \begin{cases} 1 - d(r, h) & if (1 - d(r, h) \geq \lambda) \\ 1 - d(r, h) - \lambda & otherwise \end{cases} \quad (10)$$

Definition 10 (Influence from Direct Neighbors). The influence of direct neighbors h and z of any node is

$$DI = -\left(\frac{fuc(1 - d(h, z))}{\deg(h)} + \frac{fuc(1 - d(h, z))}{\deg(z)}\right) \quad (11)$$

Definition 11 (Influence from the Common Neighbors). The influence of the common neighbor set of nodes h and z is

$$CI = -\sum_{q \in CN(h,z)} \left(\frac{fuc(1 - d(q, h)) \cdot (1 - d(q, z))}{\deg(h)} + \frac{fuc(1 - d(q, z)) \cdot (1 - d(q, h))}{\deg(z)}\right) \quad (12)$$

Definition 12 (Influence from Exclusive Neighbors). The influence of the exclusive neighbors of nodes h and z is

$$EI = -\sum_{r \in EN(h)} \frac{fuc(1 - d(r, h)) \cdot inf(r, h)}{\deg(h)} - \sum_{g \in EN(z)} \frac{fuc(1 - d(g, z)) \cdot inf(g, z)}{\deg(z)} \quad (13)$$

3 Community Detection Based on Triangle Coarsening and Dynamic Distance

3.1 Design Ideas

The proposed algorithm CDTD can be divided into three stages:

(1) *Network coarsening processing.* The network is coarsened by making use of the characteristics of triangle structure. The endpoints of each traversed triangle are combined into one node. Since the three endpoints of the triangle are completely connected and have strong community characteristics [13], the community attribute of the compound node is consistent with that of the compound node. As a significant feature of complex networks, community structure requires that the nodes in the community are closely connected and the edge density is high. A triangle is a 3-complete graph that can be regarded as a smallest stable community. In the raw network, the nodes of the triangle generally pertain to a community or the overlapping communities, which are less likely to belong to different communities. The CPM algorithm uses this feature to discover

overlapping communities [2]. Unlike the CPM algorithm, we find communities on the new network obtained from triangle coarsening. These communities are made up of the adjacent triangles in the raw network. Therefore, the communities found on the new network correspond to the communities of the adjacent triangles in the raw network.

(2) *Process based on the Overlapping-Attractor (O-Attractor) with dynamic distance.* The algorithm based on dynamic distance can detect the communities. However, they still have some shortcomings such as the inability to find overlapping communities and low time efficiency. At this stage, the communities generated by the O-Attractor with dynamic distance are optimized and merged. The boundary nodes and some similar communities are processed according to the similarity Eqs. (8) and (9) to obtain overlapping communities.

(3) *Reverse coarsening processing. The aim of* this stage is to restore the initial community structure generated by stage 2. The nodes that make up of each compound node are assigned to the community of the corresponding compound node to get the final communities.

The schematic diagram of CDTD algorithm is described in Fig. 1.

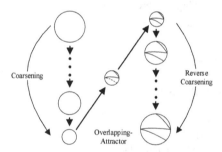

Fig. 1. The schematic diagram about CDTD algorithm.

The details of the CDTD algorithm is as follow:

Algorithm 1. CDTD
Input: $G = (V, E, W)$, threshold δ.
Output: community set C'
1. $G' = coarsening(G, \delta)$;   // Network coarsening processing stage.
2. $C = overlapAttractor(G')$;   //O-Attractor stage.
3. $C' = restore(C)$;   //Reverse coarsening processing stage.
4. OUTPUT C';

The threshold δ represents the coarsening rate of the network coarsening stage. The function *coarsening(G, δ)* is used to coarsen the orginal network based on the triangular strategy. The function *overlapAttractor(G')* is applied to discover the initial communities according to the mechanism of O-Attractor with dynamic distance. The function *restore(C)* is used to restore the raw network.

3.2 Network Coarsening Process

First, the initial network G is traversed. For each triangle encountered in the network, the endpoints of the triangle are fused into a composite node. Second, the neighbors of the composite node and the weights of its edges are updated, and the edge relationship mapping of the endpoints is fused into the composite node. Specifically, the coarsening graph G_1 is generated after the first layer is coarsened. Next, G_1 is used as the initial network for the second layer coarsening. The above steps are repeated to generate the subsequent coarsened networks. When the coarsening rate $(G_m - G_{m-1})/G$ of the mth coarsening is smaller than the given coarsening rate threshold δ, the coarsening process ends. The final coarsened graph G' is output.

Function 1. Coarsening

Input: $G = (V,E,W)$, coarsening rate threshold δ.

Output: network after coarsening stage G'.

1. $G_0 = G$; $G_{cur} = G$;
2.   WHILE $(rate_{coar} >=\delta)$ DO
3. $G_{last} = G_{cur}$;
4. $nodes_{sort} = sortByDegree(G_{cur})$;
5. $initF(G_{cur})$;
6.   FOR ALL $h \in nodes_{sort}$ DO
7.   IF $(F(h) < 2)$ THEN
8.   FOR ALL $z \in h.neighbor$ DO
9.   IF $((F(z) < 2)$ and $(z.degree > h.degree))$ THEN
10.   FOR ALL $w \in (h.nei \cap z.nei)$ DO
11.   IF $((F(w) < 1)$ and $(w.degree > h.degree)$ and $(w.degree > z.degree))$ THEN
12. $h.nei = h.nei \cup z.nei$;
13. $F(z) = 2$;
14. $F(w) = 2$;
15. $F(h)$++;
16.   BREAK;
17. $rate_{coar} = (G_{last} - G_{cur}) / G_0$;
18.   END WHILE
19. $G' = G_{last}$;
20.   RETURN G';

The input of Function 1 is a weighted Graph. If G is unweighted, the weight of each edge is regarded as 1. During the fusion progress of the triangles, function *sortBy-Degree()* is firstly used to sort the nodes in the ascending order of their degrees. Then, the nodes are traversed according to the order. For each node h and each of its neighbor z, the common neighbor w of them is found whose neighbor set is merged with h's neighbor set. Every (h, z, w) triple composes a triangle. Traverse the triangles in the network in this order. The random selection has little effect on the whole process. $F(h)$ represents the flag of node h which is used to distinguish the state of node h. At the beginning, the flags of all nodes are initialized to -1. If a node belongs a composite node such as node z and node w in Function 1, its corresponding $F(z)$ and $F(w)$ are set to 2. It will no longer participate in the subsequent coarsening process. If the node is a composite node such as node h in Function 1, its corresponding $F(h)$ is incremented by 1. If $F(h)$ is still less than 2, then node h can continue to participate in the subsequent traversal process. Otherwise, node h will not participate in the subsequent traversal process until it is reconsidered when the next layer is coarsened. At the end of Function 1, the relations of the composite nodes and their corresponding original nodes (the nodes compose the composite nodes) will be stored in a map for later inverse coarsening process.

3.3 The Stage Based on the Mechanism of Overlapping-Attractor with Dynamic Distance

At this stage, the O-Attractor mechanism with dynamic distance is used to discover the overlapping communities. First, the distances of the endpoints of all the edges are initialize according to Eq. (4).

(1) *The influence of direct neighbors DI.* It reflects the influence of direct neighbors, h and z, on $d(h, z)$, which is computed according to Eq. (11)
(2) *The influence of common neighbors CI.* It reflects the influence of the common neighbor set of node h and z on $d(h, z)$, which is computed according to Eq. (12).
(3) *The influence of exclusive neighbors EI.* It reflects the influence of the exclusive neighbor set of node h and z on $d(h, z)$, which is computed according to Eq. (13).

The distance will gradually converge to 0 or 1 finally. The nodes with distance 1 is at the boundary of communities and may belong to multiple communities. Therefore, the strategy of similarity maximization is used to deal with the community ownership of these nodes and discover the overlapping communities in the network. The details are shown in Function 2.

Function 2. OverlapAttractor

Input: the coarsened network $G'=(V',E',W')$, coarsening rate threshold δ.

Output: the initial community set C.

1.   FOR ALL $\{h,z\} \in E'$ DO
2.   Using equation (4) to caculate $d(h,z)$;
3.   FOR ALL $r \in EN(h)$ DO
4.   Using equation (4) to caculate $d(h,z)$;
5.   FOR ALL $g \in EN(z)$ DO
6.   Using equation (4) to caculate $d(h,z)$;
7. $flag$ = TRUE;   //Flag indicates whether there is a change in the distance during
                                                    the iteration. TRUE if changed, otherwise FALSE
8. $loop$ = 0;   //Number of iteration
9.   WHILE ($flag$) and ($loop < 1000$) DO
10. $flag$ = FALSE;
11.   FOR ALL $\{h,z\} \in E'$ DO
12.   Using equation (11)(12)(13) to caculate DI,CI,EI, respectively;
13. $dist = d(h,z) + DI + CI + EI$;
14.   IF ($0 < d(h,z) < 1$) THEN
15.   IF ($dist > 1$) THEN
16. $d(h,z) = 1$;
17.   IF ($dist < 0$) THEN
18. $d(h,z) = 0$;
19.   IF ($0 < dist < 1$) THEN
20. $d(h,z) = dist$;
21. $flag$ = TRUE;
22. $loop$++;
23. END WHILE
24. $Node_{over}$ = Φ;
25. FOR ALL $\{h,z\} \in E'$ DO
26.   IF ($d(h,z) < 1$) THEN
27. $d(h,z) = 0$;
28.   IF ($d(h,z) == 1$) THEN
29. $Node_{over} = Node_{over} \cup (h,z)$;
30.   IF ($d(h,z) >= 1$) THEN
31. $G' = G' - e$;
32. $C = findComponent(G')$;   //Discover the connected components on G' and add it
                                                    as a community to C
33. FOR ALL $h \in Node_{over}$ DO   //Judge the boundary points
34. $community = \arg\max_{com}\{sim(p,com)\}$;
35.   IF ($sim(h, community) >= 0.5$) THEN
36. $community = community \cup \{h\}$;
37. FOR ALL $c_1 \in C$ DO   //Merge similar communities
38.   IF ($c_1.size <= 5$) THEN
39. $c_2 = \arg\max_{com}\{sim(c_1,com)\}$; //$com$ is the element in C

40. $newc_1 = c_1 \cup c_2$;
41. Update C;   // Update the communities in the original community set C
42. RETURN C;

In Function 2, first, the original communities are generated based on the mechanism of O-Attractor with dynamic distance. Second, the judgment of overlapping nodes and the merging of similar communities are performed, where $findComponent(G')$ is a function that finds the connected components in G'. Function 2 overcomes the short-coming of the Attractor algorithm [10] that it cannot discover the overlapping com-munities. It adopts the strategy of the similarity maximization to find overlapping structures. The strategy of similarity maximization is mainly consistent with two stages. In the first stage, the judgment of overlapping community attribution of the boundary nodes corresponding to the edge with distance 1 is performed. When the affinity between a node and a community exceeds threshold, this node is added to the com-munity. Therefore, the overlapping structures in the network are discovered. After conducting comprehensive experiments, the algorithm is found to have the highest accuracy when the threshold value is set to 0.5. In the second stage, the small com-munities are merged with their most similar communities, which greatly reduces the count of orphan communities and improve the quality of the communities.

3.4   Reverse Coarsening Process

The communities of composite nodes obtained by Function 2 only reflects the network partition after coarsening. They have to be restored to the node communities in the raw network, which is called the reverse coarsening process. The stage restores the com-munities of composite nodes to the communities of nodes in raw network according to the map containing the information the relations between the coarsened nodes and the original nodes generated by Function 1.

3.5   Time Complexity

Let n be nodes' number of raw network, m be edges' number, k be nodes' average degree, n' be the number of nodes after coarsening, and m' be edges' number after coarsening, k' be the average number of exclusive neighbors of two adjacent nodes. In Function 1, the time paid for node sorting of step 5 is $O(n\log n)$. Step 11 to step 19 costs $O(k^2)$. Step 9 to step 21 costs $O(k^3)$ time. The time used for traversing triangles in step 7 to step 23 is $O(k^3 n)$ or $O(k^2 m)$. Step 3 to 25 costs $O(Tk^2 m)$ time, where T is the count of iterations of the coarsening process. Hence, Function 1 costs $O(n\log n + Tk^2 m)$ in total. In Function 2, the time for initializing the distance of nodes in step 1 to step 9 is $O(m')$. The time consumption for traversing the edges of the network in step 1 to step 2 is $O(m')$. Traversing the exclusive neighbors of two adjacent nodes in step 3 to step 9 costs $O(k'm')$ time. The time paid for iteratively updating the distance of nodes in step 12 to step 31 is $O(T'm')$, where T' is the count of iterations. The running time of step 33 to 43 is $O(m')$. The number of boundary nodes is assumed to be n_b, the number of communities is assumed to be n_c. The time of the two FOR cycles in step 45 to 56 is $O(n_b)$ and $O(n_c)$, separately. Since n_b, $n_c \ll m'$, Function 2 costs $O(2 m' + k'm' + T'm')$

in total. The stage of reverse coarsening only needs to traverse each node and restore the composite nodes, so it costs $O(n)$. In conclusion, the CDTD totally costs O ($n\log n + Tk^2m + 2\ m' + k'm' + T'm' + n$). Since $m' < m$, $k' < k$, T, $T' << m$, and $n < m$ for a general complex network, the CDTD algorithm costs O ($n\log n + m$).

4 Experiments

Multiple real networks and artificial networks are used in the experiments so as to prove the performance of the CDTD algorithm. The hardware and software of the experiments are: a PC with 3.1 GHz Pentium 4CPU, 12G RAM, 64 bit, and Windows 7 64bit. The code of all algorithm is implemented in Python 3.6.

4.1 Experiment Datasets

(1) *real-world datasets*

Five different real networks are selected to compare the CDTD algorithm with the other contemporary algorithms on the real-world datasets. They are Zachary karate club network Karate [14], the American political books network Polbooks [1], the general relativity and the quantum cosmological literature collaboration network Ca-GrQc [15], and the word adjacency network word [16]. Table 1 describes the real-world networks are described in detail.

Table 1. The details of the real-world datasets.

Real-world dataset	Nodes	Edges	Average degree
Karate	34	78	4.59
Polbooks	105	441	8.4
Ga-GrQc	5242	14496	5.53
Word	112	425	7.59

(2) *artificial datasets*

The artificial networks produced by the LFR [17] benchmark is adopted to compare the CDTD algorithm with the other contemporary algorithms. Table 2 describes the settings of the parameters of the LFR for generating the artificial networks.

Three sets of artificial networks are used in the experiments, where $k = 20$, $k_{upper} = 50$, $C_{lower} = 100$ is same at three datasets. Table 3 describes the specific selections of other parameters.

Table 2. Parameters of the artificial networks.

Parameter	Description
N	Nodes' number
k	The average degree of nodes
k_{upper}	Nodes' maximum degree
C_{lower}	Minimum number of nodes of community
C_{upper}	Maximum number of nodes of community
on	Overlapping nodes' number
om	Communities' number to which overlapping nodes pertain
μ	Mixed parameter

Table 3. Parameter settings of the artificial networks.

Parameter	Description
T_1	$N = 1000$, $C_{upper} = 100$, $\mu = 0.1$–0.6
T_2	$N = 1000$, $C_{upper} = 100$, $\mu = 0.3$, $om = 2$, $on = 10$–100
T_3	$N = 2000$–10000, $C_{upper} = 50$, $\mu = 0.3$, $om = 4$

4.2   Experimental Scheme and Evaluation Metrics

(1) *experimental scheme*

In the experiments, four contemporary algorithms are selected, namely Attractor algorithm [10], MCL algorithm [18], CPM algorithm [2], DEMON algorithm [19]. Table 4 describes the choices of algorithms' parameters.

Table 4. The settings of algorithms' parameters.

Algorithm	Parameter
CDTD	$\delta = 0.5$–0.9, $\lambda = 0.6$
Attractor	$\lambda = 0.6$
MCL	*expand_factor* $= 2$, *inflate_factor* $= 2$, *max_loop* $= 20$, *mult_factor* $= 0.5$
CPM	$k = 3$–8
DEMON	$e = 0.1$–0.5

(2) *evaluation metrics*

In the experiment, the overlapping modularity EQ [3] is selected as an evaluation metric. The closer the value of EQ is to 1, the higher the quality of the communities discovered by the algorithm. The closer the value of EQ is to 0, the worse the quality of the communities discovered. The equation of EQ is as follows:

$$EQ = \frac{1}{2m} \sum_{l=1}^{c} \sum_{z,h \in C_l} \frac{1}{O_z O_h} [A_{zh} - \frac{k_z k_h}{2m}] \tag{14}$$

where m denotes edges' number in the network, c means communities' number, C_l is the lth community, O_z means communities' number to which node z pertains, k_z is the degree of node z. A_{zk} is used to indicate the connection between node z and node h. If there is an edge connecting the two nodes, $A_{zh} = 1$, otherwise it is 0.

If the networks' true communities are given, the NMI (Normalized Mutual Information) [20] is adopted as the evaluation metric. The closer the value of NMI is to 1, the higher the veracity of the algorithm is. The closer the value of NMI is to 0, the lower the veracity of the algorithm is. The equation of NMI is as follows:

$$NMI = \frac{-2 \sum_{l=1}^{C_X} \sum_{k=1}^{C_Y} N_{lk} \log(\frac{N_{lk}N}{N_{l\bullet}N_{\bullet k}})}{\sum_{l=1}^{C_X} N_{l\bullet} \log(\frac{N_{l\bullet}}{N}) + \sum_{k=1}^{C_Y} N_{\bullet k} \log(\frac{N_{\bullet k}}{N})} \tag{15}$$

where N is the confusion matrix. N_{lk} is the element of the l-th row and the k-th column of N. Its value means the number of common nodes of community l and community k. $N_{l\bullet}$ means the sum of the elements of the lth row of matrix N. $N_{\bullet k}$ denotes the sum of the elements of the kth column of matrix N. C_X denotes real communities' number. C_Y means the number of communities discovered by the algorithm.

4.3 Experiments of Parameters

Different values of parameter δ of the CDTD algorithm will influence the veracity of the algorithm, so experiments were conducted to determine the proper value of the parameter. Network T_1 is used in the experiments. Figure 2 displays experimental results. Figure 2(a) reveals that as the value of δ raises, the accuracy of the CDTD algorithm increases rapidly and stabilizes soon. The algorithm gets high precision when $\delta = 0.2$–0.6. Figure 2(b) reveals that as the value of δ raises, the accuracy of the algorithm raises gradually. The algorithm performs well when $\delta = 0.6$–0.9. In summary, if the value of the parameter δ is 0.6, the precision of the CDTD algorithm is

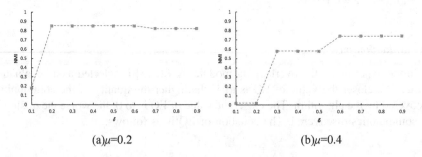

(a)μ=0.2   (b)μ=0.4

Fig. 2. The results of experiment parameter δ.

always in high level. Hence, the value of parameter δ is 0.6 in the subsequent experiments.

4.4 Experimental Results on the Real-World Datasets

Figure 3 gives the experimental results of the CDTD algorithm, Attractor algorithm, MCL algorithm, CPM algorithm and DEMON algorithm on the real-world datasets. Figure 3 reveals that, except for the word dataset, the CDTD algorithm is better than other algorithms on all datasets. Because the CDTD adhibits the mechanism of dynamic distance to update the distance between nodes, and finds overlapping community structure according to the strategy of similarity maximization. Therefore, the CDTD algorithm can find overlapping communities with high precision.

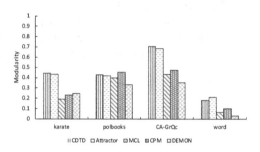

Fig. 3. The results of experiment on real-world dataset.

4.5 Experimental Results on Artificial Datasets

(1) *experiments with different values of μ*

Figure 4 gives the experimental results of the algorithms on artificial network T_1. Figure 4 reveals that, with the raise of the value of μ, the NMI values of all the algorithms gradually decrease. When the value of μ increases to a certain value, the NMI value drops dramatically because the boundaries of the communities are getting blurred as the value of μ increases, which makes most algorithms more difficult to

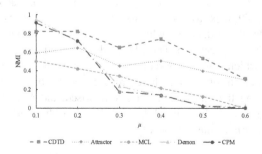

Fig. 4. The results of experiment on network T_1.

identify communities accurately. In Fig. 4, except for $\mu = 0.1$, the NMI values of the CDTD algorithm are higher than the other algorithms. The Attractor algorithm is in the second place. The other three algorithms do not perform well. As the value of μ raises, the results of CDTD are stable and the fluctuation is small because the mechanism based on the dynamic distance considers the influence of three different types of neighbor nodes when dealing with the influence of community nodes. Therefore, the robustness of the algorithm is improved.

(2) *experiments with different values of on*

Figure 5 gives the experimental results of the algorithms on artificial network T_2. Figure 5 tells us that, as the value of *on* raises, the NMI value of each algorithm lessens slightly or remain unchanged. In Fig. 5, the CDTD algorithm always gets the best results no matter how the value of *on* varies, followed by the Attractor algorithm and the DEMON algorithm. The other two algorithms perform not very well. It is because that the CDTD algorithm uses the strategy of similarity maximization for community detection. The strategy considers the similarity between the nodes and the communities, which can better discover the overlapping structures in the network.

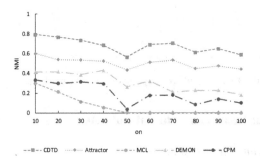

Fig. 5. The results of experiment on network T_2.

(3) *scalability experiments*

Figure 6 gives the results of the experiments of the algorithms on artificial network T_3. It reflects the time cost of each algorithm while the scale of the data set increases. Figure 6 reveals that, as the value of N raises, the cost of each algorithm rises up. The CDTD algorithm performs well. Its time-consuming raises linearly with the increase of the scale of the datasets, which is kept up with the analysis of time complexity of the algorithm in Sect. 3.5. The CDTD algorithm adopts the strategy based on triangle coarsening which can greatly reduce the size of the network while maintaining most of the community information. Therefore, the running time of the algorithm can reduce greatly. Among the other algorithms comparised, the Attractor, the CPM and the DEMON perform relatively well, while the MCL algorithm performs poorly, which is largely due to its $O(n^3)$ time complexity.

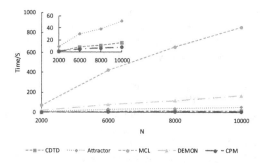

Fig. 6. The results of experiment on network T_3.

5 Conclusion

In this paper, a community detection algorithm devised upon triangle coarsening and dynamic distance is put forward. First, a triangle-based coarsening strategy is adopted to reduce the network scale. Then, the initial community discovery is implemented on the coarsened network. The mechanism of overlapping-Attractor with dynamic distance is adopted. The overlapping community is found by the strategy of similarity maximization. Finally, the final community is obtained through the reverse coarsening process. The results of the experiments reveal that the CDTD can discover overlapping communities with high precision while maintaining near linear time complexity. Next, we intend to enhance the performance of the CDTD algorithm devised upon the incremental analysis strategies to apply it to dynamic social networks. In addition, the MapReduce model will be tried to parallelize the CDTD algorithm to make it available to uncover communities in tremendous networks.

Acknowledgments. This work is partly supported by the National Natural Science Foundation of China under Grant No. 61300104, No. 61300103 and No. 61672158, the Fujian Province High School Science Fund for Distinguished Young Scholars under Grant No. JA12016, the Program for New Century Excellent Talents in Fujian Province University under Grant No. JA13021, the Fujian Natural Science Funds for Distinguished Young Scholar under Grant No. 2014J06017 and No. 2015J06014, the Major Production and Research Project of Fujian Scientific and Technical Department, the Technology Innovation Platform Project of Fujian Province (Grants Nos. 2009J1007, 2014H2005), the Fujian Collaborative Innovation Center for Big Data Applications in Governments, and the Natural Science Foundation of Fujian Province under Grant No. 2013J01230 and No. 2014J01232, Industry-Academy Cooperation Project under Grant No. 2014H6014 and No. 2017H6008. Haixi Government Big Data Application Cooperative Innovation Center.

References

1. Newman, M.E., Girvan, M.: Finding and evaluating community structure in networks. Phys. Rev. E Stat. Nonlinear Soft Matter Phys. **69**(2), 026113 (2004)
2. Palla, G., Derényi, I., Farkas, I., et al.: Uncovering the overlapping community structure of complex networks in nature and society. Nature **435**, 814–818 (2005)

3. Shen, H.W., Cheng, X.Q., Cai, K., et al.: Detect overlapping and hierarchical community structure in networks. Phys. A **388**(8), 1706–1712 (2009)
4. Raghavan, U.N., Albert, R., Kumara, S.: Near linear time algorithm to detect community structures in large-scale networks. Phys. Rev. E (Stat. Nonlinear Soft Matter Phys.) **76**(3), 036106 (2007)
5. Gregory, S.: Finding overlapping communities in networks by label propagation. New J. Phys. **12**(10), 1–26 (2010)
6. Zhang, C.L., Wang, Y.L., Wu, Y.J., et al.: Multi-label propagation algorithm for overlapping community discovery based on information entropy and local correlation. J. Chin. Mini-Micro Comput. Syst. **37**(8), 1645–1650 (2016)
7. Zhu, M., Meng, F.R., Zhou, Y.: Density-based link clustering algorithm for overlapping community detection. J. Comput. Res. Dev. **50**(12), 2520–2530 (2013)
8. He, D., Jin, D., Baquero, C., et al.: Link community detection using generative model and nonnegative matrix factorization. PLoS ONE **9**(1), 0086899 (2014)
9. Liu, Q., Liu, C., Wang, J., et al.: Evolutionary link community structure discovery in dynamic weighted networks. Phys. A **466**, 370–388 (2017)
10. Shao, J., Han, Z., Yang, Q., Zhou, T.: Community detection based on distance dynamics. In: Proceedings of 21th ACM SIGKDD International Conference on Knowledge Discovery and Data Mining, Sydney, Australia, pp. 1075–1084 (2015)
11. Meng, T., Cai, L., He, T., et al.: An improved community detection algorithm based on the distance dynamics. In: International Conference on Intelligent Networking and Collaborative Systems, pp. 135–142. IEEE (2016)
12. Chen, L., Zhang, J., Cai, L.J., Deng, Z.Y.: Fast community detection based on distance dynamics. Tsinghua Sci. Technol. **22**(06), 564–585 (2017)
13. Kumpula, J.M., Kivelä, M., Kaski, K., et al.: Sequential algorithm for fast clique percolation. Phys. Rev. E **78**(2), 026109 (2008)
14. Zachary, W.W.: An information flow model for conflict and fission in small groups. J. Anthropol. Res. **33**(4), 452–473 (1977)
15. Newman, M.E.: Finding community structure in networks using the eigenvectors of matrices. Phys. Rev. E (Stat. Nonlinear Soft Matter Phys.) **74**(3), 036104 (2006)
16. Lancichinetti, A., Fortunato, S., Radicchi, F.: Benchmark graphs for testing community detection algorithms. Phys. Rev. E Stat. Nonlinear Soft Matter Phys. **78**(2), 046110 (2008)
17. Dongen, S.: A cluster algorithm for graphs. Technical report, CWI, Amsterdam, The Netherlands (2000)
18. Palla, G., Derényi, I., Farkas, I., Vicsek, T.: Uncovering the overlapping community structure of complex networks in nature and society. Nature **435**(7043), 814–818 (2005)
19. Coscia, M., Rossetti, G., Giannotti, F., Pedreschi, D.: Demon: a local-first discovery method for overlapping communities. In: Proceedings of the 18th ACM SIGKDD International Conference on Knowledge Discovery and Data Mining, pp. 615–623 (2012)
20. Danon, L., Diaz-Guilera, A., Duch, J., Arenas, A.: Comparing community structure identification. J. Stat. Mech. Theory Exp. **09**, P09008 (2005)

Identifying Potential Experts on Stack Overflow

Zihan Ban[1,2], Jiafei Yan[1,2(✉)], and Hailong Sun[1,2]

[1] SKLSDE Lab, School of Computer Science and Engineering, Beihang University,
Beijing 100191, China
`zhban23@hotmail.com, yanjf@act.buaa.edu.cn, sunhl@buaa.edu.cn`
[2] Beijing Advanced Innovation Center for Big Data and Brain Computing,
Beijing 100191, China

Abstract. Question answering community is an online service of user-generated content, where users seek help by posting questions and help others by offering answers. In question answering community, most of high quality answers are posted by some users called experts. The early identification of experts is of great significance to the success of community, based on which we can take measures to avoid the loss of expert users and encourage them to make more contributions. Different from the related works, we put forward an efficient method of supervised learning to identify potential topical experts in question answering community. Above all, we define and quantify the concepts of expert. Then on a specific topic, we extract the user features from three dimensions, including text-feature, behavior-feature and time-feature. Finally, we use the classification algorithms in machine learning to identify whether a user is the potential expert on current topic. Based on the data of Stack Overflow, we carry out a lot of experiments and implement a potential experts identification system. The results demonstrate the excellent effectiveness of our method based on artificial neural network model. Besides, we find that expert users are inclined to interact with other expert users, providing new ideas for future research on this subject.

Keywords: Question answering community
Potential experts identifying · Feature extraction
Classification algorithm

1 Introduction

With the prosperity of the information industry, question answering communities, such as Stack Overflow[1], Quora[2], and Zhihu[3], have been recognized by more and more users. The question answering community provides users with

---

[1] http://stackoverflow.com.
[2] http://quora.com.
[3] http://zhihu.com.

© Springer Nature Singapore Pte Ltd. 2019
Y. Sun et al. (Eds.): ChineseCSCW 2018, CCIS 917, pp. 301–315, 2019.
https://doi.org/10.1007/978-981-13-3044-5_22

a convenient way to exchange knowledge and explore questions [3], where users can ask questions, provide answers and vote on questions or answers. Thousands of questions and answers are posted every day, which provide continuous growth of information resources for the communities.

In question answering community, most of high quality answers are posted by a little group of experts [8]. As a service of user-generated content, question answering community platforms' most valuable resources are users, especially the expert users. Therefore, in order to promote question answering community's development, it's necessary to take some measures to avoid the loss of expert users and encourage them to make more contributions, in particular when the experts have just entered the community. The crucial step is to identify as early as possible who will become expert users in the future.

In this research, our aim is to identify potential topical experts in question answering community, which is to determine whether an ordinary user will become an expert. We define expert users quantitatively by the best answer[4] number and the lifecycle. Users who have provided at least ten best answers on one topic in the first four years from joining the community are considered expert users. This definition allows us to clearly divide the expert users and ordinary users, and make it possible to apply supervised learning.

Unlike the previous works, we consider potential topical experts identifying problem from the viewpoint of supervised learning, which is better than the semi-supervised learning used by the Van Dijk et al. [11]. First, we extract the user features on Stack Overflow from three dimensions: text-feature, behavior-feature and time-feature, and select a total of 16 features. Then, to forecast if an ordinary user will be an expert, we apply five commonly used classification algorithms in machine learning, including Linear Support Vector Machine, Multi-Layer Perceptron, Random Forest, Gauss Bayes, Logistic Regression, and select the best classification algorithm. In the experiments, we apply supervised learning to train classifiers. Finally, we achieve the identification effect of F1-Score reaching more than 90% at the initial stage of user entry.

After that, we implement a potential experts identification system based on Stack Overflow. In our research, we also seek to explore three questions: Which classification algorithm performs best on the dataset of Stack Overflow? Which feature dimension influences the identification effect of classifier the most? If interaction relationship of users can become a new feature dimension to optimize classifier?

In this paper, our main contributions are as follows:

- We give a clearer definition of experts then previous work. Then, we use supervised learning methods: artificial neural networks model to achieve potential experts classifier.
- Based on our approach, we implement a potential experts identification system on Stack Overflow.
- We find that expert users are inclined to interact with other expert users, providing new ideas for future research on this subject.

---

[4] Answers that are accepted by the question posters.

Roadmap. The remaining parts of this paper are organized as follows. In next section, we give a literature review of previous subject, and summarize previous study according to the order of research and development. In Sect. 3, we define and quantify several important nouns, and give a detailed description of our approach and some of the important technologies used. In Sect. 4, we give the introduction and partition of the data used in the experiment, as well as the specific experimental process and results. The next Sect. 5 gives an introduction to our exhibition system. Section 6 gives our verification, analysis and exploration of the research results. At last, in Sect. 7, we give a summary of the whole research and look into the future of this subject.

2   Related Work

2.1   Text-Feature and Behavior-Feature

In 2011, Pal et al. [8] first start identifying the potential experts in Community Question Answering platforms.

They believe that the key for CQA[5] sites to succeed is a little group of experts who continue to post a lot of high quality answers. In first few weeks of expert users entering the community, finding them will bring a lot of benefits to the development of CQA, for example, community administrators can take measures to motivate and make these potential expert users stay in community. In their work, they explore how to predict these potential experts early and analyze users' behavior and quantify users' interests to help solve problems. These features make it possible for Pal et al. [8] to apply classification algorithms, including Support Vector Machine and Decision Tree, to determine users who may become experts. At last, they achieve the classification effect of F1-Score to 50%. Their research shows that potential experts in CQA can be identified effectively through their method.

In addition, Pal et al. [8] also ask TTLC[6] community managers to assess their model of identifying potential experts. The results show that many users in the TTLC community are already experts or are on the road to becoming experts.

2.2   Text-Feature and Interest-Feature

In 2013, Yang et al. [12] put forward new research methods for identifying potential experts.

For the first time, they put forward a method that topics and users both participate in feature extraction. Before that, the topics and users performance features are modeled separately. On the one hand, when the topic model is applied to question answering community, the semantic similarity between questions and answers can be quantified, thus helping to find the related questions

---

[5] Community Question Answering.

[6] http://ttlc.intuit.com.

and answers when a question is posted. They also use user historical data to build a model of users' preference, so that users and problems can be matched according to the similarity between users and topics. On the other hand, the ability of users to post answers is considered as the professional level of the user, so that questions can be better recommended to the user.

Besides, they put forward a probabilistic thematic expert model, TEM [12], which uses label to extract the topic profile and uses a gaussian mixture model to simulate the process of vote. Based on the results, they put forward an extension of the PageRank [7] - CQARank [12].

Finally, they use a large dataset from Stack Overflow to carry out a complete experimental research. Results show the identification effect of the CQARank is significantly improved compared with the previous work.

2.3   Text-Feature and Time-Feature

In 2015, Van Dijk et al. [11], based on the research of Pal et al. [8], further optimize the identification of potential experts and achieve better results.

In their methods, the professional level of users can be displayed through multiple channels, such as comments, questions, answers and best answers. The work done by Van Dijk et al. [11] has some differences from previous work on potential expert identification:

– They propose a new definition of potential experts,
– They study and demonstrate the importance of combining a large number of text-feature, behavior-feature and time-feature to identify potential experts.

They define experts based on the best answer number, and users who have ten or more best answers on one topic are considered expert users. They design three types of features to predict potential experts: text, behavior and time. In addition, they want to explore and answer the following questions through experiments.

– How does it affect the effectiveness of classification when combined with some feature sets? Can the performance be stable?
– Which is the most essential feature set of identifying potential experts in text, behavior and time feature sets?
– Which is the most essential individual feature in the whole features?

To answer these questions, they use data from Stack Overflow in the experiment. The results are significantly improved compared with Pal et al. [8], and demonstrate the effectiveness of using multiple text-features and time-features. Finally, the F1-Score of the classifier reaches 75%, indicating that they can achieve high precision prediction when users enters question answering community early on in their lifecycle.

2.4   Question-Feature and Behavior-Feature

In 2017, on the basis of previous research, Bhanu et al. [2] further consider the difficulty of questions in the question answering community to identify whether a user will become an expert user. They also introduce the difficulty of questions to the classification model. Finally, they get the result of F1-Score over 90% on three hot topics of C, Python and Java.

In the paper, they propose that when they predict experts on Stack Overflow, they consider the difficulty of a question when a user answer to the question as a new dimension of feature. And they combine it with the other features based on behavior to identify the potential experts. They use two different ideas to judge the difficulty of questions:

– Not easy to find high quality answers, that is long answer time and low number of answers,
– Asked by users many times, that is frequent occurrence.

In the experiment, they analyze the text and data produced by Stack Overflow, and apply the random forest algorithm to the extracted feature set. Then, they compare the identification effect of the classifier when four different expert labeling methods are used.

The results show that although the difficulty of questions may not be the greatest feature of predicting potential experts, the accuracy and effect of the potential expert identification is greatly improved by combining the features with users' behavioral features. Moreover, they use three programming language topics for verification, with an accuracy increase of between 5% and 16%.

3   Approach

This section gives a detailed description of our approach.

First, we define the expert quantitatively. In Van Dijk's [11] definition method, users are experts on a topic when their number of best answers is one standard deviation larger than the average number of best answers over all users on the topic. Based on that definition, we take into account the expert user's efficiency of obtaining best answers and propose stricter definition. In the paper, we optimize the definition method as: users are experts on a topic when their number of best answers is one standard deviation larger than the average and their using-time is one standard deviation less than the average over all users on the topic. Next, we get the definition on Stack Overflow that users who obtain at least ten best answers using less than four years are considered as expert users. At last, we can give the definition of potential experts - users who are not experts now, but will get at least ten best answers on a topic in their first four years.

Then, we extract three types of user features: text-feature, behavior-feature and time-feature, with a total of 16 features. Table 1 shows all the features and detailed descriptions used in the experiment.

Table 1. Three types of features we used and descriptions.

ID	Feature	Description
	Text-feature	
1	TR	Model2 with TextRank
2	BM	Model2 with BM25
3	TFIDF	Model2 with TF.IDF
	Behavior-feature	
4	Q	Number of questions
5	A	Number of answers
6	AScore	Average score of answers
7	ACom	Average comment number of answers
8	ZScore	Question-answering ratio
	Time-feature	
9	M	Months between joining and present
10	TR/M	LM/M
11	BM/M	BM/M
12	TFIDF/M	TFIDF/M
13	Q/M	Question/M
14	A/M	Answer/M
15	ZScore/M	ZScore/M
16	QA/M	Question/Answer/M

Among them, the main step of text-feature extraction is to use TF-IDF [13] to calculate the weight of all text on JavaScript topic, and select the 100 words with the highest weight as the profile of the current topic, then use TF-IDF [13], BM25 [9] and TextRank [5] respectively. The three algorithms are to extract every user's profile weight from all words. After that, we apply the idea of Model 2 [1] to calculate the text relevance between users and topics. The following formula shows how Model 2 to calculate text relevance:

$$R(t|u) = \sum_{w \in P_t} f(w, P_u), \tag{1}$$

where t denotes a topic, u denotes a user, w denotes a word, P_t is the profile of the topic, P_u is the profile of the user and $f(w, P_u)$ is the function of calculating the weight of words, that is the three text algorithms we mentioned earlier.

With regard to behavior-feature, we use the users' most basic behavioral performance, such as question number, answer number, and so on. Among them, it is worth noting that ZScore [14] is related to user question number and answer number, which is used to quantify the user's professional level, and its mathematical expression is as the formula:

$$ZScore = \frac{a - q}{\sqrt{a + q}},\qquad(2)$$

where q denotes user question number and a denotes user answer number.

Regarding the time-feature, we improve on the basis of the research of Van Dijk et al. [11], and select a total of eight features, which can be referred to the Table 1.

After feature extraction, we use five commonly used machine learning classification algorithms to forecast if a user can be an expert. The algorithms are as follows:

- Gaussian Bayesian, is an algorithm based on Bayesian theory,
- Logistic Regression, is an algorithm based on regression,
- Linear Support Vector Machine, is an algorithm based on kernel,
- Random Forest, is an improved algorithm based on decision tree,
- Multi-Layer Perceptron, is an artificial neural network algorithm.

Finally, we cross-validate the five algorithms and select the best performing classification algorithm as the final classifier.

4 Experiments

In this part, we carry out experiments to select the best classifier for potential experts identifying.

We use the dataset of Stack Overflow[7] since its inception to August 31, 2017, including questions, answers, basic user information and topic information. The data resources are quite rich, and Table 2 gives the composition of all dataset.

Table 2. Composition of the dataset from Stack Overflow.

Type	Number	Description
Question	14,458,875	Question text, best answer ID, timestamp, topic et al.
Answer	22,668,556	Answer text, question ID, timestamp, user ID, grade et al.
User	7,617,191	Name, reputation, registration time, last login time et al.
Topic	50,000	ID, name, question number et al.

In our experiments, we identify potential experts on the most popular topic on Stack Overflow - JavaScript. After selecting the JavaScript-related data, we get the dataset including 272,564 users, 1,665,483 answers, and 937,917 questions. We use these data for feature extraction, then build the data set.

---

[7] http://blog.stackoverflow.com/category/cc-wiki-dump/.

For ease of explanation and experimentation, we have a preliminary breakdown of user data:

$$User = E + NE + U, \qquad (3)$$

where $User$ denotes all users in dataset, E denotes users who are already experts, NE denotes non-expert users who don't get at least ten best answers in the first four years, and U denotes users who can't be labeled because of their short lifecycle. In addition, U can be divided as the formula:

$$U = PE + NPE, \qquad (4)$$

where PE denotes the potential expert users and NPE denotes users who are not experts now and won't be experts.

Further, we divide train set and test set based on the set of $E + NE$. So as to ensure that there are enough expert users in train set and test set, we expand the expert user data according to the N($0 \leq N \leq 9$) periods of the number of the best answers of the experts. In addition, in order to balance the number of non-experts in train set and test set, we use the downsampling [10] method for non-expert data in each period, so that the proportion of experts and non-experts in each period of both set is balanced. Finally, train set and test set are as follows:

- Train Set = 3,391 Expert × 10($0 \leq N \leq 9$) + 95,993 Non-Expert,
- Test Set = 3,390 Expert × 10($0 \leq N \leq 9$) + 95,993 Non-Expert.

The process of feature extraction and dataset construction takes about 3 hours on our experimental computer.

For finding the classification algorithm with the best classification effect, we tried five commonly used classification algorithms, and we hope to get a suitable one for the data of Stack Overflow from these algorithms, including: Gaussian Bayesian Classifier, Logistic Regression Classifier, Linear Support Vector Machine Classifier, Random Forest Classifier, and Multi-Layer Perceptron Classifier.

In the experiment, we train classifiers based on the algorithms provided by Scikit[8], no parameter optimization performed except for the Multi-Layer Perceptron algorithm. In order to get suitable parameters of the Multi-Layer Perceptron Classifier, we have separately constructed a validation set with a sample size of 1000. After many attempts, the multi-layer neural network uses 2 hidden layers with 10 neurons per layer. The model is trained using the Adam [4] optimization algorithm with a maximum number of iterations of 200.

Before getting the formal classifiers, we apply the K-fold cross-validation [6] to evaluate the effect of five classification models. When using K-fold cross-validation, we use the most common ten-fold cross-validation method for all experimental samples. The data set used is the previously divided train set.

In the process of cross-validating, the training of Multi-Layer Perceptron Classifier takes several minutes, while other classifiers' training are finished in

---

[8] http://scikit-learn.org.

seconds. The average value of F1-Score is used as the final evaluation, and Table 3 gives the result of K-fold cross-validation.

Table 3. Results of K-fold cross-validation.

Classifier	F1 average
Linear Support Vector Machine Classifier	0.724
Random Forest Classifier	0.883
Gaussian Bayesian Classifier	0.657
Logistic Regression Classifier	0.734
Multi-Layer Perceptron Classifier	0.944

According to the results in Table 3, Multi-Layer Perceptron Classifier performs best and its advantage in terms of F1-Score is quite obvious. Therefore, we choose the Multi-Layer Perceptron Classifier that best fits the Stack Overflow dataset as the final classification model. Next, we will formally train the classifier.

We continue to train the Multi-Layer Perceptron model using the Adam optimization algorithm, with a maximum number of iterations of 200. The process of training takes a few minutes. Next, we use test set is to evaluate the effect of Multi-Layer Perceptron model on JavaScript topic, and the final result is given by Fig. 1 of the best answer number as the evaluation basic unit, where the average F1-Score is 94.6%.

Fig. 1. Classification effect of Multi-Layer Perceptron Classifier on JavaScript topic.

It can be seen from Fig. 1 that the Multi-Layer Perceptron Classifier can achieve the classification effect of F1-Score more than 90% in every period of best answer number, indicating that our classifier on Stack Overflow dataset has a good fitting effect and is ideal for identifying potential experts.

Besides, we also use the Multi-Layer Perceptron Classifier to identify all users on JavaScript topic. And the results show that the number of potential experts on JavaScript topic is 1,566.

5   Prototype Implementation

After the training of classifier, we implement the potential experts identification system based on Stack Overflow. By the system, we can present the predictive result to people in a clearer and more convenient way through the web page. What's more, the system contains more comprehensive user query results and analysis charts.

Figure 2 gives the web system's architecture.

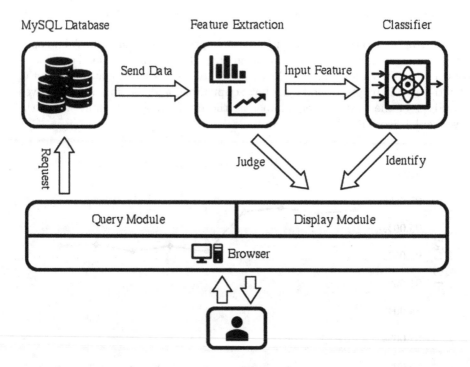

Fig. 2. Overall architecture of the potential expert identification system based on the Stack Overflow.

In our system, people can search for users by ID number or nickname, and obtain the basic information, the statistics information and the predictive result of the user in the form of tables, including: registration time, question number, answer number, best answer number, user interaction distribution, activity heat maps of each period, and the results of identification by the classifier. The results of classifier are divided into four types:

- Expert,
- Non-Expert,
- Not expert now, but will be expert,
- Not expert now, and will not be expert.

The working process of the system is that the user enters the system through the browser, queries through the search box, and then the web page sends a request to the background system. Next, system extracts data from the database for judgment and input into the Multi-Layer Perceptron Classifier for identification. Finally, the result is sent to the browser's display module.

At present, Stack Overflow community has no similar function for identifying and predicting users. Based on our system, Stack Overflow platform can better manage its users. They can not only label users with the results we provide but also take measures to motivate the expert users in the community.

6 Results and Analysis

In this part, we verify the effectiveness of the approach and explore the experimental results.

6.1 Results Verification

In previous section, we only experiment on JavaScript topic of Stack Overflow, so the experiments may have some contingency, and it cannot be said that our methods must be reasonable and correct. Therefore, we will continue to experiment on Java topic to eliminate or reduce the impact of contingency on the results of this experiment and verify the results we have achieved.

There are 244,810 users, 1,722,879 answers and 919,012 questions on Java topic. We extract three types of features of all users on Java topic in the same way as before, and get 7,307 expert users. Then, we build the test set and train set, finally use the Adam optimization algorithm to train the Multi-Layer Perceptron Classifier with the same structure and iteration number as before. The effect of the classifier on Java topic is shown in Fig. 3.

The Multi-Layer Perceptron Classifier on Java topic achieves the classification effect of F1-Score about 90% in every period of best answer number, which is a good verification of our previous results. It demonstrates that our methods can accurately identify potential experts on Stack Overflow.

Similar to on JavaScript, we use the classifier to identify all users on Java topic and results show there are 2,561 potential experts on Java topic at present.

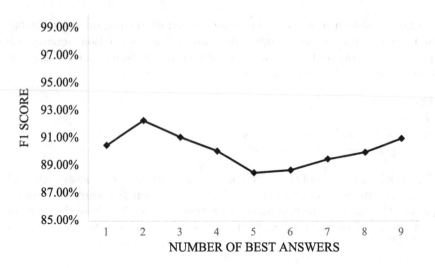

Fig. 3. Classification effect of Multi-Layer Perceptron Classifier on Java topic.

6.2 Impact of Each Feature Dimension

Before the experiments, we raise several questions. One of them is: in the process of training, which dimension features have the greatest impact on the classifiers? To solve this problem, we further set up experiments on JavaScript topic to divide the features of the three dimensions into three groups: (1) behavior-feature and time-feature, (2) text-feature and time-feature, and (3) text-feature and behavior-feature. Next, Multi-Layer Perceptron Classifiers are trained and tested through these groups of sets, and the effects are judged by comparing with the effects of original classifier.

Figure 4 shows the results. And it can be seen that in the absence of behavior-feature, the degradation of classifier identification effect is very obvious, so it can be concluded that in the experiment of identifying potential experts, behavior-feature plays the most important role. The reasons may be that behavior-feature accumulates more than other features and has stronger representation.

In addition, from the results of Fig. 4, we can also see that in the absence of text-feature or time-feature, the effects of classifier have declined to some extent, so both text-feature and time-feature has the function of optimizing the performance of the model and improving the identification effect. However, we can also see that in the absence of time-feature, the magnitude of the classifier's decline in each period is greater than in the absence of text-feature, indicating that the impact of text-feature on the identification effect should be minimal. In future research, we will try to extract the users' text-feature in a more scientific way.

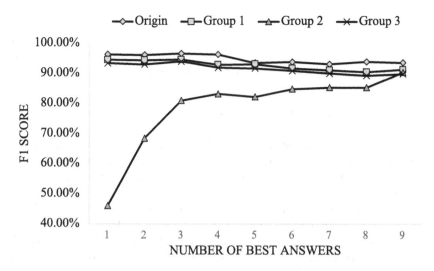

Fig. 4. Classification results of three groups of features.

6.3 Exploration of User Interaction

We explore whether the user interaction relationship can be a part of feature extraction, so we can improve the identification effect of the classifier on potential experts. In other words, we want to verify whether the user interaction distribution has a potential function of distinguishing potential experts and non-potential experts.

First, we define that the user A has an interaction with user B when the user A answers the questions posted by user B. The user interaction distribution is defined as a categories component of all users that interacts with a user. Here, we use statistical methods to get the difference between users' interactions in different categories.

We divide all users into two categories: expert-users, which consists of the potential experts obtained by classifier and users who have been experts, and non-expert-users, which consists of the non-potential experts and users who are not experts. Further statistics show that the average answer number of all expert-users on JavaScript topic is 26.47 times, and the average answer times of non-expert-users is 3.08 times; the average number of interaction between expert-users and expert-users is 7.69 times, and the average number of inter-action between non-expert-users and expert-users is 0.19 times. Furthermore, we calculate that the proportion of the interaction between expert-users and expert-users is 29.04%, while the proportion of non-expert-users and expert-users is 6.02%. The gap between the two results is very obvious, which shows that using user interaction distribution to distinguish between expert-users and non-expert-users is feasible. It can be concluded that expert-users are inclined to interact with expert-users.

The above description is only one of the many features in user interaction relationship. We can see that users' relationship is related to user category. We believe that, in the future, we can consider using the features of user relationship to obtain a better potential experts identification effect.

7   Conclusions and Future Work

In our study, we use the classification model of machine learning to complete the identification of potential experts on Stack Overflow, then implement a potential topic experts identification system, and finally explore the results of the experiment.

In the experiment, first of all, we define and quantify the concepts. Then, we extract features from three dimensions of user data. After that, the effect of five candidate classification models is evaluated by cross validation, and the Multi-Layer Perceptron Classifier with the average value of 94.6% at each time of F1-Score is selected as the final classifier. So as to eliminate the contingency of experiments, we carry out experiments again to verify the previous results. Finally, the potential experts identification system on Stack Overflow is completed based on the classifier.

After the experiments, we further explore the results to solve the questions raised before the experiment. According to the experimental results, we can see that the expert-users and non-expert-users show different behavior patterns in user relationship. Therefore, we can believe that the user interaction has the function of distinguishing the user category, and can be added to the training of the classifier as a new feature dimension in the future. Our study puts forward improvement measures and new research ideas.

Acknowledgments. This work was supported by National Key Research and Development Program of China under Grant No. 2016YFB1000804.

References

1. Balog, K., Fang, Y., Rijke, M.D.: Expertise retrieval (2012)
2. Bhanu, M., Chandra, J.: Exploiting response patterns for identifying topical experts in StackOverflow. In: Eleventh International Conference on Digital Information Management, pp. 139–144 (2017)
3. Bouguessa, M., Wang, S.: Identifying authoritative actors in question-answering forums: the case of Yahoo! answers. In: ACM SIGKDD International Conference on Knowledge Discovery and Data Mining, pp. 866–874 (2008)
4. Kingma, D.P., Ba, J.: Adam: a method for stochastic optimization. Computer Science (2014)
5. Mihalcea, R.: Textrank: bringing order into texts. In: EMNLP, pp. 404–411 (2004)
6. Moreno-Torres, J.G., Saez, J.A., Herrera, F.: Study on the impact of partition-induced dataset shift on k-fold cross-validation. IEEE Trans. Neural Netw. Learn. Syst. **23**(8), 1304–1312 (2012)

7. Page, L., Brin, S., Motwani, R., Winograd, T.: The PageRank citation ranking: bringing order to the web. In: World Wide Web Internet and Web Information Systems. Food Microstructure, pp. 1–17 (1990)
8. Pal, A., Farzan, R., Konstan, J.A., Kraut, R.E.: Early detection of potential experts in question answering communities. In: Konstan, J.A., Conejo, R., Marzo, J.L., Oliver, N. (eds.) UMAP 2011. LNCS, vol. 6787, pp. 231–242. Springer, Heidelberg (2011). https://doi.org/10.1007/978-3-642-22362-4_20
9. Robertson, S., Zaragoza, H., Taylor, M.: Simple BM25 extension to multiple weighted fields. In: Thirteenth ACM International Conference on Information and Knowledge Management, pp. 42–49 (2004)
10. Segall, C.A.: Study of upsampling/down-sampling for spatial scalability (2005)
11. Van Dijk, D., Tsagkias, M., De Rijke, M.: Early detection of topical expertise in community question answering, pp. 995–998 (2015)
12. Yang, L., Qiu, M., Gottipati, S., Zhu, F., Jiang, J.: CQARank: jointly model topics and expertise in community question answering, pp. 99–108 (2013)
13. Zhai, C., Lafferty, J.: A study of smoothing methods for language models applied to ad hoc information retrieval. In: International ACM SIGIR Conference on Research and Development in Information Retrieval, pp. 334–342 (2001)
14. Zhang, J., Ackerman, M.S., Adamic, L.: Expertise networks in online communities: structure and algorithms. In: International Conference on World Wide Web, pp. 221–230 (2007)

Predicting Students' Mood Level Using Multi-feature Fusion Joint Sentiment-Topic Model in Mobile Learning

Xianqing Wang[1], Meihua Zhao[2], Changqin Huang[2(✉)], Jia Zhu[2], and Yong Tang[2]

[1] School of Continuing Education, Guangdong Polytechnic of Science and Technology, Guangzhou 510640, China
[2] School of Computer, South China Normal University, Guangzhou 510631, China
cqhuang@scnu.edu.cn

Abstract. The absence of learning emotional support has great impact on online learning. This paper presents an adaptive students-mood prediction framework to improve learning emotion in Mobile Learning (M-Learning), in which a mechanism is adopted to detect a kind of depressed students and provide guidance for tutors to help them with intervention. To effectively predict students' mood level, we propose a novel fully-unsupervised multi-feature fusion joint sentiment-topic model and detail its inference. The proposed model adds an additional pedagogical features layer into the existing layers based on two classical models, and applies IG (Information Gain) feature selection to optimize performance. Experiments have been conducted on various students' interactive emotion texts. The results show that our approach is a robust and reliable solution for automatic students' mood prediction in M-Learning.

Keywords: Mobile learning · Educational data · Multi-feature fusion
Mood analysis · Un-supervised learning

1 Introduction

The proliferation of the Internet into every aspect of our lives has evolved rapidly over the recent years, and many new learning ways are created with the support of the Internet [1]. Taking online learning as an instance, it has an increasing growth in the 21st century, and its sub-type: Mobile learning (M-Learning), is emerging in a promising way [2].

M-Learning takes advantage of traditional E-learning, and breaks the limitation of time and space by utilizing wireless technologies, such as mobile phones, PDAs or tablets. However, like E-learning, M-Learning is still lack of learning emotion since there are no face-to-face environments [3]. Without a loose, free and positive emotion communication environment, it may reduce students' learning confidence, interest and engagement, which becomes a harmful indication of mental health status or physical health for young adults. It's commonly believed that levels of mood have significant impact to physical health [4, 5]. What' worse, in M-Learning, how to solve the emotion

© Springer Nature Singapore Pte Ltd. 2019
Y. Sun et al. (Eds.): ChineseCSCW 2018, CCIS 917, pp. 316–330, 2019.
https://doi.org/10.1007/978-981-13-3044-5_23

obstacle becomes extremely harder due to location mobility, access intermittence and short contents [6]. Thereby, as for M-Learning, we need a new way of predicting students' emotion so as to alleviate the feeling of isolation.

To tackle the limitation, and achieve an accurate prediction of students' emotion in the education field, in this paper, we investigate to build an adaptive students-emotion predicting framework in M-Learning based on the proposed Multi-feature Fusion Joint Sentiment-Topic (MF-JST) model for the first time. Note that our model is unsupervised. In addition, we fuse discriminative pedagogical features of learners into the model by using three effective approaches of feature selection, i.e., the Chi-square ($\chi2$), the Mutual Information (MI) and the Information Gain (IG). Extensive experiments based on students' interactive emotion texts show that our framework has a better performance than other baseline methods.

In a word, the main technical contributions of this work include (i) a novel fully-unsupervised MF-JST model; and (ii) an approach to integrate four pedagogical features into the model achieving overall accuracy of 84.9% in education dataset.

2 Related Work

2.1 M-Learning

As a novel paradigm of teaching and learning, M-Learning sometimes refers to 'handheld learning', associated with the "learn anytime and anywhere" motto, which means that students engage in asynchronous, ubiquitous instruction through mobile devices [7]. The previous studies investigating M-Learning are mainly divided into two research fields: building systems of M-learning and improving the effectiveness of M-learning.

On the one hand, Jing [3] introduces the mobile communication system providing a convenient and efficient mode for millions of students to obtain effective phonetics education. Sun et al. [8] design a novel application in real-time for mobile phones to enhance learners' Islamic knowledge, and observe that the software has a lots of benefits for end-users through extensive experiments. Sidan et al. [9] present a collaborative system, and they focus on how to use wireless and mobile devices in medical education and clinical cooperation practice.

On the other hand, a growing number of literatures have paid attention on other broader area: the effectiveness of M-Learning. For example, Alrasheedi et al. [10] determine the leading cause for reducing the acceptance of M-Learning, and encourage students to leverage M-Learning platform. Kechaou et al. [11] propose a conceptual framework of emotion detection and analysis for e-learning system. Al-Hmouz et al. [12] investigate the limited factors affecting students' satisfaction. They analyze students' individual data by adopting machine learning methods: regression and SVMs and so on.

However, there are still few primary literatures focusing on the absence of learning emotional support also limiting the effectiveness of M-Learning. It is crucial to conduct a variety of further research methods to explore students' mood and physical health using substantial data produced by the mobile devices in students' daily lives.

2.2 Sentiment-Topic Analysis for NLP

Great bulk of work focusing on machine learning techniques has been universally applied for emotion prediction. Among these proposed algorithms, both supervised and un-supervised outperform than other methods.

Firstly, Pang et al. [13] determine a review whether it is positive or negative with the overall supervised machine learning methods and observe that the SVMs performance exceeds all other approaches. And the accuracy of sentiment predicting continues to be further improved in their next work [14]. In addition, Whitelaw et al. [15] provide a standard annotated movie review dataset for sentiment prediction field.

However, we find that the above work has common shortcomings: (1) they only investigate sentiment without extracting the topics in the texts; (2) the aforementioned supervised approaches require labelled corpora for training.

It is deemed to be more challenging to un-supervised methods. Blei et al. firstly propose a topic model named LDA [16] based on three layer Bayesian model, in order to extract underlying topics of documents. Yut et al. have improved on this model. They propose the LDA* [17] model to offer services in topic application field to Internet companies. However, Lin et al. add a brand-new function of sentiment analysis to LDA model by proposing the JST [19] model. Similarly, Lu et al. also present a MAS [18] model in another field. The most significant improvement is that MAS model and JST model can simultaneously analyze sentiment and topics of texts.

However, all these work seems not to be applicable completely in education field. Motivated by these observations, our work is partly inspired by the JST model, whereas MF-JST model concentrate on feasibly solving the absence of emotion of education by fusing pedagogical features.

3 Methodology

3.1 Overview of Framework

As depicted in Fig. 1, the overall framework is divided into five main parts. The following gives some details of these components.

Students' Interactive Emotion Texts Collection. In the first component, a set of informative students' emotional interactive texts are firstly collected and manually annotated with positive or negative sentiments.

Textual Pre-processing. The pre-processing procedure consists of five steps: merge documents, split sentences, segment words, remove stop words and generate a MF-JST input document.

Learning Context Collections. Four characteristics of learners are collected via smartphone apps, wearable sensors.

MF-JST Model. The above four-fold discriminative features are fused into the proposed MF-JST model, then we complete the topic-word distribution using Gibbs sampling to improve work efficiency.

Students' Mood Prediction. Finally, the last step aims to determine the mood level for each student based on simultaneously extracted emotion topics.

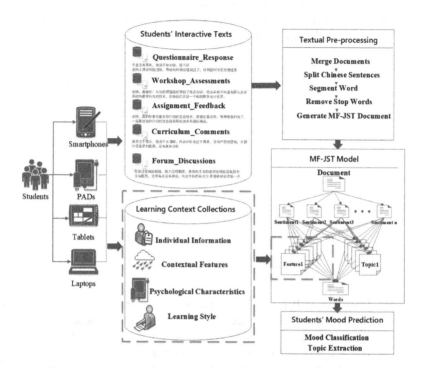

Fig. 1. Framework of MF-JST model for the students' mood prediction.

3.2 Joint Sentiment-Topic Model

The existing JST [19] model integrates an extra sentiment layer between document hierarchy and topic hierarchy based on LDA [24] model. In other words, sentiment layer is generated on the basis of document layer, topic layer is generated on the basis of sentiment layer. Finally, word layer are generated on the basis of both sentiment and topic layers. A graph of JST model is shown in Fig. 2a.

Assume we have a set of documents D, $D = \{d_1, d_2, \ldots, d_M\}$; each document d contains a sequence of N_d words, $d = (w_1, w_2, \ldots, w_{N_d})$. A word index contains V distinct elements, which each word in each d comes from it. In addition, the number of overall sentiment labels and topics labels are defined as S and T, respectively. In other words, every document contains S sentiment labels, and every sentiment label is related to T topics labels in JST model.

In JST, the whole generation step of each word w_i in document d is divided into three steps. First of all, a sentiment label l is selected from the document-sentiment distribution π_d. Secondly, the next step is to select a topic z constrained by sentiment label l from the sentiment-topic distribution $\theta_{d,l}$. Finally, a word w is selected from the sentiment-topic-word distribution $\varphi_{d,l,z}$, which is constrained by both l and z.

3.3   Multi-feature Fusion Joint Sentiment-Topic Model

In the section, we show the generation process of every word w_i in document d under MF-JST model, and we will introduce the approach how to integrate the feature layer into MF-JST model and elaborate the implementation method of MF-JST model in details. A diagram of MF-JST model is shown in Fig. 2b.

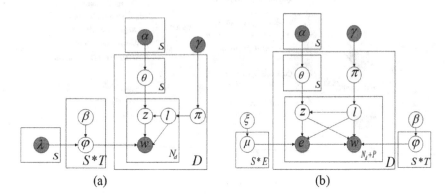

(a)   (b)

Fig. 2. (a) JST model; (b) MF-JST model.

The transformation of JST model into MF-JST model may be similar to that of LDA model into JST model. We propose the MF-JST model by integrating an additive feature layer between the document layer and the sentiment layer. Hence, the MF-JST model contains four layers. In MF-JST model, sentiment label l is related to document d. And then both topic label z and feature label e are related to sentiment label l. Finally, words w are related to the above three labels. To sum up, the generation process essentially offers methods to classify the sentiment of texts related to topics and features.

Following that, we present the formal definition of words in document d generation procedure of MF-JST model according to the graph model shown in Fig. 2b:

- For every sentiment label l, select a document- sentiment distribution $\pi_{d,l} \sim Dir(\gamma)$.
- For every topic label z, select a sentiment - topic distribution $\theta_{d,l,z} \sim Dir(\beta)$.
- For every feature label e, select a sentiment - feature distribution $\mu_{d,l,e} \sim Dir(\xi)$.
- For every word w_i:
  - Select a sentiment label $l_i \sim Mult(\pi_d)$,
  - Select a topic label $z_i \sim Mult(\theta_{d,l_i})$,
  - Select a feature label $e_i \sim Mult(\mu_{d,l})$,
  - Select a word w_i from both φ_{d_i,l_i,z_i} and θ_{d_i,l_i,e_i}, which are two multinomial distributions constrained by the above all labels: l_i, z_i and e_i.

3.4 MF-JST Model Inference

In the section, in details we will show the procedure of inference to four prior variables γ, α, β, ξ and distribution variables π, μ, θ, φ of MF-JST model.

The hyper-parameter γ in MF-JST model is defined as the prior observation counting numbers of times that it takes the sample of sentiment labels l from d. Similarly, the hyper-parameters α and ξ in MF-JST model are defined as the prior observation counting numbers of times that it takes the sample of topic labels z and features label e both related to sentiment labels l from d, respectively. Finally, the hyper-parameters β in MF-JST model is defined as the prior observation counting numbers of times that it takes the sample of words w related to the above three labels from d.

Furthermore, we present the procedure of inference to the following four distribution variables in MF-JST model, such as the document-sentiment distribution π, the sentiment-topic distribution θ, the sentiment-feature distribution μ, and the joint sentiment-topic/feature-word distribution φ. All in all, the following content will present how document-sentiment distribution π occupies an extremely significant role in classifying the polarity of texts.

The definition of the joint probability composed of w, z, e and l, is presented as the following Eq. (1):

$$P(w, e, z, l) = P(w|e, z, l)P(e|z, l) = P(w|z, l)P(e|z, l)P(z|l)P(l), \qquad (1)$$

where can be divided into four probability formula. By integrating out φ, we gain the first probability formula:

$$P(w|e, z, l) = \left(\frac{\tau(V\beta)}{\tau(\beta)^V}\right)^{S*T} \prod_l \prod_z \prod_e \frac{\prod_w \tau(N_{l,z,e,w} + \beta)}{\tau(N_{l,z,e} + V\beta)}, \qquad (2)$$

where S and T are defined as the overall numbers of sentiment labels and topics labels respectively; $N_{l,z,e,w}$ is defined as the overall number of times that words w show up under label z and label e; $N_{l,z,e}$ is defined as the overall number of times that words w are assigned to label z, label e and label l, and τ is treated as the gamma function.

By integrating out μ, we gain the second probability formula:

$$P(e|z, l) = \left(\frac{\tau(V\beta)}{\tau(\beta)^V}\right)^{E*S} \prod_d \prod_l \frac{\prod_l \tau(N_{d,l,e} + \xi)}{\tau(N_{d,l} + E\xi)}, \qquad (3)$$

where E is defined as the overall numbers of feature labels, $N_{d,l,e}$ is defined as the overall number of times that features e show up under label l, and $N_{d,l}$ is the overall number of times that labels l are assigned to d.

By integrating out θ, we gain the third probability formula:

$$P(z|l) = \left(\frac{\tau\left(\sum_{j=1}^{T}\alpha\right)}{\prod_{l=1}^{T}\tau(\alpha)}\right)^{D*S} \prod_{d}\prod_{l}\frac{\prod_{l}\tau(N_{d,l,z}+\alpha_{l,z})}{\tau\left(N_{d,l}+\sum_{j}\alpha_{l,z}\right)}, \tag{4}$$

where D is defined as the overall numbers of documents d, $N_{d,l,z}$ is defined as the overall number of times that topics z show up under label l.

By integrating out π, we gain the fourth probability formula:

$$P(l) = \left(\frac{\tau(S\gamma)}{\tau(\gamma)^s}\right)^{D} \prod_{d}\frac{\prod_{l}\tau(N_{d,l}+\gamma)}{\tau(N_d+S\gamma)}, \tag{5}$$

where N_d is defined as the overall number of w in d.

We use Gibbs sampling to build a conditional posterior distribution through taking the sample of variables: z_t, e_t and l_t, where $-t$ is defined as tth position that excludes data by the approaches of marginalizing out the distribution variables φ, θ, μ and π. Finally, the calculation formula of the distribution variables of φ, θ, μ and π are presented as the following Eq. (6):

$$P(e_t = e, z_t = z, l_t = l | w, e^{-t}, z^{-t}, l^{-t}, \alpha, \beta, \gamma, \xi)$$
$$\propto \frac{N_{l,z,w_t}^{T}+\beta}{N_{l,z}^{-t}+V\beta} \cdot \frac{N_{d,l,z}^{-t}+\alpha_{l,z}}{N_{d,l}^{-t}+\sum_z \alpha_{l,z}} \cdot \frac{N_{d,l}^{-t}+\gamma}{N_d^{-t}+S\gamma} \cdot \frac{P_{z,l}^e+\xi}{P_{z,l}+E\xi}. \tag{6}$$

The famous Markov chain is utilized to estimate joint sentiment-topic/feature-word distribution φ in this paper is

$$\varphi_{l,z,e,w} = \frac{N_{l,z,e}+\beta}{N_{l,z}+V\beta}. \tag{7}$$

And then, the estimated sentiment-topic distribution θ is

$$\theta_{d,l,z} = \frac{N_{d,l,z}+\alpha_{l,z}}{N_{d,l}+T\alpha}. \tag{8}$$

Similarly, the estimated sentiment-feature distribution μ, is

$$\mu_{d,l,e} = \frac{N_{d,l,e}+\xi}{N_{d,l}+E\xi}. \tag{9}$$

Lastly, we can easily obtain the estimated document-sentiment distribution π as following:

$$\pi_{d,l} = \frac{N_{d,l} + \gamma}{N_d + S\gamma}.$$

(10)

To sum up, the whole technological process of Gibbs sampling of proposed MF-JST model is described in Algorithm 1.

Algorithm 1 The process of Gibbs sampling of proposed MF-JST model

---

Input: α , β , γ ,ξ prior

Output: l and z distribution for all words in the document d

1: Initialize $S \times T \times E \times V$ distribution φ , $S \times E \times V$ distribution μ ,

      $S \times T \times V$ distribution θ , $D \times S$ distribution π .

2:   **for** i $1, i$ $(1, \max(sample\ iterations))$ **do**

3:     **for** D, all $d=1$ to M **do**

4:       **for** all w 1 to N_d **do**

5:         Extract every word w related to label l , label z and label e from

            variables $N_{l,z,e,w}$, $N_{d,l,e}$, $N_{d,l,z}$, $N_{d,l}$ and N_d;

6:         Sample new l , z and e through Equation (6);

7:         Update variables $N_{l,z,e,w}$, $N_{d,l,e}$, $N_{d,l,z}$, $N_{d,l}$ and N_d using the all

            new labels: l , z and e;

8:     **end**

9:   **end**

10:   **for** each 50 iterations **do**

11:     Update the prior hyperparameter α with new sampling results;

12:   **end**

13:   **for** each 100 iterations **do**

14:     Update the distribution φ , μ , θ and π ;

15:   **end**

16: **end**

---

4 Dataset Description

The Liru Online Courses [20] is a M-Learning Platform of South China Normal University. It provides the random sample of all the students' interactive emotion texts via its sample API in real time for our experiment, totally comprising 5 genre students' interactive textual data. In total, the dataset Statistics are shown in Table 1.

Table 1. Experimental datasets and polarity statistics.

Data genre	Data shape	Polarity_Distribution
Questionnaire_Response	1000 * 16	50.36% Pos.
Workshop_Assessments	1000 * 10	61.02% Pos.
Assignment_Feedback	1000 * 11	48.25% Pos.
Curriculum_Comments	1000 * 15	65.13% Pos.
Forum_Discussions	1000 * 18	48.57% Pos.

In addition, we take the first dataset as an example, showing the specification of the Questionnaire_Response dataset, in which the students are required to write the questionnaire-surveys in M-learning platform to submit in their own words, their personal feedbacks and feelings as regards the teaching, the lecture and so on. The distribution of polarity for each topic is demonstrated in Table 2.

Table 2. Example of topics in Questionnaire_Response dataset.

Questionnaire_Topics	Polarity_Distribution
Your opinion of online homework	65.59% Pos.
Your evaluation of the teachers	56.32% Pos.
The way you retrieve information	80.61% Pos.
Your opinion of group division	86.46% Pos.
Your views on the lecture	79.88% Pos.

5 Experiment Setup

In the section, we mainly introduce the experiment preparation of mood prediction in students' interactive text collections. Our dataset consists of five categories of students' interactive emotion texts. However, it should be noted that we do not use any annotated labels of the texts in experiments which just are used to assessing the experimental results of the proposed MF-JST model.

5.1 Preprocessing

The procedure for our data preprocess mainly includes 5 stages. Specific details will be described as follows:

Merge Documents. For each dataset, we merge all the documents into one document. Hence we continue to use this big corpus to in the following pre-processing process easily.

Split Chinese Sentences. The next stage is to split sentences of our datasets. It is easy to split Chinese sentences because each Chinese sentence ends with punctuations obviously, such as full stop and question marks.

Segment Words. As Chinese characters don't have any spaces to automatically separate the words in one sentence like other languages, thus it is necessary to segment the words of each sentence in dataset.

Exclude Stop Words. We use a frequently-used stop words set to remove all stop words not necessary and many other noisy signs.

Generate a MF-JST Input Document. We construct a dictionary for the remaining words. In this dictionary, the order regarding to words descend on the basis of frequencies of words. Finally we generate an input document for MF-JST model.

5.2 Hyperparameter Settings

In the section, we present the values of hyperparameters of proposed MF-JST model implementation.

Firstly, we set up the value of hyperparameter β is 0.01, another hyperparameter γ is determined to be $(0.05 * L)/S$, where S and L are defined as the overall numbers of sentiment labels and average length of document, respectively. In addition, the prior hyperparameter α is automatically updating each 50 iterations during the process of Gibbs sampling of proposed MF-JST model. The value of additive prior hyperparameter ξ will be set up to 0.01 too. To sum up, for proposed MF-JST model, we set four important prior hyperparameters $\beta, \xi = 0.01$, $\gamma = (0.05 * L)/(T * S)$ and the hyperparameter α is automatically come from sampling results in MF-JST model.

6   Experimental Results

6.1   Mood Prediction

To evaluate the performance of our proposed model in mood prediction, we compare the MF-JST model with JST model on the basis of different datasets.

Table 3. Comparison results between JST and MF-JST model on different datasets.

Dataset	F1-measure		Best accuracy	
	JST	MF-JST	JST (%)	MF-JST (%)
Questionnaire_Response	0.80 ± 0.3	0.82 ± 0.3	82.6	83.9
Workshop_Assessments	0.78 ± 0.4	0.79 ± 0.6	79.8	83.2
Assignment_Feedback	0.80 ± 0.5	0.82 ± 0.5	81.7	84.3
Curriculum_Comments	0.81 ± 0.5	0.83 ± 0.5	82.1	84.2
Forum_Discussions	0.81 ± 0.3	0.81 ± 0.3	83.0	84.9

From the above Table 3, we observe that the MF-JST model achieves the best accuracy 84.9% over the Forum_Discussions dataset, outperforming the best result 83.0% achieved by JST model. As for another Workshop_Assessments dataset, the traditional JST model only achieves 79.8%, whereas our MF-JST model still achieves high accuracy 83.2%, so we can conclude that the MF-JST model performs well in tough cases. Using F1-measure as criterion, we also observe that MF-JST model gives around 2% improvement compared to JST model over all the datasets.

Then we compare the mood prediction accuracy between some other important supervised and un-supervised models. Learning from Fig. 3, we observe that MF-JST model achieves accuracy of approximate 85%, which is a definite improvement compared with the un-supervised baseline [18, 19] accuracy of 76% and 83%, or even better than supervised in some cases [13]. In particular, it is observed that MF-JST model is only 2% lower than the best supervised study [14], which is relied on labeled datasets to train the classifiers, whereas our model doesn't need any annotated data to train the classifiers.

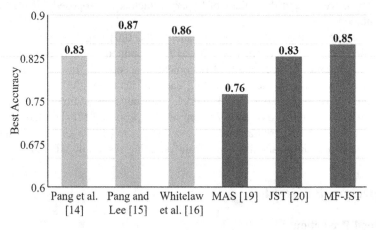

Fig. 3. Best accuracy comparison with some important existing approaches.

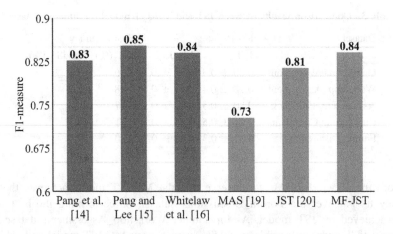

Fig. 4. F1-measure comparison with some important existing approaches.

We take F1-measure as the criteria, Fig. 4 shows this is a clear improvement over 0.73 and 0.85 achieved by MAS and MF-JST model, respectively. We observe that MF-JST model achieves comparable performance over the supervised models, even F1-measure is impressive higher than some mentioned supervised models.

We can conclude that our proposed MF-JST model is not only successful in ordinary prediction, but also predicts effectively the harder tasks, which indicates MF-JST model has a robust and reliable performance in predicting students' mood.

6.2 Topic Extraction

We show that the MF-JST model can be used to succeed in analyzing meaningful topics in education datasets, and we can evaluate the effectiveness of topics extracted by proposed MF-JST model through our manually comparison with real datasets.

As shown in Table 4, the first kind of topics are captured with positive emotions and the other kind of topics are captured with negative emotions. We only present the top 10 frequent words of each topic.

For the two positive sentiment topics, the first topic in positive sentiment label is closely related to the common topic "Homework", and the other one is likely to describe positive topic "Information retrieval".

Regarding the negative labels in Table 4, the first one under the negative sentiment label probably discusses "Effect of curriculum", while the last negative topic is mainly about the "Forum contents".

Finally, we adopt manual examination to evaluate the topic-extraction performance of MF-JST model. Manually examining results reveal that the captured topics are relative helpful and completely suitable for instructors to take corresponding intervention measures to help students. All in all, the above observations and in-depth analysis illustrate the well performance of proposed MF-JST model in capturing latent topics in students' interactive texts.

Table 4. Topic examples captured by MF-JST model with different emotions.

Positive				Negative			
Topic 1		Topic 2		Topic 3		Topic 4	
w	p	w	p	w	p	w	p
bucuo (不错)	0.0847	tushu (图书)	0.0874	wuqu (无趣)	0.0714	luntan (论坛)	0.0857
buhao (好)	0.0465	jiansuo (检索)	0.0865	laoshi (老师)	0.0662	bunneng (不能)	0.0565
taolun (讨论)	0.0441	guanjian (关键)	0.0741	rongchang (冗长)	0.0441	canyu (参与)	0.0503
zuoye (作业)	0.0366	wenxian (文献)	0.0352	wu (无)	0.0466	jishao (极少)	0.0503
xuexi (学习)	0.0289	baidu (百度)	0.0356	xiwang (希望)	0.0385	xushe (虚设)	0.0489
bangzhu (帮助)	0.0263	zhiwang (知网)	0.0316	shao (少)	0.0386	jinliang (尽量)	0.0266
faqi (发起)	0.0227	nuli (努力)	0.0212	bu (不)	0.0322	taolun (讨论)	0.0257
zhizhi (纸质)	0.0203	ganhuo (干货)	0.0180	danyi (单一)	0.0270	hudong (互动)	0.0250
jianyi (建议)	0.0174	sousuo (搜索)	0.0174	taikuai (太快)	0.0194	henshao (很少)	0.0174
xingqu (兴趣)	0.0166	jingyan (经验)	0.0126	wangji (忘记)	0.0176	meiyou (没有)	0.0156
fangbian (方便)	0.0160	shiyong (实用)	0.0120	di (低)	0.0165	duodian (多点)	0.0120

7 Discussions

In this section, for the sake of determining the most significant features and excluding the irrelevant or the less relevant features concerning the students' mood predicting task, we compute the Chi-square ($\chi 2$) value, the Mutual Information (MI) value and the Information Gain (IG) value of each feature, which are the best criterions in the research field of machine learning [14]. Table 5 shows the order of top 10 features based on the computing results. According to the results of calculation, we discuss the most discriminative pedagogical features.

Table 5. Top 10 predictive features and their discriminative power.

Rank	Feature	χ^2 value	MI value	IG value
1	Learning progress	403.25	0.1985	0.2021
2	Learning effect	393.61	0.0755	0.1507
3	Length of time on-line	384.28	0.0689	0.1211
4	Weather	305.26	0.0591	0.0851
5	Temperature	296.32	0.0434	0.0820
6	Major	111.25	0.0482	0.0563
7	Skin temperature	105.69	0.0212	0.0427
8	Frequency of login	86.39	0.0149	0.0140
9	Skin conductance	81.27	0.126	0.0182
10	Gender	46.38	0.0114	0.0139

Individual Information. Table 5 shows "Major" and "Gender" are the most significant individuals features linked with students' physical health. For example, when evaluating a curriculum to arouse the interests of students, it is prudent to examine across different majors.

Contextual Features. We observe that context features logged via the smartphone app, like "Weather", "length of on-line time" and "frequency of login". For instance, frequency of login will be higher if more routine in one day, which is explored associated with mood prediction.

Psychological Characteristics. Students can also roughly be characterized based on their different education backgrounds, living and learning experiences. According to Table 5, the most discriminative psychological characteristics used in the task of students' mood prediction include "skin temperature" and "skin conductance", which are recorded throughout the day using mobile phone APP.

Learning Style. As depicted in Table 5, we observe that the most discriminative features are the "learning progress" and "learning effect". For instance, some students like graphic representations and it is best to deepen their memory of knowledge, but others favor of audio materials or texts which are the best to deepen the memory of what they once read. Students who maintains a suitable path of learning are more likely to make greater progress and keep a positive emotion.

To understand the importance of feature selection approaches, we perform ablation experiments by removal of various features selection methods. As can be seen from Fig. 5, both chi-square ($\chi 2$) and mutual information (MI) only achieves 84%, whereas information gain (IG) achieves a higher accuracy of 85%. We observe that the IG shows better results. Hence, the IG is used for performance optimization of our proposed MF-JST model.

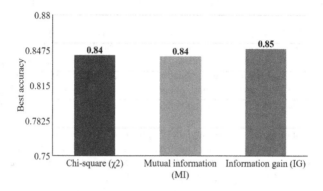

Fig. 5. Accuracy comparison with different feature selection approaches.

8   Conclusions and Future Work

In this paper, we make sense of an in-depth review of students' emotion absence status in M-Learning, therefore we propose a fully un-supervised MF-JST model based on JST model to address the absence of emotion in M-Learning environments. Firstly, by integrating pedagogical features into MF-JST model, solid experiment results show that the proposed model compares favorably with the existing supervised approaches without annotation. Furthermore, the topics detected by MF-JST model are indeed helpful and completely suitable for enhancing learning effect. To the best of our knowledge, the work is the brand-new research to approach the challenge of students' emotion prediction commendably in M-Learning with contemporary pedagogy. To sum up, this paper contributes to a development to affective computing techniques in educational field.

In the future work, we intend to collect more multi-modal students' emotional data in online learning platform with privacy preservation and look into corresponding approaches for further accurate and automatic predicting students' mood to alleviate the absence of emotion.

Acknowledgments. This work is supported by the National Natural Science Foundation of China (No. 61370229 and 61750110516), the S&T Projects of Guangdong Province (No.2016B010109008 and 2015A030401087), the GDUPS (2015), and the Innovation Project of Graduate School of South China Normal University (No.2017LKXM051).

References

1. Crompton, H., Burke, D.: The use of mobile learning in higher education: a systematic review. Comput. Educ. **123**, 53–64 (2018)
2. Sharples, M., Spikol, D.: Mobile learning. In: Duval, E., Sharples, M., Sutherland, R. (eds.) Technology Enhanced Learning, pp. 89–96. Springer, Cham (2017). https://doi.org/10.1007/978-3-319-02600-8_8
3. Jing, X.: Application of mobile learning system in phonetics teaching. In: International Conference on E-Education, E-Business, E-Management and E-Learning, pp. 19–23 (2017)
4. Chee, K.N., Yahaya, N., Hasan Ibrahim, N.H., Noor, M.: Review of mobile learning trends 2010–2015. J. Educ. Technol. Soc. **20**(2), 113–126 (2017)
5. Veenhoven, R.: Healthy happiness: effects of happiness on physical health and the consequences for preventive health care. J. Happiness Stud. **9**(3), 449–469 (2008)
6. Lopezmartinez, D., Rudovic, O., Picard, R.: Physiological and behavioral profiling for nociceptive pain estimation using personalized multitask learning **56**(2), 126–130 (2017)
7. Hwang, G.J., Wu, P.H.: Applications, impacts and trends of mobile technology-enhanced learning: a review of 2008–2012 publications in selected SSCI journals. Inderscience Publishers (2017)
8. Sun, C.Y., Chang, K.Y.: Design and development of a location-based mobile learning system to facilitate english learning. Univ. Access Inf. Soc. **15**(3), 1–13 (2016)
9. Sidan, L.I., Chen, Y., Qin, M., Wang, B., Zhou, X., Zhu, G., et al.: Mobile learning in medical education. China Medical Herald, China (2017)
10. Alrasheedi, M., Capretz, L.F.: Determination of critical success factors affecting mobile learning: a meta-analysis approach. Turk. Online J. Educ. Technol. **14**(2), 41 (2018)
11. Kechaou, Z., Ammar, M.B., Alimi, A.M.: Improving e-learning with sentiment analysis of users' opinions. In: IEEE Global Engineering Education Conference, vol. 72, pp. 1032–1038. IEEE, Shanghai (2011)
12. Al-Hmouz, A., Shen, J., Yan, J.: A machine learning based framework for adaptive mobile learning. In: Spaniol, M., Li, Q., Klamma, R., Lau, R.W.H. (eds.) ICWL 2009. LNCS, vol. 5686, pp. 34–43. Springer, Heidelberg (2009). https://doi.org/10.1007/978-3-642-03426-8_4
13. Pang, B., Lee, L., Vaithyanathan, S.: Thumbs up? Sentiment classification using machine learning techniques. In: Proceedings of EMNLP, pp. 79–86 (2002)
14. Bo, P., Lee, L.: Seeing stars: exploiting class relationships for sentiment categorization with respect to rating scales, pp. 115–124 (2005)
15. Whitelaw, C., Garg, N., Argamon, S.: Using appraisal groups for sentiment analysis. In: Proceedings of CIKM, p. 6, Springer, Berlin (2005)
16. Blei, D.M., Ng, A.Y., Jordan, M.I.: Latent dirichlet allocation. J. Mach. Learn. Res. Arch. **3**(1), 993–1022 (2003)
17. Yut, L., Zhang, C., Shao, Y., Cui, B., Yut, L., Zhang, C., et al.: LDA*: a robust and large-scale topic modeling system. Proc. VLDB Endow. **10**(11), 1406–1417 (2017)
18. Lu, B., Ott, M., Cardie, C., Tsou, B.K.: Multi-aspect sentiment analysis with topic models. In: IEEE International Conference on Data Mining Workshops, pp. 81–88. IEEE (2012)
19. Lin, C., He, Y.: Joint sentiment/topic model for sentiment analysis. In: ACM Conference on Information and Knowledge Management, vol. 217, pp. 375–384. ACM (2009)
20. The Liru Online Courses Homepage. http://www.moodle.scnu.edu.cn. Accessed 7 Aug 2018

Identification of Influential Users in Emerging Online Social Networks Using Cross-site Linking

Qingyuan Gong[1,2,3], Yang Chen[1,2,3(✉)], Xinlei He[1,2,3], Fei Li[1,2,3], Yu Xiao[4], Pan Hui[5,6], Xin Wang[1,2,3], and Xiaoming Fu[7]

[1] School of Computer Science, Fudan University, Shanghai, China
{gongqingyuan,chenyang,xinw}@fudan.edu.cn
[2] Shanghai Key Lab of Intelligent Information Processing, Fudan University, Shanghai, China
[3] SKLCS, Institute of Software, Chinese Academy of Sciences, Beijing, China
[4] Department of Communications and Networking, Aalto University, Espoo, Finland
yu.xiao@aalto.fi
[5] Department of Computer Science, University of Helsinki, Helsinki, Finland
panhui@cs.helsinki.fi
[6] CSE Department, Hong Kong University of Science and Technology, Clear Water Bay, Hong Kong
[7] Institute of Computer Science, University of Göttingen, Göttingen, Germany
fu@cs.uni-goettingen.de

Abstract. Online social networks (OSNs) have become a commodity in our daily-life. Besides the dominant platforms such as Facebook and Twitter, several emerging OSNs have been launched recently, where users may generate less activity data than on dominant ones. Identifying influential users is critical for the advertisement and the initial development of the emerging OSNs. In this work, we investigate the identification of potential influential users in these emerging OSNs. We build a supervised machine learning-based system by leveraging the widely adopted cross-site linking function, which could overcome the limitations of referring to the user data of a single OSN. Based on the collected real data from Twitter (a dominant OSN) and Medium (an emerging OSN), we show that our system is able to achieve an F1-score of 0.701 and an AUC of 0.755 in identifying influential users on Medium using the Twitter data only.

Keywords: Influential users · Emerging online social networks
Cross-site linking

1 Introduction

Online social networks (OSNs) have become very popular all over the world, and have attracted billions of users [13]. Besides supporting the interactions between

© Springer Nature Singapore Pte Ltd. 2019
Y. Sun et al. (Eds.): ChineseCSCW 2018, CCIS 917, pp. 331–341, 2019.
https://doi.org/10.1007/978-981-13-3044-5_24

people, OSNs also become platforms for information diffusion. The concept of *social influence* has been proposed to quantify the impact of different users within a selected OSN. Each OSN has a number of influential users, who could achieve a higher impact than most of the users. As discussed in [3], an influential user could be a "cool" teenager, an opinion leader or a popular public figure. Identifying influential users is quite useful for various practical scenarios, including viral marketing or making agile action to critical events. Several social influence metrics have been introduced [3,15] and studied on dominant OSNs, for example, Twitter. Meanwhile, many of the new (emerging) OSNs, such as Foursquare, Pinterest and Quora, are increasingly attracting users around the world.

An emerging OSN often offers some unique functions, instead of aiming to replace dominant OSNs such as Facebook and Twitter. For example, Foursquare provides location-centric services, Pinterest allows social content curation, and Quora acts as a question-and-answer site. Different from dominant OSNs, which offer general-purpose services, an emerging OSN typically has a special focus and only records each user's activities from limited aspects. Also, the account ages on emerging OSNs are in general younger than the account ages on dominant OSNs for same users. For example, according to our dataset, the average account age of Medium users is 3.39 years, while that of Twitter users is 7.70 years. As a result, it is harder to predict the social influence of a user on an emerging OSN due to the lack of comprehensive user activities. This problem is known as a challenging "cold start" problem [16], which appears when one user on a dominant OSN creates an account on an emerging OSN but has not added any information to her profile, or when she just plans to create an account on the emerging OSN. At this point, our goal is to predict whether she could become an influential user on the emerging OSN. Understanding the potential of the current less active users to be influentials is important to the advertisement and initial development of the emerging OSNs.

In this work, we explore the problem of uncovering influential users in "cold start" scenarios, i.e., predicting whether a newly registered user or a current inactive user on an emerging OSN would become an influential one. To solve the challenges brought by the inactiveness of the objective users, we leverage the power of the cross-site linking function [10]. We demonstrate that a user's rich demographic information and activity data on a dominant OSN could play an important role towards an accurate identification.

- We build an identification system to predict users' potential social influence in emerging OSNs. We take a story sharing social network, Medium, as an exemplified emerging OSN. We demonstrate how our system can make good use of user generated data on Twitter to achieve an accurate identification of influential users on Medium.
- We crawled the profiles and activities of 1 million Medium users, and their linked Twitter accounts. We conduct a data-driven study to evaluate our system. Our evaluation demonstrates that our system can achieve an F1-score of

0.701 and an AUC of 0.755, showing that cross-site linking could play a significant role in identifying potential influential users on emerging OSNs.

2   Background and Data Collection

2.1   Cross-site Linking on Medium

Many of the emerging OSNs, such as Foursquare [6]/Swarm [5], Quora [18] and Pinterest [12], take advantage of their users' accounts on dominant OSNs to enhance their function-orientated services. They support a *cross-site linking function* [10], allowing users to link their accounts on dominant OSNs, e.g., Twitter and Facebook. In this way, users can log into the emerging OSNs with their Twitter or Facebook accounts, avoiding the problem of managing multiple accounts. By using the cross-site linking function, a user is allowed to post the same piece of information to multiple OSNs simultaneously, copy social connections from dominant OSNs, and help people know more about her. By connecting a same user's accounts on multiple OSNs, the cross-site linking function provides opportunities to address the challenges in identifying influential users on emerging OSNs.

In this work, we select the "Medium-Twitter" pair as a case study, since Medium allows a user to link her profile to her account on Twitter. Medium is a blog sharing social network launched in August 2012. On Medium, each user maintains a profile page, showing her demographic attributes such as username and profile photo, her social connectivities including the number of followings and followers, and a paragraph of her biography. The linked Facebook and Twitter accounts are also shown on this page. Visitors to the Medium page can go to the users' Facebook and Twitter pages conveniently. A post on Medium is called a "story". If a user is impressed by a story published by other users, she can click a "Clap" button to show her appreciation or support. The profile page also provides links to three additional tabs, i.e., "Latest", "Claps", and "Responses", showing the latest stories published by the user, the stories she has clapped for, and the stories she has commented with, respectively. The stories in these tabs are organized with a reverse chronological order. In our investigation, Medium serves as the emerging OSN, and Twitter acts as the dominant OSN. Medium allows a user to link her Facebook and Twitter accounts to her Medium profile page. Users can only post tweets within 140 characters on Twitter, while Medium encourages users to post longer blogs without any character length limits.

2.2   Social Influence Definition

Users' influence on OSNs can be regarded as the power they can affect other users. The power can be quantified as P_u by various metrics depicting the user u's activeness on the website and connectivity with others. For example, Kwak et al. [15] proposed three social influence metrics, including the number of followers, the number of retweets and the PageRank value. Based on the influence value

P_u, the users can be categorized into two groups: the influential users and the ordinary users. Given a threshold p, the discrimination of these two user groups can be formularized as

$$u \text{ is } \begin{cases} \text{an influential user} & if \ P_u > p. \\ \text{an ordinary user} & if \ P_u \leq p. \end{cases} \tag{1}$$

The formularization is compatible with various metrics of social influence, since the formularization only takes the calculated value into consideration according to the definition. The threshold can be determined according to the specific requirement to the influential user. For example, it can be a percentage as top p% of the rank by the values of social influence, where a smaller p indicates that we select fewer users as influential users.

2.3   Data Collection

To obtain a dataset for our study, we need the activity records of Medium users and the data they generate on Twitter. We used Breadth First Search (BFS) to crawl the data of a number of Medium users, which has been widely used in OSN data collection, such as in [8,11,19]. We started our crawling from the user Evan Williams (https://medium.com/@ev), the CEO of Medium. To implement BFS, we maintain a queue of Medium user IDs, and put Evan Williams's Medium ID into the queue first. For each round, we picked the first Medium ID from the head of the queue, and obtained the lists of the corresponding user's followings and followers. The Medium IDs of these followings and followers, if have not been crawled, would be further added to the end of the queue. This process was repeated until the number of users we collected reached the threshold of 90 thousand. For each user in this dataset, we crawled her Medium profile and published stories. In our crawled data, 67.64% of the Medium users have linked their Twitter accounts. Accordingly, we further crawled these users' profiles and published tweets on Twitter.

3   Identification of Potential Influential Users on Emerging OSNs

The *social influence* of a user is an important concept in sociology and viral marketing [3]. In social networks, a piece of information can reach a massive number of audiences through the network via a "word-of-mouth" way of diffusion. Since users may differ substantially in their credibility, expertise and social connectivity, they could achieve different levels of social influence. Some users, known as influential users, could quickly deliver information to a large number of audiences. Researchers have made numerous efforts in quantifying users' social influence in OSNs [1,3,15]. These studies focus on identifying influential users on Twitter, given the convenience brought by its global coverage and intensive user engagement.

We build a supervised machine learning-based system to discover the potential influential users on emerging OSNs in the cold start scenario, by leveraging the power of cross-site linking. We explain the overview of our solution in Sect. 3.1, and introduce the implementation details in Sect. 3.2.

3.1   System Overview

We illustrate the system workflow by taking one user instance as an example in Fig. 1. Our goal is to predict whether this user is a potential influential user on Medium. For a user that enables the cross-site linking function and links dominant OSNs such as Twitter, we are able to access her Twitter account shown on her Medium profile page. By visiting the URL of her Twitter homepage, our system is able to use the collected information to determine whether this user will become an influential user on Medium. The data from the dominant OSNs allow us to have a better understanding of one user, extracted as feature sets to describe her. A user's features will be fed into a decision maker, powered by a supervised machine learning-based classifier. Different machine learning algorithms could be applied to implement the decision maker. In this paper, we study classic algorithms include Random Forest [2] and C4.5 decision tree (J48) [17], as well as new algorithms including XGBoost [4] and LightGBM [14]. XGBoost and LightGBM are efficient tree boosting systems. Both of them have been widely adopted in machine learning competitions such as Kaggle. The decision maker predicts whether the user will become an influential user, based on the extracted features of her.

3.2   System Implementation

Construction of the Ground Truth Dataset. A training dataset is needed to train a classifier to serve as the decision maker. For the user instances in the training dataset, there needs an explicit metric to determine the ground truth of whether each user is an influential user or an ordinary user, so that the classification performance of the decision maker can be evaluated. The ground-truth data is obtained based on the threshold defining the influential users. Our system is compatible with different kinds of metrics of social influence.

Extraction of Feature Sets. Supervised machine learning-based classifiers need a number of features to describe an instance. Leveraging the cross-site linking function, the system introduces illustrative features based on her publicly-accessible information on Twitter. We list our selected features in Table 1. Considering the services provided by OSNs, we classify users' features into 4 categories, i.e., demographic, account, social and UGC (user-generated content).

On Twitter, a user can choose to fill the information fields in her profile page, including a biography to describe herself, her current location, and the URL of her homepages. We also extract the information that describe a user's Twitter account, including the age of the account, the UTC offset she sets up, whether

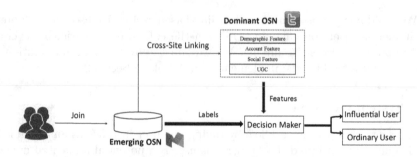

Fig. 1. Identification of potential influential users

the user has changed the default profile image and the background image, and whether this account has been verified as an account of public interest. Since Twitter supports the social networking function by endowing a user to follow anyone she is interested in, we select the number of followers and followings as the social features. Besides receiving tweets from her followings or lists subscribed, Twitter users can also post tweets, publishing original tweets and re-tweeting other users' tweets. We extract comprehensive UGC features from users' tweeting behavior, including her preference of enabling the geography tags for tweets or not, her activeness of posting tweets, and the attentions she have received from other Twitter users in the forms of "like" and retweet.

The above features are all in decimal or binary values. These values construct a numerical vector for each user finally, depicting the user from demographic, account, social, and UGC aspects from her linked Twitter account.

Generation of the Decision Maker. Fed with the feature vectors, the classifier employs a selected supervised machine learning-based classifier to learn the correlations between the extracted features and the social influence of users. We use a training dataset to get a set of "best" parameters of the decision maker. Afterwards, the trained decision maker is able to make the judgement whether one user will become an influential user on Medium, by referring to her information on Twitter.

There are several metrics to study and quantify the classification performance. In this work, we apply four representative metrics, including precision, recall, F1-score and AUC (Area Under Curve). Precision measures the fraction of users classified as influential users who are real influential users. Recall is the fraction of influential users who are correctly identified. F1-score is defined as the harmonic mean of these two metrics. AUC denotes the probability that this classifier would rank higher of a randomly selected influential user than a randomly chosen ordinary user. The performance for a selected classifier should be affected by the set of parameters in the classification algorithm, which can be attained through parameter tuning. We apply a grid search to sweep the parameters space of the given classifier, and choose the set of the parameters that could help the classifier achieve the highest F1-score.

Table 1. Subsets of features for potential influential user identification

Site	Feature set	Feature list
Twitter	Demographic features	· Length of biography
		· Has_added_location
		· UTC offset
		· Has_added_other_homepage
	Account features	· Age of the account
		· Has_profile_image
		· Has_profile_background_image
		· Has_verified
	Social features	· Number of followers
		· Number of followings
	UGC features	· Number of tweets
		· Has_geo_tags
		· Number of lists subscribed to
		· Number of original tweets
		· Number of retweets
		· Number of tweets "liked" by the user
		· Total number of "likes" received (original tweets only)
		· Average number of "likes" received (original tweets only)
		· Total number of retweets (original tweets only)
		· Average number of retweets (original tweets only)

4   Evaluation of the Influential User Identification System

In this section, we implement the proposed prediction system of influential users on Medium and evaluate its performance. The implementation and evaluations are based on the crawled data described in Sect. 2.3.

4.1   Evaluation Setup

We first construct a training dataset and build the ground truth of the influential users. In the evaluation, we consider the total number of "claps" received by a Medium user to quantify her influence. The intuition is that the "claps" can better reflect the social interactions between users than considering the following relationships only. As discussed in [19], the social interactions on Facebook are skewed towards a small portion of a user's social contacts. We rank the total numbers of "claps" received by all crawled Medium users, and take the top 10% as the threshold to divide the influential users and ordinary users in the dataset. After determining the ground truth dataset, we obtain the training dataset containing 4,624 randomly selected influential users and 4,624 randomly selected ordinary users.

To test the identification efficiency separately, another Medium dataset is introduced, called test dataset. In this dataset, there are 1,156 randomly selected influential users and 1,156 randomly selected ordinary users. Fed with the feature vectors of the users in the test dataset, the decision maker can give its judgement of whether any of them are influential users or ordinary users. In our system, we use different supervised machine learning algorithms to empower the decision maker, and train the parameters used through the approach of grid search.

4.2   Evaluation of the System Performance

Using precision, recall, F1-score and AUC, we show the performance of the identification system on the test dataset in Table 2. From this table, we see that when we feed the Twitter features into classification algorithms, the F1-score of XGBoost reaches 0.701, and the AUC value is as large as 0.755. For LightGBM, the F1-score and AUC values are a bit inferior to XGBoost, reaching 0.670 and 0.727 respectively. The F1-score or AUC will be both 0.5 if we apply a random guess to see whether one user will be an influential user, which can serve as the baseline of the prediction. This demonstrates the usefulness of our system, in particular, the usefulness of involving users' generated content on Twitter through cross-site linking.

Table 2. Performance of the identification system of influential users

Algorithm	Parameters	Precision	Recall	F1-Score	AUC
Baseline	-	0.5	0.5	0.5	0.5
Decision tree	criterion=entropy, min_samples_split=0.5, min_samples_leaf=10, min_weight_fraction_leaf=0.0	0.627	0.633	0.630	0.656
Random forest	criterion=gini, max_depth=10, max_features=20, min_samples_leaf=1, min_weight_fraction_leaf=0.0	0.668	0.698	0.682	0.744
LightGBM	learning_rate=0.05, min_child_weight=1, max_depth=0, num_leaves=15, subsample=0.4, colsample_bytree=1.0, boosting_type=gbdt, objective=binary:logistic	0.658	0.684	0.670	0.727
XGBoost	learning_rate=0.1, min_child_weight=1, max_depth=12, gamma=0, subsample=0.9, colsample_bytree=0.6, booster=gbtree, objective=binary:logistic	0.691	0.713	0.701	0.755

4.3   Feature Importance

To evaluate the contributions of the features involved in the system, we feed the trained decision maker with one subset of features at a time. In such case, the classification algorithm judges the users in the test dataset only through the corresponding feature subset. We evaluate the performance of the identification system with each subset of features listed in Table 1. The classification performance of using each feature subset is shown in Table 3. We can see that the social and UGC features of Twitter play important roles in improving the

Table 3. Contribution of each feature sets in the identification system

Feature subsets	Precision	Recall	F1-Score	AUC
Baseline	0.5	0.5	0.5	0.5
+Demographic features	0.556	0.540	0.548	0.607
+Account feature	0.622	0.213	0.318	0.561
+Social features	0.626	0.588	0.607	0.669
+UGC features	0.630	0.645	0.637	0.696

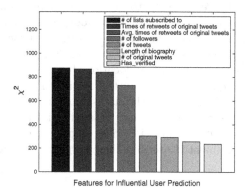

Fig. 2. χ^2 Analysis for the identification system of influential users

system performance. Demographic features are also helpful in the identification system. These results show the usefulness of Twitter features in the identification of influential users, which are based on cross-site linking.

We conduct the χ^2 analysis [20] to further measure the discriminative power of each feature of the identification system. Figure 2 shows that the top 8 features cover all four categories. The content curation features rank the top 3, with the number of followers as the fourth one. The demographic and the account features also affect the prediction performance.

5 Related Work

Identifying influential users is critical to study the information diffusion in OSNs. The Twitter platform has been widely used in studying the social influence. Cha et al. [3] explored three social influence metrics, i.e., in-degree (number of followers), number of retweets and number of mentions. These metrics represent different roles users play in OSNs. In-degree denotes the number of followers a user has, indicating how popular this user is concerning social connections. The number of retweets means how many times a user's tweets have been re-posted, showing the content value of her tweets. The number of mentions reflects the name value of a user. Existing explorations about social influence are mainly based on the rich user activities. For emerging OSNs, identifying the potential influential users is more challenging due to the lack of knowledge of users. In our work, we study the prediction of potential influential users on emerging OSNs like Medium. We make use of the cross-site linking function to introduce a user's information on established OSNs to realize the identification.

Cross-site linking is widely applied by emerging OSNs as a way to take advantage of the established social connections of users on dominant OSNs. Zhong et al. [22] proposed the concept of social bootstrapping, i.e., copying existing friends from a dominant OSN into an emerging OSN. Their study demonstrated how a new OSN evolves by referring to the cross-site linking function. There are research works trying to utilize the rich social footprints formed by users across OSNs. Zhang et al. [21] studied the relationship between social interactions on emerging OSNs and social ties on established ones. Farseev et al. [7] aggregated different kinds of information such as location, text, photo, and demographic attributes from Foursquare, Twitter, Instagram and Facebook to construct a multi-source dataset. They applied the dataset to predict users' demographic information. In our work, we make use of cross-site links between an emerging OSN and a dominant OSN. From this more informative view, we study how to discover potential influential users on the emerging OSN, even for the newly registered users.

6   Conclusion and Future Work

In this paper, we study the problem of identifying potential influential users on emerging OSNs. By introducing a user's usage and profile information on dominant OSNs, we design and implement a machine learning-based system to predict whether she will be an influential user. Based on the real data of Medium and Twitter, we demonstrate an F1-score of 0.701 and an AUC of 0.755 of our system in distinguishing between influential users and ordinary users on Medium. Note that our system can be used by both OSN operators and third-party application providers, as the system only needs to access the publicly accessible information. For the next step, we plan to expand our approach to other emerging OSNs, and examine the prediction performance of our system. Moreover, we wish to study different types of user classification problems, such as the detection of malicious users [9], instead of merely focusing on identifying influential users.

Acknowledgement. This work is sponsored by National Natural Science Foundation of China (No. 61602122, No. 71731004), Natural Science Foundation of Shanghai (No. 16ZR1402200), Shanghai Pujiang Program (No. 16PJ1400700), EU FP7 IRSES MobileCloud project (No. 612212) and Lindemann Foundation (No. 12-2016), Projects 26211515 and 16214817 from the Research Grants Council of Hong Kong. Yang Chen is the corresponding author.

References

1. Bakshy, E., Mason, W.A., Hofman, J.M., Watts, D.J.: Everyone is an influencer: quantifying influence on twitter. In: Proceedings of ACM WSDM (2011)
2. Breiman, L.: Random forests. Mach. Learn. **45**(1), 5–32 (2001)
3. Cha, M., Haddadi, H., Benevenuto, F., Gummadi, P.K.: Measuring user influence in Twitter: The million follower fallacy. In: Proceeedings of AAAI ICWSM (2010)
4. Chen, T., Guestrin, C.: XGBoost: a scalable tree boosting system. In: Proceedings of ACM KDD (2016)
5. Chen, Y., Hu, J., Zhao, H., Xiao, Y., Hui, P.: Measurement and analysis of the swarm social network with tens of millions of nodes. IEEE Access **6**, 4547–4559 (2018)
6. Chen, Y., Yang, Y., Hu, J., Zhuang, C.: Measurement and analysis of tips in foursquare. In: Proceedings of IEEE PerCom Workshops (2016)
7. Farseev, A., Nie, L., Akbari, M., Chua, T.: Harvesting multiple sources for user profile learning: a big data study. In: Proceedings of ACM ICMR (2015)
8. Gong, N.Z., Xu, W., Huang, L., et al.: Evolution of social-attribute networks: measurements, modeling, and implications using Google+. In: Proceedings of ACM IMC (2012)
9. Gong, Q., et al.: DeepScan: exploiting deep learning for malicious account detection in location-based social networks. IEEE Commun. Mag. **56**(11) (2018, in press)
10. Gong, Q., Chen, Y., Hu, J., et al.: Understanding cross-site linking in online social networks. ACM Trans. Web **12**(4), 25:1–25:29 (2018). https://dl.acm.org/citation.cfm?id=3213898
11. Gonzalez, R., Cuevas, R., Motamedi, R., Rejaie, R., Cuevas, A.: Google+ or Google−?: dissecting the evolution of the new OSN in its first year. In: Proceedings of WWW (2013)
12. Han, J., Choi, D., Chun, B.-G., et al.: Collecting, organizing, and sharing pins in pinterest: interest-driven or social-driven? In: Proceedings of ACM SIGMETRICS (2014)
13. Jin, L., Chen, Y., Wang, T., Hui, P., Vasilakos, A.V.: Understanding user behavior in online social networks: a survey. IEEE Commun. Mag. **51**(9), 144–150 (2013)
14. Ke, G., Meng, Q., Finley, T., et al.: LightGBM: a highly efficient gradient boosting decision tree. In: Proceedings of NIPS (2017)
15. Kwak, H., Lee, C., Park, H., Moon, S.: What is Twitter, a social network or a news media? In: Proc of WWW (2010)
16. Meo, P., Ferrara, E., Abel, F., et al.: Analyzing user behavior across social sharing environments. ACM Trans. Intell. Syst. Technol. **5**(1), 14:1–14:31 (2014)
17. Quinlan, J.R.: C4.5: Programs for Machine Learning. Morgan Kaufmann Publishers Inc., San Francisco (1993)
18. Wang, G., Gill, K., Mohanlal, M., et al.: Wisdom in the social crowd: an analysis of Quora. In: Proceedings of WWW (2013)
19. Wilson, C., Boe, B., Sala, A., et al.: User interactions in social networks and their implications. In: Proceedings of ACM EuroSys (2009)
20. Yang, Y., Pedersen, J.O.: A comparative study on feature selection in text categorization. In: Proceedings of ICML (1997)
21. Zhang, P., Zhu, H., Lu, T., Gu, H., Huang, W., Gu, N.: Understanding relationship overlapping on social network sites: a case study of Weibo and Douban. Proc. ACM Hum.-Comput. Interact. **1**(CSCW), 120:1–120:18 (2017)
22. Zhong, C., Salehi, M., Shah, S., Cobzarenco, M., Sastry, N., Cha, M.: Social Bootstrapping: how pinterest and Last.fm social communities benefit by borrowing links from Facebook. In: Proceedings of WWW (2014)

LSTM Sentiment Polarity Analysis Based on LDA Clustering

Zechuan Chen, Shaohua Teng, Wei Zhang$^{(\boxtimes)}$, Huan Tang,
Zhenhua Zhang, Junping He, Xiaozhao Fang, and Lunke Fei

School of Computer Science, Guangdong University of Technology,
Guangzhou 510006, China
zc_chen@aliyun.com, {shteng,weizhang}@gdut.edu.cn

Abstract. Sentiment polarity analysis is a major problem in the field of sentiment analysis, especially emotional words will have different emotional tendencies under different scenarios. This paper aims to solve the problem of emotional polarity confusion caused by polysemy of sentiment polarity in different domains, and proposes an LSTM (Long-Short Term Memory) network sentiment polarity analysis method based on LDA (Latent Dirichlet distribution) clustering. The method firstly employs LDA topic model clustering on datasets. Then, the LSTM algorithm is used to train the emotion base learners for clusters. At last, all base learners are integrated with weighting by using the topic probability distribution. Experiments are made on three datasets: (1) Unlocked mobile phone reviews on Amazon; (2) Electronic products reviews on Amazon; and (3) Movies reviews on IMDB. Our experimental result shows the classification accuracy of this method is obviously better than that of using only LSTM method.

Keywords: Sentiment polarity analysis · Natural Language Processing
LDA · LSTM · Ensemble learning method · Cluster

1 Introduction

With the rapid development of Internet technologies and applications, sentiment analysis has become an extremely important research direction in Natural Language Processing [1]. Sentiment analysis is divided into sentiment polarity analysis and fine-grained sentiment analysis. Sentiment polarity analysis, which is a binary classification problem, aims at predicting the positivity or negativity of texts. Fine-grained sentiment analysis subdivision same emotional polarity into fine-grained emotional labels. Santos et al. divided the text data into 5 sentiment classes (labels), they are "very positive", "positive", "neutral", "negative" and "very negative" [1]. User reviews may refer to multi-domains and involve different perspectives. For example, comments on the same mobile phone may aim at the appearance of the mobile phone, or the ability to continue, or the ability to calculate, or the official after sales service, and so on. Single-domain text sentiment analysis can estimate the sentiment polarity of given text by analyzing the domain-specific information (words, phrases, or special sentences) [2]. However, sentiment analysis on multi-domain text have a common problem, that is,

© Springer Nature Singapore Pte Ltd. 2019
Y. Sun et al. (Eds.): ChineseCSCW 2018, CCIS 917, pp. 342–355, 2019.
https://doi.org/10.1007/978-981-13-3044-5_25

domain-specific information may has different sentiment polarity in different domains [2]. The same word or words with similar meaning have different sentiment orientations in different domains, which may lead to classification mistake of sentiment polarity. Let us consider the following examples:

(1) The service attitudes of the staff are cold, and they often shirk their responsibilities.
(2) After playing for more than an hour, the rear cover of the mobile phone is still cold.

In the first sentence, the adjective "cold" is used with negative emotion, describes the attitude of the staff be indifferent. However in the second sentence, the adjective "cold" possesses positive feelings, describes the temperature of the phone's back cover be not hot after playing game long time.

There are amount of cases that the same vocabulary expresses the same meaning but has different sentiment polarity information in different domains. Following this two sentence where the adjective "large" with the same meaning but with different emotion polarity.

(1) This mobile phone screen is very large and it's cool to watch movies.
(2) When the phone starts to heat up, the power consumption becomes very large.

In the first sentence, the advantages of the screen are described, and the adjective "large" has positive emotion. In the second sentence, the problem of power consumption is pointed out and the adjective "large" has negative emotion.

In order to solve the problem of emotional polarity confusion caused by polysemy between different domains in sentiment polarity analysis, we propose a LSTM sentiment polarity analysis method based on LDA clustering. At first, our method train LDA topic model on entire training dataset, and uses this LDA topic model to cluster the entire training dataset to obtain multiple data subsets with same topic. Then we uses each data subset to train the LSTM base learner separately. Finally, all base learners are integrated with weighting by using the topic probability distribution. When we predict the sentiment polarity of a review, we firstly calculate its topic probability distribution using LDA topic model we had trained, and then send it to all LSTM base learners for evaluating the emotional score, finally weight all base learners based on topic probability distribution and summate their weighted predicted sentiment score as the sentiment predictive score of the review. After the sentiment predictive score of the review is obtained, we can make the sentiment polarity judgment according to the sentiment predictive score. This paper makes experiments on three data sets: (1) Unlocked mobile phone reviews on Amazon; (2) Electronic products reviews on Amazon; (3) Movies reviews on IMDB, experimental results show our method is obviously better than directly using the LSTM algorithm in judging the accuracy rate.

The contribution presented in our paper aims at reducing the influence of polysemy on multi-domains sentiment analysis. The described approach bases on the following pillars:

1. The LDA model is used to cluster the training dataset, and train LSTM base learner independently on each cluster after clustering.

2. The LDA model is used to calculate the topics probability distribution of text as dynamic weight of base learners.
3. The use of weighted summation of output of every base learner to obtain the final sentiment predictive score of text.

2 Related Work

2.1 Sentiment Polarity Analysis on Text

Sentiment Analysis is an important research direction in Natural Language Processing [3]. The methods of sentiment analysis are mainly to fall into two categories [3]: (1) lexicon-based methods; (2) machine learning methods [3].

Lexicon-based methods always need to construct sentiment lexicon of opinion words and design classification rules based on this sentiment lexicon and prior syntactic knowledge [3]. When it predicts emotional polarity of the text, it usually divides the text into sentences, then uses the classification rules and prior syntactic knowledge to calculate sentiment predictive score. Despite lexicon-based methods are well done in some sentiment analysis tasks on short text, it spends a major expenditure of time and effort on constructing lexicon and designing classification rules. And lexicon-based methods are always difficult to deal with the implicit opinions [3].

Machine learning methods commonly use classic machine learning supervised classification algorithms such as Naive Bayes [4], SVM (Support Vector Machine) [5]. These approaches convert the text into vector representations, manually label the emotion and then do supervised learning to get the sentiment classifier. Machine learning methods have an excellent performance in sentiment analysis. Recently, because of powerful storage and computational capabilities of hardware, and increasing amount of data on Internet, artificial neural network has been widely used in sentiment analysis of texts [6]. Bengio [14], Yih [15], Mikolov [16], Collobert [17] et al. proposed a method for learning word embedding representations through neural language models and performing composition over word embeddings for classification [7]. RNTN (Recursive neural tensor network) [8] was proposed by Socher et al. for semantic compositionality over a sentiment treebank, and the accuracy of dichotomy classification on stanford sentiment tree bank increased from 80% to 85.4% [8]. In 2014, Yih [18] verified that the CNN (convolution neural network) model originally invented for computer vision was effective for NLP and achieved excellent results in semantics analyze [7]. Santos and Gattit constructed the CharSCNN (Character to Sentence Convolution Neural Network) which performed significantly better in experiments than RNN (Recurrent Neural Network) and most traditional machine learning methods such as Naive Bayes and SVM [1].

However, many methods are mentioned in most literature, which focus on using whole training dataset to train one classifier. These methods lose sight of domain-specific information of documents while building sentiment model [2]. It is easily to misjudge when the model predicts sentiment polarity of the text which contains the syntactic constituent with domain-specific sentiment opinion. LSTM network, which has the ability to learn long-term dependencies, is a variant of RNN [3]. It can take contextual domain information of text into consideration. A domain is a topic on which reviewers can comment with [2]. But when the sentiment opinion word is far away from its described entities, this contextual domain information will be forgot by LSTM networks [2]. Our paper proposes a LSTM sentiment polarity analysis method based on LDA clustering, which uses the LDA topic clustering to divide documents into multiple clusters and train LSTM network to get base learner on each cluster.

The advantage of our approach is converting the multi-domain sentiment analysis problem into multiple single-topic sentiment analysis problems because the document of same topic has similar describing opinion. It is equivalent to binding domain knowledge on each base learner, and improving the accuracy of base learner by clustering documents with same topic. Another advantage of our approach is combining weak classifiers into a strong classifier helps to improve the accuracy of classification.

2.2 LDA Topic Model

LDA (Latent Dirichlet Allocation) topic model [9] was proposed by Blei, Jordan and Ng in 2003 to speculate topic probability distribution of a document. It is a 3-layers Bayes probability model containing "documents - topics – words" structure [10]. All documents written by people are conceived on certain topics. The idea of LDA design is similar. It considers that the relationship between document and topic is a one-to-many relationship, and relationship between topic and the word is also one-to-many. In another word, a document contains multiple topics, and each topic has multiple words to be chosen. The process of computer simulation of human beings conceiving a document is as follows: (1) first randomly select a topic by simple random sampling method; (2) randomly select a word from the corresponding thesaurus of the selected topic to fill into the document; (3) repeat step (1) and (2) to select the next word to fill into the document until the document is filled. After the above process, the computer successfully generated an article. The LDA topic model is the inverse of the process above, that is, obtaining a document to infer the topics of the document, and these topics are composed of words appeared in the document, so it's also necessary to infer which words are used to form these topics. The principle of the LDA topic model uses Bag of Words model, which only performs probability statistics on the appearance of words. Assuming that the number of topics appears in the document is K, including the word sequence $\{w_0, w_1, \ldots, w_i, \ldots, w_{n-1}\}$, the probability of occurrence of w_i in the document is $p(w_i)$:

$$p(w_i) = \sum_{k=1}^{K} p(z = k) \cdot p(w_i | z = k) \qquad (1)$$

Where $p(z = j)$ represents the probability of topic j is selected, and $p(w_i | z = j)$ represents the probability of selecting word w_i when topic j is selected. They all belong to a polynomial distribution, and the distribution is subject to the Dirichlet distribution. It is also known that there are a total of X documents, and the above Eq. (1) is expanded to:

$$p(w_i|d_x) = \sum_{k=1}^{K} p(z = k|d_x) \cdot p(w_i|z = k) \tag{2}$$

Inferred that:

$$p(w_i, d_x) = p(d_x) \cdot p(w_i|d_x) = p(d_x) \sum_{k=1}^{K} p(z = k|d_x) \cdot p(w_i|z = k) \tag{3}$$

Where $p(d_x)$ represents the probability of selecting the xth document, $p(w_i, d_x)$ represents the probability of the word w_i generated in the document d_x. Some words with the highest probability are chosen to combine as topic of the document.

2.3   LSTM Network

LSTM network, which is a special variant of RNN, is designed to solve the problem of gradient disappearance of RNN [3]. Subsequent time nodes lose the perceived ability to the previous time nodes in the native RNN makes the long-distance learning ability of network insufficient. LSTM receives status information from the previous time node and sets three gates: Forget Gate, Input Gate and Output Gate [11], which were used to judge whether status information is useful. So LSTM has learning ability of long-term dependence [11].

At time t, the forward feedback operation of the LSTM memory cell is as follows:

$$d_t = g(W_d x_t + U_d z_{t-1} + b_d) \tag{4}$$

$$i_t = \sigma(W_i x_t + U_i z_{t-1} + b_i) \tag{5}$$

$$f_t = \sigma\left(W_f x_t + U_f z_{t-1} + b_f\right) \tag{6}$$

$$o_t = \sigma(W_o x_t + U_o z_{t-1} + b_o) \tag{7}$$

$$c_t = i_t \odot d_t + f_t \odot c_{t-1} \tag{8}$$

$$z_t = o_t \odot g(c_t) \tag{9}$$

The $\sigma(.)$ function is the sigmoid activation function, and the $g(.)$ function generally uses the hyperbolic tangent function. All varies in $\{W_*, U_*, b_*\}_{*\in\{d,i,o,f\}}$ are LSTM model parameters. The symbol $\odot$ denotes the dot product operation, $d_t, i_t, f_t,$ and o_t separately represent outputs of neuron, input gate, forget gate, and output gate at time t [3]. c_t will be passed to next time as the current internal state of the memory cell [3]. z_t is the output of the current node [3].

For this result, we choose to use LSTM network to train base learner. The output layer of LSTM network we use the sigmoid function as the activation function.

3   LSTM Sentiment Analysis Based on LDA Clustering

In recent years, many methods in Sentiment Analysis have been proposed. These methods include document-level, sentence-level, aspect-level, word-level, and even character-level sentiment analysis. Our paper studies a method adapting multi-domain sentiment analysis based on topic-level and word-level.

3.1   Data Acquisition and Preprocessing

We obtained three public datasets: electronic product reviews dataset, unlock mobile phone reviews dataset on American Amazon website, and movie reviews dataset on IMDB, as our experimental objects, which contain user reviews, and ratings. For these datasets, we need to remove duplicate reviews, word segmentation, remove stop words, and finally weaken the rating as binary classes. The process is shown in Fig. 1.

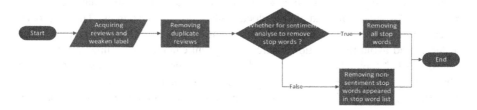

Fig. 1. The process of data acquisition and preprocessing

In order to conduct word frequency statistics and extract feature, word segmentation should be done after acquiring reviews. In English word segmentation, scholars have developed some effective word segmentation tools. We use the word segmentation tool in Natural Language Toolbox (NLTK) to develop in Python. We also need to remove stop word. Stop words generally refers to the most common words which as functional word in sentence, such as determiners likes "the", "at", and preposition express location likes "under", "above", and punctuation marks, numbers, characters, etc. Stop words have an impact on the LDA topic model which using bag of words model. In addition, the removal of stop words not only can save storage, but also be proved its necessary in sentiment analysis [12]. Note that the stop words list contains with the emotional words and non-emotional words. We especially reconstruct a new stop words list without emotional words for sentiment analysis by removing all sentiment word in the stop words list. But when training the LDA model, we still use the stop words list contained sentiment words.

While acquiring review sentences, we mark the emotional rating label for each review. The review data obtained from Amazon and IMDB contain with the emotional rating label, which represent the reviewer's emotional degree. The emotional rating label values from 1 to 5, which 5 represented as very satisfied, 4 as satisfied, 3 as neutral, 2 as unsatisfied and 1 as very unsatisfied. In this paper, we focus on the sentiment polarity prediction of documents. The ratings of review sentences become noisy information and would mislead classifier training if directly used in supervised training [3], so we adopt the weak supervision method, remove 3 points of reviews; regard the rating 5 or 4 reviews as positive and mark its' label as 1; regard the rating 5 or 4 reviews as positive and mark its' label as 0.

3.2   Integrated Learning Framework on LDA Topic Clustering

Different from the most clustering algorithms cluster using document similarity calculating [13], LDA topic clustering considers the topics probability distribution of the document as the unique feature to cluster. Whether two documents belong to the same cluster depends on whether their highest probability topic in topic probability distribution is the same.

The process of LDA topic clustering is: (1) acquired the entire training dataset which has been preprocessed to train the LDA model; (2) using this LDA model to cluster the entire training dataset. In order to make the LDA model we trained is more conducive to clustering the training set, we choose to use the training dataset itself to train the LDA model instead of the documents from other sources. This approach makes the training dataset have a certain amount of data in each training subset after clustering and avoid the situation where a document cannot find a suitable topic. The process of LDA topic clustering is: (1) while LDA model we trained has K topics, we define K topic sub-datasets; (2) obtain a text from training dataset, and use LDA model to predict topic probability distribution of this text; (3) compare the topic probability distribution of this text to get the topic with highest probability, and join this text to corresponding topic sub-dataset; (4) repeat step (2) and (3) until all texts in the training set are assigned to corresponding topic sub-dataset. The Integrated Learning Framework on LDA Topic Clustering is shown in Fig. 2.

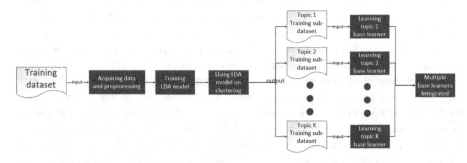

Fig. 2. The integrated learning framework on LDA topic clustering

After the LDA topic clustering, the training set is divided into several independent topic sub-datasets. We use these topic sub-datasets to train the corresponding topic base learner independently. Most machine learning or deep learning classification algorithm can be used to implement the topic base learner. Finally, all these topic base learners are integrated by ensemble learning method. This process realizes the combination of multiple weak learners into strong learners. Algorithm 1 provides pseudo code for implementing the ensemble learning method based on LDA topic clustering.

Algorithm 1:	*Ensemble Learning Method Based On LDA Topic Clustering*

Input:

1) doc_list: list contains X documents with label

Output:

1) LDA topic model

2) Topic k Base learner(k ∈ {1,2,...,K})

1   Remove duplicate document appeared in *doc_list*

2   **for** each document *doc$_i$ in doc_list* **do**

3   word segmentation for *doc$_i$* to obtain *words_sequence$_i$* of *doc$_i$*

4   remove stop words in *words_sequence$_i$*

5   add *words_sequence$_i$* into list: *wseqs_list*

6   update lexicon and word frequency statistics

7   **end**

8   **for** each *words_seq$_i$* in *wseqs_list* **do**

9   **for** each *word$_j$* in *words_seq$_i$* **do**

10   transform *word$_j$* into vector: *w_vec$_j$*

11   add *w_vec$_j$* into a list: *w_vecs1$_i$*

12   **end**

13   add *w_vecs1$_i$* into a list: *w_vecs_list*

14   **end**

15   use *w_vecs_list* and lexicon to train *LDA topic model*

16   **store** *LDA topic model*

17   **for** each *w_vecs$_i$* in *w_vecs_list* **do**

18   use LDA model to predict document topic probability distribution: *topic_probs*

19   obtain $K \leftarrow$ topic index with probability maximum in *topic_probs*

20   add   *doc_list[i]*   into   *topic_docs[k]*

21   **end**

22   **for** each *doc_list_topic$_k$* in *topic_docs* **do**

23   **for** each *doc$_i$* in *doc_list_topic$_k$* **do**

24   word segmentation for *doc$_i$* to obtain *words_sequence$_i$*

25   remove non-sentiment stop words in *words_sequence$_i$*

26   **for** each *word$_j$* in *words_sequence$_i$* **do**

27   transform *word$_j$* into vector: *w_vec$_j$*

28   add *w_vec$_j$* into a list: *w_vecs2$_i$*

29   **end**

30   add *w_vecs2$_i$* into a list: *vecs_topic[k]*

31 | **end**

32 **end**

33 **for** each w_vecs_k in $vecs\_topic$ **do**

34 | train *Topic k Base learner* using w_vecs_i

35 | **store** *Topic k Base learner*

36 **end**

37 ensemble all base learners

3.3   LSTM Sentiment Polarity Base Learner

After using LDA topic clustering to cluster the training dataset into multiple topic sub-datasets, we use each topic sub-dataset to train corresponding topic base learner independently. These topic base learners are also independent of each other.

As shown in the line 22 to line 32 of Algorithm 1, all documents in sub-dataset needs to execute word segmentation, and to remove stop words. All remaining words of each document are converted into word vectors, and putting word vectors into the sequence as the embedding representation of the document. After preprocessing, the xth document is $doc_x = \{word_0, word_1, \ldots, word_{l-1},\}$, where $word_i$, $i \in (0, l-1)$ represents the ith word in document, l represents the length of the document which is the number of words left. Assign w_{vec_i} as word vector of the $word_i$. The embedding representation of the document $resp_{doc(doc_x)}$ is:

$$resp_{doc(doc_x)} = [w_{vec_0}, w_{vec_1}, \ldots, w_{vec_{l-1}}] \tag{10}$$

Generating Word Embedding can use Bag of words model, or you can use Gensim Open Source Tool word2vec. Noted before removing the stop words, the sentiment words likes 'isn't', "would't", "good" and "very" etc., must be removed from the stop word list first. This process avoids the sentiment features of the text be removed thoughtless.

While converting words into word embedding, it is necessary to add zero padding makes the dimensionality of word embedding the same. Before training the network, we randomly divided each training sub-dataset into 80% of the internal training set and 20% of the model verification set.

Figure 3 is shown the process of sentiment analysis LSTM. And the process of LSTM model predict sentiment polarity of text: (1) text is preprocessed; (2) each word is transformed into a word embedding, and then combined word embedding sequence to get sentence embedding; (3) input the sentence embedding into LSTM networks and the predicted value is output through two layers of network.

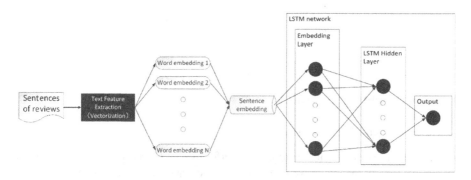

Fig. 3. The process of LSTM sentiment analysis

3.4 Ensemble Learning Classifier

Ensemble learning methods are methods of combining multiple base learners, include BAGGING, BOOSTING, STACKING, etc.

BAGGING sampling randomly with put back from the training dataset to obtain multiple sub-datasets to trained base learners. It uses the average combination or majority voting rule to integrate multiple base learners. Boosting is an optimized variant of Bagging. The first base learner is trained on dataset which is sampled randomly from training dataset, and its prediction result is feedback to weight the training dataset to make misclassified data will increase sampling weight. Then continue sampling from training dataset to train new base learner and update the weights until the end. This approach aims to strengthen the classification ability of misclassified data. STACKING is developed with a meta learning layer to re-learn the outputs of the base learner trained on dataset which is sampled randomly from the training dataset.

Ensemble learning method proposed in our paper based on LDA topic clustering. Our method clusters dataset into multiple base learning sub-datasets, and trains base learners on each sub-datasets. Suppose our topic model contains K topics and performs sentiment analysis on text X. First, we predict the topic probability distribution of text X through LDA model, and mark it as vector $probabilities(X) = (p_1, p_2, p_3, ..., p_K)$, where p_z is represents the probability of topic Z. Then we use base learners to predict the sentiment polarity of text X to obtain its sentiment polarity scores vector: $scores(X) = (s_1, s_2, s_3, ..., s_K)$, where s_z is represent predicted sentiment polarity score of X using base learner with topic Z. Finally, we obtain the final sentiment polarity score $Score(X)$ of text X by calculating the dot product between topic probability distribution vector and sentiment polarity scores vector, as the Eq. 11 is shown:

$$Score(X) = probabilitys(X) \odot scores(X) = \sum_{z=1}^{K} p_z \cdot s_z \qquad (11)$$

After calculating final sentiment polarity score of text X, we can tag the emotional label for text X. As the Eq. 12 is shown, the range of sentiment polarity values is 0 to 1, so we consider the final sentiment polarity value is greater than 0.5 means text is positive, and less than 0.5 means text is negative.

$$Label(X) = \begin{cases} 0, & 0 < Score(X) < 0.5 \\ 1, & 0.5 \leq Score(X) < 1 \end{cases} \qquad (12)$$

4 Experiments and Evaluations

4.1 Datasets and Preprocessing

In this section, we report the experimental performances of our approach. The experimental datasets in this paper we selects three large-scale social media public datasets: (1) Unlocked mobile phone reviews on Amazon; (2) Electronic products reviews on Amazon; (3) Movies reviews on IMDB. These datasets are common compose of multi-domain information. Table 1 summarizes the statistics of these three datasets.

Table 1. The statistics of the evaluation datasets

Dataset	Training dataset size		Testing dataset size	
	Positive	Negative	Positive	Negative
Unlock mobile phone reviews on Amazon	20000	20000	4000	4000
Electronic product reviews on Amazon	20000	20000	4000	4000
Movie reviews On IMDB	20000	20000	4000	4000

The preprocessing of the dataset mainly includes: (1) removing duplicate reviews; (2) word segmentation; (3) filtering of unexpected information such as non-emotional stop words and numbers; (4) converting words to numerical vector, and converting review sentence to sequence of vectors; (5) adding weak supervision to reviews.

4.2 Experimental Results and Evaluation

In order to achieve better effect of LDA clustering, we set the LDA topics number is 50. It guaranteed a smaller perplexity while having fewer topics [9]. For each dataset, we randomly divided it into 80% of internal training set and 20% of model verification set when training LSTM networks. To prevent over-fitting of the LSTM network, we set the dropout rate to 0.2. We set sigmoid function as output layer of LSTM to projection the output to the interval [0, 1], binary_crossentropy function as loss function of LSTM, and Adam function as its optimizer. The mini-batch has size of 50, and epoch limits 10 times when training LSTM networks.

As Table 2 is shown, comparing experiments between four methods on three data sets. These four methods is: (1) using entire training dataset to train LSTM sentiment polarity classifier; (2) randomly divide the training dataset into 50 data subsets and train 50 LSTM sentiment polarity base learners, and then integrated these base learners using BAGGING methods; (3) The LDA topic clustering is used to divide the training dataset into 50 topic training data subsets and 50 topic LSTM sentiment polarity base learner is trained. In the prediction, using the LDA model to derive the maximum probability topic of text, and the corresponding base learner is selected for prediction; (4) The LSTM sentiment polarity Analysis method base on LDA clustering and integrating by topic probability distribution which we propose in this paper.

Table 2. Performance comparison

Method	Accuracy		
	Unlock mobile phone reviews (%)	Electronic product reviews (%)	Movie reviews (%)
LSTM classifier	84.6	79.3	76.4
multiple base learners integrating	84.7	76.8	79.9
LDA topic cluster + multiple base learners select	85.3	80.5	81.3
LDA topic cluster + multiple base learners ensemble	86.7	83.6	82.1

The unlocked phones phone reviews focus on information related to mobile phones, but the electronic products reviews cover wider, and IMDB movie reviews contain most abundant different domain information. The performance of using only LSTM method on the unlock mobile phone dataset is significantly better than the other two datasets. Using LDA topic clustering makes the prediction accuracy on three datasets are improved, especially for the accuracy of electronic product datasets and the movie reviews dataset. Comparing to the method randomly divide the entire training dataset, using LDA clustering have more excellent performance. In addition, ensemble learning methods using topic distribution as dynamic weights of base learners are better than using probability voting. After using the LDA topic clustering on training dataset, over-fitting is more likely to occur when training LSTM base learner.

5   Conclusion and Future Work

This paper aims to solve the problem of emotional polarity confusion caused by polysemy in different domains of sentiment polarity analysis, and proposes an LSTM sentiment polarity analysis method based on LDA clustering. Our method employs topic clustering on datasets by utilizing LDA topic model, and respectively uses the LSTM algorithm to train the base learners. Each base learner integrated by dynamically achieving weights allocation using the topic probability distribution. The performance of the method has been evaluated by experiment on three large-scale social media public datasets, especially for datasets with more different domains information, the prediction accuracy of our method has significantly improved. Although our method performs excellent in sentiment polarity analysis, we also found in the experiment that this method can't achieve the desired effect in fine-grained sentiment analysis. From the idea of our method proposed in this paper, if the similarity as small as possible between texts with the same sentiment polarity but different degree, it is possible to improve the fine-grained classification accuracy of texts with the same emotional polarity. Therefore we will try to optimize our method to apply on fine-grained sentiment analysis in future.

Acknowledgements. This work is supported in part by the National Natural Science Foundation of China under Grants 61772141, 61702110, 61603100, and 61673123, by the Guangdong Provincial Science & Technology Project under Grants 2015B090901016 and 2016B010108007, by the Guangdong Education Department Project under Grants Guangdong Higher Education letter 2014 [97], 2015[133], and by the Guangzhou Science & Technology Project under Grants 201508010067, 201604020145, 201604046017, 2016201604030034, 201802030011, 201802010042, and 201802010026.

References

1. Santos, C.N.D., Gattit, M.: Deep convolutional neural networks for sentiment analysis of short texts. In: International Conference on Computational Linguistics (2014)
2. Dragoni, M., Petrucci, G.: A neural word embeddings approach for multi-domain sentiment analysis. IEEE Trans. Affect. Comput. **8**(4), 457–470 (2017)
3. Zhao, W., Guan, Z., Chen, L., et al.: Weakly-supervised deep embedding for product review sentiment analysis. IEEE Trans. Knowl. Data Eng. **30**(1), 185–197 (2018)
4. Yang, T., Teng, S.-H.: Research and application of improved Bayes algorithm for the telecommunication customer Churn. J. Guangdong Univ. Technol. **3**, 67–72 (2015)
5. Teng, S.-H., Hu, J., Zhang, W., Liu, D.-N.: The research of multi-classification based on SVM and Huffnan tree. J. Jiangxi Norm. Univ. (Nat. Sci. Ed.) **31**(2), 36–42 (2014)
6. Teng, S.-H., Tang, H.-T., Zhang, W., Liu, D.-N., Liang, L.: Identifying local rainfall type and forecasting rainfall quantity based on mixed multiple PNN and RBF neural network models. J. Chin. Comput. Syst. **37**(11), 2571–2576 (2016)
7. Yoon, K.: Convolutional neural networks for sentence classification. Eprint Arxiv (2014)
8. Socher, R., Perelygin, A., Wu, J.Y., et al.: Recursive deep models for semantic compositionality over a sentiment TreeBank (2013)
9. Blei, D.M., Ng, A.Y., Jordan, M.I.: Latent Dirichlet allocation. J. Mach. Learn. Res. **3**, 993–1022 (2003)
10. Wei, W., Yongmei, Z., Aimin, Y., et al.: Method of sentiment analysis for comment texts based on LDA. J. Data Acquis. Process. **32**(3), 629–635 (2017)
11. Chen, T., Xu, R., He, Y., et al.: Learning user and product distributed representations using a sequence model for sentiment analysis. IEEE Comput. Intell. Mag. **11**(3), 34–44 (2016)
12. Zhao, J., Gui, X.: Comparison research on text pre-processing methods on twitter sentiment analysis. IEEE Access **5**(99), 2870–2879 (2017)
13. Teng, S., Mai, J., Zhang, W., Zhao, G.: User multi-faced interests recommendation algorithm based on hybrid similarity. J. Jiangxi Norm. Univ. (Nat. Sci. Ed.) **40**(5), 481–486 (2016)
14. Bengio, Y., Ducharme, R., Vincent, P.: A neural probabilitistic language model. J. Mach. Learn. Res. **3**(6), 932–938 (2003)

15. Yih, W., Toutanova, K., Platt, J., Meek, C.: Learning discriminative projections for text similarity measures. In: Proceedings of the Fifteenth Conference on Computational Natural Language Learning, pp. 247–256 (2011)
16. Mikolov, T., Sutskever, I., Chen, K., Corrado, G., Dean, J.: Distributed representations of words and phrases and their compositionality. In: Proceedings of NIPS 2013 (2013)
17. Collobert, R., Weston, J., Bottou, L., Karlen, M., Kavukcuglu, K., Kuksa, P.: Natural language processing (almost) from scratch. J. Mach. Learn. Res. **12**, 2493–2537 (2011)
18. Yih, W., He, X., Meek, C.: Semantic parsing for single-relation question answering. In: Proceedings of ACL 2014 (2014)

Data Analysis and Machine Learning for CSCW and Social Computing

Anomaly Detection Algorithm Based on Cluster of Entropy

Wenan Tan[1,2(✉)], Xi Fang[1], Lu Zhao[1], and Anqiong Tang[2]

[1] School of Computer and Technology,
Nanjing University of Aeronautics and Astronautics, Nanjing 210016, China
wtan@foxmail.com, fa_xi@foxmail.com,
zhulu90@foxmail.com
[2] School of Computer and Information, Shanghai Polytechnic University,
Shanghai 2012209, China
aqtang@sspu.edu.cn

Abstract. To address the issue that the K-means algorithm chooses and determines the initial cluster center in a random way, which would fall into the local optimal clustering result, a way towards choosing the initial clustering center using information entropy is proposed. This proposed method divides the dataset evenly into data blocks with more than K, and then uses the entropy method to obtain the value of target function of each data block, as well as selects the centroid corresponding to the data block with the smallest value function of the first k target as the initial cluster center. By using entropy method to ensure the efficiency of the initial clustering center selection, an anomaly detection method is proposed. The result of the experiment show that this method performs better than the traditional K-means algorithm both in clustering effect and anomaly detection ability.

Keywords: Anomaly detection · Information entropy · Cluster algorithm
Cluster analysis

1 Introduction

The information technology is developing so fast in modern time, some special data that are different from most data in many fields have received extensive attention. These special data are called abnormal data. Hawkins gives the essential definition of anomaly [1]: Anomalies are unique data in the dataset, which makes people suspect that the data is not a deviation but results from a completely different mechanism. The common methods of anomaly detection include statistical methods, detection methods based on data stream algorithms, and machine learning methods based on unsupervised learning [2]. The application of data mining and machine learning in anomaly detection has received extensive attention. Data mining [3] refers to the process of searching for hidden information from massive data. It is usually combined with machine learning, pattern recognition and other methods to achieve anomaly detection. Wenke Lee [4] first applied the data mining into anomaly detection, and proposed that the anomaly detection should be classified into three kinds: classification, clustering and association rules.

© Springer Nature Singapore Pte Ltd. 2019
Y. Sun et al. (Eds.): ChineseCSCW 2018, CCIS 917, pp. 359–370, 2019.
https://doi.org/10.1007/978-981-13-3044-5_26

K-means is a type of unsupervised clustering algorithm, which has been widely used in anomaly detection field because of its high efficiency and simplicity [5]. However, the algorithm selects the initial cluster centers in a random way, it's unreason. In order to address the initialization problem, Grigorios [6] proposed a MinMax K-means algorithm. It first selects the first initial centers at random, then selects the data farthest from the first initial center as the second center from the remaining data, and so on until the K centers are selected. This method can make the initial cluster centers separate from each other, but it is not guaranteed to exclude outliers. Han [7] calculated the denseness around all the data points and selected the k highest density as the initial clustering center. However, this method of selecting initial clustering center based on the data-intensive size cannot guarantee uniform distribution.

When Zuo [8] selected the initial cluster center, it could exclude the outliers in the dataset and selected K centers evenly in the data close to avoid the defect of the local optimality caused by the random selection.

Another common detection method is anomaly detection using information entropy. Information entropy is proposed by Shannon in the 1948 [9], he introduced the core idea of entropy in thermodynamics into information theory. The greater the entropy value is, the more disordered the data in the system is. Conversely, the smaller the entropy value is, the more orderly and purer the data in the system is. If the information entropy is applied to the clustering algorithm, because it is dependent on the probability of each attribute in the data, the value of the attribute may be discrete and disordered [10]. Information entropy is suitable for dealing with the clustering problem of records with classification attributes. According to the clustering criteria, the data in the same cluster is the same as the better [11].

This paper represents a dynamic clustering method using information entropy to address the problem that the result of traditional clustering algorithm is susceptible to the selecting of initial cluster centers. The method first modifies the distance function of the object by means of the entropy method to the cluster object, the initial clustering centers with higher quality are selected by the weighting function values of the initial clusters, and the initialization process of the algorithm is optimized. Based on this, an anomaly detection algorithm was proposed. Experiments show this improved method is more accurate and practical clustering effect in anomaly detection.

2 K-Means Clustering Algorithm

The core concept of cluster analysis is that it is a process of dividing data into different clusters by using similarity criterion. In the scopes of cluster analysis, the K-means clustering algorithm which is based on distance division is commonly used. It is a typical dynamic clustering algorithm which is based on iterative modification [12].

K-means cluster algorithm [13] accepted the number of clustering K and the initial dataset, the detailed processing process is as follows.

(1) Choose K data samples from the dataset as initial cluster centers randomly;
(2) Calculate the each distance from every object in the dataset to the cluster centers, then classifying it to the cluster that is closest to the center;
(3) Recalculate step (2) after all objects are sorted in dataset;
(4) Once the cluster centers is changed, then turn to (2), otherwise turn to (5);
(5) Output Clustering results.

Since the K-means was proposed, a lot of research on this algorithm has emerged, and the drawbacks of the algorithm are revealed, including the following four points:

(1) The value of the K must be determined beforehand
    The result of clustering depends on the value of the K. Although, the value of k is not easy to determine, it is hard to figure out that the given dataset should be divided into several classes. So, in general, the value of K is given by experience according to the property of the problem and the given dataset.
(2) Clustering results will be affected by the initial centers
    At the beginning of the algorithm iteration, the initial centers are selected randomly, different iterative starting points correspond to different search paths.
(3) Results of clustering are unstable
    Clustering results are very dependent on the choice of the initial center.
(4) Vulnerable to the impact of outliers
    Outliers refer to data that is outside the data-intensive area. A small amount of such data will cause a significant influence on the results. Thus, if the K-means chooses the outliers as the cluster center, it will cause the clustering center to be far away from the real data dense area and affect the clustering results. As shown in Fig. 1, if the initial center selected is close to the true cluster center, the clustering result is more objective and real; However, as shown in Fig. 2, if the initial cluster contains outliers, the final result will produce a large error.

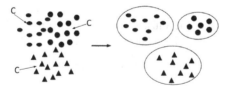

Fig. 1. The effect of outliers (reasonable)

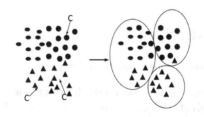

Fig. 2. The effect of outliers (unreasonable)

3 Definitions

Definition 1. Entropy

The entropy reflects the stability of the system, which is widely used in anomaly detection in recent years, and it regards each attribute in the data as a group of random events. Shannon uses the probability statistic method to give the definition of information entropy:

$$H(X) = -\sum_{i=1}^{n} p(x_i) \log(p(x_i)) \tag{1}$$

Given that $H(X)$ is the identifier of the entropy, x represents all the random variables, it contains n random events. x_i is a random event that may occur, then $p(x_i)$ represents the probability of x_i. The $0 \le p(x_i) \le 1$ can be obtained by probability theory, then $\log(p(x_i)) < 0$, so that the entropy is nonnegative.

Definition 2. Euclidean Metric

Suppose $A = \{x_i | x_i \in R^m, i = 1, 2, \ldots, n|\}$ is the given dataset, vector $x_i = (x_{i1}, x_{i2}, \ldots, x_{im})$ and vector $x_j = (x_{j1}, x_{j2}, \ldots, x_{jm})$ represent two data objects, respectively. So, the Euclidean distance between x_i, x_j is defined as follow [14]:

$$D(x_i, x_j) = \sqrt{\sum_{d=1}^{m} (x_{id} - x_{jd})^2} \tag{2}$$

Definition 3. The centroid point of a data category

$$c(T_i) = \frac{\sum_{a_j \in T_i} a_j}{|T_i|} \tag{3}$$

Given that $c(T_i)$ represents the cluster center of category i, then $T_i(i = 1, 2, \ldots, k)$ represents the category i, and $|T_i|$ represents the number of data objects in T_i.

Definition 4. Standard deviation σ of n_i data objects $x_i(i = 1, 2, \ldots, n_i)$ belonging to category T_j

$$\sigma = \sqrt{\frac{\sum_{i=1}^{n_i} (x_i - c(T_i))^2}{n_i - 1}} \tag{4}$$

4 The Improved Algorithm

4.1 Select Initial Cluster Center Based on Entropy

This paper proposes a method to choose and determine the initial clustering centers using entropy. Firstly, divide the dataset into k_1 $(k_1 > k)$ subsets equally; secondly, select a data object from each subset randomly, determine to use these k_1 data objects as cluster centers, then calculate the weighted category value function σ_i for each category, sorted them in ascending order; Finally, the centroids corresponding to the first k categories are used as the initial centers.

The following describes the steps to use the entropy method to calculate the weighted category value function.

Step 1. Construct attribute value matrix

$$
X = \begin{bmatrix}
x_{11}, & x_{12}, & \cdots & x_{1n} \\
x_{21}, & x_{22}, & \cdots & x_{2n} \\
\vdots & \vdots & & \vdots \\
x_{m1}, & x_{m2}, & \cdots & x_{mn}
\end{bmatrix}
$$

Given that n represents the number of sample data, and m represents the dimensions of each data object.

Step 2. Calculates the proportion of the jth dimensional attribute to the ith data.

The data needs to be standardized and compressed into interval $[0, 1]$, using the following method:

$$
M_{ij} = \frac{x_{ij}}{\sum_{i=1}^{m} x_{ij}} \tag{5}
$$

Given that M_{ij} represents the weight of the attribute value, x_{ij} represents property value, $i = 1, 2, \ldots, m$.

Step 3. Calculate jth dimension property's entropy

$$
H_j = -\frac{1}{\log n} \sum_{i=1}^{n} M_{ij} \log M_{ij} \tag{6}
$$

When $M_{ij} = 0$, then $M_{ij} \ln M_{ij} = 0$. If x_{ij} is equal to the all given j, then $M_{ij} = \frac{x_{ij}}{\sum_{i=1}^{m} x_{ij}} = \frac{1}{n}$, at this point the H_j takes a maximum.

Step 4. Calculate the difference function of the jth dimension attribute

$$
q_j = 1 - H_j \tag{7}
$$

For a given j, the smaller the H_j is, the larger the q_j is, and more stable the jth dimension attribute is, it means that the attribute is more import.

Step 5. Calculate the jth dimension attribute weight

$$
w_j = \frac{q_j}{\sum_{j=1}^{m} q_j} \tag{8}
$$

In the above formula, $\sum_{j=1}^{m} w_j = 1, j = 1, 2, \ldots, m, 0 \leq w_j \leq 1$.

Step 6. Using Euclidean distance to calculate the similarity between data objects, then can obtain the Euclidean distance after empowerment:

$$d_w(x_a, x_b) = \sqrt{\sum_{j=1}^{m} w_j (x_{aj} - x_{bj})^2} \tag{9}$$

Given that w_j is the weight of the jth dimension attribute. It is equivalent to making the attribute value corresponding to the weight appropriately enlarged or reduced, so that the attribute with larger weight has more clustering effect, and the attribute with smaller weight has less clustering effect.

Step 7. Using standard deviation as a standard measure function, The definition of objective value function for the weighted category is obtained by Definition 3.

$$\sigma_i = \sqrt{\frac{\sum_{x_i \in T_j} d_w(x_i, c(T_j))}{|T_j| - 1}} \tag{10}$$

Given that σ_i represents the weighted standard deviation of the ith category; The above equation shows that the value of σ_i is smaller, the larger degree of similarity of the data objects within the category is, and the more dense the data objects are, the more the centroid of the category can embody the classification decision surface.

The algorithm for generating the initial bcenter is described below:

Algorithm1 Select initial clustering centers based on entropy

---

Input:

(1) A: a dataset

(2) Number of initial centers k

Output: Initial Cluster Centers

1 Divide the dataset into $k_1 (k_1 > k)$ subsets. Select one data object randomly from each subset and use it as the clustering center.

2 Scanning all the dataset, then place each data object to its most similar cluster according to their similarity with the cluster centers (Euclidean distance after empowerment);

3 Calculate σ_i of k_1 clusters, and sort them in ascending order. Select the centroid of the cluster corresponding to the first k σ_i values as the initial center;

4 Calculate the centroid point of each category.

4.2 Anomaly Detection Based on Improved Clustering Algorithm

Due to the characteristics of the K-means, if the outliers participate in the operation of the clustering center during each iteration, the clustering results will be biased. Therefore, this paper considers the characteristic that the K-means is sensitive to outliers.

Algorithm 2 Anomaly detection algorithm

Input:

1) A: a dataset

2) k: number of initial cluster centers

3) ε: accuracy of clustering function

Output:

1) K clusters generated after the completion of the algorithm

2) exception point set U

1 Set the initial clustering criterion function value $J_0 = 0$, and the initial anomaly degree of each data point x in the dataset $Abn_x = 0$;

2 Divide the dataset into $k_1(k_1 > k)$ subsets. Select one data object randomly from each subset and use it as the clustering center.

3 Scanning all the dataset, then place each data object to its most similar cluster according to their similarity with the cluster centers (Euclidean distance after empowerment), then can get k_1 initial clusters;

4 Calculate σ_i of k_1 clusters, and sort them in ascending order of σ_i values. Select the centroid of the cluster corresponding to the first k σ_i values as the initial cluster center c_j;

5 Calculate the Euclidean Distance:

$$D(x_i, c_j) = \sqrt{\sum_{h=1}^{m}(x_{ih} - c_{jh})^2} \tag{11}$$

In the above formula, i=1,2,...,n and j=1,2,...,K, the m represents the dimension of the dataset. For a data object x, if c_j makes $D(x_i, c_j) = minD(x_i, c_j)$, j=1,2,...,K, then place x into the cluster represented by c_j;

6 After the K clusters formed, if the distance between the data object x belonging to the cluster and the center of the cluster is greater than the average distance, that is $D(x_i, c_j) \geq \frac{1}{N_j}\Sigma_{Lx=w_j} D(x_i, c_j)$, where N_j is the total number of the cluster represented by c_j, then $Abn_x + +$;

7 If $Abn_x \geq 3$, then determine x as an outlier, remove it from the dataset, and merge it into the exception set U;

8 Judging whether the clustering criterion function

$$J = \sum_{j=1}^{K} \sum_{Lx=w_j} D^2(x - c_j) \tag{12}$$

satisfies the convergence condition $|J' - J| \leq \varepsilon$ (J is the last iterative clustering criterion function value, J' current clustering criterion function value), if not, then turn to Step9 and continue iterating; If so, then the algorithm ends, output each cluster and outliers set U;

9 Recalculate cluster centers:

$$c'_j = \frac{1}{N_j} \sum_{L_x = w_j} x \tag{13}$$

then turn to Step5, the given N_j is the total number of data objects owned by the cluster represented by c_j.

The flow chart of the anomaly detection algorithm based on information entropy clustering is shown below, as shown in Fig. 3.

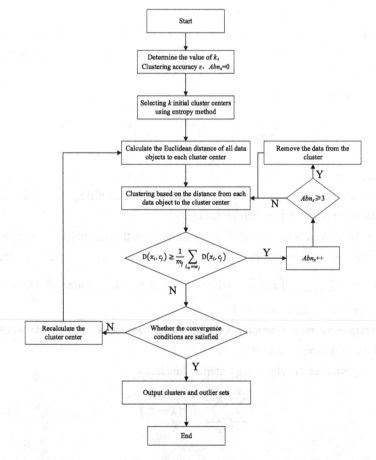

Fig. 3. Flow chart of the anomaly detection algorithm based on information entropy clustering

5 Experiment Analysis

The experiment contains two parts. The first one tests the clustering performance of the algorithm proposed in this paper. The second part of the experiment analyzes the performance of anomaly detection. The main performance evaluation indexes are: detection rate of abnormal data, false alarm rate, and average running time of the algorithm. All datasets are come from the UCI [15], which mainly includes Iris, Ecoli and Yest, and the dimensions and scale of these three datasets are enlarged in sequence. In this experiment, the clustering function convergence accuracy ε is set as 0.25, and the k values of Iris, Ecoli and Yest are 3, 8, 10 respectively.

5.1 Clustering Performance Comparison

There are many improved algorithms for traditional K-means algorithms, such as FCM algorithm based on fuzzy clustering, K-mean ++, MinMax K-means and so on. This paper selects three algorithms as comparisons: (1) the original K-means, (2) the MinMax K-means algorithm, (3) the improved algorithm proposed in this paper. The reason for choosing MinMax K-means is because it separates the initial cluster centers from each other as much as possible, and avoids the clustering result falling into local optimal. Thus the MinMax K-means is similar to the algorithm in this paper.

Table 1. Comparison of clustering performance between traditional K-mean and this algorithm

Dataset	Traditional K-mean algorithm			Improved algorithm		
	J_1	Number of iterations	Accuracy rate (%)	J_1	Number of iterations	Accuracy rate (%)
Iris	2081.2212	15	82.3	1992.32	13	84.2
Ecoli	5652.3281	17	77.9	4321.4	15	79.9
Yeast	9209.9876	28	72.3	5631.2	24	83.3

Table 2. Comparison of clustering performance between Minmax K-means and this algorithm

Dataset	Minmax K-means algorithm			Improved algorithm		
	J_1	Number of iterations	Accuracy rate (%)	J_1	Number of iterations	Accuracy rate (%)
Iris	1899.3	13	76.3	1923.5	12	88.9
Ecoli	4453.3	16	77.9	6653.9	15	84.4
Yeast	9822.7	29	69.3	7892.7	24	78.3

In order to confirm the rationality of the initial cluster center chosen by the algorithm, the experiment adopts the first cluster criterion function J_1 after selecting the initial cluster center. Before the iteration of the algorithm, if J_1 is smaller, the closer the initial cluster center is to the real cluster center, the more reasonable the selection is. Similarly, the fewer iterations, the higher the clustering accuracy and the more efficient the algorithm.

The Tables 1 and 2 show the improved algorithm uses the entropy to determine the initial clustering center, which can be closer to the real condition. Moreover, the reasonable selection of the initial clustering center reduces the iterative number and accelerates the convergence of the algorithm.

Because the Minmax K-means focuses on the uniform distribution of the initial cluster center, the algorithm can quickly reach the local optimal, the first clustering criterion function J_1 and the iterative times are better than the improved algorithm, but the clustering accuracy is inferior to this algorithm, In the process of dealing with high and large datasets, the performance of the improved algorithm is superior to Minmax K-means obviously.

Since the Minmax K-means focuses on the uniform distribution of the initial cluster center, therefore, the algorithm can quickly reach the local optimal solution, the first clustering criterion function J_1 and number of iterations are better than the improved algorithm. But the accuracy of clustering is inferior to the algorithm of this paper, and in dealing with multidimensional and huge scale data, the improved algorithm is much better than Minmax K-means.

5.2   Anomaly Detection Analysis

The performance analysis of anomaly detection in this paper mainly focuses on the detection rate, false alarm rate and average running time of the algorithm for anomaly detection of dataset. The algorithm is tested by adding a certain proportion of abnormal data in three different dimension and scale datasets. The experimental results are shown in Tables 3 and 4.

Table 3. Comparison of anomaly detection between traditional K-means and this algorithm

Dataset	Traditional K-mean algorithm			Improved algorithm		
	Detection (%)	False detection (%)	Average cost (ms)	Detection rate (%)	False detection (%)	Average spend (ms)
Iris	75.3	14.8	978	83.4	3.2	980
Ecoli	72.8	22.5	1177	79.3	10.9	1208
Yeast	68.9	28.9	1897	80.2	9.7	2032

Table 4. Comparison of anomaly detection between Minmax K-means and this algorithm

Dataset	Minmax K-means algorithm			Improved algorithm		
	Detection (%)	False detection (%)	Average cost (ms)	Detection rate (%)	False detection (%)	Average spend (ms)
Iris	71.4	18.9	862	83.6	7.8	965
Ecoli	69.6	28.7	962	75.6	10.5	1327
Yeast	60.3	36.8	1475	73.8	15.8	1872

In terms of the running time, since the improved algorithm spends more time on selecting of the initial centers, the average time is not as good as the original algorithm. Because the traditional algorithm chooses the cluster center randomly, the algorithm may choose the wrong data as the initial centers, the clustering result will produce great errors. Therefore, the improved algorithm is obviously better than the original in false detection rate. Compared with the MinMax, the improved algorithm takes more time. All in all, the performance of the Min–max is not as good as that of the improved algorithm both in detection rate and false detection rate.

6 Conclusion

The classical K-means algorithm chooses and determines the initial clustering center in random way. If the initial cluster center is not properly selected, the final clustering result will deviate from the actual situation. This paper adopts the method of determining the initial clusters centers based on entropy, selects the higher quality initial clustering center, and then proposes an anomaly detection method based on this. Through the experiment, the result show the algorithm presented in this paper perform better than the traditional K-means algorithm both in clustering effect and anomaly detection results. However, this paper also has some limitations. In the face of large data and dimension of high datasets, whether the calculation or iterative times will increase dramatically, the performance of the algorithm will be very general. The future work of this paper is to promote the comprehensive performance of this algorithm and cut down the time complexity on the basis of existing.

Acknowledgements. This paper is supported in part by the National Natural Science Foundation of China under Grant No. 61672022, Key Disciplines of Computer Science and Technology of Shanghai Polytechnic University under Grant No. XXKZD1604, and the Graduate Innovation Program No. A01GY17F022.

References

1. Hawkins, D.M.: Indentification of oufliers. Monogr. Appl. Probab. Stat. **80**(2), 321–328 (1980)
2. Agrawal, S., Agrawal, J.: Survey on anomaly detection using data mining techniques. Proc. Comput. Sci. **60**(1), 708–713 (2015)
3. Joseph, S.R., Hlomani, H., Letsholo, K.: Data mining algorithms: an overview. Neuroscience **12**(3), 719–743 (2016)
4. Lee, W.: Applying data mining to intrusion detection. ACM SIGKDD Explor. Newsl. **4**(2), 35–42 (2002)
5. Arora, P., Deepali, Varshney, S.: Analysis of k-means and k-medoids algorithm for big data. Proc. Comput. Sci. **78**, 507–512 (2016)
6. Celebi, M.E., Kingravi, H.A., Vela, P.A.: A Comparative Study of Efficient Initialization Methods for the K-Means Clustering Algorithm. Pergamon Press Inc., Oxford (2013)
7. Han, Z.-J.: An adaptive k—means initialization method based on data density. Comput. Appl. Softw. **3t**(2), 182–187 (2014). (in Chinese)

8. Zuo, J., Chen, Z.: Anomaly detection algorithm based on improved k-means clustering. Comput. Sci. **43**(8), 258–261 (2016). (in Chinese)
9. Liang, J., Shi, Z., Li, D., et al.: Information entropy, rough entropy and knowledge granulation in incomplete information systems. Int. J. Gen Syst **35**(6), 641–654 (2016)
10. Qian, P., Jiang, Y., Deng, Z., et al.: Cluster prototypes and fuzzy memberships jointly leveraged cross-domain maximum entropy clustering. IEEE Trans. Cybern. **46**(1), 181 (2016)
11. Yang, Y.-M.: Improved k-means dynamic clustering algorithm based on information entropy. J. Chongqing Univ. Posts Telecommun. (Nat. Sci. Ed.) **28**(2), 254–259 (2016). (in Chinese)
12. Har-Peled, S., Mazumdar, S.: Coresets for k-means and k-median clustering and their applications. In: Annual ACM Symposium on Theory of Computing, pp. 291–300 (2004)
13. Jia, G., Cheng, G., Gangahar, D.M., et al.: Traffic anomaly detection using k-means clustering **40**(6), 403–410 (2012)
14. Cohenaddad, V., Klein, P.N., Mathieu, C.: Local search yields approximation schemes for k-means and k-median in euclidean and minor-free metrics. In: Foundations of Computer Science, pp. 353–364. IEEE (2016)
15. UCI Homepage. http://archive.ics.uci.edu/ml/datasets.html. Accessed 07 May 2018

Abnormal Detecting over Data Stream Based on Maximal Pattern Mining Technology

Saihua Cai[1], Ruizhi Sun[1,2($\boxtimes$)], Jiayao Li[1], Chao Deng[1], and Sicong Li[1]

[1] College of Information and Electrical Engineering,
China Agricultural University, Beijing 100083, China
{caisaih, sunruizhi, Jiayao_Lee, lsc}@cau.edu.cn
[2] Scientific Research Base for Integrated Technologies of Precision Agriculture (Animal Husbandry), The Ministry of Agriculture, Beijing 100083, China

Abstract. With the rapid development of IoT and sensor technologies, data stream is more common in real life and it can provide data assurance for production. However, the abnormal data is usually existed in the collected data stream, and the presence of abnormal data will affect data-based prediction and analysis, therefore, it needs to be detected effectively. The widely distributed sensors make the volume of collected data is very huge, which results the traditional frequent pattern-based abnormal detecting method not suitable for large scale data due to the time cost in abnormal detecting process is expensive. Aimed at this problem, this paper records the data information of the collected data stream into vector structure first, and then proposes a maximal frequent pattern-based abnormal detecting method called MFPM-AD to improve the efficiency of abnormal detecting. Specifically, the maximal frequent patterns are mined instead of frequent patterns to reduce the time cost in the abnormal detecting phase, moreover, three abnormality indexes are designed to measure the abnormal degree of each detected transaction. Then, the abnormal detecting algorithm called MFPM-AD is proposed to effectively detect the implicit abnormal data based on the mined maximal frequent patterns and designed deviation indexes. The experimental results show that our proposed MFPM-AD method can effectively detect the existing implicit abnormal data over data stream.

Keywords: Abnormal detecting · Maximal frequent pattern mining
Data stream · Abnormality indexes

1 Introduction

To master the information in production more accuracy and comprehensively, the sensors are widely distributed in various fields. With the information transmitted by the sensors, people can better guide the production process of agriculture, industry, manufacturing, etc. Therefore, the collected information is critical in real life. However, the abnormal data is almost existed in all collected data due to sensor failure, external environment fluctuation and so on. The rarely appeared abnormal data would mislead

© Springer Nature Singapore Pte Ltd. 2019
Y. Sun et al. (Eds.): ChineseCSCW 2018, CCIS 917, pp. 371–385, 2019.
https://doi.org/10.1007/978-981-13-3044-5_27

data processing and affect data-based prediction and analysis, therefore, it need to be detected effectively.

Abnormal detecting is an important method that aims at examining the data with a significant difference to most data. The traditional abnormal detecting methods can be divided into: distance-based abnormal detecting methods [1, 2], density-based abnormal detecting methods [3–5], clustering-based abnormal detecting methods [6, 7] and pattern-based abnormal detecting methods [8–10]. Among these methods, the detecting accuracy of pattern mining-based method is much higher and this method is more suitable in processing large volume data. Pattern-based abnormal detecting method is usually composed of pattern mining phase and abnormal detecting stage. The core product of pattern mining stage is to mine the implicit frequent patterns, where the frequent patterns mean the occurred frequency of the patterns is large or equal the predefined minimum *support* value (*min_sup*). The abnormal data detecting phase is to detect the data that different with most data. The continuous, infinite, and fast characteristics of data stream [11] make the traditional abnormal detecting methods that directed into static data not applicable in data stream environment. Besides that, the amount of collected data stream shows an explosive growth trend in recent years, and the huge scale of collected data stream makes the abnormal detecting methods fell into a very difficult situation.

The most famous pattern-based abnormal detecting method, FindFPOF [8], can efficiently discover the abnormal transactions based on the mined frequent patterns. However, the drawback of FindFPOF method is that much time is used in abnormal detecting phase due to the scale of mined frequent patterns is very huge. Due to maximal frequent patterns can imply all the frequent patterns perfectly and the number is relatively smaller, therefore, the abnormal detecting phase can be more efficient if the frequent pattern mining process is transformed into maximal frequent pattern mining operation.

Based on the above idea, we propose a maximal frequent pattern-based abnormal detecting method called MFPM-AD to detect the abnormal data in data stream. The major contribution of this paper is generalized as follows:

(1) Design a vector structure to record the specific data information in data stream, and introduce an index structure to guide the maximal frequent pattern mining operation.
(2) Design three abnormal indexes to measure the abnormal degree of the transactions in data stream.
(3) Propose the abnormal detecting method to effectively detect the implicit abnormal transactions based on the mined maximal frequent patterns and designed abnormal indexes.

The remaining sections are organized as follows. The related work of this paper is stated in Sect. 2. The preliminaries related to this paper are given in Sect. 3. The abnormal detecting framework, maximal frequent pattern mining method and abnormal detecting method are introduced in Sect. 4. The empirical studies and analysis are stated in Sect. 5. The conclusion of our study is discussed in Sect. 6.

2 Related Work

2.1 Maximal Frequent Pattern Mining

At present, several methods were presented to mine the maximal frequent patterns from data stream. Li et al. [12] developed the SFI-forest data structure to incremental record the important information of maximal frequent patterns that embedded in the stream, and then proposed a novel algorithm called DSM-MFI to recursively mine all implicit maximal frequent patterns over data stream in one-pass using landmark window technology. Due to every sub-projection of affairs were stored in SFI-forest and some of them were not frequent at all, therefore, the occupied memory of DSM-MFI method is very large. Moreover, more time was also wasted due to some sub-projections were not frequent, and they should be deleted in pattern mining process to reduce the potential scale of extended patterns.

Mao et al. [13] proposed INSTANT algorithm to mine the maximal frequent patterns, it maintained patterns into memory with different level of support, and then the maximal frequent patterns were displayed to the users through a serious of sub-operations when the new transactions arriving. However, the amount of arrays that designing for maintaining all maximal frequent patterns was very large, besides that, the comparison times and memory usage were increased faster due to no supersets or subsets of new maximal frequent patterns have been checked.

Yang et al. [14] designed an efficient algorithm called DSM-Miner to mine maximal frequent patterns from data stream, and then used an appropriate method to reduce the effects of old transactions. The maximum frequent pattern tree was constructed to grasp the data information of latest patterns. In maximum frequent pattern mining stage, the pruning technology, the bit items group and "depth-first" search strategy were used to speed up the mining operation. With the above operations, the time cost and memory cost of DSM-Miner algorithm were very nice.

2.2 Abnormal Detecting over Data Stream

Cao et al. [1] proposed the principles of "minimal probing" and "lifespan-aware prioritization" to realize the scalable outlier detecting, and then the first general framework called LEAP was proposed to effectively handle three classic categories of distance-based outliers in data stream.

Based on the outlier factor of cluster, Jiang et al. [15] proposed an algorithm called CBOD to detect the clustering-based abnormal information in data stream. More specifically, the clustering algorithm was used to cluster the dataset in one-pass first, and then abnormal clusters were determined by the outlier factor. Although the detecting rate of aforementioned methods is relatively high, but the detected outlier can't well fit the widely recognized definition of abnormal data defined by Hawkins [16], moreover, this method was incapable in dealing with the large amounts of data.

As mentioned above, the abnormal detecting rate of frequent pattern-based detecting method FindFPOF [8] was very well, but it was a time consuming work due to the scale of mined frequent patterns was very huge, and the importance of mined frequent patterns haven't taken into their consideration. Aimed at the above problems,

Zhang et al. [9] proposed an improved frequent pattern-based outlier detecting method called LFP to detect the implicit abnormal data information, it took the longer-frequent patterns as the more important patterns due to more short-frequent patterns are contained in the longer frequent patterns. Lin et al. [10] proposed a novel abnormal detecting method called OODFP based on maximal frequent patterns to detect the implicit abnormal data in high-dimensional time-series dataset.

3 Preliminaries

To illustrate the proposed method more clearly, we provide some formal important definitions that used in this paper first, and then give the downward closure property to speed up the mining operations.

3.1 Definitions

Definition 1. *Pattern*: Pattern $P = \{p_1, p_2, ..., p_n\}$ is a set of literals. For any subset $P_t = \{p_1, p_2, ..., p_m\}$ $(m < n)$, P_t is the sub-pattern of P and P is the super-pattern of P_t.

Definition 2. *Support*: The frequency of pattern p_i in data stream (DS) in current sliding window is defined as *support*, $support = count(p_i, DS)/|SW|$, where $count(p_i, DS)$ is the appeared times of p_i in DS, and $|SW|$ is the size of sliding window.

For example, DS is $<abc, bd, acd, ade>$, then, $count(a, DS) = 3$ (a is appeared in $\{abc, acd, ade\}$) and $support(a, DS) = 3/4 = 0.75$.

Definition 3. *Frequent pattern* (*FP*): Pattern X is called frequent pattern must satisfy $support(X) \geq min\_sup$.

Definition 4. *Maximal frequent pattern* (*MFP*): Pattern X is called maximal frequent pattern must satisfy two conditions: (1) X is frequent, and (2) X is not the subset of any frequent pattern.

3.2 Downward Closure Property

Downward closure property [17] is an important theoretical basis in the whole maximal pattern mining process, it can reduce much time cost in the mining operation.

Property 1. All nonempty subsets of frequent pattern are frequent.

Property 2. The super-pattern of infrequent patterns is infrequent.

The detailed proof process can be found in literature 17.

From property 1, we can know that all *FPs* are the sub-patterns of *MFPs*, that is, each *FP* can be gained if all *MFPs* are mined, therefore, *MFPs* are the compression of *PFs*. It can be known from property 2 that if current short-pattern is not frequent, then, any longer-pattern extended by it will not be frequent, therefore, the "pattern extension" operation for the infrequent patterns is meaningless.

4   Abnormal Detecting over Data Stream

We separately present the overall framework of maximal frequent pattern-based abnormal detecting, the maximal frequent pattern mining method and abnormal detecting method in next three subsections.

4.1   Abnormal Detecting Framework

This paper mainly proposes a novel maximal frequent pattern-based abnormal detecting method to discover the implicit abnormal data over data stream. The whole method is divided into: (1) maximal frequent pattern mining phase, and (2) abnormal detecting phase. The overall framework of the proposed method is outlined in Fig. 1.

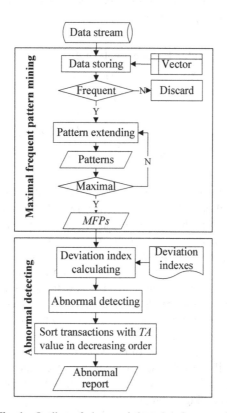

Fig. 1. Outline of abnormal detecting framework

In maximal frequent pattern mining model, the proposed method first stores the information of data stream with the vector structure, and then implements the "pattern extension" operation for the mined frequent patterns. These extended patterns are stored in maximal frequent pattern library (*MFP-L*) if they are maximal frequent, otherwise, the "pattern extension" process is continued until obtaining the maximal frequent patterns.

In abnormal detecting model, the detecting operation is conducted based on the mined maximal frequent patterns and their abnormal index, then the transactions are sorted by abnormal degree and these transactions whose abnormal degree larger than predefined minimal threshold μ are judged as abnormal transactions. Finally, the abnormal report is generated.

4.2   Maximal Frequent Pattern Mining

In this subsection, a Maximal Frequent Pattern Mining method on Data Stream called MFPM-DS is proposed to mine the *MFPs*. The whole process can be split into next 4 steps and they are explained with an example listed in Table 1. In this example, the $|SW|$ is set to 6 and *min_sup* is set to 2.0.

Table 1. An example of data stream

TID	Trans	TID	Trans
T_1	$\{a, b, e\}$	T_2	$\{a, b, c, d\}$
T_3	$\{b, c, e\}$	T_4	$\{a, b, c, e\}$
T_5	$\{a, c, e\}$	T_6	$\{a, b, c, e, f\}$
...	...	...	...

(1) Construct vector structure to record the specific data information of data stream. To detect the abnormal data over data stream, MFPM-DS method first constructs the vector structure to store the data information to overcome the shortcoming of tree structure, then, the pattern index is constructed to direct the information of stored element and to guide the "pattern extension" operation. When data stream is arriving at computer terminal, the data information is stored in the vectors in turn according the index of the vector. Once the new transactions are arriving, the old data information in vectors needs to be covered by the new ones directly. In this example, we first construct the vector structure and the corresponding index when data stream is arriving at computer terminal, then the data information is written into vectors in turn. The structure of the constructed vectors and index is shown in Fig. 2. Specially, if the calculated *support* value of current pattern is less than *min_sup* value, we need not take these infrequent 1-patterns into "pattern extension" operation according to property 2.

(2) Check and store the frequent 1-patterns. When the data information is stored in the constructed vector structure, calculate the *support* value of each 1-pattern. If the *support* value of the 1-patterns is not less than predefined *min_sup*, these 1-patterns are frequent 1-patterns and they are stored in frequent patterns library *FP-L* and *MFP-L*. In this example, the frequent 1-patterns are $\{a\}$, $\{b\}$, $\{c\}$ and $\{e\}$.

(3) Extend the frequent 1-patterns into 2-patterns and check the extended 2-patterns frequent or not. Randomly select two patterns of frequent 1-patterns from *FP-L* to extend them into 2-patterns, and then calculate the *support* value of each 2-pattern.

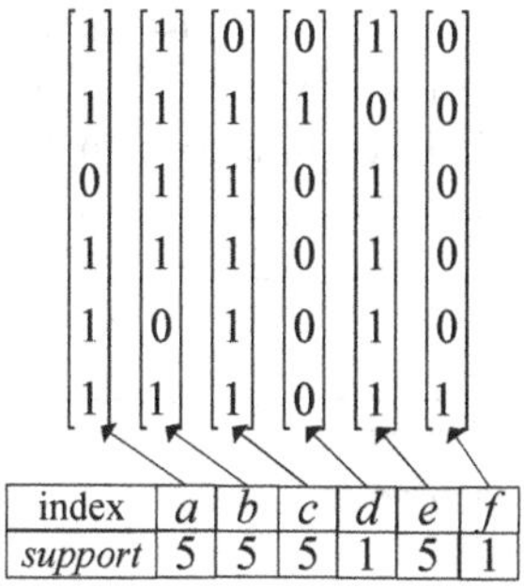

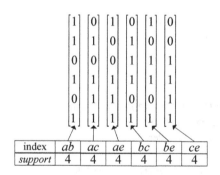

Fig. 2. The constructed vectors and index of data stream

The *support* value calculating is do "*logic and*" operation for the data information of the extended two 1-patterns guided by pattern index. When the *support* values of the extended 2-patterns are calculated, the data information of frequent 2-patterns and their index are saved to support next "pattern extension" operation. Then, the extended frequent 2-patterns are stored into *FP-L* and *MFP-L*, and the sub-patterns of the frequent 2-patterns are deleted from the *MFP-L* in turn. The vector and index of extended 2-patterns are shown in Fig. 3.

$$\begin{bmatrix} 1 \\ 1 \\ 0 \\ 1 \\ 0 \\ 1 \end{bmatrix} \begin{bmatrix} 0 \\ 1 \\ 0 \\ 1 \\ 1 \\ 1 \end{bmatrix} \begin{bmatrix} 1 \\ 0 \\ 0 \\ 1 \\ 1 \\ 1 \end{bmatrix} \begin{bmatrix} 0 \\ 1 \\ 1 \\ 1 \\ 0 \\ 1 \end{bmatrix} \begin{bmatrix} 1 \\ 0 \\ 1 \\ 1 \\ 0 \\ 1 \end{bmatrix} \begin{bmatrix} 0 \\ 0 \\ 1 \\ 1 \\ 1 \\ 1 \end{bmatrix}$$

index	ab	ac	ae	bc	be	ce
support	4	4	4	4	4	4

Fig. 3. The constructed vectors and index of extended 2-patterns

(4) Extend frequent short-patterns into long-patterns. The idea of "pattern extension" operation can be included as: for the frequent $(p - 1)$-pattern $\{p_{k1}, p_{k2}, ..., p_{k(p-1)}\}$, it can be extended into p-pattern $\{p_{k1}, p_{k2}, ..., p_{k(p-1)}, p_{kp}\}$ if $support(p_{kp})$ is not less than min_sup. Then, the column vector of the frequent 1-pattern $\{p_{kp}\}$ do "*logic and*" operation with the obtained column vector of frequent $(p - 1)$-pattern $\{p_{k1}, p_{k2}, ..., p_{k(p-1)}\}$ to get the *support* value of the extended $\{p_{k1}, p_{k2}, ..., p_{k(p-1)}, p_{kp}\}$. The extended p-pattern is a frequent pattern if the *support* value is large or equal to min_sup. Store the extended frequent p-patterns into *FP-L* and *MFP-L* and delete all the sub-patterns of the frequent p-patterns from *MFP-L*.

The maximal frequent mining phase is finished with the above 4 steps, and the mined maximal frequent pattern of the example is {*abce*}. The specific maximal frequent pattern mining algorithm is listed in algorithm 1.

Algorithm 1: MFPM-DS

Input: *DS*, *min_sup*

Output: *MFPs*

---

01. construct vector structure and index
02. write each data information into vector
03. **for each** 1-patttern $\{p_k\}$ **do**
04.   calculate *support*(p_k)
05.   **if** *support*(p_k)≥*min_sup* **then**
06.   *FP-L* and *MFP-L*←$\{p_k\}$
07.   **else**
08.   delete $\{p_k\}$
09.   **end if**
10. **end for**
11. randomly select $\{p_k\}$ and $\{p_j\}$ from *FP-L* to extend them into 2-pattern $\{p_k, p_j\}$
12. calculate *support*($p_k p_j$) // do *"logic and"* operation
13. **if** *support*(p_k, p_j)≥*min_sup* **then**
14.   save vector p_k & p_j and its index
15.   *FP-L* and *MFP-L*←$\{p_k, p_j\}$
16.   delete sub-patterns of $\{p_k, p_j\}$
17. **else**
18.   delete 2-pattern $\{p_k, p_j\}$
19. **end if**
20. **for** p=3 to *m* **do**
21.   **for** each frequent (p-1)-pattern $\{p_{k1}, p_{k2}, ..., p_{k(p-1)}\}$ **do**
22.   **if** *support*(p_{kp})≥*min_sup* **then**
23.   extend frequent (p-1)-pattern into $\{p_{k1}, p_{k2}, ..., p_{k(p-1)}, p_{kp}\}$
24.   **end if**
25.   **if** *support*($p_{k1}, p_{k2}, ..., p_{k(p-1)}, p_{kp}$)≥*min_sup* **then**
26.   *FP-L* and *MFP-L*←$\{p_{k1}, p_{k2}, ..., p_{k(p-1)}, p_{kp}\}$
27.   delete each sub-pattern of frequent p-patterns
28.   **end if**
29.   **end for**
30. **end for**

4.3   Abnormal Detecting

In abnormal detecting phase, the main work is to design an abnormal degree determining method to detect the existing implicit abnormal data accurately. Therefore, the primary task is to discover the abnormal index that will influence the abnormal detecting result.

Firstly, the length and the *support* value of mined maximal frequent patterns are two factors that will influence the abnormal degree. That is, the longer length of a *MFP* means it containing more frequent patterns, therefore, the transaction having long *MFP* is less like abnormal transaction. Similarly, the big *support* value of a *MFP* means it is appearing more frequently, therefore, the transaction containing *MFP* with big *support* value is less like abnormal transaction.

Secondly, the infrequent 1-patterns were collected in *MFP* mining process, and the containing number of infrequent 1-patterns is a main factor that will influence the abnormal degree. That is, the transactions is more like an abnormal transaction if it has more infrequent 1-patterns, the reason is that the infrequent 1-pattern is the sub-pattern of all infrequent p-patterns $(p > 1)$, and the more infrequent 1-patterns contained in the transaction, the more abnormal degree of the transaction is.

Thirdly, the length of a transaction is also a factor that will influence the abnormal degree. That is, if transactions t_1 and t_2 contain same maximal frequent patterns and $len(t_1) > len(t_2)$, of course, transaction t_1 is more likely an abnormal transaction due to its frequent density is smaller than t_2.

Based on the above analysis, we propose three definitions of abnormal indexes for each transaction to determine whether the transaction is abnormal or normal.

Definition 5. *Maximal frequent pattern abnormality index (MFPA)*: For each maximal frequent pattern X, its length is $len(X)$, then, the *MFPA* of each X is defined as:

$$MFPA(X) = \frac{1}{support(X) * len(X)} \tag{1}$$

Definition 6. *MiFPA* (*Minimal infrequent* 1-*pattern abnormality index*): For each transaction t_i, the number of infrequent 1-patterns x is $M(x)$, then, the *MiFPA* is defined as:

$$MiFPA(t_i) = M(x) + 1 \tag{2}$$

Definition 7. *Transaction abnormality index (TA)*: For each transaction t_i, its length is $len(t_i)$ and the number of contained *MFPs* is $N(t_i)$, then, the *TA* of each transaction t_i is defined as:

$$TA(t_i) = \sum_{X \subseteq t_i, X \in MFP-L} MFPA(X) + \frac{MiFPA(t_i)}{len(t_i) * (N(t_i) + 1)} \tag{3}$$

After the calculation of *TA* value, the transactions are sorting with their *TA* value in descending order. If the $TA(t_i)$ value is not less than predefined minimal threshold μ, it is judged as an abnormal transaction. Based on this idea, we propose the maximal frequent pattern-based abnormal detecting method called MFPM-AD to discover the implicit abnormal transactions in data stream. The specific steps of MFPM-AD algorithm is listed in algorithm 2.

Algorithm 2: MFPM-AD
Input: $DS, min\_sup, |SW|, \mu$
Output: Abnormal transactions
01.call Algorithm 1
02.**for** pattern X in MFP-L **do**
03. $MFPA(X)=1/(support(X)*len(X))$
04.**end for**
05.**for** $i \in [1, |SW|]$ **do**
06.   **for** pattern X in t_i and MFP-L **do**
07. $MiFPA(t_i)=M(x)+1$
08. $TA(t_i) = \sum\limits_{X \subseteq t_i, X \in MFP-L} MFPA(X) + \dfrac{MiFPA(t_i)}{len(t_i)*(N(t_i)+1)}$
09.   **end for**
10.**end for**
11.sort transactions with their TA value in decreasing order
12.**if** $TA(t_i) \geq \mu$ **then**
13.output abnormal transaction t_i
14.**end if**

5   Experimental Analysis

To test the abnormal detecting efficiency of the proposed MFPM-AD method, the classic pattern-based methods of FindFPOF [8], LFP [9] and OODFP [10] are compared in the experiment. All experiments are implementing on a machine running Windows 10 with an AMD Ryzen 7 1700 3.6 GHz processor, and the development environment is python 3.6. The performance of MFPM-AD method is analyzed by the public dataset of Wisconsin Breast Cancer Data (WBCD) [18] and real data of the collected agricultural sensor data stream. The agricultural data stream that monitoring the air temperature, air humidity, soil temperature, soil humidity and CO_2 concentration of greenhouse are transmitted from the agricultural sensors every 30 s. The experiments of MFPM-AD are conducted in the detecting efficiency and the time cost on abnormal detecting phase.

5.1   Detecting Efficiency of MFPM-AD Method

In this subsection, the detecting efficiency of MFPM-AD method is first conducted on dataset WBCD using different $|SW|$ and different min_sup value, and then the agricultural sensor data stream is also used to test the detecting efficiency with different min_sup value.

5.1.1   Detecting Efficiency on Dataset WBCD

The experimental results of abnormal detecting efficiency on WBCD are shown in Figs. 4, 5 and 6, where the bar in figures represents the number of true abnormal transactions. The "Top k transactions" of the y-axis means the top k transactions having highest min_sup value are selected when all real abnormal transactions have been detected. The "No. of sliding window" of x-axis means the serial number of the sliding window. The abnormal detecting efficiency is more excellent if the value k is closer to the number of real abnormal transactions.

It can be easily known from Fig. 4 when $|SW|$ is 20, the abnormal detecting efficiency of MFPM-AD method is the highest of the compared four methods. In most sliding window, the MFPM-AD method can discover the implicit abnormal transactions accurately and the abnormal detecting rate can reach into 100%. Accompanied with the min_sup value is increasing gradually, the abnormal detecting accuracy shows an increasing trend for MFPM-AD method. The accuracy of abnormal detecting of FindF-POF method is higher than that of LFP method and OODFP method in some window.

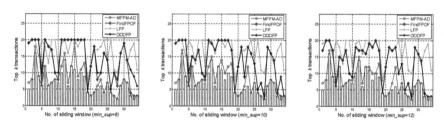

Fig. 4. The top k transactions when $|SW|$ is 20

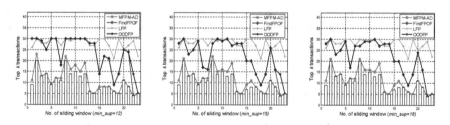

Fig. 5. The top k transactions when $|SW|$ is 30

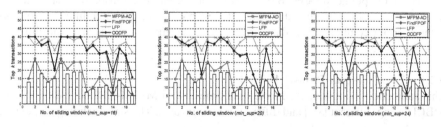

Fig. 6. The top k transactions when $|SW|$ is 40

382   S. Cai et al.

As seen in Fig. 5, the accuracy of abnormal detecting of MFPM-AD method is much higher than that of FindFPOF method, LFP method and OODFP method when |SW| is 30, and the error detecting situation is appearing rarely. Similarly, the accuracy of abnormal detecting of MFPM-AD method shows an increasing trend with the increasing of *min_sup* value.

We can see from Fig. 6 that the accuracy of abnormal detecting of MFPM-AD method is the highest of the compared three pattern-based abnormal detecting methods. When the *min_sup* value is 20, the accuracy of abnormal detecting is higher than that when the *min_sup* value is 16 and 24.

5.1.2 Detecting Efficiency on Agricultural Sensor Data Stream

Due to the number of distributed agricultural sensors is 30, therefore, the size of sliding window is kept 30 in this experiment. This experiment of detecting efficiency on agricultural sensor data stream is conducted with different *min_sup* value, and the experimental result is shown in Fig. 7.

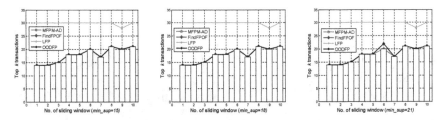

Fig. 7. Detecting efficiency on agricultural sensor data stream

The accuracy of abnormal detecting method, MPFM-AD, can reach to 100% on agricultural sensor data stream, and the accuracy of FindFPOF method and OODFP method also close to 100% except for in the six siding window when *min_sup* value is 21. The accuracy of LFP method is relatively lower, and when all abnormal transactions have been detected, the selected transactions almost close the total number of the transactions in sliding window.

5.2 Time Cost of MFPM-AD Method in Abnormal Detecting Phase

In this subsection, the time cost of MFPM-AD method in abnormal detecting phase is conducted on public dataset WBCD and real agricultural sensor data stream. For dataset WBCD, the experiment is conducted with different |SW| and different *min_sup* value. For agricultural sensor data stream, the experiment is conducted with different *min_sup* value.

5.2.1 Time Cost on Dataset WBCD

This subsection is implemented to test the time cost of MFPM-AD method on dataset WBCD using different |SW| and different *min_sup* value. The size of sliding window in this experiment is selected in 20, 30 and 40, and the ratio of *min_sup* value to |*SW*| is selected in 40%, 50% and 60%.

It can be seen for Figs. 8, 9 and 10 that the LFP method consumes lowest time in abnormal detecting phase in four pattern-based methods, and the time cost of MFPM-AD method and FindFPOF method is relatively similar in most situations. When the |*SW*| is relatively small, MFPM-AD method consumes less time than that of FindFPOF method in most situations. The time cost of MFPM-AD method is gradually larger than that of FindFPOF method with the increasing *min_sup* value.

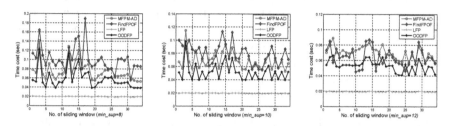

Fig. 8. Time cost in abnormal detecting when |*SW*| is 20

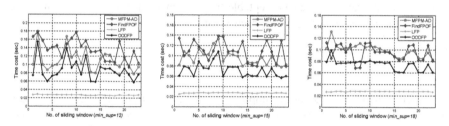

Fig. 9. Time cost in abnormal detecting when |*SW*| is 30

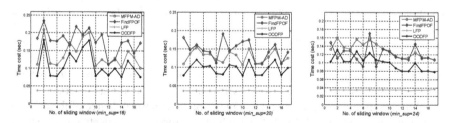

Fig. 10. Time cost in abnormal detecting when |*SW*| is 40

5.2.2 Time Cost on Agricultural Sensor Data Stream

In this subsection, the time cost of MFPM-AD method in abnormal detecting phase is tested on agricultural sensor data stream, it is conducted with different *min_sup* value. The experimental results are listed in Table 2.

Table 2. Time cost of MFPM-AD method on agricultural sensor data stream (ms)

No. SW	min_sup = 15			min_sup = 18			min_sup = 21		
	MFPM-AD	FindFPOF	LFP	MFPM-AD	FindFPOF	LFP	MFPM-AD	FindFPOF	LFP
1	0.337	10.836	0.167	0.316	7.252	0.08	0.377	1.776	0.049
2	0.227	9.813	0.106	0.426	7.913	0.091	0.413	4.176	0.065
3	0.363	8.827	0.101	0.481	8.24	0.091	0.355	2.612	0.056
4	0.965	5.378	0.074	0.683	3.458	0.064	0.459	0.85	0.046
5	1.298	5.659	0.078	0.999	3.969	0.109	0.58	0.678	0.056
6	0.497	3.85	0.066	0.39	1.747	0.051	0.354	0.639	0.041
7	0.563	6.55	0.143	0.713	3.4	0.092	0.463	0.793	0.04
8	0.668	5.233	0.073	0.825	3.792	0.08	0.449	1.189	0.048
9	0.532	6.952	0.116	0.76	2.43	0.056	0.358	0.911	0.042
10	0.85	5.183	0.074	0.833	2.342	0.052	0.546	0.839	0.043

We can know from Table 2 that MFPM-AD method uses less time in abnormal detecting phase than that of FindFPOF method, and LFP method uses the least time in the compared three methods. Although our proposed MFPM-AD uses much time than LFP method, however, it is also acceptable for abnormal detecting due to it only takes less than one millisecond to process each sliding window.

6   Conclusion

It is often difficult to discover the implicit abnormal data from data stream due to its huge scale, moreover, the frequent pattern-based abnormal detecting methods will cost much time in abnormal detecting phase due to the number of mined *FPs* is very large. Aimed at this problem, we propose an abnormal detecting method called MFPM-AD to discover the abnormal transactions based on the maximal frequent pattern mining technology. Specifically, the vector structure is constructed to record the data information of data stream in sliding window, and then long-patterns are extended by frequent short-patterns using "pattern extension" operation and the infrequent patterns are discarded directly to reduce the potential scale of extended patterns. After the frequent long-patterns are gained, the sub-patterns of extended frequent long-patterns are checked and they are deleted from *MFP-L* directly. In abnormal detecting phase, three abnormality indexes are designed to measure the abnormal degree of the detected transactions, and then the MFPM-AD method is proposed to effectively detect the abnormal data. The experimental results show that MFPM-AD method is more accurate than FindFPOF method, LFP method and OODFP method, and the time cost in abnormal detecting phase is much smaller than FindFPOF method in most situations.

In recent years, the uncertain data stream is more common in real life, and it has troubled people much for the characteristics of uncertainty. In the future, we will try our best to use the maximal frequent pattern mining technology to discover the implicit abnormal transactions from uncertain data stream.

Acknowledgements. This work was supported by Scientific and technological key projects of Xinjiang Production & Construction Corps (Grant No. 2015AC023).

References

1. Cao, L., Yang, D., Wang, Q., Yu, Y., Wang, J.: Scalable distance-based outlier detection over high-volume data streams. In: 30th International Conference on Data Engineering, Chicago, USA, pp. 76–87. IEEE (2014)
2. Kontaki, M., Gounaris, A., Papadopoulos, A.N., Tsichlas, K., Manolopoulos, Y.: Efficient and flexible algorithms for monitoring distance-based outliers over data streams. Inf. Syst. **55**, 37–53 (2016)
3. Bai, M., Wang, X., Xin, J., Wang, G.: An efficient algorithm for distributed density-based outlier detection on big data. Neurocomputing **181**, 19–28 (2016)
4. Tang, B., He, H.: A local density-based approach for outlier detection. Neurocomputing **241**, 171–180 (2017)
5. de Vries, T., Chawla, S., Houle, M.E.: Density-preserving projections for large-scale local anomaly detection. Knowl. Inf. Syst. **32**(1), 25–52 (2012)
6. Elahi, M., Li, K., Nisar, W., Lv, X., Wang, H.: Efficient clustering-based outlier detection algorithm for dynamic data stream. In: 5th International Conference on Fuzzy Systems and Knowledge Discovery, Shandong, China, pp. 298–304. IEEE (2008)
7. Huang, J., Zhu, Q., Yang, L., Cheng, D., Wu, Q.: A novel outlier cluster detection algorithm without top-n parameter. Knowl.-Based Syst. **121**, 32–40 (2017)
8. He, Z., Xu, X., Huang, Z.J., Deng, S.: Fp-outlier: frequent pattern based outlier detection. Comput. Sci. Inf. Syst. **2**(1), 103–118 (2005)
9. Zhang, W., Wu, J., Yu, J.: An improved method of outlier detection based on frequent pattern. In: 2nd WASE International Conference on Information Engineering, Beidaihe, China, pp. 3–6. IEEE (2010)
10. Lin, F., Le, W., Bo, J.: Research on maximal frequent pattern outlier factor for online high dimensional time-series outlier detection. J. Converg. Inf. Technol. **5**(10), 66–71 (2010)
11. Calders, T., Dexters, N., Gillis, J.J., Goethals, B.: Mining frequent itemsets in a stream. Inf. Syst. **39**, 233–255 (2014)
12. Li, H.F., Lee, S.Y., Shan, M.K.: Online mining (recently) maximal frequent itemsets over data streams. In: 15th International Workshop on Research Issues in Data Engineering: Stream Data Mining and Applications, Tokyo, Japan, pp. 11–18. IEEE (2005)
13. Mao, G., Wu, X., Zhu, X., Chen, G., Liu, C.: Mining maximal frequent itemsets from data streams. J. Inf. Sci. **33**(3), 251–262 (2007)
14. Yang, J., Wei, Y., Zhou, F.: An efficient algorithm for mining maximal frequent patterns over data streams. In: 7th International Conference on Intelligent Human–Machine Systems and Cybernetics, Hangzhou, China, pp. 444–447. IEEE (2015)
15. Jiang, S.Y., An, Q.B.: Clustering-based outlier detection method. In: 5th International Conference on Fuzzy Systems and Knowledge Discovery, Shandong, China, pp. 429–433. IEEE (2008)
16. Hawkins, D.M.: Identification of Outliers, vol. 11. Chapman and Hall, London (1980)
17. Cai, S., Sun, R., Cheng, C., Wu, G.: Exception detection of data stream based on improved maximal frequent itemsets mining. In: Xu, M., Qin, Z., Yan, F., Fu, S. (eds.) CTCIS 2017. CCIS, vol. 704, pp. 112–125. Springer, Singapore (2017). https://doi.org/10.1007/978-981-10-7080-8_10
18. https://archive.ics.uci.edu/ml/machine-learning-databases/breast-cancer-wisconsin/. Accessed 12 June 2018

Spatial Task Allocation Based on User Trajectory Prediction

Yun Jiang[1], Wei He[1(✉)], Lizhen Cui[1], Qian Yang[1], and Zhaohui Peng[2]

[1] School of Software, Shandong University, Jinan, China
`sdu_jy@163.com`, {`hewei,clz`}`@sdu.edu.cn`, `791907346@qq.com`
[2] School of Computer Science and Technology, Shandong University, Jinan, China
`pzh@sdu.edu.cn`

Abstract. With the rapid development of wireless communication technology and mobile intelligent terminals, location based service has been widely used for its unique features such as mobility, practicality and portability, including mobile crowdsourcing. In mobile computing environment, mobile crowdsourcing task allocation has become a focused research issue. In mobile crowdsourcing, application scenarios are in dynamic state, and workers are also willing to accept tasks. In response to these challenges, this paper proposes a mobile crowdsourcing task allocation strategy based on user trajectory prediction. First, the location points in user historical trajectory data are clustered into regions using k-means algorithm. Then the user's trajectory is analyzed and excavated to get the user's mobile pattern. On this basis, we extract mobile rules and calculate the confidence. According to the mobile rules, we predict the region that the user will reach, and finally assign the tasks in the region to him. The prediction based task allocation method proposed in this paper avoids the additional cost that platform need to pay to users, recommends user the task that more suitable for him, and improves the success rate of task allocation. Finally, based on the analysis and simulation experiments of real datasets, the proposed method can effectively predict the location region of users, and at the same time, it can achieve better results than other methods in the situation of task allocation and completion.

Keywords: Mobile computing environment · Mobile crowdsourcing
Trajectory prediction · Task allocation

1 Introduction

Nowadays, with the rapid development of Internet, location based services (LBS) can make us get mobile network services and information content anytime and anywhere, with its unique characteristics, such as mobility, practicality, portability and so on. However, mobile Internet services and information transmission are affected by mobile social networks. How to find the service that users are

© Springer Nature Singapore Pte Ltd. 2019
Y. Sun et al. (Eds.): ChineseCSCW 2018, CCIS 917, pp. 386–397, 2019.
https://doi.org/10.1007/978-981-13-3044-5_28

interested in from the vast ocean of mobile information and improve the personalized service experience of users has become a difficult problem to be solved in mobile recommendation system.

Crowdsourcing, usually refers to "a distributed problem solving model that has been outsourced in a voluntary form to a non-specific solution provider group through an open Web platform that has been performed by a full-time employee in the past" [3]. Mobile crowdsourcing is location-based service, it can not require participants to complete online, but subject to offline time and space constraints. The most important thing in mobile crowdsourcing is task allocation, which is designed to assign a spatio-temporal task to a worker set [5], the workers complete the same task in separate or collaborative manners (e.g., taking pictures or signing up at designated locations), while meeting the requirements for time, location and other constraints of the task [6].

At present, the strategy of assigning tasks is based on the current (allocation time) location of the mobile workers and pushing spatio-temporal task to the workers that close to him. This may lead workers to refuse to accept the task, because the task recommended to him deviates from the direction and intention of his movement. There are also some malicious workers who choose to accept the task in order to get the corresponding reward, but the answer he submitted is obviously wrong. All this have brought challenges to the allocation of tasks, not only the success rate of task allocation is low, but also leads to a reduction in the accuracy of the answer to the task. On the other hand, it also increases the extra travel cost that platform need to pay to workers when they perform their tasks.

Now in the big data environment, the diversity of huge amounts of data can provide us with valuable and meaningful information. Taking into account the historical trajectory data of workers, this paper analyzes the trajectory patterns, behavior habits, preferences for certain locations of workers. Then, based on the analysis, the worker's mobile position is predicted, and the task near the predicted position will be pushed to him. This will not only improve the probability of workers accepting tasks and the efficiency of completing tasks, but also reduce the extra travel expenses of workers and effectively avoid malicious workers.

The main contributions of this paper are:

(1) The discrete historical location points are clustered into regions, and an algorithm for mining workers' mobile patterns is proposed. The mobile pattern is used to describe the frequent movement trajectories of workers.
(2) On the basis of the workers' mobile pattern, the mobile rules of the workers are extracted, and the method of using the rules to predict the location of the workers is put forward, and the crowdsourcing tasks in the region are pushed to him.
(3) Experiments on real data sets verify the accuracy of the proposed algorithm based on mobile user location prediction and the effectiveness of the task recommendation strategy.

The rest of this paper is organized as follows, in second section, related work is described; in the third section, we propose the method of this paper, and introduce specific algorithms and examples; the task allocation is introduced in the fourth section; the fifth section shows the results of the experiment. Finally, in the sixth section, we draw a conclusion.

2 Related Work

The widely used predict methods are divided into sequential analysis mode prediction method [2,10], and Markov model based statistical model prediction method [4,7–9]. In paper [7], the hybrid Markov model is used to predict the mobile path, reducing the spatial cost of the 2 order Markov prediction model. But it has not effectively improved the prediction accuracy, and has insufficient consideration of historical information. Paper [8] uses a simple Markov model to predict the location of the position, which only takes into account the impact of the current location on the future position, resulting in a low prediction accuracy. In document [4], a variable order local matching Markov prediction model is proposed to reduce the prediction sparsity. However, there will be a lot of degradation in the prediction process to a simple Markov.

This paper improves the location prediction method proposed in document [9], and completely matches the trajectory of workers' recent activities with the historical mobile pattern. Mining the longest matching sequence from it. Generating the mobile rule to predict the region that worker will come to, Thus, the accuracy and adaptability of the prediction are improved.

In task allocation, Dingxiong Deng et al. [1] proposed the Maximum Task Scheduling (MTS) problem, which aims to maximize the number of tasks a worker chooses. Given a worker, a set of tasks with time and place constraints, a set of executable schedules is recommended for workers by using the range of activities of workers and the deadline of tasks. Workers perform tasks according to the schedule, which can maximize the number of tasks completed. Li et al. [11] is also a reference to the workers' historical trajectory, and recommends a route for workers to include as many tasks as possible, and the workers can finish the route to the end and get the most benefit. Compared with previous work, this paper overcomes the problem of dynamic programming path, and updates the route timely when new tasks arrive.

The above method studies the maximization of the number of tasks allocated as far as possible, without considering whether the workers are willing to accept it. It doesn't take into account the changes in the position of workers' dynamics. This paper is based on the location of the user region prediction, and then assign task to the worker, which can be more effective to allocate the tasks, improve the success rate of the distribution, and reduce the extra travel costs and reduce the cost of the workers.

3 Worker Location Prediction Based on Mobile Pattern Mining

This section describes the location prediction model of mobile workers, which mainly consists of four steps. In the first step, the location points are clustered into regions. The second step is to mine workers' mobile trajectories and form a worker mobile pattern. The third step is to generate mobile rules based on the mobile pattern. The fourth step is to use mobile rules to predict the regions where workers will go next to provide a basis for mobile crowdsourcing task allocation.

The task allocation process of crowdsourcing service platform is shown below (Fig. 1).

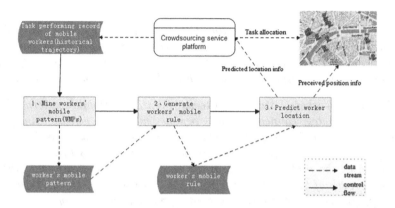

Fig. 1. Task allocation process for mobile workers.

3.1   Generate Region

It is assumed that the location of all the tasks in this paper can also be included in these regions, using the most popular clustering algorithm K-Means algorithm for the location point aggregation region, to realize the transformation of the point to region.

K-Means algorithm is an algorithm for clustering data points through the means. It partitions the similar data points through the preset K value as well as the initial centroid of each cluster and obtain the optimal clustering results through iterative refinement. Clustering is a kind of unsupervised learning to classify similar objects into the same cluster.

After clustering the location points by K-Means algorithm, we get the region and further formalize it into digraph G. As shown below, Fig. 2 is the geographical region map and Fig. 3 is regional network digraph.

3.2   Mining Workers' Mobile Patterns

This section introduces how to excavate worker's mobile pattern in detail. First, introduce some related definitions to facilitate understanding.

390   Y. Jiang et al.

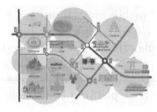
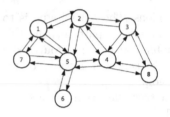

     Fig. 2. Actual regional map   **Fig. 3.** Regional network digraph

Definition 1. *Workers' Actual Paths (WAPs). Worker's actual paths WAPs is defined as* $W^{ap}(w) = <(r_1, t_1), (r_2, t_2), \ldots, (r_n, t_n)>$, *where* (r_n, t_n) *indicates that worker w reaches the region* r_i *at* t_i *time and* r_i *is the region number. A path indicates where workers w went in chronological order within a day.*

Definition 2. *Workers' Mobile Patterns (WMPs). Mobile pattern WMPs is also a route connected by region number, which can better describe workers' daily frequent mobile trajectory. Expressed as* $W^{mp}(w) = (<(r_1, t_1), (r_2, t_2), \ldots, *(r_n, t_n)>, supp)$, *where* $<(r_1, t_1), (r_2, t_2), \ldots, (r_n, t_n)>$ *is the same as the route definition of the above 1. supp indicates that the frequent occurrence of this route is based on the historical trajectory of worker w, called support,* $supp \geq 0$. *Support is used to measure how many times a route occurs in user history. The calculation method of support is consistent with the Apriori algorithm.*

    The WMPmining algorithm is described below.

    Now we explain how the algorithm CandidateGenaration() works, assume that there is already a user trajectory of length k, $C = <(r_1, t_1), (r_2, t_2), \ldots, (r_k, t_k)>$ as an input to the algorithm, in order to generate a candidate prediction trajectory based on C, consider the coverage area in the network map, first, the vertices of all the regions that can be reached from the vertex r_k are added to the set $N^+(r_k)$, where the vertices of the set represent where the worker can get away from r_k. Then, select a vertex v from $N^+(r_k)$ and add it to the candidate sequence $R' = <(r_1, t_1), (r_2, t_2), \ldots, (r_k, t_k), (v, t)>$, add R' to a candidate sequence of length $k + 1$.

    Table 1 gives an example of a worker's historical trajectory based on Fig. 3 area network diagram.

Table 1. Workers' actual path (WAP)

WAP ID	WAP
1	$<(6, t_1), (4, t_2), (5, t_3), (3, t_4), (2, t_5)>$
2	$<(1, t_1), (2, t_2), (3, t_3), (8, t_4)>$
3	$<(7, t_1), (1, t_2), (5, t_3), (4, t_4), (3, t_5), (8, t_6)>$
4	$<(6, t_1), (4, t_2), (2, t_3)>$

Algorithm 1. WMPsMining()

Input: Database of Worker's actual path, D; Threshold of support, $supp_{min}$; Regional network digraph, G

Output: Worker' Mobile Patterns($WMPs$), L

1: $C_1 \leftarrow$ the pattern whose length is one
2: $k=1$
3: $L = \phi$ //The set of patterns is empty initially
4: **while** $C_k \neq \phi$ **do**
5:     **for** $WAPa \in D$ **do**
6:         $S = \{s|s \in C_k$ and s is a subpath of a$\}$//S is the set of candidate length-k patterns which are also subpath of WAP a
7:         **for** $s \in S$ **do**
8:             s.count = s.count + s.suppInc //increment the support of c and s
9:         **end for**
10:    **end for**
11:    $L_k = \{s|s \in C_k$, s.count $\geq supp_{min}\}$ //choose the candidates which have enough support
12:    $L = L \cup L_k$
13:    $C_{k+1} \leftarrow CandidateGenaration(L, G)$
14:    k=k+1
15: **end while**
16: **return** L

Assume that the pre-set threshold for support is $supp_{min} = 1.33$, according to the actual route of the worker in Table 1. Mining the worker mobile pattern set by WMPMining() algorithm, as shown in Table 2. In order to facilitate reading, we omitted time in the table display, but the time was taken into account actually.

Table 2. A set of workers' mobile patterns

L					
Cand	supp	Cand	supp	Cand	supp
<1>	2	<5>	2	<3, 8>	2
<2>	3	<6>	2	<4, 2>	1.33
<3>	3	<8>	2	<4, 3>	1.5
<4>	3	<2, 3>	2	<6, 2>	2
<6, 4, 2>	2				

Table 3. Mobile rule set

Mobile rules	
Rule	Confidence
<2 >→< 3>	66.7
<3 >→< 8>	66.7
<4 >→< 3>	50
<6 >→< 4>	100
<6 >→< 4, 2>	75
<6, 4 >→< 2>	75

3.3 Generate Mobile Rules

On the basis of the last section of the worker mobile pattern we extract the mobile rules and give the definition of mobile rules first (Table 4).

Definition 3. *Workers' Mobile Rules (WMRs). A mobile rule, WMRs, describes the transfer relationship between regions which workers arrived at,* *expressed as $W^{mr}(w) = <(r_1, t_1), (r_2, t_2), \ldots, (r_{k-1}, t_{k-1}) > \rightarrow < (r_k, t_k) >$. $<(r_1, t_1), (r_2, t_2), \ldots, (r_{k-1}, t_{k-1})>$ is the head of the rule, representing the current path of a worker and the tail $<r_k>$ of the rule indicate the region with the maximum probability that the workers are going to go. The mobile rule is derived from the mobile pattern $(<(r_1, t_1), (r_2, t_2), \ldots, (r_n, t_n)>, s)$, and the following is an example of its rule set.*

Table 4. An example of mobile rule set

$<(r_1, t_1)> \rightarrow <(r_2, t_2), \ldots, (r_k, t_k)>$
$<(r_1, t_1)>, <(r_2, t_2)> \rightarrow <(r_3, t_3), \ldots, (r_k, t_k)>$
$\ldots$
$<(r_1, t_1), (r_2, t_2), \ldots, (r_{k-1}, t_{k-1})> \rightarrow <(r_k, t_k)>$

For a rule R: $<(r_1, t_1), (r_2, t_2), \ldots, (r_{k-1}, t_{k-1})> \rightarrow <(r_k, t_k)>$, a confidence is defined for it to indicate the accuracy of rule prediction. Confidence is defined using the following formula:

$$confidence = \frac{<(r_1, t_1), (r_2, t_2), \ldots, (r_k, t_k) >.supp}{<(r_1, t_1), (r_2, t_2), \ldots, (r_{k-1}, t_{k-1}) >.supp} \tag{1}$$

According to the above rules, we can get the corresponding mobile rules in each mobile pattern, and then calculate their confidence. If the confidence of a rule is higher than the pre-determined confidence threshold $(coff_{min})$, the rules are selected as mobile rules. The method of setting the threshold is consistent with the Apriori algorithm. If the confidence threshold $(coff_{min})$ is 50, then the mobile rule set is shown in Table 3 based on mobile pattern in Table 2.

3.4   Predict Workers' Regions

The process of regional prediction can be summarized as follows: it is known that a worker's current route is: $P = <(r_1, t_1), (r_2, t_2), \ldots, (r_{i-1}, t_{i-1})>$. Firstly, find all the rules that meet the current path prediction requirements and summarize them into the matching rule set. The set of matching rules has the following characteristics: The head of the rule is included in the current mobile route, and we can understand that it is an ordered subset of the path. The algorithm first sorted the rules in descending order according to the length of the head, and then looked for the matching rules. When matching, choose according to this principle, first match the rule head and track exactly the same, then gradually reduce the length of the rule head. Scan all the mobile rule sets to find all the rules that match the characteristics of the matching rule set. The first region number of each rule tail, the length of the rule head and the confidence of the rule form a three tuple(r, n, confidence). First, sort descending order according to the length of the rule head, and then sort again according to confidence. The first region number is selected from the ordered array as a prediction for the worker.

4   Task Allocation

The executant of tasks in crowdsourcing mode is non-specific people on the Internet, the acceptance and execution of the task are in full compliance with the principle of voluntariness, it is determined by the interests or intentions of the workers themselves and cannot be enforced, which requires a full consideration of the task allocation strategy, and even the prediction of each potential user's interests, behavioral intentions, etc., as far as possible to match the spatiotemporal task with the wishes of the mobile worker to improve the success rate of the task allocation. The location and trajectory of mobile users are constantly changing, so we propose a task allocation method based on user location prediction. First, predict the location of the workers, then assign the tasks in the region to him. The task allocation algorithm has improved real-time validity and dynamic scene adaptation ability.

In the mobile crowdsourcing application scenario, the crowdsourcing tasks and the location and quantity of workers are dynamically changing and updated in real time. Crowdsourcing platforms will receive tasks from task publishers at regular intervals, and workers will enter the platform to see if there are tasks to perform. We know that each task has a deadline, and workers can not always wait for the task. Therefore, it shows that it is impossible to achieve a global optimum. On the contrary, the platform realizes the local optimization of tasks and workers according to time segmented processing. In this paper, the goal of task allocation is to realize the local optimum of task allocation maximization over a period of time, while reducing the travel cost of workers. This paper is based on the greedy strategy of [4] to assign tasks. Given a set of workers $W_i = \{w_1, w_2, \dots\}$ and a set of tasks $T_i = \{t_1, t_2, \dots\}$ in region D, the goal is to allocate the tasks in T_i to workers in W_i for a period of time.

Since the prediction is not guaranteed to be completely correct, there may still be some unsuccessful allocation after performing a task allocation. But we can achieve a local optimal, and every other time, there will be a new increase in the workers and tasks, the distribution information will be updated, such a local optimal, will eventually form a global optimal effect.

The allocation algorithm is as follows in Algorithm 2:

Algorithm 2. Random Allocation

1: Initialize the candidate set be empty.
2: **for** task t arrives **do**
3:     Add the workers who can arrive at the location of task t into the candidate set;
4:     Choose worker w in the candidate set, if multiple, randomly select a worker. If the candidate set is empty, cancel task t;
5:     Assign task t to worker w, reset candidate set to empty;
6:     Response that task t has been accepted by worker w to user and platform.
7: **end for**
8: **End**

---

5 Experiment

5.1 Data Reduction

For verifying the performance of our method in real environment, we uses the real data set of location-based social network Gowalla, which includes user numbers, check-in time, latitude, longitude, and ID of location. It collected about six million check-in data from 2009 to October 2010. We chose 1047550 data with user numbers from 4807 to 18635 as our dataset, which contained more than 9200 users and 376000 different locations. The location and users of the data set are used to represent the location and workers of the mobile crowdsourcing task respectively. As long as the workers arrive at the specified place to sign in, they are regarded as accepting crowdsourcing tasks and completing them. Although data sets do not come directly from crowdsourcing, they provide the distribution of workers and task locations. Since the algorithm we proposed depends on location, using this dataset can draw some reasonable conclusions about the performance of the method.

This paper selects multiple class to cluster. Here is an example. Figure 4 is a clustering result when the number of class is 500, and each color represents a class.

Fig. 4. Distribution of clustered regions (Color figure online)

5.2 Experimental Evaluation

Next, we compare the WMP-methods in this paper with the UMP-methods proposed by Yavaş et al. [9] based on whether the region number predicted by the test set is correct, as shown in Fig. 5.

The accuracy is defined as follows:

$$Accuracy\#k = \frac{|hit\#k|}{|Total|} \qquad (2)$$

Accuracy#k represents the accuracy on condition that there are k-clusters; *hit#k* represents the number of data items predicted successfully; *|Total|* represents the total number of the sign-in data items by k-clusters.

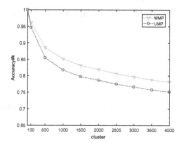
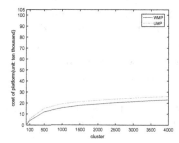

Fig. 5. Compare of WMP and UMP   **Fig. 6.** Cost of WMP and UMP

As the Fig. 5 shows, as the number of clusters increases, the accuracy of the two methods is reduced. This is because the number of clusters is small and the range of the actual region is large, and the change in the trajectory of the workers is less, the workers are basically in the fixed one or two regions, and the rate of accuracy will rise. The number of cluster is large, the actual region is small, and more and more close to the location point, the trajectory of workers begin to increase and the accuracy would be slightly reduced. When the number of cluster is 100, the accuracy is pretty high, the actual region is very large and the worker is basically in one region for a day, so predicted the result is very accurate. From Fig. 5 we can know that the method in this paper is better than the method proposed by Yavaş [9]. We consider the sequential of the historical track of the workers, the probability of users going to the first 100 locations is 0.5 larger than the last hundred thousand locations, which shows that there is a potential connection between the regional locations, not only considering the last region to predict. The method proposed by Yavaş is only to consider the last location without considering the links between regions, which will lead to a lower accuracy of prediction.

We also compared the extra cost that the platform needed to pay. If the prediction is correct, we think that the platform needed to pay is 0, otherwise is 1. We calculated the additional cost of platform need to pay under each class. As shown in Fig. 6, In terms of the cost of platform payment, the method we proposed is clearly reduced compared with the method proposed by Yavaş. Our method not only improves the probability of task allocation successful, but also reduces the additional travel cost and cut down the cost of platform.

6   Conclusion

For mobile crowdsourcing task allocation, this paper proposes a task allocation strategy based on trajectory prediction of mobile users. When crowdsourcing platform assigns tasks, it can perceive the current trajectory of users in real time. First it predicts the location of the user will arrive, then push the spatial tasks in the region to them. The task allocation method in this paper avoids increasing the extra time and travel cost when workers perform tasks. Workers are more willing to accept tasks, on the one hand, it increases the probability of assigning tasks successfully, on the other hand, the possibility of task completion is increased, and as many tasks as possible are allocated out.

Acknowledgements. This work is supported by Natural Science Foundation of Shandong Province under Grant No. ZR2017MF065 and No. ZR2018MF014.

References

1. Deng, D., Shahabi, C., Demiryurek, U.: Maximizing the number of worker's self-selected tasks in spatial crowdsourcing. In: ACM Sigspatial International Conference on Advances in Geographic Information Systems, pp. 324–333 (2013)
2. Gidfalvi, G., Borgelt, C., Kaul, M., Pedersen, T.B.: Frequent route based continuous moving object location- and density prediction on road networks. In: ACM Sigspatial International Symposium on Advances in Geographic Information Systems, Acm-Gis 2011, 1–4 November 2011, Chicago, IL, USA, Proceedings, pp. 381–384 (2011)
3. Howe, J., Booksx, I.: Crowdsourcing: why the power of the crowd is driving the future of business, pp. 1565–1566 (2008)
4. Jeung, H., Shen, H.T., Zhou, X.: Mining trajectory patterns using hidden Markov models. In: International Conference on Data Warehousing and Knowledge Discovery, pp. 470–480 (2007)
5. Kazemi, L., Shahabi, C.: Geocrowd: enabling query answering with spatial crowdsourcing. In: International Conference on Advances in Geographic Information Systems, pp. 189–198 (2012)
6. Kazemi, L., Shahabi, C., Chen, L.: Geotrucrowd: trustworthy query answering with spatial crowdsourcing. In: ACM Sigspatial International Conference on Advances in Geographic Information Systems, pp. 314–323 (2013)
7. Petzold, J., Pietzowski, A., Bagci, F., Trumler, W., Ungerer, T.: Prediction of indoor movements using Bayesian networks. In: Strang, T., Linnhoff-Popien, C. (eds.) LoCA 2005. LNCS, vol. 3479, pp. 211–222. Springer, Heidelberg (2005). https://doi.org/10.1007/11426646_20
8. Song, C., Qu, Z., Blumm, N., Barabsi, A.: Limits of predictability in human mobility. Science **327**(5968), 1018–1021 (2016)
9. Yavaş, G., Katsaros, D., Ulusoy, Ö., Manolopoulos, Y.: A data mining approach for location prediction in mobile environments. Data Knowl. Eng. **54**(2), 121–146 (2005)

10. Ying, J.C., Lee, W.C., Weng, T.C., Tseng, V.S.: Semantic trajectory mining for location prediction. In: ACM Sigspatial International Conference on Advances in Geographic Information Systems, pp. 34–43 (2011)

11. Li, Y., Yiu, M.L., Xu, W.: Oriented online route recommendation for spatial crowd-sourcing task workers. In: Claramunt, C., et al. (eds.) SSTD 2015. LNCS, vol. 9239, pp. 137–156. Springer, Cham (2015). https://doi.org/10.1007/978-3-319-22363-6_8

Study on Learner's Interest Mining Based on EEG Signal Analysis

Yonghui Dai[1], Junjie Chen[2], Haijian Chen[3], Shengqi Lu[4], Ye Fu[5], and Weihui Dai[5(✉)]

[1] Shanghai University of International Business and Economics, Shanghai 201620, China
[2] Shanghai Research Institute of Microwave Equipment, Shanghai 201802, China
[3] Shanghai Open University, Shanghai 200433, China
[4] Shanghai University of Finance and Economics, Shanghai 200433, China
[5] Fudan University, Shanghai 200433, China
whdai@fudan.edu.cn

Abstract. It is generally known that learning interest plays the key role on affecting learners' performance. Previous research methods of learning interest are mostly based on questionnaire survey and the analysis of learners' behavioral data. Considering the defects such as inaccuracy of subjective statements and limitations of samples, this paper proposed a new method for the learner's interest mining from their EEG signals through neural activity observation. It analyzed the neural activities in learning process, and designed the situational interest experiment according to learners' brain neural mechanism. Firstly, the experimental results of EEG test of thirty-six participants verify that animation, image and speech are superior to texts in terms of cognitive attention time, and provide the cognitive neural basis for the design and display of learning resources. In addition, the experimental results show that the eigenvalues of wavelet entropy and standard deviation obtained from EEG signals appear significant difference under the state of interest. When the cognitive load is higher, the relative energy of the frontal and temporal regions will be enhanced. Research findings of this paper provide the neural observation method and characteristic parameters to find learning interest more accurately and effectively than traditional methods.

Keywords: EEG · Situated cognition · Learning interest · Interest mining

1 Introduction

With the development of educational information technology, profound changes have taken place in learning methods. Although learning methods such as online learning and blended learning have made great contributions to cultivating students' innovative thinking, interpersonal cooperation and down-to-earth practicing. Various new problems like over-dependence on online teaching, higher drop-out rates and the fact of students being weary of studying still often happen. For example, a course named "Software Engineering" lectured on the Coursera Platform of University of California,

© Springer Nature Singapore Pte Ltd. 2019
Y. Sun et al. (Eds.): ChineseCSCW 2018, CCIS 917, pp. 398–409, 2019.
https://doi.org/10.1007/978-981-13-3044-5_29

Berkeley attracted over 50,000 students, while only 7% of whom stuck to it to the end. The above phenomena can be largely attributed to the students' shift of interest in addition to other objective reasons. According to the results of the investigation of the Guokr's MOOC, the three major motivations of the study are: learning interest, skill promotion, and going abroad. Among which the interest of learning is 61% in the first place [1]. All along, the study of interest in learning is a hot topic, and has attracted the attention of many scholars in their researches, such as learners' emotion mining and learning resources recommendation [2–4].

In the past years, most scholars studied learning interest usually from the learners' online browsing path and web log data, and obtained many meaningful research results. Based on the progress of cognitive neuroscience in the aspects of management [5], emotional cognition [6], memory and attention [7–9] etc., this paper introduces the internal cognitive mechanism of the formation of learners' interest in blended learning, and provides a new method for analysis and understanding of big learning behavior data [10].

The structure of the paper is as follows: Sect. 2 is written to introduce applied theories; Sect. 3 illustrates the model of neural mechanism for cognition in the aspect of text-based interest; Sect. 4 focuses on the analysis of EEG experiments and the learner's interest; Sect. 5 provides the conclusion and expectation.

2 Theories and Methods

2.1 Situational Interest

Interest is the interaction and connection between an individual and the surrounding environment, which can be interpreted as the positive attitude and emotion of an individual when he/she is involved in certain activities or exposed to certain cultural environment, usually reflecting his/her intention and choice. Interesting can be seen as a kind of psychological state under an individual tries to explore certain items, or it is regarded as a kind of mental disposition of an individual when he/she keeps himself/herself engaged in certain activities [11]. Some foreign scholars have divided interest into text-based interest and individual interest based on the interaction between individuals and the environments [12]. Among them, situational interest refers to people's concern about the task and the environment. It is an immediate emotional response from the environment that stimulates it, and its duration is short [13]. Individual interest refers to the relatively stable and persistent tendency of psychological preference expressed by an individual on a particular subject activity or thing, which is closely associated with internal motivation [14]. Situation interest can be transformed into individual interest under certain conditions. According to the source of situational interest, it includes three categories: interest based on text, interest based on task, and interest based on knowledge [15], among, situational interest based on task shows that learners can adapt to the requirements of different tasks by adjusting their own internal interests when they meet the changes in their learning tasks.

The cognition of situational interest is closely related to memory. Memory is divided into sensory memory, short-term memory and long-term memory in the field of cognitive psychology. Sensory memory refers to the memory of the external stimuli acting directly on the human sensory organ, the appearance of the sensory appearance and the instant storage. After the brain scans, the memory information is stored in the form of short memory [16]. When retelling the information of short-term memory, it can be maintained for a long time and become a long-term memory. From the process of brain activity, learners' perception of information is the first emotional response of external information to the limbic system by ingestion of sensory pathways [17]. Then it reaches the higher cortex of the brain, forming second emotional responses after cognitive activities. Specifically, the initial stimulus is transmitted to the cerebral marginal system through the various sensory organs, the selective attention mechanism and the internal sensory pathways within the brain, and the learners' cerebral cortex is selectively concerned with their advanced psychological activities, such as their own motivation, knowledge, memory, cognition, and decision-making.

The results of cognitive neuroscience have shown that human's cognitive psychological responses are stimulated by external signals and are the result of a series of neural activities under the action of the brain [18]. These processes are dominant by brain functional mechanism, and produce physiological activation in the corresponding brain regions. In recent years, the development of modern experimental observation technology, such as EEG (Electroencephalogram), ERPs (brain evoked Event Related Potentials), fNIRS(functional Near-infrared Spectroscopy) and fMRI (functional Magnetic Resonance Imaging), provides advanced technical means for the study of human emotion and its neural mechanism. The EEG test process is shown in Fig. 1.

Fig. 1. EEG test process.

2.2   Brain Neural Mechanism

In the cognitive process of situational interest, the cognitive process and interest will change with the change of situation. As a result of cognition, learners' emotional experience is also dynamic. For example, when the learners log on to the MOOCs learning platform, the design form and the information contained in the web course page will be transferred to the learner's brain edge system first through the sensory pathway of the learner's selective attention mechanism. Therefore, the first (primary) emotional response is generated, and the above reaction is produced mainly by the imagery information of the stimulus. Therefore, how to design an attractive network course interface and convey the image force of the learning interest to the learners is the first factor to be considered in the design of the MOOCs learning platform.

On the basis of the first emotional reaction, the content information in the stimulus signal will further form a secondary cognitive response to its semantic information through the cognitive activity of the learner's cerebral cortex, thus forming a further emotional experience. This is a question that the MOOCs learning platform should consider in the content of the content. Therefore, it is necessary for learners to provide attractive learning resource, and fully arouse their interest in autonomous learning.

On the basis of the above first and secondary emotional experience, the learner's brain quickly built an emotional symbol processing system for specific stimulus in the state of memory. Once the familiar imagery information or semantic information symbols appear, the learners will give specific selective attention to the above symbols according to their previous emotional experience memory. And their brain can adjust the distribution of visual, auditory and cognitive time resources. Therefore, enjoyable learning experiences play an important guidance in stimulating the learner's interest, and it can help learner to cultivate the interest and behavior of autonomous learning. From the above analysis, in MOOCs learning, the cognitive process of situational interest is systematically related to the construction of the situation, the characteristics of the cognitive neural activity of the brain, and the emotional experience of the learners. Based on the existing research results [12], the brain neural mechanism of situational learning interest is summarized in this paper as shown in Fig. 2.

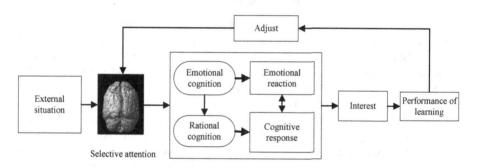

Fig. 2. Brain neural mechanism of situational learning interest.

3 Experiment of Situational Interest Brain Cognitive

Because of the rich content of emotional, mental and psychological activities in EEG signals, the study of cognition through EEG signals has become a choice for many scholars. EEG was also used to study the cognitive brain cognition of the learners in our research.

3.1 Subjects

A total of thirty-six participants were from Shanghai Open University, including twenty males and sixteen females, with an average age of 23.3 years. All the subjects signed the EEG informed consent before the test. Their physical and mental health was healthy, and their eyesight was normal.

3.2 Experimental Process

The experimental process of this study, as shown in Fig. 3, includes four stages, including experimental preparation, experimental execution, and post experiment communication and data processing. After the experiment, the experimenter refers to the subjective expression of the material at that time after the experimenter completes the EEG experiment, such as whether there is any interference. If he is disturbed during the test, he needs to eliminate the time segment of the disturbed brain waves.

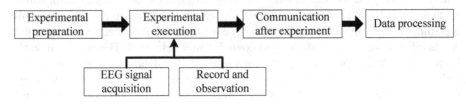

Fig. 3. Brain neural mechanism of situational learning interest.

3.3 Experimental Procedure

This experiment includes the following steps:

Step 1: the subjects are prepared. Before the experiment, the subjects kept their heads neat and tidy, and sit in a special laboratory such as sit on the sofa, and eight channel electrodes position (Fp1, Fp2, T3, T4, C3, C4, O1 and O2) have placed on the brain electric cap. It were led from the electrode wires and connected to the electroencephalogram machine for experiment.

Step 2: start the experiment. The screen is black. The distance between the test and the test screen is about 70 cm. The horizontal * vertical angle is about 3.1° * 2.2°. The stimulus is presented in the center of the screen. First, the red signal of '+' is displayed in the center of the screen. After 1 s, the experiment related material is appeared. The display time is 2 s, then after the interval of 2 s with black background screen, and waiting for the reaction of the subjects. Then enter the next test, the interval between tests is 2 s.

Step 3: data acquisition. The EEG data acquisition of the subjects is completed through the proprietary data device, which will be used for subsequent data analysis.

3.4 Experimental Task

There are two tasks in this paper: Task 1 (material browsing), task 2 (symbol information cognition time allocation). In order to obtain effective experimental data, task 2 is carried out a week after task 1, and the material of task 2 is based on the text of the tester with more than 3 of the degree of interest in task 1 plus other content. The two tasks are detailed as shown in Tables 1 and 2.

Table 1. Experiment task 1 (material browsing).

No.	Description
1	Black screen background
2	Start the test
3	The screen displays the active words and related texts for 15 s
4	The black screen is 2 s
5	Repeat steps 3–5 until 20 material browsing is completed
6	Test end

Table 2. Experiment task 2 (material browsing).

No.	Description
1	Black screen background
2	The screen presents the task 1 interest degree more than 3 of the text and animated interface, and start timing
3	The tester gives an interest response and ends the timer at 0–5 of a figure
4	The black screen is 2 s
5	The screen presents task 1 interest text and audio interface, and starts timing
6	The tester gives an interest response and ends with a count of 0–5
7	The black screen is 2 s
8	The screen presents task 1 interest text and colored interface, and starts timing
9	The tester gives an interest response and ends with a count of 0–5
10	The black screen is 2 s
11	The screen presents task 1 interested text and graphic interface, and starts timing
12	The tester gives an interest response and ends with a count of 0–5
13	The black screen is 2 s
14	Repeat steps 3 to 13 until completing task 1
15	Test end

4 Data Processing

4.1 Data Preprocessing

Since the weak electroencephalogram EEG usually with an amplitude lower than 100 μv, the EEG collected in the experiment is often mixed with many internal and external interferential noises, such as head shaking, blinking, electrocardiogram, power frequency and interference and so on. The amplitude of these noises is relatively large so that the original EEG signal is covered. Thus, it's necessary to carry out data processing to remove artifacts and restore the EEG signal as much as possible.

In terms of removing artifacts, this paper selects the average reference electrode as the reference. The average value of the voltage recorded on the all positioned EEG electrodes on the scalp is taken as the reference, and this average reference electrode is subtracted from original electrodes to get the EEG data of each electrode. The principle of this method is based on that the sum of the positive and negative electrode on the whole spherical head equals to zero. Since the artifacts are not real EEG signal, this feature is not shown. Artifacts usually present a consistent electric potential reaction, and an approximate pseudo signal can be reduced by the average of the superposition. Therefore, it's easy to remove or attenuate some artifacts through retrieving the average reference electrode, especially irregular randomly explosive artifacts.

In this paper, wavelet transform technology is adopted to de-noise EEG. To order to remove artifacts, the signals are decomposed by the wavelet packet to filter signals which is above 30 Hz and reconstructed later. The wavelet transform process is as follows

If the basic wavelet satisfies the following conditions:

$$C_\varphi = \int_{-\infty}^{+\infty} \frac{|\varphi(\omega)|^2}{|\omega|} d\omega < \infty \tag{1}$$

The continuous wavelet transform has inverse transformation, and its formula is as follows:

$$f(t) = C_\varphi^{-1} \int_0^\infty \int_{-\infty}^{+\infty} \frac{1}{\sqrt{a}} \varphi_{a,b}(t) \cdot CWT_{a,b} \frac{d_a d_b}{a^2} \tag{2}$$

Discrete wavelet transform requires discrete sample of scale factor a, and displacement factor b:

$$a = a_0^m, b = nb_0 a_0^m \tag{3}$$

Therefore, the discrete wavelet transform can be defined as:

$$DWT_{m,n} = \int_{-\infty}^{+\infty} f(t)\varphi_{m,n}(t)dt \tag{4}$$

Its reconstruction formula is as follows:

$$f(t) = \sum_{m,n} DWT_{m,n} \tilde{\varphi}_{m,n}(t) \tag{5}$$

The dual frame of $\varphi_{m,n}$ is $\tilde{\varphi}_{m,n}$.

In general, the size of a_0 and b_0 should be changed to allow the wavelet transform to perform dynamic frequency and time resolution adjustments. For convenience, the binary discrete method is usually adopted to take $a_0 = 2$. Therefore, such transformation form is also called dyadic wavelet transform. And then taking $b_0 = 1$, this transformation form is named orthogonal dyadic wavelet transform. With the corresponding scale factor is 2^k and displacement factor $2^k n$, the orthogonal dyadic wavelet is as follows:

$$\varphi_{k,n}(t) = 2^{\frac{-k}{2}}\varphi\left(2^{-k}t - n\right) \tag{6}$$

The functions represented by the orthogonal dyadic wavelet are:

$$f(t) = \sum_{k\in z}\sum_{n\in z}D_{k,n}\varphi_{k,n}(t) \tag{7}$$

In the formula, $D_{k,n}$ refers to wavelet coefficient and $\varphi_{k,n}$ is called a wavelet function.

If scale is used to measure and a certain scale is used as the boundary, then signals above this scale are characterized as basic features while signals below as detailed features; the scales above this boundary corresponds to the low-pass filter banks while the scales below this boundary corresponds to band-pass filter banks in terms of filter function. The wavelet transform can decompose the signal into the detail signal and the approximate signal on different scales, and transform them by recombining them.

In the signal processing of this paper, the preprocessed EEG signal is first loaded and then the signal is decomposed with wavelet packet decomposition function. The db10 wavelet packet base is selected to decompose the signal in 4 layers, and the fourth layers can get $2^4 = 16$ wavelet packet band S(4, I), i = 1, 2, ..., 16. The sample frequency f_s of this experimental data are 128 Hz. According to the formula $\Delta f = \frac{1}{2^4} \times \frac{f_s}{2}$, the frequency width of each of the fourth layers is about 4 Hz.

And then the Shannon entropy is used to set the threshold to decompose the wavelet signal, and its wavelet tree is shown in Fig. 4.

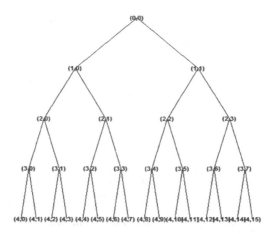

Fig. 4. Four layer decomposition of wavelet tree.

Considering the frequency range of four rhythmic waves (δ, θ, α, β), the corresponding four rhythmic waves can be obtained, such as $\delta[0.5\sim3.5\text{Hz}] : \{S(4,0)\}$; $\theta[4\sim7\text{Hz}] : \{S(4,1)\}$, which is built from the corresponding sub-band for superposition reconfiguration after de-noising the obtained wavelet packet tree.

4.2   Data Analysis

Analysis of experimental Task 1. The test data of the four-type brain waves (α, β, δ, θ) were collected by the testers after the stimulus words and neutral word browsing experiments in the task (material browsing) were completed. The results of biomedical research show that when human being is thinking or their brains are in excitement, β waves appear in large numbers, which is thought to be the main manifestation of the potential activity in the cerebral cortex the moment the cerebral cortex is in a state of tension or excitement. And the β wave is most obvious in the frontal and temporal parts. When learners take an interest in learning, their attention and emotions tend to have a change, causing β rhythmic waves. Therefore, this paper uses the relative energy ratio of beta rhythmic waves as a characteristic value to analyze the characteristics of the learners' EEG signals under different cognitive loads.

The relative energy of the beta rhythm of the learner examined by stimulus words and neutral words through eight channels is selected and plotted in a line chart, as shown in Fig. 5.

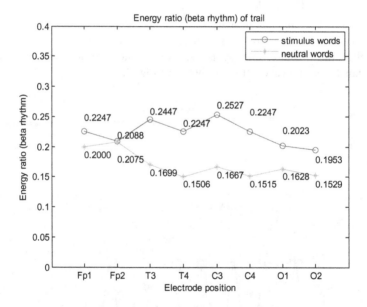

Fig. 5. Relative energy of beta rhythm.

From Fig. 5, it can be seen that when the subject is reading stimulus words, the energy ratio of the beta rhythm of positions (Fp1, Fp2, T3, T4, C3, C4, O1 and O2) is higher than neutral words. It means that stimulus words have a greater impact on the radio waves in the forehead and temple region regions. This indicates that the subject is concentrated and excited, and his/her cognitive load is increased at the time of reading stimulus words.

Analysis of experimental Task 2. Experiment Task 2 is based on the experimental Task 1, which aims to verify the words that the tester is interested in and to study the time allocation of a human brain's cognitive symbols, thus to provide learners with more trustworthy evidence for data cleanup during log data preprocessing. Task 1 has revealed the texts that each tester is interested in and interest values. Experiment task 2, therefore, focuses on each the tester's interest and selects the "text plus content types" materials. The experiment record is shown in Table 3.

Table 3. Record of experiment task 2.

Tester	Material no.	Material type	Interesting-ness score	Start time	End time
Test 1	No. 1	Text 1 + Animation	4	2018/3/2 19:00:01	2018/3/2 19:00:10
	No. 2	Text 1 + Audio	5	2018/3/2 19:00:13	2018/3/2 19:00:45
	No. 3	Text 1 + Color	4	2018/3/2 19:00:47	2018/3/2 19:01:00
	No. 4	Text 1 + Graphics	4	2018/3/2 19:01:02	2018/3/2 19:01:15
	No. 5	Text 2 + Animation	4	2018/3/2 19:01:17	2018/3/2 19:01:32
	No. 6	Text 2 + Audio	2	2018/3/2 19:01:35	2018/3/2 19:01:46
	No. 7	Text 2 + Color	3	2018/3/2 19:01:48	2018/3/2 19:01:59
	No. 8	Text 2 + Graphics	5	2018/3/2 19:02:01	2018/3/2 19:02:15
...	...	...	...	...	...

After comparing the EEG signal waveforms of the same tester in the two experiment tasks, it is found that there are indeed similar wave bands, as shown in Table 4.

Table 4. Waveforms of Task 1 and 2.

Experiment	Task 1	Task 2
Waveforms		

From Table 4, it is known that there are similar waveforms in part of Task 1 and Task 2 (within two segmentation lines), and their interesting to the material is scored more than 3, therefore, the tester is considered to be interest in this material. Another finding was that different types of materials can cause the difference cognitive time to the tester when talking to the tester after the experiment. Relatively, it takes the shortest time to focus on the "texts plus animations", and the time it takes gradually rises to focus on the "texts plus colors", "texts plus graphics" and "texts plus audios", and finally only text, as shown in Fig. 6.

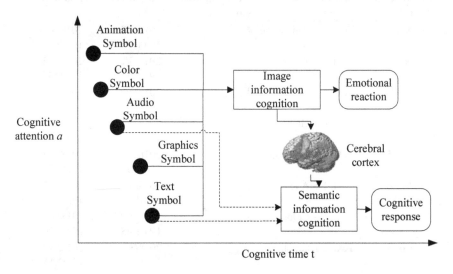

Fig. 6. Cognitive attention and cognitive time.

5   Conclusions

With the guidance of situational interest and the theory of brain cognitive mechanism, this paper puts forward a new method of neural observation to excavate the interest of the learners from the brain electrical signals. The article sums up the brain neural mechanism model, and carries out the situational interest brain cognition experiment. The results show that the analysis of the EEG signals is small. The eigenvalue of wave entropy and the eigenvalue of standard deviation show significant differences in the state of interest, and provide effective experimental means and characteristic parameters for the evaluation of learning interest.

The future research work can continue to collect and analyze the learning interest behavior data by swarm intelligent algorithm [19], eliminate the influences of different speakers through the cost-sensitive learning method [20], and consider more physiological response characteristics, such as the eye movements, infrared observation changes, etc., and enrich the means and methods of studying the interest of the learners, so as to get more comprehensive and accurate assessment of the learners' interest.

Acknowledgements. This work is supported by Humanities and Social Sciences Project of Ministry of Education of China (No. 18YJA630019), International Cooperative Program of Shanghai Municipal Science and Technology Commission of China (No. 16550720500), Shanghai Philosophy and Social Sciences Plan (No. 2018BGL023), and Association of Fundamental Computing Education in Chinese Universities (2018-AFCEC-119). Special thanks to Dr. Hongzhi Hu for her assistance to Prof. Weihui Dai who is the corresponding author of this paper.

References

1. MOOC College. http://mooc.guokr.com/post/610674. Accessed 11 June 2018
2. Dai, W.H.: Neuromangement: disciplinary development and research paradigm. J. Beijing Technol. Bus. Univ. Soc. Sci. **32**(4), 1–10 (2017)
3. Chen, H.J., Dai, Y.H., Feng, Y.J., et al.: Construction of affective education in mobile learning: the study based on learner's interest and emotion recognition. Comput. Sci. Inf. Syst. **14**(3), 685–702 (2017)
4. Liu, Z.B., Song, W.A., Kong, X.Y., et al.: Research on learner modeling and learning resources recommendation in cloud environment. Educ. Res. **7**, 58–63 (2017)
5. Kim, Z.M., Kim, S., Oh, A., et al.: An adaptive vocabulary learning application through modelling learner's linguistic proficiency and interests. In: IEEE International Conference on Big Data and Smart Computing, pp. 434–436 (2017)
6. Huang, S., Zhou, X., Xue, K., et al.: Neural cognition and affective computing on cyber language. Comput. Intell. Neurosci. **2**, 1–10 (2015)
7. Ma, Q.G., Feng, Y.D., Xu, Q., et al.: Brain potentials associated with the outcome processing in framing effects. Neurosci. Lett. **528**(2), 110–113 (2012)
8. Dai, W.H., Han, D.M., Dai, Y.H., et al.: Emotion recognition and affective computing on vocal social media. Inf. Manag. **52**(7), 777–788 (2015)
9. Ma, Q.G., Jin, J., Wang, L.: The neural process of hazard perception and evaluation for warning signal words: evidence from event-related potentials. Neurosci. Lett. **483**(3), 206–210 (2010)
10. Chen, H.J.: Study on the Interest Mining of Learners in MOOCs. Shanghai University of Finance and Economics, Shanghai City (2015)
11. Li, H.Y., He, Y.S.: Learning Ability Development Psychology. Anhui Education Press, Hefei City (2004)
12. Hidi, S.: Interest and its contribution as a mental resource for learning. Rev. Educ. Res. **60**(4), 549–571 (1990)
13. Hidi, S., Renninger, K.A.: The four-phase model of interest development. Educ. Psychol. **41**(2), 111–127 (2006)
14. Tobias, S.: Interest prior knowledge and learning. Rev. Educ. Res. **64**(1), 37–55 (1994)
15. Mitchell, M.: Situational interest: its multifaceted structure in the secondary school mathematics classroom. J. Educ. Psychol. **85**(3), 424–436 (1993)
16. Blomberg, O.: Concepts of cognition for cognitive engineering. Int. J. Aviat. Psychol. **21**(1), 85–104 (2011)
17. Simon, F., Usunier, J.C.: Cognitive, demographic, and situational determinants of service customer preference for personnel-in-contact over self-service technology. Int. J. Res. Mark. **24**(2), 163–173 (2007)
18. Grady, C.: The cognitive neuroscience of ageing. Nat. Rev. Neurosci. **13**(7), 491–505 (2012)
19. Hu, X.H., Mu, T., Dai, W.H., et al.: Analysis of browsing behaviors with ant colony clustering algorithm. J. Comput. **7**(12), 3096–3102 (2012)
20. Li, D.D., Yang, Y.C., Dai, W.H.: Cost-sensitive learning for emotion robust speaker. Sci. World J. **2014**, 1–9 (2014). Article ID 628516

Research on Cross-Media Retrieval of Collaborative Plotted Multimedia Data Based on Container-Based Cloud Platform and Deep Learning

Xiaolan Xie[1,2], Qiangqing Zheng[1(✉)], Xinrong Li[1],
Xiaochun Cheng[3], and Zhihong Guo[4]

[1] College of Information Science and Engineering, Guilin University
of Technology, Guilin, Guangxi Zhuang Autonomous Region, China
zhengqiangqing@glut.edu.cn
[2] Guangxi Universities Key Laboratory of Embedded Technology
and Intelligent System, Guilin University of Technology, Guilin, China
[3] Department of Computer Science, Middlesex University, London, UK
[4] College of Mechanical and Control Engineering, Guilin University
of Technology, Guilin, Guangxi Zhuang Autonomous Region, China

Abstract. The purpose of this paper is to solve some issues in cross-media retrieval of collaboratively plotted multimedia data. Under the premise of global dynamic heterogeneous spatial information collaborative plotting and spatial knowledge service technical support, in this thesis, the characteristics of the retrieved data is seen as a prerequisite, and combined the advantages of collaborative plots generated multimedia data, using distributed deep learning technology and container cloud in the technology, the features of the extracted data are formed into a database of data feature vectors, and the UFM-LF model is proposed to modify and filter the features of the plotted data so as to improve the accuracy of data retrieval and thus provide the user with knowledge services. The experimental data shows that under the same conditions, the computing power of the container-based cloud platform is about 2.6 times as powerful as that of the stand-alone combination, which provides a powerful computing capability for the training task; Besides, combining the deep learning model with the UFM-LF model improves the accuracy of the retrieved data significantly. The platform can provide powerful computing capabilities and improve the accuracy of cross-media data retrieval. It has good scalability and can be applied to data retrieval in other fields.

Keywords: Docker · Collaborative plotting · Deep learning · Container cloud
TensorFlow

1 Research Background

Multimedia data retrieval [1] are hot topics in recent years. At present, most of the research data are multimedia data with specific forms and semantic structure. Such as, adding metadata to the media data as a label in the earlier period, and later analyzing and researching the text data based on the text content and the analysis research based

© Springer Nature Singapore Pte Ltd. 2019
Y. Sun et al. (Eds.): ChineseCSCW 2018, CCIS 917, pp. 410–423, 2019.
https://doi.org/10.1007/978-981-13-3044-5_30

on the visual characteristics, and the multimedia data retrieval combining the two. The relevance of multimedia data analysis [2] is focused on recent research, the establishment of a common mapping space [3], or, isomorphic semantic retrieval model and so on. These source data have a certain degree of regularity, such as wikipedia, mnist, imageclef, etc. And these data sets are organized, according to a certain classification of the collection. However, the sources, contents, semantic structure, time and space, objects and so on of collaborative plotting data all have the characteristics of uncertainty, diversity and high complexity [4]. Based on the characteristics of collaborative plotting data, the paper combines container cloud with deep learning technology to search text, image, audio and video for collaboratively plotting multimedia data based on textual information.

Global Dynamic Heterogeneous Spatial Information Collaborative Mapping and Spatial Knowledge Services Platform, is based on the existing plotting knowledge. Taking Africa as an example, data mining and hot graphic generation are carried out based on this, and a customized geospatial information mapping knowledge service is developed for user applications. On the platform, users can use a different modal data format (such as text, images, audio, video, etc.) to plot a location or a specific event. As shown in Fig. 1, when describing an event that "explosion" somewhere, the user typically plots text, images, audio, video, etc. The expression is lively, informative and easy to understand. In the paper, those semantics are called cross-media data, which are similar, yet from different modalities, different perspectives, different sources, different backgrounds and other data. Cross-media data is widespread, so how to effectively understand the semantic relevance and semantic content of cross-media data has become an important research topic in the field of cross-media and pattern recognition.

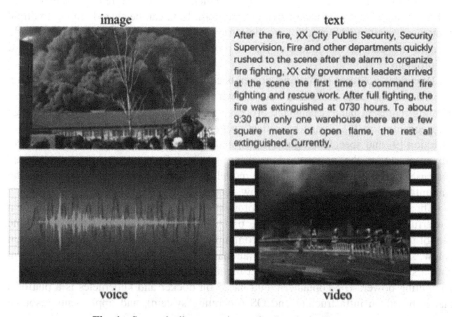

Fig. 1. Semantically approximate for "explosion" events

2   Related Technology Research

2.1   Cross-Media Technology Research and Analysis

The current cross-media data correlation modeling still faces some challenges. On the one hand, cross-media data correlation modeling to support the cross-mode data spanning needs to be realized. Although cross-media data perform are different in modal form, the heterogeneous data can be unified at the semantic level (Fig. 1). However, the traditional single media retrieval related technologies ignore the semantic commonality of heterogeneous cross-media data, so it is difficult to effectively deal with a variety of heterogeneous cross-media data coexisting with complex data. A unified understanding and analysis of heterogeneous cross-media data is required in cross-media technologies to make common use of heterogeneous data such as images, videos and texts at the high-level semantic level. Not only it's more easily for people to understand, but also contributing to the unified management of cross-media data. On the other hand, cross-media data association modeling also supports the semantic leap of homogeneous media data from different data sources. The so-called homogeneous media data refers to the same type of media data, such as multiple images are mutually homogeneous media data. Although the kind of data often has consistency in feature representation, the semantic association it contains is complicated.

2.2   Container Cloud and Deep Learning Technology Advantage Analysis

The container cloud clustering solution based on the docker container, On the one hand, it has the characteristics of quick opening and closing of containers, under modes of serial and parallel, greatly speeding the process of parallelization and serialization. On the other hand, by creating data volumes, which are used to store the data that needs to be accessed during the running of the program. Data can be shared among multiple containers, avoiding the need for parallel programs to be accessed through the network. To delay the data exchange to wait for the problem, and promote the parallelization of the program.

Providing a strong computing power becomes the basic needs of deep learning. Experiments on large-scale data have shown that the features obtained through deep learning represent natural language processing (word vector learning [5]), knowledge map construction [6], image classification [7] scene recognition [8], human motion detection [9] and speech recognition [10] and other fields showed good performance. However, under the premise of ensuring good performance, with the error rate decreases, the deeper the deep learning model is, the more parameters it takes, and the amount of computation required to grow geometrically.

Through the container layout technology and rapid capacity expansion to provide a powerful computing power. Under the premise of time efficiency, a single machine cannot meet the needs of its powerful computing capacity, especially the configuration is low, so you need a platform to integrate many common machines to form a platform with a strong computing power to meet the algorithmic debugging process consumed computing power. The container cloud based on docker and kubernetes is a platform that is based on infrastructure and OS (operating system), and implements resource scheduling through the deployment of docker engine. TensorFlow is an open source project initiated by Google. It is a graph-based deep learning framework with high performance, high efficiency and fast iteration. It meets the needs of large-scale iterative computing. With kubernetes-based container cloud for TensorFlow powerful computing support, is a good combination of innovation, based on TensorFlow framework for deep learning in the field of artificial intelligence to create a new breakthrough has a strong foundation, but also based on TensorFlow artificial Intelligent and kubernetes-based container cloud has more valuable space to play.

3 Building UFM-LF Model and Platform Technology Roadmap

Based on the idea of crowdsourcing, On the Global Dynamic Heterogeneous Spatial Information Collaborative Plot and Spatial Knowledge Service Platform, users plot their experiences of events or locations on the co-plotting system as relatively real data. Recording and sharing their own information, for other users browsing information it can be timely access to different regions of the event or human geography information, to provide knowledge services. At the same time, users are trying to search for text or images that are close to their content, or to search for relevant text, images, audio, and video using keywords and text documents. By analyzing the cross-media data correlation, we can effectively provide users with better retrieval services and further, promote the exchange and dissemination of information. Table 1 shows the amount of data stored in collaboration with the system.

Table 1. Collaborative plot system stored data scale

Classification	Text	Image	Voice	Video
Data size (item)	475711	384649	14792	87760

3.1 Building UFM-LF Model

Due to the wide range, diversity and complexity of the collaborative plot data, its characteristics are as follows:

- A wide range: Co-mapping system serves different populations from different regions of the world's users;
- Diversity: There are no restrictions on the content and place of the user's drawing. Users are free to upload the information data of any combination of text, image, audio and video at any time.
- Complexity: User-uploaded data is tag-free and has no fixed semantic structure.

According to the above characteristics, uses deep learning methods to retrieve relevant results from collaboratively-plotted multimedia data using textual information, which can be imagined to be less accurate due to data noise, so we combine deep learning with crowd-sourcing models and propose a user feedback model based on tags and features that makes efficient use of annotated data in crowd-sourcing to enhance the performance of deep learning methods that rely solely on data-driven patterns. The model is shown in Fig. 2.

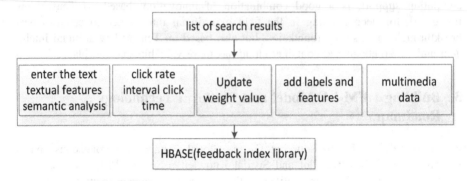

Fig. 2. User feedback model based on label and features

The label and features of the user feedback model based on tags and features are mainly built in the following five aspects:

1. The text information input by the user and the text features analyzed by the text information, semantic analysis;
2. The user clicks on the search results and the interval click time. Click-through rate is the user click rate for similar information in the text search results; The interval click time is click time for the piece of information that after the user inputs the text information to be searched and displays the result list, from the time the result is displayed until the user clicks on the information in the list;
3. Update the article information on the input text information retrieval weight value. The weight value is proportional to the size of the user satisfaction with the search results;
4. The user adds information such as tag characteristics for the piece of information data;
5. Multimedia data, which refers to the information displayed by the search results data.

When the user views the search result list, we refer to the concept of crowd-sourcing, and ask the viewer to fill out the satisfaction of the search information, and add the corresponding addition and amendment opinions. We will update the weight value of this information according to the user's filled content, and then add new tags for this information according to the user's add and modify opinions, and then build UFM-LF models. As time increases and the number of user feedback increases, the impact of data noise gradually decreases, thus improving the search Accuracy. The machine, collaborative mapping of multimedia data, labeling users and viewers, container cloud technology and deep learning technology are closely linked to achieve the infrastructure, mass data, people, advanced technology and close integration, improve the utilization of resources and deep retrieval of massive data.

3.2   Platform Technology Roadmap

When annotators use collaborative mapping system for information and data mapping, the plotted information data can be divided into seven types: text and video, video, text and audio, audio, text and image, image, text (note: under no consideration of four types of similar text, video, image of the combination of three types of multimedia data retrieval). Therefore, when we receive the text that the user needs to retrieve and perform semantic analysis and feature extraction, we need to carry out the feature matching with the 7 deep learning model. Here we introduce a user feedback model [11] based on tags and features. After using the user feedback model, we combine the results into four categories: video search result, audio search result, image search result and text search result. Among them, the first three categories are screened according to low characteristic information such as plotting time and plotting location of information data and comparison, and respectively, extracted from the four categories of the highest similarity video, audio, image and text as the user's search display list. Combined with the UFM-LF model mentioned above, we regularly update the user feedback model as well as seven deep learning models, to some extent to achieve enhanced learning of collaboratively labeled multimedia information data. The technical roadmap is shown in Fig. 3.

In the construction of the deep learning model of video texts, we adopt a content-based video learning model [12], which first extracts the key frames in the video and then extracts the features of the key frames by convolutional neural network to recognize the images and establish video index of the key frame [13], and finally match the video index and the marked information with the search term, and match the video as the learning result.

For the video data without text description, we use the content-based video learning model [14] to generate the text index of the key frame, and then find the main content of the index through the main level analysis model. The main content is tagged on the video, and then the tag content is matched with the search term [15], and the corresponding video is used as a result of the learning by matching with the retrieved text.

In the construction of the deep learning model of audio and texts, we use a deep neural network-based audio event detection model [16], which uses deep neural networks as a deep feature extractor and the event using a multi-stream and multi-layer deep neural network audio event transformation features, combined with the advantages of traditional audio features fusion, and further tap the characteristics of the new input information, the user input by the text information and audio features and retrieval of text matching information to match the audio as a result of learning.

For the audio information without textual description, we use the audio scene recognition model based on probabilistic potential semantic analysis [17]. In the sample of cooperatively-mapped data audio, the mixed voice and non-voice occupy a certain proportion. Because there is no textual information, the audio-oriented scene Identification to extract feature information. The model firstly constructs the acoustic event dictionary through the Gaussian mixture model to remove the influence of the synonymous and ambiguous acoustic events on the audio scene recognition. Then, the SVM model is used to process the audio scene processed by the probabilistic latent semantic analysis model files are classified, and the text information of the category is

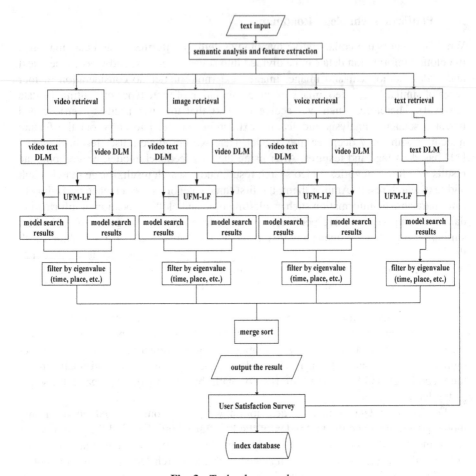

Fig. 3. Technology roadmap

matched with the search keywords, and the matched audio is used as a result of the learning.

We use a method called multi-scale orderless pooling in the construction of a deep learning model for image texts [18], which extracts features at different scales of the image by convolutional neural networks at each scale, a vector of locally aggregated descriptors (VLAD) codes are encoded. Finally, these coding results are spliced together, and the recognition result is combined with the text information of the mapping to match the retrieved text as the image feature learning result.

For the image data without textual description, we make recognition twice. The first time through deep neural network identify the subject matter in the image, and identify the results of text labels to the image [19]. Then combined with the sine basis function and the absolute distance. The background model is constructed by measuring the brightness of each pixel in the background model and the brightness of each pixel in the actual image to determine whether each pixel is a background or a foreground, and the image is segmented according to the background model or the similarity of the adjacent segments [20]. The second time Detect the background, match the corresponding scene, and label the image with the second test in text. Combined with two tags and search terms match, the picture will be matched as a result of learning.

In the construction of the deep learning model of the text, we use the LDA theme model [21], which is actually a three-level Bayesian probability model that contains the three-level structure of words, themes and documents. Through a method of "selecting a certain theme with a certain probability and selecting a certain word from the theme with a certain probability", every word in an article is stored, and then corresponding the retrieval term to the corresponding topic. The corresponding plotted text information is retrieved from the same or similar topics, and the matched text is output as a result.

4 Platform Architecture Design

Considering the characteristics of data generated by collaborative plotting, container cloud technology, deep learning algorithm and deep learning model are used to make use of text retrieval text, image, audio and video functions as a starting point. By analyzing and using container cloud and deep learning technology, multi-modal data retrieval of collaboratively-mapped multimedia data are realized. The multimedia data retrieval system architecture of collaborative plotting based on container cloud and deep learning is shown in Fig. 4.

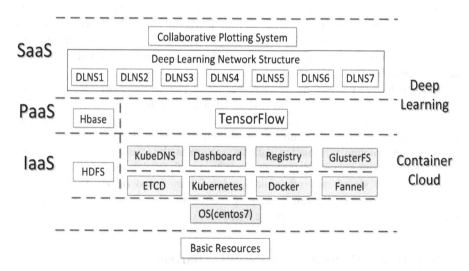

Fig. 4. The architecture of the system based on container cloud and deep learning for multimedia data retrieval and mining

Containers based on multiple low-performance computers combined with deep learning technology are set up to complete complex tasks about achieving collaborative mapping of multimedia data retrieval and mining capabilities. System architecture in accordance with the concept of cloud computing is divided into three layers, namely: IaaS: Infrastructure-as-a-Service; PaaS: Platform-as-a-Service; SaaS: Software-as-a-Service.

The IaaS layer uses container cloud technology to build a docker-based [22] container cloud cluster as the operating environment of the entire system and builds HDFS (Distributed File Storage System) on the bare metal system to provide support for HBASE [23], Use kubernetes as a cluster management tool and install the etcd and flannel components in it for real-time monitoring of service discovery and cluster network management. Deploy DNS services and Dashboard services as cluster visualization management tools. Use the GlusterFS [24] open source project as Docker's distributed storage solution. GlusterFS is an open source distributed file system [25] that uses the tcp protocol and the infiniband rdma [26] protocol for data transfer and supports up to seven file storage modes. And this considered the collaborative plotting data as training data, without the addition and deletion of data. In order to saving storage space, reducing data redundancy, and raising up the efficiency, using distributed volume storage management to store collaborative plot multimedia data.

The PaaS layer [27] uses TensorFlow, a deep learning technology framework, to analyze and extract the runtime environment of the entire informational data of the system and store the training results using the HBFS database based on HDFS. TensorFlow is an open source project initiated by Google. It is a graph-based deep learning framework with high performance, high efficiency and fast iteration. It meets the needs of large-scale iterative computing. Because our multimedia data is not regular, each data has different features and semantics, and the characteristics and semantics of the information is dynamically increased, the classification is not fixed, which requires each column of data is not fixed. It can be dynamically added, based on these characteristics we choose non-relational database HBASE as a training result of multimedia data storage solutions.

SaaS layer uses the underlying container cloud platform and deep learning technology framework TensorFlow, processing in a combination of serial and parallel methods, combined with the results of relevant researchers to find and contrasting with good results of seven deep learning network structure, as well as the four categories collaboratively plotted information data for feature analysis and extraction, and the trained features are correlated with the four types of collaboratively-mapped information data and stored in a multimedia index library based on HBASE, so as to implement text-based collaborative mapping multimedia data retrieval, and the system embedded in the collaborative mapping system.

5   Experimental Design and Results Analysis

5.1   Platform to Build

Steps and key uses outlined below:

1. Preparation of basic resources. Use the three machines in the task group and install the operating system (centos7).

2. Build docker-based container cloud, using kubernetes as the management cluster tool container cloud, etcd components to achieve real-time monitoring services, and using fannel deploy the network.
3. Install GlusterFS distributed file system, collaborative mapping of multimedia data distributed storage.
4. Select a lower-performance machine as a local mirroring repository and deploy the DNS service and the Dashboard service to implement the cluster interface management.
5. Using the existing deep learning model and method, using the combination of serial and parallel, and using the advantages of containers to run deep learning and deep learning model, the data stored in the data volume feature extraction and analysis, the information characteristics of the data are stored in the HBase data index library.
6. Embedding the entire system into the collaborative mapping system.

5.2 Container Cloud Computing Platform for the Ability to Test and Analyze

In order to ensure the consistency of the experimental environment, we use six identical hosts as the test environment. The experimental data is five groups of data in the collaborative plot multimedia database. The number of data records in each group is 2,000 data increments. On the one hand, we choose any three hosts, configure a deep learning environment, test seven training tasks for deep learning, record the elapsed time in turn, and calculate the total time; On the other hand, on the remaining three hosts, a container cloud platform based on docker and kubernetes was set up. The deep learning environment was configured by downloading mirror images, and 7 deep learning training tasks corresponding to 7 containers were started respectively. Consumption time. The experimental results are shown in Fig. 5. From this, it can be concluded that with three machines with the same hardware resources, the computing power of the container cloud platform is at least 2.6 times higher.

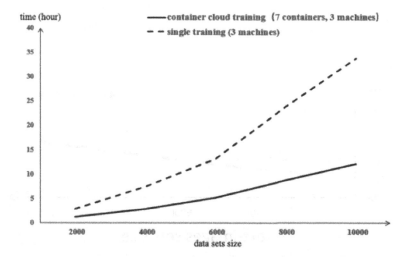

Fig. 5. Container cloud platform and stand-alone platform test capability comparison chart

5.3   Testing the UFM-LF Model

Since the platform provides retrieval as the main function, it is necessary to consider that the returned retrieval results are ordered and are sorted by relevance, so the experiment uses MAP (Mean Average Precision) as the evaluation index. Refers to the average of the average accuracy of multiple search input texts. MAP can be calculated by the following formulas (1) and (2).

$$AP = \frac{1}{c} \sum_{j=1}^{c} \frac{TP_j}{TP_j + FP_j} \tag{1}$$

$$MAP = \frac{1}{n} \sum_{i=1}^{n} AP(i) \tag{2}$$

Where n denotes the number of input search texts, c denotes the number of evaluation search sequences, TP_j denotes the correct number of result sequence j positions, and FP_j denotes the incorrect number of result sequence j positions, AP indicates that the search result is a probability value arranged according to relevance, and MAP is the mean value of AP.

Combining deep learning with crowdsourced computing, this paper proposes an accumulative test based on the UFM-LF model and the deep learning model. Here, the test object is, input text information, and search in the text-image information data to obtain the average accuracy rate. Since we use the UFM-LF model here, it is very unrealistic for users to fill in all the search results. Considering the user's experience, only the feedback for the first 10 search results is filled here. The experimental results are as follows Fig. 6.

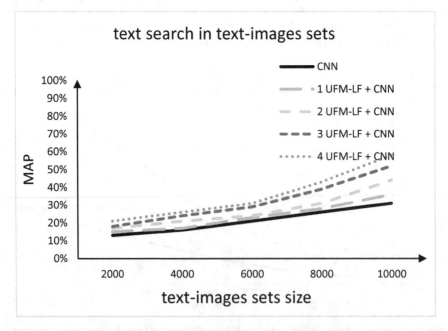

Fig. 6. UFM-LF and CNN model accumulative test results

As can be seen from Fig. 6, although CNN has a great advantage in extracting the spatial features of images and has a better effect in the conventional image annotation set, there are more noise data in collaborative plot data, which can be obtained from the figure. It can be seen that the retrieval effect is not very good; We use the UFM-LF model to further modify the eigenvector results extracted from the CNN network. With the increase in the number of feedbacks, the UFM-LF model is playing an increasingly important role in improving the average accuracy of collaborative plot data retrieval. From the above, we can also speculate that applying the deep learning technology to the container cloud platform, combined with the UFM-LF model, has a great advantage in improving the average accuracy of retrieval results in the cross-modal retrieval of collaborative multimedia data. At the same time, it can be seen in the figure that as the data volume increases, the accuracy of retrieval accuracy increases as the number of UFM-LF models increases.

6 Conclusion

In the paper, we use docker-based container cloud technology to build a platform with powerful computing power. By using a combination of parallelism and serialization, we provide powerful computing power to the platform through the ability of container layout and rapid capacity expansion to meet the requirements of deep Learn the amount of computation required to model and train a large number of samples. We use the current multi-modal retrieval of multimedia data for research and application of research results, and for the co-ordination of the characteristics of multimedia data, the deep of learning and crowdsourcing methods are combined to propose a tag and feature-based user feedback model, collaboratively labeled multimedia data retrieval. Through the experiment, the platform can retrieve four different modalities of media and obtain relatively satisfactory retrieval data.

Acknowledgements. This research work was supported by the National Natural Science Foundation of China (Grant No. 61762031), Guangxi Key Research and Development Plan (Nos. 2017AB51024, 2018AB8126006), Guangxi Key Laboratory Fund of Embedded Technology and Intelligent System.

References

1. Wu, F., Zhu, W.W., Yu, J.Q.: Researches on multimedia technology 2014—deep learning and multimedia computing. J. Image Graph. **19**(11), 1423–1433 (2014)
2. Pereira, J.C., Coviello, E., Doyle, G., et al.: On the role of correlation and abstraction in cross-modal multimedia retrieval. IEEE Trans. Pattern Anal. Mach. Intell. **36**(3), 521–535 (2014)
3. Paul, S.N., Singh, Y.J.: Unified framework for representation, analysis of multimedia content for correlation and prediction. In: International Conference on Emerging Trends and Applications in Computer Science, pp. 214–218. IEEE (2013)

4. Dua, S.: Toward integrating text and images for multimedia retrieval in heterogeneous data mining. In: Proceedings of SPIE—The International Society for Optical Engineering, p. 6015 (2005)
5. Mikolov, T., Sutskever, I., Chen, K., et al.: Distributed Representations of words and phrases and their compositionality. In: Advances in Neural Information Processing Systems, vol. 26, pp. 3111–3119 (2013)
6. Socher, R., Chen, D., Manning, C.D., et al.: Reasoning with neural tensor networks for knowledge base completion. In: International Conference on Neural Information Processing Systems, pp. 926–934. Curran Associates Inc. (2013)
7. Szegedy, C., Liu, W., Jia, Y., et al.: Going deeper with convolutions. In: Computer Vision and Pattern Recognition, pp. 1–9. IEEE (2015)
8. Farabet, C., Couprie, C., Najman, L., et al.: Learning hierarchical features for scene labeling. IEEE Trans. Pattern Anal. Mach. Intell. 35(8), 1915 (2013)
9. Tompson, J., Jain, A., Lecun, Y., et al.: Joint training of a convolutional network and a graphical model for human pose estimation. e-Print arXiv, pp. 1799–1807 (2014)
10. Hinton, G., Deng, L., Yu, D., et al.: Deep neural networks for acoustic modelling in speech recognition: the shared views of four research groups. IEEE Sig. Process. Mag. 29(6), 82–97 (2012)
11. Paredes, R., Deselaers, T., Vidal, E.: A probabilistic model for user relevance feedback on image retrieval. In: Popescu-Belis, A., Stiefelhagen, R. (eds.) MLMI 2008. LNCS, vol. 5237, pp. 260–271. Springer, Heidelberg (2008). https://doi.org/10.1007/978-3-540-85853-9_24
12. Wu, Z., Wang, X., Jiang, Y.G., et al.: Modeling spatial-temporal clues in a hybrid deep learning framework for video classification. In: ACM International Conference on Multimedia, pp. 461–470. ACM (2015)
13. Pan, Z., Liu, S., Fu, W.: A review of visual moving target tracking. Multimed. Tools Appl. 76(16), 16989–17018 (2017)
14. Ouyang, J.Q., Li, J.T., Tang, H.: Interactive key frame selection model. J. Vis. Commun. Image Represent. 17(6), 1145–1163 (2006)
15. Liu, S., Lu, M., Liu, G., et al.: A novel distance matric: generalized relative entropy. Entropy 19, 269 (2017)
16. Wang, Y., Neves, L., Metze, F.: Audio-based multimedia event detection using deep recurrent neural networks. In: IEEE International Conference on Acoustics, Speech and Signal Processing, pp. 2742–2746. IEEE (2016)
17. Li, P., Cheng, J., Li, Z., Lu, H.: Correlated PLSA for image clustering. In: Lee, K.-T., Tsai, W.-H., Liao, H.-Y.M., Chen, T., Hsieh, J.-W., Tseng, C.-C. (eds.) MMM 2011. LNCS, vol. 6523, pp. 307–316. Springer, Heidelberg (2011). https://doi.org/10.1007/978-3-642-17832-0_29
18. Ning, J., Zhang, L., Zhang, D., et al.: Interactive image segmentation by maximal similarity based region merging. Pattern Recogn. 43(2), 445–456 (2010)
19. Gong, Y., Wang, L., Guo, R., Lazebnik, S.: Multi-scale orderless pooling of deep convolutional activation features. In: Fleet, D., Pajdla, T., Schiele, B., Tuytelaars, T. (eds.) ECCV 2014. LNCS, vol. 8695, pp. 392–407. Springer, Cham (2014). https://doi.org/10.1007/978-3-319-10584-0_26
20. Liu, S., Pan, Z., Cheng, X.: A novel fast fractal image compression method based on distance clustering in high dimensional sphere surface. Fractals 25(4), 17400045 (2017)
21. Fu, X., Liu, G., Guo, Y., Guo, W.: Multi-aspect blog sentiment analysis based on LDA topic model and hownet lexicon. In: Gong, Z., Luo, X., Chen, J., Lei, J., Wang, F.L. (eds.) WISM 2011. LNCS, vol. 6988, pp. 131–138. Springer, Heidelberg (2011). https://doi.org/10.1007/978-3-642-23982-3_17

22. Negus, C.: Docker containers from start to enterprise (includes content update program): build and deploy with kubernetes, flannel, cockpit and atomic. Vaccine **19**(Suppl 1), S87–S95 (2016)
23. Bai, J.: Feasibility analysis of big log data real time search based on Hbase and ElasticSearch. In: Ninth International Conference on Natural Computation, pp. 1166–1170. IEEE (2014)
24. Yang, Y.: Distribution redundancy storage based on GlusterFS. J. Xian Univ. Arts Sci. **13** (4), 67–70 (2010)
25. Donvito, G., Marzulli, G., Diacono, D.: Testing of several distributed file-systems (HDFS, Ceph and GlusterFS) for supporting the HEP experiments analysis. J. Phys. **513**(4), 042014 (2014)
26. Liu, J., Wu, J., Kini, S.P., et al.: High performance RDMA-based MPI implementation over InfiniBand. In: International Conference on Supercomputing, ICS 2003, San Francisco, CA, USA, June, pp. 295–304. DBLP (2003)
27. Yin, X., Shang, Y.: Research and implementation PaaS platform based on Docker. In: National Conference on Electrical, Electronics and Computer Engineering (2016)

A Fast Feature Selection Method Based on Mutual Information in Multi-label Learning

Zhenqiang Sun, Jia Zhang, Zhiming Luo, Donglin Cao, and Shaozi Li[✉]

Department of Cognitive Science, Xiamen University, Xiamen 361005,
People's Republic of China
m15122329324@163.com, zhangjia_gl@163.com,
zmluo_xmu@qq.com,{another,szlig}@xmu.edu.cn

Abstract. Recently, multi-label learning is concerned and studied in lots of fields by many researchers. However, multi-label datasets often have noisy, irrelevant and redundant features with high dimensionality. Accompanying with these issues, a critical challenge called "the curse of dimensionality" makes many tasks of multi-label learning very difficult. Therefore, many method such as feature selection to solve this problem has received much attention. Among many feature selection methods, a large number of information-theoretical-based methods are developed to solve the learning issue and the results are very good. Unfortunately, most of existing feature selection methods are either directly transformed from single-label methods or insufficient in light of using heuristic algorithms as the search component. Motivated by this, a novel fast method based on mutual information with no parameter is proposed, which obtains the optimal solution via constrained convex optimization with less time. Specifically, by incorporating the label information into the feature selection process, label-correlation is taken into consideration to generate the generalized model.

Keywords: Multi-label learning · Mutual information
Label-correlation · Feature selection

1 Introduction

It is generally accepted that one instance is default to only having one semantic information or one label. However, such assumption is often at odds with the reality of the world, for example, a scene image could be labeled as "sea", "boat" and "sea mew" at the same time, it will be difficult to classify this image exactly by using single-label classification method. Thus, multi-label learning [1] emerged and got lots of excellent results in lots of reality problems such as information retrieval [2], bioinformation [3], and TCM diagnosis [4].

Comparing with single-label task, the output dimension of multi-label learning task is higher. In most cases, features of multi-label datasets are more irrelevant and redundant than single-label datasets, because in real word, multi-label

© Springer Nature Singapore Pte Ltd. 2019
Y. Sun et al. (Eds.): ChineseCSCW 2018, CCIS 917, pp. 424–437, 2019.
https://doi.org/10.1007/978-981-13-3044-5_31

datasets often exist with hundreds of features [5–7] to support multi-label problem. However, too many features may cause the *curse of dimensionality* [8] which makes multi-label tasks more ineffective and hard [9]. Therefore, it's crucial and necessary to reduce the influence of *curse of dimensionality*.

Many previous methods directly try to search relevant and best subsets from high-dimensional space for a compact and accurate representation. It is simple, interpretable, and especially needed when we face high-dimensional data or when we have limited data [1]. Meanwhile, in multi-label tasks, label-correlation usually can provide important information, and based on the order of correlation [10], it is able to be classified into three categories.

Therefore, it's important to seek a reasonable way of exploiting label-correlation for multi-label feature selection, and considering that many previous related methods based on information theory did not make effective use of label-correlation information, and the time cost of searching is relatively large. Therefore a novel method is proposed to solve these issues better. We integrate the feature correlation, feature redundancy and second-order label-correlation information into the proposed method, and the interior point penalty function method is used to try to find the best feature weight distribution, transform the previous search problem into a global optimization problem to improve the feature selection efficiency greatly. Additionally, the optimization framework does not contain any parameter, so compared with other parameters method, our method is stronger and more robust generalization performance. Conducting experiments in six real-word multi-label datasets to demonstrate the high performance of our methods.

2   Related Work

In the decades since the development of multi-label feature selection, many outstanding works have emerged [6, 11–17]. In order to better distinguish the similarities and differences of each method, the related workers have classified the existing feature selection methods into two widely recognized classifications. From the selection strategy perspective, wrapper [18–20] and filter methods [8, 21, 22], and embedded methods [8, 23, 24] are exist. From the label perspective (whether or not label information is involved during the selection phase), previous methods is able to be seen as supervised [8, 23, 25], unsupervised [24, 26] and semi-supervised [27, 28].

Our work is mostly related to mutual information (MI) and label-correlation, therefore, in the following context, we briefly introduce a few related works on these two aspects. Among those works, two representative methods are named MIFS [29], and mRMR [25] respectively. In MIFS, the author used MI to evaluate the "information content", and proposed an algorithm based on a "greedy" selection of the features. In mRMR, the authors used MI to search the best subset which satisfies the criterion "max relevance, min redundancy" proposed in their paper. In addition, Lin et al. [30] accorded the heuristic search strategy, proposed a standard method called "max-dependent" and "min-redundant"

(MDMR). Lee et al. [31] proposed a method called (PMU). Lim et al. [32] presented a fast method by improving mRMR.

There are also some excellent methods incorporating the class label information into learning methods. Zhang et al. [33] presented an effective method by combining the label-specific features and label correlations together. Wang et al. [34] presented a method by maximizing the information of independent classification. Brown [35] presented a method based on information theoretic feature selection (CMI), which is a unifying framework. Wang et al. [36] presented a supervised method by preserving class correlation. Wang et al. [37] proposed a semi-supervised method which leverages the information among labels. Spolaôr et al. [38] proposed a method called LCFS.

3   Preliminaries

3.1   Mutual Information and mRMR

Since C.E.Shannon published the famous paper "A Mathematical Theory of Communication" [39] in 1948. As an important part of information theory, MI can measure the correlation between variables [40], which means the reduction in uncertainty of one variable when another is given [41]. Formally, the mutual information of two discrete variables A and B can be defined as

$$I(A;B) = \sum_{a \in A} \sum_{b \in B} p(a,b) log(\frac{p(a,b)}{p(a)p(b)}) \tag{1}$$

Similarly, in the case of continuous variables, the equation is replaced as following

$$I(A;B) = \int_A \int_B p(a,b) log(\frac{p(a,b)}{p(a)p(b)}) dadb \tag{2}$$

Or we can be expressed the equation in another way

$$I(A;B) = H(A) + H(B) - H(A,B) \tag{3}$$

or

$$I(A;B) = H(A) - H(A|B) \tag{4}$$

where $H(a) = -p(a) \sum_{a \in A} p(a)$, $H(b) = -p(b) \sum_{b \in B} p(b)$ represent the entropy of A and B, $H(a|b) = H(a,b) - H(b)$ represents conditional entropy of the involved variables.

Since the proposed method is inspired by mRMR [25], we will introduce mRMR in detail in this subsection. As a classical method, the "minimal-redundancy-maximal-relevance" framework has been developed lots of outstanding works. In [25], Peng et al. think "the m best features are not the best m

features", this is because of the m best features may be highly correlated. There-fore, they presented the mRMR framework, and defined the equation $\Phi(D, R)$ to band the relevance and redundancy together.

$$\max \Phi(D, R), \Phi = D - R. \tag{5}$$

where D means the relevance or dependence, and it's calculated as

$$D(S, c) = \frac{1}{|S|} \sum_{x_i \in S} I(x_i; c) \tag{6}$$

and R means redundancy, it's calculated as

$$R(S) = \frac{1}{|S|^2} \sum_{x_i, x_j} I(x_i; x_j) \tag{7}$$

where S denotes feature set, and c denotes label set.

3.2 Evaluation Measures

In this paper, we select some evaluation measures in [42] to evaluate our exper-imental results. In the following description, true label set is indicated by L, $y_i \subseteq L$ means real label, y_i' is the result of classifier for x_i, N, m are the dimen-sions of the label matrix.

(1) *Average Precision* (AP):

$$AP = \frac{1}{N} \sum_{i=1}^{N} \frac{1}{|y_i|} \sum_{\Upsilon \in y_i} \frac{|\Upsilon' \in y_i : r_i(\Upsilon' \leq r_i(\Upsilon))|}{r_i(\Upsilon)} \tag{8}$$

This indicator measures the situation that the mark before the related mark is still the related mark in the tag sequence sorted by the predicted value, and the higher the value, the better.

(2) *Coverage* (CV):

$$CV = \frac{1}{N} \sum_{i=1}^{N} \max_{\lambda \in y_i} rank(\lambda) - 1 \tag{9}$$

This indicator reflects the search depth required to cover all related tags in the predicted tag sequence, and the smaller the value is, the higher all related tags are ranked.

(3) *One Error* (OE):

$$OE = \frac{1}{N} \sum_{i=1}^{N} [\![[argmax_{y_i \in L} f(x_i, y_i)] \notin y_i']\!] \tag{10}$$

This indicator calculates the proportion of the most likely marker predictive errors in the predicted results, with a value between 0 and 1, the smaller the better.

(4) *Ranking Loss* (RL):

$$RL = \frac{1}{N} \sum_{i=1}^{N} \frac{1}{|y_i||\bar{y}_i|} |(\lambda_1, \lambda_2)| \lambda_1 \le \lambda_2, (\lambda_1, \lambda_2) \in y_i \times \bar{y}_i| \tag{11}$$

Where y_i and $\bar{y}_i$ respectively represent the correlation label set and the irrelevant label set of x_i. It calculates the proportion of relevant and irrelevant tag pair error, the smaller the better.

(5) *Hamming Loss (HL)*:

$$HL = \frac{1}{N} \sum_{i=1}^{N} \frac{y_i' \oplus y_i}{m} \tag{12}$$

This indicator calculates the proportion of errors in all predictive labels, with a value between 0 and 1.

4   Proposed Method

In the following, the motivation of our method and some related formulaic representation are introduced. Then, in the second section, the solution method used in this paper is briefly introduced, and the corresponding pseudo-code description is provided.

4.1   Method Motivation and Formulaic Expression

In most multi-label datasets, label-correlation often provides important information. Inspired by this, based on the traditional method of mRMR, our method joined the label-correlation within the framework for feature selection, and turning it into a framework without parameters, makes the method can be applied in the most of related tasks. First of all, the most original framework are described as follows:

$$\max_{S} J = \frac{\sum_{f_i \in S} \sum_{l_j, l_k \in L} I(f_i; l_j) Cor(l_j; l_k) + \sum_{f_i \in S} \sum_{l_j \in L} I(f_i; l_j)}{\sum_{f_i, f_j \in S} I(f_i; f_j)} \tag{13}$$

where $I(\cdot; \cdot)$ is the mutual information, $Cor(\cdot; \cdot)$ is the label-correlation, and in this paper, we choose Jaccard-correlation ($J(l_i, l_j) = \frac{|l_i \cap l_j|}{|l_i \cup l_j|}$) to calculate $Cor(l_j; l_k)$, and if you wonder it can be replaced by any differentiable correlation measures. S and L are the same as mentioned above. However, if you wonder search the best k features, it's time complexity will be $\mathcal{O}(C_n^k(nm^3 + n^2 + nm))$.

By analyzing the calculation process of Eq. (13), we find that $I(\cdot; \cdot)$ and $Cor(\cdot; \cdot)$ are calculated many times repeatedly when searching the best subset. To solve this issue and reduce computation time, we define a matrix D and two vectors c and e, and their calculation details are as follows

$$D_{i,j} = I(f_i; f_j) = \sum_{a \in f_i} \sum_{b \in f_j} p(a,b) log(\frac{p(a,b)}{p(a)p(b)}) \tag{14}$$

where $D_{i,j}$ is each element of D, $D \in \mathbb{R}^{n \times n}$.

$$c_i = \sum_{l_j \in L} I(f_i; l_j) = \sum_{l_j \in L} \sum_{a \in f_i} \sum_{b \in l_j} p(a,b) log(\frac{p(a,b)}{p(a)p(b)}) \tag{15}$$

where c_i is each element of c, represents the correlation between the ith feature and labels, $c \in \mathbb{R}^{n \times 1}$.

$$e_i = \sum_{l_j \in L} I(f_i; l_j) \sum_{l_k \in L} Cor(l_j; l_k) \tag{16}$$

where e_i is each element of e, represents the correlation between the ith feature and labels weighted by the label-correlation, $e \in \mathbb{R}^{n \times 1}$.

By calculating D, c and e firstly, we can redefine Eq. (13) as

$$\max_{S} J = \frac{\sum\limits_{f_i \in S} e_i + \sum\limits_{f_i \in S} c_i}{\sum\limits_{f_i \in S} \sum\limits_{f_j \in S} D_{i,j}} \tag{17}$$

by doing this, the time complexity of searching first k features can be reduced to $\mathcal{O}(C_n^k)$.

However, in real-world multi-label tasks, the dimensions of many feature sets are always very high, at the same time, we usually don't know how many features should we select. So we always try to use each possible optimal number, and we will get $C_n^1 + C_n^2 \dots + C_n^n = 2^n$ subsets of all. As you can see, selecting the optimal feature subset is still need take a lot of computation time or even impractical.

For further simplification, we try to transform Eq. (17) into a numerical optimization problem. Inspired by sparse-learning based methods such as [43], it is natural to think that each feature can be assigned different weights to find the optimal subsets. So, we define a weight vector $x \in \mathbb{R}^{n \times 1}$ and x_i represents the weight of the ith feature. Then, we get the equation as

$$\max_{x} J = \frac{c^T x + e^T x}{x^T D x} \tag{18}$$

$$s.t. \ x_1, x_2, x_3, \dots, x_n \geq 0, \ \sum_{i=1}^{n} x_i = 1.$$

where the constraints on the above guarantee that each weight of features is significant.

4.2   Solution

Equation (18) is a constrained optimization problem, it contains equality and inequality constraints at the same time, so it can be solved by employing

Interior Penalty Function Method, which enables us to find the approximate optimization solution under the two constraints. First of all, we need to construct an augmented objective function as follows

$$F(x) = f(x) + r_k \sum_{i=1}^{n} \frac{1}{x_i} + \frac{1}{\sqrt{r_k}} [\sum_{j=1}^{n} x_i - 1]^2 \tag{19}$$

where $f(x)$ is minus Eq. (18), $r_k > 0$ is penalty factor. Then before we using Newton method to find global approximate optimal solution of Eq. (19), we should set the initial point of x, which is marked as x^0, and $\forall x_i^0 \in x^0 : 0 \leqslant x_i^0 \leqslant 1$. And to obtain the final solution by iteration, we also need to set some other parameters such as initial barrier factor r_0, penalty factor reduction factor $c < 1$, precision factor ε, and finally set $k = 0$.

Assume that the iteration point x^{k-1} has been obtained, we set x^{k-1} as a new initial point, and solve the new optimal solution x^k by using Newton method. If $||F(x^k) - F(x^{k-1})|| \leqslant \varepsilon$, x^k is the optimal solution, else update the parameters as follows

$$r_{k+1} = cr_k \tag{20}$$

and set x^k as a new iteration point to solve the optimal solution repeatedly until meet the precision requirement.

After obtaining the feature weight vector, the first k features with the largest weight are selected according to the weight size, which is the optimal feature subset. According to the above analysis, in order to express the algorithm steps in this paper more clearly, it is described as follows:

Algorithm 1. "Interior Penalty Function Method"

Input: Feature data matrix F, label data matrix L

Output: Feature weight vector x

   1: setting the initial point x^0 satisfying the inequality constraints, penalty factor $r_0 > 0$, shrinking coefficient $c < 1$, and precision factor $\varepsilon > 0$.

   2: calculate matrix D according to Eq.(14), calculate vector c and e according Eq.(15,16).

   3: repeat

   4:    construct augmented objective function according to Eq.(19).

   5:    get new optimal point x_1 by using Newton method.

   6:    if $|F(x^1) - F(x^0)| \leqslant \varepsilon$

   7:      break;

   8:    else

   9:      $r_0 = c \times r_0$;

  10:    $x^0 = x^1$;

  11:    back to step 4;

  12: output x^1

---

5   Experiments

Then, we will introduce some experiments detail and show the performance of our method.

5.1   Experimental Settings

In this paper, six experiments are performed on text, image, and biology datasets, which are available in the Mulan, and all of these datasets are discretized beforehand. Table 1 lists some information about theses datasets. The Arts, Business, Health, Recreation four web data sets belong to Yahoo dataset, each dataset contains 5000 samples, the extracted features represent different word frequency in the text, label data says category information; TCM dataset contains 1,146 samples, each feature represents the quantitative information of patients' symptoms. Yeast is used to describe the basic genetic functional classification of saccharomycetes, including 2417 samples. Meanwhile, for comparing our method with five contrast algorithms, i.e., MLNB [44], PMU [31], MDDMspc [45], MDDMproj [45], and MDMR [30] based on evaluation measures mentioned above. Then, as a classical multi-label classification algorithm, MLkNN [42] is used to evaluate the performance of every methods, and the number of parameter k is set as 10.

Table 1. Detailed information of multi-label datasets

Data sets	Samples	Features	Classes	Training	Test	Domains
Arts	5000	462	26	2000	3000	Text
Education	5000	550	33	2000	3000	Text
Health	5000	612	32	2000	3000	Text
Recreation	5000	606	22	2000	3000	Text
TCM	1146	461	43	606	540	Biology
Yeast	2417	103	14	918	1499	Biology

5.2   Comparison Results

To compare each algorithm's best classification result, the optimal feature subset dimension will be changed from 1 to maximum and draw curves, and the maximum dimension of feature subset of MLNB is different from other methods, but it still be comparable.

Figures 1, 2, 3, 4 and 5 are the results of six datasets in five different measures. The red line is our method. And one thing that needs to be specified is that one of the baseline algorithms MLNB mentioned above is a degenerated method, so the curves of MLNB (the pink one) for all the comparisons are truncated.

At the same time, for verifying the efficiency of our method, experiments on the same machine (configured as Intel Core i7, 2.60 G CPU 12 GB RAM,

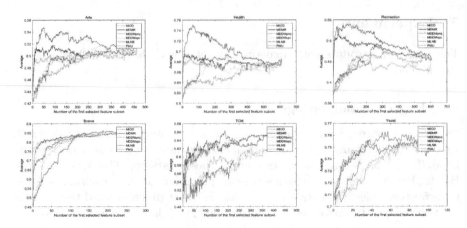

Fig. 1. Average Precision (Color figure online)

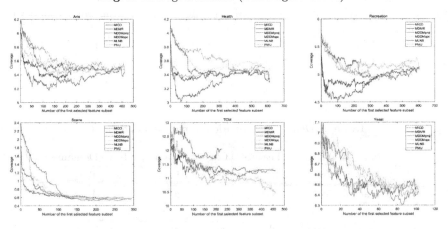

Fig. 2. Coverage (Color figure online)

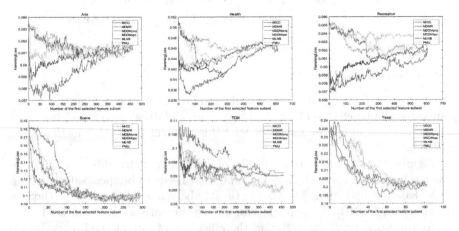

Fig. 3. HammingLoss (Color figure online)

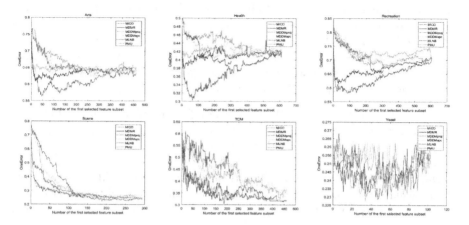

Fig. 4. OneError (Color figure online)

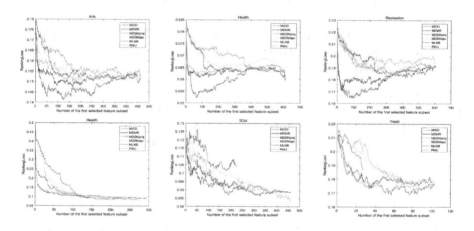

Fig. 5. RankingLoss (Color figure online)

Table 2. CPU Run time comparison of each feature selection method (second)

Dataset	Proposed	MDMR	MDDMproj	MDDMspc	MLNB	PMU
Arts	9.93	8630	0.97	0.88	10509	9373
Education	8.77	14854	1.66	1.64	12680	15643
Health	15.55	18628	1.92	1.73	14383	18739
Recreation	15.16	12738	1.68	1.71	9844	13153
TCM	4.16	2021	0.42	0.41	2448	2102
Yes	1.56	180	0.19	0.19	2460	196

the programming language is Matlab) respectively to the above time contrast, and the specific results are shown in following table. Our method compared with MDMR, MLNB, PMU, has obvious promotion in the running time, and get better feature selection results at the same time, achieves a good balance between selection results and the time consumption.

As shown in Figs. 1, 2, 3, 4 and 5 and Table 2:

- The experimental curves in the first several features show a trend of obvious up or down and remain stable after reach the optimal value or the opposite trend changes, which means that MICO is effective for many datasets and can choose the optimal feature subsets.
- Our method in the Arts, Education, Health, Recreation, TCM, Yeast datasets can achieve the optimal effect, particularly in the Arts and the effect on the Health datasets, which shows our method has obvious advantage compared with other methods.
- Because MDDM method is based on the method of matrix decomposition, so it has obvious advantage on time performance, but our method compared with MDMR, MLNB, and PMU on the time performance are two orders of magnitude shorter.
- Our method has the highest performance time ratio and can greatly improve the algorithm efficiency without sacrificing performance or even improving performance.

In general speaking, our method under the contrast indicators have good performance, and our method is a kind of no parameter feature selection method, so our method has better learning performance and generalization ability, can adapt to multiple scenarios and find the optimal feature subset.

6   Conclusion

In our paper, a fast method without parameters is introduced on the basis of traditional method "mRMR". At the same time, label correlation is integrated into the optimization framework, and the feature is weighted by label-correlation, which makes our algorithm performance more robust. Another contribution of this paper is to solve the problem of TCM diagnosis from the perspective of multi-label classification. By combining traditional Chinese medicine theories with data mining methods, a new attempt is made for the modernization of TCM diagnosis methods.

References

1. Schapire, R.E., Singer, Y.: BoosTexter: a boosting-based system for text categorization. Mach. Learn. 39(2/3), 135–168 (2000)
2. Sebastiani, F.: Machine learning in automated text categorization. ACM Comput. Surv. 34(1), 1–47 (2002)

3. Diplaris, S., Tsoumakas, G., Mitkas, P.A., Vlahavas, I.: Protein classification with multiple algorithms. In: Bozanis, P., Houstis, E.N. (eds.) PCI 2005. LNCS, vol. 3746, pp. 448–456. Springer, Heidelberg (2005). https://doi.org/10.1007/11573036_42
4. Liu, G.P., Li, G.Z., Wang, Y.L., Wang, Y.Q.: Modelling of inquiry diagnosis for coronary heart disease in traditional Chinese medicine by using multi-label learning. BMC Complement. Altern. Med. 10(1), 37 (2010)
5. Naula, P., Airola, A., Salakoski, T., Pahikkala, T.: Multi-label learning under feature extraction budgets. Pattern Recognit. Lett. 40, 56–65 (2014)
6. Zhang, L., Hu, Q., Duan, J., Wang, X.: Multi-label feature selection with fuzzy rough sets. In: Miao, D., Pedrycz, W., Ślęzak, D., Peters, G., Hu, Q., Wang, R. (eds.) RSKT 2014. LNCS (LNAI), vol. 8818, pp. 121–128. Springer, Cham (2014). https://doi.org/10.1007/978-3-319-11740-9_12
7. Zhang, J., Fang, M., Li, X.: Multi-label learning with discriminative features for each label. Neurocomputing 154, 305–316 (2015)
8. Guyon, I., Elisseeff, A.: An introduction to variable and feature selection. J. Mach. Learn. Res. 3, 1157–1182 (2003)
9. Molchanov, V., Linsen, L.: Overcoming the curse of dimensionality when clustering multivariate volume data. In: Proceedings of the 13th International Joint Conference on Computer Vision, Imaging and Computer Graphics Theory and Applications (VISIGRAPP 2018) - Volume 3: IVAPP, Funchal, Madeira, Portugal, 27–29 January 2018, pp. 29–39 (2018)
10. Zhang, M.-L., Zhou, Z.-H.: A review on multi-label learning algorithms. IEEE Trans. Knowl. Data Eng. 26(8), 1819–1837 (2014)
11. Kong, X., Yu, P.S.: gMLC: a multi-label feature selection framework for graph classification. Knowl. Inf. Syst. 31(2), 281–305 (2012)
12. Lee, J.-S., Kim, D.-W.: Memetic feature selection algorithm for multi-label classification. Inf. Sci. 293, 80–96 (2015)
13. Li, P., Li, H., Min, W.: Multi-label ensemble based on variable pairwise constraint projection. Inf. Sci. 222, 269–281 (2013)
14. Zhang, M.-L., Lei, W.: LIFT: multi-label learning with label-specific features. IEEE Trans. Pattern Anal. Mach. Intell. 37(1), 107–120 (2015)
15. Lin, Y., Qinghua, H., Zhang, J., Xindong, W.: Multi-label feature selection with streaming labels. Inf. Sci. 372, 256–275 (2016)
16. Liu, J., Lin, Y., Lin, M., Shunxiang, W., Zhang, J.: Feature selection based on quality of information. Neurocomputing 225, 11–22 (2017)
17. Teisseyre, P.: CCnet: joint multi-label classification and feature selection using classifier chains and elastic net regularization. Neurocomputing 235, 98–111 (2017)
18. Pudil, P., Novovicová, J., Kittler, J.: Floating search methods in feature selection. Pattern Recognit. Lett. 15(10), 1119–1125 (1994)
19. Reunanen, J.: Overfitting in making comparisons between variable selection methods. J. Mach. Learn. Res. 3, 1371–1382 (2003)
20. Somol, P., Pudil, P., Novovicová, J., Paclík, P.: Adaptive floating search methods in feature selection. Pattern Recognit. Lett. 20(11–13), 1157–1163 (1999)
21. Blum, A., Langley, P.: Selection of relevant features and examples in machine learning. Artif. Intell. 97(1–2), 245–271 (1997)
22. John, G.H., Kohavi, R., Pfleger, K.: Irrelevant features and the subset selection problem. In: Machine Learning, Proceedings of the Eleventh International Conference, Rutgers University, New Brunswick, NJ, USA, 10–13 July 1994, pp. 121–129 (1994)

23. Guyon, I., Weston, J., Barnhill, S., Vapnik, V.: Gene selection for cancer classification using support vector machines. Mach. Learn. **46**(1–3), 389–422 (2002)
24. Law, M.H.C., Figueiredo, M.A.T., Jain, A.K.: Simultaneous feature selection and clustering using mixture models. IEEE Trans. Pattern Anal. Mach. Intell. **26**(9), 1154–1166 (2004)
25. Peng, H., Long, F., Ding, C.H.Q.: Feature selection based on mutual information: criteria of max-dependency, max-relevance, and min-redundancy. IEEE Trans. Pattern Anal. Mach. Intell. **27**(8), 1226–1238 (2005)
26. Xing, E.P., Karp, R.M.: CLIFF: clustering of high-dimensional microarray data via iterative feature filtering using normalized cuts. In: Proceedings of the Ninth International Conference on Intelligent Systems for Molecular Biology, 21–25 July 2001, Copenhagen, Denmark, pp. 306–315 (2001)
27. Zhao, Z., Liu, H.: Semi-supervised feature selection via spectral analysis. In: Proceedings of the Seventh SIAM International Conference on Data Mining, 26–28 April 2007, Minneapolis, Minnesota, USA, pp. 641–646 (2007)
28. Sheikhpour, R., Sarram, M.A., Gharaghani, S., Chahooki, M.A.Z.: A survey on semi-supervised feature selection methods. Pattern Recognit. **64**, 141–158 (2017)
29. Battiti, R.: Using mutual information for selecting features in supervised neural net learning. IEEE Trans. Neural Netw. **5**(4), 537–550 (1994)
30. Lin, Y., Qinghua, H., Liu, J., Duan, J.: Multi-label feature selection based on max-dependency and min-redundancy. Neurocomputing **168**, 92–103 (2015)
31. Lee, J.-S., Kim, D.-W.: Feature selection for multi-label classification using multivariate mutual information. Pattern Recognit. Lett. **34**(3), 349–357 (2013)
32. Lim, H., Lee, J.-S., Kim, D.-W.: Optimization approach for feature selection in multi-label classification. Pattern Recognit. Lett. **89**, 25–30 (2017)
33. Zhang, J., et al.: Multi-label learning with label-specific features by resolving label correlations. Knowl.-Based Syst. **159**, 148–157 (2018)
34. Wang, J., Wei, J.-M., Yang, Z., Wang, S.-Q.: Feature selection by maximizing independent classification information. IEEE Trans. Knowl. Data Eng. **29**(4), 828–841 (2017)
35. Brown, G., Pocock, A.C., Zhao, M.-J., Luján, M.: Conditional likelihood maximisation: a unifying framework for information theoretic feature selection. J. Mach. Learn. Res. **13**, 27–66 (2012)
36. Wang, J., Wei, J., Yang, Z.: Supervised feature selection by preserving class correlation. In: Proceedings of the 25th ACM International Conference on Information and Knowledge Management, CIKM 2016, Indianapolis, IN, USA, 24–28 October 2016, pp. 1613–1622 (2016)
37. Wang, X., Chen, R.-C., Hong, C., Zeng, Z., Zhou, Z.: Semi-supervised multi-label feature selection via label correlation analysis with l1-norm graph embedding. Image Vis. Comput. **63**, 10–23 (2017)
38. Spolaôr, N., Monard, M.C., Tsoumaka, G., Lee, H.D.: A systematic review of multi-label feature selection and a new method based on label construction. Neurocomputing **180**, 3–15 (2016)
39. Shannon, C.E.: A mathematical theory of communication. Mob. Comput. Commun. Rev. **5**(1), 3–55 (2001)
40. Willems, F.M.J.: Review of 'elements of information theory' (Cover, T.M., and Thomas, J.A.; 1991). IEEE Trans. Inf. Theory **39**(1), 313 (1993)
41. Vinh, N.X., Epps, J., Bailey, J.: Information theoretic measures for clusterings comparison: variants, properties, normalization and correction for chance. J. Mach. Learn. Res. **11**, 2837–2854 (2010)

42. Zhang, M.-L., Zhou, Z.-H.: ML-KNN: a lazy learning approach to multi-label learning. Pattern Recogn. **40**(7), 2038–2048 (2007)
43. Zhang, M., Ding, C.H.Q., Zhang, Y., Nie, F.: Feature selection at the discrete limit. In: Proceedings of the Twenty-Eighth AAAI Conference on Artificial Intelligence, 27–31 July 2014, Québec City, Québec, Canada, pp. 1355–1361 (2014)
44. Zhang, M.-L., Sánchez, J.M.P., Robles, V.: Feature selection for multi-label naive bayes classification. Inf. Sci. **179**(19), 3218–3229 (2009)
45. Zhang, Y., Zhou, Z.-H.: Multi-label dimensionality reduction via dependence maximization. In: Proceedings of the Twenty-Third AAAI Conference on Artificial Intelligence, AAAI 2008, Chicago, Illinois, USA, 13–17 July 2008, pp. 1503–1505 (2008)

Multi-kernel Collaboration-Induced Fuzzy Local Information C-Means Algorithm for Image Segmentation

Yiming Tang[1,2]($\boxtimes$), Xianghui Hu[1], Fuji Ren[1], Xiaocheng Song[1], and Xi Wu[1]

[1] School of Computer and Information, Hefei University of Technology, Hefei 230601, China
tym608@163.com
[2] Department of Electrical and Computer Engineering, University of Alberta, Edmonton, AB T6R 2V4, Canada

Abstract. As an advanced method in the field of image segmentation, the fuzzy local information c-means (FLICM) algorithm has the problem of which segmentation performance is degraded when neighboring pixels are polluted, and it is imperfect for clustering nonlinear data. Focusing on these points, the Multi-kernel Collaboration-induced Fuzzy Local Information C-Means (MCFLICM) algorithm is put forward. To begin with, the concept of multi-kernel collaboration is introduced in image segmentation, and the Euclidean distance of the original space is replaced by multiple kernel-induced distance that are composed of multiple kernels in different proportions. Moreover, a new fuzzy factor is proposed from the viewpoints of pixel mean and local information, so as to increase the noises immunity. Finally, the multi-kernel collaboration and the new fuzzy factor are synthesized, and then the MCFLICM algorithm is put forward. MCFLICM can automatically adjust the requirements of different data points for kernel functions in the iterative procedure and can avoid the uncertainty of the selection of kernel function by the ordinary kernel algorithms. These advantages increase the robustness of the algorithm. In addition, MCFLICM has a stronger denoising performance to improve the ability to retain the original image details. Through comparing experiments with seven related algorithms, it is found that the segmentation performance of MCFLICM in binary image, three-valued image and natural image is superior to other algorithms, and the best results are achieved by MCFLICM from the viewpoints of visual effects and evaluation indexes.

Keywords: Multi-kernel · Collaboration · FCM · Image segmentation

1 Introduction

Clustering is a vital branch of pattern recognition, which is unsupervised [1–3]. The ultimate goal of clustering is to make the distance between similar samples as small as possible, and the distance between different samples as large as possible. Based on this criterion, clustering algorithms can mine the potential data structure in the dataset.

© Springer Nature Singapore Pte Ltd. 2019
Y. Sun et al. (Eds.): ChineseCSCW 2018, CCIS 917, pp. 438–453, 2019.
https://doi.org/10.1007/978-981-13-3044-5_32

Image segmentation is one of the image recognition steps, which is a method to subdivide a target image into several sub-regions with correlation characteristics but non-overlapping. Fuzzy clustering algorithms have been widely applied to this field in recent years. There are many image segmentation approaches with fuzzy clustering which have made great progress in texture and color image segmentation [4–6].

As a typical representative, fuzzy C-means clustering (FCM) algorithm was proposed by Dunn [7] and Bezdek developed it [8]. This algorithm mainly converges its objective function based upon the minimal square error method, but it is sensitive to noises. Because it does not employ the spatial relationships between pixels. Therefore, Ahmed et al. put the neighborhood mean element into FCM in [9], and proposed an improved algorithm BCFCM. However, the algorithm needs to recalculate the mean term before each iteration, thus the time complexity of it is greatly increased. In [10], Szilagyi et al. processed the image by average filter at first, then performed fuzzy clustering upon the gray level image. So they proposed a two-step enhanced FCM algorithm-EnFCM algorithm. However, average filter method may lose image details so that EnFCM algorithm get an edge blurred image. As to save the time of running the algorithm, Chen and Zhang came up with two improved algorithms of BCFCM algorithm in [11], namely FCM_S1 and FCM_S2. FCM_S1 considered the mean neighboring pixels while FCM_S2 computed the median. Since the median or mean of the neighbors can be calculated in advance, the FCM_S1 and FCM_S2 algorithms need less clustering time compared to the BCFCM algorithm. Experiments in [11] showed that kernelization increased the robustness of the algorithm. The GFCM algorithm proposed by Zhu et al. [12] got an additional membership restriction into the FCM objective function to obtain a more explicit division, so as to speed up the convergence and reduce running time of the algorithm. Zhao et al. [13] integrated spatial information into multi-objective evolutionary fuzzy clustering algorithm, and proposed multi-objective evolutionary image segmentation algorithm based on spatial information, which obtained ideal performance on noisy images.

In [14], the fuzzy local information C-means clustering (FLICM) algorithm is established. It overcomes the problem of sensitivity to parameters. Meanwhile, owing to a novel fuzzy factor, the FLICM algorithm can suppress image noises and preserve the details of the image so that it raises the accuracy of image segmentation. However, FLICM uses Euclidean distance, so it is unideal for nonlinear data clustering. When the image is seriously polluted by noise, the central pixel may be polluted. Then the spatial information of the pixel cannot play an effective and active role in the noisy image segmentation. FLICM is highly recognized as an advanced algorithm in image segmentation. However, the above problems are demanded to be resolved, so our study will start with these.

With the development of related researches, scholars gradually try to carry out fuzzy clustering at the multidimensional kernel space instead of the original space. This idea inspired our study. By introducing a kernel function, the samples are mapped into the high-dimensional feature space F, which makes it linearly separable. The problem that the cluster samples are linearly inseparable can be solved by this way. At the same time, the samples are fuzzy clustered in space F to form a kernel-based clustering strategy. In the kernel-learning space, it is possible to enlarge the difference between samples and increase the accuracy of clustering. The kernel-based fuzzy C-means

(KFCM) algorithm was established in [15]. Genton demonstrated a kernel learning approach with a statistical viewpoint in [16]. However, the single-kernel fuzzy clustering algorithms are only suitable for spherical data while not ideal for non-spherical data.

How to choose a suitable kernel function is vital in this area. Nevertheless, a single kernel sometimes cannot be sufficient to express data with various characteristics. The selected data may generate diverse similarity values matching to corresponding kernels. Therefore, uniting basic kernels becomes a way to improve single-kernel learning performance. Lanckriet et al. firstly mentioned the concept of multi-kernel in [17], which directly led to the generation of convex optimization problems of support vector machines. At the same time, the problem of validity has always existed. Bach mentioned in [18] the algorithm of order minimization optimization, and the efficiency problem of multi-kernel learning was later solved by semi-infinite linear programming. Zhao et al. raised a multi-kernel clustering strategy in [19], which was based on maximum marginal clustering. However, one obvious disadvantage is that their clustering algorithm is mostly used for hard clustering. [20] and [21] used the idea of multi-kernel to extend FCM and established the multi-kernel FCM. By adjusting the weights of each kernel, the clustering algorithm is effective to invalid kernels and unrelated features, thus it reduces the importance of kernel selection. However, it is clear that these multiple kernel clustering algorithms are hard to determine the weights of the kernels and it is difficult to achieve good kernels weights distribution.

In general, these multiple kernel clustering algorithms still have many problems. First of all, we must find the appropriate parameters. But for the selection of parameters, there is no effective method. The selection of parameters is basically experimental or guessing, and its reliability is not strong. Moreover, the lack of priority and effectiveness in the selection and adjustment of weights leads to that the experimental results are not perfect.

Aiming at these problems, this paper introduces the idea of multi-kernel collaboration to image segmentation, and derives proper proportional relationship of kernels through their internal relationships. The effect of each kernels is strengthened. Furthermore, the original fuzzy factor of FLICM is improved because it is constructed from the viewpoint of pixel mean and local information. Finally, the Multi-kernel Collaboration-induced Fuzzy Local Information C-Means algorithm (MCFLICM) is put forward by integrating multi-kernel collaboration and new fuzzy factors.

Section 2 recommends related researches. Section 3 explores the proposed algorithm and elaborates on its details. Section 4 gives experimental analyses for eight algorithms. Section 5 summarizes the whole study.

2   Related Works

The FCM algorithm mainly optimizes the objective function to obtain the optimal value, so as to cluster the image or data sample. FCM implements data partition by minimizing the objective function. However, as the FCM algorithm does not think over spatial information when processing data sets or images, the results obtained are not ideal.

FCM_S1 together with FCM_S2 [8] employs the mean of neighborhood pixels and the median in turn. FCM_S1 allows the previous image as well as the mean image to possess identical clustering result, and is robust to Gaussian noise, but it is still not suitable for denoising of pulsed images. The idea of FCM_S2 combines with median filtering to overcome this problem. FCM_S1 together with FCM_S2 effectively save the runtime.

The EnFCM algorithm [7] can speed up the clustering processing of grayscale images, which requires the mean filtering of the image firstly. Since the EnFCM algorithm only processes the grayscale image, the time complexity of the algorithm is greatly lessened. However, when the mean filtering of the image is performed, the texture features of the original image are lost, which will result in blurring of the image edges.

The GFCM algorithm [9] is an improved algorithm of FCM. It introduces a membership restriction element into FCM to obtain a further explicit division, so as to accelerate the convergence speed.

The multi-objective evolutionary (MSOFCM) algorithm for complementary spatial information [10] uses two fitness functions. One is the global fuzzy compactness function that fuses spatial information, while the other is a fuzzy separability function. However, this kind of algorithm only has a good clustering effect on the data of the convex structure, and the clustering effect of the complex form with arbitrary shape is not very good.

The FLICM algorithm [15] introduces fuzzy factors G_{ki} for the first time:

$$G_{ki} = \sum_{\substack{j \in N_i \\ i \neq j}} \frac{1}{d_{ij}+1} \left(1 - u_{kj}\right)^m \|x_j - v_k\|^2. \tag{1}$$

Here the fuzzy factor G_{ki} combines spatial structure with gray element to enhance the denoising ability. The objective function after introducing the fuzzy factor G_{ki} is expressed as:

$$J_m = \sum_{i=1}^{N} \sum_{k=1}^{c} \left[u_{ki}^m \|x_i - v_k\|^2 + G_{ki} \right]. \tag{2}$$

Then, the expressions of membership and cluster center are as follows:

$$u_{ki} = \frac{1}{\sum_{j=1}^{c} \left(\frac{\|x_i - v_k\|^2 + G_{ki}}{\|x_i - v_j\|^2 + G_{ji}} \right)^{\frac{1}{m-1}}}, \tag{3}$$

$$v_k = \frac{\sum_{i=1}^{n} u_{ki}^m x_i}{\sum_{i=1}^{n} u_{ki}^m}. \tag{4}$$

The FLICM algorithm can effectively segment most of the images contaminated by noise. But when the center pixel of the field window is noise, its processing effect will be significantly reduced.

3 The Proposed MCFLICM Algorithm

Being an advanced algorithm of image segmentation, the FLICM algorithm has the problem of degrading image segmentation performance when the central pixel of the neighborhood is polluted. And as like other fuzzy clustering algorithms, its clustering result on nonlinear data is not satisfactory. For dealing with those problems, we propose the MCFLICM algorithm.

3.1 Framework of MCFLICM

The following formula shows the idea of the MCFLICM algorithm:

$$J_{MKFILCM} = \sum_{i=1}^{c} \sum_{j=1}^{n} \left[u_{ij}^m D_{ij}^2 + P_{ij} \right], \tag{5}$$

$$D_{ij}^2 = \left\| \phi(x_j) - v_i \right\|^2 = \left(\phi(x_j) - v_i \right)^T \left(\phi(x_j) - v_i \right). \tag{6}$$

Here D_{ij}^2 represents the formula for calculating the Euclidean distance from the kernel viewpoint.

We fully consider the importance of introducing a balance factor, so we introduce a balance fuzzy factor P_{ij}:

$$P_{ij} = \sum_{\substack{p \in N_j \\ p \neq j}} \frac{\left\| x_j - \bar{x} \right\|^2}{d_{jp} + 1} \left(1 - u_{ip} \right)^m D_{ij}^2, \tag{7}$$

where $\bar{x}$ denotes the average pixel value, which can reflect the concentrated trend of the pixels distribution. And x_j expresses the j th value. P_{ij} can better reflect the local spatial information. Moreover, we consider the possibility that the pixel x_j at the neighborhood central is a noise point. The larger value of $\left\| x_j - \bar{x} \right\|^2$ indicates that the farther the pixel x_j is deviated from the overall pixel distribution, the more likely it is a noise point. We can see that the improved fuzzy factor P_{ij} makes up for the defect that the FLICM algorithm does not take account into the pixel in neighborhood center is the noise point. So the MCFLICM algorithm can improve the image segmentation performance. P_{ij} also does not introduce any other parameters, which reduces the randomness of the algorithm implementation.

Alike to the FLICM algorithm, the expressions of membership degree and cluster center for iterative updating can be as follows:

$$u_{ij} = \cfrac{1}{\sum\limits_{s=1}^{c} \left(\cfrac{D_{ij}^2 + P_{ij}}{D_{sj}^2 + P_{ij}} \right)^{\frac{1}{m-1}}}, \tag{8}$$

$$v_i = \cfrac{\sum\limits_{j=1}^{n} u_{ij}^m \phi(x_j)}{\sum\limits_{j=1}^{n} u_{ij}^m} = \sum_{j=1}^{n} \hat{u}_{ij} \phi(x_j). \tag{9}$$

In (6) and (9), $\phi(x_j)$ represents the representation of x_j, which is from the viewpoint of multi-kernel multidimensional feature space. To let the results satisfy the Mercer condition [22], we adopt a new mapping function $\phi(x_j) = \sum\limits_{k=1}^{M} \beta_k \phi_k(x_j)$ to combine kernel functions. β_k means the weight of the sub-kernel function, and M is the number of sub-kernel functions. This is the basic idea of multi-kernel collaboration.

3.2 Collaboration of Multi-kernel Function

The multi-kernel function essentially combines M kernel functions. In fact, any function can be regarded as a kernel function provided that it meets the Mercer condition. So assuming a set of basis kernel functions $\{K_k\}_{k=1}^M$, the total function can be defined as:

$$K(x_j, x_q) = \sum_{k=1}^{M} \beta_k K_k(x_j, x_q), \beta_l \geq 0. \tag{10}$$

And there are restrictions $\sum\limits_{k=1}^{M} \beta_k = 1$. The sub-Mercer kernel function can be expressed as $K_k(x_i, x_j) = \phi_k(x_i)^T \phi_k(x_j)$. As a result, the update of D_{ij} in conjunction with (6) is expressed as follows:

$$D_{ij}^2 = \sum_{k=1}^{M} \beta_k^2 K_k(x_j, x_j) - 2 \sum_{q=1}^{n} \sum_{k=1}^{M} \hat{u}_{iq} \beta_k^2 K_k(x_j, x_q) + \sum_{q=1}^{n} \sum_{q'=1}^{n} \sum_{k=1}^{M} \hat{u}_{iq} \hat{u}_{iq'} \beta_k^2 K_k(x_q, x_{q'}). \tag{11}$$

Let

$$\alpha_{ijk} = K_k(x_j, x_j) - 2 \sum_{q=1}^{n} \hat{u}_{iq} K_k(x_j, x_q) + \sum_{q=1}^{n} \sum_{q'=1}^{n} \hat{u}_{iq} \hat{u}_{iq'} K_k(x_q, x_{q'}), \tag{12}$$

So the simplified distance formula is as follows:

$$D_{ij}^2 = \sum_{k=1}^{M} \beta_k^2 \alpha_{ijk}. \tag{13}$$

Therefore, (5) is transformed into a new objective function expression:

$$J_m = \sum_{i=1}^{c} \sum_{j=1}^{n} \sum_{k=1}^{M} \beta_k^2 \alpha_{ijk} \left[u_{ij}^m + \sum_{\substack{p \in N_j \\ p \neq j}} \frac{\|x_j - \bar{x}\|^2}{d_{jp} + 1} (1 - u_{ij})^m \right]. \tag{14}$$

Let

$$S_{ij} = u_{ij}^m + \sum_{\substack{p \in N_j \\ p \neq j}} \frac{\|x_j - \bar{x}\|^2}{d_{jp} + 1} (1 - u_{ij})^m, \tag{15}$$

then the objective function (14) is converted to:

$$J_m = \sum_{i=1}^{c} \sum_{j=1}^{n} \sum_{k=1}^{M} \beta_k^2 \alpha_{ijk} S_{ij}. \tag{16}$$

By introducing a parameter λ, the constraint function is associated with the objective function to define a new function. Because $\sum_{k=1}^{m} \beta_k = 1$, the expression (16) is transformed into:

$$J_m = \sum_{i=1}^{c} \sum_{j=1}^{n} \sum_{k=1}^{M} \beta_k^2 \alpha_{ijk} S_{ij} - 2\lambda \left(\sum_{k=1}^{M} \beta_k - 1 \right). \tag{17}$$

Then, in turn, we can get the following formula:

$$\sum_{k=1}^{M} \beta_k = \sum_{k=1}^{M} \frac{\lambda}{\sum_{i=1}^{c} \sum_{j=1}^{n} \alpha_{ijk} S_{ij}} = 1, \tag{18}$$

$$\lambda = \left[\left(\sum_{i=1}^{c} \sum_{j=1}^{n} \alpha_{ij1} S_{ij} \right)^{-1} + \left(\sum_{i=1}^{c} \sum_{j=1}^{n} \alpha_{ij2} S_{ij} \right)^{-1} + \cdots + \left(\sum_{i=1}^{c} \sum_{j=1}^{n} \alpha_{ijM} S_{ij} \right)^{-1} \right]^{-1}, \tag{19}$$

$$\beta_k = \frac{\left(\sum_{i=1}^{c}\sum_{j=1}^{n} \alpha_{ijk}S_{ij}\right)^{-1}}{\left(\sum_{i=1}^{c}\sum_{j=1}^{n} \alpha_{ij1}S_{ij}\right)^{-1} + \left(\sum_{i=1}^{c}\sum_{j=1}^{n} \alpha_{ij2}S_{ij}\right)^{-1} + \cdots + \left(\sum_{i=1}^{c}\sum_{j=1}^{n} \alpha_{ijM}S_{ij}\right)^{-1}}. \tag{20}$$

In summary, we combine the multi-kernel collaboration and the new fuzzy factor concept into FCM, and combine the spatial distance and gray information of the neighborhood pixels, so we can balance the noise and detail features of the image. Using the formula to derive the weight value β_k. Because $u_{ij} \geq 0$ and $\sum_{i=1}^{c} u_{ij} \geq 0$, we have $\sum_{k=1}^{m} \beta_k \geq 0$.

3.3 Selection of Sub-kernel Functions

There are two kinds of kernel functions: global and local ones. The global one allows sample points that are far apart to affect the kernel function value, so the global kernel function has powerful generalization ability, but its learning ability is short. In contrast to the global kernel function, the local one possesses very strong learning performance, but its generalization performance is weak. Currently the most commonly used in clustering is the Gaussian kernel function, which embodies as a local one. Another famous function is a polynomial kernel function, which is a global one. Here we will use the multi-kernel function composed of these two functions to make the advantages of different types of kernel functions, so as to get better results.

The Gaussian kernel function is computed by the following formula:

$$K(x_j, x_q) = \exp\left(\frac{-\|x_j - x_q\|}{\sigma^2}\right), \tag{21}$$

where σ is its width and can be calculated by $\min_{j,q}\left(-\|x_j - x_q\|^2 / \log(0.005)\right)$. The polynomial kernel function formula is:

$$K(x_j, x_q) = \left(x_i \cdot x_q + l\right)^d, l \geq 0, d \in N. \tag{22}$$

In the experiments, the parameter l takes the value 1 and the d takes the value 2.

3.4 Algorithm Operation Framework

Algorithm 1 describes the operational steps of the MCFLICM algorithm. Figure 1 is a flowsheet of the proposed MCFLICM algorithm.

Algorithm 1. The MCFLICM algorithm.
Input: n pixels of an image I, cluster number c, fuzzy parameter $m>1$, maximum iteration number $tMax$, minimum threshold ε, combined kernel function $\{K_k\}_{k=1}^M$.
Output: A membership matrix U, weights β_k and the segmented image.

Procedure MCFLICM (Image I, Number c)
Randomly initialize the membership matrix $U^{(0)}$;
Repeat number $t=0$;
repeat
       $t=t+1$;
       Calculate α_{ijk} using Eq. (12);
       Calculate S_{ij} using Eq. (15);
       Update $\beta_k^{(t)}$ using Eq. (20);
       Calculate D_{ij}^2 using Eq. (13);
       Update $U^{(t)}$ using Eq. (8);
Until $\left\|U^{(t)}-U^{(t-1)}\right\|<\varepsilon$ **or** $t>tMax$;

Return $U^{(t)}$, $\beta_k^{(t)}$ and segmented image;
end procedure

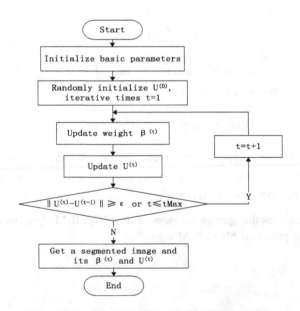

Fig. 1. The flowsheet of the MCFLICM algorithm

4   Experiment

Here we confirm the effectiveness and robustness of our proposed MCFLICM algorithm. Here, FCM, FCM_S1, FCM_S2, En_FCM, GFCM, MSOFCM, FLICM, and MCFLICM are fully compared with each other.

4.1   Evaluation Indexes

In terms of indexes, the segmentation accuracy (*SA*) and score (*R*) are used here [23, 24]. And *SA* represents the ratio which is expressed as:

$$SA = \sum_{i=1}^{c} \frac{A_i \cap C_i}{\sum_{j=1}^{c} C_j}. \tag{23}$$

Note that c denotes the number of classifications of pixels. Then A_i represents the pixel set of the i-th class computed with the strategy. Meanwhile, C_i corresponds to the i-th class derived from the reference one.

The quantitative index score (*R*) can be calculated by:

$$R = \sum_{i=1}^{c} \frac{A_i \cap C_i}{A_i \cup C_i}, \tag{24}$$

Here the notions are the same as *SA*. The index R actually indicates the degree of similarity between A_i and C_i. Then bigger R value means superior performance.

4.2   Experimental Results

In our experiments, we generally set the parameters $m = 2$, $tMax = 100$, $\varepsilon = 0.0001$, $\alpha = 6$ (for FCM_S1, FCS_S2 and EnFCM algorithm), and all neighborhood window sizes were set to 3×3. The multi-kernel in MCFLICM combines Gaussian kernel with polynomial one, and then we performs cooperative weighting processing. we use Matlab2013 Ra and VS2010 for testing. Here we focus on the application of each algorithm in two synthetic images (see Figs. 2(a) and 3(a)) as well as a natural image (see Fig. 4(a)).

Figure 2(a) with 128×128 pixels includes two clusters, in which 27 and 119 are two gray values. Figure 3(a) with 256×256 pixels is composed of three types of pixels whose gray level values are 20, 120 and 228.

First, we apply eight algorithms to Fig. 2(a) polluted by diverse levels of Gaussian together with Salt & Pepper noise, in turn. Table 1 lists the accuracy *SA* of this experiment. According to Table 1 results, we find that the proposed MCFLICM algorithm has preferred denoising property by contrast with the other seven methods. The results verifies that the MCFLICM algorithm presents robustness to all considered kind of noises and improves the classification accuracy.

Table 1. The SA% value comparison of eight algorithm on Fig. 1(a)

Algorithms	Gaussian (5)	Gaussian (10)	Gaussian (15)	Salt & Pepper (5)	Salt & Pepper (10)	Salt & Pepper (15)
FCM	88.72	86.58	84.32	93.62	90.45	89.75
BCFCM	98.67	91.35	86.57	97.74	89.58	82.69
FCM_S1	98.13	92.35	86.87	99.52	96.37	88.14
FCM_S2	99.20	90.35	86.37	99.51	89.39	87.98
EnFCM	98.13	97.36	96.97	99.60	98.42	98.01
GFCM	97.87	96.58	95.64	99.63	98.51	98.24
MSOFCM	96.11	95.47	93.91	99.63	98.51	98.24
FLICM	99.87	98.54	96.99	99.87	98.86	98.37
MCFLICM	**99.98**	**99.27**	**98.51**	**99.98**	**99.75**	**98.61**

Figures 2(c)–(j) and 3(c)–(j) together with Fig. 4(c)–(j) are the segmentation effects of eight algorithms on three kinds of images respectively. Figure (a) and (b) of Figs. 2, 3 and 4 are the previous image together with the noisy image contaminated by Salt & Pepper noise (10%). Tables 2 and 3 show the values of the indexes SA and R of each algorithms on three types of images. With the quantification analyses of the two indexes and the visual analysis of the segmented images of eight algorithms, the segmentation effect of MCFLICM is superior to the other seven algorithms. The main reason is from that MCFLICM gives consideration to the influence of neighbor pixels and adopts an adaptive multi-kernel algorithm.

Table 2. SA values of eight algorithms on various images

Algorithms	Figure 1	Figure 2	Figure 3
FCM	0.9518	0.9434	0.492
FCM_S1	0.9847	0.9632	0.4987
FCM_S2	0.9835	0.9632	0.4987
EnFCM	0.9854	0.9745	0.8826
GFCM	0.9525	0.9429	0.8711
MSOFCM	0.9689	0.9865	0.5025
FLICM	0.9951	0.9903	0.8771
MCFLICM	**0.9998**	**0.9989**	**0.9405**

Finally, let us discuss about how large the window radius is, the MCFLICM algorithm has the highest segmentation accuracy ($SA\%$). We add 10% Gaussian noise to Fig. 1(a), and get comparison as shown in Table 4. It can be seen that when the window radius is 1, the segmentation accuracy at the same level is the highest no matter how much the noise variance σ is. As the radius increases, the accuracy gradually decreases. Because the larger the radius, the more blurred the texture information.

Table 3. R values of eight algorithms on various images

Algorithm	Figure 1	Figure 2	Figure 3
FCM	0.9081	0.8931	0.5929
FCM_S1	0.9699	0.9017	0.6094
FCM_S2	0.9675	0.9407	0.5917
EnFCM	0.9711	0.9295	0.7957
GFCM	0.9094	0.8929	0.7989
MSOFCM	0.9236	0.9643	0.6182
FLICM	0.9903	0.9751	0.7801
MCFLICM	**0.9926**	**0.9971**	**0.8621**

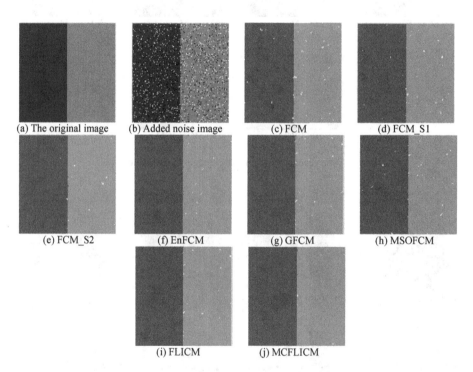

(a) The original image (b) Added noise image (c) FCM (d) FCM_S1

(e) FCM_S2 (f) EnFCM (g) GFCM (h) MSOFCM

(i) FLICM (j) MCFLICM

Fig. 2. The results of a synthetic image with two classes

And the more the noise is added under the same radius, the lower the accuracy will be. When σ reaches 50, the accuracy will decrease significantly regardless of radius. In addition, after the algorithm complexity is increased, the segmentation effect will naturally decrease. Therefore, when the noise is not large, the radius is generally selected to be 1, and when the noise is large, radius 3 is proper.

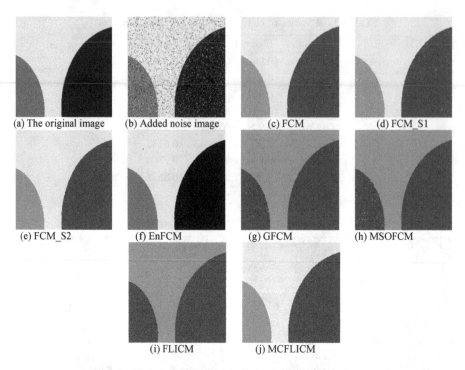

Fig. 3. The results of a synthetic image with three classes

Fig. 4. The results of a natural image

Table 4. SA% of the proposed algorithm under different radius and noise conditions

σ	Radius = 1	Radius = 2	Radius = 3	Radius = 4	Radius = 5
5	99.99	99.98	99.96	99.91	99.89
15	99.96	99.93	99.87	99.85	99.81
25	99.76	99.72	99.69	99.63	99.58
50	99.70	99.57	99.50	99.43	99.38
75	83.76	82.39	98.68	97.35	96.12
100	73.29	72.16	83.57	83.14	79.13

4.3 Running Time

Table 5 shows the running time. Each type of image adds 10% salt & pepper noise. The MCFLICM algorithm is not the fastest, but is faster than FLICM which also has good segmentation performance. FLICM recalculates the distance between each pixel and cluster center before each iteration, so it takes more time. From Sect. 4.2, we can know that MCFLICM is optimal in terms of evaluation indexes and segmentation performance, so it is worthwhile to consume more time.

Table 5. Running time(s) of eight algorithms on various images

Images	FCM	FCM_S1	FCM_S2	EnFCM	GFCM	MSOFCM	FLICM	MCFLICM
Figure 1	0.112	0.134	0.158	0.079	0.123	0.326	0.472	0.259
Figure 2	0.424	0.696	0.787	0.096	0.558	1.368	4.597	0.793
Figure 3	0.703	1.174	1.494	0.126	0.567	3.984	8.546	1.956

5 Conclusion

We put forward a fuzzy C-means image segmentation strategy derived from multi-kernel collaboration and spatial information, and apply it to the field of image segmentation. First of all, through the internal mechanism of multi-kernel, the Euclidean distance of the original space is replaced by the kernel distance composed of multiple kernels in different proportions. Secondly, a new fuzzy factor is established from the viewpoint of mean pixel and local information, so as to deal with the problem of mis-segmentation when the central pixel of the neighborhood is a noise point. Finally, the multi-kernel collaboration mechanism and new fuzzy factor are integrated, and a novel objective function is presented to establish the MCFLICM algorithm. Through comparison experiments with seven methods, MCFLICM performs best from the viewpoints of visual effects and evaluation indexes, and it has stronger denoising ability, which can better preserve the original image details.

The reasons why the MCFLICM algorithm is superior are mainly as follows:

(i) We introduce a multi-kernel based similarity metric to avoid the problem that FCM is sensitive to noise points.

(ii) We consider the case where the center pixel of the neighborhood pixels is a noise point. It solves the embarrassing situation that FLICM is easy to cause mis-segmentation when neighboring pixels are polluted.

(iii) The multi-kernel collaboration mechanism reduces the influence of the choice of the kernel on the experimental results which effectively solves the puzzle that the multi-kernel clustering algorithm is difficult for selecting the kernel function, and increases the anti-transformation of the method.

(iv) We combine the global and local kernels into multi-kernel in different proportions which gives full play to the advantages of different types of kernels and overcomes single-kernel defects. Moreover it enhances the performance of the algorithm.

In the future, we try to introduce the theory of logical reasoning in fuzzy clustering [25, 26], and establish a new collaborative system of combing fuzzy reasoning with fuzzy clustering. We aim to improve the process of optimizing iteration from the viewpoints of theoretical basis and algorithm implementation.

Acknowledgement. This work was supported by the National Natural Science Foundation of China (Nos. 61673156, 61672202, 61432004, U1613217), the Natural Science Foundation of Anhui Province (Nos. 1408085MKL15, 1508085QF129).

References

1. Tsakiris, M.C., Vidal, R.: Algebraic clustering of affine subspaces. IEEE Trans. Pattern Anal. Mach. Intell. **40**(2), 482–489 (2018)
2. Yang, M.S., Nataliani, Y.: A feature-reduction fuzzy clustering algorithm based on feature-weighted entropy. IEEE Trans. Fuzzy Syst. **26**(2), 817–835 (2018)
3. Huang, F.L., Li, X.L., Zhang, S.C., et al.: Harmonious genetic clustering. IEEE Trans. Cybern. **48**, 199–214 (2018)
4. Sarkar, J.P., Saha, I., Maulik, U.: Rough possibilistic type-2 fuzzy C-means clustering for MR brain image segmentation. Appl. Soft Comput. **8**(6), 527–536 (2016)
5. Tian, Y., Li, Y., Liu, D., et al.: FCM texture image segmentation method based on the local binary pattern. In: 12th World Congress on Intelligent Control and Automation, pp. 92–97. IEEE (2016)
6. Koundal, D.: Texture-based image segmentation using neutrosophic clustering. IET Image Process. **11**(8), 640–645 (2017)
7. Dunn, J.C.: A fuzzy relative of the ISO DATA process and its use in detecting compact well-separated clusters. J. Cybern. Syst. **3**(3), 33–57 (1973)
8. Bezdek, J.C.: Pattern recognition with fuzzy objective function algorithms. Adv. Appl. Pattern Recogn. **22**(1171), 203–239 (1981)
9. Ahmed, M.N., Yamany, S.M., Mohamed, N., et al.: A modified fuzzy c-means algorithm for bias field estimation and segmentation of MRI data. IEEE Trans. Med. Imag. **21**(3), 193–199 (2002)
10. Szilagyi, L., Benyo, Z., Szilagyi, S.M., et al.: MR brain image segmentation using an enhanced fuzzy C-means algorithm. In: Proceedings of Annual International Conference on Engineering in Medicine and Biology Society, vol. 5, no. 12, pp. 724–726 (2003)

11. Chen, S.C., Zhang, D.Q.: Robust image segmentation using FCM with spatial constraints based on new Kernel-induced distance measure. IEEE Trans. Syst. Man Cybern. Part B Cybern. **34**(4), 1907–1916 (2004)
12. Zhu, L., Chung, F.L., Wang, S.T.: Generalized fuzzy c-means clustering algorithm with improved fuzzy partitions. IEEE Trans. Syst. Man Cybern.-Part B: Cybern. **39**(3), 578–591 (2009)
13. Zhao, F., Liu, H.Q., Fan, J.L.: A multiobjective spatial fuzzy clustering algorithm for image segmentation. Appl. Soft Comput. **30**, 48–57 (2015)
14. Krinidis, S., Chatzis, V.: A robust fuzzy local information C-means clustering algorithm. IEEE Trans. Image Process. **19**(5), 1328–1337 (2010)
15. Yang, M.S., Tsai, H.S.: A Gaussian kernel-based fuzzy C-means algorithm with a spatial bias correction. Pattern Recogn. Lett. **29**(12), 1713–1725 (2008)
16. Genton, M.G.: Classes of kernels for machine learning: a statistics perspective. J. Mach. Learn. Res. **2**(2), 299–312 (2001)
17. Lanckriet, G., Bie, T.D., Cristianini, N., et al.: A statistical framework for genomic data fusion. Bioinformatics **20**(6), 2626–2635 (2004)
18. Bach, F.R., Lanckriet, G.R.G, Jordan, M.I.: Multiple kernel learning, conic duality, and the SMO algorithm. In: Proceedings of the Twenty-First International Conference on Machine Learning, Banff, Alberta, Canada, p. 6 (2004)
19. Zhao, B., Kwok, J., Zhang, C.: Multiple kernel clustering. In: Proceedings of 9th SIAM International Conference on Data Mining, pp. 638–649 (2009)
20. Huang, H.C., Chuang, Y.Y.: Multiple kernel fuzzy clustering. IEEE Trans. Fuzzy Syst. **20**(1), 120–134 (2012)
21. Zhou, J., Philip, C.L., Chen, L.: Maximum-entropy-based multiple kernel, fuzzy c-means clustering algorithm. In: IEEE International Conference on Systems, Man and Cybernetics, 5–8 October, pp. 1198–1203. IEEE, San Diego (2013)
22. Bach, F.R., Lanckriet, G.R.G., Jordan, M.I.: Multiple kernel learning, conic duality, and the SMO algorithm. In: Proceedings of 21st International Conference on Machine Learning (2004)
23. Cai, W., Chen, S., Zhang, D.: Fast and robust fuzzy c-means clustering algorithms incorporating local information for image segmentation. Pattern Recogn. **20**(3), 825–838 (2007)
24. Masulli, F., Schenone, A.: A fuzzy clustering based segmentation system as support to diagnosis in medical imaging. Artif. Intell. Med. **16**(2), 129–147 (1999)
25. Tang, Y.M., Liu, X.P.: Differently implicational universal triple I method of (1, 2, 2) type. Comput. Math Appl. **59**(6), 1965–1984 (2010)
26. Tang, Y.M., Pedrycz, W.: On the α(u, v)-symmetric implicational method for R- and (S, N)-implications. Int. J. Approx. Reasoning **92**, 212–231 (2018)

Chinese-Vietnamese Word Alignment Method Based on Bidirectional RNN and Linguistic Features

Shengxiang Gao, Haodong Zhu, Zhuo Wang, Zhengtao Yu[✉],
and Xiaohan Wang

School of Information Engineering and Automation,
Kunming University of Science and Technology, No.727 South Jingming Rd.,
Chenggong District, Kunming 650500, China
ztyu@hotmail.com

Abstract. We propose an automatically word alignment method of Chinese-Vietnamese based on bidirectional RNN and linguistic features. With the bidirectional RNN, we can obtain the context information of both forward and backward direction. Moreover, some bilingual features are also integrated. In the process of training model. The experiments show that the approach proposed outperform the previous method, and suggests that linguistic features and context information can effectively enhance the effect of word alignment.

Keywords: Word alignment · Chinese-Vietnamese
Bidirectional recurrent neural network · Linguistic features

1 Introduction

Word alignment a significant subtask in NLP, Which is to obtain the word correspondence between parallel sentence pairs during the alignment procedure. Word alignment is important to machine translation task, for example, the phrase table used in some MT model is usually extracted from the alignment result. Therefore, the quality of word alignment influences the performance of further tasks. The word alignment is always obtained automatically out of a set of parallel sentence pairs and the most classical word alignment methods include the IBM model and the Hidden Markov Model [2,12]. Yang et al., apply the context-dependent deep neural network to the Hidden Markov Model, which based on feed-forward neural networks, and the results reached the best level at the time [13]. There is an important hypothesis in the model based on feed-forward neural network: word alignment is based on first-order Markov dependence. Mo Yuanyuan proposed a novel method of Chinese-Vietnamese word alignment based on deep neural network (DNN) [14]. In this method, the Chinese-Vietnamese bilingual words

Y. Sun et al. (Eds.): ChineseCSCW 2018, CCIS 917, pp. 454–465, 2019.
https://doi.org/10.1007/978-981-13-3044-5_33

were transformed into the word vector as the input of the DNN model, meanwhile context information was integrated to construct the DNN-HMM words Alignment model. The accuracy and recall rate of this method are obviously improved compared with HMM model and IBM model 4, and the error rate of word alignment is greatly reduced.

In recent years, applying neural network especially recurrent neural network in NLP tasks has become a hot research topic [1,5–7,10], such as the alignment modeling based on feed-forward neural network (FFNN). Tamura et al. proposed a word alignment model based on the RNN [11], and also achieved good results. Akihiro Tamura et al. used Yang et al.'s method to generate word alignment as supervised training data and using Noise-Contrastive Estimation (NCE) [4,8] to train the model. However, in Akihiro Tamura et al.'s research, they only considered the effect of the information before the alignment position, and didn't take the effect of the backward alignment information into account. Moreover, studies have shown that linguistic features are also helpful in word alignment tasks. Considering the integration of alignment context and linguistic features, a bilingual word alignment model based on bidirectional RNN and linguistic feature function is proposed. In this method, the language structure difference is integrated into the loss function of bidirectional RNN training, and the alignment context information in both forward and backward directions can be captured by RNN cells. The proposed model indicate that the performances of our approaches are superior to others and both linguistic features and context information can help improve the word alignment performance.

2   Word Alignment Model Based on RNN

Akihiro Tamura et al. proposed an alignment model, which using an RNN to calculate the score, as shown in (1):

$$S_{NN}\left(a_1^J \middle| f_1^J, e_1^I\right) = \prod_{j=1}^{J} t_{RNN}\left(a_j \middle| a_1^{j-1}, f_j, e_{a_j}\right) \tag{1}$$

where f_1^J and e_1^I are two parallel sentences, a_1^J is the whole alignment information of the sentence pair, t_{RNN} is the score of a certain alignment a_j, f_j and e_{a_j} are words in the sentence pair respectively. The $j - th$ word a_j rely on all previous prediction a_1^{j-1}, which is similar to the FFNN model that used non-probabilstic score, our model show as Fig. 1. it contains three layers of lookup, hidden and output, each layer has weight matrices, which are L, $\left\{H^d, R^d, B_H^d\right\}$ and $\{O, B_O\}$ respectively. Each matrix in the hidden layer (H^d, R^d and B_H^d) depends on alignment, where d denotes the jump distance from a_{j-1} to a_j, and if d changes, the weight matrix set switch to another.

Alike the forword feed nertual network, when calculate the score of two words f_i, e_{a_j}, which are the input of the lookup layer and converting to word vector respectively, then input to the hidden layer with the form of vector concatenation. The hidden layer receive the output of the lookup layer. In the lookup

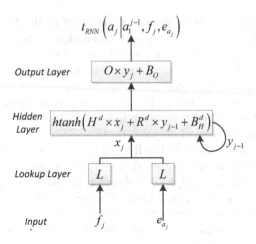

Fig. 1. The bidirectional RNN model [11]

layer, each of these words is converted to its word vector, and then the concatenation of the two vectors is fed to the hidden layer. The hidden layer receives the output of the lookup layer x_j and the output of the previous hidden layer y_{j-1}, and then computes the nonlinear relations between them. Note that unlike FFNN-based model, in this model, the weight matrices are related to the span between a_{j-1} and a_j. Besides, differ from the score in FFNN-based model consists of two components: lexical translation and alignment, the model uses only one single score. The hidden layer Y_i, and finnal output T_{RNN} as follows:

$$y_j = f\left(H^d \times x_j + R^d \times y_{j-1} + B_H^d\right) \tag{2}$$

$$t_{RNN} = O \times y_j + B_O \tag{3}$$

where H^d, R^d, B_H^d, O, and B_O are $|y_j| \times |x_j|$, $|y_j| \times |y_{j-1}|$, $|y_j| \times 1$, $1 \times |y_j|$, and 1×1 matrices, respectively. $f(x)$ is an activation function, which is a hard hyperbolic tangent, i.e., $h\tan(x)$, in this model.

In conclusion, the proposed model encodes all precious information, Therefore, better alignments can be obtained by taking advantage of the whole previous information, while FFNN-based model considers part of alignment context.

3   Chinese-Vietnamese Linguistic Differences

There are lots of differences between Chinese and Vietnamese, and here we describe two of the most significant differences. The first is the different position of modifier and central word between the two languages. In Chinese, the modifiers are usually appears before the central words, but in Vietnamese, the modifier is tend to be after the central word. The second is the differences between attributive and adverbial postposition in Vietnamese-Chinese. Mo et al. summarize and represent these two properties that integrated into [9].

3.1 Progressive Structure Feature

The progressive structure means the right branch, that is, the language level of the modifier after the central words. The inverse structure indicates the left branch, that is, the language level of the modifier before the central words. The sequence of Chinese and Vietnamese attributes and head word which most clearly manifestation of the correspondence between the bilingual. For the position of the attributive, which in Chinese is before the central language, while in Vietnamese the attributive after the central language. The sequence of multilayered incremental attributives in Chinese is: 1. predicate; 2. verb preposition; 3. adjective and other descriptive phrases; 4. adjective and descriptive noun without " 的 ".

The order of descriptive multi-layered attributive structure in Vietnamese is mirror image to Chinese. For example, The attributive order is 1-2-3-4 in the former, and 4-3-2-1 in the latter. In the chinese-vietnamese statement pairs, if the sequence of lexical markers in Chinese sentences is defined as $e = e_{1(n)} = eT_1, ..., eT_n$, the sequence of parts of speech in Vietnamese sentences is defined as $f = f_{1(m)} = fT_1, ..., fT_m$, where n, m represent the quantity of words in sentence pair e and f Then using the progressive structure of Vietnamese, Vietnamese broken up into two parts, $Q_f = fT_1, ..., fT_i, i \in \{i | 0 \leq i < m\}$ and $A_f = fT_j, ..., fT_m, j = i + 1$ Then, the probability of match between Chinese of vietnamese is expressed:

$$\Pr(A_f | e_i) = \frac{N(e_i, A_f)}{N(e_i)} \tag{4}$$

where $N(e_i)$ denotes the number of appearing of the former attribute tagger e_i, and $N(e_i, A_f)$ denotes the times e_i matched A_f of the latter sentences anterogradely. Then the anterograde structure model that the former descriptive attribute can match A_f of the latter anterogradely is defined:

$$P_r(A_f | \beta, e) = \prod_{i \in \beta} f(A_f | e_{l(i)}) \tag{5}$$

where l represents align correspondence, $\beta = \{i : e(i) \rightarrow A_f\}$ indicates the rage of the i-th word matched A_f progressively. Likewise, the progressive structure model is:

$$P_r(Q_f | \gamma, e) = \prod_{l \in \gamma} f(Q_f | e_{l(i)}) \tag{6}$$

3.2 Offset Feature of Word Sequence

Due to the scarcity of Chinese-Vietnamese corpus, In certain condition, the N-th word of the former may match that of the latter. In order to solve this problem, Mo Yuanyuan et al. proposed to add ChineseVietnamese bi-directional feature functions to reflect this statistical feature. Non-descriptive attribute is expressed as $\Pr(Q_f | Q_e)$, and descriptive attribute is expressed as $\Pr(A_f | A_e)$. For a source language descriptive or non-descriptive attribute, the probability of the position of the target language is:

$$P_r\left(Q_{fj}|Q_{ei}\right) = \frac{N\left(Q_{fj},Q_{ei}\right)}{N\left(Q_{ei}\right)} \tag{7}$$

where $N(Q_{ei})$ indicates the number of occurrences of the $i-th$ noun in the source language in the Chinese-Vietnamese bilingual corpus noun in the VietnameseChinese corpus. $N(Q_{fj},Q_{ei})$ indicates the number of times the $i-th$ $\Pr(Q_f|Q_t)$ of the former is aligned to the $j-th$ $\Pr(Q_f|Q_t)$ of the latter. Then the Chinese-Vietnamese non-descriptive attributive offset model is defined as follows:

$$P_r\left(Q_f|\beta,Q_e\right) = \prod_{l\in\beta} f\left(Q_{fl(j)}|Q_{el(i)}\right) \tag{8}$$

Where β represents the word alignment while the sentence pairs of Chinese-Vietnamese is a non-descriptive attribute In the same way, we can get the feature function of Vietnamese-Chinese bidirectional descriptive attribute:

$$P_r\left(A_f|\beta,A_e\right) = \prod_{l\in\beta} f\left(A_{fl(j)}|A_{el(i)}\right) \tag{9}$$

4   Word Alignment Model Based on Bidirectional RNN and Bilingual Features

The RNN model is capable of capturing the alignment context, and to enhance this ability, we try to apply bidirectional RNN to this model, so that new model can simultaneously capture the information on both directions. Moreover, we consider the constrain role of the Chinese-Vietnamese language feature in the alignment, and integrate the linguistic features into the loss function of the bidirectional RNN model.

4.1   Word Alignment Model Based on Bidirectional RNN

In the study of Tamura et al. [11], Only the alignment in front of the j-th position was considered. From the FFNN-based model, we can see that it is helpful to consider the alignment information after the alignment position for word alignment. Thus, we improve the model on the network structure, using an additional RNN to encode the alignment information after the current position in order to use this information to constrain the whole word alignment. In order to effectively use the forward and backward context information, we build a bidirectional RNN word alignment model, as shown in Fig. 2.

We use the RNN to encode the preceding alignment in our model that improved on the one presented by Akihiro Tamura et al. and use an output layer to calculate the currently alignment score, besides, we add a new set of RNNs to use the word alignment after the current position. For an alignment of

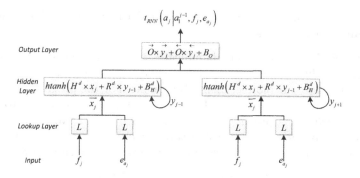

Fig. 2. The word alignment model based on bidirectional RNN

$j \rightarrow a_j$, f_j and e_{a_j} is converted to two different vectors $\overrightarrow{x_j}$ and $\overleftarrow{x_j}$ through two different lookup layers. Then the two vectors are fed to the RNN hidden layer, the former and the input from the forward arrival position cycle as the input of the forward RNN at time. The latter is the same as that calculated by the reverse arrival position Reverse RNN input at that moment. The two RNN hidden layers are taken together as input to the output layer, and the alignment of the scores is calculated by the output layer. The loss of training will be transmitted back to each RNN respectively to adjust their weight matrix. Bidirectional RNN on the word alignment and its two directions of word alignment the calculation shown in Fig. 3.

On the basis of the bidirectional RNN, the model can capture the alignment context more efficiently, which would contribute to the word alignment.

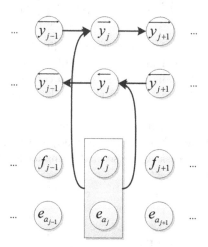

Fig. 3. A computing demonstration of the current word alignment

4.2 Word Alignment Model Based on Bidirectional RNN and Bilingual Features

The work of Mo Yuanyuan et al. indicates that linguistic features can help improve the quality of Vietnamese-Chinese word alignment. Here we also try to introduce this into our bidirectional RNN model. For the progressive structure of the lingual difference features of Chinese-Vietnamese, according to the (5) and (6), we define the probability of an alignment a_1^J of two sentences under the constraints of the progressive structure, which can be a combination of the descriptive attributive part and the non-descriptive as shown in (10):

$$P_r\left(a_1^J\,\middle|\,f_1^J,e_1^I\right) = \prod_{e\in A_e} P_r\left(A_f\,\middle|\,a_1^J,e\right) \prod_{e\in Q_e} P_r\left(Q_f\,\middle|\,a_1^J,e\right) \tag{10}$$

where A_e and Q_e represent the descriptive attributive and non-descriptive attributive parts of e_1^I respectively.

For the offset feature of word sequence of Chinese-Vietnamese, according to the formulas (8) and (9), we define the probability of an alignment a_1^J of two sentences under the offset feature of word sequence, which can be a combination of the descriptive attributive part and the non-descriptive as shown in (11):

$$P_r\left(a_1^J\,\middle|\,f_1^J,e_1^I\right) = P_r\left(Q_f\,\middle|\,a_1^J,Q_e\right)P_r\left(A_f\,\middle|\,a_1^J,A_e\right) \tag{11}$$

where A_e, A_f and Q_e, Q_f represent the descriptive attributive and non-descriptive attributive parts of e_1^I and f_1^J respectively. To integrate these features into our model, we choose to multiply the probabilistic feature functions to the loss function, and the new loss function can be defined as shown in (12).

$$S\left(a_1^J\,\middle|\,f_1^J,e_1^I\right) = \prod_{j=1}^{J} t_{RNN}\left(a_j\,\middle|\,f_j,e_{a_j}\right) \prod_{i\in H} P_{ri}\left(a_1^J\,\middle|\,f_1^J,e_1^I\right) \tag{12}$$

where H is the feature set and P_{ri} is the probability that a feature corresponds.

In this case, the linguistic features are actually used to correct the alignment score of the sentence. If the alignment satisfies a certain characteristic, the corresponding probability should be close to 1, that is, the feature is almost not corrected. If the alignment does not satisfy the characteristic, the corresponding probability should be close to 0, that is, the whole sentence score is closer to zero. This allows the wrong alignment to only adjust the network weight matrix slightly in the training process (because of the smaller loss), thus improving the network training effect.

5 Training

5.1 Unsupervised Training

Dyer et al. presented an unsupervised word alignment model based on contrastive estimation [3], taking the neighborhood of observed data as a pseudo-positive example. Introducing this idea, the loss function can be defined as (13).

$$loss\left(\theta\right) = \max\left\{0, 1 - \sum_{(f^+,e^+)\in T} E\left[s\left(a\left|f^+,e^+\right.\right)\right]\right.$$

$$\left. + \sum_{(f^+,e^-)\in\Omega} E\left[s\left(a\left|f^+,e^-\right.\right)\right]\right\} \quad (13)$$

where T is the training data set and Ω is a set of all possible alignments. $E\left(x\right)$ computes the expected value of the scores, e^+ and e^- denote the target sentence and the pseudo-target language sentence respectively. However, considering all possible alignment, the computing is prohibitively expensive. To reduce computation, Akihiro Tamura et al. employ NCE, which uses randomly sampled sentences from all target language sentences. In their work, the function show as (14).

$$loss\left(\theta\right) = \sum_{f^+\in T} \max\left\{0, 1 - E\left[s\left(a\left|f^+,e^+\right.\right)\right]\right.$$

$$\left. + \frac{1}{N}\sum_{e^-} E\left[s\left(a\left|f^+,e^-\right.\right)\right]\right\} \quad (14)$$

N indicates the count of pseudo-target language sentences per source sentence.

5.2 Bidirectional Alignment

The RNN-based model is actually a HMM-based word alignment model, so it is asymmetric of bidirectional. Previous studies have shown that it is helpful to consider the results in two directions for word alignment. Akihiro Tamura et al. used a method of consistency constraint, which introduced a penalty term to represent the difference in the search layer parameters in both directions. The training objectives are as follows: Inspired by previous work, we propose a learning model with agreenment constraint, which enforces in word embeddings by bidirections, a penalty term is introduced to represent the difference of the lookup level parameters in two directions, shown as follow:

$$\arg\min\left\{loss\left(\theta_{FE}\right) + \alpha\left\|\theta_{L_{EF}} - \theta_{L_{FE}}\right\|\right\} \quad (15)$$

$$\arg\min\left\{loss\left(\theta_{EF}\right) + \alpha\left\|\theta_{L_{FE}} - \theta_{L_{EF}}\right\|\right\} \quad (16)$$

where θ_{FE} and θ_{EF} denotes the weights of layers in both alignment direction, θ_L denotes weights of the lookup layer, and α refers to the strength of the agreement.

6 Experiment and Result Analysis

6.1 Experimental Data

We built Chinese-Vietnamese parallel sentence pairs, which collected by news, legal instruments, contracts and other texts. We use GIZA ++ to obtain "rough alignment" results on Chinese-Vietnamese parallel sentence pairs and use the "rough alignment" results as unsupervised training data; use manual alignment as supervised training data. A brief description of the data is shown in Table 1.

Table 1. Corpus statistics

Data Set			Vietnamese	Chinese
GIZA++ generated	Train	Sentences	4523	
		Words	54276	52368
		Vocabulary	2134	2315
	Dev	Sentences	380	
		Words	3369	3687
		Vocabulary	1023	1470
	Test	Sentences	450	
		Words	13673	15978
		Vocabulary	1887	1936
Manually aligned	Train	Sentences	1236	
		Words	13210	11389
		Vocabulary	1810	1728
	Dev	Sentences	120	
		Words	1445	1526
		Vocabulary	512	654
	Test	Sentences	100	
		Words	1346	1412
		Vocabulary	479	545

We use ICTCLAS to segment and annotate the test examples and develop examples of Chinese sentences, in Vietnamese sentences using VH.HUS.NIP toolkit for Vietnamese word segmentation.

6.2   Evaluation Terms

In terms of evaluation, we use Precision, Recall, F-Measure and AER as the word alignment evaluation criteria, in order to assess the results of unsupervised training and supervised training. Calculated as follows:

$$precision = \frac{|A \cap P|}{|A|} \tag{17}$$

$$recall = \frac{|A \cap S|}{|A|} \tag{18}$$

$$F - Measure = \frac{2 \times precision \times recall}{precision + recall} \times 100\% \tag{19}$$

$$AER = 1 - \frac{|A \cap S| + |A \cap P|}{|A| + |S|} \tag{20}$$

where A is the alignment results for evaluating, S and P are results manually-aligned as a fixed set and an indeterminate set respectively.

6.3 Experiments Result and Evaluation

The following model was selected as the baseline: the IBM model 4 (GIZA ++), the RNN-based model [11], and the log-linear model of with linguistic features [9]. And the Precision, Recall, F-Measure and AER of each model are shown in Table 2.

Table 2. The experimental results for word alignment

Alignment method	Precision(%)	Recall(%)	F-Measure	AER
IBM4	45.24	43.28	44.24	0.38
RNN	45.83	44.26	45.03	0.32
Multi-feature Log-Linear model	46.14	44.48	45.29	0.29
Bidirectional RNN	47.01	45.03	45.99	0.25
Bidirectional RNN with linguistic features	47.99	45.97	46.96	0.21

The result was indicative of the precision and recall rate are increased after considering the history of reverse alignment and the bilingual language, and the AER is decreased. This shows that the following alignment information and bilingual language features are helpful for word alignment.

7   Conclusion

We propose an improval RNN model of word-aligned, which introduces the encoding of the context information in the RNN and merges lingual difference features. The experiment is based on IBM model 4 and the RNN model proposed by Akihiro Tamura et al., and the logarithmic linear model of fusion language features proposed by Mo Yuanyuan et al. The experimental results show that the improved model outperforms the original RNN word alignment considers the above information, and integrated features into improve the word alignment effect.

Acknowledgment. This work was supported by the National Natural Science Foundation of China (Grant Nos.61761026, 61732005, 61672271, 61472168), the Natural Science Fundation of Yunnan Province (Grant No.2018FB104), Innovation Talent Fund For Technology of Yunnan Province (Grant No.2014HE001).

References

1. Auli, M., Galley, M., Quirk, C., Zweig, G.: Joint language and translation modeling with recurrent neural networks. In: Proceedings of the Conference on Empirical Methods in Natural Language Processing (EMNLP), Seattle, Washington, USA, pp. 1044–1054 (2013)
2. Brown, P.F., Pietra, V.J.D., Pietra, S.A.D., Mercer, R.L.: The mathematics of statistical machine translation: parameter estimation. Comput. Linguist. **19**(2), 263–311 (1993)
3. Dyer, C., Clark, J.H., Lavie, A., Smith, N.A.: Unsupervised word alignment with arbitrary features. In: Proceedings of the 49th Annual Meeting of the Association for Computational Linguistics: Human Language Technologies, Portland, Oregon, USA, pp. 409–419 (2011)
4. Gutmann, M., Hyvärinen, A.: Noise-contrastive estimation: a new estimation principle for unnormalized statistical models. In: Proceedings of the Thirteenth International Conference on Artificial Intelligence and Statistics (AISTATS 2010), Chia Laguna Resort, Sardinia, Italy, pp. 297–304 (2010)
5. Kalchbrenner, N., Blunsom, P.: Recurrent continuous translation models. In: Proceedings of the Conference on Empirical Methods in Natural Language Processing (EMNLP), Seattle, Washington, USA, pp. 1700–1709 (2013)
6. Mikolov, T., Karafiát, M., Burget, L., Černocký, J., Khudanpur, S.: Recurrent neural network based language model. In: Proceedings of INTERSPEECH 2010 11th Annual Conference of the International Speech Communication Association, Makuhari, Chiba, Japan, pp. 1045–1048 (2010)
7. Mikolov, T., Zweig, G.: Context dependent recurrent neural network language model. In: In Proceedings of IEEE Spoken Language Technology Workshop (SLT), Miami, Florida, USA, pp. 234–239 (2012)
8. Mnih, A., Teh, Y.W.: A fast and simple algorithm for training neural probabilistic language models. In: Proceedings of the 29th International Conference on Machine Learning (ICML 2012), Edinburgh, Scotland, UK, pp. 419–426 (2012)
9. Mo, Y., Guo, J., Yu, Z., Luo, L., Gao, S.: A bilingual word alignment algorithm of Vietnamese-Chinese based on feature constraint. Int. J. Mach. Learn. Cybern. **6**(4), 537–543 (2015)
10. Sundermeyer, M., Oparin, I., Gauvain, J.L., Freiberg, B., Schlüter, R., Ney, H.: Comparison of feedforward and recurrent neural network language models. In: Proceedings of IEEE International Conference on Acoustics Speech and Signal (ICASSP), Vancouver, BC, Canada, pp. 8430–8434 (2013)
11. Tamura, A., Watanabe, T., Sumita, E.: Recurrent neural networks for word alignment model. In: Proceedings of the Annual Meeting of the Association for Computational Linguistics (ACL), Baltimore, MD, USA, pp. 1470–1480 (2014)
12. Vogel, S., Ney, H., Tillmann, C.: Hmm-based word alignment in statistical translation. In: Proceedings of International Conference on Computational Linguistics (COLING), Copenhagen, Denmark, pp. 836–841 (1996)

13. Yang, N., Liu, S., Li, M., Zhou, M., Yu, N.: Word alignment modeling with context dependent deep neural network. In: Proceedings of the Annual Meeting of the Association for Computational Linguistics (ACL), Sofia, Bulgaria, pp. 166–175 (2013)
14. Yuanyuan, M., Jianyi, G., Zhengtao, Y., Cunli, M., Yitong, N.: A bilingual word alignment method of Vietnamese-Chinese based on deep neural network. J. Shandong Univ. (Nat. Sci.) **51**(1), 77–83 (2016)

Short Papers

Facial Expression Recognition Algorithm Based on Equal Probability Symbolization Entropy

Fa Zheng[1,2], Bin Hu[1,3(✉)], and Xiangwei Zheng[1,2]

[1] School of Information Science and Engineering, Shandong Normal University,
Jinan 250014, China
`1486756562@qq.com`, `binhu@sdnu.edu.cn`,
`xwzhengcn@163.com`
[2] Shandong Provincial Key Laboratory for Distributed Computer Software
Novel Technology, Jinan 250014, China
[3] School of Information Science and Engineering, Lanzhou University,
Lanzhou 730000, China

Abstract. Electroencephalogram (EEG) records brain activity using electro-physiological markers and is a comprehensive representation of the dynamic activity of human brain neurons. EEG can be used to study human facial expression recognition. In fact, entropy values of EEG can fully reflect changes in facial expressions. This paper improves the sample entropy and the permutation entropy by introducing equal probability symbolization and applies the equal probability symbolization entropy to facial expression recognition. The original permutation entropy, sample entropy and equal-probability symbolization entropy values are calculated for the three expressions of anger, fear and happiness. The results demonstrate that equal-probability symbolization entropy can distinguish human facial expressions clearly and accurately.

Keywords: Facial expression recognition · EEG signal
Equal probability symbolization entropy

1 Introduction

In recent years, with the continuous advancement of technology, human–computer interaction and artificial intelligence have been applied to many fields. The ability to recognize human emotions of computer will bring a better user experience.

The role of emotion is ubiquitous in people's daily life and work. Emotion is defined as the human response to emergencies with short duration, which is the result of the interaction of language, physiology, behavior, and neural mechanisms [1]. The realization of the automatic recognition of emotion is important in the physical and psychological fields, and it is also an inevitable requirement for the development of artificial intelligence. In fact, EEG is a very complex nonlinear signal and it has a very wide range of nonlinear dynamic characteristics. This opinion has been widely accepted by the academic community [2]. At the same time, different emotion fluctuations generate corresponding EEG signals.

© Springer Nature Singapore Pte Ltd. 2019
Y. Sun et al. (Eds.): ChineseCSCW 2018, CCIS 917, pp. 469–477, 2019.
https://doi.org/10.1007/978-981-13-3044-5_34

In fact, human brain controls human behavior and emotional perception. Human brain is the most complex information processing system in the human body. It consists of a large number of neurons and brain regions connected to each other through the role of each other to complete the various functions of the brain [3]. EEG signal is the summation of the synaptic electrical activity of cerebral cortical neurons. As a special physiological signal, it contains a large number of physiological and pathological information [4]. At the same time, the change of emotion will inevitably affect people's decision-making and communication in different degrees. Therefore, it is of great significance to analyze human emotion changes by studying EEG signal. This paper calculates and analyzes the equal probability symbolic entropy feature of EEG signal and fully exploits the multi-scale features of EEG to determine the corresponding facial expression.

2   Related Work

In recent years, a lot of work has been done in the field of sentiment calculation and many achievements have been made. Nicolaou applied permutation entropy to analyze EEG signals and classify human brain labor [5]. Jiang studied emotion characteristics based on the wave energy of P-QRS-T. The results show that this feature is closely related to changes in emotional state, especially under positive emotions such as happiness [6]. Li contrasted three features of EEG sample entropy, approximate entropy and Hurst index under positive and negative emotion states. He found that sample entropy is more suitable for facial expression recognition, especially in the study of facial expression recognition [7]. Cai studied on the speech signals and mainly researched on emotional speech recognition analysis and Putonghua sentiment analysis [8]. Guo did experiments on facial expression recognition for children with autism and revealed the main factors affecting their facial expression recognition. It provided experimental evidence for effective intervention and improvement of facial expression recognition ability of children with autism [9]. Ye studied the facial expressions of children with mental retardation from 7 to 15 years old who are happy, sad, afraid, and angry. He explored the recognition characteristics of facial expressions of mentally retarded children [10]. At present, people's understanding of objective things will always be accompanied by the recognition of facial expressions such as anger, sadness, fear, panic, through human physiological signals such as brain electrical signals [11]. Gao studied that EEG is a special physiological signal, rich in physiological and pathological information and widely used in clinical diagnosis and laboratory research [12].

This paper mainly focuses on the recognition of human facial expressions. We apply the features of equal probability symbolization to improve the sample entropy and sorting entropy so as to accurately and rapidly distinguish multiple emotions.

3   Facial Expression Recognition Algorithm Based on Equal Probability Symbolization Entropy

Permutation entropy (PE) is widely used in EEG analysis because the computation is fast and easy. Sample entropy (SE) is often used because of its high accuracy and its physical meaning reflects time series. Therefore, this paper combines the advantages of the two algorithms and proposes an equal probability symbolization entropy algorithm and verifies the effectiveness of the proposed algorithm in emotional electroencephalogram analysis.

3.1 Equal Probability Symbolization Entropy

The permutation entropy is used to symbolize the signal while the sample entropy is used when calculating the reconstructed components. The efficiency and accuracy of the calculation are considered. The specific process of equal probability symbolization entropy is as follows:

Step 1: Set the time sequence $\{x_i\}$ $i = 1, 2, 3,..., n$. The sequence x_1, x_2, x_n is sorted in ascending order, namely $X_{(k_1)} \leq X_{(k_2)} \leq X_{(k_3)} \leq \cdots \leq X_{(k_n)}$.

Where $X_{(k_1)}$ is the minimum value, $X_{(k_n)}$ is the maximum value, and k_1 and k_2 are the sequence numbers after sorted. The sorted sequence number is divided into L and the sequence number corresponding to the segmentation point is represented by n_1, n_2, n_3.

$$N_j = \frac{n - n_{j-1}}{L - (j - 1)} \quad j = 1, 2, ..., L - 1 \tag{1}$$

n_j is the segmentation point that satisfies condition 1, and the segmented sequence may not satisfy the second condition. There are the same values near the segmentation points, and they are not necessarily equal after symbolization. The following processing is required. j_1 and j_m are the first and last corresponding time sequence numbers of the same data respectively.

$$N_j = \begin{cases} n_{j1} - 1, & j \leq \frac{1+m}{2} \\ n_{j2}, & j > \frac{1+m}{2} \end{cases} \tag{2}$$

After all the segmentation point numbers have been determined and then they are symbolized: $s_{ki} = s_j$, $j = 1, 2,...L$, $i = 1, 2,..., n$, $n_{j-1} + 1 \leq i \leq n_j$.

Therefore, the symbolized sequence is obtained. When $m \neq 1$ and $j_1 \neq j$ or $j_1 \neq j$, the symbol may not be equally divided. When $n \gg L$, the number of occurrences of different characters in the reconstructed symbol sequence can be achieved equal or substantially equal.

Step 2: The converted symbol sequence is $s = \{s_{(i)}\}$, $i = 1, 2, 3,..., n$, The sequence $s_{(1)}, s_{(2)},..., s_{(N)}$ is sequenced into m-dimensional vectors, i.e.

$$s_m(i) = [s_{(i)}, s_{(i+1)}, \cdots s_{(i+m-1)}], \quad 1 \leq i \leq N - m + 1 \tag{3}$$

For each $1 \leq i \leq N - m$, count the number equal to $s_m(i)$ as n_i^m and calculate the ratio of the total number of vectors $N - m - 1$, i.e.

$$B_i^m = \frac{n_i^m}{N - m - 1} \tag{4}$$

Among them, $1 \leq j \leq N - m$, $i \neq j$. Calculate the average of B_i^m versus i,

$$B^m = \frac{1}{N-m}\sum_{i=1}^{N-m} B_i^m \qquad (5)$$

For the $m + 1$ point vector,

$$A_i^m = \frac{n_i^{m+1}}{N-m-1} \qquad (6)$$

Among them, $1 \leq j \leq N - m$, $i \neq j$. Calculate the average of A_i^m versus i,

$$A^m = \frac{1}{N-m}\sum_{i=1}^{N-m} A_i^m \qquad (7)$$

Step 3: The entropy of the sequence is:

$$ESampEn(m) = lim_{N\to\infty}\left\{-\ln\left[\frac{A^m}{B^m}\right]\right\} \qquad (8)$$

When N is a finite value and it is approximately equal to:

$$ESampEn(m,N) = -\ln\left[\frac{A^m}{B^m}\right] \qquad (9)$$

4   Algorithm Description

4.1   The Specific Steps of the Algorithm Are as Follows

Suppose $\{x_{(i)}, i = 1, 2,\dots, n\}$ is a time series.

Step 1: Classify and iterate the processed average raw data. The artifact-eliminated data is loaded using the *Load* function. Different points are used as the basis for data iterations; we start intercepting 1000 meaningful points from marker point according to the points corresponding to different markers, which are superimposed and averaged. The data after processing is separately stored in the *.mat* file using the *Save* function provided in *Matlab*.

Step 2: Load data from different expression data into *GoarseGrain.m* and average each t data and store it in a matrix. Calculate the division scale using the circulation mechanism 1–25 and select the most suitable division scale to store in *D1.mat*.

Step 3: Construct the function of permutation entropy and calculate the permutation entropy values of fear, happiness, and anger. The resulting data is stored in Excel using the *Save* function.

Step 4: Construct the function of equal probability symbolization entropy. We calculate the equal probability symbolization entropy values of fear, happiness, and anger according to formula (8). The resulting data is stored in Excel using the *Save* function.

Step 5: Analyze the data and judge the difference in different expressions based on the entropy

Step 6: Apply the *Draw* function to draw different expressions entropy images on different canvases using the *figure* function and perform comparative analysis. The images were used to distinguish the three expressions.

5 Experimental Results and Analysis

5.1 Experimental Data

Nineteen university students participated in the experiment as paid participants (9 males and 10 females, with an average age of 24 years). Five subjects were excluded due to too many artifacts or insufficient stacking times. Therefore, a total of 14 subjects (7 male and 7 female) were analyzed.

Experimental materials were selected from the Chinese Facial Affective Picture System (CFAPS). We selected 40 pictures (half of men and women) of fear, happiness, and anger face emotions with a degree of recognition above 70%. 120 pictures of calm face emotions (half of men and women) were used as filling materials.

In this experiment, the original EEG data is divided according to the markers of different emotions, and the original EEG data was overlaid and averaged; the premise of the iterative average was that the neural activities related to the time-locked events were the same for each trial. The superposition of signals is a process of non-specific EEG. After the superimposed average, 66 data difference are reduced and each derivative data contain 1000 valid data points.

5.2 The Influence of Scale Factors on Experimental Results

The algorithmic process of equalizing symbolic entropy mainly involves the selection of three parameter values, namely phase vector dimension m, division scale L, and sequence length N. In general, the vector dimension m is chosen as 1 or 2, which makes the equal probability symbolization entropy more reasonable statistically; the sequence length N determines the statistical validity of the entropy calculation.

After equal probability symbolization, the phase space is essentially divided into $L*m$ sub-regions, so when $N \gg L*m$ is satisfied, the statistical validity of the entropy calculation can be guaranteed; and with different divisions L, the resulting value will appear. The symbol interval is related to the distribution of the interval density after the original sequence is sorted. The symbol interval of the densely distributed area is small, and the symbol interval of the sparse area is large. In general, while guaranteeing sufficient amplitude domain resolution, it is also necessary to ensure that the minimum symbol interval can't be smaller than the known noise amplitude, L cannot be too small or too large.

Therefore, it will be considered to use different division scale L for analysis. As the scale L changes, the ESE signals of the fear and anger expressions change in their ESE values differently. Then, the 4th, 5th, and 6th channel ESE values were compared and analyzed. The length of the time series was 1000 and the division scale L was 1–25.

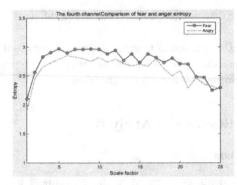

Fig. 1. Comparison of ESE entropy changes of fear and anger expression for the fourth channel.

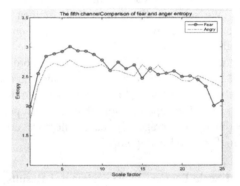

Fig. 2. Comparison of ESE entropy changes of fear and anger expression for the fifth channel.

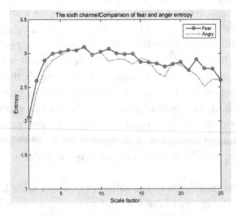

Fig. 3. Comparison of ESE entropy changes of fear and anger expression for the sixth channel.

After the above experiments, it is not difficult to see that under different electrodes, the division scale L is selected differently, which will result in differences in expression recognition. As shown in Fig. 1, when L is greater than 17, the entropy values of the anger and fear expression no longer follow the anger entropy value less than the fear entropy value. Similarly, it can be obtained that L is greater than 14 in Fig. 2, and it is a same situation when L is greater than 6 in Fig. 3. Therefore, in order to more accurately and clearly to compare the changes of the equi-probative entropy values under the three kinds of expressions, in the following experiments, the case where the division scale L is equal to 5 is selected.

5.3   Expression Recognition Analysis

In this experiment, we used the traditional permutation entropy method and the new equal probability entropy method to compare the three kinds of expressions. In order to more accurately verify the advantages of equal probability symbolic entropy, we set the vector dimension m to 2, the sequence length N to 1000, and the division scale L to 5 according to the experimental parameters discussed above, and calculated under the 66 electrode respectively. The entropy of permutation entropy and equal probability symbolization entropy are showed in Figs. 4 and 5.

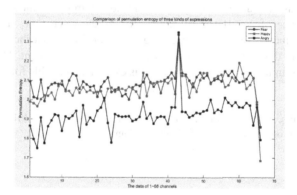

Fig. 4. The original permutation entropy for 66 channels.

It can be seen from Fig. 4 that based on the original permutation entropy method, there is no obvious numerical difference in the ranking entropy, and three expressions of anger, happiness, and fear cannot be identified. As can be seen from Fig. 5, the equal probability symbolization entropy values of the three kinds of expressions have obvious differences, and three facial expressions can be clearly and accurately identified.

By comparing the two entropy values, it is not difficult to find that equal-probability symbolization entropy can more accurately identify the three kinds of expressions, and has a significant improvement over the original permutation entropy method.

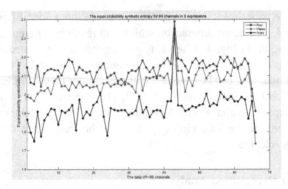

Fig. 5. The equal probability symbolization entropy for 66 channels.

6 Conclusion

In this paper, we apply the non-linear signal processing method, namely equal probability symbolization entropy, to distinguish different emotions and calculate the equal probability symbolization of each emotion. The experimental results show that the equal probability entropy algorithm can more accurately and quickly recognize human facial expressions. Equal-probability symbolization entropy method can effectively resist the influence of non-stationary mutations. At the same time, this method can eliminate the influence of the original sequence probability distribution and simply reflect the symbol dynamics of the time series information increment. This method has clear physical meaning and is easy and fast. It is extremely valuable for the feedback of EEG signals with high real-time requirements.

Acknowledgements. National Natural Science Foundation of China (61373149) and the Taishan Scholars Program of Shandong Province, China.

References

1. Fox, E.: An integration of cognitive and neuroscientific approaches, 16–17 (2008)
2. Hosseini, M.B.: Emotion recognition method using entropy analysis of EEG signals. Int. J. Image Graph. Signal Process. **3**(5), 30–36 (2011)
3. Su, J.X.: Emotion Recognition Based on EEG Signals. Nanjing University of Posts and Telecommunications, Nanjing (2015)
4. Gao, L.P., Shao, B., Zhu, L., Lu, T., Gu, N.: Maintaining time and space consistencies in hybrid engineering environments: framework and algorithms. Comput. Ind. **59**(9), 894–904 (2008)
5. Nicolaou, N., Georgiou, J.: Permutation entropy, a new feature for Brain-Computer Interfaces. In: Biomedical Circuits and Systems Conference, pp. 49–52. IEEE (2010)
6. Cowie, R., Douglascowie, E., Tsapatsoulis, N., et al.: Emotion recognition in human–computer interaction. IEEE Signal Process. Mag. **18**(1), 32–80 (2002)
7. Zhang, Y.M., Lin, J.Z., Wu, B.M., Yan, B.W.: Single guided EEG sleep staging algorithm based on EEG rhythm sample entropy. Electronics World **24**, 189–190 (2016)

8. Wen, W.H.: Research on emotion recognition method based on physiological signal. Southwest University (2010)
9. Chen, J.H., Li, Z., Qian, K.X.: Preliminary emotion recognition based on multiple physiological signal. Biomed. Eng. Res. **03**, 141–146 (2006)
10. Xie, J.L.: Multi-scale entropy algorithm and its application in emotional EEG recognition. Yanshan University (2016)
11. Yao, W.B., Liu, T.B., Dai, J.F.: Multi-scale permutation entropy analysis of EEG signals. Acta Physica Sinica. **63**(7)
12. Gao, L.P., Gu, N.: Supporting Semantic Maintenance of Complex Undo Operations in Replicated Co-AutoCAD Environments, 22–24 April 2009, Santiago, Chile, pp. 84–89 (2009)

Automatic Sleep Stage Classification Based on LSTM

Peiying Shi[1,2], Xiangwei Zheng[1,2(✉)], Ping Du[1,2], and Feng Yuan[3]

[1] School of Information Science and Engineering, Shandong Normal University,
Ji'Nan 250358, Shandong Province, People's Republic of China
xwzhengcn@163.com
[2] Shandong Provincial Key Laboratory for Distributed Computer Software
Novel Technology, Ji'Nan 250358, People's Republic of China
[3] Key Laboratory of TCM Data Cloud Service in Universities of Shandong,
Shandong Management University, Ji'Nan 250357, People's Republic of China

Abstract. Sleep stage classification is closely related to human health and plays an effective role in sleep disorders diagnose. At present, the accuracy rate of conventional automatic sleep staging system is still not high, and there is still a large space for improvement. To solve the above problems, this paper proposed an automatic sleep stage classification method based on the Long Short-Term Memory (LSTM) and fuzzy entropy. We firstly adopt fuzzy entropy to extract the feature from electroencephalography (EEG) signals, then these features are put into the designed LSTM to carry out the automatic sleep stage classification and attain the final sleep stages. To verify the validity of our experiment, we tested it on public datasets called ISRUC_Sleep. The results demonstrate that this method improves the classification accuracy of sleep stages.

Keywords: Deep learning · Recurrent neural networks
Sleep stage classification · Long Short-Term memory · Fuzzy entropy

1 Introduction

Sleep as a necessary process of life is an important part of the body's recovery, integration and consolidation of memory, and it is an indispensable part of health [1]. Increased stress in modern society and unhealthy lifestyles have led to large number of sleep disorders [2]. In order to diagnose sleep-related diseases, the first thing to solve is the classification of sleep stages [3]. The crucial step in sleep stage classification is polysomnographic (PSG). Those PSG recordings include an electroencephalography (EEG), electrooculogram (EOG) and electromyogram (EMG) [4]. PSG recordings are divided into 30 s epochs. All sleep stages are artificially classified by experts, which have certain subjectivity and require a lot of time. So, LSTM and fuzzy entropy were used for sleep stage classification in this paper. We adopt American Academy of Sleep Medicine (AASM) criterion and categorized sleep data into five stages which are wake (W), non-rapid eye movement (N1, N2, N3) and rapid eye movement (REM) [5]. Staging according to different frequencies of the signal [6].

Y. Sun et al. (Eds.): ChineseCSCW 2018, CCIS 917, pp. 478–486, 2019.
https://doi.org/10.1007/978-981-13-3044-5_35

This paper consists of the following parts. In Sect. 2, we detail the proposed LSTM architecture with fuzzy entropy for sleep stage classification. In Sect. 3, we compare it with other classification algorithms. The last section concludes our paper.

2 Proposed Method

The automatic phase staging of sleep state is divided into three parts according to the process: signal preprocessing, feature extraction, and automatic classification. The specific steps of the automatic sleep stage classification are shown in Fig. 1. First, the artifacts have a bad influence on the final sleep stage classification, so we need to do some preprocessing work [7]. Subsequently, we use a fuzzy entropy algorithm to calculate the denoized EEG signal and obtain the entropy value of the EEG signal. Finally, all the feature parameters are input into the LSTM classifier, and the sleep stage is classified into W, N1, N2, N3 and R.

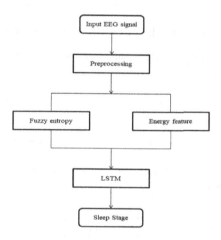

Fig. 1. Flow Chart of Automatic Sleep Stage Classification

2.1 Fuzzy Entropy

Entropy can measure the probability of a new pattern generated by time series, that is, entropy can characterize the complexity of the signal [8]. When people are in different sleep stages, the complexity of EEG is not the same, so we can use entropy to monitor the sleep depth [9]. The fuzzy entropy value transitions steadily with the parameter transformation, and has the relative consistency of sample entropy and the processing characteristics of short datasets, which overcomes the limitations of sample entropy definition [10]. Therefore, this paper uses fuzzy entropy to extract features of EEG sleep staging. The principle of fuzzy entropy algorithm is as follows.

(1) Define the sampling sequence of N points as $\{u(i):1 \leq i \leq N\}$;
(2) Reconstruct a sequence of m-dimensional vectors in sequence:

$$X_i^m = \{u(i), u(i+1), \ldots, u(i+m-1)\} - u_0(i), (i = 1, \ldots, N-m) \quad (1)$$

where $\{u(i), u(i+1), \ldots, u(i+m-1)\}$ is the value of consecutive u from the ith point, $u_0(i)$ is the mean value.

$$u_0(i) = \frac{1}{m} \sum_{j=0}^{m-1} u(i+1) \quad (2)$$

(3) The distance d_{ij}^m between the vector X_i^m and vector X_j^m is defined as the largest difference between the corresponding elements of the two:

$$d_{ij}^m = d\left[X_i^m, X_j^m\right] = max_{k \in (0, m-1)}\{|u(i+k) - u_0(i) - (u(j+k) - u_0(j))|\}$$
$$(i, j = 1, \ldots, N-m), j \neq i \quad (3)$$

(4) Define the vector X_i^m by The fuzzy function, and the similarity of X_j^m is $D_{ij}^m = \exp\left(-\left(d_{ij}^m\right)^n / r\right)$, where n and r are the gradient and width of the exponential function boundary.
(5) Define functions:

$$O^m(n, r) = \frac{1}{N-m} \sum_{i=1}^{N-m} \left[\frac{1}{N-m-1} \sum_{j=1, j \neq i}^{N-m} D_{ij}^m\right] \quad (4)$$

(6) Repeat steps (2)–(5) to regenerate a set of m + 1 dimensional vectors in sequence, defining the function:

$$O^{m+1}(n, r) = \frac{1}{N-m} \sum_{i=1}^{N-m} \left[\frac{1}{N-m-1} \sum_{j=1, j \neq i}^{N-m} D_{ij}^{m+1}\right] \quad (5)$$

(7) Define the fuzzy entropy as:

$$\text{Fuzzy En}(m, n, r) = \lim_{N=\infty}\left[\ln O^m(n, r) - \ln O^{m+1}(n, r)\right] \quad (6)$$

The fuzzy entropy values of C3-A2, C4-A1, O1-A2, LOC-A2 and X1 are calculated by using the measured sleep EEG data in 5 cases. When calculating Fuzzy En $(m, n\ r, N)$, the length of the short data N = 1000, the embedding dimension $m = 2$, $n = 2$, and $r = 0.25$SD(Standard Deviation). The entropy of the sleep EEG after denoising is extracted. Table 1 shows the values of fuzzy entropy.

Table 1. Fuzzy entropy values of different sleep stage

Subjects	W	N1	N2	N3	R
1	0.8957	0.6569	0.5683	0.5065	0.7683
2	0.7377	0.5879	0.6201	0.6203	0.7573
3	0.8310	0.6201	0.555	0.4224	0.7000
4	1.0430	0.6135	0.5498	0.4571	0.7371
5	0.8968	0.4837	0.5589	0.5244	0.6897

2.2 LSTM for ASSC

As a means of simulating biological neural networks, neural networks are most suitable for the identification of multi-class patterns. Therefore, it can be used in automatic sleep stage classification. We use the famous LSTM as a repetitive neural classifier to classify human sleep stages. LSTM is well suited for dealing with problems that are highly relevant to time series [11]. LSTM is applied to perform the information processing. Figure 2 shows the novel LSTM structure is designed specifically for sleep staging.

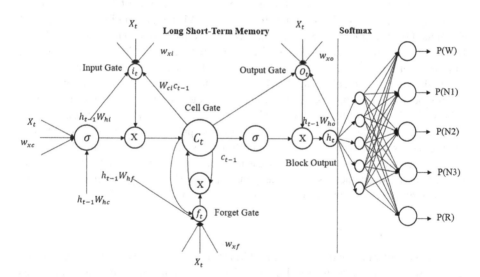

Fig. 2. The architecture of Long Short-Term Memory

The data after feature extraction is put into the LSTM for classification. After LSTM, the last fully connected layer dimension as input is classified by softmax. Softmax functions are mainly used for multi-classification problems. The output number of the softmax layer is 5. LSTM proceeds by the following functions. Most of the σ is the sigmoid function, and the σ_c and σ_h is tanh function.

$$i_t = \sigma_i(x_t W_{xi} + h_{t-1} W_{hi} + w_{ci} \odot c_{t-1} + b_i)$$

$$c_t = f_t \odot c_{t-1} + i_t \odot \sigma_c(x_t W_{xc} + h_{t-1} W_{hc} + b_c)$$

$$f_t = \sigma_c(x_t W_{xf} + h_{t-1} W_{hf} \odot c_{t-1} + b_f)$$

$$o_t = \sigma_o(x_t W_{xo} + h_{t-1} W_{ho} + w_{co} \odot c_t + b_o)$$

$$h_t = o_t \odot \sigma_h(c_t)$$

3   Experimental Results and Analysis

3.1   Experimental Data

To prove the robustness of our method, we test it on a public sleep datasets called ISRUC-SLEEP [12]. The datasets contain the overnight records of 126 subjects. Each recording contains four EEG channels (C3_A2, C4_A1, F3_A2 and F4-A1), four EOG channels (O1-A2, LOC_A2, ROC-A1 and O2-A1), three EMG channels (X1, X2, and X3) and the file with detailed events. We use the recordings of 20 subjects for testing and the recordings of the remaining 106 subjects for training and validation.

In the process of collecting EEG, due to the influence of the electromagnetic environment, the recorder itself, the subject itself, etc., a lot of noise and interference will inevitably be introduced. Those artifacts do really has a bad influence on the final sleep stage classification, so we need to do some preprocessing work. The preprocessing results are showed in Fig. 3. We both plot a sleep data of 5 s with 11 channels. It can be clearly see that our preprocessing work really remove the artifacts while keeping the basic characteristics of the signal unchanged at the same time, which will have a good effect on the sleep stages classification task.

3.2   Performance Metrics

To evaluate performance of proposed LSTM architecture, we used accuracy, precision, recall, f-score and loss defined in Eqs. (7)–(11). The evaluation metrics are defined as follows.

(1) Precision. It is the ratio of all "correctly searched (TP)" to all "actually retrieved (TP + FP)".

$$\text{precision} = \frac{\text{TP(True Positives)}}{\text{TP} + \text{FP(False Positives)}} \tag{7}$$

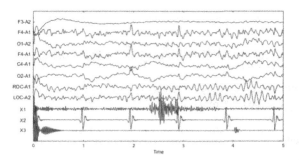

(a)   Data before preprocessing

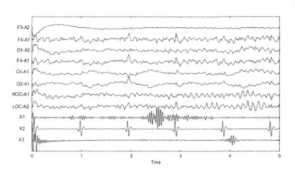

(b)   Data after preprocessing

Fig. 3. Data before and after processing.

(2)   Recall. It calculates the proportion of all "correctly searched (TP)" accounts for all "ought to retrieve (TP + FN)".

$$recall = \frac{TP}{TP + FN(\text{False Negatives})} \tag{8}$$

(3)   F-score. The harmonic mean of the exact value and recall rate.

$$f\text{-score} = \frac{2TP}{2TP + FP + FN} \tag{9}$$

(4)   Accuracy. The ratio of the number of samples correctly classified by the classifier to the total number of samples for a given set of test data.

$$accuracy = \frac{TP + TN(\text{True Negatives})}{TP + FN + FP + TN} \tag{10}$$

(5) Loss.

$$loss = -\frac{1}{M} * \sum_{i=1}^{M} y_i logf(x_i) \tag{11}$$

M is the number of training samples, x_i and y_i are the input and the expected output. $f(x_i)$ denotes the real output.

3.3   Experiments

In order to fully explore the nature of this method, we conducted the following experimental steps: (1) to show the results of the design algorithm; (2) to compare with K-Nearest Neighbor classification algorithms.

3.3.1   Experiments 1: The Performance of the Proposed LSTM

All EEG recording signal rate is 200 Hz and the time sampling points T = 200 30 = 6000. The LSTM is supplemented with fuzzy entropy extraction feature. From Fig. 4, the loss is basically stable when we add the fuzzy entropy LSTM architecture with 10000 (th) iteration. Therefore, our proposed LSTM with fuzzy entropy architecture is more efficient than original LSTM.

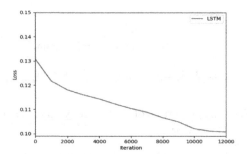

Fig. 4. The loss of LSTM

More specifically, Table 2 shows the value of every sleep stages in four measurements of accuracy, precision, recall, and f-score. We can see that the LSTM with fuzzy entropy has a higher accuracy. In a word, LSTM on sleep stage classification has a good performance.

3.3.2   Experiments 2: Compared Approach

We compare fuzzy entropy with LSTM to fuzzy entropy with KNN (K-Nearest Neighbor algorithm). The basic idea of KNN is to input new data that has not been classified. First, the features of the new data are extracted and compared with each data feature in the test set. Then, the nearest K data feature labels were extracted from the test set, and the most frequently occurring classification of the nearest K data was

Table 2. Evaluation results of our proposed LSTM with Fuzzy entropy and original LSTM

Neural Network	Stage	Precision	Recall	F-score	Accuracy
LSTM with Fuzzy entropy	W	0.91	0.81	0.88	0.85
	N1	0.89	0.73	0.90	0.90
	N2	0.80	0.89	0.70	0.87
	N3	0.82	0.71	0.84	0.88
	REM	0.79	1.00	0.89	0.80
	Average	0.85	0.83	0.84	0.86
LSTM	W	0.81	0.75	0.82	0.85
	N1	0.73	0.65	0.78	0.80
	N2	0.63	0.89	0.70	0.87
	N3	0.61	0.71	0.82	0.75
	REM	0.65	0.74	0.86	0.79
	Average	0.69	0.75	0.80	0.81

Table 3. Comparison of experimental results of LSTM and KNN

Algorithm model	Precision	Recall	F-score	Accuracy
Fuzzy Entropy with LSTM	**0.85**	**0.83**	**0.84**	**0.86**
Fuzzy Entropy with KNN	0.75	0.85	0.61	0.79

counted as the new data category. As shown in Table 3, LSTM classification is obviously better than KNN, and the fuzzy entropy feature is added to make the classification effect more obvious.

4 Conclusion

We proposed a new method for sleep stage classifiation based on LSTM with the fuzzy entropy feature extraction. We conduct experiments from three aspects. Firstly we verify the superior performance of our LSTM architecture by comparing it with our previous work. It compete an accuracy validated at confidence of 86%, which means it really successfully compete the sleep stage classification. Secondly, compared with KNN classification, our LSTM classification accuracy is higher. Finally, we verified the LSTM architecture with fuzzy entropy. The results demonstrate that excellent performance with an accuracy of 86% and it is superior to the other approach.

Acknowledgements. The NNSF of China (61373149), the NSSF of China (16BGL181) and the NSF of Shandong (ZR201702130105).

References

1. Kemp, B., Schimsheimer, R.J., De Weerd, A., et al.: Automatic classification of sleep stages. Electroencephalogr. Clin. Neurophysiol. **1**, 44 (1997)
2. Gao, L., Lu, T., Gu, N.: Supporting semantic maintenance of complex Undo operations in replicated Co-AutoCAD environments. In: International Conference on Computer Supported Cooperative Work in Design, pp. 84–89. IEEE (2009)
3. Choi, S., Jiang, Z.: A wearable cardiorespiratory sensor system for analyzing the sleep condition. Expert Syst. Appl. **35**(1–2), 317–329 (2008)
4. Huang, S., Wu, X.: Feature extraction and classification of EEG based on energy characteristics. Chin. J. Sens. Actuators **23**(6), 782–785 (2010)
5. Iber, C., Quan, S.: The AASM Manual for the Scoring of Sleep and Associated Events: Rules, Terminology and Technical Specifications. American Academy of Sleep Medicine, Darien (2007)
6. Zhang, J., Wu, Y.: A new method for automatic sleep stage classification. IEEE Trans. Biomed. Circuits Syst. **11**(5), 1097–1110 (2017)
7. Ronzhina, M., Janoušek, O., Kolářová, J., et al.: Sleep scoring using artificial neural networks. Sleep Med. Rev. **16**(3), 251–263 (2012)
8. Gers, F.A., Schmidhuber, J.: LSTM recurrent networks learn simple context-free and context-sensitive languages. IEEE Trans. Neural Netw. **12**(6), 1333–1340 (2001)
9. Liang, S.F., Kuo, C.E., et al.: Automatic stage scoring of single-channel sleep eeg by using multiscale entropy and autoregressive models. IEEE Trans. Instrum. Meas. **61**(6), 1649–1657 (2012)
10. Gao, L., Shao, B., Zhu, L., Lu, T., Gu, N.: Maintaining time and space consistencies in hybrid engineering environments: framework and algorithms. Comput. Ind. **59**(9), 894–904 (2008)
11. Haşim, S., Andrew, S., Françoise, B.: Long short-term memory based recurrent neural network architectures for large vocabulary speech recognition. Comput. Sci. **14**, 338–342 (2014)
12. Khalighi, S., Sousa, T., Santos, J.M., et al.: ISRUC-Sleep: a comprehensive public dataset for sleep researchers. Comput. Methods Programs Biomed. **124**, 180–192 (2016)

Overlapping Community Detection Algorithm Based on Spectral and Fuzzy C-Means Clustering

Xiaoshan He[1,2,3], Kun Guo[1,2,3(✉)], Qinwu Liao[4], and Qiaoling Yan[4]

[1] College of Mathematics and Computer Sciences, Fuzhou University,
Fuzhou 350116, China
`Miller_he614@163.com, guknl23@163.com`
[2] Fujian Provincial Key Laboratory of Network Computing and Intelligent
Information Processing, Fuzhou University, Fuzhou 350116, China
[3] Key Laboratory of Spatial Data Mining and Information Sharing,
Ministry of Education, Fuzhou 350116, China
[4] Power Science and Technology Corporation State Grid Information
and Telecommunication Group, Xiamen 351008, China
`{liaoqinwu,yanqiaoling}@sgitg.sgcc.com.cn`

Abstract. Community detection is the detection and revelation of the communities inherent in different types of complex networks, which can help people understand various functions and hidden rules of the complex networks to predict their future behavior. The spectral clustering algorithm suffers from the disadvantage of spending too much time for calculating eigenvectors, so it can't apply in large-scale networks. This paper puts forward the overlapping community detection algorithm devised upon spectral with Fuzzy c-means clustering. Firstly, the node similarity is calculated according to the influence of attribute features on nodes. Secondly, the node similarity is combined with the Jaccard similarity to construct the similarity matrix. Thirdly, the feature decomposition is performed on the matrix by using the DPIC (Deflation-based power iteration clustering) method. Finally, the advanced version of the traditional Fuzzy c-means algorithm can find the overlapping communities. The results of experiments reveal that it can detect communities on real and artificial datasets effectively and accurately.

Keywords: Spectral cluster · Fuzzy C-means · Overlapping community

1 Introduction

There are many complex networks in real life, such as social networks, collaboration networks of scientists, literature citation networks, protein collaboration networks, and online social networks [1–3]. The commonality of these complex networks can be abstracted into nodes and edges. Nodes represent individuals in the networks, while edges represent the connections between individuals, which can be assigned weights [4]. Communities in complex networks often require nodes inside a community to be tightly connected, while nodes among the communities are sparsely connected [5, 6]. The objective of community detection is to efficiently and accurately discover these close related communities from complex networks.

© Springer Nature Singapore Pte Ltd. 2019
Y. Sun et al. (Eds.): ChineseCSCW 2018, CCIS 917, pp. 487–497, 2019.
https://doi.org/10.1007/978-981-13-3044-5_36

Spectral method is the algorithm based on graph cut problem [7]. The graph theory's spectrum is the basis of this kind of algorithm, which transforms the clustering problem into the optimal graph partitioning problem. The data points are mapped to the graph, and the weights of the edges determines the similarity of the data points. It is a point-to-point clustering algorithm. However, its time cost is too large to be applied to large-scale networks, and the steps of calculating feature vectors are too complicated and time-consuming.

To detect community structures effectively and accurately in complex networks, the overlapping community detection algorithm devised upon spectral with Fuzzy c-means algorithm (OCDSF) is proposed. When constructing the similarity matrix, beyond that considering the adjacency relationship between the nodes, the influence of the nodes' self attributes on the similarity of the nodes is also considered. The effect of irrelevant features on the results is reduced by iteratively calculating new feature vectors when computing matrix eigenvectors. In the clustering phase, the improved Fuzzy c-means algorithm can generate communities and discover overlapping communities.

2   Basic Concepts of Community Detection

An undigraph $G = (V, E)$ can denote a social network, in which nodes' sets and edges' are represented by V and E, severally. Generally, $n = |V|$ and $m = |E|$ indicates network nodes' number and edges', severally.

Definition 1. (Jaccard Coefficient [8]) The Jaccard coefficient between two nodes is defined as

$$J_{gh} = \frac{|A(g) \cap A(h)|}{|A(g) \cup A(h)|} \tag{1}$$

where $A(g)$ can represent the neighbors sets of point g. The numerator of J_{gh} is the intersection of all the neighbor sets of the two nodes. The denominator is the union of all the neighbor sets of the two nodes. The Jaccard coefficient J_{gh} can be used for measuring the proximity of the nodes. The larger the value of J_{gh} is, the more similar the two nodes are.

Definition 2. (Node Attribute Similarity) The node attribute similarity $SD(y, m)$ between node y and node m is

$$SD(y, m) = \text{haming}(y, m) \tag{2}$$

Definition 3. (Node Similarity) The similarity between two nodes combine the Jaccard coefficient with of node attribute similarity. It is defined as:

$$S(g, h) = J_{gh} + SD(g, h) \tag{3}$$

Definition 4. (Membership) The degree of membership between each node i and the partitioned community j it belongs to is defined as

$$u_{ij} = \frac{1}{\sum_{k=1}^{C} \left(\frac{||c_i - c_j||}{||c_j - c_k||} \right)^{\frac{2}{m-1}}} \tag{4}$$

where m denotes the degree of fuzzification which needs to be determined in advance. It is usually set to 2 according literature [9].

Definition 5. (Cluster Center), Cluster center is defined as

$$c_j = \frac{\sum_{i=1}^{N} u_{ij}^m * c_i}{\sum_{i=1}^{N} u_{ij}^m} \tag{5}$$

c_i is the i-th node in the network.

Definition 6. (Value Function) The objective function used to evaluate the clustering effect. The value function is defined as

$$P = \sum_{u=1}^{c} \sum_{v=1}^{n} u_{uv}^m ||e_u - c_v||^2 \tag{6}$$

where the value function of the final communities is P [9]. The membership of community C_v for community C is updated by calculating P. C_v represents the v-th cluster center. e_u represents the u-th node in the v-th community, which indicates the degree of membership of point e_u with respect to community C_v.

3   Overlapping Community Detection Algorithm Devised upon Spectral with Fuzzy C-Means Clustering

3.1   Design Ideas

The overlapping community detection algorithm devised upon spectral with Fuzzy c-means clustering can be divided into three stages: (1) computing node similarity matrix; (2) computing feature vectors of the similarity matrix; (3) overlapping community partitioning. Firstly, the Jaccard coefficient of each node pair is calculated as the structural similarity of them, and the attribute similarity is calculated according to nodes' features. The two similarities are linearly combined to output the similarity matrix to calculate the feature vectors. Secondly, during the calculation of the eigenvectors, the DPIC method [10] is used to reduce the influence of redundant eigenvectors on the clustering results to avoid the conflicts caused by the iterative calculation. Thirdly, the fuzzy c-means algorithm is used for performing fuzzy clustering on the row vectors of the feature matrix. It is composed of the eigenvectors belonging to the similarity matrix to generate overlapping communities. The algorithm's details are shown in Algorithm 1.

Algorithm 1. OCDSF algorithm

Input: network G (V, E, F)

Output: community set C'

1. S=ConstructSimilarityMatrix()//compute node similarity matrix

2. W=CalculateEigenvector(S)//compute feature vectors of similarity matrix

3. C=GenerateCommunity(W)//overlapping community partitioning

4. Return C';

3.2   Node Similarity Matrix Calculation

Spectral clustering uses Gaussian kernel function [11] to build a similarity matrix by computing the affinity between nodes. The similarity matrix is normalized to create the Laplacian matrix. It may be over-fitting if parameter σ of the Gaussian kernel function is too large, which seriously affects the quality of the clustering results. Therefore, it is proposed to combine the topology with the node properties to calculate the similarity. Firstly, the similarity of the two neighbors of each node pair is calculated by the Jaccard coefficient. The attribute values of the nodes are converted into multi-dimensional vectors. Secondly, the attribute similarity of the nodes is calculated by comparing the degree of similarity between the multidimensional vectors. Finally, since the attributes and topology of the nodes have the same important meaning for the division of the nodes, when they are both considered to get the optimal effect. The details are shown in Function 1.

Function 1. *ConstructSimilarityMatrix()*

Input: network $G\ (V,\ E,\ F)$

Output: similarity matrix S.

1. $S=\Phi$;

2.   FOR EACH $u,\ v$ in V;

3.   Calculate J_{uv} according to equation (1);

4.   Calculate $SD\ (u,\ v)$ according to equation (2);

5. $S\ (u,\ v) = J_{uv} + SD\ (u,\ v)$;

6.   END FOR;

7.   Return S;

3.3   Calculation of the Feature Vectors of Similarity Matrix

In the stage of feature vector calculation, the time complexity of the traditional spectral clustering algorithm for calculating the feature vectors and eigenvalues of the Laplacian matrix [12, 13] is $O(n^3)$, which is only suitable for small-scale networks. Therefore, the neighboring feature vector calculation method based on DPIC algorithm is adopted. The DPIC algorithm is based on the way to build a suitable combination of pseudo-feature vectors in the case of removing redundant feature information. The degree matrix D is constructed according to the similarity matrix S, thereby generating a normalized Laplacian matrix W_0. After superimposing the similarity of each row of the matrix W_0 and converting them into a matrix of $N*1$, the normalization of the feature vector V_0 is performed. The redundant feature information is removed when vector V_1 is calculated. In this way, the effective information extraction of the feature vectors is improved. k orthogonal feature vectors are generated to form feature matrix W. The communities' number was inputted to the DPIC is k. The details are shown in Function 2.

Function 2. *CalculateEigenvector(S)*

Input: similarity matrix S, k

Output: orthogonal eigenvector matrix W

1.   Construct diagonal matrix D;

2.   Construct Laplace matrix $W_0=D^{-1}S$;

3. $V_0= (W_0*E_{n*1})/ (E_{1*n}* ||W_0||)$; // Initialize vector V_0

4.   WHILE($l>k$) DO

5. V_l =DPIC (W_{l-1}, V_{l-1});

6. W_l=DPIC (V_l, W_{l-1});

7.   END WHILE;

8.   RETURN W;

3.4   Overlapping Community Partitioning

The fuzzy c-means algorithm allows one node to belong to multiple communities, thereby it can generate overlapping communities. There is a membership degree between each node and the community to which it is assigned. The larger the degree of membership is, the greater the possibility that the node belongs to the corresponding community is. The sum of the memberships of each node to all communities is 1. The fuzzy c-means is adopt to cluster the feature matrix W's row vectors. The value of function J is reduced by continuously updating cluster core c_j of each community and the membership degree u_{ij} of each node. When the variation of u_{ij} is lower than a given threshold ε, the algorithm stops. Finally, the community detection results are return. The details are shown in Function 3.

Function 3. *GenerateCommunity(W)*

Input: eigenvector matrix W, k, ε

Output: final overlapping communities O

1. $O = \Phi$;

2.   FOR EACH i, j in W

3.   WHILE $(r > \varepsilon)$ DO

4. $u_{ijt} = u_{ij}$;

5.   Calculate u_{ij} according to equation (4);

6.   Update c_j according to equation (5);

7. $r = ||u_{ij} - u_{ijt}||$;

8.   FOR EACH i,j in W

9.   IF $(u_{ij} > 1/k)$ THEN

10. $O_j = O_j \cup V_i$;

11.   Form comunities $O = \{O1, O2, ...Ok\}$;

12.   RETURN O;

3.5   Time Complexity

Let the network have n nodes and m edges, where k is the network's average degree. In Function 1, the time for calculating the Jaccard coefficient between all pair of nodes is $O(nk)$. The calculation of the attribute similarity between all pair of nodes requires $O(n^2)$. Therefore, Function 1's time complexity is $O(nk + n^2)$. In Function 2, the sparse matrix is used to construct the normalized Laplacian matrix. When DPIC is used to solve the feature vector, the time complexity is $O(nt)$, where the iterations' number is t. Since $t \ll n$, the time complexity is approximately linear to n. Therefore, Function 2 costs $O(n)$. In Function 3, the cluster centers are used to update the membership degrees of the nodes. Hence, Function 3 costs $O(nk)$, where k is the number of feature vectors, the nodes' number is n. So the OCDSF algorithm totally costs $O(nk + n^2 + nt + nk)$. The total time complexity can be rewritten as $O(n^2)$ since n is much greater than t and k.

4   Experiments

These experiments use multiple different artificial and real networks so as to verify the performance of the OCDSF [14]. The experiments' hardware and software are: a PC with 3.2 GHz Pentium (R) CPU, 8 G RAM, and Windows 7 64 bit. The code of all algorithm is implemented in Python 3.6.

4.1   Experiment Datasets

(1) real-world datasets

The real social network dataset uses the ego-Facebook datasets from Stanford's network datasets SNAP [15]. The ego-Facebook datasets provides feature information about user-centric circle of friends and friends in social network Facebook. 0:N = 347 E = 2519, F = 224;107:N = 1045, E = 26,749, F = 576;348:N = 227, E = 3192, F = 161;1684:N = 792, E = 14,024, F = 319;1912:N = 755, E = 30,025, F = 480; 3437:N = 547, E = 4813, F = 262.

(2) artificial datasets

Since the artificially networks have its own built-in community structures, it can be used for verifying the algorithm's accuracy. The LFR benchmark [16] is a widely used benchmark network program in recent years, because the networks it generated can well represent the heterogeneity of node's degree and community's scale distribution. So the LFR benchmark is used to generate 10 artificial datasets. The datasets' parameter are set as follows:
D1:N = 200, k = 30, E = 3014, F = 40;D2:N = 500, k = 20, E = 4716, F = 140;D3: N = 500, k = 30, E = 7413, F = 110;D4:N = 1000, k = 50, E = 25,000, F = 140;D5: N = 1000, k = 30, E = 15,179, F = 260; The rest of the parameters use the same settings: $\mu = 0.1$, $k_{max} = 50$, $C_{min} = 10$, $C_{max} = 100$.
D6 $\sim$ D10:N = 1000, k = 30, $\mu = 0.1 \sim 0.6$, $k_{max} = 50$, $C_{min} = 10$, $C_{max} = 100$.
According to the heterogeneity of the communities automatically generated by the LFR benchmark, the attribute values of the simulated construction nodes are simulated by some means [17].

4.2   Experimental Scheme and Evaluation Metrics

(1) experimental scheme

In the experiment, the OCDSF algorithm is compared with multiple community detection algorithms based on spectral clustering including PIC algorithm, DPIC algorithm and SPF algorithm. By comparing the results of these algorithms running on real and artificial datasets, the precision of the OCDSF algorithm is evaluated. Many algorithms are affected by the parameter settings. Therefore, it is necessary to set the parameters of the algorithm within a reasonable range for experimentation and use the average values of multiple experiments as the final results.

(2) evaluation metrics

The algorithm uses the modularity EQ, which is proposed by Shen Huawei et al. [18] to evaluate the quality of overlapping community structures, as an evaluation index for real network partitioning. The quality of the community detection is more better if the EQ value is closer to 1, vice versa.

Normalized Mutual Information (NMI) [19] is an index which evaluates for the artificially generated networks. NMI can evaluate the community division of known standard results and is a good indicator of overlapping community detection accuracy.

4.3   Experimental Results on the Real Datasets

The ego-Facebook dataset provides feature information about user-centric circles of friends and friends in social network Facebook. Figure 1 indicates the results on the dataset of the PIC, DPIC, SPF and OCDSF algorithm.

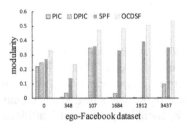

Fig. 1. The modularity results on real dataset.

As can be seen from Fig. 1, the OCDSF algorithm is superior to other algorithms in most networks. The PIC algorithm is not applicable to community partitioning based on ego-networks like Facebook. In some datasets, it settles all nodes to the same community, or there are empty communities, which leads to poor results. The DPIC algorithm is instable in the real networks. Its performance in different data sets are different. The results of the SPF algorithm is second to the OCDSF algorithm, but it cannot find overlapping communities. Calculating the similarity with combinatorial attributes strengthens the stability of the OCDSF algorithm. When calculating the feature vector, the redundant vector information is removed and the features are effectively utilized. Therefore, the OCDSF algorithm is capable of finding large-scale communities.

4.4   Experimental Results on the Artificial Datasets

10 artificial data sets were generated by using the LFR benchmark program for experiments. Since the LFR benchmark cannot generate node's properties, the properties of the constructed nodes are simulated according to the known community structures. Figure 2 indicates the comparison of the modularity and the NMI value of the algorithms on the artificial datasets.

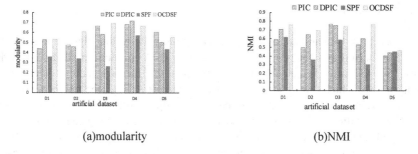

(a)modularity   (b)NMI

Fig. 2. The modularity and NMI results on artificial datasets.

Figure 2 shows that the DPIC is perform better than the PIC and SPF algorithms. And the OCDSF algorithm is significantly better than other algorithms in almost all artificial datasets. It shows that the communities found by the OCDSF algorithm are closer to the true communities than other algorithms. Therefore, combining node neighbor relationships with attribute features can reasonably improve the algorithm's clustering performance. The OCDSF algorithm effectively reduces the original spectral method's time complexity by compressing the eigenvectors. Compared with the original ones, the OCDSF algorithm improves the quality of community detection and the processing efficiency.

4.5   Scalability Experiments

The experiments on datasets were conducted with varying sizes so as to investigate the scalability of the algorithm. Figure 3 indicates the change of the running time of the algorithm on the real and artificial datasets with different sizes.

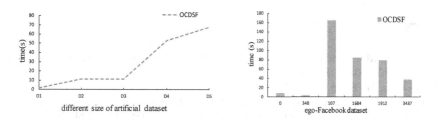

Fig. 3. The running time on the real and artificial datasets

Figure 3 indicates that the OCDSF's the running time raises nearly linear with the increase of the dataset size at first and increase sharply after dataset D3. The square time complexity of the algorithm hinders its performance on large datasets. The OCDSF algorithm uses the nearest neighbor feature vectors calculation method based on the DPIC algorithm to construct combinatorial pseudo feature vectors and removes the redundant feature information. Therefore, the time cost of the algorithm is greatly reduced, which makes the algorithm capable of accurately discovering the communities in the network.

5 Conclusion

This paper puts forward an overlapping community detection algorithm based on spectral clustering and fuzzy c-means to discover the communities of the networks. Firstly, the similarity is calculated by combining the Jaccard coefficient and node attributes, from which the similarity matrix is constructed. Then, the redundant parts of the feature vectors are removed when calculating the feature vectors. In progress of community partitioning, the fuzzy c-means is used for classifying the feature matrix formed with the feature vectors of the similarity matrix. The vectors are subjected to fuzzy clustering to generate overlapping communities. The results of experiments reveal that the OCDSF can accurately detect nodes of community and divide overlapping communities. In future, we will consider applying the methods of network characterization learning [20–22] to improve the feature solving part of the algorithm, so that it can better discover the network characteristics and the hidden information of the networks.

Acknowledgements. This work is partly supported by the National Natural Science Foundation of China under Grant Nos. 61300104, 61300103 and 61672158, the Fujian Province High School Science Fund for Distinguished Young Scholars under Grant No. JA12016, the Program for New Century Excellent Talents in Fujian Province University under Grant No. JA13021, the Fujian Natural Science Funds for Distinguished Young Scholar under Grant Nos. 2014J06017 and 2015J06014, the Major Production and Research Project of Fujian Scientific and Technical Department, the Technology Innovation Platform Project of Fujian Province (Grants Nos. 2009J1007, 2014H2005), the Fujian Collaborative Innovation Center for Big Data Applications in Governments, and the Natural Science Foundation of Fujian Province under Grant Nos. 2013J01230 and 2014J01232, Industry-Academy Cooperation Project under Grant Nos. 2014H6014 and 2017H6008. Haixi Government Big Data Application Cooperative Innovation Center.

References

1. Newman, M.E.: The structure of scientific collaboration networks. Proc. Natl. Acad. Sci. USA **98**(2), 404–409 (2001)
2. Takaffoli, M., Sangi, F., Fagnan, J., et al.: Community evolution mining in dynamic social networks. Procedia - Soc. Behav. Sci. **22**(22), 49–58 (2011)
3. Fortunato, S.: Community detection in graphs. Phys. Rep. **486**(3), 75–174 (2010)
4. Girvan, M., Newman, M.E.: Community structure in social and biological networks. Proc. Natl. Acad. Sci. **99**(12), 7821–7826 (2002)
5. Radicchi, F., Castellano, C., Cecconi, F., et al.: Defining and identifying communities in networks. Proc. Natl. Acad. Sci. USA **101**(9), 2658 (2004)
6. Clauset, A., Newman, M.E., Moore, C.: Finding community structure in very large networks. Phys. Rev. E Stat. Nonlinear Soft Matter Phys. **70**(2), 6111 (2004)
7. Luxburg, U.V.: A tutorial on spectral clustering. Stat. Comput. **17**(4), 395–416 (2007)
8. Jaccard, P.: Etude de la distribution florale dans une portion des Alpes et du Jura. Bulletin De La Societe Vaudoise Des Sciences Naturelles **37**(142), 547–579 (1901)
9. Havens, T.C., Bezdek, J.C., Leckie, C., et al.: Fuzzy c-means algorithms for very large data. IEEE Trans. Fuzzy Syst. **20**(6), 1130–1146 (2012)

10. The, A.P., Thang, N.D., Vinh, L.T., et al.: Deflation-based power iteration clustering. In: IASTED International Conference on Communications, Internet, and Information Technology, pp. 73–78. ACTA Press (2007). https://doi.org/10.1007/s10489-012-0418-0
11. Miller, F.P., Vandome, A.F., Mcbrewster, J.: Gaussian Function (2010)
12. Sonka, M., Hlavac, V., Ceng, R.B.D.M.: Image processing, analysis and machine vision. J. Electron. Imag. **19**(82), 685–686 (2008)
13. Szeliski, R.: Computer vision: algorithms and applications. Springer, New York (2010)
14. Xie, J., Kelley, S., Szymanski, B.K.: Overlapping community detection in networks: the state-of-the-art and comparative study. ACM Comput. Surv. **45**(4), 1–35 (2013)
15. Mcauley, J., Leskovec, J.: Learning to discover social circles in ego networks. In: International Conference on Neural Information Processing Systems, pp. 539–547. Curran Associates Inc. (2012)
16. Lancichinetti, A., Fortunato, S., Radicchi, F.: Benchmark graphs for testing community detection algorithms. Phys. Rev. E: Stat. Nonlinear Soft Matter Phys. **78**(4 Pt 2), 046110 (2008)
17. Guo, K., Guo, W.Z., Qiu, Q.R., et al.: Community detection algorithm based on local affinity propagation and user profile. J. Commun. **36**(2), 68–79 (2015)
18. Shen, H., Cheng, X., Cai, K., et al.: Detect overlapping and hierarchical community structure in networks. Phy. A Stat. Mech. Appl. **388**(8), 1706–1712 (2009)
19. Danon, L., Díazguilera, A., Duch, J., et al.: Comparing community structure identification. J. Stat. Mech. **2005**(09), 09008 (2005)
20. Wang, D., Cui, P., Zhu, W.: Structural deep network embedding. In: ACM SIGKDD International Conference on Knowledge Discovery and Data Mining, pp. 1225–1234. ACM (2016)
21. Liang, L.: Network representation learning and link prediction towards attributed network. East China Normal University (2017)
22. Tu, C.C., Yang, C., Liu, Z.Y., et al.: Network representation learning: an overview (in Chinese). Sci. Sin. Inf. (2017). https://doi.org/10.1360/n112017-00145

Watershed Flood Forecasting Based on Cluster Analysis and BP Neural Network

Wangsong Wang and Yan Tang[✉]

College of Computer and Information, Hohai University, Nanjing 210098, China
{wswang, tangyan}@hhu.edu.cn

Abstract. This paper makes an improvement on the traditional flood fore-casting method. There are two shortcomings in the conventional prediction process. First, it is not rigorous for clustering by selecting fixed features. Many factors affect the flood, so this leads the loss of useful information and inaccurate clustering results. Second, number of clusters is also fixed, the optimal clustering under multiple clusters is not studied. For the above problems, we propose a new approach by increasing the impact of flood properties before the fuzzy C-means clustering and improving the PCA analysis through leveraging the KMO test and Bartlett test to determine the advantages and disadvantages of the data set to extract, we utilize the gravel map to determine the number of extraction of the main components. When using our improved approach for flood prediction, it can effectively filter out useless and redundant information, and reduce the dimension of high-dimensional data. Then based on the processed data, we use pseudo-F statistics to discover optimal quantity of clusters, and use BP neural network to classify outputs online. After the improvement, we find that the system can achieve higher accuracy for the classification of floods and overcome the shortcomings of the traditional flood forecasting method.

Keywords: Flood prediction · Fuzzy C-means clustering
Principal component analysis · Pseudo-F statistic · BP neural network

1 Introduction

China is a frequent flooded country for it's vast territory with many rivers. founding brings 122 million acres of average annual affected area and 67.2 million acres of disaster area. A major flood occurs in about less than two years and causes significant losses. The annual losses caused by floods are increasing at a fast speed [3]. The flood process is complex, fuzzy [4], but at the same time show its own regularity. How to extract flood features from the historical databases and to analyze floods, and further understand the different types of floods is a vital researches direction to improve the accuracy and efficiency of flood forecasting.

In this paper, we have made improvements to the problems that exists in the traditional methods [1, 2] to overcome the original shortcomings, the general process based on improved PCA analysis of flood information extraction processing, and then use the extracted components for adaptive fuzzy C means Algorithm clustering. The clustering results are used to filter the optimal clustering using the pseudo-F statistic.

© Springer Nature Singapore Pte Ltd. 2019
Y. Sun et al. (Eds.): ChineseCSCW 2018, CCIS 917, pp. 498–506, 2019.
https://doi.org/10.1007/978-981-13-3044-5_37

Real-time information such as rainfall are input data to make the online classification process more accurate. The classification results are obtained as neural network outputs. Finally, the results are used to forecast the corresponding model parameters. Experiments show that our proposed approach outperforms traditional methods and is effective in flood prediction.

The remaining work is organized as follows: important related work are introduced in the next section; The proposed approach is described in detail in Sect. 3. The experimental results are presented in Sect. 4. In Sect. 5, the conclusions is summarized.

2 Related Work

2.1 Determination of the Optimal Clustering Number of Fuzzy C-Means Clustering

The cluster center initialization and the cluster validity problems are two important issues of the Fuzzy C-means (FCM) algorithm. FCM algorithm is sensitive the initial class center, and different initial class centers may lead to different clustering results. The quality of clustering is closely related to the number of clusters. Excessive values will make the clustering results complicated and make it difficult to interpret and analyze, while too small c value will cause the loss of information and mislead the final decision. Therefore how to get the best number of clusters has always been a key topic in the study of clustering effectiveness. For the classic FCM, people have put forward a number of validity functions, pseudo F-statistic is used to discover optimal number of clusters [5].

2.2 KMO Measure

KMO measure (Kaiser-Meyer-Olkin measure) [6] is a statistical test method provided by SPSS software to determine whether the variables of the original data set can be used as PCA analysis. The measure value compares the observed correlation coefficient between the original data set variables and the magnitude of the partial correlation coefficient, the larger the KMO measure value, the original data set is more conducive to PCA analysis.

3 Proposed Approach

3.1 Improvements the Flow Chart of the Proposed Model

Figure 1 is the flow chart of our proposed flood prediction model. The blue parts are the flow of the original model [2] and the orange part is the improvement part. The original process has been described in the literature [2], and will not be repeated here. The improvement process is as follows: first making PCA analysis in view of the original data set (including the features of the flood information), and the data is processed by PCA, this effectively reduces the data redundancy and high-dimensional dimension. Then the obtained principal components are clustered by fuzzy C-means clustering under different clustering numbers. After the clustering is completed, several kinds of clustering results will be obtained by using the pseudo-F statistic to obtain the optimal clustering number. Finally, the optimal clustering result is obtained as BP network output, the rainfall related information will be used as a network input. Finally, make an online classification of real-time floods and then according to the type of real-time flood to choose the corresponding model parameters to predict and analyze flooding data.

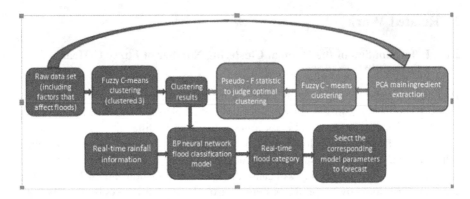

Fig. 1. Improved model flow chart

3.2   PCA Analysis

The essence of principal component analysis (PCA) is to use a certain method to reduce the high-dimensional flood characteristic variables in the flood feature data into a few new independent variables. The method of operation is to use the orthogonal transformation to convert the relevant flood feature original variable into a relatively independent new variable. And we have taken the KMO and Bartlett test and the gravel map to optimize the process, the optimized PCA analysis of the main calculation step are as follows:

(1) Normalize the n sample data $X_k = (x_{k1}, x_{k2}, \cdots, x_{kp})^t$, $k = 1, 2, \ldots$, n, where n > p under standardized selected flood characteristic index data p-dimension random vectors $X = (X_1, X_2, \cdots X_p)^T$, then construct the flood sample matrix, standardize the above-mentioned flood feature matrix:

$$Z_{jk} = \frac{x_{jk} - \overline{x_k}}{s_k}, j = 1, 2, \cdots, n; k = 1, 2, \cdots, p \tag{1}$$

$$\overline{x_k} = \frac{1}{n}\sum_{j=1}^{n} x_{jk}, x_k^2 = \frac{1}{n-1}\sum_{j=1}^{n}(x_{jk} - \overline{x_k})^2 \tag{2}$$

then a standardized flood feature matrix Z is obtained.

(2) Find out the related coefficient matrix R of the normalized matrix Z and the partial correlation coefficient and the correlation coefficient between KMO and Bartlett's test are used to determine whether Z can carry out the principal component extraction.

(3) Transformed the normalized flood characteristic index variable into the main component, and according to the judgment in 3 to select the corresponding P principal components.

$$U_{ij} = z_i^T b_j^0, \; j = 1, 2, \cdots m \tag{3}$$

3.3 Fuzzy C-Means Clustering Algorithm

Fuzzy C-means cluster algorithms (FCM) [8] is extensive used in various application fields. According the concept of fuzzy partitioning, the objective function of hard clustering is extended to soft clustering, which is called fuzzy clustering [9], at the same time, in order to avoid the objective function trapped in the local optimal solution. In the objective function, the exponential multiplication factor is added to the distance between each sample and each type of prototype, we refer to this weight as the membership degree. Based on this, there is a n × p flood characteristic data set C, which divides these flood characteristic data into c class. The center of each class is that each flood sample j belongs to the membership degree of a flood class i, then define an FCM objective function (4) with constraints (5) are as follows:

$$J = \sum_{i=1}^{c} \sum_{j=1}^{n} q_{ij}^m \|x_j - c_i\|^2 \tag{4}$$

$$\sum_{k=1}^{c} q_{kj} = 1, j = 1, 2, \cdots, n \tag{5}$$

Which the membership factor $m \in [1, \infty)$, x_j represents the j-th Attribute vector of flood samples.

3.4 BP Neural Network Online Classification

Use the characteristics of floods in terms of genesis as a training sample input for BP neural networks, using the classification results obtained by fuzzy C-means clustering as a training sample output to train BP neural network, we will get an intelligent classification model, it can classify floods timely.

4 Forecasting Process

4.1 SPSS Principal Component Extraction

We get the correlation matrix by SPSS principal component analysis. However, the correlation matrix table only shows that there is some correlation between attributes, it does not indicate whether the original data is suitable for principal component extraction. Therefore, in order to determine whether the data set suitable for the principal component extraction, KMO and Bartlett's test is desired. The test consequences are shown in Table 1.

Table 1. KMO and Barrlett checklist

Sampling enough KUII metrics	.739
Bartlett's spherical approximation of the karst test	103.959
df	28
Sig.	.000

From Table 1, we can see that the KMO test value is 0.739, which indicates that the data set is suitable for the main component extraction. The Sig value of artlett's sphericity test is less than 0.001. Consolidating the values of two variable, the original data set is suitable for principal component extraction. After determining that the data can be used to principal component analysis.

Table 2. Explain the total variance table

Ingredient	Initial eigenvalue			Extract squares and load		
	Total	Variance %	Accumulation %	Total	Variance %	Accumulation %
P1	2.429	30.358	30.358	2.429	30.358	30.358
P2	1.812	22.647	53.005	1.812	22.647	53.005
P3	1.408	17.605	70.61	1.408	17.605	70.61
P4	0.985	12.308	82.918	0.985	12.308	82.918
P5	0.493	6.156	89.075	0.493	6.156	89.075
P6	0.402	5.026	94.1			
P7	0.343	4.286	98.386			

In general, the principal component selection is the part where the correlation matrix eigenvalue greater than 1, but sometimes such selection does not meet the requirement of contribution. For example, there are three principal component eigenvalues greater than 1 in Table 2, but its contribution was only 70.61% that do not meet the requirements of more than 80%. According to the steepness of the lithograph, its principal component is selected as shown in Table 3.

Table 3. List of principal components for individual floods

Serial number	P1	P2	P3	P4
1	−0.86911	0.28464	0.49139	−1.23333
2	−0.45813	−0.13086	0.36914	1.27121
3	0.96914	1.28635	−0.62106	−0.50692
4	−1.67461	0.33643	0.12718	1.04772
...	..	...	..	...
38	1.19205	−3.3751	−0.77032	−0.27292
39	0.59993	−2.03631	−1.35546	0.47204

4.2   Fuzzy C-Means Clustering

The scores of the five principal components P1, P2, P3, P4, and P5 are taken as clustering indicators, then selecting the number of clusters $c_{min} = 2$ and $c_{max} = \text{int}(\sqrt{n})$ according to Bezdek's recommendations, where n is the sample size [10]. The sample size is 40, number of clusters are locked in classes between 2 to 6, it is divided into large, medium and small three categories based on floods, the number of flood clusters is locked in 3 to 6 categories. For each cluster number, calculate its pseudo-F statistic [7] to determining optimal number of clusters, the results are shown in Table 4:

Table 4. Pseudo-F statistic values

Number of classes c	3 classes	4 classes	5 classes	6 classes
The sum of molecules	86.98142	122.37014	137.72914	153.65180
Denominator sum	190.97158	155.58286	140.22386	124.30120
(n − c)/(c − 1)	18.5	12	8.75	6.8
Pseudo-F statistic	8.42616	9.43833	8.59433	8.40565

From the Table 4 we can see that when the number of clusters is 4, the pseudo-F statistic value is largest, and the clustering effect is the best. In order to determine the effect of the new clustering, a new method and original method for calculating the average flood value. the results as illustrated in Fig. 2.

As shown in Fig. 2, the first three points for the original clustering results, followed by four points for the new clustering results, blue line represents maximum rain intensity and red line represents average rain intensity.

It is observed that our improved model identifies one more cluster and can distinguish maximum rain intensity and average rain intensity more clearly. Therefore, the above analysis proves that the clustering effect under the improved method is better than the results under the original method. It can also be seen that the PCA analysis and the pseudo-F statistic have optimized our classification of the flood to a certain extent.

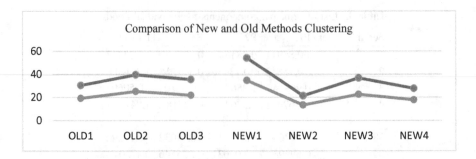

Fig. 2. Comparison of new and old methods clustering effect

4.3   Online Classification of BP Neural Network

According to the historical flood data of Cao'e river, we take rainstorm center of 30 floods, rainfall trends and other seven as training samples for BP neural network input, and the number of clusters obtained from cluster was used as training sample output.

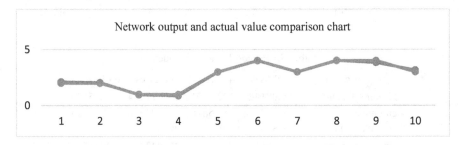

Fig. 3. Comparison of model calculated and actual values on testing data

Based on Fig. 3, where red line represents the network output value and blue line represents the actual value for flood category classification. It is observed that the output value and actual value of the network are identical. This also reflects the accuracy of our model's clustering ability from another aspect. Based on the above analysis, there is very small margin of classification error. In addition, the BP network is able to classify the data correctly, and the clustering results of PCA analysis and pseudo-F statistics are suitable and can adapt to the network.

4.4   Watershed Flood Classification Forecast

For the four types of classification floods, we use Matlab to classify the parameters of the rate, and obtained four groups of Xin'anjiang model production and production forecast parameters, corresponding to the four types of floods respectively. Then according to the relevant flood characteristics of flooding, the BP neural network online classification model is used to classify the category of real-time flood, and then the flood forecasting is carried out by using the corresponding model parameters. According to Fig. 4, we found that, compared to the old method, the flood flow prediction results of our proposed model are closer to the actual flow values, indicating that our new model achieves better prediction accuracy.

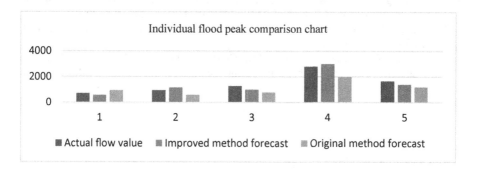

Fig. 4. Comparison of peak flow prediction results

5 Conclusion

This paper proposes a novel approach for flood prediction by increasing the impact of flood properties before the fuzzy C-means clustering and improving PCA analysis through leveraging the KMO test and Bartlett test to determine the advantages and disadvantages of the data set to extract. Gravel map is utilized to determine the number of extraction of the main components. Then based on the processed data, we use pseudo-F statistics to discover the optimal quantity of clusters, also use the BP neural network to classify outputs online. Experiment result shows that our approach can not only reduce the dimension of high dimensional data, but also eliminate the redundant information of the original data set and effectively improve the quality of clustering. In summary, compared with the traditional approach, our proposed model can effectively improve the accuracy of flood forecasting and applicable to real-time classification forecasting.

References

1. Ren, M.L.: Research on classified flood forecast based on fuzzy clustering and BP neural networks. J. Dalian Univ. Technol. **49**(1), 121–127 (2009)
2. Liu, K., Bao, W., Que, J., et al.: Application of K-mean cluster method to flood forecasting based on principal component analysis. Eng. J. Wuhan Univ. **48**, 448–458 (2015)
3. Ni, P., Bao, W., Zhang, Q., et al.: Application of hierarchical cluster analysis to flood forecasting based on principal component analysis. J. China Three Gorges Univ. 1–4 (2018)
4. Wang, C., Wei, N., Xie, J., et al.: Scheme optimization of Jialingjiang-to-Hanjiang river water transfer project based on multi-objective fuzzy optimization model. J. Water Resour. Water Eng. 144–148 (2018)

5. Vogol, M.A., Wong, A.K.C.: PFS clustering method. IEEE Trans. PAMI **1**(3), 237–245 (1979)
6. Xie, K., Zhang, J.: Short-term wind speed forecasting using PCA-WNN based on KMO-Bartlett typical wind speed selection. Power Equip. 86–91 (2017)
7. Li, H.: Evaluation on quality of medical treatment by pseudo F-statistics fuzzy clustering method. Chin. J. Hosp. Stat. **51**, 113–115 (2005)
8. Jin, J., Zhang, Y., Wang, W.: Optimal fuzzy equivalent matrix-base fuzzy clustering method for hydrological station classification. IAHS-AISH Publication, 447–458 (2007)
9. Lin, L.: Specific emitter identification based on ambiguity function. J. Electron. Inf. Technol. **31**(11), 2546–2551 (2009)
10. García, S.L., Magdalena, L., Velasco, J.R.: Cluster validity for FCM clustering algorithm using uniform data. In: Eusflat-Estylf Joint Conference, Palma De Mallorca, Spain, September. DBLP, pp. 501–504 (2009)

Academic News Text Classification Model Based on Attention Mechanism and RCNN

Ronghua Lin, Chengzhou Fu, Chengjie Mao[✉], Jingmin Wei,
and Jianguo Li

South China Normal University, Guangzhou, Guangdong, China
{rhlin,fucz,weijingmin,jianguoli}@m.scnu.edu.cn,
maochj@qq.com

Abstract. With the expeditious development of Internet technology and academic social media, massive academic news generated by academic social media have provided rich information for scholars to communicate and learn about the latest academic trends. How to effectively classify academic news data and obtain valuable information have become one of the important research directions of information science. Traditional classification methods have the problems of high dimensions, high sparseness and weak feature expression ability, etc. Deep neural network models such as CNN and RNN are also often affected by their own parameters. In this paper we present a deep neural network model based on attention mechanism and RCNN (ARCNN). We capture the context of each word and generate the word vectors with deep bidirectional LSTM layers after preprocessing. Then we use attention mechanism to calculate the attention probability distribution of news titles and contents, effectively highlighting key information. In our experiments, we use news data of academic social network SCHOLAT and Fudan University document classification set to evaluate our model and achieve better results than other widely used text classification algorithms.

Keywords: Text classification · Deep learning · Natural language processing
Attention mechanism

1 Introduction

Text classification is widely used in Natural Language Processing (NLP) tasks. At present, text classification has been used in many scenarios, such as news portal websites [2], spam filtering [3] and so on. Furthermore, academic social media networks such as ResearchGate and SCHOLAT[1] have gradually emerged. Academic exchange activities have become more frequent, generating a large amount of academic news texts. It is important that how to effectively classify and manage these news data.

Traditional machine learning algorithms, including Support Vector Machine (SVM) [4], Logistic Regression (LR) [5] and so on, have already achieved satisfying results in text classification. However, most of traditional text classification works still require feature engineering, relying on features of human design, such as dictionary [6],

---

[1] http://www.scholat.com.

© Springer Nature Singapore Pte Ltd. 2019
Y. Sun et al. (Eds.): ChineseCSCW 2018, CCIS 917, pp. 507–516, 2019.
https://doi.org/10.1007/978-981-13-3044-5_38

knowledge base and so on. In addition, most of these features may have high dimensions and be sparse.

Compared with traditional machine learning methods, using deep learning to solve large-scale text classification tasks can automatically extract features without human intervention such as feature engineering. Some deep neural network models like Convolutional Neural Network (CNN) and Recurrent Convolutional Neural Network (RCNN) can achieve better results. However, there are also some problems with CNN and RCNN. For example, the training time will be much longer and there are more hyper parameters that need to be adjusted.

In this paper, we present a text classification model ARCNN based on attention mechanism and RCNN, which can effectively extract texts features and classify the academic news data. In our works, we mainly study how to classify Chinese texts. Firstly, we use word vectors trained by the large corpus to represent the words, reducing the high dimensionality and sparsity of the data. Secondly, according to the characteristics of academic social news texts, we designed a deep neural network based on attention mechanism and RCNN for feature selection. Finally, we experiment with the academic news dataset of SCHOLAT and Fudan University document classification set. The results show that our model ARCNN is superior to other widely used text classification algorithms.

The remainder of this paper is organized as follows. Section 2 covers related work and Sect. 3 we introduce the details of our model ARCNN. Section 4 contains our experiments and results analysis. In Sect. 5 we summarize our works.

2 Related Work

2.1 Text Representation

The goal of text representation is to represent the texts or words that can be identified by a computer, using the formalization of language or mathematical descriptions [1]. The text representation methods that currently commonly used mainly include one-hot text representation and distributed text representation.

One-hot text representation is the most intuitive and commonly used method in NLP tasks [7]. The characteristics of one-hot representation is that each row in feature matrices has one and only one element is 1, and the other elements are 0. However, the biggest drawback is that the data is sparse.

Distributed text representation method will map words into a dense vectors space which is also with low dimension according to the relationship between current word and the context. In 2013, Google released the open source toolkit Word2Vec [8], which made word vectors widely used. Word2Vec is an unsupervised pre-training method, using low-dimensional vectors to represent words. It will put the similar words in close positions and map words into fixed-length short vectors. In this paper, we use the words vectors trained by Word2Vec as input to our model ARCNN.

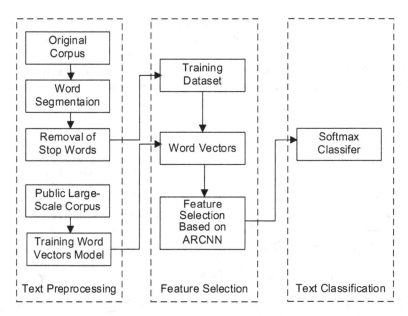

Fig. 1. ARCNN model includes three phases, (1) text preprocessing, (2) feature selection, (3) text classification.

2.2 Traditional Text Classification

Traditional text classification methods may require feature engineering before training, including text preprocessing, feature selection, and text representation. In this phase, a lot of human costs is required.

An appropriate classifier is need to be chosen after the feature engineering phase. Traditional text classification models include LR, SVM, et al. However, the learning ability of these models may be limited. They require a better feature engineering phase to analyze the effective features or feature combinations in advance, thereby indirectly enhancing the learning ability.

2.3 Text Classification Based on Deep Learning

The text classification models based on deep learning like CNN, RCNN and so on, has the following advantages [9]. Firstly, it is not required of artificial feature selection. Secondly, deep learning can utilize the features of word order well and obtain better results. Thirdly, the accuracy will be improved as the increase of training samples and the network depth.

In 2014, Kim [10] firstly applied CNN [11] to text classification. CNN model can extract deeper information from the texts. However, it is hard to set the convolutional kernel size.

RCNN model [12] obtains the context representation of each word by using the forward and backward recurrent neural networks. It can effectively extract the text features of the entire texts.

Although CNN and RCNN are effective in text classification tasks, there are still deficiencies that are not intuitive enough and poorly interpretable, especially when applied to bad situations or scenarios. Attention mechanism [13] is able to calculate the attention probability distribution for the current output, thereby highlighting the key information of the texts. Bahdanau et al. [14] used attention mechanism in translation tasks and achieved satisfying results.

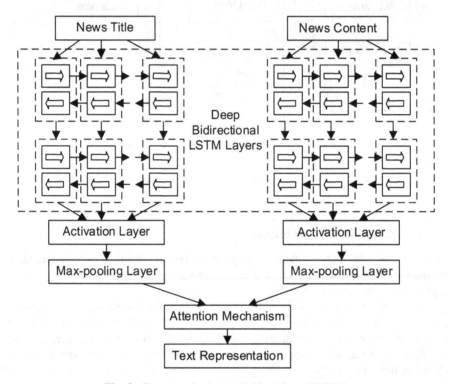

Fig. 2. Feature selection model based on ARCNN.

3 Methodology

We will then introduce the details of our model ARCNN in this section. It mainly focuses on three phases, including text preprocessing, feature selection and text classification. The pipeline is shown as Fig. 1.

3.1 Text Preprocessing

Word segmentation is an indispensable part of the Chinese text preprocessing process, which will directly determine the effect of feature selection and classification. In our works, we use the Chinese words segmentation toolkit jieba to segment Chinese texts for further processing.

We then remove stop words for texts. Stop words refer to a large number of words in a document that are meaningless for classification, such as pronouns, conjunctions, prepositions, etc.

Since the length of the texts may affect the final results of text classification, we need to normalize the length of the texts before experiment. In this paper, we determine the length of texts by double the mean value for higher samples coverage.

When using neural networks for text classification, we need to convert the text into word vectors. However, the corpus in this paper is not large enough to train word vectors. We use 2017 Wikipedia Chinese Dataset[2] as a corpus, training by Word2Vec to generate the word vectors WV (the dimension is set to 50).

3.2 Feature Selection

We design a feature selection model based on ARCNN, taking the news titles and contents after preprocessing as input according to the composition of academic social news (see Fig. 2).

Input Layer

After text preprocessing phase, we use $\{t_1, t_2,..., t_n\}$ and $\{c_1, c_2,..., c_m\}$ to represent news title (T) and content (C) respectively, where n is the number of words of title and m is the number of words of content. Each word vectors of titles v_{title} and contents $v_{content}$ in T and C are respectively constructed by searching in the word vectors WV trained by Word2Vec in advance. Those that do not appear in WV are represented by random initialization. v_{title} and $v_{content}$ are as shown in Eqs. 1 and 2, where $\mathbb{R}^{V*dim}$ is the word vectors WV and V is the size of WV.

$$v_{title} = (v_{t1}, v_{t2}, \ldots, v_{tn}), v_{ti} \in \mathbb{R}^{V*dim} \tag{1}$$

$$v_{content} = (v_{c1}, v_{c2}, \ldots, v_{cm}), v_{ci} \in \mathbb{R}^{V*dim} \tag{2}$$

Deep Bidirectional LSTM Layers

The output of input layer will be feed into a deep bidirectional LSTM layers to capture the context of each word. Taking the news titles as example, we define $t_l(w_i)$ as the left context of the word w_i and $t_r(w_i)$ as the right context. $t_l(w_i)$ and $t_r(w_i)$ are calculated as shown in Eqs. 3 and 4,

$$t_l(w_i) = f\left(W^{(l)}t_l(w_{i-1}) + W^{(sl)}v(w_{i-1})\right) \tag{3}$$

$$t_r(w_i) = f\left(W^{(r)}t_r(w_{i+1}) + W^{(sr)}v(w_{i+1})\right) \tag{4}$$

---

[2] https://dumps.wikimedia.org/.

where $t_l(w_i)$ and $t_r(w_i)$ are word vectors with $|t|$ dimension. $t_l(w_{i-1})$ is the left context of the previous word w_{i-1} of the word w_i while $v(w_{i-1})$ are the word vectors of word w_{i-1}. The left context of the first word in any document is $t_l(w_1)$. $W^{(l)}$ is a matrix that converts the hidden layer to the next hidden layer. $W^{(sl)}$ is a matrix that combines the semantic of the current word with the left context of next word. Function f is a nonlinear activation function. Equation 4 is similar to Eq. 3, where $t_r(w_{i+1})$ is the right context of the next word w_{i+1} of the word w_i, and the right context of the last word in any document is $t_r(w_n)$.

Activation Layer
We then use the activation function Rectified Linear Unit (ReLU) [15] to strengthen the learning ability of our model. ReLU function can reduce the amount of calculation and greatly shorten the learning period. Furthermore, it will make the output of a part of neurons as zero, which can effectively avoid overfitting [15].

Max-pooling Layer
After then, we further extract text features by using a max-pooling layer. We only take the feature with the largest score as the reserved of the max-pooling layer, while other are discarded.

Attention Mechanism
In our model, greater weights will be given to the more important information of the documents. We use attention mechanism [13] to re-weight the output of max-pooling layer. Firstly we connect the news titles y_t and contents y_c of each news document directly and get h, as shown in Eq. 5.

$$h_i = [y_t; y_c] \tag{5}$$

We then use a tanh function to calculate u_i which is the hidden layer representation of h_i (as shown in Eq. 6), where W_w and b_w are the weights and bias that our model learned.

$$u_i = \tanh(W_w h_i + b_w) \tag{6}$$

To further identify the importance of each word, we use softmax function to calculate the normalized attention weight matrix α_i, representing the weight of the ith word (as shown in Eq. 7), where u_w is the vectors learned during the training network.

$$\alpha_i = \frac{\exp\left(u_i^T u_w\right)}{\sum_t \exp(u_i^T u_w)} \tag{7}$$

We use α_i as weights of each word, and then weight and sum them to obtain a text representation, as shown in Eq. 8.

$$y^{(2)} = \sum_{t=1}^{m} \alpha_i h_i \tag{8}$$

3.3   Text Classifier

In this paper, we use softmax [16] classifier to finish the final classification. The softmax function can convert the output of multiple neurons into probability between 0 and 1 for each categorie of academic news. For softmax classifier, the absolute value of the classification result characterizes the probability of belonging to that category.

We use Algorithm 1 as follow to summarize our model ARCNN.

Algorithm 1 ARCNN's algorithm

Input: *dim* (dimension of vector)
Output: *label* (classification result)

1: $\mathbb{R}^{V*dim}$ (word vectors matrix)
2: V (size of word vectors matrix)
3: $Length_{title}$ (length of news titles)
4: $Length_{content}$ (length of news contents)
5: $v_{title} = (v_{t1}, v_{t2}, ..., v_{tn}), v_{ti} \in \mathbb{R}^{V*dim}$ (word vectors of news titles)
6: $v_{content} = (v_{c1}, v_{c2}, ..., v_{cm}), v_{ci} \in \mathbb{R}^{V*dim}$ (word vectors of news contents)
7: **for** i **to** n **do**
8:      $output_{title} = $ DBi-LSTM(v_{ti})
9: **end for**
10: **for** i **to** m **do**
11:     $output_{content} = $ DBi-LSTM(v_{ci})
12: **end for**
13: $output_{title} = activation (output_{title})$
14: $output_{title} = maxpooling (output_{title})$
15: $output_{content} = activation (output_{content})$
16: $output_{content} = maxpooling (output_{content})$
17: attention = $[output_{title}; output_{content}]$
18: label = softmax(attention)
19: **return** label

---

4   Experiments and Results

We use scikit-learn, Tensorflow, and Keras to implement our model ARCNN. We use the news dataset of SCHOLAT and Fudan University document classification set[3] to experiment. We initialize the training epochs as 100, and early stop until the cross entropy begin to converge. In addition, we implement and compare our model with RCNN, CNN, fastText (a Facebook open source toolkit for text classification), SVM, LR algorithms.

---

[3] www.datatang.com/data/44139 and 43543.

4.1 Datasets

In our works, we evaluate our model with two different datasets. First is the academic social news dataset of SCHOLAT, with total 8627 documents, each of which includes titles and contents. We manually label them as 6 categories, including (1) academic news, (2) admissions, (3) recruitments, (4) call for papers, (5) school notices, and (6) others. We take a fixed length of 50 words for news titles and 651 words for contents.

Second is Fudan University document classification set, with total 17481 documents and 9 categories. We take a fixed length of 137 words for news titles and 3981 words for contents.

4.2 Results and Analysis

We divide each dataset into 10 parts randomly and evenly, 9 of which are taken as training sets and 1 as test set. We measure the performance of our model ARCNN by precision (P), recall (R) and F1 score (F1) [17].

Table 1. Experimental results for SCHOLAT dataset

		RCNN	CNN	fastText	SVM	LR	ARCNN
Academic news	P	0.849	0.862	0.840	0.845	0.809	**0.882**
	R	0.905	0.872	0.867	0.896	0.902	**0.902**
	F1	0.876	0.867	0.854	0.870	0.853	**0.892**
Admissions	P	0.923	0.915	0.913	0.862	0.824	**0.932**
	R	0.774	0.761	0.778	0.806	0.452	**0.780**
	F1	0.842	0.831	0.840	0.833	0.583	**0.849**
Recruitments	P	0.810	0.795	0.773	0.773	0.800	**0.838**
	R	0.773	0.761	0.708	0.773	0.545	**0.781**
	F1	0.791	0.777	0.739	0.773	0.689	**0.809**
Call for papers	P	0.825	0.813	0.837	0.857	0.963	**0.850**
	R	0.868	0.860	0.857	0.790	0.684	**0.882**
	F1	0.846	0.836	0.847	0.822	0.800	**0.866**
School Notices	P	0.818	0.808	0.652	0.804	0.844	**0.837**
	R	0.804	0.799	0.754	0.732	0.679	**0.821**
	F1	0.811	0.803	0.699	0.766	0.753	**0.829**
Others	P	0.912	0.902	0.872	0.891	0.862	**0.932**
	R	0.867	0.851	0.836	0.865	0.867	**0.881**
	F1	0.889	0.876	0.854	0.878	0.864	**0.906**

From the results in Table 1 and Fig. 3, the classification results of neural network classification algorithms (RCNN, CNN, ARCNN) are significantly better than traditional classification algorithms (SVM, LR), since they can effectively extract text features, and therefore enhance the accuracy of classification.

Compared with RCNN and CNN, the proposed model ARCNN have improved F1 score in all categories, showing that attention mechanism can better highlight the key information in the documents and optimize the word vectors as features. Our model is also better than fastText from the results in Table 3 and Fig. 3.

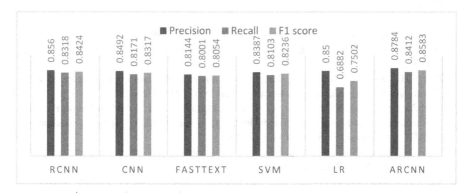

Fig. 3. The average values of precision, recall and F1 score of SCHOLAT dataset.

We also evaluate our model on Fudan University document classification set. As shown in Table 2, our model ARCNN performs better than RCNN, CNN, fastText, SVM and LR algorithms.

Table 2. Experimental results for Fudan University set

	RCNN	CNN	fastText	SVM	LR	ARCNN
P	0.944	0.937	0.931	0.935	0.929	**0.959**
R	0.946	0.937	0.924	0.927	0.907	**0.940**
F1	0.945	0.937	0.927	0.931	0.916	**0.949**

5 Conclusion

In this paper, we present a text classification model ARCNN based on attention mechanism and RCNN. We use word vectors trained by Word2Vec toolkit as text representation to avoid feature engineering phase. In the feature selection phase, we take news titles and contents as input respectively, using deep bidirectional LSTM layers and attention mechanism to further extract text features and highlight the key information in the documents. We use the academic news dataset of SCHOLAT and Fudan University document classification set to evaluate our model. The results demonstrate that our model has better performance than other text classification algorithms such as RCNN, CNN, fastText, SVM, and LR.

Acknowledgements. Our works were supported by the National Natural Science Foundation of China (No. 61772211), Science and Technology project of Guangdong (No. 2017A040405057), and "Challenge Cup" Gold Seed Cultivation Project of South China Normal University (No. 18JJKA03).

References

1. Wei, Z., Miao, D., Chauchat, J., et al.: N-grams based feature selection and text representation for Chinese text classification. Int. J. Comput. Intell. Syst. **2**(4), 365–374 (2009)
2. Zhang, H., Zhong, G.: Improving short text classification by learning vector representations of both words and hidden topics. Knowl.-Based Syst. **102**, 76–86 (2016)
3. Karthika Renuka, D., Hamsapriya, T., Raja Chakkaravarthi, M., Lakshmi Surya, P.: Spam classification based on supervised learning using machine learning techniques. ICTACT J. Commun. Technol. **2**(4), 1–7 (2011)
4. Wang, H.Y., Jian-Hui, L.I., Yang, F.L., et al.: Overview of support vector machine analysis and algorithm. Appl. Res. Comput. (2014)
5. Kurt, I., Ture, M., Kurum, A.T.: Comparing performances of logistic regression, classification and regression tree, and neural networks for predicting coronary artery disease. Expert Syst. Appl. **34**(1), 366–374 (2008)
6. Fu, C., Zeng, W., Tang, Y., Chen, L., Wei, J.: DNALS: a recommendation algorithm based on Chinese vocabulary emotion analysis of songs. Int. J. u-and e-Serv. Sci. Technol. **9**(9), 101–110 (2016)
7. Chen, X., Xu, L., Liu, Z., Sun, M., Luan, H.: Joint learning of character and word embeddings. In: International Conference on Artificial Intelligence, pp. 1236–1242. AAAI Press (2015)
8. Cui, P., Wang, X., Pei, J., Zhu, W.: A survey on network embedding. arXiv preprint arXiv: 1711.08752 (2017)
9. Aggarwal, C.C., Zhai, C.X.: A survey of text classification algorithms. In: Aggarwal, C., Zhai, C.X. (eds.) Mining Text Data, pp. 163–222. Springer, Berlin (2012). https://doi.org/10. 1007/978-1-4614-3223-4_6
10. Kim, Y.: Convolutional neural networks for sentence classification. arXiv preprint arXiv: 1408.5882 (2014)
11. Wang, P., Xu, B., Xu, J., et al.: Semantic expansion using word embedding clustering and convolutional neural network for improving short text classification. Neurocomputing **174** (PB), 806–814 (2016)
12. Lai, S., Xu, L., Liu, K., Zhao, J.: Recurrent convolutional neural networks for text classification. In: Proceedings of the Twenty-Ninth AAAI Conference on Artificial Intelligence, pp. 2267–2273. AAAI Press (2015)
13. Yin, W., Schütze, H.: Attentive convolution. arXiv preprint arXiv:1710.00519 (2017)
14. Bahdanau, D., Cho, K., Bengio, Y.: Neural machine translation by jointly learning to align and translate. Comput. Sci. (2014)
15. Glorot, X., Bordes, A., Bengio, Y.: Deep sparse rectifier neural networks. In: Proceedings of the Fourteenth International Conference on Artificial Intelligence and Statistics, pp. 315–323 (2011)
16. Memisevic, R., Zach, C., Hinton, G., Pollefeys, M.: Gated softmax classification. In: Advances in Neural Information Processing Systems, pp. 1603–1611 (2010)
17. Song, F., Lin, G.: Performance evaluation metric for text classifiers. Comput. Eng. **30**(13), 107–109 (2004)

Energy-Efficiency for Smartphones Using Interaction Link Prediction in Mobile Cloud Computing

Jiuyun Xu[1(✉)], Chao Guan[1], and Xiangrui Xu[2]

[1] College of Computer and Communication, China University of Petroleum,
Qingdao 266580, Shandong, China
jiuyun.xu@computer.org, 924484185@qq.com
[2] School of Computer, Electronics and Information, Guangxi University,
Nanning 530004, China
xiangrui.xu@qq.com

Abstract. Along With vast deployment of mobile cloud computing systems, users accessing any information on the Internet by smart phones are often based on continuous data communication. However, when the communication status is unstable, the mobile client needs to establish multiple connections with the cloud. This leads to great energy consumption, which poses a huge challenge to the usability of mobile cloud computing systems. In this article, considering the similarity of the accessibility data of strong interactive users and the predictability of user behaviour data, we proposes a link prediction method based on the maximization of user interaction behaviour (Maximize Interaction Link Prediction) in a specific environment for the mobile cloud computing: First, based on the data prediction model, we use the interaction degree method to improve the access data prediction for known users; Secondly, combining with the social network method we analyze and filter the prediction data; At last, we pre-store the above prediction data by the pre-storage mechanism. The Evaluations show that it can reduce mobile energy consumption significantly by around 20%.

Keywords: Access data prediction · Social network
Interaction times · Data pre-storage hit rate

1 Introduction

In mobile cloud computing, Energy-efficiency is particularly one of most concerning issues on mobile devices. Mobile cloud computing is a recent developed technology that combines mobile Internet and cloud computing [12]. On one hand, mobile devices, such as iphone and iwatch, are the device which have very limited computing capability and energy supply of their batteries [8]. On the other hand, mobile cloud computing can migrate data calculation and storage to the cloud to improve the disadvantages of small storage space [11].

© Springer Nature Singapore Pte Ltd. 2019
Y. Sun et al. (Eds.): ChineseCSCW 2018, CCIS 917, pp. 517–526, 2019.
https://doi.org/10.1007/978-981-13-3044-5_39

Ideally, the cloud is a critical part of mobile cloud computing which is a center as resource information service and application service for users. The mobile terminal does not need to have powerful computing storage capacity to provide users with the required services, but the mobile terminal needs to establish a connection with cloud before information exchange.

According the invegestion of the papers [3,4,7], almost 80 percent of mobile energy consumption is spent on establishing data connection and data transmission with the server in mobile cloud computing. Although a lot of research efforts have been focused on the energy-saving technologies, the current research on energy-efficiency still have to be improved.

1.1 Motivation

In this article, we aim to combine with the data pre-storage mode by mitigating the energy consumption of mobile devices in the scenario of the transmission of data between the mobile device and cloud computing system. In particular, we propose a link prediction method based on maximizing user interaction behavior (Maximize Interaction Link Prediction. MILP). Different from traditional data pre-storage modes, our solution is to combine with the interaction of social network and reduce the number of connections between mobile clients and the cloud by taking into account the similarity of the access data of strong interactive users and the predictability of user behavior data. Its main tasks are:

- Interactive behavior maximization stage: A frame structure of a mobile energy-saving model and a method for maximizing the impact based on user interaction behavior are proposed. Based on the data prediction model, we use the interaction degree method to improve the access data prediction for known users.
- Link prediction stage: An interaction random walk algorithm is proposed. In this article, the user behavior based social network method is used to analyze and filter the prediction data, it can predict as accurately as possible the current user's data information that may be accessed in the future.
- To achieve the purpose of energy-saving mobile phones, the data pre-storage mechanism is a critical part for pre-storing the above prediction data and reducing the number of communication times.

1.2 Challenges and Contributions

In the scenario of the mobile cloud computing, especially with weak signal of cellular network condition in the mountain area, much times constructing the connection between mobile device and the server of cloud computing need to consume a lot of power energy of mobile device. With the illumination of the Interaction Link Prediction in the social computing, MILP is able to mitigate mobile energy consumption in the data transmission with the server in mobile cloud computing, and thus extends the battery life so as to optimizing the user experience. More specifically, this paper makes the following contributions:

- We propose to add social network interactions to integrate with data pre-storage models to avoid using user background privacy information.
- We design an efficient Interaction Random Walk algorithm via not only utilizing interactions but also paying attention to the relationship between friends.

In the rest of this paper, a system model is presented in Sect. 2. After that, the description of maximize interaction link prediction is shown in Sect. 3. Then, the system evaluation in Sect. 4. After comparing with related work in Sect. 5, we draw conclusions in Sect. 6.

2   The Proposed System Model

To get over the challenge of energy consumption of smartphone during using mobile cloud service with bad communication condition, we propose a system model to leverage the data pre-storage architecture and prediction method. In Fig. 1, it shows the overview of our proposed architecture. In this architecture, it is based on the smart phone pre-storage model of user access data prediction combined with social network, adding interaction relationship maximization and link prediction modules to existing cloud servers which constitute the Maximize Interaction Link Prediction method proposed in this article. It includes the "Mobile Terminal" and "Cloud" levels. "Mobile Terminal" consists of mobile intelligent terminal device that can complete information exchange and data pre-storage model; "Cloud" refers to a cloud server, which is virtual resource information center that provides powerful computing storage capabilities. The "Cloud" shown in the figure consists of a server, a database, the Data Prediction Module and so on.

The core of this architecture is the Data Prediction Module. Its main task is to predict the data that may be used again in the future via the proposed MILP method and return the prediction data to the local area which acts as a local cache. The purpose of the architecture is to reduce the power consumption of multiple connection establishment due to poor communication environment. When user send data request, mobile terminal need to establish connection with Cloud firstly, and then transmit data with Cloud via wireless communication network (①). The server data storage module queries historical user access data and social activities after received the data request from mobile terminal. For the historical data, the Data Prediction Module begins to predict the data via interaction relationship maximization method (②), and then filter the data predicted before via link prediction (③). The final predicted data is returned to the local data pre-storage module via wireless communication network (①). When the user requests similar data again, app firstly sends local data request to the cache in data pre-storage module and queries corresponding results (④). The data response is returned from data pre-storage module (⑤). The process reduces the power consumption via avoiding multiple connection establishment with Cloud.

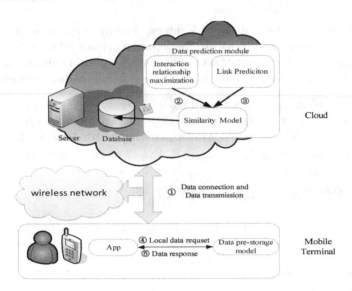

Fig. 1. The architecture of the MILP method

3   The Maximized Interaction Link Prediction

3.1   The Maximized Interaction Influence Algorithm

To avoid using user background privacy information. We add social network interactions to integrate with data pre-storage model. The basic idea is interaction relationships. The more users interact, the stronger similarity is. Target user may access the same data which have accessed by users who have a high degree of interaction similarity with them. In order to quantitatively calculate the degree of behavioral interaction, We formalize the problem with a Directed Acyclic graph (DAG) $G = \langle V, E, W \rangle$ as virtual social network, interaction relationships included. where V refers to the users, E refers to the connections between users and W refers to the number of interactions (like, comment, forward and other interactive behaviours). Each $W < v_1, v_2 >$ is defined as follows: If the number of interactions between user v_1 and user v_2 is w, edge $\langle v_1, v_2 \rangle$ has weight w; if user v_1 does not interact with user v_2, then $W_{v_1 v_2} = 0$.

After defining the social network, We also define the user request as a collection:

$Q = \{id, data, Inter, friend\}$. Where id is the unique identifier of the user when the user requests the service. The $data$ indicates the user access data information in the storage module. $Inter$ represents the collection of user interactions with other users. The $friend$ judges whether the user is a friend relationship, it is 1 when users are mutual friend relationship, else it is 0 when users are potential friend relationship.

The first for maximize interaction influence is building a neighbour group and calculate the degree of interaction. When the user u initiates a request to the server, a neighbour group is constructed according to the historical interaction times Inter. An improved degree of interaction method is used to calculate the degree of interaction of each neighbour in the neighbour group with the target user. The number of interactions between u and v is expressed as $I(u, v)$.

Based on the two factors of mutual influence between the users and the number of contacts, the calculation formula of the user interaction degree is given. The specific algorithm formula for the degree of interaction between users is as follows:

$$I_{mutual}(u, v) = \sqrt{W_{uv} + W_{vu}} + \sqrt{W_{uv} + W_{vu} - |W_{uv} - W_{vu}|} \qquad (1)$$

In this topic, the relationship between friends is regarded as undirected. The formula for the degree of interaction between users is:

$$I_{mutual}(u, v) = 2\sqrt{I_{uv}} \qquad (2)$$

As can be seen from the above formula, the higher the frequency of interactions are, the greater the number of mutual interactions are, the greater the degree of user interaction $I_{mutual}u, v$ is. The second for maximize interaction influence is calculating social influence based on interactive behaviour. Based on the formula, the interaction degree between the neighbour user and the target user in the neighbour group is deduced, but this obviously cannot be directly used to evaluate the influence between the users. In the case of complex interaction, the influence of the neighbour user on the target user is not only limited to the interaction relationship, but also includes friend relationship friend. In general, the relationship between the number of friends and the number of interactions Iu, v is not regular and cannot be directly associated with the formula for not an order of magnitude. As a result, calculating the influence of the friend relationship and interaction relationship on the target user requires a certain percentage conversion of the number of interactions $I(u, v)$. We measure the influence of interaction behaviour based on the above formula:

$$I_{mutual}(u, v) = I_{mutual}(u, v) \times \frac{I(u, v)}{W_u + W_v} \qquad (3)$$

Among them, $SI_{mutual}(u, v)$ indicates the influence of user u and user v through interactions, $I_{mutual}(u, v)$ represents the degree of interaction calculated by formula, $N(v)$ represents the set of neighbours of user v, and W_1 represents the number of total interactions between user and its total neighbours. It can be seen from formula that the number of interactions between the two users represented by $I(u, v)$ plays a decisive role for $SI_{mutual}(u, v)$, and the specific $SI_{mutual}(u, v)$ value can be calculated to measure the influence of interaction behaviour between users. The greater the $SI_{mutual}(u, v)$, the higher the degree of intimacy between u and v is, the more likely they are affected by each other's data, and the more likely user u access user v's historical access data; The greater the $SI_{mutual}(u, v)$, the more the relationship based on the interaction behaviour between them alienate, and the less the chance that the user u will access the historical access data of the user v in the future. The pseudo-code of maximize interaction influence is described in Algorithm 1.

Algorithm 1. Maximize interaction influence algorithm

Input: the user request $Q = id, data, Inter, friend$
Output: SI_{mutual}
1: **for all** Q **do**
2:     $G = (V, E, W)$ *undirected   graph* $\leftarrow Inter, friend$
3: **end for**
4: **for all** $q_i \in Q$ **do**
5:     **for all** $I_i \in Inter$ **do**
6:         build a neighbour group Q_k
7:     **end for**
8: **end for**
9: **for all** $u_i \in U$ **do**
10:     **for all** $u_j \in Q$ **do**
11:         $I_{mutual} \leftarrow I(u_i, u_j)$
12:         calculate new $SI_{mutual}(u_i, u_j)$
13:     **end for**
14: **end for**
15: **return** $SI_{mutual}(u_i, u_j)$.

3.2   Interaction Random Walk Model

For the friend selection problem, in addition to the maximization influence model based on the user interaction degree, the actual friend relationship also has critical influence on the target user. The key of the link prediction recommendation method is the calculation of users' similarity. The access data of neighbours with larger similarity is more possibility to be the data that the target user will access next. This efficient Interaction Random Walk model we proposed based on link prediction paying attention to the relationship between friends introduces interaction based on user behaviour and identifies friends with different intensities in social networks. It needs to form a weighted social network. Furthermore, it can obtain the $TOP\ K$ user access data as the data that the target user will access next via walk method trending to larger similarity node based on the weighted social network. Particularly, considering only the network of friends, the strength of the relationship w_{ij} between the users u_i and u_j is shown in the following formula. The number of mutual friends plays a decisive role.

$$w_{ij} = \begin{cases} \Gamma(u_i) \cap \Gamma(u_i) + 1, & \text{if } \langle u_i, u_j \rangle \in E \\ 0, & \text{if } \langle u_i, u_j \rangle \notin E, \end{cases} \tag{4}$$

However, as mentioned previously, the number of interactions (user behaviors such as comment, forward, and sharing) between users used to indicate the strength of their friendship can improve the actual accuracy of the network topology. If the user is more concerned about a user's data information, the user may be more likely to select this data as the next data to be accessed. Therefore, we need to utilize the interaction influence SI_{mutual} as shown in Eq. 5.1. To this end, The correlation strength w_{ij} of the users u_i and u_j is determined by the number of mutual friends and the interaction influence SI_{mutual}.

$$w_{ij} = \begin{cases} \Gamma(u_i) \cap \Gamma(u_i) + 1 + SI_{mutual}(u_i, u_j), & \text{if } \langle u_i, u_j \rangle \in E \\ SI_{mutual}(u_i, u_j), & \text{if } \langle u_i, u_j \rangle \notin E, \end{cases} \qquad (5)$$

The formula shows that the influence of interactive relationships based on interactive behavior will have a greater impact on relevance. Therefore, the symmetric adjacency matrix $\mathcal{A}' = (a'_{ij})$ can be used to represent the undirected weighted social network, where $a'_{ij} = w_{ij}$.

We assume that a walker is on the target user in the social network, the walker can randomly walk the vertices according to the network topology in traditional social network. However, the walker need to consider the influence of interactive behaviour in our model and no longer walk with equal probability like a simple topology. A local random walk process can be described using a transition probability matrix Q whose element q'_{ij} are:

$$q'_{ij} = \frac{W_{ij}}{\sum_{k=1}^{\Gamma(u_i)} W_{ik}} \qquad (6)$$

The formula shows the probability q'_{ij} that the random walker chooses from the vertex u_i to u_j, which is equivalent to the correlation strength W_{ij} based on the interaction relationship. It is important for the probability of a walker choosing a direction to bias towards users with strong interaction. In this way, the similarity of u_i and u_j can be calculated by the probability that the walker will experience multiple paths from the starting point u_i to arrive at u_j.

$$sim(u_i, u_j) = \sum_{a=1}^{b} \prod_{t=2}^{l} q'_{ij}(t) \qquad (7)$$

Among them, b represents the number of possible paths between u_i and u_j; The variable l represents the path length of every path a; t represents the step within a possible path. In summary, the above process can obtain the TOP of $sim(u_i, u_j)$ K users access data as the data that the target user will access next.

4   Energy-Consumption Evaluation

We evaluate MILP from two aspects. First, we analyze and evaluate the performance of $Top - k$ in MILP by evaluation index and the data size of pre-storage module. Second, we examine the energy saving effect of our system by simulating the Real-World Experiments.

We carried up all our experiments using a Letv X500 smartphone (with CPU 1.6 GHz and 2 GB RAM), running the Android 6.0 operating system. We use the AliCloud as the rear-end Cloud service platform. We use Spring Tool Suite 3.7.0. RELEASE to execute the MILP code and Android Studio 1.4 to develop the front-end. We deploy the remote resource proxy on a laptop computer. The connection of smartphones and the laptop computer under the different WIFI environment.

This article focuses on the predictability of user access data in the context of interactions between users. The data set uses some of the data in Tencent's Weibo data, including friends' relationships by user focuses others as *relation* field in database, interactions as interaction field in database (likes, responses, comments, etc.) and user access data as data field in database.

According to the dataset, we start from the target users and collect user friend relationships via the breadth-first strategy. A small social network is first simulated through the database *relation* field, only taking the friend relationships between these users into consideration. Then we predict the data target user will access next through the MILP method proposed in this article, integrating *interaction* field and *data* field. We can obtain K users with the highest similarity with using the amount of mutual friends and interactive influences. This process does not involve user background information and improves the hit rate of accessing data according to the user interaction behaviour.

Determining the value of K is particularly a key on solving the relationship between the amount of pre-storage data and the energy consumption of mobile phones. $Top - k$ recommendations commonly used in the evaluation are F-measure (F_m) with formula of Precision (P) and Recall (R), which are $P = \frac{N_f}{K}$, $R = \frac{N_f}{N}$ and $F_m = \frac{2 \times P \times R}{P+R}$.

According to the above index Precision, the accuracy of predicted potential friends using the MILP method is highest when $k = 5$ as shown in Fig. 2. In this way, the K value can be found. The amount of pre-storage data can satisfy the accuracy requirement and consume as little power as possible.

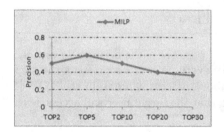
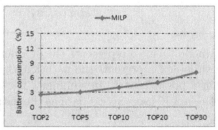

Precision for MILP   Battery consumption for MILP under $Top - k$

Fig. 2. Comparison of energy consumption with the users $k = 5$

On the other hand, only determining the value of $Top-k$ cannot we determine the relationship between the pre-stored data capacity and the mobile phone's energy consumption. The access data capacity of all friends of the target user is $10M$ and the obtained $Datasize(u)$ experiment result is shown in Fig. 2. According to the formal model of the relationship in Sect. 4, when the data capacity is about $60M$ as $\sum_{n\in \overline{K}} \mu SI_{mutual}(v_n, u) \times Size_n$, the pre-stored data can best meet the accuracy requirement and minimize power consumption.

5   Related Work

The study of energy-saving technologies in communication includes two major models: the push and pull mode. The push mode is the mobile terminal passively accepts the server data. The smart phone initiatively acquires the data block related to the current processing and operation from the server is the pull mode. Lim et al. [6] proposed an methods that active mode replaced by passive mode, Although utilizing pull mode consumes low energy, there is no guarantee that the data is latest. Based on this, Burgstahler et al. [1] found that the energy consumption of the push model is much more than that of the pull model and proposed a model instant switching method which can save energy and reduce the delay. To realize the extension of the mobile terminal's battery life, Eom et al. [2] used the hybrid coding method to improve the energy efficiency of the mobile terminal in the mobile cloud computing environment.

To benefit the performance of mobile applications, computing migration was introduced which refers to the process of moving complex computing tasks from the smartphone to the data center with high computing capability. It can minimize the energy consumed by the program for calculation and communication. Khairy et al. [3] reduced the energy consumption caused by migration by supervising learning. Paterna et al. [7] used active services to reduce the communication delay and energy consumption of mobile terminals. Daniela et al. achieved the goal of minimizing energy consumption on the basis that the mobile terminal satisfies the reasonable execution time. For the unloading scheme in mobile cloud computing, based on the load balance in the distributed system, Kumar et al. [4] provided a simple and effective calculation method to analyze the necessity of offloading computing tasks to the server. Rudenko et al. [9] verified the effectiveness of the offloading technique through experiments, and proved that the migration can indeed achieve the goal of reducing energy consumption on the mobile side through computational migration. Considering to reduce the energy consumption of computation in the mobile terminal, some scholars have studied the mobile phone energy-saving method of data pre-storage technology in mobile cloud computing paradigm, and have achieved the purpose of energy saving by predicting the data that the user may visit returned to the local area. Shen et al. [10] calculated the energy required for the passive cache data to be replaced through the energy efficiency model, and selected the pre-fetched data object with a minimum energy consumption to perform a pre-storage operation. Liu et al. [5] studied the data pre-storage method when the network connectivity was unstable. It was proposed that when the network connectivity is poor, the data frequently used by the user was pre-stored with the least energy consumption.

6   Conclusion

In this paper, a link prediction method (MILP) have been presented, which is based on the maximization of user interaction behaviour. The method considers the similarity of the accessibility data of strong interactive users and the predictability of user behaviour data. We implement the pre-storage model, and show that MILP can have 20 to 25 percent of energy saving on mobile devices.

References

1. Burgstahler, D., Lampe, U., Richerzhagen, N., Steinmetz, R.: Push vs. pull: an energy perspective (short paper), pp. 190–193 (2013)
2. Eom, B., Lee, C., Lee, H., Ryu, W.: An adaptive remote display scheme to deliver mobile cloud services. IEEE Trans. Consum. Electron. **60**(3), 540–547 (2014)
3. Khairy, A., Ammar, H.H., Bahgat, R.: Smartphone energizer: extending smartphone's battery life with smart offloading, pp. 329–336 (2013)
4. Kumar, K., Lu, Y.: Cloud computing for mobile users: can offloading computation save energy? IEEE Comput. **43**(4), 51–56 (2010)
5. Liu, F., Shu, P., Lui, J.C.S.: Appatp : an energy conserving adaptive mobile-cloud transmission protocol. IEEE Trans. Comput. **64**(11), 3051–3063 (2015)
6. Misra, A., Lim, L.: Optimizing sensor data acquisition for energy-efficient smartphone-based continuous event processing, vol. 1, pp. 88–97 (2011)
7. Paterna, F., Acquaviva, A., Benini, L.: Aging-aware energy-efficient workload allocation for mobile multimedia platforms. IEEE Trans. Parallel Distrib. Syst. **24**(8), 1489–1499 (2013)
8. Pedersen, P.E.: Adoption of mobile internet services: an exploratory study of mobile commerce early adopters. J. Organ. Comput. Electron. Commer. **15**(3), 203–222 (2005)
9. Rudenko, A., Reiher, P.L., Popek, G.J., Kuenning, G.H.: Saving portable computer battery power through remote process execution. Mob. Comput. Commun. Rev. **2**(1), 19–26 (1998)
10. Shen, H., Kumar, M., Das, S.K., Wang, Z.: Energy-efficient data caching and prefetching for mobile devices based on utility. Mob. Netw. Appl. **10**(4), 475–486 (2005)
11. Xu, Y., Mao, S.: A survey of mobile cloud computing for rich media applications. IEEE Wirel. Commun. **20**(3), 46–53 (2013)
12. Zhou, L., Yang, Z., Rodrigues, J.J.P.C., Guizani, M.: Exploring blind online scheduling for mobile cloud multimedia services. IEEE Wirel. Commun. **20**(3), 54–61 (2013)

MDIS: A Node Localization Algorithm Based on Multi-region Division and Similarity Matching

Hao Wang[1], Haixiang Chen[1], Ping Yuan[2], Feng Yin[3], Qian Luo[4], and Liangyin Chen[1(✉)]

[1] School of Computer Science, Sichuan University, Chengdu, China
124324651@qq.com, 1309924894@qq.com, chenliangyin@scu.edu.cn
[2] School of Mathematics and Information Engineering,
Chongqing University of Education, Chongqing, China
pypingyuan@163.com
[3] School of Computer Science and Technology,
Southwest University for Nationalities, Chengdu, China
yf_eagle@aliyun.com
[4] The Second Research Institute, General Administration
of Civil Aviation of China, Chengdu, China
caacsri_luoqian@163.com

Abstract. This paper proposes an improved localization algorithm called MDIS (Multi-Region Division In Shadow). The algorithm divides the traditional overlapping communication regions constructed by neighbor anchor nodes (nodes whose locations are known) into many subregions, and coordinates of centroid points in these subregions could be calculated. Furthermore, the algorithm establishes relation arrays of the unknown node to anchor nodes and centroid points to anchor nodes. Then the location of unknown nodes in subregions is determined by calculating the correlation coefficient of above relation arrays. And simulations demonstrate that MDIS algorithm increases the accuracy and stability compared to other range-free algorithms.

Keywords: Multi-Region Division · MDIS · Relation array
Correlation coefficient

1 Introduction

Sensor nodes are usually randomly deployed and perform a lot of monitoring tasks in different environment in Wireless Sensor Networks (WSNs) [1]. And location information is important for sensor nodes which monitor environmental objectives [2]. In the field of node localization, sensor nodes can be divided into two categories, one is the anchor node (location is known) whose coordinates are usually obtained by GPS or manual deployment. The other is the unknown node (location is unknown), which needs to estimate its coordinates with the

© Springer Nature Singapore Pte Ltd. 2019
Y. Sun et al. (Eds.): ChineseCSCW 2018, CCIS 917, pp. 527–535, 2019.
https://doi.org/10.1007/978-981-13-3044-5_40

information provided by surrounding anchor nodes. At present, there are two kinds of localization algorithms. One is range-based algorithm that need measure distance among nodes. The other is range-free location algorithm which only completes locating through the angle or hop information without distance measurement. Recent range-based localization algorithms [3] are mostly influenced by the environment, and it leads to large locating error and high algorithm complexity. However, one problem that cannot be ignored in the range-free localization algorithm [4] is also the large locating error. So it is proved that there is still a lot of research space for the localization method, which is worthy of further excavation and exploration. In order to reduce the locating error without raising costs, this paper proposes a range-free localization algorithm by studying the current localization algorithms. The main innovations and contributions are as follows.

(1) This paper proposes MDIS model to implement a novel range-free localization algorithm that determines the unknown node in which subregion through correlation coefficient calculated by relation arrays of the unlocated node to its neighbor anchor nodes and centroid points to these anchor nodes.
(2) The program is designed to verify the rationality of the algorithm by changing Anchor Node Rate, Number of Nodes, GPS Error and Communication Radius of the Anchor Node in simulation scenarios.

2   Related Work

In general, RSSI, TOA, TDOA and AOA are commonly used in range-based localization algorithms. And they calculate location of nodes by using the method of triangulation and maximum likelihood estimation. Some common range-free localization algorithms are introduced as follows. Convex algorithm regards the communication connection between nodes as the geometric constraint problem, and it can build a node location constraint model to locate nodes by using the connection information between nodes. Bounding Box algorithm [5] is to determine the one hop overlapping communication area, which is constituted by neighbor anchor nodes of the unknown node, then the location of centroid point in the region is considered as the position of the unknown node. DV-hop is based on distance vector routing [6]. APIT algorithm [7] is assumed that an unknown node can receive N signals from all anchor nodes. And it finds out all the combinations of three anchor nodes from N anchor nodes. Determine which triangle the unknown nodes are inside and mark such triangles. Centroid points are connected to form a polygon and then centroid point's coordinates of the polygon is regarded as location of the unknown node. And Centroid algorithm regards the centroid point of the polygon constructed by the unknown node's neighbor anchor nodes as the location [8].

3   Model Design

Node localization algorithms still exist many problems, because it is easily influenced by environment. And the cost of range-based location algorithms is still high and location efficiency is low. So MDIS algorithm introduced in this chapter is to improve the traditional range-free algorithm, unknown nodes are located more accurately without increasing the locating cost and eliminating the signal influence indirectly.

3.1 Background

Before introducing the algorithm, it is necessary to explain the concepts of the algorithm. And two concepts called relation array and correlation coefficient in this paper are introduced.

Definition 1. *Relation Array is a one-dimensional array which represents the distance array of one node to its neighbor anchor nodes.*

Definition 2. *Correlation Coefficient denotes the degree of distance between nodes, and the greater correlation coefficient, the closer location between nodes. The interval of the correlation coefficient of nodes is* $[-1, 1]$.

$$\cos\theta = \frac{\sum_{i=1}^{n}(A_i \times B_i)}{\sqrt{\sum_{i=1}^{n}A_i^2} \times \sqrt{\sum_{i=1}^{n}B_i^2}} \qquad (1)$$

$A = (A_1, A_2, \cdots, A_n), B = (B_1, B_2, \cdots, B_n)$.

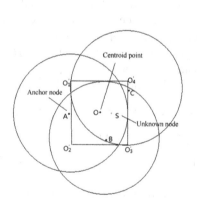

Fig. 1. Convex model

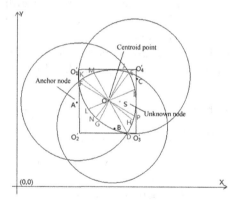

Fig. 2. MDIS model

And there are two theoretical foundations of this paper. One of the theoretical bases is from the convex algorithm, the convex algorithm regards the communication connection between nodes as the geometric constraint problem and it can build a node location constraint model to locate nodes through using the neighbor information among sensor nodes. In Fig. 1, A, B and C are three anchor nodes, S is the unknown node and O'_1, O'_2, O'_3, O'_4 are the four vertices of a restricted rectangle with overlapping communication areas of three anchor nodes. At this time, the centroid point O of $O_1'O_2'O_3'O_4'$ approximately regarded as the location of the unknown node S. Another theoretical basis is from cosine similarity formula. For two vectors, their similarity can be measured by the cosine of the angle.

In Fig. 1, there are two unknown nodes R_1, R_2 and three anchor nodes A, B, C. Meanwhile, the distances of R_1 away from A, B and C are L_{1A}, L_{1B}, L_{1C} respectively. The distances of R_2 to A, B and C are L_{2A}, L_{2B}, L_{2C} respectively. Then the relation array of R_1 is $relation - array_1(L_{1A}, L_{1B}, L_{1C})$ and the relation array of R_2 is $relation - array_2(L_{2A}, L_{2B}, L_{2C})$. So the correlation coefficient of R_1 and R_2 can be denoted by $\frac{L_{1A} \times L_{2A} + L_{1B} \times L_{2B} + L_{1C} \times L_{2C}}{\sqrt{L_{1A}^2 + L_{1B}^2 + L_{1C}^2} \times \sqrt{L_{2A}^2 + L_{2B}^2 + L_{2C}^2}}$.

3.2   MDIS Model

The core of MDIS model is to divide the overlapping communication area of anchor nodes into multiple parts. Draw parallel lines of AB, AC, BC over point O and intersect the area DEF with G, H, I, J, K, L, then connect the D, E and F to O and intersect the area DEF with M, N, P. Through the above method, the overlapping area DEF can be divided into twelve subregions in Fig. 2. In this way, the relatively complex location problems are transformed into the problem of finding the best location subregion. According to the circle equations, the intersection coordinates of three circles can be calculated. The coordinates of D, E and F can be denoted by $(x_d, y_d), (x_e, y_e)$ and (x_f, y_f). According to the feature of the circular tangent, the coordinates of O_1, O_2, O_3, O_4 are denoted by $(x_f, y_b+r), (x_f, y_d), (x_a+r, y_d)$ and (x_a+r, y_b+r). Then the coordinates of O can be calculated as $(x_f + \frac{x_a+r-x_f}{2}, y_d + \frac{y_b+r-y_d}{2})$ according to characteristics of the quadrilateral centroid point. Because HK, LI, GJ are parallel to AB, AC, BC respectively, so the slope of HK, LI and GJ can be expressed as $k_{HK} = k_{AB} = \frac{y_b-y_a}{x_b-x_a}, k_{LI} = k_{AC} = \frac{y_c-y_a}{x_c-x_a}, k_{GJ} = k_{BC} = \frac{y_c-y_b}{x_c-x_b}$. The slope of DM, EN and FP can be expressed as $K_{DM} = \frac{y_d-(y_d+\frac{y_b+r-y_d}{2})}{x_d-(x_f+\frac{x_a+r-x_f}{2})}, K_{EN} = \frac{y_e-(y_d+\frac{y_b+r-y_d}{2})}{x_e-(x_f+\frac{x_a+r-x_f}{2})}, K_{FP} = \frac{y_f-(y_d+\frac{y_b+r-y_d}{2})}{x_f-(x_f+\frac{x_a+r-x_f}{2})}$. In summary, equations of HK, LI, GJ, DM, EN, FP can be expressed. Associated with the circular equation, the coordinates of all intersections of lines and the overlapping area DEF can be calculated.

Each subregion is a graphic with a curved edge, in order to find the centroid coordinates of each subregion, the following conversion is needed. Because the subregion is small in reality, we can approximate the curved side of the subregion into a line so that the subregion is converted into a triangular region, as shown in Fig. 3. Then the problem of solving the centroid coordinate of the subregion is transformed into the centroid coordinate problem of solving the triangle. If the centroid point of the triangle OGD is O_1, the coordinates of the centroid point of the triangle OG can be expressed as $(\frac{1}{3} \times (x_O + x_G + x_D), \frac{1}{3} \times (y_O + y_G + y_D))$. So centroid points of all subregions can be calculated, and relation arrays can be denoted as $(d_{ia}, d_{ib}, d_{ic})_{12 \times 3}, d_{ij} = \sqrt{(x_{o_i} - x_j)^2 + (y_{o_i} - y_j)^2}, i \in [1, 12], j \in \{a, b, c\}$. For the unknown node S, although its location is unknown, node S can

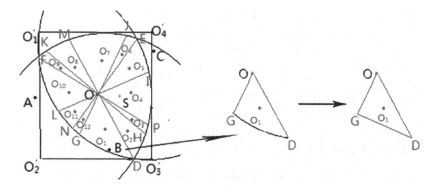

Fig. 3. Subregion approximation into triangle

obtain the signals sent by A, B, C and can calculate the RSSI. According to the RSSI distance decay model formula $d = \frac{|RSSI| - A}{10 \times n}$, where d denotes the distance between receiving sensor node and sending sensor node, and $RSSI$ is received signal strength. A is signal strength when the distance between the sender and the receiver is $1m$, and n is the environmental attenuation factor. The relation array of unknown node S can be denoted as $(10^{\frac{|RSSI_a| - A}{10 \times n}}, 10^{\frac{|RSSI_b| - A}{10 \times n}}, 10^{\frac{|RSSI_c| - A}{10 \times n}})$, where $RSSI_a, RSSI_b, RSSI_c$ represent the signal strength of S to receive the anchor nodes A, B and C respectively. Thus, formula 1 is applied to compute the correlation coefficient of the unknown node S and each centroid point of twelve subregions. According to the experimental situation, the above mentioned location area DEF is relatively small area in the actual situation, and the interference is same for any point in area DEF. So it is reasonable to denote the distance of two nodes by using RSSI signal attenuation model. According to formula 1 and the relation array, the correlation coefficient matrix between the unknown point S and each centroid point of all subregions can be denoted as,

$$r_c = \left(\frac{10^{\frac{|RSSI_a| - A}{10 \times n}} \times d_{ia} + 10^{\frac{|RSSI_b| - A}{10 \times n}} \times d_{ib} + 10^{\frac{|RSSI_c| - A}{10 \times n}} \times d_{ic}}{\sqrt{d_{ia}^2 + d_{ib}^2 + d_{ic}^2} \times \sqrt{(10^{\frac{|RSSI_a| - A}{10 \times n}})^2 + (10^{\frac{|RSSI_b| - A}{10 \times n}})^2 + (10^{\frac{|RSSI_c| - A}{10 \times n}})^2}} \right)_{12 \times 1} \quad (2)$$

The larger the correlation coefficient between the unknown node S and the centroid point of a subregion, the closer their location is. Then the location of the centroid point with the largest correlation coefficient can be regarded as the location of S. When the number of anchor nodes whose signals could be received by node S is 2, its location can be estimated as the coordinates of the centroid point of the bounding box for communication circles of these two anchor nodes. When S could only receive signals from one anchor node, its location can be estimated as the location of this anchor node. When there is no neighbor anchor node around node S, S cannot be located. In summary, the location coordinates of the node can be computed by using formula 3,

$$L_S = \begin{cases} unsure, & n = 0 \\ (x_a, y_a), & n = 1 \\ (\frac{x_a+x_b}{2}, \frac{y_a+y_b}{2}), & n = 2 \\ (x_{o_i}, y_{o_i}), \ r_{so_i} = \|r_c\|_\infty, & n > 2 \end{cases} \tag{3}$$

where n is the number of neighbor anchor nodes for S, and r_{SO_i} denotes correlation coefficient of S and O_i.

3.3 MDIS Algorithm

(1) Initialize the entire wireless sensor network, the maximum value of communication radius is r. For node k, its neighbor discovery process can use neighbor discovery algorithms [9]. When it finds its neighbor node, the set of neighbor anchor nodes is marked as $\{A(k)\}$, where $\{A(k)\} = (\cup_{i=1}^{a_k} A_i)$, and the number of neighbor anchor nodes is a_k.

(2) For a node k, when the number of neighbor anchor nodes is less than 3, the coordinates of node k can be calculated according to formula 3. And when the number of its neighbor anchors is equal or greater than 3, the coordinates of the centroid point in each subregion can be estimated by selecting 3 nodes with strongest signal strength of k neighbor anchor nodes to construct MDIS model.

(3) Calculate relation arrays of the unknown node and centroid points of all subregions, and calculate correlation coefficient matrix of the relation array of the unknown node and the relation array of the centroid point of each subregion. At last, the location of the centroid point with the largest correlation coefficient is estimated as the location denoted as $L_k(x_k, y_k)$.

(4) Take turns to locate other nodes.

4 Simulation

In this section, each experiment runs for 20 times and then calculates the average value as the result. In order to make the experimental simulation more realistic, the communication radiation model is constructed in the simulation algorithm, and nodes are deployed in $500\,m \times 500\,m$ area randomly. The degree of irregularity (DOI) is also considered in the simulation. And the main simulation parameters are Anchor Node Rate, Number of Nodes, GPS Error and Communication radius of the Anchor Node (Table 1).

(1) The impact of anchor node rate (Figs. 4 and 5)
(2) The impact of the number of nodes (Figs. 6 and 7)
(3) The impact of GPS Error (Figs. 8 and 9)
(4) The impact of anchor node communication radius (Figs. 10 and 11)

Table 1. Simulation parameters

Parameter	Value
Length of area	500 m
Width of area	500 m
Number of nodes	0–300
Anchor node rate	0.1–0.2
DOI	0.015
GPS error	10–40 m
Radius of the unknown node (r)	$r = r_{max}(1 - DOI), r_{max} = 100\,\text{m}$
Radius of the anchor node (r_a)	$r_a = \beta r, \beta \in [1, 4]$

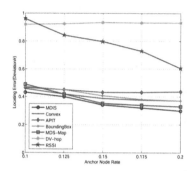

Fig. 4. Impact on locating accuracy

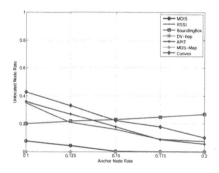

Fig. 5. Impact on unlocated node rate

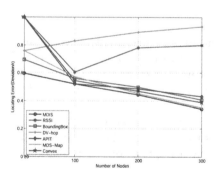

Fig. 6. Impact on locating accuracy

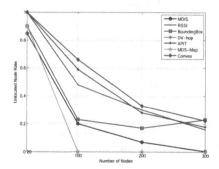

Fig. 7. Impact on unlocated node rate

534   H. Wang et al.

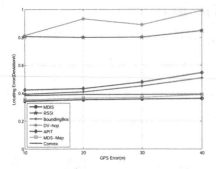

Fig. 8. Impact on locating accuracy

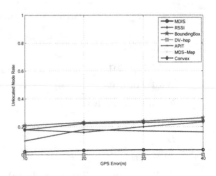

Fig. 9. Impact on unlocated node rate

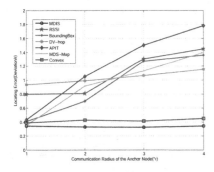

Fig. 10. Impact on locating accuracy

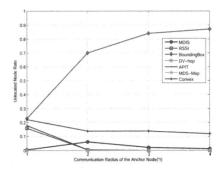

Fig. 11. Impact on unlocated node rate

5 Conclusion

In conclusion, the main idea of MDIS algorithm is to segment the overlapping localization area. And then position of the unknown node can be estimated by constructing relation arrays of nodes and calculating correlation coefficient of nodes. According to (1), (2), (3), (4) of Sect. 4, MDIS algorithm is applied in locating scenarios with different parameters. Compared to other range-free and RSSI based localization algorithms, the locating error of MDIS algorithm is the smallest, and the unlocated node rate is less than 10%. In the future, security of nodes will be considered in this algorithm by using hop count information.

Acknowledgements. This paper is supported by the NNSFC (grant number 61373091); Civil Aviation Airport United Laboratory of Second Research Institute, CAAC && Sichuan University of Chengdu (grant number 2015-YF04-00050-JH); the Collaborative Innovation of Industrial Cluster Project of Chengdu (grant number 2016-XT00-00015-GX); NNSFC&CAAC U1533203; the key Technology R&D program of Sichuan Province (grant number 2016GZ0068).

References

1. Chen, L., Xiong, X., Liu, K., et al.: POPA: localising nodes by splitting PLA with NTH-HOP anchor neighbours. Electron. Lett. **50**(13), 964–966 (2014). https://doi.org/10.1049/el.2013.4046
2. Rodriquez, R.Y., Julcapoma, M.R., Jacinto, R.A.: Network monitoring environmental quality in agriculture and pisciculture with low power sensor nodes based on ZigBee and GPRS technology. In: IEEE Xxiii International Congress on Electronics, Electrical Engineering and Computing, pp. 1–6. IEEE (2017). https://doi.org/10.0.4.85/INTERCON.2016.7815578
3. Qiang, R., Wang, W., Wang, H., et al.: 3D maximum likelihood estimation positioning algorithm based on RSSI ranging. In: Advanced Information Technology, Electronic and Automation Control Conference, pp. 1311–1314. IEEE (2017). https://doi.org/10.1109/IAEAC.2017.8054226
4. Shahzad, F., Shaltami, T., Shakshukhi, E.: DV-maxHop: a fast and accurate range-free localization algorithm for anisotropic wireless networks. IEEE Trans. Mob. Comput. **PP**(99), 2494–2505 (2017). https://doi.org/10.1109/TMC.2016.2632715
5. Simic, S.N., Sastry, S.: Distributed localization in wireless ad hoc networks (2001). https://doi.org/10.1145/1653760.1653768
6. Niculescu, D., Nath, B.: DV based positioning in ad hoc networks. Telecommun. Syst. **22**(1–4), 267–280 (2003). https://doi.org/10.1023/A:1023403323460
7. He, T., Huang, C., Blum, B.M., et al.: Range-free localization schemes for large scale sensor networks. In: International Conference on Mobile Computing and Networking, pp. 81–95. ACM (2005)
8. Kim, K.Y., Shin, Y.: A distance boundary with virtual nodes for the weighted centroid localization algorithm. Sensors **18**(4), 1054 (2018). https://doi.org/10.3390/s18041054
9. Wei, L., Zhou, B., Ma, X., et al.: Lightning: a high-efficient neighbor discovery protocol for low duty cycle WSNs. IEEE Commun. Lett. **20**(5), 966–969 (2016). https://doi.org/10.1109/LCOMM.2016.2536018

An Efficient Graph-Search Algorithm for Full Link Application Suggestion

Haijie Zhang[1], Nan Zeng[2], Hu Song[3], Menghan Xu[3], Huiyu Wang[3], Bo Yang[4], and Chen Lyu[1,5(✉)]

[1] School of Information Science and Engineering, Shandong Normal University, Jinan, China
[2] State Grid Corporation of China, Beijing, China
[3] Information and Telecommunication Branch, State Grid Jiangsu Electric Power Co. LTD., Nanjing, China
[4] Jiangsu Electric Power Information Technology Co. LTD., Nanjing, China
[5] Luoyang Institute of Information Technology Industries, Luoyang, China
lvchen@sdnu.edu.cn

Abstract. One common issue in reusing an existing library is that there is often a requirement to write a full link application that can instantiate a required destination class type according to an object of a given source class type. Recently, various code suggestion methods have been proposed to help programmers to address this issue by striving to recommend much more (good recall) and correct (good precision) solutions. However, for most of current methods, it is very difficult to balance the recall ratio and precision. Thus, a practical code suggestion method is expected to make trade-off between these two terms. In this study, a novel graph-search algorithm for efficient code suggestion is introduced to address the above issue. Our method obtain better experimental effect compared to the most related studies.

Keywords: Full link application · Graph theory · Code suggestion

1 Introduction

Reusing existing libraries can effectively enhance the quality and productivity of software [8]. Nevertheless, such a work is challenging for the reasons that the usage of the library is versatile and the APIs' number is tremendous. One challenge problem involved in reusing libraries is to suggest a full link application for object instantiation. This term has been coined in the work [13], which defines a task that inputs a query (*Source, Destination*) that represents the start point (Source type) and the end point (Destination type), outputs the full link application that is comprised of API invoking chains from Source type to Destination type.

This problem mentioned above is still very difficult once we have to use a new library. For example, in order to seek out the required APIs, it is required to

© Springer Nature Singapore Pte Ltd. 2019
Y. Sun et al. (Eds.): ChineseCSCW 2018, CCIS 917, pp. 536–545, 2019.
https://doi.org/10.1007/978-981-13-3044-5_41

read ponderous documents, which is a difficult and baldness work without any hints. According to the study [6], to search and learn API usage, two-fifths of the time for software development will be consumed. If we can conduct this object instantiation task automatically and suggest related full link applications to programmers, a great deal of programmers' efforts will be saved. Thus, automated full link application suggestion has attracted much attention [3, 5, 9, 13].

Most of the existing works [3, 5, 9, 13] collect the relevant library or code examples with the usage of a query (*Source, Destination*), and represent the API dependencies in them via different graph-based models. After that, by virtue of such graphs, they can generate a subgraph from Source to Destination, which corresponds to a full link application that can instantiate the Destination type according to the object of Source type. In this paper, we call this subgraph as the full link solution (this term will be defined in Definition 1).

Definition 1 *(Full Link Solution). It is a subgraph linking from the source node (source class type) to the destination node (destination class type) in a certain graph-based model. More specially, such a subgraph is either a path or a DAG (Directed Acyclic Graph). The above two different shapes of full link solutions are referred to path-link solution and DAG-link solution separately.*

Essentially, if a solution requires invoking some methods with multiple class type parameters, it would be formed as a DAG-link solution. Otherwise, it would be formed as a path-link solution.

The performance of a full link application suggestion method depends on the recall ratio and precision. Our observation is that the existing methods [3, 5, 9, 13] either achieves good recall ratio or good precision, but not both owing to improper data model and less effective searching algorithm applied to getting DAG-link solution.

In this study, we introduce a novel graph-search algorithm to suggest the full link application. First, it proposes to represent API dependencies in the library via a new global view model, in which the APIs are specified as the nodes, the parameter dependencies are specified as the edges, and the weights represent the frequency of each API method retrieved from relevant projects. Second, based on this graph, it proposes a new graph-search algorithm to explore desirable solutions for suggesting the full link application. The contributions include: (1) we propose a new graph model that can represent all the available API dependencies in the relevant library that is reusing and (2) we present an efficient graph-search algorithm that can support searching correct DAG-link solution.

2   Related Work

2.1   Code Suggestion Methods Based on Graph

The methods in [3, 5, 9, 13] can suggest codes of the full link applications. According to the employed data model, they can be divided into two categories, global view based method [3] and local view based method [5,9,13]. Briefly, for a given query of the form *(source, destination)*, the former method explores the full link solutions on a single global view graph, and the latter explores the full link solutions on many local view graphs. The detailed descriptions of these two methods are as follows.

Global View Based Method: The global view based method [3] models all of the API dependencies involved in a library as a single graph. It treats class type as node, and API that transforms from one class type to another as edge. This graph can be treated as a global view of API dependencies. Based on this graph, the work models the full link application suggestion issue as a conventional graph search problem, shortest paths problem. The standard graph search algorithm is used to explore the full link solutions. Such a method achieves good performance on recall. This is because all the possible solutions can be retrieved on the global view. However its performance on precision is not so good. Because it can only search the path-link solutions directly, but is not suit to search the DAG-link solutions.

Local View Based Method: The local view based methods [5,9,13] model the API dependencies into many smaller graphs. Each such a graph corresponds to the code in a specified unit, such as a class files in the library [13] or an API method in the relevant code examples [5,9]. These graphs can be treated as a set of local views of API dependencies. Similar to CSCA [3], XSnippet [13] and GRAPLE [5] also model the object instantiation issue as a shortest path problem. They explore solutions by common graph search algorithms on the exploited local views. Different from the works in [5,13], GraPacc [9] models the full link application suggestion as a pattern matching problem. By using a specific tool, called GrouMiner [12], it extracts the sub-graphs frequently appearing in the local views as patterns. Those patterns can be used to match with a query *(Source, Destination)*. Then, a graph-based code completion algorithm is used to select the best matching patterns and generate the subgraphs from source to destination by such patterns. The performance of these methods on recall ratio is not so good. This is because they are only able to represent the API dependencies in the isolated local views, but ignore the interconnections across the local views. This causes many possible correct solutions could not be recommended for lack of the valid API dependencies across the local views.

2.2   Other Code Suggestion Methods

The works to be discussed focus on recommend code examples according to uses' requests. However, they do not aim at suggesting the full link applications. Even so, the ideas in these works still have positive referential significance for us. Thus, we will discuss them as follows.

CodeBroker [17] and Strathcona [10] analysed the code under development to retrieve context information. Then, related code examples are extracted from code repository based on the context information. The researches in [2,4,11,14] addressed library reusing problem by data mining technology. Among them, the researches in [2, 4, 11] mine some rules such as inheritance relations or association rules to recommend the related example codes; and the research in [14] finds related functions based on a random walk approach. Instead of static codes based above, the research in [16] mines temporal patterns from the change history of API client program.

Other approaches adopt the technology of Web search engines. There are many specialized code search engines now with different scale of source files, such as Codease, Google Code Search, Krugle. Generally, code search engines index existing source files from various open source code repository, e.g., source Forge, Apache. Then, they retrieve related code examples by information retrieval techniques, e.g., keyword matching. A comparison of 13 typical code search engines is presented in [1]. The works in the works of [7, 15] belong to this category. Furthermore, test-driven code search is provided in the work of [1]. However, to acquire the best-fit solution in the massive result pages is a tough work.

3   General Terms

In this section, we define some terms used in this paper.

QoS: Non-functional properties of API method. In this paper, it refers to the used frequency information of the API method from relevant projects in code repository.

Query: Two class types (*Source, Destination*). Source refers to the class type that the user can provide its object/instance, and Destination refers to the class type that the user requires instantiating.

Method (M_i): $M_i(1 < i < N) = I_{M_i}, O_{M_i}, QoS_{M_i}$. I_{M_i} (inputs of M_i) refers to the receiver and parameter types of M_i, O_{M_i} (output of M_i) refers to the return type of M_i and QoS_{M_i} refers to the QoS of M_i.

Method Match: Given two methods M_a and M_b, if M_a's output matches with one of M_b's inputs in terms of type, we say M_a match with M_b.

Solution: It refers to the full-link solution defined in Definition 1.

4   Directed QoS API Graph

In this section, we introduce our data model, Directed QoS API graph (abbr, DQA graph). It is built with in two phases. We explain them as follows.

4.1   Phase1: Graph Construction

We construct an API dependency graph by retrieving all the API signatures in the relevant library that is reusing. As shown in Fig. 1, each node in this graph corresponds to an API method. An edge will be built from node M_a to M_b, if M_a's output matches with one of M_b's inputs in terms of type. In this graph, the query is represented as two virtual nodes, Source and Destination. Each node has one or more inputs (receiver and parameter types), but only one output

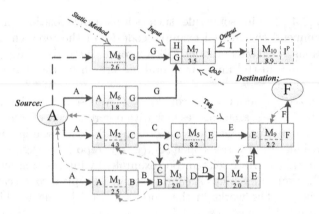

Fig. 1. Directed weight API graph.

(return type). $M_1 - M_{10}$ and $H - I$ is used to represent the nodes and their inputs/outputs respectively. Two cases must be treated in particular as follows. (1) **Virtual node.** A virtual node represents an always right operation, upcast that casts the subclass's object to its parent class's object, e.g., the node M_{10} in Fig. 1 where its output I_P is the parent class of its input I. It may corresponds to a method invocation: $I_P \, i_p = new \, I()$. (2) **Virtual edge.** A virtual edge is built from source node to the node of static method, e.g., the edge from A to M_8. This is due to M_8 can be invoked without any objects.

Furthermore, we acquire the downcast information from the relevant projects. For each line of downcast code, a virtual node is created in the DQA Graph, whose input is the parent class type and output is the available subclass type[1].

4.2 Phase2: QoS Calculation and Assignment

After step 1, we extract the information of API history usages from the relevant projects, e.g., the times of each API method invoked by the developers. Based on this information, we calculate the QoS of each method M_i, M_i.self by Eq. 1.

$$M_i.self == \begin{cases} Log \frac{Max-Min}{M_i.count-Min} & M_i.count > Min, \\ +\infty & M_i.count = Min. \end{cases} \qquad (1)$$

In Eq. 1, $M_i.count$ refers to the invoking times of method M_i. We use Max and Min to represent the maximum and minimum invoking times among all the methods of the library that are reusing.

Essentially, the QoS value calculated by Eq. 1 is a normalization form of the method's invoking times. This value is the smaller the better, which means that the methods frequently used are more likely to be adopted compared to the less

---

[1] To avoid the flood of downcast, the method invoking sequences that contain downcast with small frequency will not recommended to users by our system. In the future work, the strategy to handle downcast codes proposed in the paper of [3] can be used to refine the DQA graph.

frequently used methods. Finally, we assign this value as QoS to each node, eg., the number at the bottom of each node in Fig. 1.

5   Graph-Search Algorithm for DAG-Link Solution

We give a novel graph-search algorithm for exploring full link applications on the DQA graph. The algorithm is described as follows. Concretely, we use a priority queue, *enabledNodes* to store the unprocessed nodes whose statuses are enabled. The property of *enabledNodes* is that the item/node with more optimal/minimum overall QoS in this queue will be popped first. *EnabledNodes* is initialized with Source node. Then for each output of each popped node M_i, if the class type of this output (par) has not been stored in RPT[2], we will add an entry $(par, M_i.\text{all}, Mi)$ to RPT. Meanwhile, for each successor node M_s of M_i, let M_s's count value minus one. This means that one of the inputs of these nodes has been instantiated. Thus, M_s's status will be set to enabled if the count equals to zero. In this way, we can recursively obtain new enabled nodes and put them into *enabledNodes*. This process will not terminate until the queue is empty. After this process, we use a priority queue, $CQkp$, to store the optimal main path and the non-optimal main paths. The property of $CQkp$ is: the main path with more best/minimum overall QoS in this queue will be popped first. If the $CQkp$ is empty, we will retrieve the optimal main path first, and then $CQkp$ is initialized with the optimal main path. After that, we iterate over the main paths in $CQkp$. At each iteration, we do the following two jobs: we construct the corresponding DAGs by the popped main path. If the DAGs's number is smaller than a specified threshold, we generate new non-optimal main paths by loosing on each node of the popped main path. These generated non-optimal main paths will be push into $CQkp$.

6   Evaluation

We have tested our method with three mainstream methods. In Sect. 6.1, we elaborate experiment setting. In Sects. 6.2 and 6.3, we focused on comparing the number of queries that can be addressed by our method with global view method and local view method, respectively. In Sect. 6.4, we compared the performance on accuracy, results examination times and efficiency.

6.1   Experiment Setting

All experiments were carried out on a 3.3 GHz CPU machine with 4 GB RAM running Microsoft Windows 7. The conventional methods for comparison involves one global view based method, CSCA [3], and two local view based methods, GRAPLE [5] and GraPacc [9].

---

[2] RPT is a inverted index table which is used to store the optQoS for each input/precondition and its optimal provider.

542   H. Zhang et al.

Table 1. Comparison results with 12 queries' task from GRAPLE

No.	Query Source	Destination	CSCA	GRAPLE	Our method	Time (ms)
1	IPageSite	EditorInputTransfer	✓	✗	✓	130
2	IShowInTarget	MultiEditor	✓	✓	✓	160
3	IPage	PageSite	✓	✓	✓	150
4	ViewPart	WorkbenchPart	✓	✓	✗	120
5	ICache	IFileTypeInfo	✓	✗	✓	90
6	ViewPart	ISelectionService	✗	✗	✓	150
7	IViewCategory	IEditorPart	✓	✗	✓	140
8	IInPlaceEditor	IStartup	✓	✓	✓	110
9	IWorkbenchPage	PerspectiveAdapter	✓	✓	✓	150
10	AbstractDecorated TextEditor	ProjectViewer	✗	✗	✗	120
11	ITextEditor	IDocument	✓	✗	✓	160
12	ITextEditor	ITextSelection	✓	✓	✓	140

Table 2. Comparison results with 10 queries' task from the Eclipse Plug-in Project

No.	Query Source	Destination	CSCA		GRAP		Our method		
			No	Ra	No	Ra	No	Ra	Time (ms)
1	IPageSite	IActionBars	2	2	5	3	12	1	80
2	ActionRegistry	IAction	4	3	6	Nil	12	2	120
3	ActionRegistry Provider	ContextMenu	Nil	Nil	3	1	12	1	100
4	IPageSite Provider	ISelection	3	1	5	Nil	12	1	190
5	IPageSite Manager	IToolBar	5	1	6	1	12	1	130
6	String	ImageDescriptor	2	1	3	1	12	1	60
7	Composite	Control	6	1	4	Nil	12	1	170
8	Composite	Canvas	7	5	5	1	12	2	80
9	GraphicalViewer Thumbnail	Scrollable	5	1	2	2	12	3	120
10	GraphicalViewer	IFigure	4	Nil	8	Nil	12	10	70

Meaning. GRAP: GRAPLE, No: Number, Ra: Rank

Table 3. Comparison results with 10 queries' task from Eclipse & JDK Utility

No.	Query Source	Destination	GraPacc			Our method		
			No	Ra	Time (ms)	No	Ra	Time (ms)
1	LookupEnvironment	WildcardBinding	8	Nil	60	5	1	180
2	LookupEnvironment	BinaryTypeBinding	4	1	60	7	5	180
3	Scope	MethodBinding	13	1	40	12	1	130
4	StubUtility2	MethodDeclaration	15	1	60	16	1	150
5	ASTNode	BodyDeclarationRewrite	12	Nil	40	7	1	180
6	FileInputStream	DataInputStream	25	3	80	3	1	130
7	File	Scanner	19	Nil	80	26	1	110
8	Pattern	MatcherTimestamp	5	1	90	9	4	200
9	Timestamp	Date	46	Nil	60	6	1	150
10	URLConnection	OutputStream	3	Nil	40	3	1	110

Meaning. No: Number, Ra: Rank

6.2 Comparison with Global View Based Method

We compared our method with CSCA by the queries from the studies of [3,5]. The results are shown in the relevant columns in Tables 1 and 2. As shown in Tables 1 and 2, CSCA is able to address 10 and 8 queries, while our method can address 10 and 10 queries. Obviously, our method performed better than CSCA on the size of support queries. The reason behind the better performance is that our method can suggest the DAG-link solutions while CSCA cannot suggest. Another reason is that our method can avoid generating many irrelevant solutions (with worse overall QoS) as those of CSCA by using the QoS on each node as search directives. Our method cannot address only one query *(AbstractDecoratedTextEditor, ProjectViewer)* in Table 1. The reason we found is that the class *ProjectViewer* are not exist in the GEF. Thus, the other evaluated methods also cannot address this query.

6.3 Comparison with Local View Based Method

We compared our method with GRAPLE by the queries from the work of [5]. The results are shown in the relevant columns in Tables 1 and 2. As seen in the two tables, GRAPLE can correctly address 6 and 6 queries, while our method can correctly address 10 and 10 queries. The results demonstrate the strength of our method as it can leverage all the API dependencies in the library that is reusing. However, GRAPLE cannot utilize the API dependencies across the exploited local view models. Therefore, many queries relied on these missing dependencies cannot be addressed by GRAPLE. Moreover, GRAPLE is limited to analyzing partial code examples.

We also compared our method with GraPacc [9]. As presented in Table 3, our method is able to suggest all the solutions, whereas GraPacc only suggests 5 solutions. The results show that GraPacc is inferior to our method for the reasons that GraPacc cannot make use of the API dependencies across these patterns. Moreover, GraPacc is heavily dependent on the already exploited patterns. Whenever the desired solutions are not involved in the exploited pattern base, it would fail to address the corresponding queries. For example, for the query (File, Scanner), since the solution codes were not found in the pattern base, it is impossible for GraPacc to address this query.

6.4 Performance

We analyzed the experimental effects of the three methods in the following aspects: accuracy and efficiency. In the experiment, we compared our method with CSCA, GRAPLE and GraPacc on accuracy. The results in Table 4 demonstrate that, our method can raise the effectiveness of API recommendation by 45% on average on Recall compared to the two local view based approaches, and 30% on Precision compared to the global view approach. Moreover, our method achieves higher F-score value than the other approaches, which verifies that our approach can make a more satisfactory trade-off between recall and precision.

Table 4. Performance comparison

Data set	Queries in Table 1		Queries in Table 2		Queries in Table 3	
Approach	Our method	CSCA	Our method	GRAPLE	Our method	GraPacc
Recall	0.83	0.83	1.00	0.6	1.00	0.50
Precision	0.95	0.59	0.60	0.67	0.80	0.80
F-score	0.89	0.69	0.75	0.63	0.89	0.62

The results demonstrate that although we use a global view modeling strategy, we still achieve good performance on precision. This benefits from the ability of original DAG search and QoS based search directives mechanism.

We evaluate our method on response time by the column Time in Tables 1, 2 and 3. Experimental results indicate that the average cost time of our approach is less than 200 ms, which is very efficient.

7   Conclusions

In this study, we introduced a novel graph-search algorithm for full link application suggestion task. Experiments on real library data sets demonstrate that APISynth achieves better performance with regard of both recall and precision compared with other typical approaches.

Acknowledgment. The work is financially supported in part by the Project of Science and Technology of State Grid (No. SG[2017]179), Natural Science Foundation of Shandong Province, China (ZR2016FB13), National Natural Science Foundation of China (61602286) and a Project of Shandong Province Higher Educational Science and Technology Program (J16LN09).

References

1. Bajracharya, S., Ossher, J., Lopes, C.: Sourcerer: an infrastructure for large-scale collection and analysis of open-source code. Sci. Comput. Program. **79**(79), 241–259 (2014)
2. Bruch, M., Schäfer, T., Mezini, M.: FrUiT: IDE support for framework understanding. In: Proceedings of the 2006 OOPSLA Workshop on Eclipse Technology eXchange. pp. 55–59. Eclipse 2006. ACM, New York (2006). https://doi.org/10.1145/1188835.1188847
3. Feng, Y., Martins, R., Wang, Y., Dillig, I., Reps, T.W.: Component-based synthesis for complex APIs. In: ACM SIGPLAN Symposium on Principles of Programming Languages, pp. 599–612 (2017)
4. Fowkes, J., Chanthirasegaran, P., Ranca, R., Allamanis, M., Lapata, M., Sutton, C.: TASSAL: autofolding for source code summarization. In: IEEE/ACM International Conference on Software Engineering Companion, pp. 649–652 (2017)
5. Henderson, T.A.D., Podgurski, A.: Sampling code clones from program dependence graphs with GRAPLE. In: International Workshop on Software Analytics, pp. 47–53 (2016)

6. Maalej, W., Tiarks, R., Roehm, T., Koschke, R.: On the comprehension of program comprehension. ACM Trans. Softw. Eng. Methodol. **23**(4), 1–37 (2014)
7. Matsumoto, Y.: A software factory: an overall approach to software production. In: Software Reusability, pp. 155–178. IEEE Computer Society, March 1987
8. Mojica, I.J., Adams, B., Nagappan, M., Dienst, S., Berger, T., Hassan, A.E.: A large-scale empirical study on software reuse in mobile apps. IEEE Softw. **31**(2), 78–86 (2014)
9. Nguyen, A.T., Nguyen, T.N.: Graph-based statistical language model for code. In: IEEE/ACM IEEE International Conference on Software Engineering, pp. 858–868 (2015)
10. Nguyen, A.T., Nguyen, T.D., Phan, H.D., Nguyen, T.N.: A deep neural network language model with contexts for source code. In: IEEE International Conference on Software Analysis, Evolution and Reengineering, pp. 323–334 (2018)
11. Nguyen, H.A., Dyer, R., Nguyen, T.N., Rajan, H.: Mining preconditions of APIs in large-scale code corpus. In: ACM SIGSOFT International Symposium on Foundations of Software Engineering, pp. 166–177 (2014)
12. Nguyen, T., Nguyen, H., Pham, N., Al-Kofahi, J., Nguyen, T.: Graph-based mining of multiple object usage patterns. In: Proceedings of the the 7th Joint Meeting of the European Software Engineering Conference and the ACM SIGSOFT Symposium on The Foundations of Software Engineering. ESEC-FSE 2009, pp. 383–392. ACM (2009)
13. Osera, P.M., Zdancewic, S.: Type-and-example-directed program synthesis. In: ACM SIGPLAN Notices, vol. 50, no. 6, pp. 619–630 (2015)
14. Saul, Z., Filkov, V., Devanbu, P., Bird, C.: Recommending random walks. In: Proceedings of the the 6th Joint Meeting of the European Software Engineering Conference and the ACM SIGSOFT Symposium on The Foundations of Software Engineering, pp. 15–24. ACM (2007)
15. Sirres, R., et al.: Augmenting and structuring user queries to support efficient free-form code search. Empir. Softw. Eng. **1**, 1–33 (2017)
16. Uddin, G., Dagenais, B., Robillard, M.: Analyzing temporal API usage patterns. In: 2011 26th IEEE/ACM International Conference on Automated Software Engineering (ASE), pp. 456–459. IEEE (2011)
17. Ye, Y.: Supporting component-based software development with active component repository systems. Ph.D. thesis, University of Colorado (2001)

An Adaptive k-NN Classifier for Medical Treatment Recommendation Under Concept Drift

Nengjun Zhu, Jian Cao$^{(\boxtimes)}$, and Yan Zhang

Department of Computer Science and Engineering,
Shanghai Institute for Advanced Communication and Data Science,
Shanghai Jiao Tong University, Shanghai, China
{zhu_nj,cao-jian,zy1992}@sjtu.edu.cn

Abstract. In the real world, concept drift happens in various scenarios including medical treatment planing. Traditional approaches simply eliminate/dilute the effect of outdated samples on the prediction, leading to a less confident (based on fewer samples) prediction and a waste of undiscovered information contained in past samples. With the knowledge of how concepts change, outdated samples can be adapted for up-to-date prediction, which improves the confidence of prediction, especially for medical data sets of which the scale is relatively small. In this paper we present an adaptive k-NN classifier which can detect the occurrence of target concept drift and update past samples according to the knowledge of the drift for better prediction, and assess the performance over simulated and real-world categorical medical data sets. The experiment results show our classifier achieves better performance under concept drift.

Keywords: k-NN classifier · Recommendation · Concept drift
Medical treatment

1 Introduction

Concept drift was originally observed in streaming data, where the relation between the target class and features changes over time in unforeseen ways. The phenomenon also exists in other fields such as medical diagnosis. For example, Fig. 1 shows that the chemotherapies being used in breast cancer diagnosis are changing as time goes on, over different molecular subtypes [8,9] (e.g., Luminal-A), and the patients of some molecular subtypes receive different chemotherapies in different periods of time.

However, most state-of-art concept-aware learning algorithms focus on streaming data but medical diagnosis data. They achieve good performance using techniques such as ensemble learning, transfer learning, etc. For example, a novel algorithm named DETL [12] utilizes each preserved historical model as an initial model which is further trained with the new data via transfer learning. Even

© Springer Nature Singapore Pte Ltd. 2019
Y. Sun et al. (Eds.): ChineseCSCW 2018, CCIS 917, pp. 546–556, 2019.
https://doi.org/10.1007/978-981-13-3044-5_42

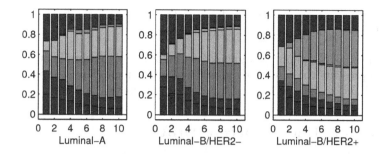

Fig. 1. Distribution of samples for different molecular subtypes, where the x-axes represent samples in temporal order, and the y-axes represent a proportion of the seven chemotherapies in each period of time.

though DETL can effectively handle concept drift in both synthetic data (e.g. SEA [11], STAGGER [7]) and real-world data streams. However, it is not easy to port this kind of algorithms directly to process such medical diagnosis data without transforming categorical data into numerical.

The medical diagnosis data is very limited compared with other fields, so that it is natural to process it with case-based approaches, i.e., the *k* Nearest Neighbors algorithm (*k*-NN). The *k* Nearest Neighbors algorithm is a non-parametric method used for classification and regression, and it has been applied to various areas [1]. To deal with concept drift, based on the idea of 'forgetting' old samples, previous work uses sliding windows to filter the historical samples for reference [13], or applies an age-related weight to each sample to dilute the influence of older samples [4,5]. However, simply forgetting old samples is not suitable in medical treatment recommendation. For small-scale data sets such as medical diagnosis data, each sample is precious and contains invaluable information due to the individual variation in patients. During the process of prediction, we should take as many samples into account as we can. And the prediction result based on more samples is more confident and more resistant to noises.

To tackle the problems introduced by concept drift, and to make better use of old samples, we propose a new *k*-NN based classifier using the paired learner technique [2]. In this approach, we discover knowledge of how an old concept changes to a new one. Instead of discarding outdated samples, we create a replica of them to preserve the original information, and then revise the labels according to new concepts for future predictions. To study the effectiveness of the approach, we compare it with two baseline methods over both simulated and real-world data, and analyze the influence of the parameters in the proposed approach. Focusing on medical treatment recommendation, the contribution of the paper is list as follows:

1. We improve the concept-drift detection method based on the paired learner technique.
2. We propose an adaptive *k*-NN classifier for concept-drifting data.

3. Extension experiments over both simulated and real data sets prove our approach has better performance against baselines.

The rest of the paper is organized as follows: Sect. 2 details our approach.
Section 3 presents the results of our experiments using different approaches over
simulated and real-world data sets. Section 4 concludes the paper.

2 Learning Under Concept Drift

In this part, we first put forward a modified *overlap* similarity, and then illustrate
in detail a k-NN based adaptive classifier which behaves well under concept drift.

2.1 Notations

For a data set D containing N samples, we define A as the set of d attributes
where A_k denotes the kth attribute, and define C as the set of all types of target
class. Temporally, let t^{th} sample in data set D be represented as follows:

$$D_t = < x^{(t)}, y^{(t)} > \tag{1}$$

where $x = (x_1, x_2, x_3, ..., x_d)^T$ denotes an attribute vector of a sample, and $y \in C$
is the labeled class of D_t. For convenience, we use $\mathbb{N}_a^b$ to represent $\mathbb{N} \cap [a, b]$, which
is the set of integers from a to b inclusive.

Similarity measure is a key issue of classifiers such as k-NN. For numerical
attributes, the Mahalanobis distance [6] is as follows:

$$Dist(x^{(a)}, x^{(b)}) = \sqrt{(x^{(a)} - x^{(b)})^T S^{-1} (x^{(a)} - x^{(b)})} \tag{2}$$

where S is the covariance matrix. We then convert this distance measure to a
similarity measure with the scale from 0 to 1 using the following formula:

$$Sim(x^{(a)}, x^{(b)}) = \frac{1}{1 + Dist(x^{(a)}, x^{(b)})} \tag{3}$$

Further, during classification, the sample will be labeled by a class according to
the labeled classes of its neighbors as well as its similarity with its neighbors,
i.e., for a sample x, the similarity is used as a weight for each neighbor, and
then, the sample will be labeled by a class with the largest linear combination of
weight among the neighbors, rather than simply assigning the majority of class
labels in its k nearest neighbors to the target case.

$$\hat{y} = \arg \max_{y_c \in Y} \sum_{D_i \in S(x,k)} [\![y^{(i)} = y_c]\!] \cdot Sim(x, x^{(i)}) \tag{4}$$

where $[\![\cdot]\!]$ is an indicator function, where $[\![true]\!] = 1$ and $[\![false]\!] = 0$, and $S(x, k)$
represents the set of k-nearest neighbors of a sample x.

2.2 Similarity Definition for Categorical Features

Since the value of categorical features is discrete, it prevents application of the Mahalanobis technique. The similarity value between two samples $D_a = \;< \boldsymbol{x}^{(a)}, y^{(a)} >$ and $D_b = \;< \boldsymbol{x}^{(b)}, y^{(b)} >$ in this context is usually synthesized by similarities in all attributes as follows:

$$Sim(\boldsymbol{x}^{(a)}, \boldsymbol{x}^{(b)}) = \Sigma_{k=1}^{d} \omega_k Sim_k(x_k^{(a)}, x_k^{(b)}) \qquad (5)$$

where $Sim_k(x_k^{(a)}, x_k^{(b)})$ denotes the similarity between single attribute A_k of sample D_a and sample D_b, and the weight ω_k indicates the importance of each attribute A_k.

Overlap [10] is a method to define the similarity between two categorical attributes. It calculates the similarity by counting the number of matched attributes, e.g., 0 represents not matching, and 1 represents matching, during the measurement of the similarity of a pair of samples on a single attribute. Thus, the proportion of the number of attributes in which they match is considered as the similarity between two multivariate categorical samples. However, in real data sets, missing the value in some attributes is very common. Consider three samples D_a, D_b and D_c having the following properties:

$$x_k^{(a)} \neq x_k^{(b)} \;\text{ and }\; x_k^{(c)} \text{ is missing}, \forall k \in \mathbb{N}_1^d \qquad (6)$$

Notice that D_a and D_b are completely different because they do not match in any attribute, while the similarity between D_a and D_c should be neutral since we do not know any of the attributes of D_c. Hence, it follows that the heuristic, $Sim(x^{(a)}, x^{(b)})$ should be the minimum while $Sim(x^{(a)}, x^{(c)})$ should be defined as a compromised value. To deal with cases where the data set has missing values, the modified overlap measure is defined as follows:

$$Sim_k(x_k^{(a)}, x_k^{(b)}) = \begin{cases} 1 & \text{if } x_k^{(a)} = x_k^{(b)} \\ 0.5 & \text{if } x_k^{(a)} or x_k^{(b)} \text{ is missing} \\ 0 & \text{otherwise} \end{cases} \qquad (7)$$

$$\omega_k = \frac{1}{d} \qquad (8)$$

Equation 8 shows that the weights of all attributes are the same. However, the experimental results in a past study [3] suggest that there is no one best performing similarity measure, hence we choose overlap to measure similarity for the sake of convenience.

2.3 Adaptive Classifier and Concept-Sensitive Detector

Similar to the paired learner, we equip the k-NN classifier with a concept-sensitive detector with a fixed-size sliding window to enable it to adapt to concept drift. Denote the adaptive classifier as AC and the concept-sensitive detector as CSD_{sw} with a sliding window of size sw. AC classifies new samples based on

---

Algorithm 1. Adaptive k-NN Classifier

Input: D, N_{init}, sw, k
Output: predicted class for each object
$\quad D = \{< \boldsymbol{x}^{(i)}, y^{(i)} >\}_{i=1}^{N}$: training data
$\quad N_{init}$: initial training sample number
$\quad sw$: sliding window size of concept-sensitive detector
1: $AC \leftarrow$ an adaptive k-NN classifier
2: $CSD_{sw} \leftarrow$ a concept-sensitive detector of window size sw
3: **for** $i \leftarrow 1$ **to** N_{init} **do**
4: $\quad$ AC.train(D_i) & CSD_{sw}.train(D_i)
5: **end for**
6: **for** $i \leftarrow N_{init} + 1$ **to** N **do**
7: $\quad$ $\hat{y}_{AC} \leftarrow AC$.classify($\boldsymbol{x}^{(i)}$)
8: $\quad$ **output** $\hat{y}_{AC}$
9: $\quad$ $\hat{y}_{CSD} \leftarrow CSD_{sw}$.classify($\boldsymbol{x}^{(i)}$)
10: $\quad$ **if** concept drift detected **then**
11: $\quad\quad$ revisePastSamples(AC)
12: $\quad$ **end if**
13: $\quad$ AC.train(D_i) & CSD_{sw}.train(D_i)
14: **end for**

---

all historical samples while CSD_{sw} makes use of the most recent samples within sw. So the effectiveness of the paired learner is based on the following heuristics:

1. Based on more knowledge, the result is more reliable.
2. Based on more recent knowledge, the result is more reactive.

As shown in Algorithm 1, the input is a data set D of N samples, the number of initial training samples N_{init}, the sliding windows size sw, and the number of nearest neighbors k. To initialize AC and CSD_{sw}, the algorithm trains them with $\{D_i | i \in \mathbb{N}_1^{N_{init}}\}$ independently (line 3–5). Note that, different from AC, CSD_{sw} keeps at most sw training samples, and will forget the earliest sample if the size of the training samples exceeds sw. After initialization, the classifier predicts new samples via AC (line 7–8) and in the meantime both classifiers learn from the sample (line 13). During the prediction, if the algorithm has observed the occurrence of concept drift, the main classifier AC will be updated, so as to maintain its performance under the new concept (line 10–12). Note that we always create a replica to preserve the original labels before revising outdated samples.

In common cases, AC should behave no worse than CSD for its abundant knowledge of both recent and past data. At the very beginning of the occurrence of concept drift, new samples are classified according to outdated knowledge, thus performance degradation for both classifiers is observed. But CSD's performance can return to a normal level soon, because the historical data of CSD is replaced with those under the new concept due to its abandoning of past samples. Based on this heuristic, the occurrence of concept drift can be observed by monitoring the performance of the paired classifiers. That is, when CSD performs better than AC for a period of time, we assert an occurrence of concept drift, and then revise the historical data of AC for better adaptation to the new concept.

2.4   Sample-Based Drift Detection and Adaptation

Instead of detecting concept drift by comparing the accuracy of each classifier in the paired classifiers for a batch of recent samples, we explore a sample-based drift detection and adaption method, since the batch accuracy comparison method cannot handle concept drift in small local part of the original data. Intuitively, we can separate the feature space into many small zones or apply clustering on the original data, and monitor concept drift independently in each zone or cluster. More extremely, we regard each sample as a single zone, in other words, we keep monitoring each sample during the classification and then we can judge for each historical sample whether the labeled class should be changed to ensure better prediction of future samples. Meanwhile, based on information of misclassification for each sample we have logged during classification, the new class to which a drifted sample should be revised can be decided simultaneously along with the detection, as shown in Algorithm 2.

Denote the sample being processed at the moment as D_{now}, if AC incorrectly classifies it but CSD_{sw} correctly classifies it (line 4). Then the training samples in AC, based on which the prediction was made, are marked as conflicting with the current sample D_{now}, for they are considered to have provided wrong implications (line 5). For each training sample in AC, if it satisfies certain conditions (line 6), e.g. being observed frequently conflicting with recent samples, it is regarded that its features fall in the zone where concept drift occurs. In this case, AC revises this sample with a new class according to its *confliction records* (line 8). The confliction records for sample D_t contain tuples of samples in future predictions which select D_t as one of the nearest neighbors for reference but receive a negative effect due to the difference in their actual classes. The definition of *confliction records* $C[t]$ is as follows:

$$\{(i, y^{(i)}) | i > t \wedge \boldsymbol{x}^{(t)} \in AC.\text{nearest}(k, \boldsymbol{x}^{(i)}) \wedge y^{(i)} \neq y^{(t)}\} \tag{9}$$

Note that we have $y^{(i)} \neq y^{(t)}, \forall (i, y^{(i)}) \in C[t]$, once D_t contributes to a correct classification for D_i, we clear the former confliction records of D_t to avoid a false alarm caused by noise (line 11). The concept-drift condition (line 6) is a key point to this algorithm, which directly decides whether to declare an occurrence of concept drift so as to revise the historical samples. We use a score-based indicator in our algorithm.

What we are most concerned about are the target classes for present and future samples, thus for tuples in the confliction records $C[t]$, conflicts with recent samples are apparently more valuable than those with older ones. In addition, responses that are too fast always cause false alarms, and conflicts in stable periods are much more meaningful than those in unstable periods. To differentiate between stable and unstable periods, according to the confliction records, we say it is stable if there is no conflicts in a fixed period of time, otherwise it is unstable. Based on these heuristics, we assign scores for each conflict which appears in $C[t]$ with a function having a positive correlation with *time*, so that confliction records in stable periods have higher scores. Then we add the scores for each class as its measure.

The function $Score(y)$ can be defined in a variety of ways, as long as it has a positive correlation with *time*. The following is one candidate for the function using the exponential technique:

$$Score(y) = \sum_{(i,y) \in C[t]} 1 - e^{(-(i-t))} \tag{10}$$

If the score of a certain class dominates among the candidates, we assert that D_t is affected by concept drift and we know exactly the trend of its change.

Algorithm 2. Sample-based detection and adaptation method

Input: $D, C, k, S, \hat{y}_{AC}, \hat{y}_{CSD}, < x^{(now)}, y^{(now)} >$
Output: Whether concept drift detected
    $D = \{< x^{(i)}, y^{(i)} >\}_{i=1}^{now-1}$: training data of AC
    C: a dict of conflicting records for training data
    $\hat{y}_{AC}$: class predicted by AC
    $\hat{y}_{CSD}$: class predicted by CSD
    $< x^{(now)}, y^{(now)} >$: current sample.
    nearest(k, x): returns a set of x's k nearest neighbors
1: $S \leftarrow \{t | D_t \in AC.\text{nearest}(k, x^{(now)}) \wedge y_t = \hat{y}_{AC}\}$
2: $flagOfDrift \leftarrow$ False
3: **for** $t \in S$ **do**
4:     **if** $\hat{y}_{AC} \neq y_{now}$ and $\hat{y}_{CSD} = y_{now}$ **then**
5:         $C[t].\text{append}((now, y_{now}))$
6:         **if** $C[t]$ satisfies concept-drift conditions **then**
7:             $flagOfDrift \leftarrow$ True
8:             revise D_t
9:         **end if**
10:    **else**
11:        $C[t].\text{clear}()$
12:    **end if**
13: **end for**
14: **return** $flagOfDrift$

---

3 Experiment Study

To verify the effectiveness of our adaptive k-NN classifier, we compare it with several baseline approaches over two data sets. Since finding the best k in the k-NN classifier is not within the scope of this paper, we simply use $k = 10$ in all the following experiments. Commonly the value of k should be an odd number to avoid tied votes, but it does not matter if we set $k = 10$ in our approach, as we choose the final class according to the sum of similarity instead of the plain count for each candidate.

3.1 Evaluation Metrics

We assess the performance of our approach and conduct comparison experiment with following two metrics: **Accumulative accuracy** and **Next-n accuracy**. Accumulative accuracy is defined as follows:

$$\text{Accuracy}_{accum}(t) = \frac{1}{t - N_{init}} \sum_{i=N_{init}+1}^{t} [\![\hat{y}^{(i)} = y^{(i)}]\!] \tag{11}$$

where t and N_{init} denote the index of current sample and that of the last sample in initial training set, respectively. Accumulative accuracy evaluates the ratio of samples which are correctly classified *to the current moment*, while Next-n accuracy evaluates the ratio of samples which are correctly classified *among the next n samples*, and it is defined as follows:

$$\text{Accuracy}_n(t) = \frac{1}{n} \sum_{i=t+1}^{t+n} [\![\hat{y}^{(i)} = y^{(i)}]\!] \tag{12}$$

A curve of accumulative accuracy reveals long-term trends in the classifier performance, while a curve of next-k accuracy shows short-term changes in performance. For both metrics, the larger the value of accuracy, the better performance of the classifier.

3.2 Comparison Classifiers

- k-**NN:** This is a basic k-nearest neighbor classifier playing the role of baseline, using the *modified overlap* similarity measure mentioned in Eq. 7.
- k-**NNSW:** This is a window-based extension of k-NN in order to deal with concept drift by learning knowledge from the most recent samples within a sliding window.
- Ak-**NN:** This is an adaptive k-NN classifier mentioned in Algorithm 1. To study the influence of different concept-drift indicators in Algorithm 2, we implement all three indicators respectively and compare them in the experiments.

3.3 Data Sets

To verify the performance of our algorithm, we perform experiments over an artificial data set with concept drift, named **Simulated Data (SD)**. Moreover, we also compare different methods over a real medical data set named **Breast Cancer Chemotherapy Data (BCCD)**, where we use the classifiers to recommend chemotherapy for breast cancer patients according to historical cases.

Table 1. Data sets overview

Name	Entries	Attributes	Classes	Drift position	Name	Entries	Attributes	Classes	Drift position
SD	3000	6	4	1000	**BCCD**	2770	12	8	unknown

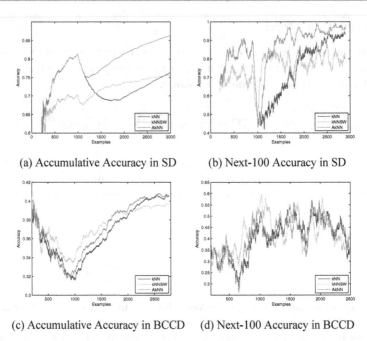

(a) Accumulative Accuracy in SD   (b) Next-100 Accuracy in SD

(c) Accumulative Accuracy in BCCD   (d) Next-100 Accuracy in BCCD

Fig. 2. Results for k-NN, k-NNSW, Ak-NN

Samples in both data sets are arranged in temporal order, where indices of each sample also represent the time. Characteristics of these two data sets are summarized in Table 1. For the simulated data set SD, there is an explicit drift position of 1000 (the first 1000 samples are labeled according to their attributes using a different linear function from the remaining 2000 samples), representing the position where concept drift occurs, while for the real data set BCCD, samples are collected from real cases, thus we cannot declare any explicit drift positions.

3.4   Experimental Results

On the simulated data set, we apply the classifiers and calculate the accumulated accuracy of all predictions, and the average accuracy of the next 100 predictions. The results of the two metrics are shown respectively in Fig. 2a and b. Both k-NN and Ak-NN exploit the whole historical data, and thus they are more accurate on average than k-NNSW as shown in Table 2. For long-term learning, k-NNSW is not a good choice.

We knew in advance that there is an occurrence of concept drift at the 1000th sample in SD. As shown in Fig. 2a, from the 1000th sample onwards, affected

Table 2. Overall accuracy over SD

sw	k-NN	k-NNSW	Ak-NN	sw	k-NN	k-NNSW	Ak-NN	sw	k-NN	k-NNSW	Ak-NN
100	0.7598	0.7212	**0.8634**	150	0.7637	0.7451	**0.8662**	200	0.7634	0.7573	**0.8631**

by the new concept, all the classifiers experience degradation in accuracy. The basic k-NN classifier takes a long time to get its accuracy back to the former level, while k-NNSW and Ak-NN both adapted to the new concept reactively. The effect on the accuracy of all the classifiers is shown more clearly in Fig. 2b, where Ak-NN and k-NNSW rebound rapidly soon after concept drift. However, to return to the former accuracy, the plain k-NN classifier learns as many as 1000 new samples. If we have more samples before concept drift, the k-NN classifier has to learn even more new samples to dilute the influence of outdated historical samples.

The results over BCCD look slightly complicated and the concept shifts slowly over time instead of changing suddenly. Rapid drops in accuracy for both k-NN and Ak-NN are observed in Fig. 2d around the 500th sample, while k-NNSW reacts well and maintains its accuracy at the former level. Due to the concept-drift detection mechanism, Ak-NN's accuracy rebounds slightly faster than k-NN's. Note that k-NNSW's accuracy exceeds the other two at the very beginning, but Fig. 2c shows the downward trend of using only the most recent samples for reference and that k-NNSW will be defeated as more samples are learned. The defect of k-NNSW is shown more clearly in Fig. 2d. At around the 1800th and 2300th samples, k-NNSW suffers from its narrow window and has an obvious degradation of accuracy while the other two classifiers remain stable. Even though it can recover very soon, its over reactivity harms the overall accumulated accuracy.

4 Conclusion

We have proposed an adaptive k-NN classifier (Ak-NN) to tackle the concept drift in medical treatment recommendation, which performs better than baseline methods on both simulated data set and real data set. Derived from k-NN, our approach is also non-parametric as it does not rely on the knowledge of distribution of the input data. Instead of discarding outdated samples, the approach discover the knowledge of concept drift, based on which it revises the old samples for better prediction under the new concept.

Acknowledgments. China National Science Foundation (Granted Number 61272438,61472253), Cross Research Fund of Biomedical Engineering of Shanghai Jiao Tong University (YG2015MS61), and Research Funds of Science and Technology Commission of Shanghai Municipality (Granted Number 15411952502, 14511107702) support this work.

References

1. Altman, N.S.: An introduction to kernel and nearest-neighbor nonparametric regression. Am. Stat. **46**(3), 175–185 (1992)
2. Bach, S.H., Maloof, M.A.: Paired learners for concept drift. In: 2008 Eighth IEEE International Conference on Data Mining, ICDM 2008, pp. 23–32. IEEE (2008)
3. Boriah, S., Chandola, V., Kumar, V.: Similarity measures for categorical data: a comparative evaluation. Red **30**(2), 3 (2008)
4. Klinkenberg, R.: Learning drifting concepts: example selection vs. example weighting. Intell. Data Anal. **8**(3), 281–300 (2004)
5. Koychev, I.: Tracking changing user interests through prior-learning of context. In: De Bra, P., Brusilovsky, P., Conejo, R. (eds.) AH 2002. LNCS, vol. 2347, pp. 223–232. Springer, Heidelberg (2002). https://doi.org/10.1007/3-540-47952-X_24
6. Mahalanobis, P.C.: On the generalized distance in statistics. Proc. Natl. Inst. Sci. (Calcutta) **2**, 49–55 (1936)
7. Minku, L.L., White, A.P., Yao, X.: The impact of diversity on online ensemble learning in the presence of concept drift. IEEE Trans. Knowl. Data Eng. **22**(5), 730–742 (2010)
8. Perou, C.M.: Molecular stratification of triple-negative breast cancers. The Oncol. **16**(Suppl. 1), 61–70 (2011)
9. Prat, A., Perou, C.M.: Deconstructing the molecular portraits of breast cancer. Mol. Oncol. **5**(1), 5–23 (2011)
10. Stanfill, C., Waltz, D.: Toward memory-based reasoning. Commun. ACM **29**(12), 1213–1228 (1986)
11. Street, W.N., Kim, Y.: A streaming ensemble algorithm (SEA) for large-scale classification. In: Proceedings of the Seventh ACM SIGKDD International Conference on Knowledge Discovery and Data Mining, pp. 377–382. ACM (2001)
12. Sun, Y., Tang, K., Zhu, Z., Yao, X.: Concept drift adaptation by exploiting historical knowledge. arXiv preprint arXiv:1702.03500 (2017)
13. Widmer, G., Kubat, M.: Learning in the presence of concept drift and hidden contexts. Mach. Learn. **23**(1), 69–101 (1996)

Evaluating the Impacts of Concurrency Control over User Experience in Feature-Based Collaborative Designing

Yuan Cheng[1], Fazhi He[2($\boxtimes$)], Xiao Lv[2], and Weiwei Cai[2]

[1] School of Information Management, Wuhan University,
Wuhan 430072, Hubei, China
[2] School of Computer Science, Wuhan University,
Wuhan 430072, Hubei, China
fzhe@whu.edu.cn

Abstract. Collaborative CAD is the trend for the next generation of CAD systems. A concurrency control approach is the fundamental leveraging tool for resolving design conflicts. Although several algorithms are proposed, seldom study has been carried out for evaluating the correctness and user satisfaction. This paper presents an experimental study to investigate users' satisfaction level over both pessimistic and optimistic concurrency approaches. Based on the experimental results, we also discuss propose implications for developing both concurrency control approach and collaborative designing platforms.

Keywords: Collaborative designing · Concurrency control · User satisfaction
Intention preservation

1 Introduction

The trends of the next generation of CAD systems can be characterized 4 C's, which are collaborative, creative, cognitive and conceptual. Collaborative CAD sets a multi-user designing environment where collective intelligence emerges and thus helps to improve creativity, cognition and efficiency in developing complex products. Bouras also described the usefulness of collaborative designing environment [1]:

> "The need to support collaboration among users for the facilitation of everyday tasks, communication, work, and training has been identified since the early stages of computer usage. This need became more critical when computer networking became available".

Concurrency control approaches serve as an important leveraging tool in resolving design conflicts among operations and achieving data consistency [2–4]. Bringing collaborative CAD to industry needs to provide expected behavior for users so that there is less confusion and less of a learning curve [5]. For feature-based collaborative designing, data consistency methods must appeal to the designer both visually and functionally [6]. Concurrency control approaches need to be both simple enough to easily understand and use, while versatile enough to provide useful and flexible functionality for convenient UX (user experience) and user satisfaction. The UX of concurrency control must allow it to "blend transparently" into the existing multi-user

© Springer Nature Singapore Pte Ltd. 2019
Y. Sun et al. (Eds.): ChineseCSCW 2018, CCIS 917, pp. 557–566, 2019.
https://doi.org/10.1007/978-981-13-3044-5_43

experience and feel natural to users. The optimistic concurrency control approach definitely meets this requirement of free, natural and concurrency collaboration [7, 8]. On the contrary, the pessimistic concurrency control approaches aim at achieving hard data consistency by restricting file editing access to a single user using access control mechanisms [9, 10].

Hardly can a concurrency control approach capable of achieving the requirements of both free-natural concurrency and hard consistency maintenance. However, this paper is not aiming at proposing a solution to fulfill the task that no previous work has finished. Its real intention is to find out to which extent a concurrency control approach can be accepted. With this motivation, we carried out an experiment by selecting two concurrency control approaches which represent optimistic and pessimistic concurrency control respectively and made a comparison from the perspective of user satisfaction. The participants volunteered for the experiment are asked to finish a questionnaire over user satisfaction and a group interview. By analyzing the data, we propose some implications over concurrency control for collaborative designing with helps to gain better user experience.

2   Related Works

Literature researches over the concurrency control approaches in the feature-based collaborative CAD will be presented in this section.

An optimistic approach is an approach where no obligatory and restrictive actions were posed on designers or locking of the data is adopted. The approach has a good wish of bringing users with free and concurrent real-time design by handling conflictive operations in a transparent way, but also creates the potential for more challenges in data consistency management. According to the definition of a modeling operation and the pipeline for executing a modeling operation, the implementation of any optimistic concurrency control approach depends on the appropriate correspondence of topological entities. Augustina exclaimed such an approach is not possible using traditional collaborative data transfer technology because many data objects could have both multiple parents and multiple children, thus not allowing the use of traditional operational transform technology to manage data as is done in the multi-user text editors [11].

The second approach is the pessimistic approach. It locks parts of the entire part model, sometimes even locking the entire designing session completely, to control designers' accesses to a part so as to prevent data inconsistencies. Advantages of pessimistic approaches to data consistency are easy implementation plus the effectiveness in preventing even both update and delete conflicts in collaborative CAD platforms [12]. Several other approaches for data consistency management in a collaborative CAD environment have already been proposed in current research. Jing used a local locking mechanism, based on operational transforms, which helps avoid conflicts by distributing locks to local features in a model in a replicated collaborative CAD system [13]. Chen applied three coordination rules embedded in e-Assembly to satisfy collaborative assembly constraints in a client-server environment [14]. Lin considered collaborative locking, masking, and time stamped methods when constraints are applied to design operations and users manipulating the same object would confuse the constraint relations [15]. Marshall recommended a task-based method that will allow hierarchal administrative control over nearly the entire design process. This system is very intricate and requires significant planning and setup to be effective [16]. Cera recommended a role-based system that only provides necessary geometry of a collaborative CAD model according to participants' roles. Additionally details of the model can be obscured to protect proprietary information in the model [17].

A more realistic method proposed uses a token-based session, which only one user can edit the part at one time [18, 19]. A softer "traffic light" method which visually warns users when it is ok to edit model features was proposed by Bidarra to pose some strict restrictions by token pass [20].

3 Experiment

3.1 Material and Participants

The experiments were conducted by recruiting a group of undergraduate students with previous experience in parametric solid modeling using single-user CAD platforms. Each student is trained until s/he can use the prototype we developed skillfully. Each participant was equipped with a desktop PC running a collaborative modeling proto-type we developed with ACIS and Microsoft Visual C++. Both optimistic and pes-simistic concurrency control methods are implemented within the prototype.

A total of 54 volunteers participated in this experiment. These volunteers are divided into 18 groups, labeled from G1 to G18, where each group contains 3 par-ticipants equally. Each team is asked to perform a design task by randomly choosing a concurrency control mode. The operations issued by one designer during the process are logged according to their generation sequences. Afterwards, the same group is asked to perform the same design task by issuing operations according to the recorded operation sequence and using another concurrency control method which is not chosen firstly. After the whole experiment is performed, each participant will finish the same questionnaires twice as to test user satisfaction towards each concurrency control method respectively. In order to evaluation the capability of user intention preservation, we conducted a focus group interview to further inquiry their suggestions over the performance of concurrency control mechanism in a feature-based collaborative designing environment.

The optimistic approach we selected is published in the literature [21]. This approach is based on the uniquely naming mechanism with topological entity changing tracking. The approach tried its best to guarantee that an operation can be executed in any context at any site. It followed the entity identity propagation so as to determine in which fashion an entity is changed by its concurrent operations. It also did an inves-tigation over the intention of when entity is referenced so as to determine how to preserve the operation's intention in the circumstance of entity change. The semi-pessimistic approach we selected is to prevent conflicts by avoiding them using some warning messages and group negotiation. The approach is part of a strict pessimistic one because users are allowed to issue modeling operations freely and concurrently. However, when conflicts among the modeling operations occur, the approach intends to invite the corresponding designers to make decisions. Hence, the modeling process is hindered and deferred. The details of the approach is presented in our conference paper [22]. Figure 1 exemplifies the conflict resolving process of both optimistic and pessimistic approaches adopted in this paper.

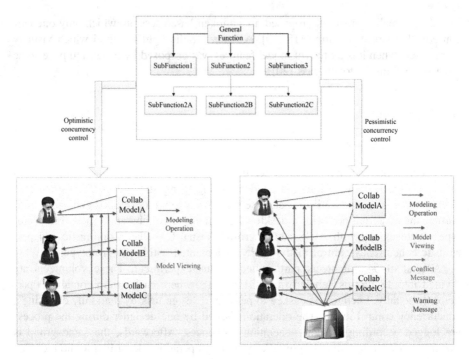

Fig. 1. The computer-human interaction and human-human interaction under the selected concurrency control approaches

3.2   Evaluation Model

Satisfaction over User Experience. To evaluate individuals' subjective experiences of different concurrency control approaches in feature-based collaborative designing, we designed a post-questionnaire adapted from the psychometrically validated usability questionnaire given in [23, 24].The questionnaire was intended to evaluate both the levels of user satisfaction over both concurrency control approaches.

After the experiment, each participant will take the questionnaire twice regarding their perceptions over both concurrency control approaches. Each question contained in the questionnaire is presented using a ten-point Likert scale ascending from 0 on the left to 9 on the right and anchored at both endpoints with adjectives. It is designed from the perspective of screen, terminology and information, learning, capability and a user's overall experience towards the investigated concurrency control approach.

Questions fall into the screen group is to let participants make an evaluation over a part model's evolution and designers' interaction process with a part affected by a concurrency control approach. Questions fall into the system information and terminology group is to acquire designers' real demands over the human-computer communication. Questions fall into the learning group is to judge which of the two types of concurrency control approaches are more acceptable. Questions fall into the capability group aims at investigating participants' response over the performance and functionality of bringing the system to a consistent state eventually. These levels are measured using the means of the data obtained from the participants' responses.

Methodology. After an extensive study, we adopt the clean-sheet design mode, which is the process of designing a part from scratch, for participants to work collaboratively. Therefore, this experiment seeks to obtain new insights on CAD collaborative designing strategies that will help us to figure out how the optimistic and the pessimistic concurrency control methods contribute separately.

In this scenario, designers are only informed with the concept and function requirements of an artifact while no detailed instructions on how the artifact will be built step by step are given, as it is also illustrated in Fig. 1. The function requirement is distributed to participants in a decomposition and hierarchical form. After an overall functional description of the artifact is obtained, it is then split into several function-based descriptions. Likewise, each of these sub–functions can become a root function for a specific sub-artifact. The main functions of every current level sub–artifact are furtherly partitioned in into smaller sub-functions at lower levels. The decomposition process stops at a logical point when the designer reaches an elemental mechanical function [25]. This elemental mechanical function may be defined as a "distinctive, generic characterization of the basic function of a machine part without reference to the specific application for which it is used" in literature [25]. Therefore, for participants involved, the designing process can then be applied to every elemental function which reduces the complexity of the overall designing process significantly. We use the case of the simple machine component exemplified in Fig. 2.

Fig. 2. An example of a simple machine component

4   Results

At the end of this experiment, we collected and made analysis over data from the feature-based collaborative designing prototype, including data from the question-naires, as well as the transcribed interview data from the focus group. In this section, we are going to explain our results from the analysis of these different sources of data.

4.1   User Satisfaction and Intention Preservation

The investigation over designers' satisfaction level towards user experience is obtained based on the above mentioned post-questionnaire listed. The comparison is given in Fig. 3.

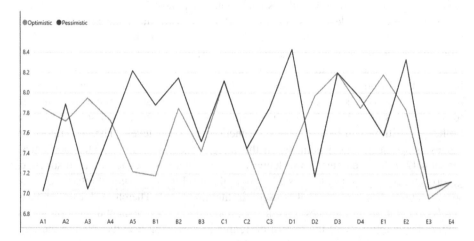

Fig. 3. Comparison of user satisfaction over pessimistic and optimistic concurrency approaches

By comparing the means, we draw the conclusion that there is no significant difference in the participants' perceptions between the optimistic approach and the pessimistic approach. According to the investigation over the focus group aiming at designers' satisfaction level with intention preservation, we summarize and categorize participants' perceptions over both approaches into the following items:

1. During the clean-sheet design, the designers have no specific anticipations aiming at what the result part model will be. At the beginning, they shall be more focused on whether their modeling intentions are preserved by examining carefully on whether the operations they issued have the effects they expect. However, accompanied by the incrementally construction of the part, they are more likely to think about if the part is evolving towards the ideal status they were wishing for. Meanwhile, designers begin to use more updates and issues undo/redo to modify the features they added.

2. Most of the participants agree that the pessimistic approach gives more opportunity for their group members to negotiate on whether to issue an operation right now or later. It is the designer who can make the decision according to the prompted confliction warning which is more meaningful in preserving each user's modeling intention.

3. The participants have positive comments over the optimistic concurrency approach. A group of them appraise the fashion that the approach helps to preserve each user's intention in a transparent way. Quotes from the focus group include, "It is good for the approach to resolve the conflicts silently so I can be more focused on the working I am doing right now.", "The performance of the approach is acceptable because it seems my designing procedure was not interrupted", "...I was not aware of the existence of any conflictive operations... May be I was a little dull...".

4.2 Suggestions

Surprisingly, we also received some comments and suggestions over the concurrency control approaches and the prototype we presented in this experiment during the interview on the selected focus group. It is about the improvement of group awareness, especially when the optimistic concurrency control approach is adopted. One participant says that "I don't think working collaboratively means that we need to work quietly. Sometimes, I will think about what my partners are doing so I can try my best to prevent conflicts.", another participant says "...It will be more helpful to prevent conflicts if I have chance to know what other designers are doing...", "You cannot expect we all reach an agreement by modifying the model at the beginning and then we all stopped suddenly at the same time. We need to know if others are thinking the way I am. There should be a tunnel for us to communicate and afterwards we can all agree to stop working".

5 Discussion

Based on the experimental results mentioned above, in this section, we will discuss several implications for developing both concurrency control approach and collaborative designing platforms.

1. In terms of intention preservation, more designer involvement is needed. Users intentions get ripen along with the collaborative designing procedure. Even if requirements are presented in a top-down manner, people have different opinions, considerations and expectations over the result model regarding to their background knowledge, experiences and etc. Because of the collaborative working environment, the result model is expected to represent every designer's intention ideally. The process of preserving users' intentions is more likely to be the process of intention presentation, communication, negotiation and compromise. The pessimistic concurrency control approach gives designers' a chance to letting them what other designers' are doing and thus presents a way to communicate and negotiate. Since the optimistic concurrency approach dedicates to build up a free and concurrent

collaborative designing environment, a designer will be more focused on his/her own task. In this way, users' intentions are preserved by a pre-set built-in rule.

2. Designers were eager to know and easily influenced by co-workers' presence and designing intentions. They trend to avoid conflicts by delaying his/her operation actively. In our experiment, workers were co-located in the same space, which made possible for them to share the work progress. However, in reality, most workers are geographically dispersed and work remotely over the Internet, which makes it hard for them to be aware of or interact with each other. Collaborative designing involves human beings who have thoughts and conscious, not merely machines who are endowed with artificial intelligent. Regardless of the method of implementation, it is critical for a collaborative designing platform to allow a target group to "easily access the application and reduce the support cost" [6]. It should "help collaboration take place with one user's awareness of others' activities" [6].

3. We also noted that the occurrence of a certain portion of conflicts is not because of operations concurrency but due to designers' different perceptions over a part's functional requirement. Such kind of conflict may not cause any troubles which violate the modeling intention of any specific operation. However, the successful execution of modeling intention preserved operations will still result in the violation of design intention. Still, it quite hard for such kind of conflicts to be detected or resolved by any of the above mentioned concurrency control mechanisms but the perceptions of human being. A useful collaboration communication channel for letting co-designers share their ideas by sketching, texts would be helpful in detecting such kind of conflicts and finally resolving them by negotiation.

6 Conclusion

Concurrency control approaches are one of the core components of a feature-based collaborative platform. In this paper, we present an experimental study over the level of user satisfaction and intention preservation over the effects of optimistic and pessimistic concurrency control approach. By recognizing that there is not a formal way for representing user satisfaction and intention preservation over collaborative designing, the research is carried out in a methods of social science. We adapt a questionnaire over user satisfaction during the human-computer interaction to evaluation the level of user satisfaction and we carried out a group interview to collection participants' comments over intention preservation. We confirmed that either concurrency approach has its advantage but more support is needed to for user experience optimization. Finally, several implications are put forward for future development of both concurrency control and collaborative designing.

Acknowledgement. The work is supported by the National Natural Science Foundation of China (NSFC Grant Nos. 61472289 and 61502353) and Youth Innovation Corps Fund of Humanities and Social Sciences, Wuhan University. The authors would like to thank all the reviewers for their constructive comments and suggestions.

References

1. Bouras, C., Giannaka, E., Tsiatsos, T.: E-collaboration concepts, systems, and applications. In: Encyclopedia of Internet Technologies and Applications, pp. 165–171 (2008)
2. Gao, L.P., Shao, B., Zhu, L., Lu, T., Gu, N.: Maintaining time and space consistencies in hybrid engineering environments: framework and algorithms. Comput. Ind. **59**(9), 894–904 (2008)
3. Gao, L.P., Gu, N.: Supporting semantic maintenance of complex undo operations in replicated Co-AutoCAD environments. In: 13th International Proceedings on Computer Supported Cooperative Work in Design 2009, pp. 84–89. IEEE Computer Society (2009)
4. Gao, L.P., Lu, T.: Achieving transparent and real-time collaboration in Co-AutoCAD application. J. Univers. Comput. Sci. **17**(14), 1887–1912 (2011)
5. Moncur, R.A.: Data consistency and conflict avoidance in a multi-user CAx environment. Master degree thesis paper 3675, Brigham Young University (2012)
6. Nuss, J.E.: Assessing User Expectations of Undo in a Multi-User CAD Environment. Master degree thesis, paper 5875, Brigham Young University (2016)
7. Gao, L.P., Lu, T., Gu, N.: CLAF: solving intention violation of step-wise operations in CAD groupware. Adv. Eng. Inf. **24**(2), 121–137 (2010)
8. Red, E., Holyoak, V., Jensen, C.G., Marshall, F., Ryskamp, J., Xu, Y.: V-CAx: a research agenda for collaborative computer-aided applications. Comput. Aided Des. Appl. **7**(3), 387–404 (2010)
9. Xu, Y., Red, E., Jensen, C.G.: A flexible context architecture for a multi-user GUI. Comput. Aided Des. Appl. **8**(4), 479–497 (2011)
10. Gao, L.P., Yu, F.Y., Chen, Q.K., Xiong, N.X.: Consistency maintenance of Do and Undo/Redo operations in real-time collaborative bitmap editing systems. Cluster Comput. **19** (1), 255–267 (2016)
11. Agustina, A., Liu, F., Xia, S., Shen, H.F., Sun, C.Z.: CoMaya: in coporating advanced collaboration capabilities into 3D digital media design tools. In: CSCW 2008 Proceedings of the 2008 ACM Conference on Computer Supported Cooperative Work 2008, pp. 5–8. ACM, New York, USA (2008)
12. Urbano, R.: Oracle Database Advance Replication. Database issue 33 (2007)
13. Jing, S.X., He, F.Z., Han, S.H.: A method for topological correspondence in a replicated collaborative CAD system. Comput. Ind. **60**(7), 467–475 (2009)
14. Chen, L., Song, Z.J., Feng, Z.J.: Internet-enabled real-time collaborative assembly modeling via an e-Assembly system: status and promise. Comput. Aided Des. **36**(9), 835–847 (2004)
15. Lin, K., Chen, D., Sun, C.Z., Dromey, G.: Maintaining constraints in collaborative graphic systems: the CoGSE approach. In: 9th Proceedings on the European Conference on Computer-Supported Cooperative Work 2005, pp. 185–204 (2005)
16. Marshall, F.: Model decomposition and constraints to parametrically partition design space in a collaborative CAx environment. Master degree thesis, paper 3184, Brigham Young University (2011)
17. Cera, C., Braude, I., Comer, I.: Hierarchical role-based viewing for secure collaborative CAD. In: 23rd Proceedings on the ASME International Design Engineering Technical Conferences and The Computer and Information in Engineering Conference 2003, pp. 965–974. ASME digital collection (2003)
18. Chan, S., Wong, M., Ng, V.: Collaborative solid modeling on the WWW. In: 14th Proceedings of the 1999 ACM Symposium on Applied Computing, pp. 598–602. Association for Computing Machinery, New York, United States (1999)

19. Li, W.D.: An Internet-enabled integrated system for co-design and concurrent engineering. Comput. Ind. **55**(1), 87–103 (2004)
20. Bidarra, R., van den Berg, E., Bronsvoort, W.F.: A collaborative feature modeling system. J. Comput. Inf. Sci. Eng. **2**(3), 192–198 (2002)
21. Cheng, Y., He, F.Z., Wu, Y.Q.: Meta-operation conflict resolution for human–human interaction in collaborative feature-based CAD systems. Cluster Comput. **19**(1), 237–253 (2016)
22. Cheng, Y., He, F.Z.: A Unified conflict prevention framework for feature based 3D collaborative designing environment. In: 22nd Proceedings on the IEEE International Conference on Computer Supported Cooperative Work in Design 2018, pp. 50–56. (2018). (In publishing)
23. Chin, J.P., Diehl, V.A., Norman, K.L.: Development of an instrument measuring user satisfaction of the human-computer interface. In: CHI 1988 Proceedings on the SIGCHI Conference on Human factors in Computing Systems 1988, pp. 213–218. ACM, Washington, USA (1988)
24. Dix, A., Finlay, J., Abowd, G., Russell, B.: Human-Computer Interaction, 3rd edn. Prentice Hall, New Jersey (2003)
25. Kirschman, C.F., Fadel, G.M.: Classifying functions for mechanical design. J. Mech. Des. **120**(3), 475–482 (1998)

A Concurrency Benchmark Tool for Cloud Storage

Weiwei Cai$^{(\boxtimes)}$, Agustina Ng, and Chengzheng Sun

School of Computer Science and Engineering,
Nanyang Technological University, 639798 Singapore, Singapore
{caiweiwei,Agustina,CZSun}@ntu.edu.sg

Abstract. File sharing and collaboration is a common functionality in cloud storage systems, which allow multiple users to concurrently manipulate files in shared folders or workspaces. However, in the face of concurrent updates, existing cloud storage systems may deliver confusing or even inconsistent results to end-users. In this paper, we present a concurrency benchmark tool, which can automatically run concurrency test cases in major cloud storage systems, including Google Drive, Microsoft OneDrive, Dropbox, and Box. This concurrency benchmark tool contributes to discovering consistency issues in existing cloud storage systems and revealing the consistency guarantees delivered by these systems.

Keywords: Consistency · Concurrency benchmark · Cloud storage

1 Introduction

With the increasing use of multi-devices, cloud storage systems, such as Google Drive, Microsoft OneDrive, Dropbox, and Box, have become very popular. Users not only can store files on cloud storage servers but also can replicate files on multiple devices and share files/folders with others. The replicated and shared workspaces are automatically synchronized by the underlying cloud storage systems among users' devices and with cloud storage data centers as well. Moreover, the front-ends are usually well integrated into users' devices. Users can access and manipulate the replicated files like the normal files on the devices.

To support collaboration, multiple users may share and replicate a workspace, and concurrently create new files, delete existing files, change file names, and update file contents in the replicated workspace. In such replicated environments, concurrent updates of replicated common data objects, such as shared documents in collaborative editing, and shared workspaces in cloud storage systems, may cause conflicts and produce inconsistent results [4]. Indeed, we have discovered that the results produced by cloud storage systems in concurrency scenarios may be undesirable or confusing to end-users, or even inconsistent [1].

Prior research [2, 3] on benchmarking front-end cloud storage mainly focused on the performance aspect. In contrast, this work is to benchmark the user-visible results achieved by cloud storage systems in concurrency scenarios, which focuses on the

© Springer Nature Singapore Pte Ltd. 2019
Y. Sun et al. (Eds.): ChineseCSCW 2018, CCIS 917, pp. 567–573, 2019.
https://doi.org/10.1007/978-981-13-3044-5_44

correctness of consistency maintenance techniques for replicated and shared workspaces.

The goal of this research is to discover the consistency issues in major cloud storage systems and reveal consistency guarantees delivered by these systems in the face of concurrent manipulating replicated and shared workspaces. Particularly, we are interested in the results of synchronizing the replicated workspaces manipulated by a pair of basic file operations concurrently, which are generated from the same workspace state. To achieve this objective, we have devised a concurrency benchmark suite [1], which covers a comprehensive set of concurrency test cases, made up of user-generated file operations in real-world collaboration scenarios. In this paper, we present a concurrency benchmark tool, which can automatically run the comprehensive set of concurrency test cases in the cloud storage systems (Google Drive, One Drive, Dropbox, and Box) and record the final results achieved by these systems.

2   Concurrency Benchmark Suite

A workspace can be modeled as a tree of nodes, representing files or folders. Each tree node has a name attribute, which is a string of characters. A file cannot have a child but has a data attribute, which represents the contents of this file. A folder can contain other folders or files. We assume two nodes, regardless whether they are files or folders, cannot have the same name under the same parent node. Such constraint is imposed in most real-world file systems. In a workspace, a pathname, which is usually represented by a sequence of folder and file names separated by a delimiter, can uniquely identify a node. The pathname of a node is the string of names of the nodes on the path from the root node to the target node.

Cloud storage end-users may generate one of the four basic operations to manipulate the replicated workspace: a *CR* (*Create*) operation creates a subtree, referred by a pathname, where the subtree can be a single file and folder, or an existing subtree; a *DL* (*Delete*) operation deletes a subtree referred by a pathname; a *RN* (*Rename*) operation changes the name of a folder/file, referred by a pathname, to a new name; an *UP* (*Update*) operation modifies the content of the file referred by a pathname. The four basic operations are sufficient to express other complex operations for manipulating workspaces provided by cloud storage systems. Each operation has a precondition for successfully generating it in a workspace. For example, to generate a CR operation in a workspace, it is required that the existing files/folders in the workspace are not on the path of the target node.

The concurrency benchmark suite provides a comprehensive set of testing cases, which is derived by the following steps: (1) enumerate all combinations of a pair of concurrent file operations along three dimensions of variation: *operation type* (i.e. CR, DL, RN, or UP), *target pathname relation* (i.e. whether the pair of targets are dependent, meaning they are the same or on the path of each other, or independent, meaning they are different and not on the path of each other), and *target type* (i.e. whether the target is a file or folder), which could affect the final results; (2) combine all variations in the three dimensions and eliminate the redundant and impractical cases.

In conclusion, the concurrency benchmark suite consists of 63 distinctive test cases for a pair of concurrent file operations generated from the same workspace state, which forms the foundation for the generation of concrete test cases.

3 Concurrency Benchmark Tool

3.1 Test Case Instantiation

To apply a general test case from the concurrency benchmark suite in a cloud storage system, we need to instantiate the test case, which gives the pair-wise concurrent operations with suitable parameters and an initial workspace for holding the preconditions of the operations.

Consider a general test case RN-RN: O_1 = RN, O_2 = RN, O_1 and O_2 rename two different sub-folders under the same folder to the same name. The two concurrent operations target dependent nodes, as their target nodes are on the same path. According to the test case specification, we can create a concrete test case: O_1 is to rename the folder A to X and O_2 is to rename the folder B to X, generated from the initial workspace T_1, as described in Fig. 1. The parameters of the two operations respect the test case specification, and the operations are executable in the initial workspace T_1.

T_1	State with the effect of O_1	State with the effect of O_2

Fig. 1. A concrete test case for RN-RN. The symbol ◢ denotes the root folder of the replicated workspace, and the symbol ◢ denotes a folder named A.

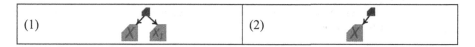

Fig. 2. The test results for the concrete test case.

In this concrete test case, OneDrive, Box, and Google Drive would produce the consistent final workspaces (1)[1], whereas Dropbox would produce the consistent final workspaces (2), as shown in Fig. 2.

---

[1] X_1 is constructed by appending system-dependent identifiers after the original name X.

3.2   Test Case Execution

To concurrently execute file update operations, we install the desktop clients of the four cloud storage systems on two computers, which host a replicated and shared folder and are connected to the Internet for accessing cloud storage services.

For each concrete test case, four steps are carried out one by one (either manually by human testers or automatically by using a benchmark tool)

- Step 1: create the same initial shared workspace in the target cloud storage system, which is replicated on the two computers.
- Step 2: execute two operations concurrently in the replicated workspaces. For ensuring concurrency of the two operations, the file synchronization functionality should be disabled during execution of individual operations.
- Step 3: let the target cloud storage system combine the effects of concurrent operations, by enabling the cloud file synchronization function after Step 2.
- Step 4: record the final states of replicated workspaces on different computers achieved in this testing case for further analysis.

Manual Testing. We briefly describe how two human testers may manually execute the concrete test case described in Fig. 1. Two testers work on the two computers.

In Step 1, tester 1 may create folder A and folder B in the replicated and shared folder of the target cloud storage system, which will trigger the cloud storage system to synchronize these two folders to the other replicated folder; tester 2 may wait for the notification of synchronization termination from the cloud storage desktop client; once tester 2 gets the notification, tester 1 and tester 2 go to Step 2.

In Step 2, the testers disable the file synchronization with the support of the cloud storage desktop client; afterward, tester 1 renames the folder A to X and concurrently tester 2 renames the folder B to X; then, they go to Step 3.

In Step 3, the testers enable the file synchronization with the support of the cloud storage desktop client; afterward, they may wait for the notification of synchronization termination from the cloud storage desktop client like in Step 1; once they get the notification, they go to the last step.

In Step 4, the testers may dive into the two replicated workspaces and record all the files/folders and file contents

Automated Testing. The concurrency benchmark tool is designed to automate the testing process. Two programs (called *Coordinator* and *Client*), establishing a TCP connection, are run on the two computers for simulating end-users, as shown in Fig. 3.

In Step 1, *Coordinator* creates the initial workspace of a test case in the replicated and shared folder of the target cloud storage system, which will trigger the cloud storage system to synchronize the created files/folders; then, *Coordinator* sends a message to *Client* for detecting the termination of synchronization; when *Client* gets the termination notification from a customized protocol, *Client* sends a message to *Coordinator* and proceeds to Step 2; after receiving the message, *Coordinator* also proceeds to Step 2.

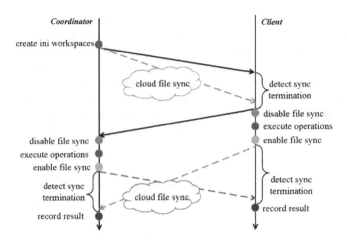

Fig. 3. Execution flow of the tool, where the solid black lines denote the communication between the two applications, and the dashed grey lines denote the cloud file sync.

In Step 2, *Coordinator* and *Client* disable the file synchronization functionality by suspending the processes of the cloud storage desktop client; then *Coordinator* and *Client* concurrently generate file operations; afterward, they proceed to the next step.

In Step 3, *Coordinator* and *Client* enable the file synchronization functionality by resuming the processes suspended in Step 2, leading the target cloud storage system to synchronize the replicated workspaces; we designed a protocol to detect the termination of synchronizing the replicated workspaces in this situation, which is capable of detecting the synchronization termination *precisely and as soon as possible*; when *Coordinator* and *Client* get the notification from the protocol, they proceed to Step 4.

In Step 4, *Coordinator* and *Client* record the states of the two replicated workspaces by invoking the low-level file operations.

The concurrency benchmark tool totally removes the human involvement in the testing process and can be applied to different cloud storage systems. Using the concurrency benchmark tool, people can easily and quickly acquire the test results of concurrency test cases in a specific cloud storage system and repeat the tests at any times.

4 Discussion

Recall the example illustrated in Sect. 3.1. From the test results in Fig. 2, it can be seen that all four cloud storage systems can achieve consistent and reasonable results. However, if we run a more complicated test case, without changing the operation types, pathname relations, and target types, we may see different consistency guarantees delivered by the cloud storage systems. For example, O_1 is to rename the folder A to the name X and O_2 is to rename the folder B to the name X, generated from the initial workspace T_2, as shown in Fig. 4. In the second test case, OneDrive and Box may produce the consistent final workspace (1); Dropbox may produce the consistent final workspace (2); and Google Drive may produce the inconsistent final workspaces (3) on the two devices, as described in Fig. 5. Compared to the test results of the first test case, the test results of the second test case reveal the inconsistency issues existed in Google Drive, and provide more details about the consistency guarantees achieved by OneDrive, Box, and Dropbox, in such a concurrency scenario. The result delivered by OneDrive and Box is desirable to end-users, as it can preserve the effects of both the two concurrent operations. However, the result delivered by Dropbox may be confusing to end-users, as the merged folder is not the effect of the two concurrent operations.

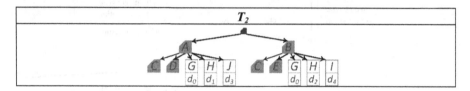

Fig. 4. The second concrete test case for RN-RN, $\boxed{G\,d_0}$ marks a file named G with data d_0.

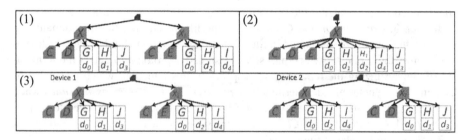

Fig. 5. The test results for the second concrete test case

From the above case study, it can be seen that testing different instances of a general test case is necessary to accurately reveal the consistency guarantees delivered by cloud storage systems. The automated concurrency benchmark tool can help repeat running various test cases, regardless of the simple test cases or the complicated test cases, to make the test results more reliable.

It is clear that cloud storage systems may achieve different final results in a concurrency scenario, some of which may be consistent and desirable to end-users, however, some others may be confusing to end-users, or even inconsistent. The automated concurrency benchmark tool can provide both the past test results and the recent test results at any time, which contributes to analyzing and comparing the test results of different cloud storage systems.

5 Conclusions and Future Work

This work presents a concurrency benchmark tool for automatically testing the results produced by major cloud storage systems under a comprehensive set of concurrency test cases. The automated benchmark tool can contribute to discovering the consistency issues in existing cloud storage systems and consistency guarantees (but never explicitly specified) delivered by existing cloud storage systems. In future, we plan to extend the functionality of the concurrency benchmark tool and to make it publically accessible so that people can freely use the concurrency benchmark tool, compare and analyze test results acquired by different cloud storage systems at anytime from anywhere.

Acknowledgment. This work is partially supported by an Academic Research Grant (MOE2015-T2-1-087) from Ministry of Education Singapore. The authors wish to thank anonymous reviewers for their insightful advice and comments.

References

1. Agustina, N., Sun, C.Z.: Operational transformation for real-time synchronization of shared workspace in cloud storage. In: ACM GROUP, pp. 61–70 (2016)
2. Bocchi, E., Drago, I., Mellia, M.: Personal cloud storage benchmarks and comparison. IEEE Trans. Cloud Comput. **5**(4), 751–764 (2017)
3. Gracia-Tinedo, R., Artigas, M.S., Moreno-Martinez, A.: Actively measuring personal cloud storage system. In: IEEE CLOUD, pp. 301–308 (2013)
4. Sun, C.Z., Ellis, C.: Operational transformation in real-time group editors: issues, algorithms, and achievements. In: ACM CSCW, pp. 59–68 (1998)

Task Assignments in Complex Collaborative Crowdsourcing

Wei He, Lizhen Cui$^{(\boxtimes)}$, and Cheng Huang

School of Software, Shandong University, Jinan, China
{hewei,clz}@sdu.edu.cn

Abstract. At present, crowdsourcing platforms are mainly developed for Micro-tasks such as data annotation and image recognition. However, complex collaborative crowdsourcing tasks, which usually contain multiple interdependent subtasks, are emerging and require a variety of workers with different skills to cooperate with each other. To solve the worker-task matching problem in the complex collaborative crowdsourcing, we propose a complex crowdsourcing task assignment algorithm (C^3TA), which models the complex collaborative crowdsourcing task assignment problem as a combinatorial optimization problem based on the maximum flow and compute the optimal solution to task assignment with a Slide-Container Queue (SCP). The experimental results show that the algorithm can effectively assign complex collaborative crowdsourcing tasks with the constraint of multi-skill workers and sequential subtasks and maximize the number of assigned tasks.

Keywords: Complex collaborative crowdsourcing
Crowdsourcing task assignment · Task dependency · Task sequence

1   Introduction

Micro-tasks refer to the predefined tasks on the crowdsourcing platforms which can be distributed to any registered user. These simple and independent tasks are mainly focus on image recognition, data annotation and online manual translation, etc. As Internet resources tend to be more open, shared and collaborative, crowdsourcing is applied to the tasks which are difficult to be accomplished independently by a computer and the complex collaborative crowdsourcing tasks (hereinafter referred to as Complex Task) which contain multiple sequential subtasks of different types and require workers with different skills. A Complex Task can be decomposed by the publisher as required, or by the crowdsourcing platform automatically according to the task target and some strategy before being accomplished by multiple workers. The characteristics of a Complex Task are summarized as follows:

(1) A Complex Task is implicitly or explicitly composed of multiple subtasks of different types and each subtask requires workers with specific professional skills.

© Springer Nature Singapore Pte Ltd. 2019
Y. Sun et al. (Eds.): ChineseCSCW 2018, CCIS 917, pp. 574–580, 2019.
https://doi.org/10.1007/978-981-13-3044-5_45

(2) There are time dependencies between subtasks.
(3) A Complex Task requires collaboration between crowdsourcing workers.

All above features of a Complex Task are challengeable for the crowdsourcing task assignment. So far, there are relatively few researches on Complex Tasks. Related researches mainly focus on workers' organizational structure and the number of Complex Tasks being assigned [2,4,5,7], rather than how to appropriately assign the tasks based on the availability and collaboration of workers while taking into account of the subtasks of multiple types and the time dependency. In this paper, it is defined as the Complex Collaborative Crowdsourcing Task Assignment Problem (C^3TA).

All above features of a Complex Task are challengeable for the crowdsourcing task assignment. So far, there are relatively few researches on Complex Tasks. Related researches mainly focus on workers' organizational structure and the number of Complex Tasks being assigned [1,2,4,5,7], rather than how to appropriately assign the tasks based on the availability and collaboration of workers while taking into account of the subtasks of multiple types and the time dependency. In this paper, it is defined as the Complex Collaborative Crowdsourcing Task Assignment Problem (C^3TAP). This paper studies the worker-task matching problem in the complex collaborative crowdsourcing task assignment. Based on the C^3TAP model, while satisfying the time dependency between sub-tasks, we propose the C^3TA, which models the complex collaborative crowdsourcing task assignment problem as a combinatorial optimization problem based on the maximum flow and compute the optimal solution to task assignment with a Slide-Container Queue (SCP).

An outline of this paper is as follows. We devote Sect. 2 to a discussion of related researches on crowdsourcing task assignment. Section 3 presents the Complex Collaborative Crowdsourcing Task Assignment Problem Model and Sect. 4 describes the complex crowdsourcing task assignment algorithm aiming at maximizing the number of assigned tasks. In Sect. 5, we verify the method proposed in this paper through simulation experiments. Finally, we draw a conclusion and introduce the future direction of our research.

2   Related Works

A complex task differs a micro task mainly in the complexity of the task, requirement for workers' skills and level of tasks. Besides, there is time or logic dependency between the subtasks of a Complex Task. Some subtasks can be dealt with in parallel, while others need to be processed by serial. With regard to the decomposition of a Complex Task, Kitter et al. [3] studied how to accomplish a Complex Task through workers on a Micro task crowdsourcing platform by decomposing a Complex Task into several independent subtasks based on the MapReduce programming framework. As to the task assignment under the requirement for multi-skills, Shen et al. [6] determined how to combine workers based on the fuzzy set theory to achieve a high quality of task completion. Cheng et al. [1]

studied the task assignment under the requirement for multi-skills in spatial crowdsourcing and proposed some heuristic optimization algorithms to find an answer proximate to the optimal solution in limited time. For the process of a Complex Task, Retelny et al. [5] studied the worker organization model and worker collaboration in Complex Task crowdsourcing, developed a crowdsourcing system named Foundry and applied to the design crowdsourcing and engineering crowdsourcing. However, these studies did not focus on the impact of the time and sequential dependencies among multiple subtasks on task allocation and execution.

3   Collaborative Crowdsourcing Task Assignment Problem Model

The assignment algorithm in collaborative crowdsourcing aims to find a suitable task allocation scheme, that is, to generate a task-worker matching set, which meet the demands for workers with multiple-skills and subtasks with time dependency. We define some of the terms in this paper as follows.

Definition 1. *Complex Task. Complex Task is represented by τ. The publisher publishes a Complex Task τ. Its subtasks are featured by atomicity and Complex Task τ is modeled as $<V_\tau, E_\tau, T_\tau, q_\tau>$.*

Definition 2. *Subtask Set of Complex Task. Subtask Set of Complex Task is represented by S_τ, a set of all subtasks: $S_\tau = \{s_{\tau 1}, s_{\tau 2}, \ldots, s_{\tau i}, \ldots\}$, where $S_{\tau i}$ indicates the subtask i in the subtask set. The time for completing each task while guarantee the quality is represented by $\delta_{\tau i}$.*
  V_τ represents the subtask set of the complex task $<v_1, v_2, \ldots, v_i, \ldots>$, $v_i \in S_\tau$. Each subtask is atomic, that is, workers cannot only complete a part of a subtask. E_τ denotes the relational dependency between subtasks and is formed by a tuple (v_1, v_2), which indicates that has v_1 an edge pointing to v_2, namely, v_1 depend on v_2. $T_\tau = \{<st_1, et_1>, \ldots, <st_i, et_i>, \ldots\}$ represents the time for each subtask while meeting their relational dependency. st_i denotes the earliest start time for subtask i, st_i indicates the latest end time, and q_τ represents the quality requirement for each task.

For example, suppose that a complex task has seven subtasks, represented by $V_\tau = \{0, 1, 2, 3, 4, 5, 6\}$, and the time dependencies between subtasks are expressed as $E_\tau = \{(0, 1), (0, 2), (0, 3), (3, 4), (1, 5), (2, 3), (4, 3), (5, 6)\}$. According to the time and sequence dependencies, subtasks 1, 2 and 3 can be parallel, subtask 4 should start after subtask 3 being completed, and subtask 5 should start after subtasks 1, 2 and 4 being completed.

Definition 3. *Complex Collaborative Crowdsourcing Task Assignment Problem, C^3TAP. In the crowdsourcing system, given a Complex Task set $T = \{\tau_1, \tau_2, \ldots, \tau_m\}$ and a worker set $W = \{w_1, w_2, \ldots, w_n\}$, the platform selects workers from W based on a certain strategy to form a set $S_w = \{w_1, w_2, \ldots, w_i\}$*

and assigns the subtasks in the Complex Task τ_j to workers in S_w. w_i satisfies the demand for skills and the expected time for completing the task satisfies the relational dependencies between subtasks. A Complex Task is not assigned successfully unless all the subtasks are assigned successfully. The worker-task matching set $<t_j, S_w>$ forms the $CS\{<t_1, S_{w1}>, <t_1, S_{w2}>, \ldots, <t_m, S_{wm}>\}$. MDCTP is to find select a suitable RS from CS and organize qualified workers to form an online team to satisfy the actual demands of the crowdsourcing platform.

Among all optimization objectives, we focus on maximizing the number of tasks being assigned to achieve the optimal task assignment efficiency. sum_t represents the total number of tasks assigned to workers by the assignment algorithm within time t. The algorithm proposed in this paper aims at maximizing the sum_t.

4   Assignment for Complex Crowdsourcing Tasks with Relational Dependencies

We firstly design a data structure based on the temporal sequence of a Complex Task and define it as the Slide-Container Queue (SCP). This structure can model the Complex Task assignment problem as the maximum flow problem of the graph. The most basic element of SCP, a slide-container is a set of dependent subtasks. v_i represents the sequential subtasks of a complex task, which can be expressed as $<v_1, \{v_2, v_3, v_4\}, v_5>$. The location of each element in the container indicates its dependency.

To assign a Complex Task is to sequentially assign its subtasks to suitable workers based on the dependencies between subtasks. Due to the isomorphism of the problem model, the Complex Task assignment problem can be simplified to the maximum flow problem of the graph to achieve assignment optimization. We construct the graph $G = \{V, E\}$, where the point set V consisting of the subtasks to be assigned and the edge set E consisting of the available workers forms a bipartite graph through the edge. We add a source point and a sink point to the graph, so the point set contains $2 + |TA| + |W|$ points. The subtask point set consisting of $|TA|$ points represents the subtasks τ_{ij} to be assigned.

Similarly, $|W|$ points represent $|W|$ available workers and worker w_i can be mapped to point $v_{|TA|+i}$ on the graph. The source points and the points representing the subtasks to be assigned are connected by $|TA|$ edges. Since each subtask needs to be assigned only once, the capacity of each edge is set to be 1 and the total sum of the capacity of all edges equals to the number of subtasks to be assigned. As the worker w can accept at most c_w tasks, suppose the number of tasks accepted yet unfulfilled is num_w, then the capacity of this edge is set to be $c_w - num_w$, indicating the number of tasks this worker can still accept.

Figure 1 gives an example of a complex collaborative crowdsourcing task, which contains a total of 8 complex tasks and 10 subtasks to be assigned. We

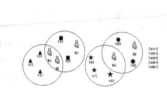

Fig. 1. Example of a complex collaborative crowdsourcing task assignment

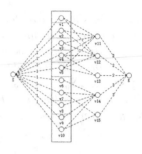

Fig. 2. The graph model for the assignment of the subtasks in a complex task

use different shape icons to represent the four task types and the Vern diagram
to indicate which type of task workers can accept.

We construct the graph model for the example in Fig. 1 by using the previous
mapping mode, as shown in Fig. 2. Combined with the SCQ, the 10 subtasks are
mapped to the points v_1 to v_{10} and the workers w_1 to w_5 are mapped to the
points $v_{11} \sim v_{15}$. In the example, the workers have not accepted any task, so the
capacity of w_4 is $c_{w4} - 0 = 3$ and the capacity of the edge between the worker
w_4 and the sink point is 3.

Based on the above model, we proposes the C^3TA, which firstly construct
a graph model $G_x = \{V, E\}$. Given the set of Complex Tasks T_p and the set of
available workers W, the points representing the subtasks in the graph model
are denoted by $V_{ta} \in$ V, which indicates the points representing the available
workers. For each (w, i), where $i \in V_{ta}$ represents a subtask to be assigned and
$w \in V_w$ represents an available worker. The cost of the such an edge is set as
$\triangle EI <i, j>$, which indicates that this assignment can bring efficiency gains, and
the costs of other edges are set to 0. Through this modeling process, the problem
of the maximum subtasks to be assigned in a Complex Task is transformed into
the maximum flow problem of the graph, which can be solved by many mature
algorithms.

5   Experimental Evaluation

We use two simulation data sets, which are generated by referring to the requirements for the data of the garment industry and the data in the crowdsourcing sys-
tem, to form a set of subtasks as $S_\tau = \{s_{\tau1}, s_{\tau2}, \ldots, s_{\tau11}\}$. There are three types
of subtasks, which can be expressed as A $= \{s_{\tau1}, s_{\tau2}, s_{\tau3}, s_{\tau4}\}$, B $= \{s_{\tau5}, s_{\tau6}, s_{\tau7}\}$
and C $= \{s_{\tau8}, s_{\tau9}, s_{\tau10}, s_{\tau11}, s_{\tau12}\}$. The SYN-Random simulation data set uses
random methods to generate various types of tasks and workers, and ultimately
the probabilities of occurrence for all types of tasks and workers are the same.
The SYN-Design simulation data set also uses random methods, but unlike the
SYN-Random, it can set the number of workers of various types.

We conduct an experiment on the SYN-Random and observe the effect of an
increasing number of tasks on the efficiency of task assignment with the number

of workers unchanged. We compare the MDTCP-Greedy algorithm based on the greedy strategy with the graph matching Naive algorithm and the C^3TA algorithm in this paper.

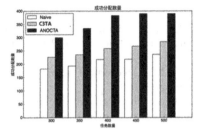
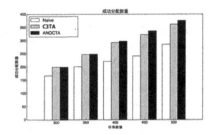

Fig. 3. Number of complex tasks successfully assigned on the SDY-Design data set

Fig. 4. Number of complex tasks successfully assigned on the SDY-Random data set

Figure 3 shows the number of Complex Tasks successfully assigned in the SDY-Design data set by using different algorithms with the number of workers being 2000. It can be seen that the performance of the Naive algorithm is the least ideal, because it does not consider the global optimization after each assignment; therefore the number of tasks successfully assigned is only about half of the total number of tasks. The MDTCP-Greedy algorithm is able to iteratively find the optimal feasible solution for each Complex Task, but it also does not take into account of the global optimization. Compared with the former two algorithms, the C^3TA algorithm optimizes the feasible solution based on the graph algorithm and thereby increasing the number of tasks successfully assigned. We can see that the C^3TA algorithm outperforms the greedy algorithm by approximately 30% in terms of the number of successful assignment on the SYN-Design data set.

The run time of each algorithm on the SYN-Random data set is similar to that on the SYN-Design. The number of successful assignment by each algorithm is shown in Fig. 4.

Figure 4 shows the number of Complex Tasks successfully assigned on the SDY-Random data set by using different algorithms with the number of workers being 2000. The C^3TA algorithm outperforms the MDTCP-Greedy algorithm in terms of the number of successful assignment.

6   Conclusion

We propose the complex collaborative crowdsourcing task assignment problem (C^3TA) model and the complex collaborative crowdsourcing task assignment algorithm (C^3TA) based on the combinatorial optimization theory. The C^3TA models the Complex Task assignment problem as the maximum flow problem of the graph to achieve the maximum task assignment. We design a simulation scene for a complex crowdsourcing task in garment industry and simulate the process of crowdsourcing.

Acknowledgements. This work is supported by Natural Science Foundation of Shandong Province under Grant ZR2017MF065 and No. ZR2018MF014.

References

1. Cheng, P., Lian, X., Chen, L., Han, J., Zhao, J.: Task assignment on multi-skill oriented spatial crowdsourcing. IEEE Trans. Knowl. Data Eng. **28**(8), 2201–2215 (2016)
2. Kim, J., Sterman, S., Cohen, A.A.B., Bernstein, M.S.: Mechanical novel: crowdsourcing complex work through reflection and revision (2018)
3. Kittur, A., Smus, B., Khamkar, S., Kraut, R.E.: CrowdForge: crowdsourcing complex work. In: Proceedings of Annual ACM Symposium on User Interface Software and Technology, pp. 1801–1806. ACM (2011)
4. Long, T.T., Huynh, T.D., Rosenfeld, A., Ramchurn, S.D., Jennings, N.R.: Crowdsourcing complex workflows under budget constraints. In: Twenty-Ninth AAAI Conference on Artificial Intelligence, pp. 1298–1304 (2015)
5. Retelny, D., et al.: Expert crowdsourcing with flash teams. In: ACM Symposium on User Interface Software and Technology, pp. 75–85 (2014)
6. Shen, M., Tzeng, G.H., Liu, D.R.: Multi-criteria task assignment in workflow management systems. In: Hawaii International Conference on System Sciences, p. 9 pp. (2003)
7. Zheng, Q., Wang, W., Yu, Y., Pan, M., Shi, X.: Crowdsourcing complex task automatically by workflow technology. In: International Workshop on Management of Information, Processes and Cooperation, pp. 17–30 (2016)

A Collaboration Services Scheduling Method Based on Intelligent Genetic Algorithm

Wei Guo[1,2], Meng Xu[2,3], Weixia Xu[1], and Lizhen Cui[1,2(✉)]

[1] School of Software, Shandong University, Jinan 250100, China
{guowei,clz}@sdu.edu.cn, xwx@mail.sdu.edu.cn
[2] Key Laboratory of Shandong Software Engineering, Jinan 250100, China
xumeng_wf@163.com
[3] School of Computer Science and Technology, Shandong Technology and Business University, Yantai 264005, China

Abstract. The optimization problem of collaboration services scheduling is a major bottleneck restricting the efficiency and cost of collaboration services executing. Correct and efficient handling of scheduling problems contributes to reducing costs and increase efficiency. The traditional GA solves this multi-objective problem more comprehensively than the random algorithm such as stochastic greedy algorithm, but it still has some one-sidedness compared with the actual situation. This paper enhances the flexibility and diversity of the algorithm on the basis of traditional genetic algorithm. In the process of initial population selection, it adopts the method of determining the preliminary internal point internal modification, and optimizes the selection process in the iteration as the selection method based on population exchange to achieve the choice. Mutation factors in the variation based on the individual's innate quality of adaptive selection enhance the diversity of the population. In the experiments, this algorithm can not only maintain individual diversity, increase the probability of excellent individuals, speed up the convergence rate, but also will not lead to the ultimate result of the local optimal solution.

Keywords: Genetic algorithm · Multi-objective optimization
Collaboration services scheduling · Self-adaption

1 Introduction

Web Services technology is now entering a rapid development and popularization stage, which has brought rapid development and application of collaborative services within and between enterprises. In the collaborative service execution, an efficient scheduling scheme needs to be obtained according to the current available resources. This enables the execution efficiency and cost of the collaborative service to meet the need of the user.

Therefore, in the process of collaborative service execution, the collaborative service needs to be scheduled based on the user's QoS (Quality of Service) requirements to obtain an optimal execution plan [1–3].

© Springer Nature Singapore Pte Ltd. 2019
Y. Sun et al. (Eds.): ChineseCSCW 2018, CCIS 917, pp. 581–587, 2019.
https://doi.org/10.1007/978-981-13-3044-5_46

This paper proposes an intelligent genetic algorithm based collaborative service scheduling algorithm iGA (intelligent Genetic Algorithm). The proposed iGA algorithm not only remains the diversity of individuals and the high probability of excellent individuals, but also speeds up the convergence. And it does not cause the final result to tend to a local optimal solution. It has certain advantages in solving such optimization problems. It is aimed at the collaborative service scheduling problem, which can greatly reduce the cost while ensuring the quality of service.

Section 2 of this paper briefly introduces the research progress of collaborative service scheduling based on Qos attribute calculation. Section 3 discusses in detail the proposed genetic algorithm including cost model, mutation strategy and fitness function. Section 4 introduces the simulation experiment results; Sect. 5 gives the conclusions and points out the following research plan.

2 Related Works

When the collaborative service is scheduled to obtain the optimal execution plan, the ant colony algorithm, the particle swarm optimization algorithm and the genetic algorithm can be used to manipulate the above kind problems.

Solnon [4] proposed an improved ant colony algorithm that aimed to handle multi-objective optimization problems. On this basis, Stutzle [5] proposed the MMAS (MAX-MIN Ant System) algorithm to limit the information on the path. Xia [6] proposed a multi-phenomenological dynamic update ant colony algorithm. However, there is only one pheromone in these algorithms, which cannot solve the problem of finding the optimal solution under the condition of multiple constraints.

Wang [7] proposed multi-objective optimization of multi-target groups collaborative differential evolution algorithm. The algorithm has M single-objective optimization subgroups and an archive group of M target optimization problems. An adaptive differential evolution algorithm is applied to each subgroup to optimize the corresponding objectives of the multi-objective optimization problem. Handle multiple targets by using multiple subgroups. Each subgroup only processes one target, and the subgroups cooperate to approximate the overall optimal solution. Antonio [8] also proposed applying scalable decision variables to multi-objective optimization problems. However, in view of the sequence of processes in each of the constraints in this problem, the presented methods are not able to echo these problems well.

Li [9] optimized the traditional genetic algorithm by defining a local search operator to achieve a better community structure. However, this method has obvious advantages for solving network problems and is not suitable for solving such optimization problems.

In summary, the existing methods have certain limitations in solving the collaborative service scheduling problem described in this paper. In solving the multi-objective sequential optimization problem, there will be problems of being trapped in the local optimal solution and unable to solve many variables. The solution to the problem of multi-objective optimization scheduling [10] described in this paper.

3 Adaptive Genetic Algorithm Model

3.1 Problem Modeling

Users need to comprehensively evaluate the combination scheme in terms of cost, time and quality of service (user QoS requirements) when performing collaborative service scheduling. Therefore, this section includes the cost model, time model, and service quality when modeling collaborative service scheduling.

Cost Model
Cost of collaborative service execution is the sum of the costs of executing each web service. The cost per web service executed on all available resources can be expressed as a matrix *Quote*, where $Quote_{ij}$ represents the cost of web service j executing on available resources i. Defining the collaborative service array X The web service j is executed on the available resources i, and the total cost of the final execution of the collaborative service can be obtained:

$$\text{Cost} = \sum\nolimits_{j=1}^{M} Quote_{ij}, \quad X_j = i \tag{1}$$

Time Model
In the collaborative service scheduling problem, the start execution time T_s of the first web service in the collaborative service is set to zero. The completion time T_f of the last web service can be obtained according to the partial order relationship between the collaborative service array X and the Web services in the collaborative service, and the required length of time T_{ij} required to execute different web services. Matrix T stores each available resource to execute each web service. The completion duration matrix T is an N*M matrix, where T_{ij} is the available resource i to complete the completion time of the web service j. The M columns of the matrix T correspond to M web services, and the M web services have a temporal topology. The total time required for the execution of the entire collaborative service is:

$$\text{Time} = T_f - T_s \tag{2}$$

Quality of Service Model
In view of the differences in computing power, memory, and network bandwidth of available resources, the quality of service of each available resource is different when performing the same Web service. The quality of service when the available resources are executed in the web service is represented as a matrix T, where T_{ij} indicates that the available resource i performs the quality of service of the web service j, and the quality of service *quality* corresponding to the coordinated service array X is as follows:

$$\text{Quality} = \sum\nolimits_{j=1}^{M} T_{ij} \quad X_j = i \tag{3}$$

Model Goal
The goal of collaborative service scheduling is to reduce costs and reduce the execution time of collaborative services under the premise of ensuring service quality. Thus, the objective function is established as follows:

$$\text{Fitness} = \min(a \cdot \text{Cost} + b \cdot \text{Time} + (1 - a - b) \cdot \text{Quality}) \tag{4}$$

Equation (4) needs to satisfy the formulas (2) and (3) above. Fitness's parameters a, b are based on the user's emphasis on each factor.

3.2 Intelligent Genetic Algorithm

The i-GA algorithm consists of four parts: (1) Retaining individuals with low fitness. (2) Individual mutation is performed as an adaptive mutation rate, and the mutation rate of newly generated individuals is dynamically determined by the fitness of the parents.

Retaining Individuals with Low Fitness and Adaptive Mutation Rate
The adaptive mutation rate method proposed in the i-GA proposed in this paper dynamically determines the mutation rate of individuals and further increases the diversity and evolutionary rate of the population. When determining the mutation rate of an individual, the father of the individual and the mother (two individuals who cross-produce the individual) are searched, and the mutation rate of the individual is determined according to the fitness of the parents.

The initial mutation rate is defined as S. For any individual Entity, its father and mother are *F_Entity*, *M_Entity*, then the mutation rate of *Entity* obtained is as follows (Table 1):

Table 1. Determination rules for adaptive mutation rate

	F_Entity has high fitness	*F_Entity* has low fitness
M_Entity has high fitness	S/2	S
M_Entity has low fitness	S	4S

4 Simulation Experiments and Results Analysis

4.1 Experimental Setup Instructions

This section will compare the iGA algorithm proposed in this paper with the traditional genetic algorithm. The experimental environment is Inter(R) Core(TM)2 Duo 3.20 GHz, RAM 16 GB, hard disk 500 GB, 1000 MB network bandwidth.

(1) GA: Genetic algorithm, implemented by traditional genetic algorithm.
(2) iGA: The improved intelligent genetic algorithm proposed in this paper.

4.2 Similar Algorithm Comparison Experiments

This section uses five algorithms, GA, iGA, for comparative experiments. The experiment took the number of services that need to be coordinated to be 15, 30, 45, 60 for comparison. The mutation rate is 0.07. The crossover rate is 0.8. The number of variant genes is 1.

The number of services for this experiment is 15, 30, 45, 60, and the specified fitness is 500, 650, 1150, and 1500. Evolutionary duration of different algorithms under different service numbers is shown in Fig. 6.

As showed in Fig. 1, comparison between iGA and GA, iGA reduced the evolutionary time by 43% on the basis of GA.

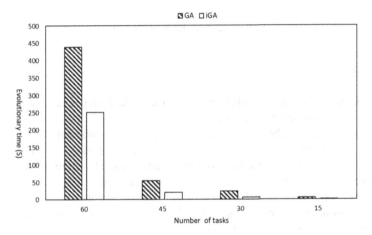

Fig. 1. Evolutionary time of different algorithms

In the case where the number of coordinated services is 15, 30, 45, 60 respectively, the corresponding target evolution time is 1, 3, 6, 50, respectively, and the actual experiment is performed according to the condition, and the obtained fitness is shown in Fig. 2.

It can be clearly seen from Fig. 2 that under the same evolutionary time, the iGA algorithm obtains a better fitness than GA for different number of cooperative services, and the fitness is 10% higher than that of GA.

It can be seen from the above comparison experiments that the iGA algorithm has obvious improvement effects on the GA algorithm, and both evolutionary time and the fitness are significantly improved.

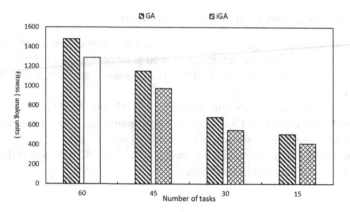

Fig. 2. Fitness of different algorithms

5 Conclusion

The optimization problem of collaborative service scheduling is an important factor that restricts the efficiency and cost of collaborative service execution. Proper and efficient processing of scheduling issues can help reduce costs and improve the efficiency of collaborative service execution. This paper enhances the flexibility and diversity of the algorithm on the basis of traditional genetic algorithm. In the process of initial population selection, it adopts the method of determining the preliminary internal point internal modification. When the intelligent genetic algorithm processes multiple populations, there may be problems such as insufficient solution speed. Such problems will be addressed in subsequent studies.

Acknowledgment. Research was supported by: (1) the National Key Technologies R&D Program No. 2016YFB1000602, No. 2017YFB1400102; (2) the National Natural Science Foundation of China under Grant, No. 61572295; (3) TaiShan Industrial Experts Programme of Shandong Province, No. tscy20160404.

References

1. Cheng, Y., Bi, L., Tao, F., Ji, P.: Hypernetwork-based manufacturing service scheduling for distributed and collaborative manufacturing operations towards smart manufacturing. J. Intell. Manuf., 1–14 (2018)
2. Hvolby, H., Setger-Jensen, K.: Technical and industrial issues of advanced planning and scheduling (APS) systems. Comput. Ind. **61**(9), 845–851 (2010)
3. Shi, L., Fu, X., Li, J.: Mobility prediction-based service scheduling optimization algorithm in cloudlets. In: Proceedings of Cloud Computing and Security, Nanjing, China, pp. 619–630 (2017)
4. Solnon, C.: Ants can solve constraint satisfaction problems. IEEE Trans. Evol. Comput. **6** (4), 347–357 (2002)

5. Stutzle, T., Hoos, H.: MAX-MIN ant system and local search for the traveling salesman problem. In: Proceedings of IEEE International Conference on Evolutionary Computation, Indianapolis, USA, pp. 309–314 (1997)
6. Xia, Y., Cheng, B., Chen, J., Cheng, B.: Optimizing services composition based on improved ant colony algorithm. Chin. J. Comput. **35**(2), 270–281 (2012)
7. Wang, J., Zhang, W., Zhang, J.: Cooperative differential evolution with multiple populations for multiobjective optimization. IEEE Trans. Cybern. **46**(12), 2848–2861 (2015)
8. Antonio, L., Coello, C.: Use of cooperative coevolution for solving large scale multiobjective optimization problems. In: Proceedings of IEEE Evolutionary Computation, Cancun, Mexico, pp. 2758–2765 (2013)
9. Li, S., Chen, Y., Du, H., Feldman, M.: A genetic algorithm with local search strategy for improved detection of community structure. Complexity **15**(4), 53–60 (2010)
10. Ide, J., Köbis, E., Kuroiwa, D.: The relationship between multi-objective robustness concepts and set-valued optimization. Fixed Point Theory Appl. **2014**(1), 1–20 (2014)

Author Index

An, Chunyan 100

Ban, Zihan 301

Cai, Saihua 176, 371
Cai, Weiwei 557, 567
Cao, Donglin 424
Cao, Jian 213, 546
Chen, Haijian 398
Chen, Haixiang 163, 527
Chen, Jia-Hui 50
Chen, Jing 115
Chen, Junjie 398
Chen, Liangyin 163, 527
Chen, Siqi 66
Chen, Yang 331
Chen, Yanru 163
Chen, Zechuan 342
Chen, Zhigang 115
Cheng, Xiaochun 410
Cheng, Yuan 557
Cui, Lizhen 386, 574, 581

Dai, Weihui 398
Dai, Yonghui 398
Deng, Chao 371
Dong, Minggang 77
Du, Ping 478

Fang, Xi 359
Fang, Xiaozhao 342
Fei, Lunke 342
Fu, Chengzhou 507
Fu, Xiaoming 331
Fu, Ye 398

Gao, Liping 20, 87, 201
Gao, Shengxiang 454
Gong, Qingyuan 331
Gu, Ning 32, 272
Guan, Chao 517
Guo, Kun 285, 487

Guo, Wei 581
Guo, Zhihong 410
Guo, Ziyu 241

Han, Yanbin 129
Hao, Shangbo 176
He, Fazhi 557
He, Junping 342
He, Liang 188
He, Wei 386, 574
He, Xiaoshan 487
He, Xinlei 331
Hu, Bin 469
Hu, Xianghui 438
Huang, Changqin 316
Huang, Cheng 574
Huang, Li 3
Hui, Pan 331

Jiang, Wei-Jin 50
Jiang, Yun 386
Jing, Chao 77

Li, Fei 331
Li, Jianguo 507
Li, Jiayao 371
Li, Liang 129, 257
Li, Shaozi 424
Li, Sicong 176, 371
Li, Taoshen 146
Li, Xinrong 410
Liao, Qinwu 285, 487
Lin, Ronghua 507
Liu, Guang-peng 257
Liu, Hong 115, 129, 257
Liu, Peng 272
Liu, Shijun 241
Liu, Zhanghui 285
Lu, Dianjie 115
Lu, Shengqi 398
Lu, Tun 32, 272
Luo, Qian 163, 527

Luo, Zhiming   424
Lv, Xiao   557
Lyu, Chen   115, 536

Mao, Chengjie   507
Mou, Zefeng   100

Ng, Agustina   567

Pan, Li   241
Peng, Zhaohui   386

Qian, Shiyou   213

Ren, Fuji   438

Shi, Peiying   478
Song, Hu   536
Song, Xiaocheng   438
Sun, Chengzheng   567
Sun, Hailong   301
Sun, Ruizhi   176, 371
Sun, Weijie   163
Sun, Yuling   188
Sun, Zhenqiang   424

Tan, Wenan   3, 359
Tang, Anqiong   359
Tang, Huan   342
Tang, Shan   3
Tang, Yan   498
Tang, Yiming   438
Tang, Yong   316
Tao, Changqing   20, 87
Teng, Shaohua   342
Tong, Lyuyang   77

Wang, Dan   20
Wang, Haiquan   228
Wang, Hao   527
Wang, Huiyu   536
Wang, Liqiang   241
Wang, Shanshan   20
Wang, Wangsong   498
Wang, Xianqing   316

Wang, Xiaohan   454
Wang, Xin   331
Wang, Yafang   241
Wang, Yang   50
Wang, Zhuo   454
Wei, Jingmin   507
Wei, Liangxiong   163
Wu, Lei   241
Wu, Xi   438

Xia, Chunhe   228
Xiao, Yu   331
Xiang, Bingjie   285
Xie, Xiaolan   410
Xu, Jiuyun   517
Xu, Meng   581
Xu, Menghan   536
Xu, Weixia   581
Xu, Xiangrui   517
Xu, Xiaofang   20, 201
Xu, Yu-Hui   50

Yan, Jiafei   301
Yan, Qiaoling   487
Yang, Bo   536
Yang, Qian   386
Yao, Yan   213
Ye, Hengzhou   146
Yin, Feng   163, 527
Yu, Fangyu   32
Yu, Zhengtao   454
Yuan, Feng   478
Yuan, Lichun   66
Yuan, Ping   163, 527

Zeng, Nan   536
Zhang, Cheng   228
Zhang, Guijuan   115
Zhang, Haijie   536
Zhang, Jia   424
Zhang, Wei   342
Zhang, Yan   546
Zhang, Zhenhua   342
Zhang, Zili   66
Zhao, Lu   3, 359
Zhao, Meihua   316

Zheng, Fa   469
Zheng, Qiangqing   410
Zheng, Xiangwei   115, 469, 478
Zhou, Beisi   32
Zhou, Jian-tao   100

Zhou, Jie   188
Zhu, Haodong   454
Zhu, Jia   316
Zhu, Nengjun   546
Zhu, Sizheng   20

Printed in the United States
by Publishers

Printed in the United States
By Bookmasters